Japanese Animation Film Directory & Resource Guide

Trish Ledoux
Doug Ranney

Edited by Fred Patten

Second Edition

Issaquah, Washington

Published by:
Tiger Mountain Press
P.O. Box 369
Issaquah, WA 98027 USA

First Printing, February 1997

Book design and layout by Doug Ranney
Cover design by Yoshiyuki Higuchi and Doug Ranney

Ledoux, Trish, 1963—
        The complete anime guide; Japanese animation film
directory & resource guide [by] Trish Ledoux [and] Doug Ranney.
Edited by Fred Patten. Second edition. Issaquah, WA, Tiger
Mountain Press [1997]
        viii + 214 p. illus. 27 cm

        1. Animated films—Japan—History and criticism. 2. Television pro-
grams—Japan. 3. Television programs—United States. I. Ranney, Douglas
Mackay, 1954— , II. Patten, Frederick Walter, 1940— , ed.
III. Title.

NC1766.J27L46 1997   791.4330952
ISBN 0-9649542-5-7

Contents

Acknowledgements

This book is a work in progress, and so, as we revise each edition, we as its authors become more and more indebted to those who assist us in its completion. This time 'round, special thanks go to our expanded editorial staff—not only to Fred Patten, but to Senior Contributing Editor **Julie Davis** (*"Softcore porn. Fairies. Whatever"*), Contributing Editors **Carl Gustav Horn** (*"Gainax? I'll tell you about Gainax"*) and **James Teal**, and Contributors **Robert Fenelon** (*Leader Dessler Lives!*) and **Kit Fox** (*"Samurai Let-Down"*)—as well as to those whose shoulders we stand upon, most notably **Frederik L. Schodt**, who, as always, remains to English-speaking anime and manga fans as the true One Who Must Be Kept. Thanks must also go to another anime tiki-head, *Yamato*, *Macross*, and *Megazone* director **Noboru Ishiguro**, who wrote our Foreword; to translator/interpreter **Takayuki Karahashi**, for translating Mr. Ishiguro's text; to employers **Seiji** and **Satoru**, for turning the usual blind eye to my late-a.m. appearances in the office after late-a.m. writing sessions; and finally, to Significant Other **Toshifumi Yoshida**, as much for his invaluable research assistance (*"So why did a film like ODIN ever get made?"*) as for his ever-excellent espresso.

— *Trish Ledoux*

In a book of this type, the assemblage of information and materials is a daunting task, and it would have been an impossible one if not for the generous assistance of many people who shall *not* remain nameless. For their assistance with information and materials: thanks to Rita Acosta at Saban Entertainment; Jonathan Lupo at Central Park Media; Yvette Rodriguez at Live Home Video; Matt Nigro at Manga Entertainment; Hiroe Tsukamoto at Pioneer LDCA; Chad Kime at U.S. Renditions; Janice Williams at A.D.V. Films; Samuel Liebowitz at Software Sculptors; and Gustav Baron, Robin Leyden, James Long, Mark Merlino, Craig Miller and Don Yee. Thanks to Steve Pearl for keeping such detailed lists of anime clubs, conventions, and electronic resources. Extra-special thanks to **Fred Patten** (*"The Patten Conspiracy to make you watch cartoons in a language you don't understand"*) for his generous and tireless help with information and materials— far above and beyond what could be expected of any editor. My sincerest apologies go to my family for my being present but unavailable for months on end during this project. And of course my deepest thanks of all go to my unfailingly patient, loving and supportive wife, Laurie— who never hesitates to remind me when my priorities get out of whack .

— *Doug Ranney*

Senior Contributing Editors

Julie Davis
Fred Patten

Contributing Editors

Carl Gustav Horn
James Teal

Contributors

Hal Erickson, Robert Fenelon, Kit Fox, Fred Ladd, Barbara Edmunds, Shawne Kleckner, James Long, Mark Merlino, Gustav Baron, Jeff Roady, Jerry Shaw

The Chapter One essays on *Astro Boy, 8th Man, Gigantor, Prince Planet, Marine Boy, Speed Racer, Battle of the Planets, Star Blazers, TranZor Z, Macron 1, SuperBook* and *Dragon Warrior* are based in part on the descriptions researched and written by Hal Erickson in *Television Cartoon Shows: An Illustrated Encyclopedia, 1949 through 1993* ©1995 Hal Erickson, McFarland & Company, Inc., Publishers, Jefferson NC 28640, and used with permission of the publisher.

Preface to the Second Edition

When Doug Ranney called me in 1995 and asked if I "knew anyone who might like to co-author a book on anime," I could hardly restrain my enthusiasm. After having been a wild-eyed anime fan myself for the fifteen years prior, it seemed a heaven-sent opportunity to combine my own hard-won knowledge of Japanese animation with Doug's extensive knowledge of American animation. The addition as editor of the estimable Fred Patten—one of the first people in this country to become involved in organized anime fandom—seemed the perfect balancing touch for the project.

Since the first edition of *THE COMPLETE ANIME GUIDE* was published in 1996, Doug and I have learned quite a lot. We knew going into the project that it would be difficult to include all the reference and resource information which seemed important and necessary; what we didn't know was *how* difficult that task would prove to be.

In its original conception, *The Complete Anime Guide* was intended (as was explained on the cover) as a "video directory and resource guide." If this had been our only criteria, then success was achieved. At the time, no other book covering the close to 1,000 Japanese-animated home video titles in release had been published in English, and *The Complete Anime Guide* was (and still is) the only book to extensively focus on Japanese-animated videos as released in the U.S. home video market. With additional indices/glossaries covering TV series animated in Japan but broadcast in America, a brief look at anime genres, the history of anime fandom in the U.S., and other resources, it seemed our goal of creating a "complete anime guide" had been met.

One criticism which we have received regarding the first edition was that information on currently Japan-only titles was lacking. Because the original focus of *The Complete Anime Guide* was Japanese animation in America, fewer resources were devoted to covering those TV series, movies, and direct-to-home-video titles which had yet to be exported to the U.S.

Although both Doug and I felt this was an appropriate (and necessary) "narrowing of the focus" for a book which states its mission as covering Japanese animation in the U.S. (as compared to Japanese animation in Japan, or Japanese animation exported in untranslated form to America), we're beginning to wonder if perhaps our original vision was a little shortsighted, and if in fact we hadn't deprived ourselves of an excellent opportunity to explore the incredibly rich world of Japanese animation with our readers.

Thus, the 1997 Edition. Although we're still an edition or two away from our goal of cataloguing each Japanese-animated TV, OAV, and movie currently available on home video in Japan, in this edition you will find much of what's already proven popular with readers of the first edition, in addition to newly revised and improved features such as up-to-the-minute home video listings for the close to 1300+ anime titles currently available in the U.S.; completely revised entries for each video, while of course retaining all the essential info (TV, OAV, movie, U.S. release label, price), any advisories for content (nudity, violence, language), etc.

Perhaps the biggest change to the 1997 Edition of *The Complete Anime Guide* is the inclusion of a more critical and analytical viewpoint. One of the criticisms made of the first edition (and rightfully so) was that a lack of opinion in the "video directory" made the book feel more like a catalog than the hoped-for "complete guide." To this end, in the video directory, you'll now find series summaries augmented with critical evaluation, served with (we hope) a modicum of wit, with additional production notes supplied as appropriate.

Additionally, for each entry you will now find the complete series title under which it was first released in Japan, with translation, as well as the year of Japanese release. For those more experienced anime hands who may already be familiar with these Japanese release titles, all videos have been extensively cross-referenced with their U.S. release titles, meaning that inexperienced and experienced anime fans alike can readily access the information provided in this edition.

Doug and I are proud to present what we hope will prove to be an invaluable addition to your animation reference library, not only for this year, but for many years to come. Lest we forget, thanks go to the many kind people who took the time to write us with their comments and suggestions, without whose help this book would not have been possible.

—*Trish Ledoux*

Foreword by Noboru Ishiguro

The idea that there are Americans interested in Japanese animation first crossed my mind almost 20 years ago, when I was watching a certain TV show. It was the year of *Star Wars*, back when the mainstream was just beginning to realize what the term "special effects" was all about. The show was a documentary, on NHK, about special effects. In it, one of the Star Wars production staff had proudly displayed a treasured cel, from Toei's animated science fiction series, *Captain Future*.

It was an unremarkable cel. In fact, it didn't even have a background. The *Captain Future* series itself had never been particularly popular, and I thought at the time that no one would ever want to buy it, which is why I noticed it in the first place. You see, I had thought the staffer had gotten the anime cel as a novelty, or perhaps because he had a professional interest in Japanese animation. Sure, there was a rumor back when *Star Wars* first came out that its production staff had bought plastic models from Japan and used the parts to build their spaceships. Later, after Em*pire* had been released, I'd even discussed with friends how reminiscent of a Japanese animation story was the part in the second movie where Darth Vader tells Luke that he is his father.

What I never thought, however, was that Hollywood would *ever* be interested in Japanese culture...let alone the existence of Japanese TV animation. Back then, shows such as *Tetsuwan Atom*, *Gatchaman*, and *Mach Go Go Go* had already been on their air as *Astro Boy*, *Battle of the Planets*, and *Speed Racer*, but how many people were even aware that all three of them had been first animated in Japan?

When it came to culture, for a long time after the end of WW II, the U.S. and Japan were like father and son. In many ways, it was a happy era, when Japanese media culture was nurtured on American movies, animation, and comics. Young Japanese people who haven't lived through these years may find it hard to understand, but there was once a time in Japan when it was considered perfectly all right to borrow liberally from American and other foreign movies.

For example, *Astro Boy* and *Kimba the White Lion* creator Osamu Tezuka used to have in his manga a character named "James Mason," who, not uncoincidentally, also resembled the movie star of the same name. These days, Tezuka might very well be sued for infringing without permission upon the likeness. Back then, however, the public took it for the caricature it was, and no one considered things such as rights and lawsuits.

The Japanese movies of this time had *many* ideas taken from foreign movies. I don't know if this is true, or just a rumor, but a certain manga artist presumably had a subscription to a science fiction magazine which he'd have a college student translate so that he could use the stories in it for his own manga. Just as bootleg versions of D*oraemon* are popular in Southeast Asia today, there was no sense of guilt associated with those kinds of activities back then.

The Japanese manga culture was nurtured in this type of generous shadow of the U.S. I still remember those days, and thus tend to overvalue American movies, while undervaluing our own Japanese works.

As I mentioned earlier, just when S*tar Wars* was a hit in Japan and the word "science fiction" was gaining currency, *Space Cruiser Yamato* had begun an anime boom. TV anime fans had become activists, and had finally achieved recognition by society. I was really surprised when something similar was going on in the U.S. Popular anime TV shows in Japan, I was told, were being mailed to the U.S. A day or so later, U.S. fans would be gathered together to watch them. As it turns out, the C*aptain Future* cel that I caught on TV wasn't a coincidence it all, but a foreshadowing.

Twenty years later, Japan's economy was riding the big wave, and Japanese culture was exported around the world, starting with the U.S. Among the old familiar faces of Judo, karate, and zen, not only sushi bars and karaoke but Japanese animation as well was being shown on TVs worldwide. When I saw *Maison Ikkoku* at a hotel in Italy, for example, I couldn't help wondering how they were ever going to explain the concepts of "*kotatsu*" heated tables and "*yojôhan*" four-and-a-half-mat apartments to the locals.

I credited this phenomenon not just to Japanese TV anime being good, but also as a result of successful marketing, backed by the powerful Japanese economy. Years before *Maison Ikkoku* was on TV in Italy, however, it was being avidly watched and promoted by English-speaking anime fans in U.S. For that reason alone, I must acknowledge a sense of gratitude, and renew my respect for everyone who helped pave the way for the popularity anime enjoys today in America.

That the target age for an American television-viewing audience is five years of age is a point which I need not belabor. There are strict rules against violence, for example, and the recent institution on U.S. television of voluntary "ratings" by broadcasters is a reflection of this. Japanese television, which does not have (and, in fact, has never had) these sorts of restrictions, has traditionally provided much more room to develop various sorts of expression. In that respect, it's only natural that Japanese TV as a medium is able to produce visuals which are more provocative and spectacular than those that are made in America. Add to this relatively more relaxed creative atmosphere the genius of artist Osamu Tezuka, who transplanted his innovative storytelling methods from manga directly to anime. And so, with the addition of a rarely seen depth of character development, a unique medium that was neither film, TV drama, nor manga, grew up.

To be fair, the kind of statements I'm making are the kind that can only be made in retrospect. Back when I and the other animators I worked with were doing our work on *Yamato, Macross,* and *Megazone,* we had no time to imagine how we'd be perceived on the outside (much less in other countries), and all we really worried about was making our deadlines from week to week.

When asked how Japanese animation differs from American animation, the brief answer is that U.S. theatrical features and TV programs have clearcut heroes and villains. They're easy to categorize, just like technicolor westerns. In that sense, perhaps it's fair to say that Japanese animation has more nuances. While the American product is all logic, the Japanese product appeals more to sentiment. In a manner of speaking, the former is dry, while the latter is wet. This may have more to do with a difference of national character, but the first generation of American anime fans surely must have found this "wetness" a novelty. Of course, this is only a hypothesis on my part. From the view-point of a culturally heterogeneous society like America, the Japanese custom which holds that stating one's mind openly is rude must make for an interesting analysis.

For example, drafting up a feature-length Japanese anime film centering around a protagonist who agonizes over whether or not to confess his love to a girl is the easiest thing in the world to an anime writer. I think the first generation, or "wave," if you will, of American anime fans, surely must have been able to understand this sort of sentiment.

Another thing. I saw a story on an American news program once, in which they were showcasing the teenage lifestyles of today's high school students. The girls said something along the lines of, "I envy the girls who came before us. The only thing they agonized over back then was what kind of dress to wear for the prom…. It must have been so peaceful, relatively. These days, your life's constantly at stake, due to things like guns and rape and AIDS." These words must ring so true to the modern American woman.

While these sorts of thoughts are going around the U.S., meanwhile, in Japan, we've got anime which treats the most frivolous of issues as life-or-death material, as though the world were still as it had been in the '60s. Japan certainly has been among the more peaceful countries in the world (although this has started to change recently), and perhaps American anime fans subconsciously see the good old days of America in Japanese anime. Or do I read too deeply? Then again, it's those same "good old days" of forty or so years ago which are imprinted so strongly in my mind, which certainly must hold a strong subconscious influence on my work. In other words, whose culture is influencing whose…?

In 1985, a new medium called the "OAV" or "Original Animation Video" began. Anime, which had already subdivided itself into so many different genres, became even more micro-marketed and specialized for the hardcore. Baptized by the explosive growth of SF movies since Star Wars, anime became even more obsessed with mecha, perhaps not unrelatedly increasing the number of American fans. To label Otomo's *Akira* as the apex of this mecha trend is no more than a natural conclusion.

On the other hand, the genesis of the adult and "Lolita" animation which began in Japan with the late-night *Cream Lemon* anime TV series must have struck home with another segment of American anime youth. I can't necessarily speak for young American men, but back here in Japan, many young men have become gynephobic, contributing to an observed overall decline in population.

Perhaps the biggest change in the last twenty years is the American acceptance of anime's stereotypically big-eyed characters. Looking at the *Sailor Moon* reader's art sent in to ANIMERICA magazine, for example, I can tell that there's real love for these characters, especially among the next generation—the younger readers. What a change from mainstream articles which have no other basis for comparison regarding anime's "otherness" than the size of their orbs…!

Shifts in sentiment are something which we see in Japanese life regularly. The old cultures of Japan disappear by the day, and are replaced by the new. It's a little sad, maybe, but since culture is a living thing, supposed to resonate and evolve, it might be even sadder if culture were unchanging. At the entropic heat-death of the cultural future, Disneyland may be ubiquitous, and exotic cuisines may be available the world over, but that won't be reason to worry. There will *always* be new subcultures that will go against the establishment; that's the nature of history.

And so, we come at last to the discussion of recent developments in the Japanese anime industry. The truth of the matter is, Japanese TV and OAV animation is being watched all over the world, but, with certain limited exceptions, that fact has little or no bearing on the industry in Japan. Here, the most notable characteristic of the '96-97 TV season was the increase in the number of late-night anime. Consider the fact that the sponsors of these late-night programs tend to be the same music publishing and recording companies which back most of the home video animation market; i.e., OAVs. This means that, the moment these TV shows go off the air, these companies are prepared to remarket them as OAVs, cleverly recouping original production costs.

This has become an established system, actually, and the result is that animators will be required more and more to produce OAV-quality work on TV-level budgets. On top of that, an increasing reliance on fantasy stories generated by video games and the like mean that characters become less and less distinct. In other words, count on seeing plenty of shows which can't be told apart one from the other, once you've shuffled their titles and characters.

The trend this year, for example, is that all characters must have razor-sharp cheekbones. I wonder if they'll find a ready audience with you, the American audience…? In another example, last year's *Evangelion* excited everyone and was the big breakthrough hit. Will there be another like it this year? The same Japanese character trait that doesn't like prominence also discourages originality. Big Japanese corporations and the media have the common behavior of not starting something until someone else proves its worth. I worry that none of this year's new TV anime will be distinct.

There's no mistake that puny shows made with puny budgets are going to become more common. A lack of enthusiastic, committed producers may be the cause; who knows? I have to wonder if there's an energetic American producer out there who'll come to Japan and stir things up.

—*Noboru Ishiguro*

A veteran animator who began his career in 1963, the same year *Astro Boy* went on the air in Japan, **Noboru Ishiguro** has worked on some of the most classic series in Japanese animation, including *Star Blazers*, *Robotech* and *Megazone 23*. A resident of Japan, he currently writes a monthly column for ANIMERICA, ANIME & MANGA MONTHLY called "Anime Memories," in which he shares his vast knowledge of the industry's most inner workings.

Introduction

Say hello to the next big Japanese import: an introduction to the wonderful world of Japanese animation

"M y name...is Tetsuo."

As *Akira*'s Neo-Tokyo went up in a ball of cyberpunk apocalyptic fire, a new genre was being born to the American pop culture landscape: Japanese animation, "*anime*" (say "Annie-May") for short, known to many Americans as "that *Speed Racer* stuff." These days, it seems everyone is getting into the act—a recent Sci-Fi Channel CD-Rom trivia game's got questions about *Ranma 1/2*, on *The Simpsons*, there's jokes about "Kimba...uh, I mean Simba," and Speed Racer and the gang are shilling for Volkswagon ("drivers needed"). Although anime has yet to achieve the kind of widespread recognition enjoyed by more traditional Disney fare, U.S.-broadcast series such as *Sailor Moon* and *Dragon Ball Z* have gone a long way toward introducing the anime "look" into the vocabularies of the generation next, if the number of *Sailor Moon* halloween costumes and *Dragon Ball* action figures sold at Toys R Us are any indication.

Say hello to the next big Japanese import.

Japan's Hollywood

"Japan's first really big cultural export," said technoBible *Wired* magazine. "The counterpart of American movies," stated *The New York Times*. "An emblem of cool," cooed *Newsweek*. Of all the hype and publicity surrounding the mainstream media's growing interest in Japanese animation, truer words were never spoken. Aside from the tried-and-true Japanese film directors beloved of the critics at *The New York Times*—samurai epic director Akira Kurosawa, contemporary satirist Juzo Itami—the hottest directors in Japan today aren't working in live-action, but in animation. In an industry where the country's most successful domestic films in recent years have been, more often than not, animated features such as director Isao Takahata's **Pom Poko**[1], can it even be doubted that anime is the forum for Japan's most cutting-edge creative talents—Japan's Hollywood, in fact?

Osamu Tezuka, **Astro Boy** creator, known in his native Japan as the "God of Comics" (*Manga no Kami-Sama*), had always openly acknowledged that his own animation efforts were inspired by animators such as Max Fleischer and Walt Disney. But comparing Tezuka to Disney is like...well, like comparing da Vinci to Rembrandt. Both created immortal, world-class works of art; both were acknowledged as masters in their respective fields. Rembrandt and da Vinci were painters; Disney and Tezuka were animators. But the processes of their creativity were vastly different.

The groundbreaking animated feature film *Akira* is generally credited for the recent breakthrough of Japanese animation into American popular culture.

[1] A thoughtful yet hilarious take on the environmental side of urban sprawl, *Grave of the Fireflies* director Isao Takahata's *Pom Poko* (1994) was the top-grossing Japanese film of the year, as well as Japan's Oscar entry for that year's "Best Foreign Film" category (it didn't make it). The antics of the anthropomorphic *tanuki* (a species of raccoon-dog indigenous to Japan) and their amazing shape-shifting testicles are among the film's most charming—if a bit startling—elements. Other films from Japan's Studio Ghibli include *My Neighbor Totoro*, which was released in the U.S. during 1993 by Fox Home Video.

[2] Translator, interpreter, manga historian and author, San Francisco Bay Area-based Frederik L. Schodt is widely acknowledged as one of the U.S. anime and manga industry's leading authorities. His book *Manga! Manga! The World of Japanese Comics* (Kodansha) remains the definitive resource on the subject, with his latest book—*Dreamland Japan: Writings on Modern Manga* (Stone Bridge Press)—a brilliant update on the always fascinating doings of this multibillion-dollar Japanese industry. Schodt's long friendship and association with Tezuka has yielded several fascinating insights into the brilliant creator and his works over the years; with any luck, perhaps someday, Schodt will publish the definitive Tezuka biography.

Photo by Robin Leyden

Osamu Tezuka (circa 1978) with a model of his creation, "Astro Boy."

[3] Beating *Tetsuwan Atom* to the airwaves by a good half year was *Otogi Manga Calendar* ("Manga Stories Calendar"), which debuted in Japanese households on 25 June 1962. Basically a series of unconnected vignettes, each five-minute episode focused on memorable events in history. By the time the series ended in 1964, over three hundred black and white episodes were eventually produced and broadcast.

[4] Generally agreed by anime and manga historians to have begun with Tezuka's original manga, 1953's *Ribon no Kishi* ("Princess Knight"), *shôjo* anime is a particularly stylized, even abstract subgenre more devoted to exploring the complexities of feeling, emotion, and relationships than the unabashedly straightforward action narrative of most *shônen* or boys' stories. Current animated examples of the genre include Osaka-based four girl super-*shôjo* team Clamp's *Tokyo Babylon*; *shôjo* manga founding mother Moto Hagio's *They Were 11*; *RG Veda*, another work based on the manga by Clamp; and Kei Kusunoki's mythological, gothic fantasy, *Ogre Slayer*. *Please Save My Earth*, a three-volume direct-to-home-video or "OAV" series based on one of the *shôjo* genre's most popular contemporary manga series, is also now available on home video.

Like Disney, Rembrandt presided over a studio of artists. Though clearly a master painter, even if Rembrandt did not, in some cases, personally brush every stroke with his own hand, even if his involvement was limited to the supervision of the other artists who worked under him in his studio, the works which were produced there are known by his name.

Leonardo da Vinci, on the other hand, was the archetype of a renaissance man, both an artist and a scientist, even an animator. In addition to being a comic artist and animator, Tezuka was also a licensed physician and a pioneer in his field whose stories and style are just as fresh (and still just as widely imitated) as they were thirty years ago. A comic artist who began his career in 1946 with a newspaper strip, Tezuka was an incredibly prolific creator who by the time of his death in 1989 had drawn an estimated 150,000 pages of comics, or *manga* (say "MAHN-gah") in his lifetime.

Like da Vinci, Tezuka was, in the words of longtime friend and manga scholar Frederik L. Schodt, a "one-man dream factory."[2] Tezuka was a creative dynamo whose comics tackled nearly every possible subject: science fiction, action/adventure, romance, horror, and adult drama, creating a readership which encompassed every possible age group. In 1963, already a successful artist, Tezuka pioneered the field of Japanese TV animation with **Tetsuwan Atom** or *Astro Boy*, for most intents and purposes the first half-hour animated series ever to be broadcast on Japanese television.[3] But Tezuka's animation efforts didn't end there—like his comics, Tezuka's animation projects pushed the envelope of the existing art form.

In addition to creating Japan's first regular animated television series, Tezuka also produced his country's first color animated series, **Jungle Taitei** or "Jungle Emperor," better known in the U.S. as **Kimba the White Lion**. Tezuka premiered his first modern-day full-length animated feature, the beautifully animated, two and a half hour **One Thousand and One Nights** (*Senya Ichiya Monogatari*) in 1969.

Tezuka made *One Thousand and One Nights* with the express desire to elevate animation into a serious medium which could be enjoyed not only by children, but by adults as well. Almost twenty-five years later, Disney would go on to animate their own version of the story with 1992's *Aladdin*, but the resemblance ends there. Despite the brief flurry of controversy provided by the film's infamous "cut off your hand" lyrics, Disney's *Aladdin* is for children, while Tezuka's version is for a decidedly more sophisticated audience. Taking almost a year and a half to animate, the animation of the *Arabian Nights* story reportedly required some 70,000 cels to achieve Tezuka's vision of bare-breasted

©1969 Tezuka Production/Mushi Films

Tezuka's **One Thousand and One Nights**

maidens, wily serpents, and blue-complected viziers (in Disney's version, only the genie is blue).

This is not a book about Tezuka, and so the story of his profound effect not only on Japan's animation industry but on its cinema and literature as well must be saved for another day. For now, it is enough to know that during the course of his career he produced one revolutionary work after another, founding several of today's most frequently seen anime genres in the process, including the increasingly more popular genre of *shôjo* manga or Japanese women's comics, which are today created almost exclusively by women, but enjoyed by everyone.[4] In Japan, most anime videos are based on manga, and manga-artist-turned-animator Tezuka constantly strove to expand the full potential of animation, producing in his later years several pieces of experimental animation seldom seen outside Japan, yet unforgettable to anyone who has ever had the privilege to view them. Tezuka's influence left an indelible mark on the inextricably linked animation and comics industry which almost surely would never have become what it was without him.

Yet Tezuka was not the *only* inspiration for ambitious animators. Noboru Ishiguro, animation director on one of Japan's most influential and beloved animated series, **_Space Battleship Yamato_**[5], remembers the times after World War II as years when "there was no TV…movies were the only form of entertainment. All the American movies banned during wartime came back in a flood, both new ones and old ones. It would have been strange for me *not* to have overdosed on them. I must have been seeing something like 300 films a year." Ishiguro, whose animation career almost exactly parallels the entire history of animation on TV in Japan, reflectively points to Hollywood as much of the inspiration for many of his generation, and to the work of Osamu Tezuka as the catalyst which lit that spark.

During his high school and college years, Ishiguro says there was a "spontaneous reaction felt throughout a nation of boys and girls who were inspired by the genius of Osamu Tezuka…. I was one of those inspired by his brilliance."

In post World War II Japan, Hollywood as a whole provided inspiration for an entire generation of artists and animators unable to realize their visions any other way. For obvious reasons, Japan's economic state after WW II was hardly capable of supporting a domestic film industry of any size. Filmmaking in any era has always required investors with deep pockets and a substantial "pioneer spirit" (that is, the willingness to risk it all for an artistic vision or dream). Unlike America's film boom of the Depression Era 1930s, Japan's post-war economy was concentrated on rebuilding the nation's entire infrastructure, not simply reorganizing its economy and politics. Filmmaking, for most creators, was out of reach.

"So many manga artists of my generation got into animation because they were all enchanted with Hollywood, just like me," says Ishiguro. "All those people who started drawing manga back then no doubt wanted to make their own movies. But that was easier said than done, so they recreated the images in their heads with paper and ink. If circumstances had allowed, the majority of those who became manga artists would probably have become film directors. That they did not, in my opinion, is an unrecoverable loss to the Japanese film industry." The good part is, as Ishiguro points out, that Japanese animation has recently returned to American shores to influence Hollywood in a kind of "reverse feedback."

These motion picture aspirations go a long way toward explaining the difference in *appearance* between most western-produced animation and Japanese animation. Aside from "style" factors such as variations in character design (including the oft-mentioned "big eyes" of Japanese animation and comics), the most significant difference lies in the abundance of cinematic techniques used to tell the story. A Japanese-animated TV show such as **_Star Blazers_**, created in the 1970s (which today hardly qualifies as state-of-the-art) absolutely overflows with tracking shots, long-view establishing shots, fancy pans, unusual point-of-view "camera angles" and extreme close-ups. In contrast, most American-produced TV animation tends to thrive in an action-obsessed middle-distance. Rarely in an American production do you ever see a significant "director's" influence on the finished 'toon.[6]

The next most obvious difference between much western animation and Japanese animation is the use of color. Most western animation uses flat, bright color almost exclusively, whether in a superhero-style action show, a "funny animals" comedy, or a sci-fi adventure.

The Japanese-animated series **_Teknoman_** (which once aired on Paramount's UPN network) is a fascinating study in contrast with its partner in the programming schedule, **_Space Strikers_**, which aired just before it. Although both series pursue amazingly similar plotlines—an alien invasion, and a heroic team of freedom fighters in

[5] Broadcast on American television as *Star Blazers*, the series known in Japan as *Uchū Senkan Yamato* or "Space Battleship Yamato" is, like *Speed Racer* and *Astro Boy*, one of those enduringly popular series which many people never suspected were even Japanese during their initial U.S. broadcasts. Heroic, romantic, and always epic, in Japan the *Yamato* series eventually produced three separate seasons of half-hour TV episodes, a TV movie, and four theatrical features. *Yamato 2520*, which U.S.-based Voyager Entertainment had originally announced for release in 1996, has yet to make it to American shores.

Noboru Ishiguro, animation director for some of Japan's most popular anime series, including *Space Battleship Yamato, Macross, Thunderbirds 2086, Megazone 23*, and more.

The space battleship *Yamato*, in two views.

[6] The mood-suffused *Batman: The Animated Series* is one obvious exception to this rule. Although it clearly takes hints from the Fleischer Brothers' animated *Superman* shorts of previous decades, *Batman: The Animated Series'* excellent cinematic storytelling style and film noir lighting would never have come about if Tim Burton's successful *Batman* movie had not placed such a high emphasis on atmosphere. Love it or hate it, Burton's *Batman* finally made the chief factor in the "Dark Knight's" popularity clear to the public at large.

7 It's worth noting that *black and white* comics, whether the pre-war newspaper action strips or the sci-fi adventures of the British magazine *2000 AD*, habitually trade in atmosphere that color comics can rarely match. The starkness of black and white lends itself more easily in many ways to creating mood, something that black and white film aficionados have been saying for years, and animation that clearly draws from those sources—including the Fleischer *Superman* cartoons of the 1940s, or the later *Jonny Quest*—in addition to getting a lot of mileage out of dramatic lighting effects, handle *color* more skillfully, as well. Also of note is MTV's *Aeon Flux*, the exceptional color sense of which hews closely in style to the flat-color French comic masterworks such as those of Jean "Moebius" Giraud…despite the popular misconception that *Aeon Flux* is somehow "anime" due to its dynamic pace, weird-looking characters, unusual storylines, and Asian surnames in the production credits.

Teknoman

a spaceship battling the menace—the disparity in style is beyond striking. Every scene in *Teknoman* seems to have been filmed in a dark room—the lighting is harsh, and the color muted…in other words, it's downright film noir. *Teknoman* is trading in the same kind of subject matter and tone that drives movies such as *Alien* or *Outland*—should we be surprised that the resulting animation has a distinct Ridley Scott feel? That the cinematic aspect is so strong in Japanese animation is a logical progression of its origins in Japanese comics and the influence of Hollywood cinema…but it also speaks of the animators' commitment to creating a believable, visually stimulating world.

Space Strikers, on the other hand, thrives in a world of perpetual bright light and primary color—even scenes set in a presumably dark cave, lit only by a flickering fire, are identical in every nuance of color and tone to those occurring at high noon on the open desert. That there is so little emphasis on creating distinct cinematic mood or sense of place is perhaps an indicator of the homogenous approach with which presumably more adult-oriented animation and comedy "kiddie" cartoons alike are approached.[7]

So much of American animation seems to utilize the same bright, primary palette, regardless of subject. Even today, when live-action filmmakers wish to invoke the "innocent" era of cartoons, the results are brightly colored to the point of parody, as in the case of the *Dick Tracy* film starring Warren Beatty. Calling a film—or anything else, for that matter—"cartoony" tends to automatically imply either garish, bright colors, or an exaggerated, hyper-dramatic style. Being "child-like" isn't the same thing as being "childish," for example, and when you're talking about animation, even if you're "cartoon-like" instead of "cartoonish," you're still the same thing: **cartoon** *n. predictable; never believable as real.*

In a recent interview with *Film Threat* magazine, master American comic artist Will Eisner (*The Spirit*) pointed out that "a lot of people…don't fully understand the difference between film and comics. They seem on the surface to be alike because they both deal with images, but film is a spectator medium and comics is a participant medium." The same thing can be said for animation. While a comics reader is able to use his/her own imagination to fill in the blanks of a story (a phenomenon comic artist and analyst Scott McCloud examines at length in his excellent book *Understanding Comics*), animation is like live-action filmmaking in that everything that transpires has to be created for the viewer; fail to provide enough information, or not *convincing* enough an illusion, and disbelief refuses to suspend.

In the case of comedy, of course, broad exaggeration is not only appropriate, but is often the point. One of the funniest cartoons on American TV today, *The Tick*, trades in *exactly* the same kind of lampooning that made the '60s *Batman* TV series so hilariously successful. Comedy animation makes few demands in the way of atmosphere, with only parody requiring the subject to in any way resemble what's being parodied. Even then, much of the comedy lies in how "reality" as we know it is either distorted or accurately mirrored, such as in *The Simpsons*. Bright color in this case does its job well by drawing more attention to the parody, making the subjects bigger, brighter and more ridiculous. But to approach all animation—even more adult-oriented animation—as though it were comedy is to do animation (and the viewers of animation) a disservice. Must all animation be regarded as "only for children"…? Even if you don't count yourself as a fan, the consistently on-target social commentary of animated series such as *Beavis and Butt-Head* and even the more recent *King of the Hill* would seem to suggest otherwise.

Disney has, by and large, been one of the few exceptions to this rule. Their earliest feature-length production, *Snow White* (1937), used cinematic techniques neatly approximating the live-action films of the day—motion pictures themselves being a very young art form at time. *Snow White*'s Prince Charming has the distinct look of a 1930s movie idol, right down to his neatly combed-back hair and rouged lips, and the wicked Queen's villainy is shrouded in muted color and stark shadows borrowed from the period's many gangster films. Other Disney features such as *Fantasia* use the cinematic approach to great effect[8], .and such technically impressive films are one of the reasons Disney holds the reputation it does today (the Happy Meals probably don't hurt, either).

But although Disney impressed the world with the feature-length *Snow White*, animation in the U.S. did not suddenly shift to a long-form medium. Most animation produced in the U.S. today descends less from the legacy of *Snow White* and, and more from the overwhelming repertoire of seven-minute comedy shorts such as *Bugs Bunny* or *Tom and Jerry*, created as opening acts for theatrical live-action films.[9] The animated television series which make up most of America's Saturday morning animated programming are still overwhelmingly comedic, despite a recent resurgence in superhero-style action. In contrast, very early on, Japan began building a tradition of feature-length animated films to take the place of the live-action films they couldn't create, and subsequent Japanese-animated television programs are built on that long-form tradition.

Other than the household name of Walt Disney, how many people on the street can name the preeminent talents in the American animation field? Perhaps a handful would recognize Chuck Jones, Ralph Bakshi, or Don Bluth, but even the name Tex Avery (legendary to students of animation worldwide) would most likely draw a blank stare. Despite the talk in places such as *Premiere* magazine about Disney's fabled "star animators," how many people outside the American animation industry itself can name more than one or two persons working in the field?

Compare this with the excitingly *individual* field of anime, where the top talents of Japan's filmmaking industry aren't busy churning out yet another *Godzilla* sequel (leave it to Hollywood to do that!), but rather, they're creating contemporary masterpieces comparable to the wonder of Spielberg, the gritty, lurid thrill of Tarantino, or the dead-on characterization of Scorsese.[10] Japanese animators are forging ever forward with new techniques, new approaches, new subjects and an infinite number of new styles. Even today, while live-action directors such as Kurosawa scramble for overseas investors to finance their films, anime directors such as **My Neighbor Totoro**'s Hayao Miyazaki, **Wicked City** and **Ninja Scroll**'s Yoshiaki Kawajiri, and **Ghost in the Shell** and **Patlabor**'s Mamoru Oshii are able to assemble top creative talents to put the finishing touches on animated films which put some higher-budgeted U.S. live-action films to shame in terms of artistic scope and sheer creative brilliance.

In a tradition stretching back even before *Astro Boy*, Japanese animators have adapted manga (which have always embraced a wider range of subjects than America's predominantly superhero comics), novels, folktales, world literature and history, moving further out with each new project until, like Hollywood's movies today, they've created their own traditions and specific genres.

Like movies, and comics, and novels, the stories of Japanese animation are as diverse as they are many: drama, comedy, action, adventure, romance. But unlike these other storytelling media, anime has developed its own language, its own *visual grammar*.[11] Naturally this grammar parses itself to certain kinds of stories, some of which are done better—and indeed, *only*—in Japanese animation.

— *Trish Ledoux*

---

[8] The similarity in choreography between *Fantasia*'s acid-trippy musical sequences to Hollywood's technicolor musicals is an interesting thing to compare. Under the influence of Gene Kelly in the 1950s, the Hollywood musical reached its apex with *Singing in the Rain*, *An American in Paris* and most importantly *Invitation to the Dance*, which utilized the best in experimental theater effects, color lighting and modern-art set design with Kelly's own innovative modern dance choreography. Watching *Invitation to the Dance* and *Fantasia* back to back makes it clear that Disney in its heyday had a much stronger feel for the trends of the time, just as anime does now.

---

[9] With the exception of the occasional Disney features, since the '60s American animation has largely been half-hour TV series and specials, with a few non-Disney feature attempts such as those by Don Bluth and Ralph Bakshi. What is *not* done in American animation are serialized stories that carry over through multiple episodes. This is the province of anime that is unique!

Mamoru Oshii's *Patlabor*.

---

[10] American critics and reviewers are, perhaps understandably, quick to label Osamu Tezuka as "Japan's Walt Disney," but keeping in mind that anime is "Japan's Hollywood," they might be well-advised to extend the simile and regard Hayao Miyazaki as "Japan's Spielberg," Yoshiaki Kawajiri as "Japan's John Carpenter," and Mamoru Oshii as "Japan's Scorsese." Thinking of anime not as Japanese for "cartoons," but rather as Japanese for "Hollywood," makes the true scope of this dynamic storytelling medium that much clearer.

---

[11] "Visual grammar" is a term borrowed from *shôjo* manga or Japanese women's comics scholar Matt Thorn, anime/manga columnist and prospective Ph.D. candidate currently finishing his doctoral dissertation on *shôjo*. (For more on *shôjo* manga, read on.)

Chapter One
Animated Television Series
made in Japan and broadcast in America

The year 1995 marked the arrival of the third wave of Japanese TV animation to American television. Going into 1997, it does not look as though this has proven to be the tidal wave for which anime fans had hoped. However, it has not completely ebbed yet.

The first wave included the classics of the 1960s, beginning with **Astro Boy** in 1963 and ending with **Speed Racer** in 1967. (Syndication kept them on TV until the late 1970s.) Fans at the time did not realize that they were from Japan, or think of them as being in any special category. There were many TV cartoons in the 1950s and 1960s from small studios that the public had never heard of: *Crusader Rabbit*, *Space Angel*, *The Mighty Hercules*, *Roger Ramjet*, etc. So nobody wondered in particular about the origins of **Gigantor** or **Marine Boy**. These Japanese cartoons were in the American format of self-contained, interchangeable episodes, so they did not especially stand out. There were similar cartoons from American studios (for example, 1967 saw both Joe Oriolo's *Johnny Cypher in Dimension Zero* and Hanna-Barbera's *The Mighty Mightor*), so the public was not aware when American television stopped buying Japanese cartoons after 1967. They seemed like any other TV cartoons: they appeared with little publicity, they lasted for a year or two, and they faded away.

The second wave started in 1978 with **Battle of the Planets**, and lasted until the late 1980s with the "combo-programs" created by editing together two or more separate anime titles. Some fans consider this as two separate waves, with the first ending with **Force Five** in 1980 and the next starting with **Voltron, Defender of the Universe** in 1984. However, there were a couple of anime titles in the interim to link them. More importantly, they shared a style which stood out from American TV animation of the '80s more than '60s anime had stood out from '60s American TV animation.

Basically, they were more genuinely dramatic. American TV had its own dramatic syndicated cartoons by this time, from *G.I. Joe* and *He-Man and the Masters of the Universe* to *ThunderCats* and *Transformers*. But somehow the drama was always more superficial, the villains less convincingly nasty, and the stories less complex than their anime counterparts. And even when American producers tried to disguise the fact, as in *Battle of the Planets* or *Force Five*, it was usually obvious that there was a continuing story in progress from one episode to the next. The best programs such as **Star Blazers**, *Voltron* and **Robotech** were actually adventure serials — unlike any American TV animation at this time.

But the second wave did not last, either. Why not? Basically, the TV entertainment industry of those days considered anime in the same way that they consider American TV animation today— as advertising to sell toys. To them, the purpose of the giant-robot anime dramas was to sell transforming robot toys. Once the market for transforming robots peaked and receded after 1985, interest in importing new anime also receded.

The third wave splashed on our shores in 1995, and it is still swirling around. During Summer and Fall 1995, there were reports in *Newsweek*, *USA Today*, *The New York Times*, and *The Hollywood Reporter* that anime was finally being accepted by American TV. The Sci-Fi Channel and The Cartoon Network began showing anime features like **Vampire Hunter D** and TV programs like the old and new **Gigantor**. **Ronin Warriors**, **Sailor Moon**, **Dragon Ball**, *and* **Teknoman** came to network or syndicated TV with high expectations.

So far, those expectations have not really been met. Those 1995 programs usually played briefly and then disappeared. What happened to *Sailor Moon* has been the most enlightening. The 65-episode program won a devoted-enough following to garner newspaper articles about its cult fandom. But that fandom did not get high enough ratings to keep it on the air. A "Save Our Sailors" campaign started on the Internet around mid-1996, complaining that poor time-slots such as 4:30 a.m. were responsible for the bad ratings. By late October, they claimed that they had collected over 30,000 signatures to put *Sailor Moon* back on the air in better time-slots. But by the end of 1996, Sailor Moon had faded away, to be replaced by *Eagle Riders* and *Samurai Pizza Cats*.

What has happened? The syndicated TV market of the mid-1990s has plenty of new, high-quality cartoons from major American animation studios from which to choose. Those studios were not producing TV cartoons during the anime waves of the 1960s and 1978 to '87, so there was an opening for cartoons from Japan. Today's TV sponsors would rather put their money behind the proven name-appeal of Disney and Warner Bros., rather than cartoons from unknown studios—American or Japanese.

This does not mean that the third wave has completely receded. The waves are not exact duplicates of each other. At least, the reputation of anime seems to be secure now. In the 1960s, American TV tried to disguise or downplay the fact that TV anime was not an American product. In the 1980s, American TV did not care whether the public was aware of anime's Japanese origins as long as the programs could be hammered into seemingly standard American childrens'-TV fare. Today, thanks in part to the growing demand for animation for older viewers (*Duckman*, *Batman: The Animated Series*, *The Ren & Stimpy Show*, *Aeon Flux*), there is less concern about the violence or the Japanese cultural aspects inherent in anime. It is simply a case of a surfeit of American cartoons filling the available time-slots. As the number of cable and satellite-broadcast channels grows, hopefully the demand for more anime cartoons to fill them will also grow.

In this chapter you'll find a more-or-less comprehensive guide to Japanese animated programs airing on American television, from *Astro Boy* in 1963 to *Eagle Riders* and *Samurai Pizza Cats* in 1996-'97. Some programs broadcast for only brief periods and/or in limited areas are not included; neither are the numerous juvenile-targeted programs broadcast on cable TV's Nickelodeon over the years such as *Belle and Sebastian*, *The Little Koala*, or *The Mysterious Cities of Gold*. With any luck, future editions of this book will include entries on these shows and more.

— Fred Patten

Astro Boy

Syndicated: 1963—1964. Mushi Productions/Video Promotions, Inc./NBC Enterprises and Screen Gems. Created and produced by Osamu Tezuka. English adaptation written and directed by Fred Ladd. Music by Tatsuo Takai; lyrics by Don Rockwell. Voices: Billie Lou Watt (Astro Boy/Astro Girl); Ray Owens (Dr. Elefun); Gilbert Mack (Mr. Pompus); Peter Fernandez.

© 1963 Tezuka Productions/ Mushi Productions

Mention *Astro Boy* to any middle-aged Japanese male and you're likely to get a quizzical or even a hostile look. Mention *Tetsuwan Atom* and you'll witness the same warm glow that comes over the face of most middle-aged American males when they're reminded of *Li'l Abner*, *Steve Canyon* or *Buz Sawyer*. For long before it was rechristened *Astro Boy* for the American market, artist Osamu Tezuka's *Tetsuwan Atom* (lit., "Iron-arm Atom") was the most popular comic book in Japan, as well as one of the longest-running newspaper strips (1951-1968) in the country's history.

The project began as **Atom Taishi** ("Ambassador Atom"), but soon adopted its more familiar title, which can also translate as "Mighty Atom." The plotline, set in the year 2000, concerned the Institute of Science's Dr. Tenma, who out of grief over the traffic accident death of his own young son, built a rocket-powered robot in the dead boy's image. The robot, *Tetsuwan Atom*, had in addition to the usual super-strength and ability to fly the capacity for human emotions. But Dr. Tenma soon became irritated that his mechanical "son" would never grow into manhood, and eventually sold the creature to a circus (shades of *Pinocchio*). Atom was brutalized in the Robot Circus by greedy Ringmaster Hamegg. He was rescued by kindly Dr. Ochanomizu, who adopted him and took him to the Institute of Science. Already programmed by Dr. Tenma to be "a good little boy," Atom was influenced by Dr. Ochanomizu's goodness and altruism into adopting a life of crimefighting—a not inconsiderable task, since his foes included mad doctors, space aliens, mind control freaks and an evil giant robot known as "Colosso."

Though his work went in a diametrically opposite direction, Osamu Tezuka was a big fan of American animators Walt Disney and Max Fleischer. As an homage to these cartoon giants, Tezuka drew nearly all his manga characters with huge, saucer-like eyes— a style soon adopted by virtually every other Japanese animator. It is for this reason, and not because of a distorted Asian perspective of how Occidental eyes are shaped (as has sometimes been suggested), that the characters in *Astro Boy* and other anime efforts all seem to have optical elephantiasis.

Astro Girl leaving her robot family's home.

The animated cartoon version of *Tetsuwan Atom*, which served as the premier attraction of Osamu Tezuka's then-recently established Mushi Productions, debuted on Fuji TV on 1 January 1963, as Japan's first true animated TV series*, and later moved to the NHK Network. In all, 193 half-hour episodes were produced. When NBC Enterprises purchased the series for American TV, rights were initially secured for 52 installments; ultimately, a total of 104 programs made it to the States— still more than enough for a Monday-through-Friday syndicated strip. Like the other non-Japanese distributors among the twenty nations carrying the series, NBC Enterprises adapted the project for domestic consumption. Dr. Ochanomizu was renamed "Dr. Packadermus J. Elefun," a tribute to his impressive nasal appendage; *Tetsuwan Atom* was named "Astro Boy"; and "Astor Boynton III," who in the NBC Enterprises version was the son of Dr. Boynton (formerly Dr. Tenma), was derived from "Astro Boy." In most other countries, the series was rechristened *Mighty Atom* (with Dr. Tenma renamed "Dr. Atom"), but a conflict with an obscure American comic book character of that name prompted NBC Enterprises to break with international tradition. (As the series progressed, Dr. Ochanomizu/Elefun constructed a

1963

Also on TV in 1963:

Beany & Cecil
The Flintstones
The Jetsons
Lippy The Lion
The Mighty Hercules
Quick Draw McGraw
Space Angel
Tennessee Tuxedo
Touche Turtle
Wally Gator

L to R: Jetto (Astro Boy's big brother), Astro Girl, Astro Boy, their robot parents.

---

* *Astro Boy* was preceded by *Otagi Manga Calendar*, a 312-episode series of 5-minute shorts that premiered June 25, 1962—slightly more than 6 months prior to the debut of *Astro Boy*.

Clockwise from lower right: Dr. Packadermus J. Elefun, Astro Boy, Astro Girl, Nip, and Tuck.

Astro Boy uses his own energy to recharge one of the robot clowns at the Robot Circus.

The **Astro Boy** voice cast (l to r): Ray Owens, Billie Lou Watt, Gilbert Mack.

©1963 Kazumasa Hirai/Jiro Kuwata/Eiken

robot family for the titular hero, starting with a mother and father, and later a little sister, Astro Girl, and a big brother, Jetto.)

While *Astro Boy* was re-edited and redubbed to conform to American broadcast policies, much of the casual sadism of the original remained intact. Surprisingly, considering the youth market for which it was aimed, the morbid opening episode sequence involving the death of Astor Boynton was left untouched, as was the curiously cruel "black" humor surrounding Dr. Boynton's eventual descent into gibbering madness. These and other no-nonsense touches elevated *Astro Boy* from the usual kiddie adventure cartoon rut, encouraging adults to join in on the excitement.

Dr. Elefun, Astro Boy, and Dr. Boynton.

Although the animation was primitive to the point of nonexistence— the series popularized the Japanese animation technique of simulating movement by flat-cutting and lap-dissolving from pose to pose, rather than using inbetween or "smear" animation— *Astro Boy* moved with swiftness, vigor, intelligent plot development, and a welcome dash of knockabout humor. It became a major syndication hit, knocking the competition out of the box in major markets like New York and Los Angeles. Even in smaller markets where the lack of independent television channels confined the series to weekly rather than daily exposure, *Astro Boy* performed exceedingly well. The series prompted an onslaught of Japanese-made cartoons on the U.S. market, enriching Mushi and establishing the careers of many other aspirant animation houses.

The grandaddy of all lovable robot cartoon series, *Astro Boy* isn't seen too much today, due to its black and white status in a color-hungry TV world and the fact that Mushi's bankruptcy in 1972 somewhat bollixed up U.S. distribution rights (Osamu Tezuka tried to make a 1980s comeback with a new, full-color *Astro Boy*, but the spirit was gone and the updated series failed miserably; Tezuka died in 1989). It can safely be said, however, that no matter what one's personal feelings are regarding such Japanese products as *Speed Racer*, *8th Man*, *Kimba the White Lion*, *Battle of the Planets*, *Robotech* and *Voltron* (see individual entries on these series), chances are none of these projects would have made a dent outside their home base had it not been for the pioneering popularity of *Astro Boy*.

8th Man

Syndicated: 1965—1966. TCJ Animation Center/ABC Films. American adaptation by Gene Prinz.

8-Man was the title of a Japanese manga series or comic strip which first appeared on a weekly basis in April of 1963. Written by science fiction specialist Kazumasa Hirai and drawn by Jiro Kuwata, the strip was the story of Detective Rachiro Azuma, who after being killed by the notorious gangster Mukade, was recreated by the brilliant Dr. Tani in the form of a humanized robot. The new creation, 8-Man, retained Azuma's memory, sense of justice, and range of emotions, as well as his personal appearance; the difference was that the "new" Azuma was an atomic-powered marvel with approximately one thousand times the strength of any ordinary mortal. To maintain his power, 8-Man recharged his atomic energy supply with tiny strength pills, which in keeping with the relatively adult approach of the original strip were in the form of cigarettes. The android was also able to confound criminals by changing his facial features; according to Japanese comic strip historian Hisao Kato, 8-Man's favorite disguise was as the villain's gun moll!

In addition to greatly influencing the "friendly robot" Japanese comic strip creations to come, *8-Man* was converted into a 56-episode, half-hour animated TV series. These were shown in their home country and 52 of them were picked up for

American distribution by ABC Films. At that time, the title was changed to *8th Man* (the original title must have sounded too much like "8-Ball" for ABC Films' taste), the dialogue redubbed and the episodes re-edited, and the character names changed. Detective Rachiro Azuma became "Peter Brady" and his robot alter ego was imaginatively called "Tobor" (spell it backwards); the evil Mukade was rechristened "Saucer

Lip" (there's a name to strike fear in the hearts of law enforcement officers everywhere!); Dr. Tani was given the new name "Professor Genius"; and Police Chief Tanaka of "Metro City" was known as "Chief Fumblethumbs."

Battling local crooks, international spies and superhuman beings with stiff-armed impunity in such episodes as "The Horrible Honeybees," "The Gold Beetle of the Orient" and "Evil Jaw and the Devil Germs," *8th Man* remained in syndication until the early 1970s; in this respect, it outlasted the original *8-Man* comic strip, which ended in 1968. If *8th Man*'s concept sounds familiar, it's because the whole "android detective" idea was successfully applied to the popular 1973-1978 TV series *The Six Million Dollar Man*. The concept was again resurrected to spectacular effect by the 1985 theatrical feature film *Robocop*— which in turn was itself converted into a weekly cartoon series.

Gigantor

Syndicated: 1966. TCJ Animation Center/Delphi Associates Inc. American producers/adapters: Fred Ladd and Al Singer. Theme created by Lou Singer and Gene Raskin. Music coordinators, Dan Hart and George Craig. Supervising editor, P. A. Zavala. Titles designed by Robert E. Lee. Sound recording, Titra. Voices: Billie Lou Watt (Jimmy Sparks), Peter Fernandez (Dick Strong), Gilbert Mack (Bob Brilliant), Cliff Owens (Inspector Ignatz Blooper).

Gigantor. Sci-Fi Channel: 1993. Tokyo Movie Shinsha Co. Ltd. Produced by Fred Ladd. Animation producers, Yasuji Takahashi, Shigeru Akagawa. Directed by Tetsuo Imazawa, Shigeo Hasegawa, Kazuyuki Hirokawa, Minoru Okazaki.

©1963 Mitsuteru Yokoyama/Eiken

Gigantor was the American name for *Tetsujin 28-go*, a Japanese manga character created in 1958 by Mitsuteru Yokoyama. The character's name translates literally as "Iron Man No. 28"; he (it?) was developed during World War II as a flying battle machine designed to combat Allied troops. The U.S. Air Force bombed the robot lab into rubble, and after the war the scientists responsible for Tetsujin 28, Dr. Kaneda and Dr. Shikashima, decided to rebuild their creation as an instrument of peace rather than war (which didn't stop the robot from mercilessly blasting villains out of the sky). The giant, helmeted flying robot became an agent of the Japanese police; the mechanism was operated by Dr. Kaneda's young son Shotaro. (Some of the elements prevalent in this concept resurfaced, uncredited, in the 1967 Hanna-Barbera cartoon series *Franken-stein Jr. and the Impossibles*.)

Tetsujin 28 had a great deal of influence on the "giant robot" school of Japanese comic art; the property was spun off into a radio series, a brief live-action television program, and in 1963, a weekly half-hour animated adventure from TCJ Animation Center, which ran on Japanese network TV for four seasons. American producers Fred Ladd and Al Singer, who spent much of their careers mining Japanese animation for domestic distribution, secured the rights for 52 episodes of *Tetsujin 28* in 1965. The producers went the *Astro Boy* route of editing out excessive violence— though the implied offscreen deaths of several bad guys were retained— as well as portions of the plotlines that wouldn't appeal to American fans. The character names were then

1965

Also on TV in 1965:
Atom Ant
The Beatles
The Flintstones
Jonny Quest
Linus the Lionhearted
Mr. Magoo
Roger Ramjet
Underdog

11

©1963 Mitsuteru Yokoyama/Eiken

Jimmy Sparks races to meet a new threat with Gigantor's control unit in hand, followed by Bob Brilliant, Inspector Blooper, and Dick Strong.

"westernized": Inspector Otsuka became "Inspector Blooper"; Dr. Kaneda's son Shotaro became "Jimmy Sparks"; Dr. Shikashima became "Bob Brilliant"; and finally, since Producer Fred Ladd felt that the literal translation of "Iron Man No. 28" didn't sound modern enough, *Tetsujin 28-go* was completely rechristened as **Gigantor**.

Like *Astro Boy*, *Gigantor* was chock full of futuristic thrills both in this world and in the Outer Limits; its character designs ranged from the "straight" secret agent Dick Strong to the "silly" Inspector (who sounded like comic actor Frank Nelson in the American version), and it moved along briskly, satisfying viewers who were bored by the comparatively languid pace of many home-grown cartoons available in 1966. Most effective was *Gigantor*'s breathtaking variety of offbeat camera angles, including at least one point-of-view shot from inside the villain's mouth!

Only its black and white photography prevented *Gigantor* from becoming as enduring an American hit as its companion Japanese imports **Speed Racer** and **Marine Boy**. Cable TV's Sci-Fi Channel broadcast the full-color remake **New Gigantor** in September 1993 ("new" to the U.S., though it was actually produced in Japan in 1980). While the character designs and voice-work of this latest *Gigantor* were on a par with the 1965 version, the animation was fuller and the violence level was amplified to suit the tastes of the 1980s. Thankfully not altered for *Gigantor*'s revival was the original series' familiar calypso theme music. American producers had learned just how attached anime addicts were to favorite theme songs when the new *Speed Racer* of 1993 came a cropper by eliminating its beloved "Here He Comes/Here Comes Speed Racer" musical signature.

For those who need more convincing of the franchise's endurance, there is even a third iteration of the series: the 1992 **Tetsujin 28FX**, which has not yet made it across the Pacific to American televisions. Despite the apparent enthusiasm of the series' producers in mounting this '90s revival, however, it should probably be noted that ratings for this *Tetsujin 28* retread when it debuted in Japan on 5 April 1992 were abysmal, eliciting a mere 5.5 share and dropping to an even worse 1.9 by the fourth week. (Compare with **Dragon Ball**, then airing its 134th episode and also on-air in Japan at the time, which held strong at 20.3 during the same ratings week.)

1966

Also on TV in 1966:

Atom Ant
Batman
The Flintstones
George of the Jungle
Gumby
Magilla Gorilla
The Marvel Superheroes
The Mighty Heroes
The Monkees
Roger Ramjet
Space Ghost & Dino Boy
Star Trek

Prince Planet

Syndicated: 1966—1967. TCJ [Eiken Studios]/American-International. Created by Dentsu Advertising Ltd. and K. Fujita Associates. English-language version: Executive producers, James H. Nicholson and Samuel Z. Arkoff. Dialogue by Reuben Guberman. Music by Ronald Stein. Title song by Guy Hemrie and Jerry Styner. Vocals by the Carol Lombard Singers. Voice credits unavailable.

Prince Planet was standard-issue Japanese animation: A 21st century setting, plenty of outer space hardware, characters with rounded eyes that appeared to be buttoned to the heads, and (in the U.S. version) a peppy theme song chanted by an all-kid chorus. Prince Planet, a preteen who hailed from the pacifistic planet Radion, was a member in good standing of the Universal Peace Corps. The Galactic

Prince Planet.

©1965 Eiken

Council of Planets chose Prince Planet as their delegate to Earth; the Council wanted to invite Earth to join up, but couldn't do so until the third planet from the sun was purged of warmongers and criminals. The Prince was selected as ambassador because of his advanced intelligence and his heightened sense of right and wrong.

After his spaceship crashed in the American southwest, Prince Planet was befriended by Diana Worthy, daughter of a wealthy but kindly oil tycoon. It was Diana who suggested the "ordinary everyday name" of Bobby as an alias for the Prince, who wanted to pass as an Earth boy when not on duty in order to avoid being pinned down as an "alien." Relocating in New Metropolis, Prince Planet carried on his fight against evil and cruelty, armed by a special pendant round his neck. Marked with a personalized "P," the pendant was powered by atomic energy from planet Radion which endowed the Prince with supernatural powers, extra body strength and the ability to fly. Maintaining his peacekeeping stance, Prince Planet avoided fisticuffs, preferring to use strategy and speed to conquer his foes. From time to time, the Prince was spelled by two volunteer helpers, Arabian magician Ajababa and ex-champion wrestler Dan Dynamo. The chief villains were weighted down with giveaway names like Warlock the Martian and Krag of Kragmire.

Prince Planet with his friend Diana Worthy.

Broadcast in Japan during 1965 as *Yûsei Shônen Papii* (Planet Boy Papii), as with most Japanese imports, *Prince Planet* was clearly patterned after *Astro Boy*, but with more elaborate background art and with better dubbing and script-adapting from the English version production team. Syndicated by American-International Pictures (whose head men James H. Nicholson and Samuel Z. Arkoff generously bestowed upon themselves an "executive producer" credit), *Prince Planet* performed best in big cities with large Asian populations. Elsewhere the half-hour, 52-week *Planet* was handicapped by its retrogressive black and white photography, which has kept this exuberantly entertaining property off the videocassette shelves of the 1990s, and has confined its present existence to the dusty closets of private anime collectors.

Marine Boy

Syndicated: 1966—1967. Japan Telecartoons/K. Fujita Associates/Seven Arts. Produced by Minoru Adachi. Directed and written by Haruo Osanai. Background design by Akira Tomita. Art director, Yuichi Fukuhara. Music by Kenjiro Hirose and Setsuo Tsukabara. Theme music by Kenjiro Hirose. English version executive producer: Stanley Jaffee. English theme lyrics by Norman Gimble. Music by Norman Gould. Dubbing by Zavala/Riss. Dialogue adaptation by Peter Fernandez. Voices: Corinne Orr (Marine Boy/Neptina/Cli Cli); Jack Curtis (Dr. Mariner/various villains), Jack Grimes (Piper/Splasher/Dr. Fumble/Commander/more various villains); Peter Fernandez (Bulton).

The Japanese series *Kaitei Shônen Marine* (Seabottom Boy Marine), produced between 1965 and 1968 by Minoru Adachi for Japan Telecartoons and distributed in its homeland by K. Fujita Associates, was intended from the beginning to be sold to other countries. Oddly enough, the series, based on *The Dolphin Prince*, was seen in America well before it aired in Japan, from 1969 to 1971. The title character (possibly patterned after DC's comic book character *Aquaman*) was the redheaded preteen son of underwater scientist Dr. Mariner, who under the aegis of the 21st century Ocean Patrol fought crime and oppression beneath the ocean waves. To sustain his air supply, the hero carried a supply of "Oxygum"— oxygen-packed gum which when chewed would allow the chewer to breathe underwater (this element was left unexplained in many episodes, leading casual viewers to surmise that the human characters had all grown invisible gills). Marine traversed the briny in his P-1 minisub in the company of crew members Bulton and Piper— who like all the other common seamen on this series incongruously wore French-style berets— as well as a hyperintelligent dolphin named Splasher. He also had a vital underwater ally in the person of Neptina, a young mermaid who might well have been the first female TV cartoon character to appear "topless" (though the viewer was denied a glimpse of her breasts as her strategically arranged hair was always in the properly modest position). Neptina was the owner of a pearl necklace that allowed her to see into the future and warn Marine of impending danger. To better battle his enemies, Marine carried a lot of *Batman*-style hardware, notably his sonic boomerang, propeller-equipped boots, and electronic listening devices.

Marine and Splasher in *Secret of the Time Capsule.*

In its abundance of larger-than-life characters and florid dialogue exchanges, *Marine Boy* was as "sheer camp" as its American ad copy promised (after the premiere of *Batman* in 1966, the term "camp," once a vague reference to a film or TV series being corny or ridiculous without intending to be, was used as an umbrella term to describe any form of deliberately exaggerated entertainment). It wasn't hard, then, for the American translating firm of Zavala/Riss to come up with dialogue that matched the dizzy exuberance of the Japanese scenarists. Nor was it hard to match the lip movements of the original cartoons, since the Japanese dialogue had adopted the same measured, deliberate pace as the animation, bypassing the usual translating problem of having the English-speaking actors talk at a super accelerated pace to match the Japanese cadence.

Seven Arts Television domestically distributed the result, as had been planned by American producer Stanley Jaffee from the inception of *Kaitei Shônen Marine*; the U.S. title was *Marine Boy*. Unlike Japanese distributor K. Fujita, Seven Arts did not offer the series in a single package. To test the profitability of the syndicated market, only 26 episodes were offered at first, with a promise of 26 more should *Marine Boy* click. As it turned out, 75 half-hour color episodes made it into syndication, which many markets telecast on a Monday-through-Friday basis. *Marine Boy* enjoyed the formidable sponsorship of a major midwestern hamburger restaurant chain and might have been the most successfui Japanese import of the 1960s had not *Speed Racer* — also packaged in Japan by K. Fujita, though using different animation personnel— broken that record.

Marine and Tim Tim in *The Gigantic Sea Farm*.

Little was changed beyond the spoken language when the series made its Pacific crossing; the only significant alteration was in the character names of the hero and of Whitey the Dolphin, who became "Splasher" in the American version. Audiences in the U.S. were more than satisfied with *Marine Boy*. The series' limited animation techniques and production design often exceeded American TV standards, with extra points scored by the elaborate undersea background art by Akira Tomita. The one main problem with domestic distribution of *Marine Boy* was the dilemma usually facing Japanese cartoons in the States— namely, that the violence, even the comic violence, was more intense than what was usually permissible in the late 1960s. Seven Arts was in fact compelled to remove three episodes from the original 78-program manifest due to excessive mayhem (these episodes were restored for later syndication runs in the 1970s). What was left was still allegedly potent enough for the National Association for Better Broadcasting to complain that *Marine Boy* was "one of the very worst animated shows. Child characters in extreme peril. Expresses a relish for torture and destruction of evil characters." In this instance, NABB chose to see only what it wanted to see. Rather than luxuriating in the demise of the villains, Marine Boy invariably tried to rescue his enemies from the perils that their own perfidy had gotten them into. When the baddies would ungratefully attempt to kill Marine Boy all the same, any fate that befell them was richly deserved.

Kimba The White Lion

Caesar and Kimba

Syndicated: 1966—1967. Mushi Productions/NBC Enterprises. Created and produced by Osamu Tezuka. Directed by Eiichi Yamamoto. Music by Isao Tomita. American version: Executive Producer Fred Ladd. Editorial supervision by Zavala-Riss Productions. Theme song by Bernie Baum, Bill Grant, Florence Kaye. Voices: Billie Lou Watt (Kimba, Gypsy, Dodie Deer); Cliff Owens (Dan'l Baboon, Bucky Deer, Tom, Cassius); Francine Owens (Kitty); Gilbert Mack (Pauley Cracker, Tab, Claw); Hal Studer (Roger Ranger, Cheetah).

Leo the Lion. Mushi Productions/ Sonic International. Available 1966; not released until CBN premiere 1984.

Kimba the White Lion was an Americanization of *Jungle Taitei* ("Jungle Emperor"), an animated series based on a Japanese manga series by Osamu Tezuka (see *Astro*

Claw vs. Kimba

Boy). Tezuka's storyline, which began unravelling in October of 1950, was set in the African jungle. Its protagonist was Leo the white lion, son of "Jungle Emperor" Panja. After his mother Eliza was captured by the evil hunter Hamegg (who subsequently killed Panja), Leo was born in in the hold of the ship taking them to a European zoo. When the ship sank in a storm off the coast of East Africa, Eliza drowned. Leo, though, swam ashore in Aden and was adopted by a human boy named Kenichi, who raised the cub. Leo found himself balancing his predator instincts with lessons of beneficence and kindliness learned from his human master. After a long interlude with Kenichi, Leo returned to the jungle. The result was an animal civilization modelled after human

Kimba and Kitty help the animals plan an amusement park. Among the crowd are Dodie Deer (above Kitty), the evil hyenas Tab and Tom, and the (barely seen) Cassius, the panther.

society (of the "Utopian" variety), which dispensed justice among the creatures and formed an allied front against future human despoilers of the jungle. A mystical note was introduced with the Moonlight Stone, a strange and powerful energy source coveted by animals and humans alike.

Jungle Taitei ended its run in 1954, but remained popular enough in reprint form to inspire a 1965 animated series of the same title, produced by Osamu Tezuka's own Mushi Studios. Tezuka contacted NBC Enterprises when he first decided to produce the TV series. NBC liked the idea, and even put up the money to convert Mushi Productions from black & white to color production for the series.

NBC also took advantage of its position to insist on some major changes in the story. They did not want the long interlude in Aden, so the pilot episode ends up with Kimba swimming away from the sunken ship towards shore, and the next episode (which NBC numbered #8) opens with him walking ashore just in time to save Bucky Deer from Tab & Tom, Claw's hench-hyenas. Kimba had also suddenly grown from the babyish cub of the first episode to the adolescent lion of the rest of the series. The excision of the Aden period necessitated several flashbacks in subsequent episodes to explain how Kimba had attained his knowledge of human civilization. NBC also nixed Tezuka's idea of watching Kimba grow into adulthood, preferring him to remain an adolescent throughout the series. This was what forced Tezuka to make **Leo The Lion** a separate sequel series. When the 1989-'90 **Jungle Emperor** TV remake premiered on Japanese TV, the advertising said (in effect), "Now! See *Jungle Taitei* the way Osamu Tezuka intended it — without American interference!"

The **Kimba** production crew. Standing (l to r): Fred Ladd, Cliff (Ray) Owens, Hal Studer, Gilbert Mack. Seated (L to R): Eileen Ladd, Billie Lou Watt, Rose Mack, Francine Owens.

As with *Astro Boy*, the U.S. scenarists took it upon themselves to Americanize all the character names, coming up with such Yankee sobriquets as "Dan'l Baboon," "Pauley Cracker the Parrot," "Roger Ranger" and "King Specklerex"; Leo himself was now known as "Kimba the White Lion," which was also this series' American title.

The Kimba backstory is a fanciful soufflé about an ancient Egyptian "wisdom formula" passed on to an African tribe called the Kickapeels. The vessel of this passage was a white lion to whom Pharaoh "Tut Tut" had fed the formula. Handed down from generation to generation for nearly 4000 years, the animal kingdom founded upon high human intelligence was finally inherited by young Kimba. This story was gradually revealed in flashbacks during the total of 52 half-hour episodes.

The adult Kimba had his name restored to Leo in the sequel series **Leo The Lion**.

Claw's hench-hyenas, Tab and Tom.

Immediately after its initial Japanese run, *Jungle Taitei* was followed by a similarly titled sequel, ***Jungle Taitei Susume Leo!*** (Jungle Emperor Go Leo!), which charted the progress of the adult Leo/Kimba, his mate, and his two sons. This 26-week offering didn't get to the United States until purchased by the CBN cable service in 1984. Christian Broadcasting Network restored the main character's original name, and the sequel was run daily under the title ***Leo the Lion***.

In 1994, Disney studios released the theatrical animated feature ***The Lion King***, which although promoted as an "original story" was perceived by many anime buffs to be more than a little beholden to Tezuka's *Kimba the White Lion*. Both stories are tales of young male lions taking up the reins of power after their fathers are murdered; both include anthropomorphic talkative birds ("Zazu" in Disney's, "Pauley Cracker" in Tezuka's); both provide wizened baboon sages for their young protagonist (Disney's "Rafiki", Tezuka's "Dan'l Baboon"), not to mention the cackling evil hyena henchmen; both feature morale-boosting visages of ghostly pater lions in the clouds above.

Disney issued a statement that none of their animation staff had ever heard of Kimba (*or* Osamu Tezuka!), despite a statement from Simba voice actor Matthew Broderick that he thought he was being cast for a remake of Tezuka's classic TV series. Coincidence? You be the judge.

Speed Racer

Syndicated: 1967—1968. MTV: 1993. Tatsunoko and Yokino/K. Fujita/Trans-Lux, then Alan Enterprises. Produced, directed and created by Tatsuo Yoshida. Music by Nobuyoshi Koshibe. Animation and art direction by Ippei Kuri and Hiroshi Sasagawa. English adaptation written and directed by Peter Fernandez. Japanese production supervision by K. Fujita. American production supervision by Zavala-Riss. Voices: Peter Fernandez (Speed Racer); Corinne Orr (Trixie/Spridle/Mrs. Racer); Jack Curtis (Racer X/Pops Racer)

The New Adventures of Speed Racer. Syndicated: 1993. Fred Wolf Films/Speed Racer Entertainment/MWS Inc./Group W. Executive producer Fred Wolf. Produced by Walt Kubiak and Michael Algar. Supervising director, Bill Wolf. Story editor, David Wise. Sequence directors: Kent Butterworth, Bill Hutten, Tony Love, Neal Warner. Music score by Dennis C. Brown and Larry Brown. Theme music by Dennis C. Brown and Maxine Sellers. Overseas animation supervisors, Mik Casey and Shivan Ramsaran.

Once seen in childhood, ***Speed Racer*** is never forgotten, which can be a bogey or a blessing depending on one's attitude. Devotees of the daily, half-hour series can't get enough of Speed Racer and his adventures both on and off the race track. Non-fans find the program ridiculous in the extreme, its "funny" artwork jarringly at odds with its "straight" plotlines. Either way, the series has remained in healthy distribution since its simultaneous 1967 Japanese/American release— representing for many viewers the quintessential Japanese animated import.

The archaeology of *Speed Racer* has been meticulously traced by anime historian Fred Patten. In the original 1960s Japanese comic book created by Tatsuo Yoshida, Speed Racer's high-tech car was the star as indicated by the title ***Mach Go Go Go***; *Go* being the Japanese word for "Five," which explains the number 5 emblazoned on the side of the auto. Speed's original name was Go Mifune, after legendary Japanese film star Toshiro Mifune, and that explains the letter "M" on Speed's helmet and jacket. Go Mifune competed in worldwide racing events on behalf of his father Daisuke's Mifune Motors. Working on behalf of Daisuke's organization was his wife Aya, Go's kid brother/mascot Kuo, and an extended family of close friends and coworkers: Go's girlfriend Michi Shimua, mechanic Sabu, and a comedy-relief monkey (complete with cute cap) named Senpei. Casting an ominous shadow over the action was a mystery figure, the Masked Racer, who popped up sporadically to save Go Mifune from the various dishonest racers, master criminals and foreign spies that plagued the

1967

Also on TV in 1967:
Batfink
Batman
Birdman & The Galaxy Trio
The Fantastic Four
George of the Jungle
Magilla Gorilla
The Marvel Superheroes
The Mighty Heroes
The Monkees
Shazzan!
Space Ghost & Dino Boy
Spider-Man
Star Trek
Superman/Aquaman Hour

hero. Unbeknownst to Go, the Masked Racer was actually his older brother Kenichi, who for a complexity of top-secret reasons (including an implied death sentence from his own government!) was compelled to divorce himself from the rest of the Mifune family.

The serialized program, distributed by K. Fujita Associates, ran in prime-time on Japanese television, then was picked up by American distributor Trans-Lux for stateside distribution in 1967, in hopes of matching the U.S. success of another Fujita animated release, the previously discussed **Marine Boy**. As was usually the case with made-in-Japan cartoonery, Trans-Lux retained only the physical series, altering all the character names for domestic consumption. Go Mifune, as mentioned, was transformed into "Speed Racer"; his girl Michi became "Trixie"; mechanic Sabu was changed (logically) into "Sparks"; little brother Kuo was changed into "Spridle"; and Senpei the monkey was now "Chim Chim." The mysterious Masked Racer was altered to the mysterious "Racer X," while parents Daisuke and Aya Mifune were left with merely "Pops and Mom Racer" (evidently Trans-Lux lost its "name the baby" dictionary).

Once the names were changed, Trans-Lux began to recondition *Speed Racer*'s interior. The Japanese version piled steaming heaps of tense violence atop its standard intrigues of gangsters and secret agents. The really rough stuff would have to be weeded out for the American version, a job entrusted to writer/actor Peter Fernandez, a former radio juvenile performer and a "regular" in the world of redubbed Japanese animation. More than two decades later, Fernandez is still proud of the fact that in his variation of *Speed Racer*, no one is ever killed. (This may explain those arbitrarily inserted shots of prone and supine bad guys with comic book planets and stars circling around their heads, indicating that although they were down, they were not permanently out.)

The one aspect of *Speed Racer* blessedly left intact was Speed's car, known in the U.S. version as the Special Formula Mach Five. If you can't quite remember the function of each button on the Mach Five's steering wheel, the pilot episode, "The Great Plan," lays it all out. Button "A" activated the auto's jets; "B" handled the special grip tires for tough roads; "C" operated the rotating saws that could cut a swath through wooded terrain (hmmm—not very pro-ecological, there); "D" activated the deflecting mechanism, principally the bulletproof and crashproof windshield; "E" provided long-range headlight illumination; "F" was for underwater driving, operating the oxygen and peri-scope (Boy! was this *the neatest!*), and "G" released a little birdlike robot, ideal for sending and receiving messages. The most remarkable feature of the Special Formula Mach Five was that it boasted the only push-button transmission in the history of the automobile industry that never jammed.

Speed has to ride the guardrail to pass his foe in "The Sword Mountain Race."

As mentioned at the outset, virtually everyone who's seen it has vivid memories of the 52-episode *Speed Racer*, notably of its insistent theme song ("Here he comes/Here comes Speed Racer/He's a de-mon on wheels. . ."), but it's much harder to find anyone unequivocably in love with its production values. Even its truest fans are hard put to justify fully *Speed Racer*'s dizzying kaleidoscope of clumsy anima-tion, inordinately wide-eyed character designs, ragged bursts of violence, comic characters uneasily rubbing shoulders with deadly serious opponents, and that ear-drum-piercing voice given the allegedly amusing kid brother Spridle. The one firm element in *Speed Racer*'s everlasting favor is that it truly lived up to its American title—the damned thing never stopped moving, making it an ideal recent entry in the schedule of the MTV cable network, a service specializing in rapid-fire, "short attention span"

Left to right: Spridle, Sparks, Trixie, Speed Racer, Chim Chim, and of course, the fabulous Mach 5.

musical material.

In the early 1990s, plans were formed to update *Speed Racer*. A live-action feature film directed by Richard (*Lethal Weapon*) Donner was promised, but the most immediate result of these plans was the 13-week, syndicated *New Adventures of Speed Racer*, from Fred Wolf Films (Wolf's previous big-money cartoon entry had been *Teenage Mutant Ninja Turtles*). The characters and the Special Formula Mach Five were given a new, streamlined design courtesy of artist George Goodchild, and a fresh sci-fi angle was introduced with Speed's ability to travel through time. Unfortunately, either out of necessity or misguided homage, the animation quality was on the level of the original series. This might have been forgivable, and *New Adventures of Speed Racer* might have had a better chance at survival past its first season, had not the series committed the ultimate sacrilege: It changed the theme music!

The Amazing 3

Syndicated 1967—1968. Mushi Productions/Erika Productions. Created by Osamu Tezuka. Voices: Corinne Orr (Bonnie Bunny); Jack Grimes, Jack Curtis. Premiered on Japanese TV in 1965 as *W3 (Wonder 3)*.

Clockwise from lower left: Randy Carter, Zero Duck, Ronnie Horse, Bonnie Bunny, unidentified baddie, and Kenny Carter.

Created by Osamu Tezuka (see notes on *Astro Boy*), *W3* was a weekly sci-fi/adventure manga series which made its debut in *Shônen Magazine* (Boys' Magazine) in March 1965. In June of that year, a weekly, half-hour animated version of *W3* premiered on Japanese television, where it remained in distribution for the next twelve months. The "W" in the title stood for "Wonder"; the Wonder Three was a trio of extraterrestrials sent by the Galactic Congress to chart the future of the warmongering planet Earth. Should they determine Earth to be too dangerous for the rest of the galaxy to survive, the game plan was to destroy the planet. Once earthbound, the three aliens assumed the forms of a rabbit, a horse and a duck, but their secret was discovered by a young boy, Kenny Carter, younger brother of Randy Carter, an agent of an international anti-crime organization. Kenny persuaded the trio to help improve Earth instead of merely observing its problems. Setting aside their original intentions, the Wonder Three united with the Earth boy to combat evil.

In the wake of the earlier successful American runs of the Osamu Tezuka/Mushi Productions animated series *Astro Boy* and *Kimba the White Lion*, it was decided to bring *W3* to the states. Joe Oriolo Productions re-edited and rescripted the 52 episodes of the Japanese production to conform with American time limits and broadcast standards (though the violence quotient was still impressive). The major characters were given Americanized names. Major Boko the rabbit was now "Bonnie Bunny," Lance Corporal Noko the horse was "Ronnie Horse," Lieutenant J.G. Poko the duck was "Zero Duck," the boy Shinichi Hoshi was "Kenny Carter," and his older brother, Secret Agent Koichi Hoshi was "Randy Carter." The voices of the characters were dubbed into English, and the series was retitled ***The Amazing Three***. Sales were respectable in the larger TV markets, but *Amazing Three* never managed to match the popularity of earlier Tezuka/ Mushi imports.

The Amazing 3: Ronnie Horse, Bonnie Bunny, and Zero Duck.

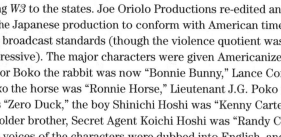

The Amazing 3's "Big Lorry" land vehicle — whipped up by Ronnie Horse from junkyard parts.

Battle of the Planets

Syndicated: 1978—1979. Gallerie International/Tatsunoko Productions/Sandy Frank. Japanese credits: Created and character designs by Tatsuo Yoshida. Series planning by Jinzo Toriumi and Satoshi Suyama. Produced by Ippei Kuri. Mecha design by Mitsuki Nakamura and Kunio Okawara. Animation directed by Sado Miyamoto. Music by Bob Sakuma. American version credits: Executive producer, Jameson Brewer. Produced and directed by David Hanson. Script adaptation: Jameson Brewer, Alan Dinehart III. Written by Jameson Brewer, Harry Winkler, Sid Morse, Howard Post, William Bloom, Richard Shaw, Kevin Coates, Alan Susin, Muriel Germano. Music by Hoyt Curtin. Voices: Alan Young (7- Zark-7/Keyop); Keye Luke (Zoltar); Casey Kasem (Mark); Janet Waldo (Princess); Ronnie Schell (Jason); Alan Dinehart III (Tiny).

G-Force. TBS: 1986. The Cartoon Network: 1995. Gallerie/Tatsunoko/Turner Program Services. American version written and directed by Fred Ladd. Voices: Sam Fontana (Ace Goodheart) Cameron Clarke (Dirk Daring): Jan Rabson (Hootie); Barbara Goodson (Agatha June/Pee Wee); Bill Capizi (Galactor).

Kagaku Ninja-Tai Gatchaman (Science Ninja Team Gatchaman) was a well-received Japanese animated series which ran in its own country from October 1972 to September 1974. Where *Gatchaman* differed from all the other "Earth is invaded" adventures was that it featured a team of five costumed heroes instead of a hero piloting a giant robot, and that the heroes battled the space invaders all around the world instead of just defending their home town each week.

The fantastic popularity of the first *Star Wars* film in 1977 put the sci-fi genre in great demand, and soon several American animation companies were drawing up plans to get their characters suited up, helmeted, and rocketed into the stratosphere. The first producer on the syndicated scene was gameshow distributor Sandy Frank, who acquired the ready-made *Gatchaman*, hired Hanna-Barbera veterans Jameson Brewer and Alan Dinehart III to adapt the scripts into English, edited out the more graphically violent passages, commissioned new animation of an R2D2-like robot character named "7-Zark-7" (and his "dog," 1-Rover-1) to narrate and bridge the continuity gaps left by the trimming, and retitled the whole package ***Battle of the Planets***. Total cost to Sandy Frank: $4.5 million. It was, as *TV Guide* reported in 1985, more than was necessary, but Frank was a man willing to overspend if he foresaw a gigantic return.

Set in the 21st Century, the Sandy Frank version of *Gatchaman* centered around the exploits of G-Force: five young heroes who sported bird costumes and traveled the cosmos in their supership. The fact that all the *Gatchaman* action took place on Earth didn't deter Frank — one of his additions was a stock shot of the team's fighter aircraft, the *Phoenix*, now called a spaceship, which was often shown flying through space. The narrator would intone, "G-Force has now arrived on the planet (whatever)" for that week's adventure. If that week's planet happened to look like Paris or Moscow or London or New York, then so be it. G-Force was a protective squad commanded by Mark (the characters did not have last names) the Eagle, and consisting of four war orphans: Jason the Condor, Tiny the Horned Owl, Princess the Swan and Keyop the Swallow. Headquartered beneath the seas of Earth at Center Neptune, the G-Force spent the better part of its time rallying together with the cry "Transmute!" (translation: get on your uniforms!), the better to stem the megalomaniacal inclinations of Zoltar, insidious leader of the Spectra monsters trying to conquer the galaxy, and the mysterious Luminous One, leader of the planet Spectra.

Eighty-five half-hour episodes of *Battle of the Planets* (whittled down from the 105 original *Gatchaman* episodes) were ready for Monday-through-Friday telecasts by

The *Phoenix* fighter aircraft / "spaceship."

1978

Also on TV in 1978:

Battlestar Galactica
The Bionic Woman
The Incredible Hulk
Nelvanamation
The Six Million Dollar Man
Tarzan & The Super Seven
Wonder Woman
The Wonderful World of Disney
Young Sentinels (Space Sentinels)

Mark and Jason (out of uniform) horsing around.

The G-Force take wing.

the spring of 1978. However, the kiddie TV market's swing back to violence and suspense by the end of the '70s rather mitigated the bowdlerized *Battle*'s impact, the end result being that Sandy Frank nearly lost his original heavy investment. Commenting on his mistimed nonviolent approach, Mr. Frank, the distributor of *The Dating Game* and *The $1.98 Beauty Show*, ascribed the error to "my damn high ideals." Still, thanks to a razzle-dazzle promotional push ("I sold it like the Second Coming"), the producer was able to clear $15 million in sales.

Although ratings weren't bad, *Battle of the Planets* had only a so-so first run, regularly beaten out by older cartoons and network reruns. The mild reaction to *Battle* effectively halted American distribution of the sequel to *Gatchaman*, which premiered on Japanese television in 1978 under the title ***Gatchaman II***. *Gatchaman II* finally made it onto the American airwaves in 1996 (see the ***Eagle Riders*** entry on page 39), and it's rumored that the recent three-volume high-quality *Gatchaman* OAV remake (featuring a soundtrack produced by Earth, Wind & Fire's Maurice White and Bill Meyers) has been optioned for future U.S. home video release.

In 1986, Turner Program Services acquired the series and set to work making a completely new Americanized version. Turner chose a different selection of 85 (of 105) episodes than earlier producer Frank had chosen, this time leaving in all but the most violent shows — and some episodes are indeed violent, with characters dying on screen. In this new incarnation, dubbed ***G-Force***, the bogus 7-Zark-7 character was dispensed with, and Turner grafted on new soundtracks and renamed the leading characters once again: Mark was now "Ace Goodheart," Jason was "Dirk Daring," and the Princess "Agatha June," indicating the generally derisive tone of the new adaptations. Although the substantially unedited new version was much truer to its original Japanese incarnation, as *G-Force*, *Gatchaman* failed to make any impact whatsoever in America, lasting only five episodes on TBS. The property languished until January of 1995, when it finally aired in its entirety on Turner's new Cartoon Network.

Star Blazers

Syndicated: 1979—1980. Office Academy and Sunwagon Productions/Westchester. Produced by Yoshinobu Nishizaki. Directed and created by Leiji Matsumoto. Music by Hiroshi Miyagawa.

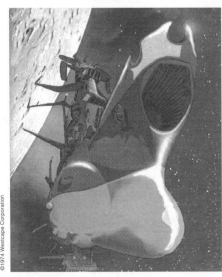

The *Argo* (or space battleship *Yamato* in the original version).

Star Blazers began in Japan in 1974 as a serialized weekly under the title **Space Battleship Yamato** (*Uchû Senkan Yamato*), the titular vehicle named for the legendary World War II Japanese warship. Leiji Matsumoto, later the guiding force behind the animated ***Captain Harlock***, created the half-hour series and the manga series upon which it was based; both were set in the year 2199.

The plot: the Earth is being radiation bombed by the planet Gamilas, led by the despotic Dessler. The faraway planet Iscandar, headed by good Queen Stasha, offers help to our beleaguered globe in the form of a "cosmic cleanser" which can protect Earth from the radiation, but she has no way to deliver it. Earth has to send an expedition to Iscandar to get it, but Iscandar is on the far side of the galaxy, with the entire Gamilas Empire in the way. Gamilas space cruisers have Earth under surveillance, so any attempt to build a starship will be detected. However, Gamilas attacks have also dried up Earth's oceans, exposing the wreck of the giant WWII battleship *Yamato*. So the Earth government secretly tunnels up from below and builds a state-of-the-art spaceship within the *Yamato*'s hull. In the American version, the *Yamato* is rechristened the *Argo*. Earth's Star Force, led by Admiral Juzo Okita and his aide Susumu Kodai, set out for Iscandar in the *Yamato*. The Star Force also includes Daisuke Shima, chief of operations; ship's doctor Sado; and Kodai's lady friend, radar operator Yuki Mori. The crew also includes a comic-relief robot, Analyzer, and a cyborg mechanic,

Captain Avatar and Leader Desslock

Sandor (these characters, incidentally, were created long before the
Star Wars films, so Matsumoto
cannot be accused of rip-off, unlike
many of his contemporary
animators).

Also on TV in 1979:
Battlestar Galactica
Buck Rogers in the 25th Century
The Incredible Hulk
Tarzan & The Super Seven
Wonder Woman
The Wonderful World of Disney

The first 26 episodes of *Space
Battleship Yamato*, subtitled for U.S.

Derek Wildstar and Nova.

release as "The Quest for Iscandar," chronicled the battle to save Earth. This *Yamato* package performed admirably on Japanese TV, despite general pessimism among Japanese TV producers that sci-fi animation (as compared to the more prevalent giant robot or costumed hero shows of the time) could never attract the generally juvenile viewers who were thought to make up most of Japan's cartoon-viewing audience in those days. In other words, *Yamato* changed the way people thought about animation—especially relatively serious sci-fi animation—in Japan. In 1978, *Space Battleship Yamato* was revived with a new group of 26 half hours, subtitled "The Comet Empire" for the U.S. release, wherein the evil Dessler aligns with Prince Zordar, ruler of Empire City, a cometlike metropolis which draws its strength from devouring other planets for fuel. This time it's the Earth Defense Fleet which sends out the *Yamato* rescue team, prompted by a cry for help from the planet Telazart (one of whose residents, the beauteous Trelaina, later becomes Daisuke Shima's sweetheart).

It was the above-mentioned 52 episodes which Claster Studios, envisioning marketing tie-ins on behalf of its Hasbro Toys division, bundled together in 1979 and syndicated to selected big cities in the U.S. as a Monday-through-Friday strip. The title *Star Blazers* was not the first choice: Claster dallied briefly with *Star Force*, which was vetoed as sounding a shade too much like *Star Wars*.

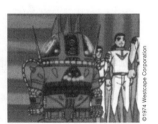

Dr. Sane and the robot IQ-9.

Claster toned down the more violent passages of *Space Battleship Yamato* and redid the character names. Admiral Okita was now "Captain Avatar"; Susumu Kodai was "Derek Wildstar" (prophetic in that Wildstar would later be the name of Claster's music division); Daisuke Shima was "Mark Venture"; Dr. Sado was "Dr. Sane"; Yuki Mori was "Nova"; Leader Dessler was "Leader Desslock"; and Queen Stasha became the more stellar-sounding "Queen Starsha." The planet Gamilas became "Gamilon," and the robot Analyzer was redubbed "IQ-9," an obvious derivative of *Star Wars*' comic-relief robot C-3PO.

Wisely, Claster avoided some of the less judicious cuts that producer Sandy Frank made in adapting **Gatchaman** into the Americanized **Battle of the Planets**. *Star Blazers* retained the plot and character complexities that were trademarks of *Space Battleship Yamato*, and as such was welcomed enthusiastically by the anime fans who'd been so sorely disappointed by *Planets*.

Queen Starsha of the planet Iscandar.

Unfortunately, the decision to limit syndication to only the most important markets resulted in a lukewarm ratings showing for *Star Blazers*. The series didn't really pick up steam until it went out in the 1980s to medium-sized cities with substantial Asian populations. At that time, Claster included 25 more episodes to the *Star Blazers* manifest, comprised of the final *Space Battleship Yamato* story arc of 1980, called "The Bolar Wars" in U.S. release. Originally telecast in Japan during 1980-'81 as **Uchû Senkan Yamato III**, "Bolar Wars" was named after the Bolar Federation, whose war with the Gamilons over the conquest of the Milky Way threatened to annihilate the Earth and all other "peaceful" planets.

1980

Also on TV in 1980:
Buck Rogers in the 25th Century
Heathcliff
The Incredible Hulk
Thundarr The Barbarian

Go Nagai's **Grandizer**, from the **Force Five** series.

Princess Aurora from Leiji Matsumoto's **Spaceketeers**, part of the **Force Five** series.

Leiji Matsumoto's **Dangard Ace**, from the **Force Five** series.

Currently, the three *Star Blazers* TV series, plus several theatrical-quality movie features, live on in America through a series of home video releases. *Yamato 2520*, a current OAV remake featuring a newly redesigned *Yamato* by none other than *Blade Runner*'s Syd Mead, has yet to make it to American shores.

Force Five

Syndicated 1980—1981. Toei Animation Co., Ltd./Jim Terry Productions. Music by Shunsuke Kikuchi. American adaptation: Directed by Kenneth Feuerman. Written by Mike Haller. Produced by Jim Terry. Voices: Greg Kirkelie; Collins Walker; Laura Cummins; Bob Linda King; Betty McIvor; Pearl Terry; Sean Faherty; Jim Terry, Jr. and Mr. Angelo.

This syndicated TV program consisted of *five* different Japanese series: **Dangard Ace, Grandizer, Gaiking, Spaceketeers,** and **Starvengers.** It was designed as a weekday cartoon package with each sub-series to be shown on the same day of the week. This setup allowed viewers to watch **Force Five** as a daily program, or to pick any one of the five and watch it on a weekly basis. The five original programs were all much longer sci-fi serials (*Grandizer* alone ran 74 episodes), produced in Japan by Toei Animation. Each episode usually stood alone, but there was a gradual continuity of story from the first episode to the last. However, American TV standards at this time (1980) required episodes which could be shown interchangeably with no story development. When American producer Jim Terry secured the rights to these Toei shows, he had no problem culling 26 essentially generic episodes from each of the five series to make up a total of 130 episodes for the entire package.

Gaiking, from the **Force Five** series.

Grandizer (**UFO Robot Grandizer**—created by Go Nagai; 74 episodes, 1975), *Gaiking* (**Ôzora Maryû** or "Demon Dragon of the Heavens"; 44 episodes, 1976*)*, and *Starvengers* (**Getta Robo G**—created by Go Nagai; 39 episodes, 1975) each featured heroes in giant robots who fought to keep Earth free from demonic space invaders who attacked with their own evil giant robots. Most of the villains had horns, befitting "foreign devils" (the Allied soldiers in Japanese WWII propaganda cartoons had foreign-devil horns). The fans' favorite was *Starvengers*, in which the invaders were the Pandemonium Empire, led by Emperor Ramzorch. His trusted commander was Captain Führer, who looked amazingly like a tall Adolf Hitler with a longhorn steer's horns.

In *Dangard Ace* (**Wakusei Robo** or "Planetary Robot" **Dangard A**—created by Leiji Matsumoto; 56 episodes, 1977), Earth discovered a new paradisical planet, Promete, out beyond Pluto. It was just what was needed to save overcrowded, resource-depleted Earth. Unfortunately, a tyrannical space empire discovered Promete at the same time, and it became a race to colonize it first. Dangard Ace was the giant-robot escort warship which fought off the Krell Corps' monsters with which sinister Dr. Monocle sought to destroy Earth's scientific space expedition flying there.

In the more humorous *Spaceketeers* (**SF Saiyûki** or "Sci-Fi *Saiyûki*" **Starzinger**—created by Leiji Matsumoto; 64 episodes, 1978), our heroes on the *Cosmos Queen* flew across the galaxy toward the Decos Star System to get a desperately needed power system, with only vague hints as to what their mission was or how close they might be to getting there. The leader of the expedition was lovely but inexperienced Princess Aurora. The three wisecracking, boastful space heroes who cockily promised to protect her were Jesse Dart (Saiyûki), Porkos (the Pig Demon, usually called Pigsy in transla-

tions) and Aramos (the Sand Demon, usually called Sandy). As should be obvious from these character names, Jim Terry tried to make this a spacegoing *Three Musketeers* with a futuristic D'Artagnan, Porthos, and Aramis.

Prior to broadcast of *Force Five*, the giant/flying/transforming robot craze had not fully hit American shores. In 1979, Mattel introduced a line of giant-robot action toys known as the *Shogun Warriors*, which featured most of the robot characters from the *Force Five* collection. These toys were a wild success in and of themselves, despite the absence of the television programs they were derived from. Ironically, by the time Jim Terry was ready to sell the syndicated TV package, Mattel had already lost the rights to the characters—creating an unfortunate situation wherein the toys and the TV shows were unable to reinforce each other. As it turned out, the toys were probably more successful than the *Force Five* TV shows themselves, but within three years, America was knee-deep in giant-robot culture anyway, including *Voltron*, *Transformers*, *Gobots*, *Orbots*, and a raft of other imitators of various degrees of quality.

Starvengers, from the *Force Five* series.

SuperBook

Syndicated: 1982. CBN/Tatsunoko Productions. Produced by Warren Marcus and Jason Vinley. English version by Echo Productions. Theme music: Live Oak Sound. Written by Ray Owens and Billie Lou Watt. Voices: Billie Lou Watt, Sonia Owens, Helene Van Koert, Ray Owens, Hal Studer, Gil Mack. Original animation by Tatsunoko Production Co., Ltd.; Screenplay by Akiyoshi Sakai. Directed by Masakazu Higuchi, Kenjiro Yoshida. Character Design by Akiko Shitamoto. Music by Masahito Maruyama.

The Flying House. Syndicated: 1982. CBN/Tatsunoko Productions. Production supervised by Warren Marcus, Ned Vankervich. Production associate, Greg Cummings. English version by Echo Productions. Written by Ray Owens. Theme music: Live Oak Sounds. Voices: Billie Lou Watt, Sonia Owens, Hal Studer, Helene Van Koert, Peter Fernandez, Ray Owens, George Gunneau. Original animation by Tatsunoko Production Co., Ltd.; Screenplay by Akiyoshi Sakai. Directed by Masakazu Higuchi, Mineo Fuji. Character Design by Hajime Fukuoka. Music by Hiroshi Takada.

Syndicated in 1982 by the Christian Broadcasting Network and cablecast at the same time over the CBN service (now known as The Family Channel), *SuperBook* and *The Flying House* were the first nationally distributed religious cartoon series since 1960-65's *Davey and Goliath*. The two interrelated CBN series originally aired on Japanese television, where the 26-episode *SuperBook* had been titled **Anime Oyako Gekijô** ("Animated Parent and Child Theatre") and the 52-episode *The Flying House* was called **Tondera House no Dai Boken** ("Great Adventures of Amazing House"). Both programs involved two precocious children— Chris and Joy— and their "R2D2" style talking robot, Gizmo, who wore a cross on his chest so we wouldn't lose track of the theological throughline. In both series, the kids and the robot were transported to biblical times. *SuperBook* transported them through the Old Testament by way of a huge, fourth-dimensional Bible, while in *Flying House*, the titular residence, actually a scientist's combination laboratory/spaceship, whisked the protagonists back to the events of the New Testament.

The twin series were animated by Tatsunoko Production Co., the same Japanese studio responsible for *Robotech* and *Speed Racer*, and as a result *Superbook* and *Flying House* shared a strong artistic resemblance to those more sectarian projects. The children were wide-eyed, chipmunk-toothed "cartoony" characters while the Biblical personalities were drawn realistically, though still with eyes far rounder than those found among residents of Jerusalem. The episodes evoked the bizarre, unsettling atmosphere common to viewers unfamiliar with anime, with quirky tidbits of inappropriate (especially for the Christian religious theme) humor, sudden jolts of violence, stop-and-go animation, grotesque facial expressions, and offpaced editing.

And as for the dialogue, during the *Flying House* scene in which Jesus is nailed to the cross (yes, that was in there, too), the Son of Man murmurs, somewhat ahead of schedule, "Father, forgive them. They know not what they do." Whereupon one of the

1982

Also on TV in 1982:
Adv's of the Little Prince
Blackstar
The Love Boat
Mork & Mindy
The New Fat Albert Show
Scooby and Scrappy-Doo Hour
Spider-Man & His Amazing Friends

Chris, Joy and Gizmo from *SuperBook*.

© 1982 Tatsunoko Productions

Roman officers (who looks like a *Speed Racer* villain) stops hammering, glares at Jesus and snarls, "Are you implying that we don't know our job?"

SuperBook and *Flying House* seldom cracked the major TV commercial outlets, but can still be seen on local UHF religious channels and on such Christian cable services as the Trinity Broadcasting Network. A third biblical series produced in 1983 by Tatsunoko, the 26-episode **Pastcon Travel Tantei Dan** ("Pastcon Travel Detective Team") featured the same leading characters as in *SuperBook* and *Flying House*, but was never shown in the U.S.

1983

Also on TV in 1983:

Dungeons & Dragons
He-Man & The Masters
of the Universe
Inspector Gadget
Pole Position
Walt Disney

Thunderbirds 2086

Showtime: 1983-1986. Syndicated: 1986. ITC Entertainment. Executive in charge of production, Robert Mandell. Executive producers, Banjiro Uemura and Shinji Nakagawa. Technical supervisor, David Gregg. Dialogue recording supervision by Peter Fernandez. Storymen: Owen Lock, Robert Mandell. Music composed by Kentaro Haneda. Theme music composed by Koji Makaino. Performed by the Columbia Symphony Orchestra. Produced in cooperation with ITC Entertainment (Japan) Ltd. Voices: Joan Audiberti, Paollo Audiberti, John Belluci, Laura Dean, Earl Hammond, Ira Lewis, Keith Mandell, Alexander Marshall, Lori Martin, Terry Vantell.

The original 1966 *Thunderbirds* series was a Gerry and Sylvia Anderson "Supermarionation" production, featuring a marionette process combining the traditional strings with electronic impulses that allowed the plastic puppets to move their eyes, blink, raise their eyebrows and move their lips in a reasonably lifelike fashion. *Thunderbirds* was set in the 21st century, and detailed the exploits of International Rescue, an impossible missions force located on a farflung Pacific atoll. Jeff Tracy headed the Thunderbirds team, which embarked in high-tech vehicles loaded with super-sophisticated equipment to rescue those unfortunates trapped in seemingly inextricable circumstances, and to prevent interplanetary criminals from pulling off their "foolproof" crimes.

© Toei Animation Co. Ltd./ITC Entertainment, Inc.

The three primary craft — TB1, TB2, and TB3 — interlock to form the nucleus of International Rescue's Thunderbirds team.

Thunderbirds 2086, the long-delayed animated version of this property, was telecast daily over Showtime pay-cable in the U.S. in 1983. First broadcast in Japan in 1982 as **Kagaku Kyûjo-Tai TechnoVoyager** ("Science Rescue Team TechnoVoyager"), no mention was made of Gerry and Sylvia Anderson in the credit titles, and none of the original characters appeared in the animated version. In place of the all-W.A.S.P. Tracy family, the new Thunderbirds International Rescue Organization was a five-person team of unrelated, multicultural adventurers: Jesse Rigel (red-haired), Dylan Beyda (dark-haired), Jonathan Jordan Jr. (African American), Gran Hanson (silver-haired, middle-aged authority figure), and Kallan James (blonde-haired girl). The squareheaded, beady-eyed Anderson character designs were skipped for standard anime renditions: attractive, wild-haired characters with round or almond-shaped eyes.

Operating (per the series' title) in 2086, this *Thunderbirds* crew all had personalized shuttle vehicles and versatile backpacks. As in the Supermarionation *Thunderbirds*, five main vehicles were utilized for search and rescue: Thunderbird-l was a shuttle, TB-2 a hypersonic transport, TB-5 a drilling vehicle, etc. While this holdover from the original was maintained, the cliffhanger structure was not; all stories on *Thunderbirds 2086* were self-contained half-hours, packing in plenty of action and suspense while keeping a well-measured pace.

The technological advances presented on the series were logical given the present rate of spaceware progress, so that the futuristic ambience of *Thunderbirds 2086* looks more like intelligent speculation rather than farfetched "sci-fi." Plots were cut from the *Star Trek* cloth, but were well-enough constructed to avoid imitation. The strictly business storylines allowed for a bare minimum of spectacular effects and resorted to violence only as a logical extension of the action, something well-suited to the series' limited animation.

International Rescue's Earth Base Command Center: the Arcology, a specialized city built on a Pacific island.

© Toei Animation Co. Ltd./ITC Entertainment, Inc.

In keeping with the Andersons' original *Thunderbirds*, the characters in the animated version behaved coolly and professionally, with none of the unnecessary histrionics or gratuitous kidding around which often weakened American-produced extraterrestrial cartoons. Teamwork was emphasized, as opposed to the maverick types in anime efforts like **Robotech** and **Captain Harlock**. Under the direction of actor/writer Peter Fernandez, the voice acting on the English-language version was realistic, more so than that on previous Fernandez projects such as **Speed Racer**.

©1982 Toei Animation Co. Ltd./ITC Entertainment, Inc.

The Thunderbirds team (l to r): Dylan Beyda, Kallan James, Gran Hanson, Jonathan Jordan Jr., and Jesse Rigel.

All in all, the 24 episodes of *Thunderbirds 2086* were capably done, and a significant improvement on the already commendable Supermarionation version. But though its level of maturity fit right in with the Showtime schedule, *Thunderbirds 2086* was less successful opposite such child-oriented competition as *He-Man* and *G.I. Joe* when syndicated commercially in 1986 and 1987.

Tekkaman the Space Knight

Syndicated: 1984—1985. William Winckler/Tatsunoko Production Co. Ltd. American version: Directed by Dianne Foster. Produced by William Winckler. Written by Frederick Patten and William Winckler. Music by Bob Sakuma. Original animation by Tatsunoko Production Co., Ltd. Created by Kenji Yoshida and Ippei Kuri. Written by Jinzo Toriumi. Voices: Bill Hederly, Jr. (Barry Gallagher); Reginald Greg Bennett (Andro); Kathy Pruitt (Patricia Richardson); Robert O'Keefe (Dr. Edward Richardson/Emperor Devoral); Clancy Syrko (Commander Randrox, Narrator); Jean Veloz (Mutan); Ken Kamp.

©1975 Tatsunoko Production

Building upon their success with **Gatchaman** was Tatsunoko "Home of the Heroes" Production's **Uchû no Kishi Tekkaman** (Space Knight Tekkaman), which in 1975 followed *Gatchaman* by three years. In the 21st century, humanity had begun its exploration of the Solar System, establishing bases as far out as Uranus. Earth's swelling population and diminishing resources gave rise to the U.N. Space Development Center, an agency funded and supervised by a now-unified planetary government dedicated to locating and terraforming a new homeworld for the planet's five billion-odd inhabitants. Humanity encounters its first outside threat in the form of the evil Waldstar aliens, also searching for inhabitable planets, and it's in a confrontation with them that the space exploration craft *Space Angel* and its brave captain are lost.

Eighteen-year-old Joji Minami, hot-shot pilot and even more hot-headed leader of the Space Knights, dons a magnificent battlesuit made of a mysterious "Tekka" alloy to become the heroic "Tekkaman." As his weapon he wields the "TekkaLance," capable of extending a full ten meters; as his craft, he rides the "Pegase," more like the giant robot Gigantor than the fabled steed of legend, which holds the Tekkaman armor when Joji isn't wearing it. On Joji's team is the beautiful teenaged Hiromi Amachi, systems engineer of the Space Knights' vessel, *Blue Earth*, and daughter of the inventor of the first interstellar spaceship; Andro Umeda, a humanoid alien who is suspected as an enemy spy but ends up throwing in his lot with the Space Knights once he sees Joji's true "burning spirit" in action; and Mutan, an aptly named mutant from the planet Sanno, full-time teleporter and part-time pet to the girlish Hiromi.

©1975 Tatsunoko Production

Unlike *Gatchaman*, the action in *Tekkaman* takes place not on Earth but in outer space. Syndicated by William Winckler (who also produced and shared a writing credit) in 1984 as a weekly television series, Winckler reportedly hoped to use the proceeds from the syndication of the first 13 episodes to purchase the remaining 13, but was unable to realize a sufficient profit.

For the English-language adaptation of the series, the title was subtly rearranged from "Space Knight Tekkaman" to **Tekkaman the Space Knight**, including a by-now expected Anglicizing of cast names: Joji Minami to "Barry Gallagher"; Hiromi Amachi and her father to "Patricia and Dr. Edward Richardson"; and the evil Waldstar aliens to

Tekkaman astride the robot Pegase.

©1975 Tatsunoko Production

the evil "Waldarians." However, other names remained the same, such as suspected spy-turned-ally Andro, the psionically talented pet Mutan, and Tekkaman's transport/storage locker, Pegase. Most importantly, Tekkaman remained Tekkaman.

On-air in Japan at roughly the same time as another Tatsunoko "hero" show, **Hariken** or "Hurricane" **Polymer**, the production of *Tekkaman* suffered from a lack of personnel and resources and, as a result, suffered an unusual fate in the world of Japanese-animated TV series: It was canceled in mid-story. This was unfortunate, as producers had been planning a much longer story wherein the Space Knights would eventually find their second Earth, and Joji/Barry would find the father he had long thought dead. The ending, producers say, would have been "even more tragic than *Gatchaman*," a reference to a plot twist wherein the long-sought-after father of the series' main character turns out to be the leader of the bad guys the Gatchaman team has been fighting all along.

Tekkaman the Space Knight premiered in Toronto in September 1984, but never achieved more than a dozen syndicated sales during 1984-'85. In Japan, the series lives on in a recently U.S.-syndicated once-a-week remake, under the title **Uchû no Kishi Tekkaman Blade**, formerly broadcast here on UPN as **Teknoman** (see the entry later in this chapter).

1984

Also on TV in 1984:

Challenge of the Gobots
Danger Mouse
Dungeons & Dragons
Fat Albert & The Cosby Kids
He-Man & The Masters
   of the Universe
Inspector Gadget
The Mighty Orbots
Pole Position
Thundercats
Transformers

Voltron: Defender of the Universe

Syndicated: 1984—1985. World Events Productions. Executive producer, Peter Keefe. Produced by Steve Sterling. Written by Jameson Brewer, Howard Albrecht, Coslough Johnson, Stan Oliver, Jack Paritz, Michael Walker and Sol Weinstein. Music by Dale Schacker. Original animation by Toei Co. Ltd. Voices: Jack Angel, Michael Bell, Peter Cullen, Neil Ross, B. J. Ward, Lennie Weinrib.

Voltron consists of two separate Japanese giant-robot serials from Toei Co. Ltd.: the 52-episode **Hyakujû-Ô Go-Lion** ("Hundred-Beast King Go Lion," renamed **Lion Force Voltron**), broadcast in Japan during 1981-'82; and the 56-episode **Kikô Kantai Dairugger-XV** ("Armored Fleet Dairugger-XV," renamed **Vehicle Team Voltron**), broadcast in Japan during 1982-'83. Both storylines were set in a far future in which Earth was the headquarters of a federation of peace-loving planets, the Galaxy Alliance, whose defense force was the Galaxy Garrison.

In *Lion Force Voltron*, the GG sent a team of young Space Explorers to the planet Arus, which had recently been devastated by the evil reptile King Zarkon (who wore French Court dress, like the rest of the "nobles" on this series) of planet Doom. The Explorers' mission was to learn the secret of Arus' greatest defense, five robot lions which could merge into the super-robot Voltron, which resembled a medieval knight with a stylized lion-head helmet. The five young Earth heroes (Sven, Keith, Lance, Pidge and Hunk) discovered that Princess Allura had survived the destruction, and from her base in the Castle of Lions was attempting to free her world from Zarkon's lash. They became the new pilots of the robot lions, and when Sven was wounded (killed outright in the Japanese version), Allura herself replaced him. The *Lion Force* storyline followed the continuing fight of the five against the Doom robeasts of Zarkon and his cunning son, Prince Lotor, and the black magic of Zarkon's witch-advisor, Haggar.

The *Vehicle Team Voltron* story was set a few years later. After Zarkon was defeated, the Space Explorers brought the Voltron technology back to Earth and used it to build their own even larger Voltron, composed of fifteen smaller robots instead of only five. This Vehicle Team Voltron was sent on the spaceship *Explorer* to search for habitable new planets. At the time, one of the enemies of the Galaxy Alliance was Drule, a planetary dictatorship which was dying from pollution and exhausted resources. Rather than sending out their own space expeditions to search for a new planet, they just followed the *Explorer* and attempted to claim-jump any worthwhile planets it might find.

©1981 Toei Co. Ltd./World Events Productions

Five robot lions, piloted by five heroes, are required to form **Lion Force Voltron**.

The *Vehicle Team Voltron* episodes trace the adventures of the fifteen pilots of the Vehicle Team (three teams of five vehicles each for Air, Land, and Sea), plus the crew of the *Explorer*, as they search for new planets. They would either do battle with natural perils like volcanoes, etc., or they would have to form Voltron to fight off the claim-jumping Drule invaders. Eventually, the Drule commander Hazar saw the folly of all this, and urged the emperor to join with the humans rather than fight them. Imprisoned for his treason, Hazar later escaped and joined a popular revolt against the government's tyranny. When planet Drule began to self-destruct like Krypton, Voltron arrived just in time to rescue the "good" Drules before the planet exploded.

Fifteen special vehicles drawn from Land, Air and Sea teams combine to form **Vehicle Team Voltron**.

The project was test-marketed in the U.S. as a 90-minute special in 1983 then syndicated by World Events Productions as a half-hour daily to 76 markets the following season. The series followed the *Transformers* and *He-Man* pattern of being built into the merchandising of such toy weaponry as the "Electrothermo Blaster," but the *Vehicle Team* episodes were never as popular as the *Lion Force* episodes (in Japan as well as in America). *Lion Force Voltron*, on the other hand, was *so* popular that *Voltron* became the first Americanized Japanese series to commission new episodes from the original Japanese studio. In one of the new episodes, the "recovered" Sven rejoined the other four Space Explorers just in time for the final battles against Zarkon. The previously built-up *Star Wars* momentum enabled the 125-episode *Voltron* to enjoy good success, both in first run and as a weekend rerun attraction on cable's Family Channel into the l990s.

TranZor Z

Syndicated: 1985. Toei Animation/3B Productions/T. E. N. Executive producer, Bunker Jenkins. Directed by Chris Henderson. Written by Dick Strome, Sandy Childs and Bunker Jenkins. Music by Doug Lackey. Voices: Gregg Berger, Mona Marshall, Paul Ross, Willard Jenkins, Pat Pinney, Robert A. Gaston, James Hodson, Willard Lloyd Davis.

TranZor Z was the Americanized version of the legendary Japanese series *Mazinger Z*, created by Go Nagai. This was the first giant robot TV cartoon — the one that started the entire giant/transforming robot toy craze. The toy manufacturers then fed the anime craze by sponsoring dozens of animated series from *Mazinger Z* in 1972 through well into the '80s.

Aphrodite A comforts TranZor Z after a rough day.

Mazinger Z was so popular in Japan that it lasted for 92 episodes, from December 1972 to September 1974, and was immediately followed by two sequels, **Great Mazinger** (56 episodes, 1974-'75) and **UFO Robo Grandizer** (74 episodes,1975- '77). All featured Go Nagai's trademark of extremely weird (even perverted when he could get away with it) villains, who delighted in sadistically slaughtering as many innocent bystanders as possible. Not surprisingly, the American version left out Aphrodite A's battle cry of "Fire breast missiles!" (There is even a rumored unsold TV pilot of Nagai's *Testicle Boy*, who washes away monsters by super-urinating on them.)

Tommy at the controls of TranZor Z.

Dr. Demon was an amazingly Moses-like evil sorceror who told anyone who would listen that he planned to rule the world. For this purpose, Demon fortified himself with the "Fork of Fury," a magic staff, and the Doom Machines—evil giant robots. He also had at his disposal the submarine fortress Barracuda (which sucked battleships into a vortex) and the Air Fortress (which used a deadly cloud to destroy aircraft). Evidently this fiend could be stopped only by kindly Dr. Wells, an American scientist who'd found a way to harness volcano energy. Wells was also the inventor of Alloy Z, an impenetrable metal. But Dr. Demon's minions eventually burned down Wells' lab, destroying most of his equipment. Found dying in his cellar by nephews Tommy (handsome hero) and

1985

Also on TV in 1985:
Care Bears
Challenge of the Gobots
Danger Mouse
Fat Albert & The Cosby Kids
G.I. Joe
The Mighty Orbots
She-Ra, Princess of Power
Thundercats
Transformers

©3B Productions/Toei Animation Co. Inc.

TranZor Z, Bobo-bot, and Aphrodite A battle two of Dr. Demon's Machine Beasts.

©3B Productions/Toei Animation Co. Inc.

Left to right: Bobo, Jessica and Tommy.

Toad (tousle-haired kid), Wells revealed his creation of the volcano powered, Alloy Z-crafted giant "super robot" TranZor Z.

Though mortally wounded, Wells delivered a spirited five-minute expository speech. TranZor Z, he explained, had detachable rocket fists, a boomerang breast plate, atomic hurricane breath which disintegrated the enemy, a flying scrambler which attached wings to the robot, and laser rays emanating from its finger tips and eyes. Wells stubbornly managed to stave off death until he'd had a chance to utter the obligatory "If this should ever fall in the wrong hands...." The right hands, it turned out, belonged to Tommy, who became the flying TranZor Z's pilot.

The remainder of *TranZor Z* was Tommy vs. Dr. Demon. On TranZor Z's side were female robot (with breasts!) Aphrodite A, operated by Tommy's girl friend Jessica; and Mobilbot, a hot rod operated by funny tough-guy Bobo. The humans were capable of being injured or kidnapped, and their hardware was prone to damage and breakdown, but TranZor Z himself was so invulnerable that he became a dullard very early on.

The plotlines were unsettling combinations of starkly realistic action with downright silliness. Campy, ripe acting and character design were juxtaposed with grisly scenes of wholesale slaughter of innocent bystanders. But if one could manage to sidestep its splotchy production values and confusing point of view, *TranZor Z* could be a lot of fun, especially if one concentrated on the villainy. For example, Dr. Demon didn't waste time exercising the typical cartoon villain prerogative of speaking in double meanings or euphemisms: "Destroy every city in America!" he'd command with admirable directness.

TranZor Z's best moments were such oddball vignettes as having one of Demon's henchmen being haunted by the "ghosts" of all the Doom Machines destroyed by TranZor Z. And although conceived in comic-opera terms, Demon's lieutenants were fascinating. Dr. DeCapito was a Nazi type who screamed all his lines and whose monocled, goateed head was disembodied, floating independently as DeCapito skulked about.

Unique in the annals of Japanese cartoons released to mainstream American television was Demon's other assistant: Devilene the "She-Man." Not only was Devilene half man and half woman—divided down the middle, carnival style—but "with the worst elements of both!," or so the narrator told us. (Does this mean that Devilene left the toilet seat up *and* stockings hanging on the shower curtains?) The character spoke in two voices and was addressed by his/her hopelessly confused flunkeys as "Sir Ma'am." (Even the transvestite nightclub singer in **Robotech** wasn't this kinky.)

Its childish dialogue at odds with its grim wanton violence, and with whacked-out characters the like of which may never pass this way again, the daily *TranZor Z* never quite found a "base" audience. Perhaps it would have worked with a demographic group comprised of giant, conscience-stricken transvestite Nazi robots...?

Macron 1

©1981 Ashi Production

Syndicated: 1985. Saban/Tamerline Publishing/Orbis. Executive producers: Haim Saban, Shuki Levy. Writing supervision and direction: Robert V. Barron. Creative supervisor, Dennys McCoy. Associate producer, Jonathan Braun. Production coordinators, Alex Dimitroff and Jeff P. Rubinstein. Written by Robert Barron, Greg Snow, Winston Richard, Richard Miller, Jason Klassi, Mike Reynolds, John Rust, Max Pynchon, Pam Hickey, Joe Hailey, Bob Cowley, Benjamin Lesko. Edited by Jonathan Braun, Mick Kollins, Sheila O'Callaghan. Editing facilities: Video Transitions. Music by Haim Saban, Shuki Levy; Top 40 music by original artists. Theme song "Reflex" performed by Duran Duran. Voices: Angela Rigamonti, Bill Laver, Christopher Eric, Octavia Beaumont, Tamara Shawn, Rich Ellis, Susan Ling, Oliver Miller.

Macron 1, a daily half-hour sci-fi syndie, was cobbled together from two separate Japanese-animated series, though American distributor Saban/Orbis did its best to hide this fact, removing all Japanese names from its production credits. The original series involved were the 1981 ***Sengoku Majin Go-Shogun*** (26 episodes, Ashi Productions) which translates roughly as "Demon-God of the War-Torn Land Go-Shogun," and the 1983-'84 ***Aku Dai Sakusen Srungle*** (53 episodes, International Film Co.) which translates as "Great Military Operation in Subspace Srungle." The two programs were linked thematically by a futuristic outer space setting and a "rebellion against oppression" throughline. Despite the Westernization efforts of its English-language adaptors, *Macron 1*'s country of origin was evident in its production and character designs, and in its similarity to the like-vintage ***Robotech*** —which in the manner of *Macron* had been patched together by its American distributor from three separate Japanese series.

The mighty Macron 1 flying space robot.

Set in the year A.D. 2545 (not in the 41st century that the series' publicity described), *Macron 1* was the story of a misguided teleportation experiment which hurled Earthling test pilot David Jance into a parallel universe— and in exchange, the evil Dark Star, leader of a terrorist cyborg-dominated army known as GRIP, wound up in our universe. From this point onward, David Jance and his *Star Wars*-like crew of rebellious teenagers and mutants—including a "Chewbacca" type first mate named Nok—flew on behalf of the parallel world's heroic Beta Command, led by Dr. Chagall. Beta Command's personnel (which received a lot more screen time than nominal hero Jance) included Nathan Bridger, the brilliant preteen son of late computer expert Dr. Bridger, whose scientific expertise placed him in a command post for which he was intellectually ready but psychologically ill-prepared. Also among the Beta group were several characters who, like the crew of Jance's "Flying Macstar," were echoes of *Star Wars*— right down to a cute "R2D2" robot named An-D and an erudite "C-3PO" computer brain named Hugo.

"Macron 1" itself was a huge, flying space robot, formed whenever the Beta Command combined its energy and weaponry with the Flying Macstar. This Macron metamorphosis took place whenever the villains threatened to outpopulate the heroes— not all that distant a danger, since the GRIP contingent included the aforementioned Dark Star, the covetous Prince Maharn (who in the tradition of *Robotech* villain Lord Khyron sounded like British actor James Mason), the "avast, swabs!" space pirate Dr. Blade, a Nazi-like mad scientist, and numerous skullheaded robot slaves.

Like *Robotech* at its best, *Macron 1* exuded a cocky wiseguy attitude, with its younger characters forever disregarding and mocking their superiors. Also like *Robotech*, *Macron* excelled in nailbiting outer-space battles, accomplished as much through rapid editing and bizarre camera angles as through clever limited animation. A major selling point to American markets was Saban/Orbis' inclusion of contemporary Top 40 tunes in *Macron 1*'s soundtrack. These were illustrated in MTV fashion with flashy montage sequences, generically constructed to conform with any song that happened to be hot at the moment (the "neutral" quality of the montages came in handy when the distributors were forced by copyright restrictions to remove some of the songs when *Macron 1* was released to home video). The "rock" motif was often carried over into the straight action sequences; some of the most effective space battles contained no sound effects at all, merely musical accompaniment.

The cyborg hordes of GRIP.

Macron 1 scored where a lot of other Japanese imports struck out, combining the more sober and straightfaced characteristics of anime with the cheerful Yankee Doodle cheekiness of Hollywood's best action-adventure films. But like its spiritual twin *Robotech*, *Macron 1* suffered from scheduling in inappropriate early morning and early afternoon fringe timeslots— and by its nearly exclusive distribution to big city markets, leaving most potential southern and midwestern fans out in the cold.

© 1982 Big West

Hot-shot pilot Hikaru Ichijo ("Rick Hunter" in the American version) in his transforming Valkyrie mecha.

Robotech

Syndicated: 1985. Tatsunoko Productions/Harmony Gold/ZIV International. Executive producer, Ahmed Agrama. Produced by Carl Macek. Supervising director, Robert Barron. Written by Gregory Snegoff, Robert Barron, Greg Finley, Steve Kramer, Mike Reynolds, Jim Wager, Steve Flood. Music editor, John Mortarotti. Music by Ulpio Minucci, Arlon Ober, Alberto Ruben Esteves. For Tatsunoko: Producer, Kenji Yoshida. Director, Ippei Kuri. Voices: Greg Snow (Khyron, Scott Bernard); Reba West (Lynn Minmei); Jonathan Alexander (Breetai); Drew Thomas (Angelo Dante); Deena Morris (Sammie); Thomas Wyner (Jonathan Wolf); Brittany Harlow (Claudia Grant); Don Warner (Roy Fokker); Axel Roberts (Rico); Tony Oliver (Rick Hunter); A. Gregory (Robotech Masters); Penny Sweet (Nova Satori, Miriya); Aline Leslie (Lisa Hayes); and Sandra Snow, Guy Garrett, Jimmy Flinders, Anthony Wayne, Eddie Frierson, Leonard Pike, Shirley Roberts, Wendee Swan, Jeffrey Platt, Larry Abraham, Mary Cobb, Celena Banas, and Chelsea Victoria.

Perhaps **Robotech** never played any of the TV stations in your city, but that didn't stop the Japanese cartoon series from achieving cult status. In fact, for many years its very unavailability helped fire the "legend."

The property was developed by Carl Macek, who wanted to take one of the recent wave of Japanese serialized cartoons and compose a faithful translation for American audiences—more faithful than the recent watered-down **Battle of the Planets**. The distribution firm Harmony Gold contracted Macek for the purpose of preparing the Japanese science fiction weekly **Super-Dimensional Fortress Macross** (*Chô Jikû Yôsai Macross*; 36 episodes, 1982-'83) for English-language consumption. Macek worked with Harmony Gold President Frank Agrama, who was already familiar with anime from dubbing it into French, Italian and Spanish for European and Latin American sales, and who wanted to break into the American market.

© 1984 Big West

A scene from the "second" **Robotech** series, **Southern Cross**.

The problem was that *Macross* ran only 36 episodes, falling short of the 85 episodes desired for a daily strip. Carl Macek decided to incorporate two other series, **Super-Dimensional Cavalry Southern Cross** (*Chô Jikû Kidan Southern Cross*; 23 episodes, 1984) and **Genesis Climber Mospeada** (*Kikô Sôseiki Mospeada*; 25 episodes, 1983-'84), to fill out the manifest with an additional 49 half-hours. This was not the artistic stretch it might have been, since all three series were produced by Tatsunoko Studios and shared similarities in character, background design and story material. Macek conjured up a throughline about an ancient scientific method of generating and utilizing robotic personnel and weaponry for extraterrestrial combat. Revell Toys, which owned the merchandising rights to *Macross*, came up with the name for this futuristic technology: "Robotech." Carl Macek rechristened the three separate series as **The Macross Saga**, **The Robotech Masters** and **The New Generation**, bridging the stories together by developing interlocking family and fraternal ties among the principal characters.

© 1982 Big West

Captain Gloval of the *SDF-1*.

The Macross Saga began when a gigantic unmanned alien spaceship, the *SDF-1*, crashed on Earth in 1999. Ten years later, a scientific community had almost made the ship operational when the alien Zentraedi came to reclaim it. Automatic weapons on the *SDF-1* fired on the Zentraedi, who retaliated against Earth. An attempt by the humans to get *SDF-1* airborne resulted in the ship making a "spacefold" to the orbit of Pluto, with the whole community on board. The ensuing story was a soap opera of the developing personal relationships among the large, multi-racial cast: fighter Rick Hunter; Lisa Hayes, commander of the *SDF-1*'s bridge crew; Lynn Minmei, a teenage girl who becomes an entertainer and symbol of the humans' will to win; Max and Miriya, human and Zentraedi lovers; and many more. Major characters died and the Earth itself was devastated during the war.

In *The Robotech Masters*, a generation later, Earth was rebuilding itself when the Robotech Masters, creators of the now-destroyed *SDF-1*, came to recover the ship's Protoculture energy source. A new war resulted. This story followed the exploits of the young soldiers of the 15th Squadron of Alpha Tactical Armored Corps commanded by

Dana Sterling, the daughter of Max and Miriya. The humans and the Robotech Masters essentially exhausted each other, leaving Earth defenseless against an invading alien species, the Invid, who came to cultivate the Protoculture as food.

In *The New Generation*, a liberation armada returning to occupied Earth after a generation in exile on Mars was annihilated by the Invid. The single survivor was Scott Bernard, who rallied a guerilla fighting force among the dispirited humans to renew the war against the Invid, until the main space fleet under Admiral Rick Hunter returned.

Breetai, officer of the alien Zentraedi forces.

With innumerable characters and honeycomb-like storylines, this self-described "Multi-Generational Space Soap Opera" offers no middle ground: you either love it or hate it. *Robotech* fans tend to be those who feel that anime, with its shattering of TV taboos with nudity, overt sexuality, and death scenes, is inherently better than American TV simply because it is so different. One could certainly revel in the somewhat perverse aura of *Robotech*, whose creators delighted in confounding all the plot and character predictability that American viewers have been lulled into. It was not uncommon for major, sympathetic characters to be killed off without warning. And never had there previously been the literal equivalent on American afternoon television of the "New Generation" character Lancer, a young man who, when not warding off enemy aliens, enjoyed a career as a female entertainer named Yellow Dancer!

A scene from the second episode of **Robotech**, "Countdown."

A protective cult has built up around *Robotech*, part of it predicated by the assumption that the show would have been much better received if it had only been shown in an appropriate time slot. In fact, Harmony Gold did the best promotional job possible, but the scheduling decisions were ultimately the province of the individual TV stations. Too many of these decided, for reasons known only to themselves, to stash the series in the early morning or early afternoon "kiddie" time slots.

Unique and challenging though it was, *Robotech* never soared as a syndicated daily. Its success in the United States has rested primarily in the form of videocassette rentals and sales, allowing the series' hard core fans to luxuriate in each twist and turn of plot with a steady finger on the pause button, and in ancillary sales of *Robotech* comic books and script novelizations.

Additionally, some of those aforementioned *Robotech* fans have recently gotten into the driver's seats of the major animation studios. The most conspicuous *Robotech* devotee in the past few seasons has been Jeff Segal, mentor of the weekly 1993 Universal Cartoon Studios syndie *Exo Squad*, often cited by anime fans as the most "anime-like" of the American animated TV series.*

Robotech/Macross remains one of the most influential anime series ever created, featuring one of the most talented production staffs ever assembled: mecha designer Shoji Kawamori, character designer Haruhiko Mikimoto, chief director Noboru Ishiguro, animation director Toshihiro Hirano, and more. Currently, there are two sequels available in the U.S. on home video, the three-volume *Macross II* from U.S. Renditions/L.A. Hero and the four-volume *Macross Plus* from Manga Entertainment. *Macross 7*, a television series focusing on the exploits of Max and Miriya's pink-haired guitar-playin' daughter Mylene, recently ended broadcast on Japanese TV and is currently available only through import.

Captain Harlock and The Queen of a Thousand Years

Syndicated 1985. Harmony Gold/Ziv International. Created by Leiji Matsumoto. *Space Pirate Captain Harlock* produced by Toei Animation Co., Ltd. *The Queen of A Thousand Years* produced by Sen-Nen Jô'o Seisaku I-inkai.

Every thousand years, the nomadic planet Millenia searches the universe for a new home, and the preferred target this millenium is Earth. An advance contingent of pilgrims, known as the L'Metaal, have traveled to Earth to pave the way for the coming invasion. Their leader is the beautiful Princess Olivia, who will become the new Queen of A Thousand Years upon the successful completion of the invasion.

Earth's only hope against this alien threat is Captain Harlock. As the captain of an interstellar space galleon, the *Arcadia*, Harlock has dedicated himself to protect and defend his home planet. The discovery of the alien invasion plot propels Captain Harlock into action. He battles the Mazone (read Amazons), a mercenary army hired by the Ruler of Millenia to assist the L'Metaal. As Harlock gets the upper hand against the sisterhood of Mazones, these mercenaries search for any means to keep a path open for the invasion. They resort to extraordinary tactics to draw Harlock away from Earth on

Leiji Matsumoto's Space Pirate Captain Harlock.

a mission of mercy to the far corners of the universe, while the fate of Earth hangs in the balance.

Much of the plot is revealed by following a teenager whose scientist father is killed by the Mazone. He initially blames Harlock and goes after him for revenge, but after learning the truth, becomes one of Harlock's crew on his ship the *Arcadia*. Far from becoming the underground hero and iconoclast one might expect, Harlock finds himself constantly being framed as a terrorist. His rebellious shaggy-haired, eyepatched charisma isn't wasted on the all-female Mazone, at least one of who throws herself at his booted feet in a vain quest to earn his affection (he ends up shooting her at her own request).

© 1978 Leiji Matsumoto/TV Asahi/Toei

La Mime ("Melody") interprets a message from the Mazone for Captain Harlock

The two original series were the 42-episode ***Space Pirate Captain Harlock*** (*Uchû Kaizoku Captain Harlock*; Toei Animation Co. Ltd., 1978-'79), and the 41-episode ***The Queen of a Thousand Years*** (*Shin Taketori Monogatari Sennen Jo'ô*; Sen-Nen Jô'o Seisaku I-inkai, 1981-'82). As with *Robotech*, Harmony Gold needed to expand the 42-episode *Harlock* to 65 episodes to fill up a daily syndicated strip. Carl Macek was assigned to find a way to tie the two series (not even from the same studio) into something resembling a coherent storyline. It was edited so that scenes from both programs are juxtaposed and connected by dialogue, even though the major characters do not appear together. The serial becomes, in effect, the story of a vast war, with the scene switching constantly between the two fronts. The American title was ***Captain Harlock and the Queen of a Thousand Years***.

Fans of the original *Harlock* bemoaned the editing process as damaging the integrity of the project. General audiences, confused by the murky continuity of the abridged version, tuned out in droves, and *Captain Harlock and the Queen of a Thousand Years* was a failure in the U.S., killing a multitude of tie-in merchandising deals that had been in the planning stages. But as in the case of other cult animated favorites like *Robotech*, *Captain Harlock*'s true disciples kept the torch lit in the form of comic books and extensive background articles in the anime fanzines catering to Japanese animation devotees... one of who would later go on to co-author this book.

1987

Also on TV in 1987:
Advs of The Galaxy Rangers
Beauty & The Beast
Bravestarr
Ducktales
Ghostbusters
Mighty Mouse:The New Adventures
Real Ghostbusters
Silverhawks
Star Trek: The Next Generation
Teenage Mutant Ninja Turtles

© 11984 Studio Pierrot/NTV

A scene from the outer-space western, ***Saber Rider and the Star Sheriffs***.

Saber Rider and the Star Sheriffs

Syndicated: 1987. Calico/World Events. For Calico: Executive producer, Peter Keefe. Produced and directed by Franklin Cofod. Executive story editor, Marc Handler. Music by Dale Schacker. For Studio Pierrot Co., Ltd.: Produced by Yousi Nunokala, Yoshitaki Suzuki. Animation directors, Akira Shigino, Yorifusa Yamaguchi, Shigonori Kageyama. Voices: Townsend Coleman, Peter Cullen, Pat Fraley, Pat Musick, Rob Paulsen, Jack Angel, Michael Bell, Brian Cummings, Diane Pershing, Hal Smith, Alison Argo, Art Burghardt, Tress MacNeille, Neil Ross, B. J. Ward, Len Weinrib.

When ***Saber Rider and the Star Sheriffs*** first ran in Europe and Asia in 1984, it was titled ***Bismarck the Star Musketeers*** (***Sei Jûshi Bismarck***; 1984-'85). The English translation played up the "cowboy" trappings of the series' 52 half-hour episodes, which were released in the U.S. for daily syndication during the brief outer-space western cartoon spate of 1986-'87 (i.e. *Adventures of the Galaxy Rangers* and *Bravestarr*).

The plotline of *Saber Rider* was set in the extraterrestrial New Frontier, an untamed land where the law was in the hands of the Star Sheriffs, headquartered at space station "Cavalry Command." The characters were aristocratic, blond Saber Rider, whose personal mecha suit made him look like a robotic Royal Hussar from *The Charge of the Light Brigade*; laid-back teenage cowboy Colt, who sported a 10-gallon hat and a six-shooter; April, the blonde, teenage team member who spent most of her time mooning over the boys; and Fireball, the daredevil (and obviously Japanese) race car driver.

The villains were the renegade Outriders, led by such hombres as Vanquo, Nemesis and Razzle. Forming a united front against the Outriders, the Star Sheriff team piloted the "Ramrod," a sheriff-shaped space vehicle. (You read that right. The vehicle was in the shape of a sheriff.)

The good guys were outfitted with electronic badge units, which were supposed to provide an interactive connection with the home viewers—that is, those kids who'd bought the necessary tie-in electronic *Star Sheriff* merchandise. The unluckier youngsters were left to scratch their heads and wonder why the program had so many gratuitous closeups of those badges. Outside of this distinctly American aspect, *Saber Rider and the Star Sheriffs* betrayed its overseas origins by being more trigger-happy than the general run of weekday cartoons.

When the series was being "Americanized," the producers wanted the main character switched from the Japanese kid, Fireball, to the American cowboy, Colt. The original *Bismarck* was designed so that the team were nominally equals, but in reality it was Fireball (Shinji Hikari in the original) who was the center of the action, and the de facto leader. The writers' attempts to make Colt the focus (and the one April favored) resulted in some weird scenes where everyone would be looking at Fireball (Shinji), but apparently listening and talking to Colt. The original series also had lots of humor based on the teenagers getting drunk. The American version edited out all scenes showing drunken behavior, and since many scenes took place in Western saloons, the heroes ended up appearing to spend time in lots of "coffee shops" and "soda fountains," drinking "lemonade" or "root beer."

Though it didn't survive past its first Monday-through-Friday season, *Saber Rider and the Star Sheriffs* was a valuable freshman lesson in cartoon syndication for Calico Entertainment, who'd later forsake distribution of readymade cartoons in order to develop its own projects: *Denver the Last Dinosaur, Widget, the World Watcher, Mr. Bogus, Bucky O'Hare and the Toad Wars* and *Twinkle the Dream Being.*

Saber Rider, probably the first anime show to feature a giant robot with a cowboy-hat head and sixgun-shaped hands.

©1984 Studio Pierrot/NTV

Dragon Warrior

Syndicated: 1990. Saban/LBS. Executive producer, Haim Saban. Supervising producer, Winston Richard. Associate producer, Eric S. Rollman. Story editor, Robert V. Barron. Music by Haim Saban and Shuki Levy. Animation facilities: Nippon Animation Studios. Voices: Long John Baldry, Jay Brazeau, Jim Byrnes, Gary Chalk, Marcy Goldberg, Sam Kouth, Shelley Lefler, Duff McDonald, Richard Newman.

Unveiled by Nintendo in 1986, ***Dragon Quest***, a combination of two personal computer games, was the company's most complicated and costly videogame to date. Its debut was heralded by a sword-and-sorcery backstory in a Japanese boys' magazine to tantalize video addicts, and its resultant big sales prompted Nintendo to create three *Dragon Quest* sequels. A 32-episode cartoon series followed, produced by Japan's Nippon Animation Studios in 1989-'90 and released in the U.S. by LBS Communications the following year, under the title ***Dragon Warrior***.

The thirteen serialized *Dragon Warrior* episodes emulated the videogame format by being titled as "Levels." The first installment was "Level One: Ariahan Village," the second was "Level Two: Departure," the third "Level Three: Leebe Village," and so on until "Level Thirteen: Najimi Tower." Introduced in Level One was 16-year-old Abel, who was compelled by circumstance to seek and destroy Baramos, a huge, horrible winged creature who bore the "Voice of Doom." Baramos had threatened to expose mankind to the apocalyptic fury of the Great Dragon by means of a magical amulet called the Red Stone.

Daisy, the so-called "Macho Miss."

©1989 Enix/Shueisha/Fuji TV/NAS

©1989 Enix/Shueisha/Fuji TV/NAS

1990

Also on TV in 1990:
Beetlejuice
Captain Planet
The Ren & Stimpy Show
Tale Spin
Tiny Toon Adventures
Magical World of Disney
The Simpsons

Look familiar? It should. Character designs for **Dragon Warrior** are by Akira Toriyama of **Dragon Ball** fame.

1995

Also on TV in 1995:

Animaniacs
Batman Animated Series
Gargoyles
Swat Kats
The Maxx
Taz-Mania
Tiny Toon Adventures
X-Men

Ringo (left) and the mysterious "D-Boy."

It's likely that Abel would have steered clear of all this had not his closest childhood friend, 15-year-old girl Tiala, been the latest descendant of the family charged with guarding the Red Stone— making her subsequent kidnapping by Baramos all but inevitable. (If you're wondering why some one in Tiala's family hadn't simply tossed the Red Stone in the dumpster to avoid potential disaster, the answer is simple: Then there wouldn't have been any *Dragon Warrior*.)

Various good and bad characters peopled the series, but outside of Baramos and his coward-bully servant Moor (who looked like an ulcerated toad), most of the regulars were "good." There was Abel's close pal MocoMoco, larger than Abel but not quite as athletic. There was Daisy, described by *Dragon Warrior*'s press release as a "macho miss," introduced in "Level 4: Girl Warrior Daisy." And for the sake of grizzled humor, there was Janac the wizard, a mustachioed, pipe-puffing old soak with not a few eccentric character flaws.

Written and produced with traditional anime ebullience, and blessed with a solid premise aimed squarely at the 11- to 14-year-old market, *Dragon Warrior* should have been at least a modest success. Sadly, the series was vanquished after six months—not by Baramos or the Great Dragon, but because of generally weak timeslots (most independent stations, overloaded with product in 1990, shunted the series to the least accessible of the Sunday-morning hours) and an overall drop of public interest in the original Nintendo videogame.

Teknoman

Syndicated: 1995. Saban Entertainment, Inc. and Saban International N.V. Executive Producer, Eric S. Rollman. Produced by Tom Wyner. Written by Tom Wyner. Music by Shuki Levy, Kussa Machi. Original animation by Tatsunoko Production Company, Ltd. Voices: Bob Bergen (Teknoman, Slade); Michael McConnohie (Ringo Richards); Barbara Goodson (Star Summers); Michael Forrest (Commander Jamison); Julie Magdalena (Tina Corman); Mari Devon (Maggie Matheson); Richard Epcar (Mac Mackelroy); Simon Prescott (Darkon); Tom Wyner (Narrator,Teknobot); Mike L. Reynolds (General Galt); Steve Bulen (Balzac St. Jacques); Paul L. Schrier II (Saber); John Vickery (Gunnar); Wendee Lee (Shara).

Debuting in Japan on 18 February 1992, the Japanese television series ***Space Knight Tekkaman Blade*** is a remake/sequel to the 1975 TV show ***Space Knight Tekkaman*** from the venerable "Home of the Heroes," Tatsunoko Productions. *Tekkaman Blade* considerably updated the premise of its predecessor while keeping on familiar ground to those who remembered the original *Tekkaman* legend—the heroes defending the Earth are still called the "Space Knights," led by a hot-shot pilot and a beautiful girl equipped with a spaceship called the *Blue Earth*. But *Tekkaman Blade* rung a number of significant changes on the original Tekkaman premise, especially regarding the origin of the Tekkaman armor.

In the 1975 *Tekkaman*, when the hero Joji Minami dons his protective Tekkaman armor, there's no particular significance—he's simply a traditional superhero fighting the alien baddies who are muscling in on his territory. But when "D-Boy," the mysterious, brooding hero of *Tekkaman Blade*, appears to help the Earth fight off an invasion by spider-like space aliens called the "Radom," the Earth forces are at first unwilling to trust him…and for good reason. In this universe, there's more than one Tekkaman, and they are *evil*—the Tekkaman armor itself causes a change to come over the wearer if it is inhabited for more than brief periods. D-Boy ("D" meaning "danger-ous," a nickname given to the surly young hero by the other Space Knights) is the only Tekkaman in known existence to actually be on the side of good, and that only because he is careful to monitor the length of time he spends merged with the Tekkaman armor. In a nicely handled nod to the original show, D-Boy's emerald crystal—which he uses to change into his protective Tekkaman armor—is damaged in a fight against another Tekkaman, and the giant robot carrier "Pegase" is built in order to augment the power of the shattered crystal so D-Boy can still transform into his armor. As in the original

Tekkaman, this new Pegase also provides a mount for Tekkaman Blade to stand dramatically on whilst fighting against the onrushing alien menaces.

The plot of *Tekkaman Blade* is considerably more sci-fi than its predecessor—the futuristic Earth is surrounded by a stationary orbital ring, which the alien hordes quickly capture and use to rain destruction on the helpless Earth below. The overriding grimness of the storyline is well complemented by a dark, harshly lit film noir animation style which summons up images of Ridley Scott's *Alien*.

Obtained for U.S. distribution by Saban Entertainment, *Tekkaman Blade* was retitled **Teknoman** for its weekly American television broadcast on Paramount's UPN network in the summer of 1995. The musical soundtrack was completely replaced with technotronic-style background music (presumably to better fit the new title) and the heroes names are, in the traditional manner, Americanized. D-Boy becomes "Slade," cocksure pilot Noa is known as "Ringo," and Aki becomes "Starr." The invading Radom are known as the "Venomoid," although typically referred to as "Spider-Crabs," a fairly descriptive moniker overall.

A natural follow-up to Saban's success with the live-action *Mighty Morphin Power Rangers*, *Teknoman* provides an animated version of **Ultraman**-esque combat set against a well-realized science fiction background... all of which makes it that much more unfortunate that the series was able to last on U.S. television less than a year.

Unlike the Japanese version, Saban's **Teknoman** features a "house-music"-style techno-beat soundtrack.

Ronin Warriors

Syndicated 1995. Sunrise Inc./Graz Entertainment. American producer, Michael Hack. Script supervisor, Barry G. Hawkins. Written by Barry G. Hawkins, Michael Adams, Karen Kolus. Theme music by Tom Keenlyside, John Mitchell, David Iris. Original animation by Sunrise Inc. Produced by Hironori Nakagawa. Directed by Sei Ikeda, Mamoru Hamazu. Voices: Matt Hill (Ryo); Jason-Gray Stanford (Kento); Ward Perry (Rowen); Michael Donovan (Sage, Cye); Lalainia Lindjberg (Mia); Christopher Turner (Ully); Richard Newman (Dr. Koji, the Ancient, Cale); Mina Mina (Talpa); Paul Dobson (Anubis); Matthew Smith (Dais, Dynasty Soldier); David Kaye (Narrator); Jane Perry (Lady Kayura); Teryl Rothery.

Yoroiden Samurai Troopers (1988-89) details the exploits of a group of five young men who have been gifted with mystical, superpowered samurai armor in order to fight against an otherworldly invasion from the "Phantom World," a dark dimension headed by the evil warlord Arago. Arago (who in his initial incarnation appears as a giant spectral, glowing helmet, and later grows to gigantic size) was originally vanquished centuries ago in his first invasion attempt by a holy man who later appears in the series to counsel the heroes. Arago's henchmen also wear mystical armor, each with different weapons and a different specialty. It is revealed later in the series that both the heroes' and the villains' mystical armor are parts of the same ultra-powerful suit of armor that was broken up when Arago was originally defeated, creating an interesting good vs. evil dichotomy in the warriors' own arms and armor.

Imported to the U.S. by Graz Entertainment under the title "Ronin Warriors" so as not to conflict with two live-action battle-team shows on-air at the same time which also included the words "Samurai" or "Troopers" in their titles, **Ronin Warriors** was first broadcast on U.S. television during Summer 1995. The show's "Americanization" was fairly light—though most of the names were changed. Arago, King of the Phantom World is changed to "Talpa," and his evil kingdom is known as "The Dynasty." The leader of the Ronin Warriors' team retains his original name, Ryo, while his teammates changed from Shin to "Cye"; Seiji to "Sage"; Toma to "Rowen" and Shu to "Kento."

Each warrior has his own special attacks and weaponry, each linked to the elemental-based powers of their individual armor, helpfully color-coded. There's Ryo's (red) Armor of Wildfire; strongman Kento's (orange) Armor of Hardrock; Cye's (blue) Armor of Torrent (accompanied by a suitably Neptune-like trident); Sage's (green) Armor of Halo; and Rowen's Armor of Strata (dark blue, for the upper atmosphere).

Sage of the Halo (top) and Cye of the Torrent.

Ronin Warriors artwork ©Sunrise, Inc./Graz Entertainment

The Ronin Warriors, clockwise from lower left: Cye of the Torrent (light blue armor); Sage of the Halo (green armor); Ryo of the Wildfire (red armor - shown here transformed into Hariel of the Armor of Inferno); Rowen of the Strata (dark blue armor); Kento of the Hardrock (orange armor).

Leader Ryo eventually gets a powered-up version of his armor which combines the powers of all five fighters (though at the cost of great exhaustion to the wearer), which is titled Hariel's White Armor of Fervor (white hot!).

Talpa's henchmen, the Dark Warlords, are equally equipped, such as Anubis, Dark Warlord of Cruelty (whose battle cry is "Quake With Fear!" as he hurls a scythe attached to a length of chain); Dais, Dark Warlord of Illusion; the spider-like Cale, Dark Warlord of Corruption; and so forth. The show's format of continuing quest-and-battle against shadow spirits who have effectively conquered the world is dark and quite gripping, with a level of violence still rather unusual on American TV, though there are few flesh-and-blood casualties on-screen (the Dynasty's chief forces consisting mostly of zombies and ghosts). The heroes tagalong companions, the young and independent woman Mia and little boy Ully (Nasutei and Jun in Japanese) are continually captured and menaced by the Dark Warlords—at one point, they're dropped into an active volcano, only to be saved just in time by Ryo—though both get their chance to save the heroes from time to time with a help of mystic talisman given to them by "the Ancient," the holy man who originally defeated Talpa.

Though its broadcast run on U.S. TV was short, *Ronin Warriors* was one of the few examples of a U.S. adaptation of a Japanese animated show to not even bother to hide its Japanese origin—no attempt was made to reanimate or cut the scenes where, as each warrior launches his special attack, the Japanese characters describing the attack appear glowing on the screen, or the moments when one of the heroes is reminded of the virtue his armor represents, and the corresponding character appears on his forehead, such as truth, wisdom or justice. Phenomenally popular in Japan, especially with teenage girls (for the five handsome heroes, natch), after the series ended its television run in Japan, several direct-to-video or OAV stories were produced, but it is yet to be seen if these will be imported to the U.S. market.

Dragon Ball

Syndicated: 1995—1996. Funimation Productions, Inc. American version produced by Seagull Entertainment. Executive Producers, Gen Fukunaga, Cindy Brennan Fukunaga. Written by Christopher Neel, Ian Corlett, Terry Klassen, Barry Watson, Cliff MacGillivray. Music by Peter Berring Griffiths, Gibson & Ramsay Productions. Original animation by Toei Animation Ltd., Japan. Voices: Ted Cole (Yamcha); Jim Conrad, Michael Donovan (Turtle Hermit); Saffron Henderson (Goku); Lalainia Lindjberg (Bulma); Kathy Morse, Doug Parker, Teryl Rothery, Alec Willows.

Dragon Ball Z. Syndicated 1996. Funimation Productions, Inc. American version produced by Seagull Entertainment. Same credits as *Dragon Ball*.

©1986 Bird Studio/Shueishinsha/Fuji TV/Toei

Based on the popular manga series by Akira Toriyama, ***Dragon Ball*** (1986) became a worldwide phenomenon from almost the moment it was first animated. The story's origin in the traditional Chinese *Saiyûki* or "Legend of the Monkey King" has long been familiar to many an Asian child, and the superpowered martial arts update and mischievous humor of *Dragon Ball*'s story came as a welcome diversion.

The story of Goku, a little "monkey-boy" with superpowers taught to him by his grandfather, who sets out on a search for the seven mystical dragon balls which, when all of them are brought together, will grant the bearer one wish for anything at all. During his travels, Goku has many adventures, and meets many other adventurers who are recognizable as variations on the traditional characters in the Monkey King legend. Humor is interjected continually throughout the series, as nearly all the main characters are named after some kind of food or clothing item. For example, a diminutive, evil king named "Pilaf" is served by henchmen named "Shao" and "Mai," which together spell out the name of a certain popular Chinese takeout dish.

In Japan, the *Dragon Ball* manga (as serialized in SHÔNEN JUMP, the world's bestselling manga weekly) only recently ended. Its animated incarnation, which had progressed from the initial *Dragon Ball* TV series to the more fighting-focused ***Dragon***

Ball Z, ended in 1996 after a decade-long broadcast run. A multimillion-dollar merchandising hit, *Dragon Ball* toys, posters and every other possible form of merchandise have been a continuing feature of Asian life ever since the series first saw print, but its entry into Western market was considerably impeded by the animated show's casual nudity, and what, by Western standards, amounted to a certain level of "naughty" humor on the level of *The Benny Hill Show*.

Obtained for American distribution by Funimation Inc., *Dragon Ball* finally began broadcast as a weekly series on U.S. airwaves in 1995. The names of the characters are essentially unchanged, although the English adaptation missed the boat completely when it came to the joke behind the lead female's name, "Buruma," meaning "Bloomer," as in the gym shorts Japanese girls wear at school (her English name is perhaps the unavoidable result of the T-shirt she wears throughout the series with her name inscribed in pseudo-English as "Bulma"). Young Goku's tendency to romp around naked, which posed no particular taboo for Asian viewers, was dealt with by digital retouching. Where Goku once appeared in the buff, in the English version he now wears a modest pair of digital underwear, and the "naughty" and bathroom-type humor has been delicately edited.

Despite the care taken to ensure a high-quality adaptation, due to poor timeslots in most areas, *Dragon Ball* did not perform as well as was perhaps expected by its American producers. Only 26 episodes of *Dragon Ball* were finally produced and aired in America before the show left syndication in 1996 after frequent reruns.

Continuing the story begun in *Dragon Ball*, **Dragon Ball Z** gives us young Goku now a full-grown man, married and with children of a monkey-tailed son, Gohan. Instead of the "Monkey King" legend on which the original series so humorously played, *Dragon Ball Z* turns its energies instead to continually escalating fights between the main cast and increasingly more powerful opponents, with some individual combats stretching over weeks and even months of real-time broadcast.

In *Dragon Ball Z*, Goku is revealed to be an alien being called a Saiyan, sent to Earth as a baby in a spaceship—almost an exact replica of Superman's origin story. Like Superman, after being discovered by a kindly local, Goku is discovered to be super-strong. Unlike Superman, however, Goku is also super violent, the reason being that Goku was actually sent to destroy all life on the planet Earth, clearing the planet for colonization by other races. This is apparently business-as-usual for the Saiyans, super-powered beings so strong that it only takes one Saiyan to destroy the populace of an entire planet. But in Goku's case, a near-fatal head injury as an infant scrambled his programming, and instead of a bloodthirsty, rampaging killer, he grew up as a pure-hearted, good-natured innocent, defender of his adopted world.

In the wake of the first *Dragon Ball* TV series' disappointing showing in the ratings, *Dragon Ball*'s American licensers, Funimation Inc., made the bold decision to skip ahead in the *Dragon Ball* saga to its second series, *Dragon Ball Z*, bypassing a lengthy segment of over 100 TV episodes of the *Dragon Ball* series which detailed the young Goku's growth from a small boy into an adult. *Dragon Ball Z*'s focus on martial arts action and superhero-like battles between alien races fit in somewhat better with the traditional American Saturday morning lineup, and combined with increased marketing power of distributor Saban Entertainment, *Dragon Ball Z* premiered on U.S. TV in Fall of 1996, for its initial 26-episode run to high ratings, registering as the top-rated children's show in some areas.

The same voice-cast was used for *Dragon Ball Z* as from the previous series *Dragon Ball*, with the addition of a new voice for the adult Goku. The names were essentially unchanged from the Japanese, though in some cases shortened, such as "Tien" for the character most often known as "Tenshinhan" ("Tien" is an alternate reading of the Chinese characters which spell out the character's name). Other names—such as "Kami-sama," or "Kami"—were simply left untranslated, no doubt

The *Dragon Ball* cast, clockwise from lower left: Bulma, Puar, Yamcha, Oolong, Goku.

Mutenroshi, the Turtle Sage.

because one translation of the name is "god."

The violence in *Dragon Ball Z* was a quantum leap from *Dragon Ball*'s simple martial arts combat—in *Dragon Ball Z*, the Saiyans casually destroy worlds and level cities. In fact, one of the first events in *Dragon Ball Z* is the death of Goku himself, who then spends a great many of the following episodes in the afterlife, sporting a halo over his head and trying to find his way back to the living world to help his friends fight the coming Saiyan attack. Like *Dragon Ball*, the more overt violence is carefully edited, but the main story of *Dragon Ball Z* remained intact—Goku's death is handled in a straightforward manner, perhaps helped by the fact that *Dragon Ball Z*'s version of the afterlife is not particularly recognizable to most Western viewers, and was therefore more easily masked. The age of Goku's son Gohan, who undergoes intensive martial arts training in Goku's absence, was upped in the English version, due to concerns about small children under age five being menaced on television. At the time of this writing, *Dragon Ball Z* is still showing in North American markets.

Sailor Moon

Syndicated: 1995. Toei Animation Co. Ltd./DIC Productions, L.P./SeaGull Entertainment Inc. Directed by Junichi Sato. Original Music: Takanori Arisawa, Tetsuya Komuro, Kazuo Sato. American version by DIC Productions, L.P. Executive Producer: Andy Heyward. English adaptation produced by Mycheline Tremblay, Gary Plaxton, and Lisa Lumby. Production Creative Consultant: Fred Ladd. Voices: Dennis Akayama, Karen Bernstein, Kirsten Bishop, Tony Daniels, Naz Edwards, Jill Frappier, Katie Griffin, Terri Hawkes, Julie Lemieux, Mary Long, Kevin Lund, Colin O'Meara, Stephanie Morgenstern, Rolans Parliament, Toby Proctor, Nadine Rabinovitch, Susan Roman, Reno Romano, Ron Rubin.

Left to right: Sailor Jupiter, Sailor Mercury, Sailor Moon, Sailor Mars, and Sailor Venus.

Sailor Moon premiered in Japan in March 1992 as the 46-episode *Bishôjo Senshi Sailor Moon* (Pretty Soldier Sailor Moon), and produced four additional sequel series thereafter: *Bishôjo Senshi Sailor Moon R* (1993-'94, Eps. 47-89); *Bishôjo Senshi Sailor Moon S* (1994-'95 Eps. 90-131); *Bishôjo Senshi Sailor Moon Supers* (1995-'96); and finally, *Bishôjo Senshi Sailor Moon Sailor Stars* (1996-'97). True to its origin as a *shôjo* manga or "girls' comic" from creator Naoko Takeuchi, *Sailor Moon* is a television series aimed chiefly at teenage girls, featuring like-aged gals in lead roles fighting against an invasion from another dimension. Queen Beryl, the Snow White-like wicked queen who leads the Negaverse, spends a great deal of the initial series hovering over a crystal ball making menacing gestures with her long red fingernails and ordering around her handsome, mostly male, lieutenants.

The main character of the show is a ditzy blonde named Usagi Tsukino, with long, top-knotted ponytails which the other characters frequently tease her about (the usual appellation: "Meatball head"). Usagi is given a brooch that can transform her into the superhero Sailor Moon by a talking cat named Luna, who periodically doles out new magical weapons for Usagi and the other girls to use.

Usagi and her fellow fighters—Sailor Mercury, Sailor Mars, Sailor Jupiter and Sailor Venus—wear an idealized version of the traditional Japanese schoolgirl outfit, a sort of "sailor suit" dress, abbreviated into what resembles a figure-skating costume. Each girl's powers differ according to her corresponding planet. Sailor Moon fends off her opponents with her crescent-shaped tiara (which seems to slice opponents like a lethal, glowing frisbee); Sailor Mercury fires a fog of disorienting bubbles; Sailor Mars hurls fireballs; Sailor Jupiter fires lighting from an antenna in her tiara; and Sailor Venus' weapon is a powerful beam of energy in the form of two crescent moons.

Released for daily U.S. broadcast in the summer of 1995 by D.I.C. Entertainment, the English version of *Sailor Moon* anglicized the main characters' names,

©1992 Naoko Takeuchi/Kodansha

though to a much lesser extent than many shows prior to it. Usagi became "Serena" (still a pun on the moon but now in English, with its similarity to the Greek Selene, goddess of the moon); Sailor Mercury's Ami was changed to "Amy"; Mars' Rei became "Raye"; Jupiter's Makoto to "Lita"; and Venus' Minako to "Mina." The English *Sailor Moon* even translated the Japanese show's signature opening song—written by former TM Network member Tetsuro Komuro—more or less intact, one of the few anime adaptations since *Star Blazers* to do so.

Aside from the girls' duties as "Sailor Scouts" (a neat term that summons up an image of Girl Scouts), the plot revolves around the everyday schoolgirl concerns of the endearingly klutzy Serena and her friends—most notably, their crushes on various boys in the neighborhood. A recurring romantic character in the show also helps them in their battles against the Negaverse, a nattily dressed fighter in complete evening wear and cape, the aptly named Tuxedo Mask.

From the advertising which accompanied the show's initial Japanese run ("First Mama" toy kitchen appliances and the like), the target audience for *Sailor Moon* was clearly young girls. But with the show's sure sense of parody for various types of animated shows—the time-tested live-action *sentai* or costumed battle-team show among them—the plotline provided interest for older anime viewers as well. The climax of the story actually descends into deadly seriousness—in the Japanese version, all of the girls except for Sailor Moon herself are killed one by one in the build-up to the climactic battle (which in the English version is carefully explained away as their being "captured"), and the continuing romance between Sailor Moon and Tuxedo Mask is revealed to be the result of their being reincarnated lovers from the past. (The future child of their love who returns to the past, the diminutive pink-haired Rini, is introduced in the second series as Sailor Moon's cousin!)

A multimillion-dollar merchandising hit in Japan, the English version of *Sailor Moon* produced merchandise tie-ins such as dolls and replicas of Sailor Moon's magical weapons which sold quite well in toy stores across the country, though perhaps not as well as its sponsors might have liked. Although the English version of *Sailor Moon* enjoyed enough popularity to progress into the show's second series (originally titled *Sailor Moon R* in Japan), *Sailor Moon* did not perform as well as hoped in the U.S. by either its Japanese producers or its American release company. After frequent reruns it was dropped from North American syndication, even though the show had done much better in the Canadian market than America due to its more fortuitous timeslot. *Sailor Moon*'s departure from the air in mid-storyline left quite a few broken-hearted fans, mostly among the target teenage girl audience, and spawned many petitions and letter-writing campaigns (including on the Internet) to the U.S. producers in hopes of bringing the show back for more seasons, but their effect has yet to be seen.

Eagle Riders

Syndicated: 1996. Tatsunoko Production Co., Ltd./Saban Entertainment, Inc. English adaptation credits: Executive Producer: Eric S. Rollman; Producer and Story Editor: Rita M. Acosta; Music by Shuki Levy and Kussa Mahchi; Voices: Richard Cansino (Hunter Harris); Bryan Cranston (Joe Thax); Heidi Lenhart (Kelly Jenar); Mona Marshall (Mickey Dugan); Paul L. Schrier II (Ollie Keeawani); Greg O'Neill (Dr. Keane); Dena Burton (Auto); Lara Cody (Dr. Aikens); Peter Spellos (Cybercon); R. Martin Klein (Mallanox).

Nineteen years after *Science Ninja Team Gatchaman* first debuted on U.S. television as "Battle of the Planets," 1978's *Gatchaman II* finally made it to U.S. shores. Picked up for distribution by Saban Entertainment, which had seen recent success with its Americanization of the Japanese live-action show *Jû Ranger* ("Beast Ranger") as the **Mighty Morphin Power Rangers**, and also distributor of such American comics-based animated shows such as *The X-Men, Gatchaman II*, retitled **Eagle Riders**, debuted on network TV in fall of 1996 as part of a new children's morning package of

·1996

Also on TV in 1996:

Animaniacs
Batman Animated Series
Beavis and Butt-Head
Casper
Doug
Gargoyles
The Simpsons
Swat Kats
Taz-Mania
The Tick

©1978 Tatsunoko Production

The brave and handsome Hunter Harris from
Eagle Riders.

The **Eagle Riders**, counterclockwise from lower left: Hunter Harris, Kelly Jenar, Ollie Keeawani, Joe Thax and Mickey Dugan,

shows, broadcast on Sunday mornings in some areas rather than the traditional Saturday morning.

Saban's version of the show gave the Gatchaman team yet another set of names: the "Eagle Riders," led by the brave and handsome "Hunter Harris " (in Japanese, Ken the Eagle), while Joe the Condor became "Joe Thax," Jun the Swan, "Kelly Jenar," Ryu the Owl changed to the Hawaiian-themed "Ollie Keeawani," and young Jinpei the Swallow to "Mickey Dugan." The Eagle Riders are called in by "Dr. Thadeaus Keane," a respected scientist who formed the Eagle Riders to assist the "Global Security Council" in their fight against the nefarious "Vorak"—aliens dedicated to the total domination of Earth, and the enslavement of its inhabitants.

As Keane tells the council in a stirring speech at the beginning of the show, the Eagle Riders and their ship, the "Ultra Eagle," are always ready to fly into action instantly to anywhere on Earth or space, "for the global good." The Vorak aliens are actually behind the scenes for the first several episodes, pulling the strings of a splashily dressed and rather effeminate villain "Mallanox" and the powerful organization he kowtows to called Cybercon. One of the key emotional touchstones of *Gatchaman II*, that of the team dealing with the loss of Condor Joe, who had died a melodramatic death at the end of the first series, and his eventual return as a cyborg, is dealt with in a fairly straightforward manner by the English adaptation.

In late 1996 Saban released an initial 13 half-hour episodes of *Eagle Riders'* projected 65-episode package. Since the 1978-79 *Gatchaman II* was only 52 episodes, it is expected that Saban will have to dip into the subsequent 1979-80 *Gatchaman F* Japanese series to complete its *Eagle Riders* strip.

Samurai Pizza Cats

Syndicated: 1996. Tatsunoko Production Co., Ltd./Saban International. English adaptation credits: Executive Producer: Winston Richard; Producer: Andy Thomas; Music by Shuki Levy and Haim Saban; Voices: Terrence Scammel, Rick Jones, Michael O'Reilly, A.J. Henderson, Pauline Little, Dean Hagopian, Mark Camacho, Sonja Ball, Susanne Glover.

Tatsunoko's original program ran for 54 half-hour episodes, from February 1, 1990 through February 12, 1991. The Japanese title, *Cats Toninden Teyande*, is one of the Yoshidas' beloved multilingual puns. "Cats" is English; "Toninden" is Classic Japanese or Chinese (or both) for "Tales of the Spy Squad" (the "nin" is the same "nin" as in "ninja"), and "teyande" is/was current 1990 Japanese teen slang for a challenge to a fight (since Speedy, the main Pizza Cat, is a hothead who is always rushing into trouble).

The show is animated in a comical, "super-deformed" style, and centers on the characters who congregate around Little Tokyo's Samurai Pizza Cats Pizza Parlor. The original Japanese concept was that the characters were "animaroids," and their home town was called both "Mecha-Edo" and "Edopolis" (Edo was the feudal name for Tokyo). The Japanese name for the heroes was the "Nyankees"; a pun on "nyan" (Japanese for "meow") and "Yankees" (note that the costumes of the three leads are red, white, and blue).

The Good Guys (l to r): Polly Esther, Speedy Cerviche, and Guido Anchovi.

Naturally, the American syndicated version has been given an extensive makeover. The fast-talking, joke-cracking, streetwise leader of the pack, Yataro, is now "Speedy Cerviche" (get it?); Sukashi, a suave, romantic ladies' cat, is "Guido Anchovi" (*groan*); and pretty kitty Pururun (a pun on purring) is "Polly Esther" (*wince*). Assisting the three lead characters are the ditzy but loveable Francine, the beautiful Lucille, the likeable Emperor Fred, and his temper tantrum-throwing daughter Princess Violet. The Pizza Cats' mentor is Big Al Dente, a kind-hearted Saint Bernard who calls them to action through secret messages from his home computer.

The minute the cats get a call for help, their eatery transforms into a state-of-the-art crimefighting headquarters. Pizza ovens morph into high-tech tubes leading into transformation chambers, where the cats jump into their superhero garb. Each Pizza Cat slips into his/her individual color-coordinated projectile and is shot up and away via a giant gun at the top of the parlor (a parody of the giant gun in the Japanese live action sci-fi movie, *Cyber Ninja*, which was a popular hit when the series was first aired)

The Bad Guys (l to r): Jerry Atrick, Bad Bird, and Big Cheese.

Invariably, trouble involves the cats' nemesis Konnokami, renamed "The Big Cheese." In the Japanese version, he's a fox who is the Shogun (always trying to overthrow the Emperor). In the American version, he's an oversized rodent mobster who's head of the Little Tokyo Big Business Association. Big Cheese is assisted by Bad Bird (Karamaru in the original version) and Jerry Atrick, and utilizes a myriad of wacky mutants, robots and monsters to terrorize the town, including a Sushi Robot who converts innocent citizens into California rolls.

Samurai Pizza Cats entered entered the syndication market in 1996 with 26 half-hour episodes.

Chapter Two

Anime Genres

Animation comes of age: it's not just for kids anymore (if it ever was)

"That Speed Racer Stuff"

Japanese animation has been familiar to American viewers since the days of *Astro Boy*, the first-ever Japanese-animated series on American television, but because so many people grew up never knowing—or even suspecting—the series' Japanese origins, true awareness of Japanese animation as something distinctly different from most American cartoons would not come for another thirty years.

Today, even though the visibility of Japanese animation is increasing with occasional mainstream media attention (no small amount brought about by the controversy over Disney's *The Lion King*, which many people in the U.S. anime and manga industry feel was directly influenced—if not lifted outright—from Osamu Tezuka's *Kimba the White Lion*[1]), to most people all anime is indistinguishable from the one series almost all Westerners can immediately identify, even if they've never seen any other Japanese animation: *Speed Racer*. Even though it could be argued that the stereotypical image many people hold of Japanese animation is that of giant, flying robots such as *Gigantor*, it wasn't *Gigantor* episodes rebroadcast on late-night MTV, nor was it *Astro Boy* shown on a T-shirt worn by Eric Stolz in director Quentin Tarantino's *Pulp Fiction* that sticks in people's minds, but *Speed Racer*.

What exactly was it about *Speed Racer* that made such an impression on American viewers? Was it the violence, fairly shocking for its era? Kiddie television shows—and in 1960s America, animation was already long-established as being almost entirely for children—did not typically have villains screaming out their deaths in flaming car wrecks, but the vigilante tradition in American comics hardly ruled it out, as early superhero comics were often very violent, faithful to their roots as offshoots of the hard-boiled crime dramas published in the lurid pulp novels of the day.

By and large, what set *Speed Racer* apart was its frenetic, breathless pace, and imaginative supply of seemingly endless permutations on the series' main attraction— the requisite car race. No one can argue that the themes of *Speed Racer* were sophisticated, but by intensely focusing on the tantalizing thrill of the super-powered Mach 5 race car and its clean-cut macho hero, Speed, the series had a surprising vitality.[2]

Speed Racer also showcased one of the strongest elements in Japanese animation: namely, its ability to create solid characters capable of carrying the show on their own. The characters of Speed, Trixie, and Spridle are so distinct and well, *real*, that even in the tongue-in-cheek English version, they're cult heroes in their own right, as much celebrities as any of their kitschy live-action brethren. This aspect of Japanese animation, more than any other, explains its cult appeal.

[1] In Japan, indignation over perceived similarities between Disney's *Lion King* and Tezuka's *Jungle Taitei* or "Jungle Emperor" was so great, manga artist Machiko Satonaka circulated a petition demanding that Disney acknowledge its debt to Tezuka. "I cannot call it a coincidence," Satonaka told the Japanese newspaper *Yomiuri Shimbun*. "As a person who admires Disney, I think it's a shame. Tezuka's works are a part of Japanese culture, and I'd hate to see their value diminished. At the very least, (Disney) should have inserted 'In appreciation of Osamu Tezuka' or something like that." At the time of the *Yomiuri Shimbun* article, over four hundred persons had signed Satonaka's petition, over eighty of them fellow manga artists.

Here he comes, Here comes *Speed Racer*.

©1967 Tatsunoko Productions

[2] First airing in Japan during 1967, *Speed Racer* is one of Japanese animation's most enduringly popular series, recently rerunning to popular acclaim on MTV and even inspiring a frantic "house" music dance hit remix by Alpha Team. Asked if he was familiar with the song (which samples Speed's urgent "Trixie!"s and Trixie's breathy cries of "Oh, SPEED—!," set against a suggestive one-two backbeat which leaves little to the imagination), Peter Fernandez, the English voice of Speed, could only smile, murmuring something under his breath about "no residuals."

Ataru and Lum having a lover's quarrel, from the **Urusei Yatsura** TV series.

3 Yasuo Yamada, one of Japan's most popular—and beloved—voice-actors, contributed his voice to the animated version of creator Monkey Punch's sly caper about a gentleman thief, **Lupin III**. In addition to his fame as Lupin, Yamada was a versatile and active actor well-known to Japanese audiences as the official voice of international stars such as Clint Eastwood, Peter Fonda and Jean-Paul Belmondo in the many theatrical releases dubbed into Japanese for television broadcast. Although he has since been replaced in the continuing Lupin III videos by another actor, when Yamada passed away in March 1995 of a brain hemorrhage, anime fans on both sides of the Pacific felt as though they had lost an old friend. (And they had.)

Ranma 1/2's Ranma Saotome, doing the yin-yang thing.

From **Urotsuki Dôji: Legend of the Overfiend**.

More Real Than Real

Like the American pop culture icons **Star Trek**, **Batman**, or **Superman**, it is the essential cast of characters that truly drives the stories of anime, no matter how silly or derivative the premise. When fictional characters from any particular medium—be it comics, movies, or television shows—take on their own life, then that work can truly be said to have entered pop culture. No one wonders what the immaculate princess Snow White does after the story ends (*Why, she lives happily ever after, of course!*), but when it comes to their favorite series and characters, that is exactly what fans of Japanese animation do—wonder what happens when the show ends.

Rumiko Takahashi, the Japanese creator of the wacky love comedies **Lum * Urusei Yatsura** and **Ranma 1/2**, visited the United States for the San Diego ComiCon in 1994. One fan who had stood patiently in line for several hours to enter the question-and-answer period asked with a tremble in his voice if Ms. Takahashi would ever publish a story in which the main characters of *Urusei Yatsura*, the bikini-clad alien Lum and the luckless schoolboy Ataru, would ever marry. The note in the fan's voice and the tears in his eyes illustrated just how important this question was for him, just as it would be for anyone who had breathlessly followed the adventures of two such characters in any live-action serial or soap opera.

This breathless anticipation regarding the "reality" of favorite characters isn't endemic to the U.S., of course; in Japan, amateur fan-created parody/homage comics called *dôjinshi* have been and will continue to be briskly traded back and forth for years, while small cults are formed around the actors who breathe life into popular animated characters. In Japan, many voice-actors are major celebrities in their own right, forever after associated lovingly with a famous role.[3] In terms of mainstream—as compared to cult—appeal, America's fan scene is still only in its infancy. And yet, the cult aspect of anime and manga is already flourishing, all of which attests to the power of the Japanese animators' ability to make their stories and their characters come alive.

Unlike so much of American animation, anime constantly strives to make its characters real and essential, not single-note comedic props or symbolic animated role models. To that end, characters grow and change throughout the story...even die. Disney has built a tradition upon striving for perfectly preserved, stiflingly *safe* fairytale-based storylines (more often than not yielding "sympathetic" characters who are interchangeable ciphers, while villains, interestingly enough, are strikingly well-defined), whereas Japanese animation—like current American productions such as **The Simpsons**, **Animaniacs**, and **Tiny Toon Adventures**—pushes for a sense of *immediacy*, unafraid to be dated, unafraid to surf the fashion of its era. Like the little girl with the curl in the middle of her forehead, when anime is dated, it's very *very* dated, but when it's current, it can be *torrid*.

Animation For Adults, Not Just "Adults-Only" Anime

With the range of styles and subjects encompassed in the entire spectrum of Japanese animation, it's possible even within the ever-expanding cornucopia of anime-in-English videos released so far to find something for every imaginable taste: horror, science fiction, fantasy, comedy or "adults-only" tentacle sex fests. Unlike the bulk of animation currently seen on weekday afternoons and Saturday morning "kiddie prime-time" viewing hours, Japanese animation manages to appeal to adults—and not always by focusing on the "adults-only" material.

Of course, it's inevitably the "adults-only" stuff which seems to garner the lion's share of mainstream media attention. In his "Japan, a Superpower Among Superheroes," the Japanese pop culture-savvy Andrew Pollack couldn't resist peppering his otherwise balanced *New York Times* article on anime with references to **Urotsuki Dôji: Legend of the Overfiend** ("an adults-only cartoon that was a popular midnight movie…it features grotesque monsters from another world forcing bizarre sex on cute teen-age earthlings") and the infamous manga series *Rape Man* ("featuring a hero who commits rape for hire").

No matter the sensationalistic aspects of certain titles, what's important to remember is that the bulk of Japanese animation isn't demonic rape fantasies or even rape fantasies of demons; like any storytelling medium, anime is infinitely variable. It's telling of anime's incredible diversity that the U.S. distributor of *Urotsuki Dôji: Legend of the Overfiend*—New York-based Central Park Media—is also responsible for bringing to America director Isao Takahata's **Grave of the Fireflies**, the critically acclaimed, heart-wrenching saga of two children amidst the fire-bombing of Kobe in World War II Japan.[4]

Like dismissing all American comics as "violent" or "erotic" due to a few high-profile, notorious examples, it's unfair to the staggering potential of the anime art form to mention "erotic grotesques" (CPM's term) such as *Urotsuki Dôji: Legend of the Overfiend* without also mentioning *Fireflies*. For every Tsutomu Miyazaki serial killer in Japanese society, there's a Hayao Miyazaki world-beloved Japanese animator.[5] In fact, given the enormous amount of animation which is produced by the Japanese industry (as cited by Pollack, in 1994 more than half of the box-office revenues of Japan's entire movie industry came from animation), the animation which is also pornographic is relatively small. Is it the fact that the pornography is *animated*, a *cartoon* (which, in this country, tends to automatically imply targeted at children) which is giving the sensationalists the heebie-jeebies?[6]

"Why would anyone say, 'I once saw or just heard of a Japanese animation called *Legend of the Overfiend* and all Japanese animations are pornographic smut and I'll never watch another one'?," asks CPM's John O'Donnell rhetorically. "How realistic is that? 'I once had a restaurant meal and it was bad, so I'll never eat in a restaurant again.' That's the level of logic which is encapsulated in those comments."

Granted, this is not to say that *Urotsuki Dôji: Legend of the Overfiend* isn't pornographic. (It is.) And it's hardly within the scope of this book to come up with a justification for what basically really does amount to "grotesque monsters from another world forcing bizarre sex on cute teen-age earthlings." Then again, especially in comparison with such live-action misogynist charmers as *I Spit On Your Grave*, *Urotsuki Dôji: Legend of the Overfiend* is both no worse and no better. The only difference is, it's animated.

By the same token, in Japan it's implicitly obvious that anime videos such as *Urotsuki Dôji: Legend of the Overfiend*, **Legend of Lyon: Flare**, **La Blue Girl** and all their adults-only brethren are for *adults*, pro-duced by adults and meant to be *seen* by adults. Nowhere in that equation does "animated" equal "for children," and so it's that much more ironic that films such as *Urotsuki Dôji: Legend of the Overfiend* set box-office records at American theaters, while acknowledged—yet woefully underpublicized—director Hiroyuki Yamaga's animated masterpiece **The Wings of Honneamise** barely raises eyebrows, or, as has been the case far too often, generates reviews written by film critics whose only frame of Japanese animation reference is *Speed Racer*. (Worse yet is when said reviewers cite *Wings'* lack of the somehow-expected explicit sex and violence as reason to ignore the film's more ambitious achievements.) Because it is true, after all—important as *Speed Racer* is to spreading mainstream awareness of anime, saying *Speed Racer* is representative of all anime is like saying, as O'Donnell puts it, that *The Terminator* is representative of all American cinema.[7]

©1992 Toshio Maeda/Daiei Co., Ltd.

One of the more outrageous examples of tentacle-porn is *La Blue Girl*.

©1989 Akira Committee

Like other media such as live-action cinema, television, literature or comic books, Japanese animation covers a wide range of interests, everything from action-packed adventure, video game-based martial arts, witty and sophisticated crime capers, darkly stylish animated noir, live-action style "battle team" or *sentai* heroes, fastidiously detailed robots and mechanics (known by those in the know as "mecha"), post apocalyptic cyberpunk, wacky romantic comedies, classic sci-fi, full-blown space operas, dramatic *tours de force*, films which appeal to children of all ages, and yes, the above-mentioned "adults-only" shockers.

The genres of storytelling in general and animation in particular are many, and so too are the genres of Japanese animation. And yet of all the animation existing in the world today, only Japanese animation owns the four most exciting, *least-easily-achievable-in-live-action* genres: cyberpunk, giant robots, the anime noir thriller, and the romantic "love" comedy. With a few notable exceptions (nobody does a fairytale or folklore-based musical comedy like Disney, after all), only in Japanese animation have these four genres evolved into distinctly recognizable subgenres, each with their own conventions, character archetypes and easily identifiable formulas, each brought to life by the unique vision or style of one individual—be that individual a director, an original creator, or even a character or mecha designer.

Nothing you've seen in American animation has prepared you for this.

Technology Run Amok: Growing Up Cyberpunk in Neo-Tokyo

The word's been in the popular vocabulary since writers such as William "*Neuromancer*" Gibson and John "*Vacuum Flowers*" Shirley published their dark, dystopian novels in the mid- to late-'80s, but "cyberpunk" is far from limited to American science fiction. With stories showcasing the cutting edge of science and technology, set in the distant-yet-closer-than-we-think world of tomorrow, anime is admirably suited to telling the kinds of stories that could only be done in animation.

Director and creator Katsuhiro Otomo's *Akira* (1988)[8] is set against the backdrop of the sprawling megalopolis Neo-Tokyo in the Year 2019 A.D. In the film, roving, bloodthirsty delinquents terrorize the streets of Neo-Tokyo on their souped-up cycles, rumbling with rival gangs and popping pills by the handful while taking disciplinary beatings from wrathful guidance counselors. After bike gang member Tetsuo almost runs down a rather special escapee from a government lab, he and his gang leader Kaneda become involved in a political and metaphysical struggle to contain—if not actually *control*—a frighteningly powerful government psychic project known only as "Akira." Wild-eyed religious cult leaders roam the streets with prophesies of doom, while the movie's soundtrack throbs with a hypnotic marimba beat and obscure and little-heard ethnic woodwinds complement the frenzied chanting of an Okinawa-influenced main title theme performed by Japan's prestigious Geinoh Yamashiro Group.

Disney it most definitely ain't.

Created, directed, and featuring character designs by Japanese manga artist Katsuhiro Otomo, upon its 1989 U.S. theatrical release by Los Angeles-based Streamline Pictures, *Akira* became a huge cult success, going on to gross nearly US$1 million at the domestic box office. In April of 1992, *Siskel & Ebert* named *Akira* a "Pick of the Week." Later, the *San Francisco Chronicle* wrote, "*Akira* is an astonishing piece of animation," while the *Washington Post* agreed, "A visceral example of the future of animation." On the occasion of *Akira*'s release in the bells 'n' whistles-added three-disc Criterion laser disc format in 1993, *Time* magazine wrote, "A virtuoso piece of speculative fiction, a violent adventure tale, a head-bending sci-fi morality play."

For many anime fans (and those who were soon-to-become anime fans), *Akira* was a first taste of the amazing, heretofore unseen potential of Japanese animation to not only capture, but *keep* the interest of the mature, sophisticated filmgoers who

[8] I debated for quite some time over whether, as I've done here, the *Japanese* release date should be listed, or the U.S. release date. Ultimately, I came to the conclusion that the date of the video's first release would prove most helpful, providing a much-needed sense of chronology—what comes before what—as well as neatly dodging the "Was that the *English* release date or the *subtitled* release date?" question.

©1989 Akira Committee

A scene from *Akira*.

patronized the film festivals and art theaters where *Akira* was primarily screened during its English-language theatrical run. It was dark; it was unsettling; it was unlike any science fiction story—animated or otherwise—anyone had ever seen before. It wasn't the first Japanese-animated film to be released theatrically in the U.S., but for many, *Akira* was the film which would make that crucial break into the American pop culture mainstream. Its technical and artistic credentials were unassailable, it was "as good as Disney" (or even better), and the subject matter was definitely *not* for kids.

Although *Akira* was arguably the one to do it the biggest and most beautifully, by no means is it the only anime video to focus on a dark and uncertain—yet frighteningly possible—future. Director Mamoru Oshii's ***Patlabor 1: The Movie*** (1989) has often been described as a mix of *Hill Street Blues*-style cinéma vérité and the topical, sociological commentary found in the works of *The Andromeda Strain* author Michael Crichton. In this world, advanced giant robots called "Labors" begin to be used for construction, much as bulldozers are today. But Labors, like guns, don't discriminate— in the wrong hands, these mechanical behemoths are powerful weapons of destruction, as easily turned on the innocent as the guilty.

A robot from ***Mobile Police Patlabor***.

To combat the increasingly common Labor crimes, law enforcement officers are equipped with Labors—the Patlabors, or "Patrol Labors" of the series title. Not a robot show in the mold of ***Gigantor*** (more on that later), *Patlabor* qualifies as a cyberpunk show not only for its "intelligent sci-fi" approach, but for its view of the future as a confused, complicated place. *Patlabor* habitually addresses topics such as the future of law enforcement and the morality of technology, where cyberpunk hackers cause robots to run amok and political coups arranged by technological terrorists threaten the public safety. Meanwhile, the black sheep of Japan's "Special Vehicles Section 2" or SV2 are caught in the middle, often able to perform little more than damage control. It's a future with which any frustrated corporate employee, held hostage to a power larger than him or herself, can sympathize.

[9] ***Patlabor 1: The Movie*** is one of two feature films inspired by a long-running animated series, including a seven-volume *Patlabor* OAV series, a 48-episode TV series, and then, a second, sixteen-episode OAV series. As of this writing, both the two ***Patlabor*** theatrical features as well as the TV and OAV series are available on home video in North America. Look to Manga Entertainment for the two films, and to U.S. Manga Corps for the OAV series (the TV series has been announced for '97).

Plot-wise, the film bears a certain similarity to other tales of a scourge upon a technological society such as author Neal Stephenson's *Snow Crash*. However, unlike the novel, the world of *Patlabor 1: The Movie* isn't an unrecognizable blur of Stephenson's overlapping city-states and law-unto-themselves "franchulates," but the world the day after tomorrow, all the more frightening because it's all the more recognizable.[9]

Ghost in the Shell (1995), Oshii's latest film, has been described by some as the "first truly integrated film of SF's cyberpunk genre," combining liberal doses of Biblically allusive musings on the spirit and the flesh (the "ghost" and the "shell," respectively) with the trademark high-tech look fans have come to expect from original story creator Masamune Shirow (see below).

As has been suggested previously by others, the imagery here is not Shirow's, however, but Oshii's, who approaches Shirow's original manga story from an angle wholly his own, replacing the slick, techno-fetish look of Shirow's Major Motoko Kusanagi with a deathly pale, unblinking automaton, perhaps, as anime critic Carl Gustav Horn says, "meant to reflect the lack of essential vitality of even a perfect body in an age where they are but shells, manufactured to order, that one's essential ghost slips in and out of as needed."

Cybernetic agent Mokoto Kusanagi from ***Ghost in the Shell***.

The first anime video to place No. 1 on *Billboard* magazine's sales chart in the U.S., *Ghost* is the first film since *Akira* to duplicate the 1989 film's widespread main-stream visibility—in fact, *Ghost* has gone the latter one better, as *Akira* has yet to be offered as a "premium selection" on an in-home satellite channel, as *Ghost* has. Although fans of the manga complained at the time of the film's first release that an already confusing story had become even *more* confusing (Oshii directing a Shirow story? whose idea was that?), that the animation is among the best anime has ever seen is a fact which remains undisputed.

The dystopian city again rears its head in the eight-volume OAV series ***Bubblegum Crisis*** (1987), this time with a different focus. "Neo-Tokyo" becomes "Mega-Tokyo," but the basic concept is still the same: Technology runs rampant, society is in turmoil, and no one is sure what tomorrow will bring.

The four-woman vigilante team, the Knight Sabers, decked out in full battle-gear —from the ***Bubblegum Crisis*** OAV series.

According to producer Toshimichi Suzuki, the *Bubblegum Crisis* or *BGC* series was written to express the fear that rapid technological innovations will make people apathetic as to how these new innovations could be used, and the series' sleek characters and stylish, decaying cities (strongly reminiscent of Ridley Scott's *Blade Runner*, in more ways than one) support this theory.

In the world of Mega-Tokyo, an all-female team of super-suited beauties known as the "Knight Sabers" battle a megalithic corporation and its evil henchmen, the bio-tech menaces, artificial lifeforms called "Boomers." Originally intended for work in space, the Boomers, like Labors, have been used and abused by the wrong people, and the Knight Sabers vigilante group is formed to put a halt to their rampages. Like a superhero team, each member of the four-woman team has a distinct personality—each one, possessed of a special skill essential to the team's success, even hard-rockin' singer Priss, leader of her band, The Replicants. With the series' carefully produced '80s-style rock opera numbers providing a driving score to the action scenes, *BGC* had all the elements needed to make it one of the most popular OAV series of its day.

Off-duty Knight Saber Priss, dressed in more casual attire.

Three years after its Japanese release, a *BGC* spinoff series, ***A.D. Police*** (1990), was produced. Based on the manga series by Tony Takezaki, *A.D. Police* is set in the same Mega-Tokyo of *BGC*, but introduces a (mostly) new cast of characters including cybernetically enhanced female A.D. Police officer Jeena Malso (Leon McNichol, a minor character from *BGC*, assumes a larger role in *A.D. Police*). In the series, the violence is upped, and the characters are tougher; unlike the original "girls with guns" of *BGC*, Jeena Malso is a bionically enhanced female warrior more in the mold of *Die Hard*'s Bruce Willis or *Terminator 2*'s Linda Hamilton than the gum-snapping, wise-cracking riot grrrl of *Tank Girl*'s Lori Petty.

BGC is notable not only for its oh-so-'80s cyberpunk story, but for the many creative talents associated with the series who would later go on to greater fame with other programs. It's a testament to the popularity of anime characters that even the character designers for animation can claim fame for their creations. Kenichi Sonoda, the justly famed character designer for *BGC*, also created the characters for the sci-fi thriller ***Gall Force*** (1986) and the *Blues Brothers*-influenced action-comedy ***Riding Bean*** (1989), but it's the sexy, distinctive look he created for the Knight Sabers that assured him his place in anime history. Mecha designer Masami Obari eventually became a much bigger name with his character designs for the martial arts action/adventure ***Fatal Fury*** (1992), but it was his animation direction and mecha design skills which brought his uniquely hyperkinetic, hyper-muscled style to the attention of many fans.[10]

[10] In the anime world, the title "mecha designer" typically applies to the designer not only of robots, but machinery of all types, including futuristic cars, guns, and other paraphernalia. Truly devoted mecha fans know their mecha designers the way film critics know their directors, giving rise to the appellation "mechahead" for those fans who know their Gundams from their Layzers, and their Gerwalks from their Battloids.

Just as New York has long since become a sort of cultural slang for a metropolis teeming with uncontrollable crime and a frightening sense of anarchy (such as in director John Carpenter's *Escape From New York*), so do many videos in Japan share the popular "Neo-Tokyo" concept. However, to date only one animated film has adopted the name as its own: ***Neo-Tokyo*** (1987), an anthology video featuring three short animated pieces by three acclaimed Japanese directors, Katsuhiro Otomo's **"The Order to Stop Construction,"** Rin Taro's **"Labyrinth,"** and Yoshiaki Kawajiri's **"The Running Man."**

Both "The Order to Stop Construction" and "Labyrinth" have strong sci-fi/fantasy elements, but it's the sense of hopelessness regarding technology's increasing chokehold on society which makes "The Running Man" fit most strongly into the cyberpunk genre. ("The Running Man" also has a touch of horror which adds, rather than subtracts, from the segment's decidedly cyberpunkish grim tone.)

In "The Running Man," psionically enhanced race-car driver Zach Hugh has been at the top of his profession for ten years. When it comes to the Death Race circuit, nobody's better than Zach, although success has its price. When you've been in the race as long as Zach, how do you stop? *Can* you stop…? Frequently seen on the ubiquitous, pop culture touchstone (and increasingly anime-aware) MTV, Kawajiri's "The Running Man" bears no resemblance to the "Richard Bachman" (a.k.a. Stephen King) short story of the same name, other than its title.

Or…does it? Both bear testament to the human will, even when stretched to the bitter end; both feature a man who runs…and runs…and runs, until he's powerless to stop. Whether Kawajiri was aware of the Bachman story or not, the fact remains that his animated version is, intentionally or unintentionally, closer in spirit to the original story than the 1987 film of the same name starring Arnold Schwarzenegger.

It's this feeling of humanity enslaved and despairing in the maw of remorseless progress which is the most affecting part of *Appleseed* (1988), based on the long-running manga series of the same name by dystopian comic visionary (and real-life teacher in hiding), Masamune Shirow.[11]

"It was in that year that the flames of war broke out simultaneously in every corner of the globe," reads the English version of Shirow's *Appleseed* comic. "To the vast movement of armies, conflict spread, merged, grew, escalating into world war.

"Knowledge was lost. Confusion reigned. New powers rose to displace the old nations. Nuclear weapons themselves were never used. But even without them, the Earth became a quieter planet."

Quieter, perhaps, but not necessarily *better*. In the post WWIII world of *Appleseed*, an omnipresent supercomputer called "Gaia" controls electricity, transportation, water, communications, and all other essentials which keep the mega-city of Olympus running smoothly. And things *do* run smoothly, *too* smoothly, perhaps, as discovered by ESWAT ([E]xtra-[S]pecial [W]eapons and [T]actics) officers Deunan and her cyborged-out partner Briareos when they investigate the death of a woman named Fleia, a woman who had everything…except the will to live. Like one of those episodes of *Star Trek* where everything has gone horribly wrong, *Appleseed* is a world out of balance, where everything *seems* to be perfect, but nothing is. Is there such a thing as being *too* safe?

Shirow is one of the most visible—if not the most consistent—of cyberpunk anime creators. His ***Black Magic M-66*** (1987), featuring an original story, screenplay, and direction by Shirow himself, remains one of the most visually stunning animated videos produced by the anime industry to date. (In the *Appleseed* animation, Shirow is credited with "original story" only... and it shows.)

In *Black Magic M-66*, tough-as-nails freelance journalist Sybel gets in over her own freewheeling head when she unveils a military operation and cover-up involving two rogue android assassins created by a more than slightly mad scientist, Dr. Matthews. The doctor's granddaughter, the more than slightly ditsy Ferris, has been programmed as a "test target" during the early stages of the androids' testing. Unfortunately, Dr. Matthews has forgotten to *remove* his granddaughter's data from the memory banks of the robotic albino assassins, and it's up to Sybel to protect Ferris from the most relentless and terrifying soldier since *The Terminator*.

Like *The Terminator*, the message of *Black Magic M-66* is that part of the miracle of advancing technology also includes its greatest threat; that is, that it may eventually

The futuristic Olympus Police Force team of Briareos Hecatones and Deunan Knute, from ***Appleseed***.

---

[11] Masamune Shirow is both one of cyberpunk anime's most prolific creators and one of its most enigmatic luminaries. A teacher by trade, Shirow works on his blackly humorous, technologically obsessed comics under a pen name. Shirow's actual name (or even what he *looks* like, as no photo has ever been published) is known only to a select few, unknown to the public at large.

A scene from ***Black Magic M-66***.

[12] Released in April '95, a three-volume ***Dominion*** sequel series, ***New Dominion Tank Police***, picked up where U.S. Manga Corps' first ***Dominion*** OAV series left off, with more Leona, more of her beloved tank Bonaparte, and more Puma Sisters than ever before. The new series is currently available in English from Manga Entertainment.

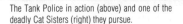

The Tank Police in action (above) and one of the deadly Cat Sisters (right) they pursue.

[13] The original Japanese series title is ***Gunnm***, literally meaning "gun" + "dream," but was released in English under the title ***Battle Angel Alita*** by Viz Comics. Anime company A.D. Vision chose to release their subtitled version of the video under the name ***Battle Angel***, but retained in their script the main character's Japanese name, Gally, rather than the English name, Alita. Other differences between the two versions include the floating city of Zalem (Tiphares in the comic), the character of Yugo (Hugo), and the name of the squalid junk heap where most of *Battle Angel*'s action takes place, Scrap Iron City (the Scrapyard). Although rumors of a second video focusing on the "Motorball" story arc have circulated among fans for months, it would seem that for now, at least, the only way to experience creator Kishiro's bloody paean to director Norman Jewison's ***Rollerball*** is through the manga.

outpace its creators. Shirow's latest anime feature—the big-budget blockbuster ***Ghost in the Shell*** (see above)—continues to explore this theme of technology as an onrushing juggernaut humans may find themselves having to battle for the right to survive.

Shirow's most dystopian city of the future to date is the Newport City of ***Dominion Tank Police*** (1988), a heavily armored animated "black" comedy which still manages to address some very serious issues.[12] In the Year 2010, the Earth has been encircled by a toxic cloud so noxious that wearing gas masks when walking the city streets isn't just an option, but a necessity. Perhaps in response to the escalating population (and the escalating population pressures), crimes in Newport City are out of control, with one being committed every 36 seconds.

In response to the ever-more-frequently occurring crimes, a new kind of police force is created, one certain to put the "terror" back into "interrogation": the Tank Police, gung-ho zealots to whom civil liberties pose no more threat than the pavement the treads of their stupifyingly armored tanks tear up every time they travel the streets. The rounded edges of the city's skyscrapers—more like *corroded* edges, with strange, barnacle-like encrustations bulging out from their sides—compete with the almost-total darkness in which all *Dominion*'s exterior shots are lit, creating an urban landscape even less welcoming than *Blade Runner*, if such a thing is possible. Little touches of black humor such as the interrogation of a suspect via a game of grenade golf, or the obsessive-compulsive (dare we say Freudian?) attachment of the Tank Police officers to their beloved tanks have the funny, yet suspiciously "This-Can't-Possibly-Be-Good-For-Me, But-I'm-Laughing-Anyway" twisted appeal of typically Tarantino black comedies such as *True Romance*, or *Pulp Fiction*, or even the gleefully Franco-phobic *Killing Zoe* by Roger Avary.

This atmosphere is taken a step further (minus the comedy) in ***Battle Angel*** (1993), based on the manga series by creator Yukito Kishiro.[13] *Battle Angel* is a dark, hyper action-packed tale of a young cyborg girl working as a bounty hunter in a crumbling junkyard city existing beneath a far distant, utopian city in the clouds. Found broken and discarded on the scrap heap, Gally is rescued from the refuse by cyborg physician/part-time bounty hunter/father-lover substitute Dr. Ido. In Scrap Iron City, life is cheap and human body parts are even cheaper. Many of the people on the streets of the city are themselves cyborgs of one stripe or another, while others are completely mechanical except for their organic, human brain.

Cyborg bounty-hunters, known as "Hunter-Warriors," are contracted by "The Factory," the only authority recognized by Scrap Iron City. The Factory is controlled from the floating city of Zalem above, with robot drones issuing the rules and orders by which all those who live below must exist. The floating city which hovers eternally above is an inescapable reminder of the vast difference in the lives of those who live above, and those who live below. With its cybernetic warrior-heroine, *Battle Angel* treads firmly on the ground that the live-action feature *Tank Girl* stumbled so ineptly upon, even with its gum-snapping, wisecracking riot grrrls.

Silent Möbius (1991) is, again, set in the nearer-than-you-think world of Tokyo, where a six-woman team known as "AMP"—"Attacked Mystification Police" or "Abnormal Mystery Police," depending on whom you ask—battle nasties from beyond while confronting their own tangled and troubled mystical pasts. While *Silent Möbius* may more properly be described as a supernatural thriller, the cyberpunk composition of AMP's crack team of capable women are unmistakable: Team leader Rally Cheyenne, a half-human, half-supernatural "Entity"; Katsumi Liqueur, daughter of a master sorcerer; kimono-clad Nami Yamigumo, a Japanese high priestess; Yuki Saito, troubled product of genetic engineering; the cyborg Kiddy Phenil; and Lebia Maverick, a super-hacker and priestess of sorts at the temple of technology.

Lebia in particular fits the cyberpunk label in the *Johnny Mnemonic* mode; as she sends out her consciousness into the global computer network, she must struggle to maintain her own identity while using her other abilities to battle terrifying creatures from beyond. Director Michitaka Kikuchi's design sense is without equal, and unlike so many Hollywood films these days, every cent of the film's budget is up on the screen—much more so than the low-budget, live-action version currently available only in Japan, *A.M.P. and the Last Days of the Shogunate*, filmed using voice-actors from the animated video in the film's title roles. Perhaps tellingly, Kikuchi himself has dismissed the live-action version as "juvenile," and while one can argue that the animated *Silent Möbius* is not an entirely successful film for anyone not already at least passingly familiar with the manga version, it hardly comes across as "for children."

The cast of *Silent Möbius*.

If anime really is "Japan's Hollywood," nowhere else is the ability to create stories not possible in any other medium so obvious as in the cyberpunk genre. Other anime genres have their demands—the sci-fi and/or "giant robot" genres in particular—but short of the Hollywood-sized budgets of films such as director Terry Gilliam's *Brazil* and yes, Ridley Scott's *Blade Runner*, where else could the sweeping cityscape panoramas and glittering carpets of light such as those found in *Akira* be possible? Even the Sylvester Stallone blockbuster *Judge Dredd* relied extensively on computer graphics to recreate the multi-tiered aviaries of the story's sprawling Mega-City; would it even have been possible using old production values such as models and mattes? Probably not.

Bubblegum Crisis creator Toshimichi Suzuki remembers that when he created his animation studio, Artmic, he'd just wanted "a place where we could indulge our imaginations. Animation or movies; anything would have been fine. But what could have cost millions in a special-effects movie, we could do in animation."

Ultimately, the value of a sci-fi or cyberpunk film is not in its special effects, but in how well it entertains or intrigues its audience. Anime videos such as *Akira* and *Bubblegum Crisis* and *Battle Angel* are popular not because of the animated bells and whistles (although there are those in abundance), but rather, because they successfully posit a world-view—dark, dystopian—and cleverly convince a sometimes-uncaring audience to care about what happens there. Cyberpunk isn't the sum and total of Japanese animation—not by a long shot—but you've got to admit, anime does it better than just about anyone else.

Mechatopia: The Role of The Robot in Anime

Remember that female comedian a few years back who had that joke about the latest centerfold in the Japanese edition of *Playboy* being a Toyota pickup? Japan's passion for technology has often been a source of humor, but nowhere else does its unabashed fascination for clever gadgets shine more clearly than in the robots of Japanese animation.

In the Robot Circus, Astro Boy is brutalized by the greedy Ringmaster Hamegg.

Robots go back to the very beginning of anime. In 1963, the robot show that *Manga! Manga! The World of Japanese Comics* author Frederik L. Schodt once described as starring "the most famous Japanese robot character of all time" made its appearance on American and Japanese TV screens: ***Astro Boy***, also known as "Mighty Atom," beloved of children of all ages the world over.

In his book ***Inside the Robot Kingdom: Japan, Mechatronics, and the Coming Robotopia***, Schodt says that *Astro Boy* creator Osamu Tezuka's true genius lay not in giving his creation superhuman powers (although Astro Boy did have those),

The Complete Anime Guide

[14] When Tezuka was in fifth grade, the story goes, a friend showed him an insect encyclopedia. From that point on, Tezuka became obsessed with insect-hunting. The mania continued until junior high school, eventually becoming the source of the pen name he would use for the rest of his life: "Osamushi," which added the Chinese character *mushi* or "bug" to the single-character name "Osamu" given to him by his parents in honor of Emperor Meiji. Immediately signing his insect diaries and school art projects with the pen name, at age 22, Tezuka began officially requesting that the two-character "Osamushi" name be read as "Osamu," just as it's read to this day.

Mitsuteru Yokoyama's **Gigantor**.

Yasuhiro Imagawa's version of **Giant Robo**.

but in placing him with a "family of robots who were all androids and normal in most respects. This had the brilliant effect of making him immediately identifiable to all the children of Japan. Atom became the little boy next door, except he lived in the future where science and technology had created a world of clever gadgets and a standard of living that the Japanese can only dream about."

Astro Boy was a revolutionary new comic, and its animated version was no less revolutionary—debuting in Japan on 1 January 1963, it was exported to the U.S. and broadcast on NBC nine months later. In Japan, 193 half-hour episodes of **Tetsuwan Atom** were produced by Tezuka's Mushi Productions[14]; 104 of them were acquired by NBC Enterprises for concurrent broadcast in the U.S. Although many of the names in the series were changed for the English version (Atom's surrogate father, Dr. Ochanomizu, was changed to "Dr. Elefun," for example), the charm of *Astro Boy* was no less powerful, and a generation of children grew up thinking the world would be a much nicer place with Astro Boy in it.

Quite unlike Tezuka's lovable *Astro Boy* series is **Gigantor** (1963), the creation of manga artist Mitsuteru Yokoyama, one of the earliest pioneers of what would soon become a robot tradition. Distributed in the U.S. by The Right Stuf, *Gigantor* is the story of an armored and aloof robot whose awesome might can be used for good or ill, depending on who holds the remote control at the time. While Astro Boy was the perfect child substitute—friendly, bright, eager to please—Gigantor was more like the dream toy every Japanese child longed to possess: unlimited power on command, the ideal size/age equalizer, utter and total obedience. Whatever nefarious plots the latest mad inventor might hatch, Gigantor and Jimmy would be there to set things right. This was, and still is, one of the most attractive aspects of the robot genre to many fans, this image of the robot as powerful enough to crush any enemy at your command.

Director Yasuhiro Imagawa's **Giant Robo** (1992), also based on the original manga by the creator of *Gigantor* himself, Mitsuteru Yokoyama, is a loving homage to those powerful robots of old, enhanced by an original story by Imagawa which paints a much bleaker world than the 1960s cartoony menaces of Yokoyama's original. The story of a boy, his giant robot, and a crime-fighting organization known as the "Agents of Justice," *Giant Robo* is a retro yet futuristic redux of a past and future where, in the words of director Imagawa, "world domination would be possible, a world with today's morality and tomorrow's look." The characters of *Giant Robo* are purposefully old-fashioned in style, with round faces, perpetual bad hair days and those big clunky shoes seen so often in *Astro Boy*. Carried off with today's more sophisticated animation techniques, the simple styles of yesteryear have a startling fluidity and power.

Fueling the seven-volume *Giant Robo* OAV story is the Shizuma Drive, the world's first perfect energy source. When the Drive is tested prematurely, the spike-haired, lab-coated Dr. Shizuma (one of the Drive's five inventors and namesake for the final device) is wracked with constant, inescapable guilt for his role in the "Tragedy of Bashtarlle," an event which cast the world into darkness for seven days and caused the deaths of countless people. The megalomaniacal organization "Big Fire," determined to use the Shizuma Drive for their own ends, send their psionically powered agents against the Agents of Justice, and the fight for world domination is on.

Anime isn't produced in a vacuum. Aside from *Giant Robo*'s source material in Mitsuteru Yokoyama's comics, there's a context behind the robots, explosions, and gags just like U.S.-produced animated series such as *Rocky & Bullwinkle* or *The Flintstones*. Disney influenced Tezuka, and Tezuka's **Jungle Emperor** influenced Disney's **The Lion King**, and so continues the endless creative cycle which Ishiguro calls "a kind of feedback." *Giant Robo* director Imagawa is a self-described *Rocky Horror Picture Show* fanatic, and admitted in a recent interview that the film has had a strong influence on his own work, other titles of which include the out-and-out parody of the venerable giant robot show genre in **Mobile Fighter G-Gundam** and the comedy TV series about a chef preparing to take over the family diner, *Mr. Ajikko* (both currently available in Japanese import only).

"*Giant Robo* is itself an homage to *Rocky Horror*," confesses Imagawa cheerfully. "(As an animator) I've always wanted to work on something I believe in, and so working on *Giant Robo* was for me like (*Rocky Horror*'s) 'Don't dream it, be it' line come true." In addition to naming main *Giant Robo* character (and thoroughly mad scientist) Dr. Franken von Vogler after *Rocky Horror*'s "Dr. Frank-N-Furter," Imagawa admitted to one other American pop culture reference in his work during a recent visit to the U.S.: *Twin Peaks*. If you watch very carefully during *Giant Robo*'s "Seven Days of Fire" montage, Imagawa says, one of the buildings you'll see destroyed in an explosion will be the Great Northern Hotel. Who influenced whom? Perhaps when it comes to creative influences, it really is like Ishiguro's "feedback."

While *Giant Robo* revisits the ground first tested by shows such as *Gigantor* and gives it a new, serious spin, other anime series such as **Ambassador Magma** (1993), based on the manga series by Osamu Tezuka, have tried to hearken back to the good ol' days of robot anime, when *Gigantor* tin toys sold in the stores and the world was more innocent, but most have not managed to capture the same atmosphere that *Giant Robo* achieves so skillfully.[15] At its best when presenting Tezuka's arresting, giant golden savior-robot in majestic poses, the animated *Ambassador Magma* falls a little short not only of Tezuka's manga, but surprisingly, the live-action version as well (why is it that the rubber-suited henchmen seemed so much more realistic, life-like and convincing in the live-action version?).

One animated project that did manage to successfully turn back the clock is **Kishin Corps** (1993), directed by Tatsunoko veteran animator Taka'aki Ishiyama. "My true goal in making the series was to create something akin to the 'giant robot' shows of old," he says. "(I'm talking about) a show such as *Gigantor*, where a big object moves, and not in the smooth and graceful way it's popular for robots to move these days, either. I'm talking about a big *KA-THUMP!* with each and every step."

Like *Giant Robo*, part of the *Kishin Corps* appeal lies in the series' deliberate, nuts 'n' bolts look. You won't find style and speed here. What you will find, however, is size and power, even a kind of grandeur. In *Kishin Corps*, robots don't just move, they *lurch*. The *Kishin* story itself serves up a weird blend of historical fact and pure, unadulterated fiction. Based on the novel series by Masaki Yamada, *Kishin Corps* is set in an alternate, WWII-influenced "What if…?" world.

The story of a squadron formed to protect the Earth from invading aliens, in *Kishin Corps* the four members of the Kishin Corps squadron pilot massive, approximately 15 meter-tall machines with names evocative of their form and function: Kishin Thunder, Kishin Wind, Kishin Dragon. Powering the massive Kishin machines is a top-secret energy source developed by the brilliant Tatsushi Takamura. Pursuing it is a motley crew of Nazis, aliens, even an evil scientist by the unlikely name of Eva Braun. In *Kishin Corps*, Einstein is a master of Kishin technology, and Hitler is in league with the aliens. And then the Americans begin to consider dropping the A-bomb on a nest of aliens sheltered by the Nazis…. Even though its style is clearly influenced by its animated forebears, *Kishin Corps* is not, as the commercial goes, your father's giant robot show.

Armored Trooper Votoms (1983) is in many ways one of the most classic "giant robot" robot shows of them all (although the robots in question are, admittedly, rather small). As part of a small group of directors who helmed the majority of the giant robot shows which dominated the airwaves in 1980s Japan, *Votoms*' Ryosuke Takahashi is among those responsible for injecting the dark, gritty feel which characterizes television anime from that era, although he protests that he's "not necessarily fluent in mecha."

Osamu Tezuka's **Ambassador Magma**.

[15] Broadcast in Japan under the same name as Tezuka's original manga, **Magma Taishi** is no doubt better known in the U.S. as the live-action **Space Giants**.

Kishin Thunder encounters the fearsome Panzer Knight in **Kishin Corps**.

53

A scene from **Armored Trooper Votoms**.

©1983 Sunrise, Inc.

A scene from the *Deprive* segment of **Robot Carnival**.

©1990 A.P.P.P. Co., Ltd.

A scene from the *A Tale of Two Robots* segment of **Robot Carnival**.

©1990 A.P.P.P. Co., Ltd.

Asked where he got his inspiration for *Votoms*, Takahashi replied in a recent interview, "Well, at the very beginning was an American movie—it was a rodeo story, *Junior Bonner*. (The movie's characters) would travel from town to town in a trailer doing rodeo shows…. From my own experience, right after the end of WW II, there were a lot of jeeps in town. Although they were war vehicles, they showed up in town as daily-use vehicles, and were used for wilderness driving and for construction. I've always had that picture in mind. I wanted to make a story about robots that were made for war but ended up being used in non-war places."

Seamlessly integrating its lovingly engineered robots against a classic sci-fi/ western backdrop, *Votoms* is one of those shows whose toy models you may have seen on the floor of a comic book or anime convention. Because the series was originally on-air back when toy manufacturers created their models around the show's mecha— rather than having mecha created around their toys—the models from *Votoms* sport a high degree of detail and an almost plausible verisimilitude.

As mecha fan and anime commentator James Teal remarks in his introduction to the Takahashi interview published in ANIMERICA magazine, it wasn't that long ago that tanks and aircraft weren't a part of military armament, offering an interesting argument in favor of the feasibility and practicality of mano a mano robot combat in favor of today's "fire and forget" strategic defense initiative mentality. In *Votoms*, the robots go right along with the rawhide (the series' main character is even a dead ringer for Steve McQueen).

What happened in the years between *Astro Boy* and *Votoms* to bring about such a shift in attitude, from wide-eyed visions of a utopian future to cogs-and-gears natural- ism? The '60s idealism slowly faded from the scene to be replaced by darker, more serious themes and questions. No better example of the kind of distance between yesterday's robots and today's exists than **Robot Carnival** (1987), an animated robot anthology featuring segments by nine of Japan's top directors including Katsuhiro Otomo, Hiroyuki Kitazume, and Yasuomi Umetsu. Begun with a request from animation producer Kazufumi Nomura to "show robots in some manner," *Robot Carnival* tells its stories "through visual action," each director with their own unique and particular vision of just what that means.

In an opening sequence animated by Otomo and Atsuko Fukushima, an impla- cable, unstoppable juggernaut lumbers across a barren wasteland amid a fantastic light show complete with swarms of tiny robotic ballerinas and musicians. In Kitazume's **"Starlight Angel,"** a pretty young girl plays at romance with a handsome android jongleur, only to be confronted with a hideous, demonic robot. In Umetsu's poignant, unforgettable **"Presence,"** a brilliant scientist created a beautiful android…too beautiful, perhaps, as he can't seem to let her go.

Other memorable segments include Chinese animator Mao Lamdo's **"Cloud,"** an exquisitely paced story inspired by his book *Snow and the Young Boy*, a thoughtful panorama unfolding in surreal, fleecy white clouds; director Hiroyuki Kitakubo's **"A Tale of Two Robots,"** one of the film's most memorable segments, in which a gigantic, creaking *wooden* robot is all that stands between one small 19th century Japanese town and certain doom in the form of one mad genius; and finally, **"Nightmare,"** directed by Takashi Nakamura, a menacing, heavily atmospheric thriller.

Whimsical, frightening, hilarious, breathtaking, and quixotic by turns, *Robot Carnival* is like having your own in-home animation art festival. "Not all the stories hit the bull's eye," says film critic Leonard Maltin in his *Movie and Video Guide*, "but the best are quite good." Even with the uneven offerings of the varied segments, no one walks away from *Robot Carnival* thinking that they just saw another hackneyed take on an old formula. The segments offer allusions to the estab- lished robot traditions, but the stories themselves end up where you might not expect.

One of *Robot Carnival*'s segments, **"Deprive,"** portrays a robot avenger, a man who has become a cyborg to fight evil. It wouldn't be out of the question to argue that the cyborg element alone qualifies "Deprive" as falling firmly within the robot genre, even without the giant, lurching mecha so crucial to the usual definition of a robot show. Like the eponymous Astro Boy, the android 8 Man (seen on American TV in the 1960s as *8th Man*) is a robot, but he leads the double life of a human man. *8 Man After*, the recent '90s update of the classic '60s TV series, gives us a detective killed in the line of duty, transplanting his stripped-down personality into the 8 Man cybernetic body, à la *Robocop*. The new 8 Man then does his best to save the city from cybernetically enhanced criminals addicted to a dangerous, power-boosting drug (shades of *Robocop 2*).

The eponymous robot avenger of **Casshan: Robot Hunter** (1994) has an even more pointed reason for his transformation—he chose to do it to himself, to right the injustices passed on to him by his brilliant robotic scientist father, who created the most sophisticated android ever, the "Black King." Unfortunately, this most advanced of robots then leads a robot uprising against humanity, enslaving all humans and installing a totalitarian robot regime. Casshan is essentially a one-man terrorist team, striking at strategic points to bring an end to the Black King's reign.

Recently seen on increasingly more frequent cable television "Japanimation" festivals, production on this new *Casshan* is headed by character designer and animation director Yasuomi Umetsu (*Robot Carnival*). It's a beautifully animated follow-up to a classic 1970s series.[16]

In a more standard sci-fi action mode is director Toshihiro Hirano's **Dangaio** (1987), featuring the story of four young espers robbed of their identities and scheduled for sale to the notorious "Bunker Pirates" as psionically enhanced pilots of the powerful transforming mecha, the Danfighters. As they struggle to remember enough of their pasts to escape their so-called "creator," in order to fight against the pirates the four are forced to learn to trust each other enough to combine their separate units into one enormously powerful giant robot, the Dangaio.

Dangaio was one of the first anime videos to be released commercially in the United States, and yet, despite the years which have passed since it was first offered for sale, from a technical standpoint it still holds up as one of the better uses of the advantages the OAV format offers.[17] Director Hirano keeps the suspense and thrills coming, while animation director Hideaki Anno (**Vampire Hunter D**, **Nadia**) provides a sharp-edged, distinctive look for the series' mecha designs (**MD Geist**'s Koichi Ohata joins designers **Robotech**'s Shoji Kawamori and **Detonator Orgun**'s Masami Obari as of the second volume).

Rather than a tale of four lesser robots working together to form one, more powerful robot, the Hirano-directed **Hades Project Zeorymer** (1989) goes back to the essentials: giant robots beating each other to a pulp. Based on a manga series written and illustrated by Morio Chimi published in Japan's *Lemon People* magazine several years ago, *Hades Project Zeorymer* is the story of Masato Akitsu, a boy taken from his family one day and told some startling news—namely, that his family isn't really his family, he isn't who he thinks he is, and that fate has something much more important in store. A clever story with more surprises and double-crosses than a spy thriller, Hirano's dynamic direction and character designs by *Silent Möbius*'s Michitaka Kikuchi make the two-volume *Hades Project Zeorymer* OAV series a welcome return to the most fundamental roots of a classic genre.

At an amazing 250 meters, one of the very largest giant robots of them all is the eponymous star of **Aim For the Top! Gunbuster** (1988). *Gunbuster* was a natural follow-up for Los Angeles-based U.S. Renditions' ground-breaking *Dangaio*, and to this day it remains one of anime fandom's most beloved—and technically accomplished—OAV series.

Tatsunoko's *Casshan: Robot Hunter*.

©1994 Tatsunoko Production Co., Ltd.

[16] Often referred to as the "Home of the Heroes," Tatsunoko Productions is the company responsible for some of the greatest anime hits for the past thirty years, including the time-tested *Speed Racer* and a heavily edited version of *Science Ninja Team Gatchaman* (broadcast in the U.S. as *Battle of the Planets*). Currently, Tatsunoko is making headlines on American syndicated television with a brand-new robot hero with roots as old as Japanese animation itself: *Teknoman*, the '90s remake of the '70s series, *Space Knight Tekkaman* (see TV chapter for more info).

[17] Released in the U.S. by Los Angeles-based U.S. Renditions (a division of Japanese importer Nippan Shuppan Hanbai), **Dangaio** joined **Aim For the Top! Gunbuster**, **Bio-Booster Armor Guyver** and **Super Dimension Century Orguss** as some of the country's first-ever anime home video releases. Until U.S.-based companies such as U.S. Renditions, AnimEigo, and Central Park Media began releasing anime on subtitled home video, anime had been available in American primarily through television reruns, or in heavily edited, English-dubbed home video versions.

Psychic teen Mia Alice from Toshihiro Hirano's *Dangaio*.

©1988 Emotion/A.I.C./Artmic

Noriko Takaya and the giant robot *Gunbuster*.

[18] The title of the series is itself a joke, a reference to the hearts and flowers animated TV sports drama, 1973's **Ace o Nerae!** ("Aim For the Ace!"). Of course, the biggest in-joke of all is the inclusion of a character fated to become Noriko's first love, Smith Toren. In real life, Canadian expat Toren Smith (now living in San Francisco) is a longtime anime and manga fan currently heading up his own manga-in-English production facility, Studio Proteus. In **Gunbuster**, Toren's doomed to a tragic death during Noriko's first space sortie (real-life Toren also voices an anonymous bridge operator in this episode, much as I would later do in **Macross II**). Perhaps it's an unavoidable occupational hazard, but many members of the anime-in-English community have given in to temptation and voiced various ADR roles—Streamline Pictures president Carl Macek in **My Neighbor Totoro**, A.D. Vision general manager Matt Greenfield in **Guy**, myself in **Outlanders,** The Complete Anime Guide's own Fred Patten in **Tekkaman the Space Knight**— but as far as I'm concerned, Toren was definitely the first, and so it's all his fault.

[19] A very particular grasp of cinematic style is, of course, one of the primary requirements of noir, animated or otherwise. Aside from the typical hard-boiled subject matter, the trademark, high contrast light and shadow interplay of live-action film noir sets a psychological tone for the story, usually *very* pessimistic. Film noir is *expressionistic* cinema, and the overriding style is paramount.

One of the nastier creatures from the Black World in *Wicked City*.

Teenage schoolgirl Noriko Takaya has a dream. Clumsy and lacking in confidence, Noriko nevertheless aspires to go into space someday just like her beloved "Papa," the renowned captain of the space vessel *Luxion*. The target of envy and scorn from the other girls at the Okinawa Space High School For Girls, no one quite believes it when Noriko is chosen over other applicants to pair with the most popular girl in school to pilot the massive Gunbuster mecha. Constantly forced to justify her role in the top-secret Gunbuster project, Noriko must overcome her own insecurities while mastering the most important lesson of all: Believing in herself.

With an alien invasion story that echoes Orson Scott Card's Hugo and Nebula Award-winning *Ender's Game*, *Gunbuster* is animated by the fans-turned-pros studio Gainax and features all the talent of the *Dangaio* video and then some. Direction is by Hideaki Anno, with character designs by Haruhiko "**Robotech**" Mikimoto and mecha designs by Koichi Ohata. The story for all six episodes of the *Gunbuster* OAV series is by then-top dog Toshio Okada of Gainax.

Because *Gunbuster* is the product of some of the industry's most feverishly inventive talents, those viewers who are new to Japanese animation are often bewildered by the series' many in-jokes, references to *otaku* culture, and bogus physics which many fans speculate was invented out of whole cloth by Okada himself (main character Noriko herself is an anime *otaku*, and has posters of **Space Battleship Yamato** and **Nausicaä of the Valley of Wind** on her walls). Don't let the light-hearted, self-referential fun fool you, though, as **Gunbuster** has more than its fair share of three-hankie scenes, not to mention one of the most poignant, bittersweet endings in anime history.[18]

Whether it's a child substitute like in *Astro Boy*, an ultimate toy like in *Gigantor*, the transforming four-robot team of *Dangaio*, or the whirling, whimsical mechanical fantasies of *Robot Carnival*, the role of the robot in Japanese animation is an important one. In anime, robots are our friends, our enemies, our tools, our adversaries, and our heroes. Like the machines covered by Isaac Asimov's famous "Three Laws of Robotics," the robots of Japanese animation are not only inextricably linked to our lifestyles, but are our friends.

At what point does a cyborg become an android? At what point does one cease to become human, crossing over into the land of the robot? One definition holds that when life is no longer sustainable except through mechanical devices, the line between "man" and "machine" has been crossed. A person with a prosthetic limb can still function (albeit less efficiently) without it, but what about a person with a pacemaker? Remove it, and life is no longer sustainable—and isn't that, according to the above definition, a cyborg?

Naturally, we're just splitting fine semantic hairs here; no sane person would call someone with a pacemaker a cyborg. But it does cause us to reassess the role of the robot in our lives...doesn't it?

Memorable Nightmares: The New Anime Noir

Every movie patron (even those who *aren't* film students) know the conventions of film noir. Characterized by a dark, brooding atmosphere, noir fiction and films tell hard-edged tales with harsh messages. The hero, generally a cop or detective, usually has few illusions left, as life's little lessons have knocked any optimism out of his (and it usually is "his" rather than "her") psyche, leaving only cynicism and what, in his world, can only be described as a healthy sense of paranoia.

Like cyberpunk, noir in many senses is an ideal genre for the animated medium. Animation's total control over light and setting provide any live-action director's ideal dream for creating a unique atmosphere.[19] But beyond the typical hard-boiled gunplay to which live-action noir typically aspires, animators have long since seized upon the advantage of the medium to inhabit strange and wonderful new worlds with their dark visions, worlds accessible only through animation. Anime noir overflows with supernatural elements, and it isn't just the system, the government, or organized crime that these heroes and anti-heroes have to worry about, but otherworldly monsters, demons, and aliens from beyond.[20]

Director Yoshiaki Kawajiri is one of the most brilliant directors working in the field today, and his films reflect an remarkably eloquent, darkly *sensual* sensibility that would find itself beloved of film critics were it in any medium but animation. *Wicked City* (1987) is a gothically erotic (erotically gothic?) psycho-thriller (the Japanese magazines called it *supurattâ* or "splatter" action) based on the novel by Hideyuki Kikuchi, detailing the adventures of a hard-edged, elite cop and his gorgeous partner, an otherworldly beauty who looks like she just stepped out of a Nagel lithograph. Together, the two struggle to prevent the invasion of some vicious demonic shape-shifters into our reality, while fighting against their own mutual attraction. When you and your lover's species are at war, can Earth guys ever be easy…?

"Human beings have stumbled through history occasionally making contact with what we call the Black World," narrates ruggedly handsome Taki Renzaburo in true noir style after a sexual encounter with a Black World woman guaranteed to make any casual Casanova give serious thought to abstinence. It seems most of the people on both sides of the continuum have wanted to share insights, information, and live peacefully with one another. But, in spite of their best intentions, bloody fights are breaking out between the two sides, and things look to get worse before they get any better.

"Things got so bad," he continues, "that finally representatives from both worlds ironed out a contract that allowed everyone to live together without stepping on each other's toes—sort of a non-aggression pact; a treaty. And every so often, that treaty is renewed and the cease-fire continues without a break. So here we are at the end of the 20th century, and we're about to conclude a new peace treaty, right here in Tokyo."

Kawajiri handles direction, character design, and animation direction in the film, and with its hard-boiled detective action, hallucinatory special effects and menacing, gnashing sexuality[21], *Wicked City* has the noir feel of Raymond Chandler, combined with the rollercoaster horror thrill of John Carpenter and the sordid thrill of Ken Russell. The only difference is, the surprisingly sophisticated *Wicked City* is animated.

Director Kawajiri has such an identifiably unique gothic touch that, even without the traditional Chandler-esque detectives to set the mood, his works always seem to thrive in a world lit by noir shadows and creeping menaces, no matter *where* the action happens to take place. *Ninja Scroll* (1993) rolls back the noir genre all the way back to feudal Japan, where a masterless ninja by the name of Jubei is coerced into mounting an attack against Gemma, immortal leader of the Eight Devils of Kimon, already once-slain by Jubei. Like *Wicked City*'s 300-year-old sorcerer, Giuseppe Maiart, *Ninja Scroll*'s wizened Dakuan is always at hand to keep Jubei focused on his mission; also like *Wicked City*, the main character's love interest—the beautiful ninja and poison-taster, Kagero—is an otherwise strong and independent career girl who falls to pieces at a word from her would-be lover and who's menaced sexually by the bad guys every time she leaves his side.

In addition to the air of intrigue and mystery provided by the presence of the ninja themselves, the noir feel of *Ninja Scroll* is enhanced by an array of Kawajiri-eque demons and monsters, the kind usually reserved for the very best (or very worst,

Jubei, the masterless ninja of **Ninja Scroll**.

[20] In his analysis of horror, **Danse Macabre**, horror über author Stephen King was actually talking about radio when he cited the effectiveness of the Orson Welles **War of the Worlds** broadcast by pointing out that "…in radio, there were no zippers running down the Martians' backs." This is also true of anime, where the world is created from the ground up. In anime, there is no "reality" to overcome. If the production's "set of reality," as King puts it, is sufficiently convincing, anime can pull off scare-the-pants-off-you special effects as well as the *Ee-Yuk!* monsters that live-action movies would be hard pressed to copy.

[21] When I say "gnashing," I do mean *gnashing*. The image of the spider woman and her labia dentata has got to be one of anime's most memorable scenes.

©1992 Toei Co. Ltd.

The evil sorcerer Kato in
Doomed Megalopolis.

[22] Director Ridley Scott's **Blade Runner** (1982), one of the most acclaimed noir films of all time, has proven a source of inspiration for more than one Japanese animator. Although no one pays more homage to Scott's film than **Bubblegum Crisis**—main character and rock opera diva Priss has a band called "The Replicants," while the gartered-stocking look of the series' mecha designs hearken back to the film—the decaying, somehow baroque cities of other anime videos such as **AD Police** and **Dominion** also suggest **Blade Runner**'s profound anime influence.

[23] Unfortunately for truly jaded thrill-seekers, most of the "adults-only" anime videos available subtitled or in English these days are of the "Lolita" variety, featuring slim-hipped (albeit large-breasted), doe-eyed prepubescent girls, the bloody-nosed beaus who adore them (in the Japanese cultural idiom, a sudden male nose bleed in the presence of the erotic is a sign of arousal and sexual naiveté), and some relatively tame sexual hijinx. Let's face it, when it comes to shock value, **Urotsuki Dōji: Legend of the Overfiend** is a tough act to beat, even without the infamous "Nazi Rape Machine" of later volumes.

©1993 Hideyuki Kikuchi/Asahi Sonorama

The tyrannical Levi Rah of
Demon City Shinjuku.

depending on your take on the subject) of Hong Kong occult action cinema such as director Tsui Hark's cult hit *A Chinese Ghost Story*. There's Tessai, the leering beast with the skin of stone; Benisato, the Mistress of Snakes; Mushizo, who controls a deadly swarm; Utsutsu, blind swordsman reminiscent of another famous entry in Japanese cinema, the warrior-masseur from *Zatoichi*; Shijima, the demon of shadows; Zakuro, who uses gunpowder to make walking bombs of the living dead; and Yurimaru, too aware of his own beauty, who kills with wires and his own self-generated electrical charge.

Good and evil, light and shadow, much of *Ninja Scroll* is "filmed" during the blue twilight hours, when the light is at its most beautiful…and its most poignant. Gorgeously animated, graphically violent, wistfully romantic, *Ninja Scroll* claimed the 1993 Yubari City International Adventure Fantastic Film Festival award. It's possibly the only film in the history of international cinema to combine elements from Fleming's *Goldfinger*, Carpenter's *Halloween*, and Clavell's *Shogun* with the only seeming death-by-head-butt scene in recent memory.

Although film noir tends to find refuge in the dark corners of specific eras—the hard-boiled 1940s and '50s, for example—like *Ninja Scroll*, anime noir can reach back further in time to a more "gaslight" brand of horror without losing its sense of atmosphere.[22] ***Doomed Megalopolis*** (1991) is based on the novel series, *Capital City*, by award-winning occult author Hiroshi Aramata. Here, the clock is turned back not to feudal Japan, but to the Japan of 1912, where a mysterious sorcerer named Kato is attempting to awaken the powerful spirit Tairo no Masakado, believed to have died during a rebellion against the Imperial Court 2000 years earlier, now popularly believed to be the guardian spirit of Tokyo. If he can awaken the guardian spirit, Kato will gain great power, but there's also the chance that all of Tokyo will be destroyed in one apocalyptic blast, Either way, Kato's sorceries are tearing the city—and some of its unfortunate citizenry—apart at the seams.

Like the *Nightmare on Elm Street* movies, *Doomed Megalopolis* features powerful dream sequences and prophetic visions which contribute to the spooky atmosphere of the story as a whole. Like *Wicked City*, *Doomed Megalopolis* also features some potent sexual imagery. Other themes such as madness, demonic possession, and incest contribute to the "R" rating *Doomed Megalopolis* would no doubt receive if it were ever to be screened by the MPAA. But despite a fairly explicit sexual content, *Doomed Megalopolis* is a good example of animation for adults (as compared to *adult* animation) which handles mature themes without going the exploitation route of the many hackneyed "tentacle porn" flicks now available.[23]

Like cyberpunk, noir often centers around the cities in which they take place. ***Demon City Shinjuku*** (1988) brings back many of the staff of *Wicked City* (including director Kawajiri) to tell the story of a battle between good and evil, with nothing less than the fate of the world of stake. Peopled with freakish inhabitants and with death hiding around every corner, the streets of Kawajiri's Shinjuku rival Carpenter's New York for sheer menace and brutality. Main character Kyoya is no Snake Pliskin, but the hardened survivors of *Demon City*'s Shinjuku cling to life just as tenaciously.

The story is a fairly simple tale of how the evil sorcerer Levi Rah defeats and kills his most powerful rival, Genichiro, taking complete control of the former downtown Tokyo business district and delivering it to the dark forces which he serves. Levi Rah then begins his long preparation for the time when the demons of the netherworld will make the Earth their own. Ten years later, Genichiro's now-teenaged son Kyoya has no intentions of becoming a hero, but then again, that's the thing about heroes—they show up when you least expect them. Possibly even more powerful than his father, Kyoya braves roving gangs, hellish creatures, and certain death to accept his destiny, regain his father's sword, and prevent Levi Rah from making Earth into a second hell.

Kurosawa's *Hidden Fortress* is often cited as an inspiration for *Star Wars*; if so, surely the creative influences have come full circle. *Demon City Shinjuku* is alive with mythic resonance, and its characters and story bear more than a passing resemblance to George Lucas' epic. Cast Levi Rah as the dark rival who must be vanquished, Darth Vader; Genichiro as the fallen father-figure, Anakin Skywalker; their master as the wizened spiritualist Yoda; Kyoya as the reluctant savior; the beautiful Sayaka as the selfless and noble Princess Leia…. Perhaps it's fair to say that *Demon City Shinjuku* is a swashbuckling sort of film noir, where the heroes may fight within a dark and insane landscape, without actually feeling that darkness inside their own souls.

Creator Go Nagai's ***Devilman*** (1987) is just the opposite. On the surface, it may seem to be just another one of those ho-hum demons taking over the Earth, enslaving the natives, and using humanity as its own private larder tales, but in *Devilman*, a young student named Akira Fudo actually *becomes* a demon himself in order to save the world from their evil. Devilman's battle to save humanity is only part of what makes his story so compelling, because it's the human Akira's struggle against the demon which rages inside his own soul that allows him to transform into Devilman, giving the series its surprising power.[24]

This concept of the hero's struggle against his own gothic identity also appears in ***Vampire Hunter D*** (1985), featuring character designs by renowned illustrator/video game character designer Yoshitaka Amano.[25] In the wastelands of a post-apocalyptic Earth inhabited by vampires and unearthly creatures of all stripes, a dark, mysterious man known only as "D" comes to the rescue of the beautiful Doris, already earmarked as the next victim of the sinister, vampiric Count Magnus Lee. To save Doris, D has to fight not only the Count's monstrous forces but, like Devilman, his own dual, inhuman nature.

Vampire Princess Miyu (1988) is, despite the potentially misleading title, a far cry from the heroics of *Vampire Hunter D* and *Devilman*. Directed by *Dangaio*'s Toshihiro Hirano, *Vampire Princess Miyu* is the tale of an unearthly beauty with golden eyes named Miyu who fulfills her family's generations-long duty to return the supernatural beings known as *shinma* to their own world. Lyrical, haunting, enchanting and frightening in turn, the four-volume *Vampire Princess Miyu* series brings a refreshing sense of *restraint* to its horror, which always reveals just enough to keep the viewer interested, never more.

Why these titles qualify as noir rather than horror lies in the magnetism of their title characters, unmistakable noir heroes, who exist in a world of hostile forces in which only they can provide salvation. Perhaps the ultimate extension of this concept is the hero of ***Ogre Slayer*** (1994). Born from the corpse of his traditional Japanese ogre or *oni* mother, the eponymous anti-hero of *Ogre Slayer* is known only by the name of his sword, *Onikirimaru*.[26] Believing he can stop being an ogre and become human only when all the other ogres in the world are gone, Ogre Slayer travels Japan, sword in hand, daring to dream…and hacking his own kind into itty bitty pieces along the way. Of course, the true irony—and the true tragedy—of the series as expressed by *shôjo* manga or girls' comics creator Kei Kusunoki is that ogres are constantly being born from the sins of humanity, making the Ogre Slayer's quest the ultimate exercise in futility.

"My theme for *Ogre Slayer* isn't necessarily the horror of the *oni*, but the vicious human karma that drives humans to producing them. Ultimately, in my story, the most horrible creatures of all are the human themselves." Like another famous monster story written by a young woman, Mary Shelley's *Frankenstein*, Kusunoki's *Ogre Slayer* explores the overwhelming attraction—not to mention the overwhelming *cost*—of striving for true humanity, something the title characters of neither *Devilman* nor *Vampire Hunter D* have to face. Both have found a way to embrace their dark selves and continue their fight against true evil, and have no real hope of regaining their lost

[24] Currently the subject of increased awareness among American comic book fans thanks to the Verotik Comics adaptation (the comic book line owned by heavy metal rocker Glenn Danzig), Go Nagai is also the creator of the infamous ***Harenchi Gakuen*** ("Shameless School") manga series condemned by the Japanese PTA for introducing erotica into children's comics and for mocking the national education system. In his ***Manga! Manga!***, author Fred Schodt writes, "***Harenchi Gakuen*** was a fantastic school of bedlam, where the main preoccupation of both male students and teachers was not study but catching glimpses of girls' underwear or contriving to see them naked." In his native Japan, Nagai still enjoys a reputation for naughtiness, a reputation proved out by the release of his animated ***Kekko Kamen***, the tale of a masked female avenger "whose body everyone knows, while no one knows her face." ***Kekko Kamen*** is currently available subtitled from A.D. Vision.

[25] An accomplished illustrator, Amano is also the conceptual designer for the popular "Final Fantasy" role-playing video game series available for both U.S. and Japanese systems.

Go Nagai's ***Devilman***.

©1987 Dynamic Planning/Kodansha/Bandai Visual

[26] Lit., "ogre" + "cut," with the nominative suffix "-*maru*" (as in the *Kobayashi Maru* of *Star Trek II: The Wrath of Khan*). *Oni* are an important part of Japanese folklore, showing up in anime videos as diverse as ***Urusei Yatsura*** (as evidenced by the cute li'l horns on her head, tiger-striped bikini-clad Lum is herself an *oni*) as well as the adults-only ***Adventure Kid***.

Curse of the Undead Yoma.

©1989 Toho Co. Ltd./MPS

27 Released by Toho as two separate theatrical features, the original Japanese title of A.D. Vision's **Curse of the Undead Yoma** is the distinctly less exciting, single-word **Yoma** (lit., *yô-*, "ghost; apparition" + -*ma*, "demon").

humanity, a theme which also occurs in creator Yuzo Takada's ***3x3 Eyes*** (1991), the tale of a young man made into the unwilling zombie servant of a supernatural, three-eyed master.

The twist in *3x3 Eyes* is that the supernatural monster also wants to become human herself, and the story revolves around their mutual quest to gain (and regain) humanity. *3x3 Eyes* has both the noir lighting and atmosphere in spades—nearly every scene of the video seems to feature sharp, indirect lighting, while the world the main characters inhabit teems with spooky mythological creatures lurking around every corner.

Like *Ninja Scroll*, the setting for the rather luridly titled ***Curse of the Undead Yoma*** (1989)[27] is feudal Japan during *sengoku jidai* or "civil war period" Japan, pitting loyal ninja against hellish demons from beyond. The hero, the noir ninja Hikage, wanders the land in search of his lost comrade Maro, now under the control of the "Yoma" or undead monster-demons of the video's title. Like *Ogre Slayer, Curse of the Undead Yoma* is based on the manga by Kei Kusunoki, one of a generation of young female manga artists who came to prominence during the '80s for their work in *shônen* manga or young men's comic magazines. Both titles share Kusunoki's uniquely female perspective on the horror genre, where the horror of the events, no matter how gruesome, is actually the story's least frightening aspect. The real terror lies in the cause and effect of the carnage, especially on the psyche, where the wounds are the hardest to heal.

Rumiko Takahashi, best known for her romantic comedies (see below), has also dabbled in noir horror, usually by giving her romantic perspective a dark twist. Created to provide a forum in which she could explore the shorter-length stories which couldn't—or shouldn't—fit into a longer-running continuing series, Takahashi's "Rumic World" series showcases pieces from several different genres, and her grim, fairy-tale like "Mermaid" stories shine with a dark brilliance all their own. Twice animated—***Mermaid Forest*** (1991) and ***Mermaid's Scar*** (1993)—Takahashi's mermaid stories take advantage of the "wandering stranger" motif which unifies such diverse TV shows as *The Fugitive, The Incredible Hulk* and even *Highway to Heaven*.

According to legend, if you eat the flesh of a mermaid, you shall be granted life eternal. But what happens when you don't want to be immortal anymore…? Yuta, a seemingly fresh-faced young man, is a 500-year-old immortal waiting to discover the secret. Together with Mana, his immortal traveling companion, the two travel across Japan, meeting all sorts of strange and macabre beings along the way.

But Takahashi's "Mermaid Saga" isn't her only entry in the horror genre—***Laughing Target*** (1987) offers up the story of Azusa and Yuzuru, two Japanese youths betrothed to one another at the tender age of six. When Azusa's mother passes away (and under mysterious circumstances, yet), the now-teenaged Azusa comes to Tokyo in search of her fiancé. Azusa intends to keep the promise her mother made on her behalf, but Yuzuru has moved on with his life, and there is now another girl to whom he has turned his attention. Yuzuru has yet to learn the fury of a woman scorned, especially now that Azusa seems to be possessed of strange, supernatural powers. In a scene reminiscent of *Cat People*, Azusa stalks her rival through a darkened locker room, and when the shock comes, it's not so much from the manifestation of her unearthly powers, but from their terrifying, unnatural origin.

Iczer-One (1985) trades in horror of a more blatant sort. Described by Japanese magazines as a blend of "science fiction, beautiful girls, and mecha-action," *Iczer-One* is a difficult story to categorize, but is nonetheless an important video because it seamlessly showcases several long-established genres of anime in one video series (one take is that it's an animated homage/parody to the giant robot/battle-team shows of old). Imagine a combination of *Alien, Mighty Morphin Power Rangers* and *Gigantor* all in one, and you'll begin to appreciate the wonderful irony of the story's premise. The

Hell hath no fury like that of Azusa in Rumiko Takahashi's ***Laughing Target***.

©Rumiko Takahashi/Shogakukan

alien-busting mecha contribute strongly to the video's appeal to giant robot fans, and while the saga of alien invasion ultimately thwarted by the unification of an Earthling schoolgirl and an alien battle android doesn't seem strictly "noir" on the surface, because the horror elements are such an important part of the story, perhaps it may be useful to think of *Iczer-One* as "mecha horror," with an emphasis on the horror aspect.

Indeed, the video's tentacled "Cthuwulf" aliens, straight out of H.P. Lovecraft, demand *Iczer-One*'s inclusion into this category, even if the main story seems to parody them along with all the other elements that make up the video. The product of an all-star animator team, *Iczer-One* is produced by *Dangaio* and *Zeorymer*'s Toru Miura, and features the talents of **Vampire Princess Miyu**'s creator, Narumi Kakinouchi and *Fatal Fury*'s Masami Obari as animation directors. In addition to his direction duties, *Vampire Princess Miyu*'s Toshihiro Hirano also provides the video's screenplay and character designs.

Bad girl Iczer-Two from the horror/mecha/sci-fi thriller **Iczer-One**.

The anime noir takes many forms. Sometimes it comes in the guise of traditional monsters—ogres, vampires, demons and devils—while other times, it may take a less traditional form, such as mermaids or tentacled Lovecraftian aliens. Either way, the anime noir mines the same lodes as horror has always done, those sensitive spots which tingle at the thought of some extraordinary entity or event outside ourselves, that something which Stephen King describes as "the other."

Often managing feats of imaginative skills unlikely or even impossible in traditional live-action storytelling, and just as with the best and most unique of anime's many genres, the anime noir takes full advantage of the medium's ability to show us visions we may not want to remember, but which we can never forget.

Wacky Hijinks: The Romantic Comedy

Animated love stories are nothing new. Nearly all of Disney's feature films center around romance, specifically musical-comedy romance in the classic Hollywood tradition. But Japanese animators have made the romantic comedy genre their own by bringing in a distinctly unique perspective to animated romance tales.

The established forms and formulas of current Japanese-animated "love comedies" (so-called because they inevitably center on the wacky hijinks which hinder—or in some cases, advance—the developing romance between the target couple) are built on a long tradition of romance tales in Japanese literature, most of them tragically serious, such as the first-ever novel in recorded existence, Lady Murasaki Shikibu's **The Tale of Genji**. Written in the 11th century and featuring as its protagonist a Casanova-type courtier and his many loves, *Genji* offers a different, all-too-*human* perspective on Japan's Heian Era.

Gentle courtier Genji and one of his many loves, from **The Tale of Genji**.

Noh, kabuki, and other modern-day Japanese dramatic forms abound with stories of tragic lovers and doomed relationships; at best, the traditional Japanese outlook of romance might be described as "unavoidable." The tradition of arranged marriages in Japan, still a powerful trend in Japanese society to this day, also make the ideal of "love matches" not always sustainable in present-day society. Because the pressure put upon young men and women to make the right match and carry on family traditions is so heavy, perhaps it is fair to say that the idea of falling in love with the "wrong" man or woman carries more weight in Japan than it does the U.S. Thus, the genre of "romantic comedy" is born.

Osamu Tezuka is often credited with pioneering romance comics in Japan with the publication of his **Ribon no Kishi** ("Princess Knight"), the story of a young girl born to a royal family in the classic European fairy tale mold. Desperate for a male heir, the family decides to rear young Princess Sapphire as a boy. Although she secretly longs to wear pretty dresses and act feminine—just as scullery maid Cinderella imagined dancing the night away with a handsome prince—the difference between

The alien princess Lum and her Earthling boyfriend Ataru, from **Urusei Yatsura**.

---

28 The release of No. 34 of the *tankōbon* or compiled manga volume of Rumiko Takahashi's **Ranma 1/2** series marked the sale of *100 million of her comics sold in Japan alone*. At the gala celebration held to commemorate the occasion by her publisher, several female pro wrestlers were invited to participate in a special exhibition starring Asia Kong (the warm-up match, they say, was between the panda from **Ranma 1/2** and the ghostly "*kotatsu-neko*" or "heated-table cat" from **Urusei Yatsura**). Emcees for the event were Toshio Furukawa and Fumi Hirano…the Japanese voices of **Urusei Yatsura**'s Ataru and Lum, respectively.

Ataru's former girlfriend Shinobu and Lum, from **Urusei Yatsura**.

---

29 The word *dōjinshi* literally means "same-person publications," referring to the special interest groups which are formed to create and later publish these largely parody/homage editions. Similar (if only in spirit) to America's "APAs" or "amateur press associations," many *dōjinshi* feature production standards and deluxe printing which would make many of America's smaller comic publishers weep in envy. In the U.S., the *dōjinshi* tradition is beginning to take root, with 'zines such as the **Sailor Moon**/**Ranma 1/2** parody "Sailor Ranma" and the continuing adventures of the **KOR** gang in "Kimagure Orange College" among the best produced (note that, also in keeping with Japanese tradition, these publications are almost always published without the permission of their U.S. copyright holders).

Ribon no Kishi and *Cinderella* is that, before *Ribon no Kishi*'s eventual happy ending, where she finds her handsome prince and settles down to a more traditionally feminine lifestyle, Sapphire completely embraces her masculine life, acting out the part of the sword-wielding Crown Prince in public with gusto, energetically battling the kingdom's enemies.

Latter-day artists expand this theme of gender-identity confusion even more, such as in Riyoko Ikeda's beloved *Berusaiyu no Bara* ("The Rose of Versailles"), wherein the main character is really a woman in male drag, held up as an object of desire by both men and women alike. In *shōjo* manga founding mother Moto Hagio's **They Were 11**, one notable character is a sexual neuter who struggles for the right to become male…but eventually opts for womanhood, instead.

Many romance tales in Japanese animation follow the formula of the strong, individualistic female who eventually finds love despite a seeming disregard for tradition. The element of comedy in such animation often comes from the absurd magnification and exaggeration of just this anime tradition. Like television sitcoms, anime romantic comedy has its own set of conventions and accepted gags, which parody "real" life, romance, heartbreak, relationships, sexual stereotypes, cultural taboos, which—just like sitcoms—depend upon the ability of the show's creative team to sustain believable, endearing characters with whom the viewer can not only identify, but become passionately involved.

Comic artist Rumiko Takahashi is indisputably the Queen of Romantic Comedy. While her body of work also includes other genres—the gothic horror of *Mermaid Forest* and *Mermaid's Scar*, or the time-travel fantasy of *Fire Tripper*—it's the animated versions of her comedic love stories which always seem to generate the most enthusiasm (and the most diehard loyalty) among her U.S. anime fans. Whether it's the shocking tale of the tiger-skin bikini-clad alien princess and her dopey lecherous boyfriend, the overeating boxer and the Catholic nun who tries to keep him on the straight and narrow, or the half-boy, half-girl martial artist cursed with just too much sex appeal for his/her own good, Rumiko Takahashi has a way of bringing out the heartwarming humanity in even the most preposterous of situations.

Urusei Yatsura (1981) has long since been established as one of the most enduringly popular animated comedy series of all time. First published in comic form when Takahashi was only 21 years old, the manga version of *Urusei Yatsura* (usually translated as "Those Obnoxious Aliens," with a playful pun involving *urusai*, "obnoxious; troublesome" and *-sei*, "planet; star") eventually went on to sell over 22 million copies in Japan alone, establishing her as one of the comic world's preeminent storytellers.[28] The animated version of *Urusei Yatsura* was almost as popular, airing on Japanese television from 1981-'86 and going on to produce some 197 half-hour television episodes, eleven direct-to-video OAVs, and six animated movies. Meanwhile, in the fan sector, passions for an animated series had been kindled as never before; countless fan-produced comics called *dōjinshi* had been published, many of which were offered and sold proudly by costumed attendees at the 200,000+ member Comic Market, by far the largest comic convention/swap meet in the world.[29]

The story of *Urusei Yatsura* is as follows: Japanese schoolboy Ataru Moroboshi, oft-described as the "world's unluckiest teenager," is randomly chosen by computer one day to be Earth's champion in a game of intergalactic tag with the princess-daughter of the invading aliens, the tiger-skin bikini-clad Lum. If Ataru can catch her, the Earth will be spared. If he fails, then it's an eternal time-out for humanity. Adding to the mayhem is an unusual cast of friends, enemies, and relatives, many of who are inspired by stories and characters from traditional Japanese folklore, such as the unique monsters of Japanese folklore, the *oni* (it should be noted, however, that the wacky *oni* of *Urusei Yatsura* are a far cry from the murderous carnivores of *Ogre Slayer*). Just as King Arthur and the Knights of the Round Table are enduring symbols which surface again and again in western fantasy, so do the folklorish origins of otherworldly creatures repeat as themes in anime videos of all genres.

But nothing is ever played completely straight in Takahashi's stories, and Lum is no different—the only prey this *oni* is interested in is Ataru, her would-be fiancé and "darling." Over the course of the series, we follow the antics of her naive seduction, Ataru's relentless pursuit of other women (any woman but Lum, as a matter of fact), plus an ever-expanding cast of aliens, mystics, monks, and more.

The zaniness of the story and its army of wacky characters are only the surface of *Urusei Yatsura*, however, as the main driving force or engine of the story is really the developing relationship between the hotly jealous Lum and the fumbling, lecherous Ataru. The appeal of a bikini-clad beauty like Lum is obvious, but what's Ataru's appeal? By presenting Ataru as a loser among losers, not necessarily a bad person but definitely one who can't seem to help making all the wrong choices, Takahashi creates a story which is touching and somehow resonant to anyone who's ever wished for an attractive, unconditionally loving mate to appear from out of nowhere and change their life forever.

Tenchi Muyô! (1992) is another wacky love-comedy featuring beings from outer space, most notably intergalactic fugitive Ryoko, imprisoned for some 700 years beneath the shrine of the Masaki family in another tip of the hat to the monsters of Japanese folklore. They say that curiosity killed the cat, and that's what almost happens to young Tenchi Masaki when he awakens Ryoko from her centuries-long slumber. She chases him throughout the schoolyard and through his home, hurling powerful bolts of lightning (just like Lum!) from her hands. When she isn't trying to kill him, she's trying to seduce him, and—also like Lum—she's also brought along some powerful friends and enemies to add to the confusion.

Tenchi Muyô! (one translation of which is "No Need For Tenchi!") has much of *Urusei Yatsura*'s slapstick sensibility, especially once other cast members begin to show up such as Ayeka and Sasami, royal princesses of the planet Jurai; Mihoshi, the bubble-headed blonde Galaxy Police Officer whose antics put science fiction author Keith Laumer's tragi-comedy *Retief* books to shame; Washu, a brilliant scientist and inventor with much more to her than it seems; not to mention the lovable mascot Ryo-Oh-Ki, a cuddly cross between a cat and a rabbit (call it a "cabbit"), who has also been known to transform into a spaceship from time to time.

Although *Tenchi!* director Hiroki Hayashi admits to cribbing many of the series' elements from a host of other series (among them *Tom and Jerry* cartoons[30]), the series nevertheless manages to achieve a fresh look by casting odd-looking new characters in comfortable, old roles. Much like following a favorite soap opera, part of the pleasure of *Tenchi!* is anticipating—and successfully predicting—what each character will do next.

In *Urusei Yatsura*, Rumiko Takahashi ensured her series' success by including along with the romance all the wacky action and comedy her viewers could handle. In ***Kimagure Orange Road*** (1987), creator Izumi Matsumoto keeps his love alive by keeping the romance front and center. Originally published in comic form in the globally bestselling weekly manga anthology *Shônen Jump*, *Kimagure Orange Road* follows the adventures of Kyosuke Kasuga, an extraordinary teenager with ordinary problems—fitting in at a new school, making new friends, and falling in love with the "wrong" girl.

Kyosuke and his family possess amazing psychic powers. You'd think being an esper would make your life a breeze, but all Kyosuke and his two sisters seem to do is get deeper and deeper into trouble, forcing the entire family to regularly pull up stakes and move to a new town where the neighbors won't gossip about them. After a brief readjustment period, things usually settle down for the Kasuga family as everyone gets used to their new surroundings, but then Kyosuke meets Hikaru and Madoka.

The lovely alien princess Lum, from ***Urusei Yatsura***.

The legendary and capricious demon Ryoko, from ***Tenchi Muyo!***

30 "I love comedy movies and slapstick movies," says director Hayashi in a recent interview. "Those really silly American movies, those super-ridiculous ones…. In live-action, I like ***Top Secret*** and ***Hot Shots*** and ***The Naked Gun***." Hayashi recalls that he often watched ***Tom and Jerry*** cartoons as a child. "In Japan, the MGM cartoons were on in the afternoons year-round," he says. "I used to watch them every day."

Sisters Sasami and Ayeka, from ***Tenchi Muyo!***

Kyosuke admires the charms of beautiful Madoka in **Kimagure Orange Road**.

Hikaru is bubbly and sweet; the perfect girl next door. Madoka is standoffish and often brusque; a girl with a past. Throughout the entire *Kimagure Orange Road* series, Kyosuke is torn between the two, unable to choose between them in a classic love triangle (the *kimagure* of the title, often translated as "whimsical; capricious," aptly reflects Kyosuke's dilemma, as well as the series' dramatic engine). Right up until the last minute, viewers are kept on the edge of their seats as Kyosuke leans first one way and then the other.

As countless American *KOR* fans will attest, the true joy of the series lies not in finding out who Kyosuke ends up with, but in following along with the thrills and heartbreak of vicarious romance. Although Kyosuke's powers are often the catalyst for events (some might say his entire family's powers are plot-determined, as they seem to vary from episode to episode depending on the needs of the story), *Kimagure Orange Road* isn't an anime version of *The X-Files*; rather, it's one of the most beloved anime series ever created, a true romantic comedy in its most warm and wonderful sense.

Like many of the early anime TV series circulated on tape here in U.S. among proto fans, Rumiko Takahashi's **Maison Ikkoku** (1986) already had a huge, built-in fan audience by the time it was finally released domestically on home video in 1996, thanks to extensive word of mouth.

Godai and Kyoko in **Maison Ikkoku**.

The story of a would-be college student named Godai and Kyoko, the wistful, beautiful manager of the rundown boarding house Maison Ikkoku (lit., "house of one moment"), the series is among the most popular anime love-comedies of all time, producing 96 half-hour TV episodes, several direct home videos, and even a full-length theatrical feature which neatly wraps up all the story's loose ends (don't see it until after you've watched all the TV episodes). Although only a dozen or so TV episodes have been released to date in English, the steady pace at which the series' U.S. distributor is also releasing English-subtitled versions of the same episodes seems pleasing to its many hardcore fans, and plans are reportedly in the works to release at least one of the *Maison* OAVs, as well.

If one had to compare between Takahashi's two other "big" series, the previously mentioned *Urusei Yatsura* and the more recent *Ranma 1/2* (see below), it would probably be most fair to say that *Maison* falls somewhere between the two: more character-driven than either *UY* or *Ranma*, yet less all-out bizarre or frenetically paced, respectively. Additionally, while both *UY* and *Ranma* are built around almost entirely self-contained episodes, *Maison* more or less tells one contiguous story over its 96 episodes…the effect of which can't be understimated when it comes to building an emotionally resounding dramatic climax.

Ranma 1/2's Ranma and Genma Saotome.

Reflecting the fact that its characters and themes are targeted at an older audience (one early episode even includes a condom joke!), today, *Maison* seems most popular among English-speaking fans of high school and college age, who perhaps can identify not only with Godai's thwarted romantic passion, but his struggles to establish an adult identity, to become *worthy* of his older building manager's affection. Like the best romantic comedies, *Maison* has its soap opera elements, but perhaps, in this case, those elements aren't something which prejudice the series' male fans against it—for if anyone knows the secret heart of young men, it's Takahashi.

In **Ranma 1/2** (1989), Takahashi takes her own *Urusei Yatsura* formula—an unwilling romance set amidst a cast of zany characters—and refines it even further. *Ranma 1/2* is the story of a young martial artist named Ranma Saotome, only son of martial artist Genma, who spirits the boy away from home and his mother's arms to train him to become "a man among men." This so-called training involves any number of harebrained schemes, the worst of which results in the pivotal dunking at the cursed training grounds of Jusenkyo, China.

Even though he doesn't speak a word of Chinese, Genma insists on taking Ranma to Jusenkyo to train, where falling into one of the area's many springs transforms the unlucky swimmer into whoever—or whatever—drowned there last. And then there's this little *accident*.... From now on, a splash of cold water will change Genma into his new alter ego, a roly-poly giant panda, while Ranma becomes an incredibly proportioned female version of himself. Hot water will reverse the effect, but only until the next time. What's a half-boy, half-girl to do?

Even with the outrageous martial arts motif, the dramatic engine of *Ranma 1/2* is undoubtedly the reluctant romance between Ranma and Akane, one of the daughters of fellow martial artist Soun Tendo. It seems every other character who shows up in the series has some sort of romantic longing for and/or attachment to either girl-type or boy-type Ranma while Akane, widower Soun's youngest daughter, has suitors of her own. But as every fan of the series can attest, the only *real* relationship in *Ranma 1/2* is that between Ranma and Akane who, despite their parents' best efforts, actually do care for each other.[31]

In the best Osamu Tezuka-inspired *Ribon no Kishi* tradition, Akane is a tomboy anointed by her father to carry on the family dojo. When Genma shows up on Soun's doorstep to make that long-ago betrothal between the families a reality, it's Akane who's nominated for bridal duty by her older and wiser sisters. Strong-willed, independent, and no slouch at martial arts herself, Akane has little patience for the thoughtless, cocksure Ranma. No leering buffoon like Ataru, Ranma straddles that fine line when boys start turning into men and girls into women, a gender line blurred considerably by his own frequent transformation from boy into girl and vice versa.

The enduring appeal of *Ranma 1/2* comes not only from the insane martial arts comedy, but in the characters' growing closeness. Even if neither of them retain any of the lessons they learned in the previous episode, each new installment of *Ranma 1/2* leaves the viewer feeling as though the romance between Ranma and Akane is as essential—and as timeless—as the concept of yin and yang itself.

Graduating from the high school love comedy is **Oh My Goddess!** (1993), featuring a fumbling college freshman named Keiichi Morisato and a literally divine girl by the name of Belldandy, based on the manga by creator Kosuke Fujishima.[32] While calling for takeout one evening from his college dorm, Keiichi somehow gets patched through to the heavenly agency of the Goddess Relief Office. Not just anyone can pick up the phone and let their fingers do the walking—to reach the GRO, you've got to be pure of heart, and if the mysterious "Ultimate Force" finds you worthy, an actual goddess may come down to Earth and grant you exactly one wish.

Fame? Fortune? Keiichi thinks only a moment before deciding that what he *really* wants is a girlfriend *just like Belldandy*, and that's what he gets, at least for the time being. If the two of them can survive being kicked out of Keiichi's all-men dorm, taking up residence in an abandoned temple, suffering through the visits of relatives on *both* their sides of the family, they may stand a chance of living happily ever after. Of course, nothing in life is ever that easy, and when you're dealing with the genre of romantic comedy, you can bet that there'll be lots of complications thrown in just to make things interesting.

In an industry where "adults-only" anime videos such as the hyper-violent crime drama *Angel Cop* or the graphically explicit sexual violence of the tentacle-porn fest *Urotsuki Dôji: Legend of the Overfiend* are sure-fire licenses to print money, Fujishima's sweet, even naive *Oh My Goddess!* is a welcome relief. Asked about the lack of more mature themes in his works, Fujishima says, "One way of looking at it is that I haven't drawn any explicit sex or violence because it hasn't been necessary. It

Boy-type Ranma and girl-type Ranma, from
Ranma 1/2

[31] This is actually one of the questions which came up during a question and answer session held during a recent Takahashi appearance at the 1994 San Diego Comic Con in California. Other interesting quotes included the essential, *Is Ranma a jerk, or what?* ("He's a boy lacking in delicacy") and the persistent fan question, *What really would happen if Ranma got pregnant?* ("I don't want to think about that, and you shouldn't, either").

College freshman Keiichi Morisato and the divine Belldandy, from ***Oh My Goddess!***

[32] Asked where he got the concept for the series, ***Oh My Goddess!*** creator Fujishima replies, "I thought it might be an interesting idea if being a goddess was a job, an occupation. I based it on Norse mythology, which is relatively unknown in Japan." In Scandinavian mythology, Verdandi (Japanese traditionally substitutes "b" for "v," as in *baiorin* for "violin") is the goddess of the present, while Urd is the goddess of the past and Skuld is the goddess of the future. It should go without saying that it doesn't take long for Fujishima to work Belldandy's sisters Urd and Skuld into the story.

happens often enough in real life and besides, sex isn't something evil." In treating the romance between a human being and an actual, goodness-to-gracious goddess, *Oh My Goddess!* can be said to have brought the "magical girlfriend" trend of romantic comedy that begun with *Urusei Yatsura* to its logical apex.

Unlike the literal divinity of the romance between Keiichi and Belldandy, Rumiko Takahashi's **One-Pound Gospel** (1988) focuses on the somehow more taboo romance between a boxer and a novitiate nun. Pro boxer Kosaku Hatanaka, the first pro ever produced by Mukaida's Gym, can't just strive to be the best; he has to overcome his constant craving for the Japanese junk food constantly pushing him over his weight limit. Junior bantamweight, bantamweight, junior featherweight—every time his weight class moves up, his coach's hopes move down. Then there's the saintly Sister Angela, a novice nun who just can't help helping others to help themselves. This includes her faith in the bumbling boxer Kosaku, because whether he believes it or not, she believes in *him*.

Aside from the *Rocky*-like boxing aspect of Takahashi's story (*"Angela-a-h!"*), it's Kosaku's willingness to do anything for the love of the beautiful Sister which gives the story its edge. As in *Ranma 1/2*, Takahashi never shies away from the brink of social taboos when deciding on the subjects for her romantic stories—many times, it's the power of the taboos themselves which gives her stories that special *frisson* of forbidden love that forms such a large part of the genre's appeal.

The romance comedy genre is, by definition, more open than most to parody. By holding up traditional values, mores, and relationships to the light of gentle scorn, the romance comedy paves the way for even broader parodies of life experiences, including work. **Maris the Chôjo** (1986), another Takahashi title, is described by its Japanese distributors as an "action comedy".[33] It's the story of a super-powered girl named Maris, a native of the planet Thanatos, where the people are six times stronger than Earthlings. Because their strength is so frequently (and unintentionally) destructive, Maris and her fellow Thanatosians are obliged to wear "power-suppression casts," elaborate harnesses which bring down superhuman strength to the merely human.

Sometimes, though, accidents happen even when you're wearing your power-suppression cast, and so mighty Maris is obliged to work as a "human taxi" to pay for all the things she's broken. Adding to her miseries are her reckless parents back home, constantly wracking up debt and expecting her to pay for it; not to mention her partner, the nine-tailed fox Murphy, who can become exactly nine of anything he wants (*how annoying!*). Maris has also been known to work as a stringer for the Space Patrol's "Special Police," and she's the one they call in to solve the case when a zillionaire named Koganemaru is kidnapped.

Some people have many loves in their lives, but for Maris there is only one—*money*, lots and lots of it. If Maris can rescue the handsome (*and wealthy! did she mention he's wealthy!?*) Koganemaru from the evil kidnappers, the idea is that he'll fall over her in gratitude, giving her his love (*and his money!*). "It's all because I'm poor!" is what she cries out whenever something goes badly for her, but anyone can see that Maris' only *real* problem is that she's inhabiting a Takahashi universe where, like Murphy's Law, nothing goes as it should.

The title is a pun on a famous film by Hong Kong action star Jackie Chan, but that isn't the only joke to be found in **Project A-Ko** (1986), a hilarious send-up of just about every anime cliché in the book, where some of anime's greatest stars show up in cameo roles. Again, this is romantic-comedy parody, hitting—on one level—the same sci-fi buttons as *Maris the Chôjo*, but deep down, it's still essentially romantic.

The very favorite friend of super-powered schoolgirl Eiko Magami is sniffling crybaby Shiko Kotobuki. But hoity-toity poor li'l rich girl Biko Daitokuji also has special feelings for Shiko, and it's this three-way rivalry which fuels the six-volume

The super-strong Thanatosian **Maris the Chojo**.

[33] Originally released under the title **The Supergal**, trademark worries involving the Gotham City-based holders of the "super" franchise caused fellow New Yorkers U.S. Manga Corps to change the title to **Maris the Chôjo**, going back in part to the original Japanese title **Za Chôjo (Sûpâgyaru)**, or "The *Chôjo* (Supergal)." Written with the characters for "super; ultra" + "girl," *chôjo* means just what you think it means: "supergal."

A-Ko, the high school student with incredible superpowers, from **Project A-Ko**.

Project A-Ko series. Directed by Katsuhiko Nishijima, it's the influence of character designer (and later, character designer/animation director/director) Yuji Moriyama which most colors *Project A-Ko*. When asked about the meaning of the girls' names, Moriyama is typically forthcoming.

"The first draft of the screenplay said 'A-Ko (tentative name)'," Moriyama says. "Likewise for the rest of them: Girl B, Girl C… You get the idea. Eventually, we came up with more elaborate Japanese character readings for their names, but they were all retrofitted. It was so tedious trying to come up with the names that we decided to just get it over with and go with A-Ko, B-Ko, and C-Ko."

In a traditional romantic comedy, the three-way rivalry is predictably two (or more) girls fighting it out over one guy. In *Urusei Yatsura*, it's Lum and his Earth girlfriend Shinobu arguing over Ataru; in *Maison Ikkoku*, it's Godai and tennis coach Mitaka vying for the affections of Kyoko; in *Ranma 1/2*, it's Shampoo, Kodachi and Ukyo competing for boy-type Ranma's attention; in *Kimagure Orange Road*, it's Kyosuke meandering between Hikaru and Madoka; in *Tenchi Muyô!*, it's Ryoko, Ayeka, Sasami and Washu, all trying to get Tenchi's attention for their own reasons. But in *Project A-Ko*, it's two bouncy, big-eyed schoolgirls squabbling over a third bouncy (and even bigger-eyed) schoolgirl, but that makes their rivalry no less serious. Long a topic of amused speculation among anime fans, *Project A-Ko*'s presumed homoerotic theme (*homo-* as in "same sex," not necessarily male-male) is screenplay writer Moriyama's unique spin on a timeless romantic comedy anime genre theme.

Aside from the unusual schoolgirl romance angle, one of the things people most remember about the *Project A-Ko* series is the frequency of cameo appearances by anime characters from other series—mostly sci-fi and action series—such as the hyper-violent ***Fist of the North Star***'s Ken as Mari, the burly schoolgirl bully with the Adam's apple; angst-ridden space opera ***My Youth in Arcadia***'s Captain Harlock as cross-dressing, d.t.-ridden Captain Napolipolita; even American comic book icons Clark Kent and Diana Prince make an appearance as A-Ko's parents.[34]

When considering the many in-jokes and parodies in *Project A-Ko*, the important thing to remember is that the humor depends less on the appearances by Superman and Wonder Woman, and more on the well-established archetypes these characters parody. Take one of the video's funniest scenes.

A-Ko and C-Ko go to a movie theater. The clip they watch at the theater is recognizably Katsuhiro Otomo's ***Harmagedon*** (1983), but there's a difference: Instead of the nefarious villain the scene leads you to expect, the dreaded monster shuffling out of the darkness is none other than KFC's own finger-lickin' good mascot and spokesperson, the ice cream-suited, walking stick-thumping Colonel Sanders.

We laugh not just because an American pop culture icon has just made an unexpected appearance in a Japanese-animated video (although it *is* funny), but because with that build-up, just about anything would have been remarkable in that scene. Would we have laughed any less hard if it had been Sanrio godhead Hello Kitty shuffling out of that darkness? Many of the other jokes in *Project A-Ko* are the same way. Captain Napolipolita is funny not just because he's a parody of creator Leiji Matsumoto's one-eyed alcoholic wanderer, the depressive-depressive (as compared to manic-depressive) Captain Harlock, but because, in this romantic comedy setting, *the Captain Harlock archetype itself* is somehow amusing.

Romantic comedy is about relationships and characters, lives and loves. It's like "soap opera plus," with some kind of hook added to appeal to different kinds of viewers—martial arts, psychic powers, or crazy cut-ups. At its most fundamental level, however, romantic comedy is all about people, about how everyone is the same inside, and how they all want the same thing—to love and be loved.

Left to right: B-Ko, A-Ko and C-Ko.

©1987 Soeishinsha/Final-Nishijima/Pony

34 "The **Wonder Woman** show was on-air in Japan at the time," Moriyama says when commenting on his use of American icons Wonder Woman and Superman as A-Ko's super-powered parents. "It was the second season. I always did like the second season." The first season was the one with the Nazis. The second season **Wonder Woman** was set during the '70s, where Diana Prince worked a government job at one of those **Man From U.N.C.L.E.**-type agencies.

Arcadia of My Youth's depressive-depressive Captain Harlock.

©1982 Toei Company, Ltd

Anime in America: The Next Step

People exploring the world of Japanese animation for the first time often don't really know what to expect. Perhaps motivated by a news article, a chance viewing on cable TV, or on a recommendation from a friend, one day you probably found yourself picking up an innocuous-looking box off a shelf, noted the stylized, brightly colored characters, took it home, and let it play.

Maybe you ended up with romantic comedy, or anime noir, or robot heroics, or a cyberpunk thriller. Despite the video you selected, it's important to remember that no matter what year it was produced, that video is the product of a long tradition of other animated shows, building and refining the genres we know today.

Despite the tremendous number of titles which have been released either subtitled or in English in the U.S. in recent years, anime in America is still in its infancy. Compared to the Japanese animation which has yet to be brought over, what's available now is only a drop in the bucket…but at least it's a start. Here in America, with our music and movie industries that creators all over the world look to for inspiration, it's easy to forget that other countries have their own creative traditions, some as old as our own, and many even older.

Today's Japanese animation may have grown and flourished out of admiration for Hollywood, but it has long since surpassed its original forebears in the animation realm, gone past America's epitome of the animated art, the animation of Walt Disney and Max Fleischer and Don Bluth and Ralph Bakshi to embrace animation's unique storytelling ability to travel to realms which would never—or could never—exist otherwise. The cutting edge of animation in America[35] has moved on to computer animation, as evidenced by the astounding technical leaps forward made in movies such as *Jurassic Park* and the more recent *Jumanji*. It could easily be argued that both of these titles are more animated films than live-action, given their extensive effects—both include major characters that are, in fact, completely animated. TV shows such as *Reboot* and *Transformers: Beast Wars*—as well as the completely computer-animated feature *Toy Story*—are the logical next step in this progression away from traditional cel-based animation in America. When, twenty years after the fact, George Lucas can make something like *Star Wars: The Special Edition*, inserting a scene with a character who never appeared as such in the original film, it seems the sky's the limit when it comes to animation as a storytelling tool. The thought seems to be, as far as traditional animation goes, what more can be done?

The answer is, of course, as much as you can imagine. Determined to take the animated art to its highest possible form, Japanese animators have never been satisfied with one version of how animation should be. The notion that animation could be used only for fairy tales and slapstick comedy was a notion they left behind long ago when they went on to stretch the boundaries of each new idea, defining and redefining the genres we see today. Today's cutting-edge Japanese directors haven't neglected computer animation as an option, but instead of creating totally computer-generated worlds, they've worked to seamlessly incorporate computer 3-D modeling into traditional, cel-based features to create even more startling effects in projects such as *Macross Plus* as well as the gorgeous, technically accomplished *Ghost in the Shell*. Even when sophisticated, polygon-based computer games such as *Virtua Fighter* or the more recent *Battle Arena Toshinden* are produced as cel-based animated shows, it's not the state-of-the-art computer animation of the games by which the show will succeed or fail, but by whether or not the shows give their characters a history, style, and stories worth the devotion of their audience. In technique, style, and above all, maturity… Japanese animators have long since gone where no American animators have gone before.

They've gone beyond.

—Trish Ledoux

[35] This is not to forget the incredible clay animation being done by Britain's Nick Park, creator of the 1993 Academy Award-winning animated short, ***The Wrong Trousers***.

A combination of computer graphics and cel animation make for a striking look in ***Macross Plus***.

©1994 Big West/Macross Plus Project

Chapter Three
Video Directory
Listings of anime home video titles available in America

One of the core reasons for writing this book was to help sort out and describe the burgeoning array of home video titles available. For the purposes of this Guide, we've restricted the domestic title listings to home videos released in America that were generally available (whether still in print or not) on 1 January 1995 or later. Titles no longer available as of 1 January 1995 and titles scheduled for release after 1 January 1997 are not listed. Due to the vagaries of the "art" of translation, there are often variant spellings of names, such as Lupin III/Rupan III; Iczer-One/Iczer-1; Harmagedon/Harmageddon; etc. We have generally listed the most commonly used spelling, and included a "See" reference for the alternate spelling. When a TV series has been imported and "Americanized" (like *Astro Boy, Battle of the Planets*, etc.), we list the number of episodes of the *domestic* version of the show, and include a mention of the number of original Japanese episodes. Whenever possible, individual episode titles and episode summaries (as provided by U.S. distributors) are included.

Key to supplier codes:
Each domestic video listing has a supplier code prefix in front of the supplier's order number. Information on each supplier is contained in the Resources chapter later in this book.

A18	Anime 18 (*see Central Park Media*)	PRV	Parade Video
ADV	A.D. Vision	RS	The Right Stuf
ANI	AnimEigo	SAE	Star Anime Enterprises
BFV	Best Film & Video	SMV	Sony Music Video (Sony Wonder)
CEL	Celebrity Home Entertainment	SPV	Streamline Pictures
CFX	Fox Home Video	SS	Software Sculptors
CM	Critical Mass (*see The Right Stuf*)	STM	Starmaker Video
CPM	Central Park Media	TFV	Tyndale Family Video
CQC	CQC Pictures	UAV	United American Video
DIC	DIC Toon Time Video	USM	U.S. Manga Corps (*see Central Park Media*)
FHE	Family Home Entertainment	USR	U.S. Renditions
ID	Image Entertainment	VEI	Voyager Entertainment
LDV	LD Video Productions	VMM	Vidmark
LUM	Lumivision	VOY	The Voyager Company
MGV	Manga Video	VR	Video Rarities (*see Central Park Media*)
PBE	Palm Beach Entertainment	VT	Video Treasures
PI	Pioneer Animation	VV	Viz Video

Key to title listings:
Each listing gives the title, subtitle (if any), copyright notice, production credits, program synopsis, and running time. All programs are color unless specifically indicated as black & white. Episode titles within the synopsis appear in all capital letters. An individual program may be available in several different versions, such as VHS and laserdisc, subtitled and dubbed, and so forth. In these cases, the program information is given just once, with the various formats available listed as separate ordering lines.

The ordering line contains the following information:

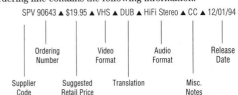

SPV 90643 ▲ $19.95 ▲ VHS ▲ DUB ▲ HiFi Stereo ▲ CC ▲ 12/01/94

Ordering Number — Video Format — Audio Format — Release Date

Supplier Code — Suggested Retail Price — Translation — Misc. Notes

VIDEO FORMAT
VHS .... VHS, Standard Play, NTSC
VHS-EP ... VHS, Extended Play, NTSC
LD .... Laserdisc, CLV (Extended Play)
LD-CAV ... Laserdisc, CAV (Standard Play)

TRANSLATION
DUB .... Dialogue dubbed in English
SUB .... Japanese dialogue with English subtitles
HYBRID ... 2 complete versions of program included (dubbed & subtitled)
M/A .... Multi-Audio: one audio track dubbed in English, one audio track in Japanese, subtitles via Closed Captioning
SPAN .... Dialogue dubbed in Spanish
ND .... No dialogue

AUDIO
Mono, Stereo, HiFi, Surround, etc.

MISC
W/S .... Widescreen version
LTBX .... Letterboxed version
CC .... Closed captioned
CP .... Copy protected

All laserdiscs have CX noise reduction and digital audio
Out of Print means this video is permanently discontinued by this supplier
Moratorium means this video is temporarily unavailable from this supplier

 Violence   Profanity   Nudity   Sexual Situations    Adult Viewers Only - content is extreme and/or explicit

3x3 Eyes

OAV series, 4 volumes

(1991-92) ©Yuzo Takada/Kodansha/Plex/Star Child

Based on the comic series by: Yuzo Takada *Director*: Daisuke Nishio *Written by*: Akinori Endo *Music*: Kaoru Wada

In search of a way to become human, Pai, an immortal, three-eyed monster in the shape of a young girl, takes the soul of a luckless young Japanese man, Yakumo Fujii, and makes him into her eternal, zombie protector (if he'd only gotten some superpowers to go along with his new immortal status, maybe being killed over and over in increasingly messy ways wouldn't be so bad, but...). At times very bloody, the atmosphere of ancient, legendary magic and monsters is carried off well; gains additional atmosphere from superlative mythically flavored music by Kaoru Wada (KISHIN CORPS). Artifacts and costumes sport interesting Tibetan details. Script for the video series is by DOOMED MEGALOPOLIS' Akinori Endo. Based on the comic series by Yuzo Takada (published in English by Dark Horse Comics). Released in Japan under the title "3x3 (Sazan) Eyes" by Kodansha/Bandai Visual; available in North America through Streamline Pictures. Followed in Japan by 3x3 EYES: SEIMA DENSETSU (Holy-Demon Legend), an as-yet continuing sequel OAV series (not yet available in English).

3 x 3 Eyes Part 1: *Altered State*

Journeying from Tibet to Tokyo, the 300-year-old "adolescent" is looking for Yakumo Fujii, the son of an archaeologist who devoted his life to learning the secrets of the Sanjiyan - the "immortal ones." Pai hopes Yakumo will help her. Yakumo is skeptical until Pai's berserk spirit guide accidentally kills him in front of the horrified girl. Using the powers of the Sanjiyan, Pai resurrects Yakumo. Now convinced of her story, Yakumo agrees to join Pai in her fantastic quest. Their only clue leads them to Hong Kong. They soon find themselves in the middle of a secret war between opposing occult forces vying for possession of the powerful artifact. What complicates matters even more is the fact that Pai has no conscious knowledge of her dual personality and is often unable to use her awesome powers at will. **30 min.**

3 x 3 Eyes Part 2: *Who Needs Enemies*

Pai's quest for mortality is temporarily put on hold while Yakumo tries to get his "life" back together by reestablishing ties with his schoolmates. But even the best of plans can fall apart when a demon enters the picture. The dream of eternal life has a strong pull, and like a moth drawn to a flame, a demonic interloper throws a monkey wrench into this domestic interlude as he threatens to destroy Yakumo's friends unless he betrays Pai and helps the demon possess her immortal soul. **30 min.**

3 x 3 Eyes Part 3: *Life and Death*

In order to save his life, Pai takes control of Yakumo's soul, causing him to become similarly immortal. As long as she lives, he lives. Now, both must find the statue to survive. Their incredible journey for the "Statue of Humanity" finally ends in a Hong Kong high-rise luxury hotel. The artifact - currently in the hands of evil demon worshippers - is the centerpiece of a human sacrifice. The ritual will result in the death of a new ally, Meishin, and bring about the resurrection of the demon lord Kaiyan Wang. Yakumo must muster all of his courage and resolve in order to stave off the murder of his new friend, rescue Pai and keep the statue from calling up Kaiyan Wang. **30 min.**

3 x 3 Eyes Part 4: *Blind Flight*

Making their way to safety following an epic battle at Kaiyan Wang's hidden temple, Pai and Yakumo begin to ponder the inevitability of their growing attraction for each other. Thus occupied, the star-crossed lovers fail to notice the appearance of a new menace until it is almost too late. Under the protection of the mysterious Madam Hoan, the group try, but fail, to unravel the mysteries of the "Statue of Humanity." In an attempt to destroy Pai, Benares, one of Kaiyan Wang's most powerful disciples, possesses the rotting carcass of Pai's feathered familiar Takuhi and gains mind control of their new ally Meishin. Realizing that there is no other choice but to face her demons, both real and imagined, Pai calls upon the inner strength of her immortal alter ego. One last psychic battle ... to the death. But Yakumo does not like the odds. Unwilling to let her face this danger alone, the valiant youth races against time to aid his endangered love. If they cannot survive this final challenge, then at least Yakumo hopes they will be able to face death together. **30 min.**

Domestic Home Video:

3 x 3 Eyes Part 1
SPV 90303 ▲ $9.95 ▲ VHS ▲ DUB ▲ Stereo ▲ 11/01/92

3 x 3 Eyes Part 2
SPV 90323 ▲ $9.95 ▲ VHS ▲ DUB ▲ Stereo ▲ 03/22/93

3 x 3 Eyes Part 3
SPV 90493 ▲ $9.95 ▲ VHS ▲ DUB ▲ Stereo ▲ 06/06/93

3 x 3 Eyes Part 4
SPV 90593 ▲ $9.95 ▲ VHS ▲ DUB ▲ Stereo ▲ 06/06/93

3 x 3 Eyes Perfect Collection: *Special Collector's Edition*
Contains all four episodes of the 4-part OAV series. (110 min.)
SPV 91213 ▲ $19.95 ▲ VHS ▲ DUB ▲ Stereo ▲ CC ▲ 02/21/95
LUM 9382 ▲ $39.95 ▲ LD ▲ MULTI-AUDIO ▲ Stereo ▲ 08/24/94

1-Pound no Fukuin *See* ONE-POUND GOSPEL

8th Man

TV series, 56 half-hour episodes

(1963-64) ©TCJ Animation Center/ABC Films

Created by: Kazumasa Hirai and Jiro Kuwata *American adaptation by*: Gene Prinz

Based on the manga series of the same name by Kazumasa Hirai and Jiro Kuwata, as serialized in publisher Kodansha's SHÔNEN MAGAZINE manga anthology. All-time classic TV series produced in Japan during the early '60s—the same time ASTRO BOY was on the air—featuring a super-powered, super-fast android called "8-Man" (retitled "8th Man" for its 1965 U.S. broadcast), based on the Hirai-Kuwata manga series (see above). Similar to the origin of American comic book character The Spectre, 8-Man is a former detective who, after being killed for unwisely poking into the business of the wrong people, comes back to a new life of super-powered crime fighting (The Spectre came back as a ghost; 8-Man, *Robocop*-like, comes back as a robot). The series' b&w TV animation—possibly seen as primitive to some—builds remarkably on the futuristic technology established in ASTRO BOY (see entry), giving it a dark, almost *noir* look to go along with its *Dick Tracy*-like villains and Fleischer *Superman* plots; i.e., plenty of mad scientists and evil monsters. A live-action film has also been released, but be warned—production values are on the same par as American-broadcast superhero TV movies (the live-action *Spider-Man* comes to mind). Released in Japan under the title "Eight Man" by Toei Video; available in North America through Video Rarities.

8th Man Vol. 1
5 uncut original episodes. In DR. SPECTRA, the evil Dr. Spectra, agent of Intercrime, wants to disassemble 8th Man to discover his robot secrets. Using the Nerve Shocking Stick and Mini-Missiles, he causes 8th Man to lose his memory! In EVIL JAW AND THE DEVIL GERMS, the Black Butterfly Gang sends its agent Evil Jaw to capture the space-based, metal-eating Devil Germs and use them for evil! In BARON STORMY, a weather machine is stolen by Baron Stormy, the Weather Wizard, and used to extort ransoms from entire cities. 8th Man must face the baron and his Lightning Gun! In ATTACK OF THE HORRIBLE HONEY BEES, the buzzing of gigantic, radioactively mutated bees causes destructive, killer sound waves. 8th Man must destroy the hive and kill the giant Queen Bee. In POUNCE THE ROBOT TIGER, 8th Man's atomic motor is running down due to depletion of its uranium power source. He must face a destructive Robot Tiger in order to take back the stolen uranium being held on Intercrime Island. **120 min. B&W**

8th Man Vol. 2
5 original uncut episodes. In THE BATTLE OF THE BROTHERS, an enemy robot masquerading as 8th Man comes looking to eliminate 8th Man and Professor Genius. In THE MONSTROUS EELER, an experiment gone wrong spawns a gigantic electric eel, who goes on a rampage of terror and attempts world conquest! In THE ATOMIC GHOST, an agent of the Black Butterfly Gang is irradiated by an exploding cyclotron and gains the ability to dematerialize. He lures 8th Man to a desert island to destroy him. In THE GOLD BEETLE OF THE ORIENTIA, flying robot beetles drill into bank vaults so a villain can use an atomic vacuum to clean them out. They have many devices to destroy 8th Man as well! In THE RETURN OF NAPOLEON BONAPARTE, two countries seeking a peace treaty are disrupted by a power-mad tyrant who thinks he's Napoleon! **120 min. B&W**

8th Man Vol. 3
5 original uncut episodes. In TARGET 8TH MAN, the Black Butterfly Gang creates an armored assassin who sets out to destroy 8th

 Made for Television Broadcast    Made for Home Video Release   Made for Theatrical Release

Man. Using the kidnapped Chief Fumblethumbs as bait, Bird the assassin lures 8th Man into a trap. In THE PASSENGER ROCKET ADVENTURE, 8th Man investigates sabotage in a secret new rocket factory. A test pilot is hypnotized by Dr. Light Ray who plans to use him as a human bomb. In THE THREAT OF DISASTER, Sam Dorian kidnaps 8th Man's secretary to prevent 8th Man from interfering with his plans to smuggle neutron bomb plans to a foreign government. In THE BELLIGERENT BODYGUARD, The President of Domestica, arrives in the US with Princess Precious. Tobor, disguised as a hotel maid, prevents a political assassination. In THE FREEZING RAY, Mr. Blizzard requires uranium to operate his freeze gun. With a huge flying saucer, he attacks Earth's cities and only 8th Man can stop him! **120 min. B&W**

8th Man Vol. 4

5 original uncut episodes. In THE SOLAR SATELLITE, Intercrime has fashioned a huge pool in the ocean. When a solar satellite is aimed at it, the ocean is boiled away to recover gold and silver. 8th Man knows that arch villain Dr. Spectra is responsible. In RASCAL FISH AND HIS PIRATE SUB, the evil Rascal Fish and his pirates try to prevent 8th Man from recovering a crashed planeload of uranium. In THE ARMORED MAN, 8th Man discovers a robot with a human brain and internal organs. Trained as a soldier, the robot-human can't stand being a monster and aims to destroy his creator and the world! In THE ELECTRONIC TYRANT, 8th Man rescues a girl from thugs only to see her fall into a coma. Dr. Genius discovers a remote control device in her brain, planted there by Brainatron who plans to turn humanity into mindless slaves! In BAT MASTER & HIS ROBOT BATS, Bat Master plans to kidnap all the brilliant scientists, transfer their brains to a brain bank, and use their genius for the evil purposes of Intercrime. **120 min. B&W**

Domestic Home Video:

8th Man Vol. 1
VR 001 ▲ $29.95 ▲ VHS ▲ DUB ▲ Mono ▲ 06/01/90

8th Man Vol. 2
VR 002 ▲ $29.95 ▲ VHS ▲ DUB ▲ Mono ▲ 06/01/90

8th Man Vol. 3
VR 003 ▲ $29.95 ▲ VHS ▲ DUB ▲ Mono ▲ 06/01/93

8th Man Vol. 4
VR 004 ▲ $29.95 ▲ VHS ▲ DUB ▲ Mono ▲ 01/15/94

8 Man After [OAV] 💥 ◎

OAV series, 4 volumes

(1993) ©Kazumasa Hirai/Jiro Kuwata/Act Co.Ltd.

Based on characters by: Kazumasa Hirai, Jiro Kuwata *Director*: Sumiyoshi Furukawa *Screenplay*: Yasushi Hirano *Music*: Michael Kennedy

Four-volume direct-to-video sequel (all released in Japan during 1993) to the 1960s animated TV series (see above) created by Kazumasa Hirai and Jiro Kuwata, better known in the U.S. by the title under which it was broadcast: 8TH MAN. 8 MAN AFTER fast-forwards from the heroic world of the '60s to the bleak view of today. The city's hero, the robotic 8 Man (who possesses super-speed just like American comic book character The Flash) has been missing for years, and the city is now populated with big-time corruption, murder, crazed junkies, and roving cybernetic gangs. When a new 8 Man appears (due to a *Robocop*-like plot device), he must face not only this corrupt city, but the ghosts of his own dark past and those of a body not his own. In a topical update of the original premise, 8 Man recharges by inserting some kind of energy capsule into his body instead of puffing away at cigarettes. Look for key characters from the '60s series to reprise their original roles. English version features new, moody, techno-flavored music by Michael Kennedy. Released in Japan under the title "8 Man After"; available in North America through Streamline Pictures.

8 Man After Vol. 1: *City in Fear*

Since the recent disappearance of 8 Man, a mysterious cyborg superhero created by Professor Tani, the city reels under terrorist assaults by murderous, drug-crazed street gangs. Daigo, a powerful industrialist, plans to run for mayor on a platform of law and order. Hazama, an ex-cop who now runs a private detective agency, is hired to track down a missing scientist alleged to have made off with cybernetics from Professor Tani's laboratory. The missing hardware is reappearing as psycho-activated weapons grafted onto the bodies of the rogue "cyber-junkies." It's up to Police Chief Tanaka to stop the crime wave without the aid of 8 Man. **29 min.**

8 Man After Vol. 2: *End Run*

In the grisly aftermath of 8 Man's apparent return to duty, the focus of current police effort centers around the investigation of the theft of weapons-grade computer components capable of turning vicious gangbangers into deadly cyber-junkies. Dr. Tani suspects that his own technology has been pirated and used to create these monstrosities. Chief Inspector Tanaka and Dr. Tani

are the only ones who know that Hazama, a P.I. murdered by a cybernetically-enhanced thug, has been used as a bio-template to replace the missing 8 Man. As a cover, 8 Man maintains his original persona as the human detective. A brutal finale pits 8 Man against a drug-crazed team of football players illegally enhanced by Tani's misused cybernetic wizardry. The team goes berserk during an exhibition game staged by would-be mayoral candidate Daigo. The players become homicidal maniacs and begin a rampage which, if left unchecked, will result in massive death and destruction. **29 min.**

8 Man After Vol. 3: *Mr. Hallowe'en*

While the city recovers from a brutal massacre at the football stadium, young Sam O'Connor struggles with the realization that his father has been turned into an unwilling cyber-junkie. Hazama and Sachiko try to break the ex-football player of a dependency on cybo-mechamine - yet the question remains whether there will be anything left of the addict's sanity once the drug wears off. Making matters worse is the fact that Hazama must struggle with his own demons. His cyborg body holds trace memories of Azuma-san, the original 8 Man. Add to this the agony accompanying the senseless murder of his sister by Tony Gleck, and this latest 8 Man finds himself suffering from serious emotional trauma. His first response is to run amok. The bitter reality of 8 Man's precarious grasp on his own self-control, as evidenced by his participation in the stadium massacre, could snap once again without warning. **29 min.**

8 Man After Vol. 4: *Sachiko's Decision*

The murder of underworld boss Mr. Hallowe'en leaves his cyber-junkie gang in the hands of his psychotic former henchman, Tony Gleck. With 8 Man closing in, Tony has his underlings kidnap Sachiko, seemingly to use her as a hostage. Tony's real motive is to draw 8 Man to his hideout. Tony's flawed cyber-junkie body is failing, and he plans to capture 8 Man and have his criminal brain transplanted into 8 Man's invincible super-body! Hazama faces a dilemma. Cold robot logic tells him that Sachiko's safety is less important than destroying Tony without revealing his secret identity. But he's still controlled by his human emotions, and he gladly lets them take over now. In the final battle, Sachiko realizes that Hazama is 8 Man now, and her previous love, whom she loved, is dead. Her decision about her feelings toward Hazama will determine whether the new 8 Man discards the last vestiges of his humanity. **29 min.**

Domestic Home Video:

8 Man After Vol. 1
SPV 90783 ▲ $9.95 ▲ VHS ▲ DUB ▲ Mono ▲ CC ▲ 06/01/94

8 Man After Vol. 2
SPV 90853 ▲ $9.95 ▲ VHS ▲ DUB ▲ Mono ▲ CC ▲ 10/10/94

8 Man After Vol. 3
SPV 90903 ▲ $9.95 ▲ VHS ▲ DUB ▲ Mono ▲ CC ▲ 11/25/94

8 Man After Vol. 4
SPV 90933 ▲ $9.95 ▲ VHS ▲ DUB ▲ Mono ▲ CC ▲ 01/10/95

8 Man After Perfect Collection
Contains all four episodes of the OAV series. (116 min.)
SPV 91173 ▲ $19.95 ▲ VHS ▲ DUB ▲ Mono ▲ CC ▲ 08/16/95

801 T.T.S. Airbats [OAV] 💥 ◎

(1994-96) ©Toshimitsu Shimizu/Tokuma Shoten/JVC

Created by: Toshimitsu Shimizu *Character Design*: Yuji Moriyama *Directors*: Yuji Moriyama, Osamu Mikasa, Junichi Sakata, Tohru Yoshida

AIRBATS follows the misadventures of a young man assigned (only half-seriously) as mechanic for Japan's first all-female jet-pilot squad. After getting off to a rocky start by walking in on his undressed fellow squad members, he becomes the center of a love triangle with two rival female pilots at the other points. Mostly slapstick comedy, but with some interestingly enlightened commentary on the treatment of women in the military, and some cool jet sequences. Created by Toshimitsu Shimizu, creator of the lighthearted sex romp REI REI (but without, thankfully, the tentacles); directed by Yuji Moriyama of PROJECT A-KO/MAISON IKKOKU fame. A major highlight is the hero's daydream in which a rampaging monster swats down aircraft with its extendable eyeballs. Released in Japan under the title "Aozora Shōjo-Tai 801 T.T.S."; available in North America through A.D. Vision. **85 min.**

Domestic Home Video:

ADV AB/001 ▲ $34.95 ▲ VHS ▲ SUB ▲ HiFi Surround ▲ 09/25/95

 Violence Profanity Nudity Sexual Situations  Adult Viewers Only - content is extreme and/or explicit

982, '85 Otaku no Video *See* OTAKU NO VIDEO
A-Ko the Vs. *See* PROJECT A-KO
Aa, Megami-sama *See* OH MY GODDESS

The Abashiri Family

(1992) ©Dynamic Planning, Inc./Studio Pierrot/Soeishinsha/NEXTART

Written and Directed by: Takashi Watanabe *Based on Story and Characters by:* Go Nagai *Music:* Takeo Miratsu

One-shot OAV based on the original manga by creator Go Nagai, as serialized in publisher Akita Shôten's WEEKLY SHÔNEN CHAMPION. A Japanese gangland family wants to raise their daughter to be a perfect little princess instead of the Japanese mafia princess she really is, and enrolls her in an elite boarding school. Unfortunately, the competition's already in attendance, and they want to see her take the big sleep, if you follow the drift. But even a fine finishing school can't erase the fact that pretty young Kukunosuke is still daddy's little girl, and eventually, her knee-capping roots show through. Violent, sexy comedy by one of the Japanese PTA's favorite targets, DEVILMAN's Go Nagai. Released in Japan under the title "Abashiri Ikka" by Nexstar/Pony Canyon; available in North America through A.D. Vision. **75 min.**

Domestic Home Video:
ADV AF/001 ▲ $29.95 ▲ VHS ▲ SUB ▲ HiFi Surround ▲ 01/30/96

Abashiri Ikka *See* ABASHIRI FAMILY

AD Police
OAV series, 3 volumes

(1990) ©Artmic, Inc./Youmex, Inc.

Directors: Takamasa Ikegami (File 1), Akira Nishimori (Files 2&3) *Planning:* Toshimichi Suzuki, Shin Unozawa *Original Story:* Toshimichi Suzuki, Tony Takezaki *Screenplay:* Noboru Aikawa *Character Design:* Tony Takezaki, Fujio Oda, Toru Nakasugi.

Three-volume OAV series (all released in Japan during 1990) set in the world of BUBBLEGUM CRISIS with a notable lack of crossover cameos by the Knight Sabers, AD POLICE is ultraviolent police fare with little to redeem it, bearing virtually no resemblance to creator Tony Takezaki's stylish manga story of the same name, although Takezaki himself is credited with character design and original story for the video series. The streets of Mega Tokyo teem with oversexed "boomer" androids with death wishes, blood, guts, guns and gore. Not for the squeamish. With vicious murders, disemboweled prostitutes, and female executives artificially augmented to get ahead in business, the best that can be said is that the series' female characters make Priss from Ridley Scott's *Blade Runner* (the movie from which so much of the BUBBLEGUM CRISIS and satellite series are so heavily influenced) look like the girl next door. Released in Japan under the title "AD Police" by Bandai Visual; available in North America through AnimEigo.

AD Police File 1: *The Phantom Woman*

MegaTokyo 2027 A.D. - Relentless technological development has resulted in the creation of Boomers, artificially intelligent androids with the potential to free mankind from physical labor. But anything that can be used can also be misused. AD Police rookie Leon McNichol gets his first lesson in the school of hard choices when he and his partner Geena are given the job of tracking down the cause of several incidents of Boomers running amok. They soon discover that a defective Boomer is illegally reactivating Boomers which have been scrapped. One of these Boomers has a vivid memory locked in her mind: the image of the man who destroyed her. The image of Leon McNichol. **40 min.**

AD Police File 2: *The Ripper*

Detective Ailis Kara doggedly investigates a string of vicious murders. All the victims have two things in common: they are all prostitutes, and they have all been disemboweled. Along the way, she meets a female executive who has had herself artificially augmented to get ahead in business. Is there a connection between the newly available implants and the murders? At what point does one stop being human and become a machine? Ailis Kara is about to find out. **40 min.**

AD Police File 3: *The Man Who Bites His Tongue*

After being critically wounded battling a runaway Boomer, AD Police officer Billy Fanword becomes the recipient of an experimental cyber-operation, and is reborn as an invincible Cyborg Policeman. But Billy, who can only confirm his humanity by biting his tongue, soon finds out that invincibility isn't all it's cracked up to be. **40 min.**

Domestic Home Video:
AD Police File 1
ANI AT093-005 ▲ $24.95 ▲ VHS ▲ SUB ▲ HiFi Stereo ▲ 09/01/93
ANI ET095-012 ▲ $19.95 ▲ VHS ▲ DUB ▲ HiFi Stereo ▲ 11/29/95
AD Police File 2
ANI AT093-006 ▲ $24.95 ▲ VHS ▲ SUB ▲ HiFi Stereo ▲ 10/27/93
ANI ET095-013 ▲ $19.95 ▲ VHS ▲ DUB ▲ HiFi Stereo ▲ 11/29/95
AD Police File 3
ANI AT093-007 ▲ $24.95 ▲ VHS ▲ SUB ▲ HiFi Stereo ▲ 12/29/93
ANI ET095-014 ▲ $19.95 ▲ VHS ▲ DUB ▲ HiFi Stereo ▲ 11/29/95
AD Police Files 1, 2 & 3
All three OAVs on one laserdisc. (120 min.)
ANI AD094-001 ▲ $39.95 ▲ LD ▲ SUB ▲ HiFi Stereo ▲ 02/23/94
AD Police 3-Pack: *Files 1, 2 & 3*
All three OAVs in a special pre-pack (120 min.)
ANI AS095-015 ▲ $49.95 ▲ VHS ▲ DUB ▲ HiFi Stereo ▲ 11/29/95
AD Police Files Hybrid LD #1: *The Phantom Woman & The Ripper*
Episodes 1 and 2 on a Hybrid LD. (55 min.)
ANI AD096-004 ▲ $39.95 ▲ LD ▲ HYBRID ▲ HiFi Stereo ▲ 07/10/96
AD Police Files Hybrid LD #2: *Man Who Bites His Tongue & Music Videos*
Episode 3 plus dubbed AD Police music videos on a Hybrid LD. (81 min.)
ANI AD096-005 ▲ $39.95 ▲ LD ▲ HYBRID ▲ HiFi Stereo ▲ 07/10/96

Adventure Kid
OAV series, 3 episodes

(1992-93) ©Toshio Maeda/West Cape Corp.

Based on the comic by: Toshio Maeda *Screenplay:* Atsushi Yamatoya *Music:* Masamichi Amano *Director:* Yoshitaka Fujimoto

WW II-era scientist resurrects his body as a computerized demon to get revenge for his wife's rape by a sadistic army officer in years past...by raping young girls himself. If that makes no sense to you, neither will this two-volume "absolutely not for children" OAV. Low-end animation takes the bite out of this production's erotic shock value—after a while, it's simply a tiresome (albeit revolting) parade of tentacles and squealing girls. The most awful thing is, the flashback sequence of the wife's rape is the only scene with any conviction. A lesser effort from the producers (and original creator, Toshio Maeda) of UROTSUKI DÔJI infamy. Released in Japan under the title "Yôjû Sensen (Demon-Beast Battle Lines) Adventure Kid 1-3" (the third episode sports the unlikely subtitle, believe it or not, of "L'Elisir d'Amore," as in the opera by Donizetti) by Sôbi Entertainment; available in North America through Anime 18.

Adventure Kid Vol. 1: *Episodes 1 and 2*

In Midori, Masago has a perfect proxy for his long dead wife and only Norikazu's love for her can save them both from an existence of eternal atonement for the sins of Masago's own failed life. **75 min.**

Adventure Kid Vol. 2: *Episode 3*

As the mad Masago has been destroyed, delivering the real world from his computer-generated nightmare, life can now revert back to normal. Not quite... Masago's universe still exists and Norikazu's computer can still open a doorway into it. Embarrassed that his own son is now the servant of a mere human, the King of Hell dispatches his inept agent Mephisto to bring Kingan home. **40 min.**

Domestic Home Video:
Adventure Kid Vol. 1: *Episodes 1 and 2*
A18 1243 ▲ $29.95 ▲ VHS ▲ SUB ▲ Stereo ▲ 02/01/95
Adventure Kid Vol. 2: *Episode 3*
A18 1244 ▲ $29.95 ▲ VHS ▲ SUB ▲ Stereo ▲ 04/04/95

Ai City (Love City)

(1986) ©Toho Co. Ltd./KK Movic/Ashi Productions

Producer: Hiroshi Kato *Director*: Koichi Mashimo

Based on the comics of the same name by Shuho Sakabashi, as serialized in publisher Futabasha's ACTION COMICS manga anthology. *X-Men*-like story of two young people with psychic powers being chased by supervillain-like corporate baddies who want to control them. A good example of the mid-'80s flair for combing stock sci-fi elements such as psychic powers, chase scenes, and ultraviolent gore with ruminations on forced evolution and the genetic destiny of mankind. Neat details include psychic power levels being measured by digital readouts on the users' foreheads, a villain that swells up into a fleshy blob that encompasses the entire city (!), and a female character dressed like a *Playboy*-style "bunny-girl" for no particular reason. The "lab" where the psionics are created is an homage to the 1978 film *Coma*. Nice '80s animation, effectively directed. (The "*ai*" city, or "love" city of the title, is a not-very-accurate New York.) Released in Japan under the title "Ai City" by Toho; available in North America through The Right Stuf. **86 min.**

Domestic Home Video:
RS 9004 ▲ $24.95 ▲ VHS ▲ SUB ▲ Stereo ▲ W/S ▲ CP ▲ 07/11/95

Akai Hayate

OAV series, 4 episodes

(1991-92) ©NEXTART/Osamu Yamazaki/Minamimachi Bugyosho

Director: Osamu Tsuruyama *Original Story and Screenplay*: Osamu Yamazaki *Music*: Takashi Kudo

A secret society of ninja assassins called "the Shinogara" have controlled Japan since ancient times, but rebellion is finally breaking their ranks. Hayate kills his father (the leader of the group) and flees, but is mortally wounded. Before he dies, however, he transfers his spirit into his sister Shiori. Especially accomplished ninja warriors sport "shadow armor"—a sort of spiky redux on samurai armor, drawn mystically from the wearers' own shadows, with neat individual armoring details. An interesting combination of ninja thriller and superhero story, nicely animated over four OAV volumes, but ultimately confusing, with an array of subplots focusing everything from boxers to the Shinogara's internal politics. Originally released in Japan as part of the continuing "magazine"-style anime video series ANIME V COMIC: RENTAMAN (which also featured a first look at creator Go Nagai's ABASHIRI FAMILY). The series is also available in Japan in two, two-episode "Special Edition" compilation volumes. Released in Japan under the title "Akai Hayate" by Walkers Company/Polydor; available in North America through U.S. Manga Corps.

Akai Hayate Vol. 1

Shiori is wandering the streets of Tokyo, under the alias "Yukiko." Assassins still search for her, unaware of her new powers. But each time Shiori calls up her brother, she sacrifices a part of herself. After all, two souls cannot occupy the same body - for long. **60 min.**

Akai Hayate Vol. 2

A bitter power struggle has begun. The battle now moves to the board room and corporate office, as the master strategist Shuri consolidates his hold over Nanso, at the eastern edge of Tokyo. It's a battle that will pitch the tools of technology against the ancient mystic arts, as Shuri fights to the death to keep the freedom he's so recently acquired. Whatever the outcome, the real showdown must come at Shinogara's heart — at the palatial headquarters hidden at the base of Mt. Fuji. Here, all questions will finally be answered: The reason Hayate murdered his own father, an explanation of Genbu's mysterious powers, and the secret of the mystic shadow armor. **60 min.**

Domestic Home Video:
Akai Hayate Vol. 1
USM 1308 ▲ $29.95 ▲ VHS ▲ SUB ▲ Stereo ▲ 06/06/95
Akai Hayate Vol. 2
USM 1309 ▲ $29.95 ▲ VHS ▲ SUB ▲ Stereo ▲ 10/03/95
Akai Hayate 2-Pack
USM 1353 ▲ $49.95 ▲ VHS ▲ SUB ▲ Stereo ▲ 10/03/95

Akai Hikari-Dan Zillion *See* ZILLION

Akai Kiba Blue Sonnet *See* BLUE SONNET

Akira

(1988) ©Akira Committee

Character Design, Script and Direction: Katsuhiro Otomo *Scenario*: Izo Hashimoto *Art Director*: Toshiharu Mizutani *Chief Animator*: Takashi Nakamura *Music*: Geinoh Yamashiro Gumi

In 21st Century "Neo-Tokyo," a drag-racing biker named Tetsuo is chosen for experimentation by the army in the theory that his unusual mental aura may prove a key to perfecting the long-buried "Akira Project." But like *The Fury* or *Carrie*, his newly awakened power quickly grows out of control, and a lifetime of resentment over his second-place existence lashes out with psychic vengeance. Though the story is extremely condensed compared to Otomo's original comic (which had not yet been finished when the film verison was produced), the overall effect is stunning and masterful, despite the inexplicable ending, and truly deserves to be called a masterpiece. Based on director Otomo's own magnum opus manga series (published in English by Epic Comics) with an incredible chorale and percussion soundtrack by Shoji Yamashiro's Geinoh Group. Fabulously animated in painstaking detail, AKIRA is one of the more widely seen anime films in the United States, being both the first anime film to have a successful, widespread screening tour in the United States, and the first to receive significant respect from American critical sources such as THE WASHINGTON POST and some of America's own giants of SF film and literature, such as James Cameron, William Gibson, and Bruce Sterling. Criterion Widescreen Special Edition three-laserdisc set includes first issue of the AKIRA graphic novel, English and Japanese trailers, original storyboards, production drawings and cels, behind-the-scenes footage, original pencil tests, and more, while Pioneer LDC's AKIRA: SPECIAL COLLECTION (not to be confused with the AKIRA PRODUCTION REPORT, below) features a bilingual Japanese/English soundtrack, thousands of continuity sketches from the film, as well as a 30-minute interview with creator/director Otomo. Additionally, in Japan there is also available a nineteen-minute video called the AKIRA SOUND CLIP BY GEINÔ YAMASHIRO GUMI (Group) which sets seven tracks from Shoji Yamashiro's stunning soundtrack to scenes from the film. Released in Japan under the title "Akira" by Bandai Visual; available in North America through Streamline Pictures. **124 min.**

Domestic Home Video:
SPV 90473 ▲ $39.95 ▲ VHS ▲ SUB ▲ HiFi Stereo ▲ 03/30/94
SPV 90643 ▲ $19.95 ▲ VHS ▲ DUB ▲ HiFi Stereo ▲ CC ▲ 12/01/94
SPV 90002 ▲ $29.95 ▲ VHS ▲ DUB ▲ HiFi Stereo ▲W/S ▲ 12/01/90
VOY 1435 ▲ $59.95 ▲ LD ▲ M/A ▲ HiFi Surround ▲ W/S ▲ 11/22/95
VOY 1294 ▲ $124.95 ▲ LD-CAV ▲ M/A ▲ HiFi Surround ▲ W/S

Akira Production Report

(1987) ©Akira Committee/Streamline Pictures

Documentary of the creation of Katsuhiro Otomo's animated masterpiece. Released in Japan under the title "Akira Production Report: Otomo Katsuhiro no Sekai to Eiga 'Akira'" (The World of Katsuhiro Otomo and the Film "Akira") by Asmic/Pioneer LDC; available in North America through Streamline Pictures. **52 min.**

Domestic Home Video:
SPV 90001 ▲ $24.95 ▲ VHS ▲ DUB ▲ HiFi Stereo ▲ 02/01/90

Alakazam The Great

(1960) ©Toei Animation

Director: Taiji Yabushita *Music*: Les Baxter *Original Author*: Osamu Tezuka

A retelling of the Chinese Monkey King legend so oft retold not only in Japanese animation, but even in the U.S. (a local theatre production was recently staged in the San Francisco Bay Area), ALAKAZAM THE GREAT is a bright and cheerful Hollywood musical-style blowout, featuring re-recorded songs to suit, voices of Frankie Avalon, Dodie Stevens, Jonathan Winters, Sterling Holloway, and Arnold Stang, winsomely fluid animation, and a strong dramatic storyline by the creator of ASTRO BOY himself, Osamu "God of Manga" Tezuka. Released in Japan under the title "Saiyûki" (traditionally translated as "Journey to the West") by Toei/Bandai Visual; available in North America through Orion Home Video. **84 min.**

Domestic Home Video:
OHV 50030 ▲ $14.95 ▲ VHS ▲ DUB ▲ HiFi Mono ▲ CC ▲ 02/13/96
OHV 50031 ▲ $24.95 ▲ VHS ▲ DUB ▲ HiFi Mono ▲ CC, Widescreen ▲ 02/13/96
ID 3398 ▲ $39.95 ▲ LD ▲ DUB ▲ HiFi Mono ▲ CC ▲ 03/13/96

 Violence   Profanity   Nudity   Sexual Situations  Adult Viewers Only - content is extreme and/or explicit

Ambassador Magma

OAV series, 13 episodes

(1993) ©Tezuka Productions/Plex.

Original Creator and Author: Osamu Tezuka *Director*: Hidehito Ueda *Produced by*: Tezuka Productions, Bandai Visual *Composer*: Toshiyuki Watanabe

Created by Osamu Tezuka (and based on the 1966 live-action TV series of the same name, broadcast in the U.S. as "Space Giants"), AMBASSADOR MAGMA is the story of a magnificent, lion-maned golden robot who, together with a handful of youths, protects Earth against the invading forces of the evil Goa empire. Retro in style, but sadly lacking in animation quality (even for a modest OAV series), this modern-day thirteen-episode production is, unfortunately, a less-than-inspiring tribute to Tezuka's genius. Released in Japan under the title "Magma Taishi" through Bandai Visual; available in North America through U.S. Renditions.

Ambassador Magma Episode 1: *My Name is Goa*
Fumiaki Asuka and his daughter Miki are keepers of Goa and Ambassador Magma's spirits. After Fumiaki is captured by aliens and releases Goa's spirit, Miki is pursued and finds protection in Atsushi Murakami's house. She discovers the true purpose of her life and must decide what to do. **30 min.**

Ambassador Magma Episode 2: *The Gold Giant*
Goa's attempt to capture Miki fails and Ambassador Magma returns to Earth. However, this does not stop Goa's plan for conquest and he sends humanoid creatures to quietly begin his plan. Mamoru meets with the protector of the Earth and gains insight into Goa and Magma. **30 min.**

Ambassador Magma Episode 3: *Silent Invasion*
As Atsushi and Junya try to uncover evidence of Goa's existence, a mysterious stranger appears. Mamoru and Tomoko are attacked by a savage canine and must fight to stay alive. **30 min.**

Ambassador Magma Episode 4: *The Two Mamorus*
Determined to find "Earth," Goa captures Mamoru and sends one of his creatures to terrorize Atsushi and Junya. **30 min.**

Ambassador Magma Episode 5: *The Government Strategy*
The Defense Intelligence Agency (DIA) is eager to discover what the aliens plan for planet Earth. Meanwhile, Mamoru is attacked by a creature but receives help from "Earth's" new rocket-humanoid assistant, Gamu. **30 min.**

Ambassador Magma Episode 6: *The Questionable Warrior*
Acting on the advice of his father, Mamoru follows Kunisaki to the Defense Intelligence Agency headquarters to learn about the origin of Earth. The government is convinced that Ambassador Magma is responsible for a deadly tsunami created by Goa. Believing in Magma's innocence, Mamoru risks his life to help a friend. **30 min.**

Ambassador Magma Episode 7: *Gigantic Task*
While searching for Onitono Shrine, Atsushi and Sekita find a girl who may lead them to Goa. As Mamoru and Umemura investigate a government installation, they are abducted by Udo - a deadly being. Mamoru learns a powerful lesson as he and his comrades escape into the forest. **30 min.**

Ambassador Magma Episode 8: *Hunted Whistle*
Goa's evil assistant Jagobu sends alien assassins to retrieve Mamoru's mystic whistle. In a desperate fight for life, Mamoru and his mother vanquish one of the alien menaces with the help of Mr. Imai, a new friend. Believing they are safe, Mamoru and Tomoko accept Mr. Imai's invitation to a barbeque. There they meet Midori, the Imais' only daughter who makes Tomoko very uncomfortable. When Hilda crashes the barbeque looking for the whistle, she reveals a secret that shocks everyone. **30 min.**

Ambassador Magma Episode 9: *The Resurrection of Udo*
Mamoru blames Goa for the deaths of those that were close to him. When it appears that his mother may be the next target, he decides to go after the evil Goa. Finding an ominous cave under a questionable shrine, Mamoru, the intelligence bureau and Gamu face off against the newly resurrected Udo. **30 min.**

Ambassador Magma Episode 10: *Mother and Her Love*
When Mamoru's life is threatened, he is saved by a guardian angel. Discovering the identity of his rescuer, Mamoru becomes enraged and confused. When Udo uses Atsushi, Sekida, and Umemura as bartering tools to capture Magma, the stranger appears again. **30 min.**

Ambassador Magma Episode 11: *Rage of the Earth*
Along with the battling Ambassador Magma and Udo a group of people are transported

back in time. While the two titans clash, Magma is aided by a former opponent. A temporal distortion with a path returning back to their period appears, but will everyone be able to return? **30 min.**

Ambassador Magma Episode 12: *Death of Magma*
Udo and Ambassador Magma clash till death, but when Goa becomes involved, who is the real victor? When Udo is about to demolish Ambassador Magma, he suddenly turns on Goa and attacks him instead. Has the world turned upside-down? Or is there some reason to this madness? **30 min.**

Ambassador Magma Episode 13: *The Planet of Love*
Mamoru learns the shocking origin of mankind. With Magma gone who will save the humans from Goa? Watch this final climactic episode and find the answers. Last volume of the series. **30 min.**

Domestic Home Video:

Ambassador Magma Vol. 1: *Episodes 1-3*
USR DIE02 ▲ $19.95 ▲ VHS ▲ DUB ▲ HiFi Stereo ▲ 06/01/93
PI 33652 ▲ $34.95 ▲ LD ▲ M/A ▲ HiFi Stereo ▲ 03/23/94

Ambassador Magma Vol. 2: *Episodes 4 and 5*
USR DIE06 ▲ $19.95 ▲ VHS ▲ DUB ▲ HiFi Stereo ▲ 12/01/93
PI 33900 ▲ $34.95 ▲ LD ▲ M/A ▲ HiFi Stereo ▲ 06/29/94

Ambassador Magma Vol. 3: *Episodes 6 and 7*
USR DIE08 ▲ $19.95 ▲ VHS ▲ DUB ▲ HiFi Stereo ▲ 12/13/94
PI 34113 ▲ $34.95 ▲ LD ▲ M/A ▲ HiFi Stereo ▲ 11/09/94

Ambassador Magma Vol. 4: *Episodes 8 and 9*
USR DIE09 ▲ $19.95 ▲ VHS ▲ DUB ▲ HiFi Stereo ▲ 04/19/95
PI 34335 ▲ $34.95 ▲ LD ▲ M/A ▲ HiFi Stereo ▲ 01/11/95

Ambassador Magma Vol. 5: *Episodes 10 and 11*
USR DIE11 ▲ $19.95 ▲ VHS ▲ DUB ▲ HiFi Stereo ▲ 11/07/95
PI 34473 ▲ $34.95 ▲ LD ▲ M/A ▲ HiFi Stereo ▲ 03/23/96

Ambassador Magma Vol. 6: *Episodes 12 and 13*
USR DIE12 ▲ $19.95 ▲ VHS ▲ DUB ▲ HiFi Stereo ▲ 11/07/95

Angel Cop

OAV series, 6 volumes

(1989-94) ©Ichiro Itano/Soeishinsha

Original Story & Director: Ichiro Itano *Character Design*: Nobuteru Yuki *Screenplay*: Noboru Aikawa *Animation Directors*: Yasuomi Umezu (Part 1), Satoru Nakamura (Parts 2&3), Yasuhiro Seo (Parts 4&5)

Ultraviolent "hard action" anime which, halfway through the six-volume OAV series' release, was delayed completion for nearly five years due to increasing sensationalism surrounding a string of child murders committed by Japanese serial killer and devoted anime fan Tsutomu "No Relation to Hayao" Miyazaki. Aside from its infamous backstory and some lovely character designs by RECORD OF LODOSS WAR's Nobuteru Yuki, ANGEL COP is an otherwise largely forgettable bullets 'n' blood police drama—more notable for the gleeful abandon in which violent crime and terrorism are "realistically" portrayed than for its in-depth character development or involving storyline—and the inclusion of some rather odd religious/racial overtones (wisely toned down in the English version) only increase confusion regarding where it's all supposed to be going. Released in Japan under the title "Angel Cop" by Pony Canyon; available in North America through Manga Entertainment.

Angel Cop Part 1: *Special Security Force*
The Red May, possibly the most dangerous terrorist organization in the world, have targeted Japan as a wave of bombings and murders sweep through the streets of Tokyo. The Special Security Force are summoned, and as they close in on the terrorists, it becomes clear that the situation is more complicated than it first appeared. **30 min.**

Angel Cop Part 2: *The Disfigured City*
The Red May threat is growing, and a shadowy government organization has its eye on the members of the SSF. Angel's partner disappears, and a trio of hunters with amazing psychic powers are killing the terrorists before the Special Security Force can get to them. A strange super-powered cyborg appears just as the situation seems desperate. Is he a friend or an enemy? **30 min.**

Angel Cop Part 3: *The Death Warrant*
With the leader of The Red May in the custody of the SSF, details begin to emerge of a sinister high-level, governmental conspiracy that threatens the future of Japan from within. The mysterious "H-File" could be the key to the safety of Japan — or it could mean the death of every member of the SSF! Meanwhile, the three enigmatic psychic "hunters" also target the SSF and Angel has found her missing partner, Raiden, transformed into an incredibly powerful armored cyborg! **30 min.**

  Made for Television Broadcast    Made for Home Video Release   Made for Theatrical Release

Angel Cop Part 4: *Pain*
With the government assassination team hot on their heels, the SSF race to conceal their last living witnesses to the secret "H-File" project, one of who is the only survivor of the terrorist group The Red May. If the truth behind the "H-Files" is ever released, it could mean the end of corrupt forces within the Japanese government, and there are men who would kill to prevent it. To add to the SSF's problems, the psychic Hunters are still on their trail, and their leader - the incredibly powerful Lucifer - has decided that not only do the terrorists deserve to die, but so do the members of the SSF. **30 min.**

Angel Cop Part 5: *Wrath of the Empire*
The army closes in on Angel and the last remaining members of the SSF who are trapped within Doctor Ichihara's research facility. It's up to Raiden's combat-enhanced cyborg body to save them. As the battle rages throughout the research center, Raiden and the SSF hold their own, until the mad "psychic hunter" Lucifer appears to finish the job she started. Nothing can stop this menacing foe once and for all? As the body count grows, the stakes revenge on the "psychic hunter" who betrayed her, and the remnants of the SSF. **30 min.**

Angel Cop Part 6: *Doomsday*
With most of the members of the SSF now either missing or dead, Angel is left alone to face the insane fury of the deranged psychic hunter, Lucifer. Will Angel have what it takes to destroy this menacing foe once and for all? As the body count grows, the stakes heighten and this desperate struggle concludes. Completes the series. **30 min.**

Domestic Home Video:
Angel Cop Part 1
MGV 635317 ▲ $9.95 ▲ VHS ▲ DUB ▲ HiFi Stereo ▲ 07/25/95
Angel Cop Part 2
MGV 635487 ▲ $9.95 ▲ VHS ▲ DUB ▲ HiFi Stereo ▲ 08/22/95
Angel Cop Part 3
MGV 635489 ▲ $9.95 ▲ VHS ▲ DUB ▲ HiFi Stereo ▲ 09/26/95
Angel Cop Part 4
MGV 635491 ▲ $9.95 ▲ VHS ▲ DUB ▲ HiFi Stereo ▲ 10/24/95
Angel Cop Part 5
MGV 635493 ▲ $9.95 ▲ VHS ▲ DUB ▲ HiFi Stereo ▲ 11/21/95
Angel Cop Part 6
MGV 635496 ▲ $9.95 ▲ VHS ▲ DUB ▲ HiFi Stereo ▲ 02/27/96

Angel of Darkness
OAV series, 3 volumes
(1990-91) ©Pink Pineapple

Produced by: Jiro Soka *Planning*: Kotaro Ran *Story/Supervision*: Yukihiro Makino *Character Design and Art Direction*: Kazunori Iwakura (Part 1), Yuji Ikeda (Parts 2&3) *Directors*: Kazuma Muraki (Part 1), Suzunari Joban (Parts 2&3)

A girls' school falls prey to the many-tentacled carnal demons (they need the emanations of young girls to survive, doncha know) housed in the building's basement, presided over by the possessed professor who released the menace in the first place, and by an evil S&M mistress. The unusual heroes of this video are a lesbian couple and, oddly enough, forest pixies; bondage gear is depicted with what one must assume is an unusual attention to detail. The second video substitutes plant monsters with the same motif (this time, it's female "bodily fluids" they need in order to survive), with a new heroine of by-now traditionally squealing variety; most odd of all is the fact that the story seems a bit tame compared to its predecessor, all of which credit UROTSUKI DÔJI's Toshio Maeda with "original story." Released in Japan under the title "Yôjû Kyôshitsu" (Bewitcher-Beast Classroom) by Daiei/Tokuma Japan Communications; available in North America through SoftCel Pictures, a division of A.D. Vision.

Angel of Darkness
In ultra-graphic animation, Atsuko and Sayaka must use their own bodies to trap and defeat an entity older than mankind itself, and even with the supernatural aid of an unexpected ally, it's going to take everything they've got just to survive this ultimate close encounter with evil! **50 min.**

Angel of Darkness 2
The teacher at the end of the hall and his collection of plants have similar tastes; the plants like to consume the lifeforce of small insects, while the teacher prefers slightly larger prey ... Isn't it convenient how the teacher's job keeps such a large supply of nubile young women so close at hand? **50 min.** *(Edited version 45 min.)*

Angel of Darkness 3
Getting rid of your enemies the old fashioned way can be a hard habit to break. When Hiromi is abused by a malevolent gang of young women, she lures them into the lair of the resurrected Professor Shimazaki. **50 min.** *(Edited version 45 min.)*

Domestic Home Video:
Angel of Darkness
ADV AD/001 ▲ $34.95 ▲ VHS ▲ SUB ▲ HiFi Surround ▲ 02/07/95
Angel of Darkness 2
ADV AD/002U ▲ $29.95 ▲ VHS ▲ SUB ▲ Uncut ▲ HiFi Surround ▲ 11/28/95
ADV AD/002G ▲ $29.95 ▲ VHS ▲ SUB ▲ Edited ▲ HiFi Surround ▲ 11/28/95
Angel of Darkness 3
ADV AD/003U ▲ $29.95 ▲ VHS ▲ SUB ▲ Uncut ▲ HiFi Surround ▲ 04/09/96
ADV AD/003G ▲ $29.95 ▲ VHS ▲ SUB ▲ Edited ▲ HiFi Surround ▲ 04/09/96

Animated Classics of Japanese Literature
TV series, 35 episodes
(1986) ©Nippon Animation Co. Ltd.

Multi-volume series (originally aired in Japan as a 35-episode weekly television series) animating famous works from Japanese literature—such as "Botchan" by Natsume Soseki and "Izu Dancer" by Nobel prize-winning Yasunari Kawabata—as interpreted by various directors, including Noboru Ishiguro (SPACE CRUISER YAMATO, SUPERDIMENSIONAL FORTRESS MACROSS, MEGAZONE 23), who adapts Yukio Mishima's "The Sound of Waves" as well as Takeyama Michio's "The Harp of Burma." Fifteen volumes in all; aired in Japan under the title "Seishun Anime Zenshû" (Collected Works of "Seishun" Anime). The most painless way known for an anime fan to ace that Japanese Lit exam. Not available on home video in Japan; available in North America through Central Park Media.

A.C.J.L.: *Ansunaro Story*
Original Story: Yukio Togawa *Director*: Akiko Matsushima *Script*: Shizuyo Kuriyama *Character Design*: Masami Abe

13-year-old Ayuta is about to experience the most important lesson of his life: 19-year-old Saeko has come to live with his family. A "bad girl," Saeko is unashamed of her expulsion from school. She sends Ayuta to deliver a letter to the man she loves, Kajima, who turns out to be Saeko's antithesis as a student. Kajima acts fatherly toward Ayuta and advises him to study hard. **26 min.**

A.C.J.L.: *Botchan Parts 1 and 2*
Director: Eisuke Kondo *Script*: Akira Miyazaki *Character Design*: Hiroshi Motomiya *Music*: Hideo Shimazu *Original Story*: Natsume Soseki *Animation Directors*: Takeo Kitahara, Hiroshi Wagatsuma, Hiroaki Ishino, Hideaki Shimada

PART 1: Botchan, a recent graduate, sets out for his first teaching assignment ... never anticipating what awaits him. He must contend with students who spy on him and pull nasty stunts and with a landlord who constantly tries to sell him worthless antiques. While on a fishing trip, Botchan suspects Hotta, his one friend in the village, as the cause of all his misery. PART 2: During a meeting to discuss the students' disrespectful behavior towards Botchan, the proposed punishment is surprisingly mild despite the severity of the acts. Yet, Botchan's suspected adversary defends him! Were the other faculty members lying about Hotta? Botchan may soon discover the truth, for when evidence of the dean's activities surfaces, Botchan and Hotta must team up to corner the dean in his own scandalous game! **52 min.**

A.C.J.L.: *The Dancing Girl*
Original Story: Mori Ogai *Director*: Noboru Ishiguro *Script*: Kenji Yoshida *Character Design*: Hideaki Shimada *Music*: Koichi Sakata

Berlin — the early 1900s. Toyotaro Ota has accepted an assignment for his government. Educated and talented, he makes a good living ... until he meets Elise. The daughter of a tailor, she lives with her widowed mother and earns a meager living as a ballet dancer. She is forced to borrow money from a loan shark — until she meets Toyotaru. Soon he must choose between his career and Elise. **52 min.**

A.C.J.L.: *Friendship*
Original Story: Mushanokoji Saneatsu *Script*: Haruhiko Mimura, Shozo Matsuda *Director & Character Design*: Taku Sugiyama *Music*: Junnosuke Yamamoto

Nokima is a young author who is beginning to be noticed by his colleagues. However, this becomes inconsequential when he spots Sugiko and immediately falls in love. Nojima confesses his love for Sugiko to his friend Omiya, who agrees to help get him a proper

 Violence   Profanity   Nudity   Sexual Situations    Adult Viewers Only - content is extreme and/or explicit

introduction. Time passes, but Nojima and Sugiko can't seem to get past impersonal exchanges. Still, Omiya encourages him to pursue Sugiko. It isn't until Omiya writes to him that Nojima finds out the shocking truth about Sugiko. **26 min.**

A.C.J.L.: *The Fruit of Olympus*
Original Story: Hidemitsu Tanaka *Director*: Akiko Matsushima *Character Design*: Norio Yazawa *Music*: Junnosuke Yamamoto

Just prior to World War II, several Japanese teams are training for the Olympics. On the trans-Pacific voyage to America, boyish rowing team member Sakamoto notices Akiko, a girl high-jumper. No sooner do they hit it off, than the coaches declare members of the opposite sex off-limits! As they compete in America, Sakamoto's team fares poorly, and Akiko seems to have taken a liking to a foreigner. How will they fare? **26 min.**

A.C.J.L.: *A Ghost Story*
Original Story: Koizumi Yakumo *Director*: Isamu Kumada *Script*: Akira Miyazaki *Character Design*: Isamu Kumada *Music*: Koichi Sakata, Kinji Tsuruta

800 years ago, the Heiki family suffered a terrible defeat at the hands of the Genji family. Houchi, a lutist, lives at a temple near the battle site. His talent for chanting old legends gains him notice by the ghosts of the Heiki family, and the blind Houichi soon finds himself performing for the dead. The chief priest fears for Houichi and devises a plan to make him invisible to the ghosts, but will it happen in time? **26 min.**

A.C.J.L.: *The Grave of the Wild Chrysanthemum*
Original Story: Ito Sachio *Director*: Isamu Kumada

Masao Saito is 15 and lives with his sickly mother on their farm. His cousin Tamiko, who is 17, comes to live with them. Masao and Tamiko get along exceedingly well. As time passes, their feelings intensify, but Tamiko is to be married in an arranged wedding—though not to Masao—yet her mind and spirit are focused on only him. **26 min.**

A.C.J.L.: *Growing Up*
Original Story: Higuchi Ichiyo *Director*: Isamu Kumada *Script*: Chisako Kuki *Character Design*: Isamu Kumada *Music*: Leijiro Koroku

Amongst the small street gangs that inhabit the red light district of Yoshiwara, Shinnyo and Midori were on good terms ... that is, until news spread that Shinnyo had joined a rival gang. Midori is the sister of an Oiran and is often teased and called a whore by the street rascals. Yet she maintains herself with pride and tries desperately to retain her individuality. Now unfriendly gang members are making trouble for Midori and her friends ... and she blames Shinnyo, mistakenly believing that he is behind the trouble. **26 min.**

A.C.J.L.: *The Harp of Burma Parts 1 & 2*
Original Story: Takeyama Michio *Director*: Noboru Ishiguro *Script*: Kenji Yoshida *Character Design*: Susumu Shiraume *Music*: Koichi Sakata *Animation Direction*: Takeo Kitihara, Hiroshi Wagatsuma, Hirokazu Ishino, Hideaki Shimada

The end of World War II is approaching. A platoon of Japanese soldiers is struggling through the mountains of Burma when notification of the war's end and of Japan's surrender is received. But high up on Triangle Mountain, where the news is greeted with disbelief, the fighting continues. Captain Inoue sends Private Yasuhiko Mizushima to the mountain to persuade the soldiers to stop fighting and dying in vain. Meanwhile, Captain Inoue's troops are moved to a concentration camp at Muson and await Mizushima's return. While the Inoue Platoon anxiously counts the days until their release, Mizushima's absence weighs heavily on their minds. As time passes, their worst fears are realized when news of Mizushima's death is received. The news is especially difficult to accept when the soldiers recall their strange encounter with a monk during the first days in the concentration camp — a monk who bore a striking resemblence to Mizushima! **52 min.**

A.C.J.L.: *The Incident in the Bedroom Suburb*
Director: Eiji Okabe *Script*: Ryuzo Nakanishi *Character Design*: Mio Murao *Music*: Hideo Shimazu *Original Story*: Jiro Akagawa *Animation Direction*: Takeo Kitahara, Hiroshi Wagatsuma, Hirokazu Ishino, Hideaki Shimada

As the Mabuchi family has learned, life in the suburbs can be harrowing if you're not accepted by your neighbors. Their troubles start when their daughter, Noriko, gets into an "accident" and their apartment complex's rabbit is mysteriously poisoned. When Mr. Mabuchi is asked by his employer to soothe his neighbors' angry feelings concerning a nearby construction project, the family faces its greatest challenge yet. **26 min.**

A.C.J.L.: *The Izu Dancer*

Original Story: Yasunari Kawabata *Director*: Katsumi Takasuka *Script*: Kenji Yoshida *Character Design*: Yoshio Kabashima *Music*: Koichi Sakata

Mizuhara, a student from Tokyo, takes a few days off to travel through the countryside and happens upon a family of strolling players — a troupe of entertainers who perform at small inns. He is taken with Kaoru, a young dancing girl who is part of this troupe. The feeling is

mutual but he must go back to school and she is just a strolling dancing girl. Written by Nobel Prize winner Yasunari Kawabata.

A.C.J.L.: *The Martyr*
Original Story: Ryunosuke Akutagawa *Script*: Shizuyo Kuriyama *Director*: Katsumi Takasuka *Character Design*: Yoshio Kabashima

When Ine, daughter of an umbrella maker, takes a liking to Lorenzo, rumors begin to spread. He knows nothing of Ine. But when she becomes pregnant and places the blame on Lorenzo, he is excommunicated by the church and shunned by the entire village. A year passes, and Lorenzo is ridiculed for not taking responsibility for the child. When tragedy strikes, the townspeople are finally confronted with the truth. **26 min.**

A.C.J.L.: *The Priest of Mt. Kouya*
Original Story: Izumi Kyoka *Script*: Masahiro Yamada *Director & Character Design*: Eisuke Kondo

His journey interrupted by flood waters, a priest contemplates following an alternate route taken by a peddler. When a passing peasant warns him of the danger facing the peddler, the priest hurries to catch up with him. Barely surviving the perils of the journey, the priest finally stumbles upon a lone house buried in the terrain. So intrigued by the voluptuous owner of the house, the priest is unaware of the danger that he faces. **26 min.**

A.C.J.L.: *A Psychological Test*
Original Story: Edogawa Rampo *Character Design*: Shotaro Ishinomori *Music*: Junnosuke Yamamoto *Director*: Eisuke Kondo *Script*: Kenji Yoshida

Seiichiro Fukiya spent a year planning the perfect crime. He set up his friend to be the fall guy, and arranged for himself to receive the victim's money. It would have worked perfectly but for private eye Kogoro Akechi. He devised a clever psychological test to flush out the real perpetrator. **26 min.**

A.C.J.L.: *A Red Room*
Original Story: Edogawa Rampo *Character Design*: Shotaro Ishinomori *Music*: Junnosuke Yamamoto *Director*: Takeo Kitahara *Script*: Mitsuo Wakasugi

Seven rich men share one common attribute: they are bored with life. A guest at their gathering shocks them with his story of murdering strangers to relieve his own boredom. Now it appears he wants to commit suicide with their assistance ... or is there really more to it? **26 min.**

A.C.J.L.: *A Roadside Stone Parts 1 & 2*
Original Story: Yuzo Yamamoto *Director*: Eiji Okabe *Script*: Kenji Yoshida *Character Design*: Yasuji Mori *Music*: Hideo Shimazu *Animation Direction*: Takeo Kitahara, Hiroshi Wagatsuma, Hirokazu Ishino, Hideaki Shimada

Goichi Aikawa is a poor boy who lives in the country. Unable to accept such a fate for the rest of his life, Goichi is driven by ambition to better himself. When the prospect of entering a new junior high school presents itself, Goichi suggests to his mother that he use his own savings for his schooling. But she is secretly broken-hearted as Goichi's father has already used the money to pay a debt. When his mother becomes ill, Goichi is forced to abandon his plans and enters into a degrading apprenticeship for a local merchant. Humiliated by everyone in the shop, Goichi fights to remain strong. Tragedy strikes when his mother dies and the truth about his father's debts becomes known. He realizes that he is now working as an indentured servant. Goichi has every intention of repaying this debt, but he will do it in his own way from now on. **52 min.**

A.C.J.L.: *Sanshiro the Judoist Parts 1, 2 & 3*
Script: Akira Miyazaki *Character Design*: Tetsuya Chiba *Music*: Hideo Shimazu *Original Story*: Tsuneo Tomita *Director*: Shoji Sato *Music*: Koichi Sakata *Animation Directors*: Takeo Kitahara, Hiroshi Wagatsuma, Hirokazu Ishino, Hideaki Shimada

Part 1, AN AMBITIOUS GUY FROM KODO-KAN: Sanshiro Sugata aspires to become a master of the art of Jujutsu. Training under several masters, he learns that there is more to the art than just fighting. He also becomes aware of the rival art of Judo. When his Jujutsu master is defeated by a Judo master, he becomes a pupil of Shogoro Yano, the Judoist. Part 2, UNAVOIDABLE CONFLICT: Now a well-established Judoist, Sanshiro meets Otomi, daughter of a Jujutsu master joining the police. Defeating his former Jujutsu master in an exhibition, Sanshiro does not realize his next opponent will be Otomi's father! Part 3, FIGHT IN UKYOGAHARA FIELD: As it turns out, if Otomi's father loses to Sanshiro, he will be forced to resign from the police. Not only that, Otomi will be forced to marry Sanshiro's most despicable opponent, Gennosuke Higaki. **78 min.**

A.C.J.L.: *The Season of the Sun*

Original Story: Shintaro Ishihara *Director*: Noboru Ishiguro

Tatsuya Tsugawa boxes at the university sports club, which makes him very popular with the ladies. He has one casual affair after another until he meets Eiko. They soon fall in love, but will he be able to express his love for her before it's too late? **26 min.**

A.C.J.L.: *The Sound of Waves, Parts 1 & 2*
Original Story: Yukio Mishima *Director*: Hidehito Ueda *Script*: Ryuzu Nakanishi *Character Design*: Susumu Shiraume *Music*: Hideo Shimazu *Animation Directors*: Takeo Kitahara, Hiroshi Wagatsuma, Hirokazu Ishino, Hideaki Shimada *Art Directors*: Shohei Kawamoto, Shukei Ito, Mukuo Takamura

Part 1, THE AWAKENING OF SPRING: In a small fishing village on the island of Utajima, 18-year-old Shinji Kubo works on a tiny fishing boat. Honest and dedicated, he works hard and prays for a good wife someday. He begins to notice Hatsue, daughter of a wealthy fisherman. She notices him too, but she is rumored to be betrothed to Yasuo Kawamoto. As rumors abound, the two agree to meet privately in a place where Shinji gets an eyeful! Part 2, THE STORM OF SUMMER: Shinji and Hatsue face each other across a blazing campfire. Their encounter threatens to become intimate when she confesses she wants to be his bride. Days later, a jealous Yasuo tries to take Hatsue by force and then by blackmail. Hatsue's father makes both men sailors on his fishing boat, and devises a test to determine which one really deserves his daughter. **52 min.**

A.C.J.L.: *Student Days*
Original Story: Masao Kume *Director*: Akiko Matsushima

Kenkichi knows he must study hard if he is to be accepted at the prestigious Ichiko School. He meets Sumiko, a flamboyant young woman who accidentally drops a good luck charm. He's concerned that the incident might bring her bad luck. He is surprised to learn that he is the intended recipient of the good luck charm. How will the results of the exam be affected by his superstition? **26 min.**

A.C.J.L.: *The Story of Koyasu Dog*
Original Story: Yukio Togawa *Director*: Akiko Matsushima *Script*: Shizuyo Kuriyama *Character Design*: Masami Abe

Hisao admired the pure-blood Koyasu dog which was thought to have died out in the Showa era. But one Koyasu dog still lives: Shiro, an aging dog living with his master in the mountains. Hisao sees that the ailing Shiro needs an operation to survive, and takes him to a far off town. But the steadfastly loyal dog cannot bear to be away from his master, escaping and beginning a perilous journey back to his mountain top home. **26 min.**

A.C.J.L.: *The Tale of Shunkin*
Original Story: Junichiro Tanizaki *Director*: Akiko Matsushima *Script*: Kenji Yoshida *Character Design*: Shigetaka Kiyoyama *Music*: Masako Tsukamoto, Koichi Sakata

After losing her sight at age nine, Shunkin studied to play the koto and the shamisen, becoming so skilled that her songs were enchanting to all who listened. Sasuke, who has faithfully taken care of her for many years, secretly saved his money and bought a shamisen. When Shunkin discovers that Sasuke has a shamisen, she takes him on as her student and a stronger bond develops between the two. But their relationship is soon put to the ultimate test. **26 min.**

A.C.J.L.: *The Theatre of Life*
Original Story: Shiro Ozaki *Director*: Eiji Okabe *Script*: Ryuzo Nakanishi *Character Design*: Mio Murao *Music*: Hideo Shimazu

In 1905, most are celebrating a war armistice, except the family of Hyokichi Aonari, whose livelihood as tobacco merchants has come to an end under new government controls. They must now sell trees off their land to survive. To overcome his image as a sissy, Hyokichi learns to climb a ginko tree, with the encouragement of Orin, the girl next door. As grownups, he goes off to school and she becomes a Geisha. Missing her, he is driven toward a goal of success even his father couldn't imagine. **26 min.**

A.C.J.L.: *Voice From Heaven*
Director: Eiji Okabe *Script*: Ryuzo Nakanishi *Character Design*: Mio Murao *Music*: Hideo Shimazu *Original Story*: Jiro Akagawa *Animation Direction*: Takeo Kitahara, Hiroohi Wagatsuma, Hirokazu Ishino, Hideaki Shimada

Not long after his appointment to officer of his housing development, Mr. Kasai faces his first challenge. A new family has moved into Unit 303. The problem: this unit is directly above the one occupied by old man Nakakita who can't tolerate even the slightest noise. Frequent, nasty run-ins with Nakakita eventually lead to the family's hasty "evacuation" from the premises. Kasai's solution to the problem may be extreme, but after all hasn't Nakakita been unreasonable? **26 min.**

A.C.J.L.: *A Walker in the Attic*
Original Story: Edogawa Rampo *Character Design*: Shotaro Ishinomori *Music*: Junnosuke Yamamoto *Director*: Takeo Kitahara *Script*: Ryuzo Nakanishi

Goda was fascinated by crime. He often crawled around the attic, spying on other residents of his boarding house. He hated Endo, and plotted the perfect crime of murder, planning to make it look like suicide. Since his plan avoided any obvious

point of entry, who would ever suspect him? **26 min.**

A.C.J.L.: *Wandering Days*
Original Story: Fumiko Hayashi *Director*: Eiji Okabe *Script*: Akira Miyazaki *Character Design*: Hirokazu Ishino *Music*: Junnosuke Yamamoto

In the early 1900s earning a modest income was a struggle for most. As a young girl, Fumiko wandered the countryside with her parents who earned their livelihood peddling medicine. Moving from town to town, the young Fumiko knew deep inside that there was more that she wanted out of life. Dreams of becoming a writer were Fumiko's salvation during these difficult times. **26 min.**

A.C.J.L.: *The Wind Rises*
Original Story: Tatsuo Hori *Director*: Hiromitsu Morita *Character Design*: Momoko Tsutsui *Music*: Koichi Sakata

A young novelist stops in Karuizawa in search of a place to write. He is struck by the beauty of Mt. Yatsugatake and dreams of someday living with a pretty girl in such a place. He chances upon Setsuko, a beautiful young lady staying at the same hotel. Being the only two guests, they become well acquainted. She reveals she has tuberculosis, but his passion is not dissuaded by the news. He writes his novel as their love blossoms. **26 min.**

Domestic Home Video:
A.C.J.L.: Ansunaro Story/Koyasu Dog
CPM 1149 ▲ $29.95 ▲ VHS ▲ SUB ▲ Mono

A.C.J.L.: Botchan Parts 1 & 2
CPM 1151 ▲ $29.95 ▲ VHS ▲ SUB ▲ Mono ▲ 04/04/95

A.C.J.L.: A Ghost Story/The Theater of Life
CPM 1142 ▲ $29.95 ▲ VHS ▲ SUB ▲ Mono ▲ 04/06/94

A.C.J.L.: The Harp of Burma Parts 1 & 2
CPM 1140 ▲ $29.95 ▲ VHS ▲ SUB ▲ Mono ▲ 04/06/94

A.C.J.L.: Incident in the Bedroom Suburb/ Voice From Heaven
CPM 1154 ▲ $29.95 ▲ VHS ▲ SUB ▲ Mono ▲ 04/04/95

A.C.J.L.: The Izu Dancer/The Dancing Girl
CPM 1139 ▲ $29.95 ▲ VHS ▲ SUB ▲ Mono ▲ 04/06/94

A.C.J.L.: A Roadside Stone Parts 1 & 2
CPM 1152 ▲ $29.95 ▲ VHS ▲ SUB ▲ Mono ▲ 04/04/95

A.C.J.L.: Season of Sun/Student Days/Wild Chrysanthemum
CPM 1141 ▲ $29.95 ▲ VHS ▲ SUB ▲ Mono ▲ 04/06/94

A.C.J.L.: Sanshiro the Judoist Parts 1, 2 & 3
CPM 1147 ▲ $29.95 ▲ VHS ▲ SUB ▲ Mono

A.C.J.L.: The Sound of Waves, Parts 1 & 2
CPM 1146 ▲ $29.95 ▲ VHS ▲ SUB ▲ Mono

A.C.J.L.: Tale of Shunkin/Friendship
CPM 1153 ▲ $29.95 ▲ VHS ▲ SUB ▲ Mono ▲ 04/04/95

A.C.J.L.: The Martyr/The Priest of Mt. Kouya
CPM 1155 ▲ $29.95 ▲ VHS ▲ SUB ▲ Mono ▲ 04/04/95

A.C.J.L.: Walker in the Attic/Psychological Test/ Red Room
CPM 1150 ▲ $29.95 ▲ VHS ▲ SUB ▲ Mono

A.C.J.L.: Wandering Days/Growing Up
CPM 1143 ▲ $29.95 ▲ VHS ▲ SUB ▲ Mono ▲ 04/06/94

A.C.J.L.: The Wind Rises/The Fruit of Olympus
CPM 1148 ▲ $29.95 ▲ VHS ▲ SUB ▲ Mono

Appleseed
(1988) ©Masamune Shirow/Seishinsha/TBM

Original Story: Masamune Shirow *Director and Screenplay*: Kazuyoshi Katayama *Character Design and Animation Director*: Yumiko Horasawa *Mecha Design*: Kiyomi Tanaka *Art Director*: Hiroaki Ogura *Music*: Norimasa Yamanaka

Single-shot OAV based on the manga by Masamune (GHOST IN THE SHELL, DOMINION) Shirow (published in English by Dark Horse Comics), this video unfortunately captures little of the original comic's atmosphere or style; main character Deunan is nearly unrecognizable, with low-end production values and an oversimplified plot (not that there was much plot in the original manga, come to think of it) making for a disappointing experience overall, especially to those who were really looking forward, for a change, to seeing some sense in their Shirow (by changing the color of the manga's "gun platforms" from black to red, for example, most of the machines' spider-like menace is completely lost). Released in

---

 Violence   Profanity   Nudity   Sexual Situations   Adult Viewers Only - content is extreme and/or explicit

Japan under the title "Appleseed" by Tohoku Shinsha/Bandai Visual/Movic; formerly available in North America through U.S. Renditions, now available through Manga Entertainment. Fans of the series may be interested to note that a 20-minute "behind the scenes" documentary-style look at the making of the live-action film of the same name is currently available in Japan only under the title "Appleseed: Special Prologue" through Sony Music. **68 min.**

Domestic Home Video:
MGV 633887 ▲ $19.95 ▲ VHS ▲ DUB ▲ HiFi Stereo ▲ 02/28/95
USR VD4 ▲ $19.95 ▲ VHS ▲ SUB ▲ Stereo ▲ 08/01/91 ▲ Out of Print

---

Aozora Shôjo-Tai 801 T.T.S. *See* 801 T.T.S. AIRBATS

Arcadia of My Youth

(1982) ©Toei Animation Co. Ltd./Tokyu Agency

Planning and Original Stories: Leiji Matsumoto *Director*: Tomoharu Katsumata *Screenplay*: Yoichi Onaka *Animation Director*: Kazuo Komatsubara *Art Director*: Iwamitsu Ito *Music*: Toshiyuki Kimori

Filled with all the manly angst one would expect from the mastermind behind SPACE CRUISER YAMATO/STAR BLAZERS, this theatrical "origin story" of creator Leiji Matsumoto's grim space pirate Captain Harlock is also Matsumoto's definitive anime film for adults. The Earth has been utterly conquered by an alien power, and Harlock is forced to surrender his ship to the invasion force. But nothing can make this surly space pirate bow his head in subjugation; after enduring abuse, disfigurement, and the crucifixion of the woman he loves, Harlock and his allies sacrifice nearly everything for freedom. Though obvious parallels can be drawn to the occupation of Japan that Matsumoto grew up under, ARCADIA is interestingly devoid of nationalistic or even "humanistic" causes; both humans and aliens are judged admirable or not according to their individual actions, for which they must take full responsibility, no matter how bitter an end to which events may come. Visually and in terms of narrative pacing, ARCADIA still holds up remarkably well. Art director Iwamitsu Ito conjures space warfare as a night battle between 18th century ships; the thunderbolt broadsides of Harlock's great ship *Arcadia* and the sight of doomed craft flaring and burning out in the ocean of vacuum are still thrilling to the eye. Those now drawn to the Gen-X angst of a NEON GENESIS EVANGELION (see below) might be intrigued to explore the existential darkness of Captain Harlock as well, a character who proves Matsumoto's previous-generation works are more complicated than one might realize at first or even second glance. This film contains facts on Harlock's lineage all the way back to the WWI ace who also bears his name. Released in Japan under the title "Waga Seishun no Arcadia" by Toei Video; available in North America from AnimEigo, and from Best Film & Video (titled "My Youth in Arcadia"). **130 min.**

Domestic Home Video:
ANI AT093-009 ▲ $39.95 ▲ VHS ▲ SUB ▲ HiFi Mono ▲ 12/01/93
ANI AD095-003 ▲ $59.95 ▲ LD-CLV/CAV ▲ SUB ▲ HiFi Mono ▲ 04/12/95
BFV 969 ▲ $19.95 ▲ VHS ▲ DUB ▲ Mono

Area 88

OAV series, 3 episodes

(1985-86) ©Project 88

Director: Eiko Toriumi *Executive Producer & Production Designer*: Ren Usami *Original Story*: Kaoru Shintani *Screenplay*: Akiyoshi Sakai *Character Design and Chief Animator*: Toshiyasu Okada *Art Director*: Mitsuji Nakamura *Music*: Ichiro Nitta

Based on the original manga by longtime Leiji Matsumoto assistant Kaoru Shintani (whom Matsumoto affectionately parodies in his currently import-only 1978 TV series "Uchû Kaizoku (Space Pirate) Captain Harlock" in the guise of the model kit-crazed character, Yattaran), AREA 88 shares Matsumoto's obsession with military hardware and his view of the hopelessness and lonely romance of the battlefield. Mercenary pilot Shin Kazama, tricked into pledging himself in service to the (fictional) Middle Eastern nation of Asran, flies a jet in their bloody civil war. Kazama's only goal is to earn enough money—1.5 million dollars—to buy his way out of Area 88 and return to his girlfriend Ryoko before his three-year contract is up. Over time, though, Shin becomes such an efficient killer (the only way to make money is to shoot down enemy planes) that it's less a question of his survival and more whether he can hold onto his innocence. Great aerial sequences, and beautifully detailed jet fighters make this a must for military buffs. Portions of Shintani's 23-volume manga have been released in English (in an on-again-off-again fashion) up through the fifth story in Volume Eight by Viz Comics. Released in Japan on VHS under the title "Area 88" by King Record; available in North America from U.S. Manga Corps.

Area 88 Act I: *The Blue Skies of Betrayal*

Shin is haunted by memories of the night his friend, Kanzaki, tricked him into joining the Asran mercenary Air Force. Now Shin is out of the picture leaving Kanzaki with one less obstacle between him and Ryoko, Shin's girlfriend. As a fighter pilot at Area 88, Shin must learn to kill for pay. There are only three ways to leave the Mercenary Air Force: to serve for three years, pay a 1.5 million dollar penalty, or... desertion. As he flies to earn his freedom, Shin realizes that killing is becoming easier. The question is no longer whether he can survive and return home; it has become whether he can keep his soul from being consumed by the fires of Asran's war. **50 min.**

Area 88 Act II: *The Requirements of Wolves*

After being shot down in what was to be his final air battle, Shin Kazama begins to seriously contemplate going AWOL when three escaped killers confront him. Rescued by his comrades, Shin opts to safeguard the bond with his squadron and abandons his plan. Back in Japan, Ryoko remains steadfast as her father pleads with her to accept Kanzaki's marriage proposal. Meanwhile, Kanzaki is busy making shady deals to buy large quantities of Yamato Airlines' stock. Ryoko learns that Shin is still alive, which further enrages Kanzaki, who hires a professional killer to eliminate Shin once and for all. A further twist of fate brings Ryoko, Kanzaki, and Area 88 commander Saki Vashutarl together on a passenger jet flying to the Middle East. Saki has been targeted for assassination by Asran's anti-government forces, and bombs have been set on the plane. As Shin and Mick race to save the plane, a team of professional mercenaries is moving into the region. Their ultimate target - Area 88. **57 min.**

Area 88 Act III: *Burning Mirage*

Like a Phoenix, Shin Kazama is back at the controls of his F-20 Tiger Shark. During battle, a pilot in his squadron is blinded by shrapnel, and panic-stricken and unable to eject from his plane, begins to fire blindly. Shin is forced to kill the man, rather than let him risk the lives of the rest of the squadron. While Shin ponders when it was that he grew accustomed to killing the enemy, Kanzaki, now president of Yamato Airlines, has brought the company to the brink of financial ruin with his purchase of cheap, defective jets. Ryoko sells her airline stock to raise money to buy Shin's freedom from the Asran military. Finding the market unfavorable, she resigns herself to seeking help from Kanzaki, but his terms are more than she can bear. Can Ryoko resist his offer to free Shin ... for the price of one evening together? **96 min.**

Domestic Home Video:

Area 88 Act I
USM 1047 ▲ $29.95 ▲ VHS ▲ SUB ▲ Mono ▲ 08/04/93
USM 1529 ▲ $14.95 ▲ VHS ▲ DUB ▲ Mono ▲ 10/08/96
ID 2225CT ▲ $34.95 ▲ LD ▲ SUB ▲ HiFi Mono ▲ 08/17/93

Area 88 Act II
USM 1048 ▲ $29.95 ▲ VHS ▲ SUB ▲ Mono ▲ 09/01/93
ID 2226CT ▲ $34.95 ▲ LD ▲ SUB ▲ HiFi Stereo ▲ 10/12/93

Area 88 Act III
USM 1049 ▲ $29.95 ▲ VHS ▲ SUB ▲ Stereo ▲ 10/06/93
ID 2227CT ▲ $39.95 ▲ LD ▲ SUB ▲ HiFi Stereo ▲ 10/20/93

Ariel

(1989-91) ©Yuichi Sasamoto/Ariel Project

Character Design: Masahisa Suzuki *Director*: Junichi Watanabe *Screenplay*: Junichi Watanabe, Muneo Kubo *Original Story*: Yuichi Sasamoto *Music*: Kohei Tanaka

It all begins when a scientist talks his five pretty daughters into piloting a giant robot (with suitably female silhouette and candy-pink color scheme) against an alien threat in this parody of the giant transforming robot genre. (The acronym "ARIEL," by the way, stands for [A]ll-[A]round [I]ntercept and [E]scort [L]ady.) Released in Japan as two, two-volume series—"Ariel" and "Deluxe Ariel"—for a total of four import volumes (the U.S. version combines the first two OAVs onto one 60-minute tape) by Pony Canyon; available in North America through U.S. Manga Corps. **60 min.**

Also see *Deluxe Ariel* entry.

Domestic Home Video:
USM 1368 ▲ $29.95 ▲ VHS ▲ SUB ▲ Stereo ▲ 03/05/96

Armitage III

OAV series, 4 parts

(1994) ©AIC/Pioneer LDC Inc.

General Director & Character Design: Hiroyuki Ochi *Screenplay:* Chiaki Konaka *Director:* Takuya Sato *Designer:* Atsushi Takeuchi *Animation Directors:* Kunihiro Abe (1,3,4), Koichi Hashimoto (Part 2), Shinya Takahashi (3), Naoyuki Onda (3), Hiroyuki Ochi (4) *Art Director:* Norihiro Hiraki (1,2), Tokuhiro Hiragi (Part 3), Hiroshi Kato (4) *Music:* Hiroyuki Namba

Four-volume OAV series featuring a futuristic Mars where human-appearing androids serve their homo sapiens masters (as in *Blade Runner*'s unseen "off-world colonies"). In an ironic twist on the concept, the Harrison Ford-esque cop protagonist, Ross Sylibus, is actually the reluctant partner of such a Martian android, Armitage. Their case is to solve a string of murders carried out by a maniacal killer who is systematically destroying the next stage of android development—"Thirds," robots so lifelike they can "pass" for human in society, and indeed are doing so. Obvious similarities to *Blade Runner* aside, the story goes off in a different direction, focusing sharply on the feelings of the title character, Armitage (both "the" and "a" Third), hearkening back to ASTRO BOY's Pinocchio-like tone. The animation has a distinctly noir feel; director Ochi also handles the character designs, with animation direction by Kunihiro Abe, Shinya Takahashi and Naoyuki Onda. The design of the Martian city of St. Lowell (!) is quite interesting; constructed inside a domed crater, buildings sprout from either the basin or the roof, creating a suitably claustrophobic mood. The series' industrial-style soundtrack music is by Hiroyuki Namba (including a music video-style opening directed by Hiroyuki "MOLDIVER" Kitazume), and a movie version—ARMITAGE III: POLY-MATRIX (1996)—combining the OAV episodes with about five minutes of new footage (a not-uncommon practice in anime) was produced in 1996 with an English-only voice-over cast (the film was shown in Japan in English, with Japanese subtitles), including Hollywood actors Elizabeth Berkely (*Showgirls, Saved By the Bell*) as Armitage, and Kiefer Sutherland (*Flatliners, Young Guns*) as the Earth cop, Ross. New Hollywood-quality sound effects by Serafine Studios were engineered specifically for the film version. Released in Japan under the title "Armitage III" by Pioneer LDC; available in North America through Pioneer LDCA (America).

Armitage III Part 1: *Electro Blood*

As soon as Detective Ross Sylibus arrived at the spaceport, he got involved in a murder. The victim was Kelly McCanon, the popular singer. Ross discovered something shocking: the fact that the corpse was not a human, but a "Third," a much more advanced robot than the "Seconds" which are currently in common use. Ross must team up with Armitage of the MPD (Martian Police Department) to chase the killer, Rene D'anclaude, who is destroying the "Thirds" one by one. **50 min.**

Armitage III Part 2: *Flesh & Stone*

A new mystery unfolds when another bullet-ridden Third, Lavinia Whately, is found dead at an industrial power plant. However, Armitage is still missing. "Yet ... isn't D'anclaude supposed to be in the police hospital?!" Another victim brings new confusion to the MPD. Still echoed by D'anclaude's mocking laughter. And now, Armitage's mysterious disappearance places her under immediate suspicion. **30 min.**

Armitage III Part 3: *Heart Core*

The MPD decides to drop the investigation of the Third Type murders. They are now focusing all operations into a full time investigation of a terrorist case involving the Seconds. Ross instead heads to Shinora General Hospital to find out if the true D'anclaude is really there. Meanwhile, Armitage discovers a video still photograph of D'anclaude and Asakura together in earlier days. What secret do they hold together involving the development of the Thirds? **30 min.**

Armitage III Part 4: *Bit of Love*

Armitage and Ross finally find Dr. Akasura, the developer of "Third Type" robots. But Akasura's memory has been erased and he can't remember Armitage. Can Armitage and Ross find the purpose of "Thirds"? And can they win a battle against the Martian Government Army? The concluding episode of the series. **30 min.**

Domestic Home Video:

Armitage III Part 1
PI VA-1221D ▲ $24.95 ▲ VHS ▲ DUB ▲ HiFi Stereo ▲ CC ▲ 03/29/95
PI VA-1221S ▲ $29.95 ▲ VHS ▲ SUB ▲ HiFi Stereo ▲ 03/29/95
PI LA-1221A ▲ $39.95 ▲ LD-CAV ▲ M/A ▲ HiFi Stereo ▲ CC ▲ 03/29/95

Armitage III Part 2
PI VA-1222D ▲ $19.95 ▲ VHS ▲ DUB ▲ HiFi Stereo ▲ CC ▲ 06/27/95
PI VA-1222S ▲ $24.95 ▲ VHS ▲ SUB ▲ HiFi Stereo ▲ 06/27/95
PI LA-1222A ▲ $34.95 ▲ LD-CAV ▲ M/A ▲ HiFi Stereo ▲ CC ▲ 06/27/95

Armitage III Part 3
PI VA-1223D ▲ $19.95 ▲ VHS ▲ DUB ▲ HiFi Stereo ▲ CC ▲ 09/05/95
PI VA-1223S ▲ $24.95 ▲ VHS ▲ SUB ▲ HiFi Stereo ▲ 09/05/95
PI LA-1223A ▲ $34.95 ▲ LD-CAV ▲ M/A ▲ HiFi Stereo ▲ CC ▲ 09/05/95

Armitage III Part 4
PI VA-1224D ▲ $19.95 ▲ VHS ▲ DUB ▲ HiFi Stereo ▲ CC ▲ 02/27/96
PI VA-1224S ▲ $24.95 ▲ VHS ▲ SUB ▲ HiFi Stereo ▲ 02/27/96
PI LA-1224A ▲ $34.95 ▲ LD-CAV ▲ M/A ▲ HiFi Stereo ▲ CC ▲ 02/27/96

Armored Trooper VOTOMS

TV series, 52 episodes

(1983-88) ©Sunrise, Inc.

Original Story and Director: Ryosuke Takahashi *Music:* Hiroki Inui *Script:* Toshi Gobu (Eps. 1-3,5,6), Ryosuke Takahashi (4), Soji Yoshikawa (7,10,11), Jinzo Toriumi (8,9,12,13)

A centuries-long subtle breeding program finally produces the perfect soldier, but by the time of this discovery, the war has ended. Covert machinations from various political factions struggle against each other to either manipulate and control his destiny or kill him. Why was all of this done? Why was he chosen? He *will* have his answers. Notable for its gritty, blood-in-the-sand approach to futuristic warfare and its realistic mecha look—thanks to mecha designer Kunio Okawara (MOBILE SUIT GUNDAM, SCIENCE NINJA TEAM GATCHAMAN)—VOTOMS takes the *Universal Soldier* concept as popularized by live-action stars Jean-Claude Van Damme and Dolph Lundgren and transplants it to an outer space war with all the grit of a Steve McQueen movie. (Not uncoincidentally, main character Chirico Cuvie is also a dead-ringer for McQueen.) Of the OAVs (as compared to the TV series), "Roots of Treachery" and "The Last Red Shoulder" flesh out Chirico's past as a member of an elite military unit, "Big Battle" is a harmless diversion, and the more recent OAV series details his further adventures. A spinoff series, ARMORED TROOPER MELLOWLINK, features further drama in the VOTOMS world. Released in Japan under the title "Sôkô Kishi Votoms" by Toshiba Eizô Soft; available in North America through U.S. Manga Corps.

STAGE 1: "UOODO CITY" (13 Episodes)

A.T.V. Stage 1, Vol. 1: *Episodes 1-3*

Episode 1, WAR'S END: Chirico unwittingly helps his unit on a renegade mission to steal a military prototype. He is blasted into space and picked up by a ship where he is interrogated relentlessly. Episode 2, UOODO: He escapes to Uoodo, where he's kidnapped by the Boone family and forced to work in their mine. Episode 3, THE ENCOUNTER: During his breakout, the leader of the family is killed and Chirico is believed to be responsible. He finds a junk VOTOM and uses it to face the Boones. **72 min.**

A.T.V. Stage 1, Vol. 2: *Episodes 4-6*

Episode 4, THE BATTLING, Episode 5, THE TRAP, and Episode 6, PROTOTYPE. The Secret Society is watching Chirico's every move, waiting for an opportunity to strike. Meanwhile, Chirico's new friends have plans for his unique talents. Gotho pushes Chirico to compete in the Battling, a futuristic form of gladiatorial combat using modified Armored Troopers. But the contest turns deadly when Chirico discovers that his opponent is one of the commanders from the Lido mission—and he's fallen into their trap! **72 min.**

A.T.V. Stage 1, Vol. 3: *Episodes 7-9*

Episode 7, THE RAID, Episode 8, THE DEAL, and Episode 9, THE RESCUE. Chirico is finally ready to launch a serious strike against the conspiracy that destroyed his career and made him a fugitive. With the assistance of Gotho, Vanilla, Coconna and a fully-armed Scopedog, Chirico plans to hijack an entire shipment of jijirium meant for the pockets of the Secret Society. Vastly outnumbered and outgunned, Chirico will need all of his battlefield-honed skills to eliminate the armed escort. **72 min.**

A.T.V. Stage 1, Vol. 4: *Episodes 10 & 11*

Episode 10, RED SHOULDER and Episode 11, COUNTERATTACK. It's payback time! After being chased from their homes, the idea of fighting back is starting to sound really good. But to take the fight to the police, they're going to need some serious firepower—and the Battling arena is fully stocked with Armored Troopers. Meanwhile, the Phantom Lady is having serious reservations about returning to battle. The solution: she must kill Chirico! **50 min.**

A.T.V. Stage 1, Vol. 5: *Episodes 12 & 13*

Episode 12, THE BONDS, and Episode 13, THE ESCAPE. Chirico must fight his way out of Police Headquarters—with Proto-One at his side. But the entire city has been plunged into chaos. As Chirico's companions fight to rescue him, Melkian forces parachute into the city for a full-scale invasion—courtesy of Captain Rochina. But the conspirators have reinforcements of their own, and as the inhabitants race to evacuate Uoodo, will Chirico be able to escape with Proto-One? **50 min.**

 Violence   Profanity   Nudity   Sexual Situations   Adult Viewers Only - content is extreme and/or explicit

The Complete Anime Guide

STAGE 2: KUMMEN JUNGLE WARS (14 episodes)

Director: Ryosuke Takahashi *Screenplay:* Toshi Gobu (Ep.1), Jinzo Toriumi (Eps.1,4,5,8,9,11), Soji Yoshikawa (Eps.1-3,6,710,12,13,14) *Original Story:* Ryosuke Takahashi *Music:* Hiroki Inui

A.T.V. Stage 2 Vol. 1: *Episodes 1-3*

Episode 1: FYANA (recap of Stage 1: Uoodo City), Episode 2: ASSEMBLE EX-10, and Episode 3: DOUBTS. Separated from his friends—and Fyana—after the fall of Uoodo, Chirico travels to the war-torn jungles of Kummen, where he signs on as a mercenary Armored Trooper pilot in a bloody civil war. Chirico's hopes are raised when he encounters a mysterious, blue AT aiding the rebels. Who else but Fyana could be so fast and deadly? But when he attempts to contact the pilot, the blue AT launches a devastating attack! **72 min.**

A.T.V. Stage 2 Vol. 2: *Episodes 4-6*

Episode 4: CLEAN SWEEP, Episode 5: REUNION, and Episode 6: TURNABOUT. After his last confrontation with the mysterious, blue Armored Trooper, Chirico comes to a startling conclusion: the pilot MUST be a Perfect Soldier... but it isn't Fyana! With his Scopedog AT damaged in battle, Chirico escapes into the jungle, where he is captured and taken to the rebels' secret base. There, Chirico is not only reunited with Fyana, but he also comes face-to-face with the pilot of the blue AT! **72 min.**

A.T.V. Stage 2 Vol. 3: *Episodes 7-9*

Episode 7: INTENTIONS, Episode 8: UPRIVER, and Episode 9: CONTACT BLAST. Chirico is ordered to lead a joint Kummen-Melkian operation against the rebel forces, beginning with an assault against Prince Kanjelman's stronghold. Their objective: the capture of a live Perfect Soldier! But Borough has plans of his own. He believes that if Ypsilon kills Chirico—and Fyana is forced to watch—the Secret Society will finally break Chirico's hold over her. **72 min.**

A.T.V. Stage 2 Vol. 4: *Episodes 10-12*

Episode 10: COMPLICATIONS, Episode 11: INTERSECTION, and Episode 12: INFILTRATION. Fyana is now on the run from Borough and the Secret Society... but Chirico has no intention of losing Fyana again. As the rebel soldiers and Chirico's squad stand poised for battle, Ypsilon prepares to exact his revenge upon Chirico. And as the mercenaries of Assemble EX-10 are air-lifted to join the fight, Prince Kanjelman is forced to make a decision that will shake the faith of even his most ardent followers. **72 min.**

A.T.V. Stage 2 Vol. 5: *Episodes 13 & 14*

Episode 13: CLOSING IN and Episode 14: DARK CHANGE. Prince Kanjelman's palace is turned into a blazing ruin as all the forces converge in a fiery finale! Chirico's squad mate searches for the treasonous Prince—determined to make him pay for the devastation he brought to Kummen. Meanwhile, Ypsilon bursts forth in a powerful new AT. His sole objective: kill Chirico! And as the forces of Assemble EX-10 prepare to crush the rebels, the Melkian forces move in to eliminate whomever stands between them and their stolen Perfect Soldier—Fyana! **50 min.**

Domestic Home Video:
Stage 1: UOODO CITY

A.T.V. Stage 1 Vol. 1
USM 1476 ▲ $24.95 ▲ VHS ▲ SUB ▲ Stereo ▲ 09/03/96
A.T.V. Stage 1 Vol. 2
USM 1477 ▲ $24.95 ▲ VHS ▲ SUB ▲ Stereo ▲ 09/03/96
A.T.V. Stage 1 Vol. 3
USM 1478 ▲ $24.95 ▲ VHS ▲ SUB ▲ Stereo ▲ 09/03/96
A.T.V. Stage 1 Vol. 4
USM 1479 ▲ $24.95 ▲ VHS ▲ SUB ▲ Stereo ▲ 09/03/96
A.T.V. Stage 1 Vol. 5
USM 1480 ▲ $24.95 ▲ VHS ▲ SUB ▲ Stereo ▲ 09/03/96
A.T.V. Stage 1 Box Set: *Episodes 1-13*
Tape vol's 1-5 in a collector's case, with liner notes. (316 min.)
USM 1481 ▲ $99.95 ▲ VHS ▲ SUB ▲ Stereo ▲ 09/03/96

STAGE 2: KUMMEN JUNGLE WARS

A.T.V. Stage 2 Vol. 1
USM 1482 ▲ $24.95 ▲ VHS ▲ SUB ▲ Stereo ▲ 12/03/96
A.T.V. Stage 2 Vol. 2
USM 1483 ▲ $24.95 ▲ VHS ▲ SUB ▲ Stereo ▲ 12/03/96
A.T.V. Stage 2 Vol. 3
USM 1484 ▲ $24.95 ▲ VHS ▲ SUB ▲ Stereo ▲ 12/03/96
A.T.V. Stage 2 Vol. 4
USM 1485 ▲ $24.95 ▲ VHS ▲ SUB ▲ Stereo ▲ 12/03/96
A.T.V. Stage 2 Vol. 5
USM 1486 ▲ $24.95 ▲ VHS ▲ SUB ▲ Stereo ▲ 12/03/96
A.T.V. Stage 2 Box Set: *Episodes 1-5*
USM 1487 ▲ $99.95 ▲ VHS ▲ SUB ▲ Stereo ▲ 12/03/96

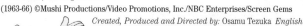

Arslan Senki *See* HEROIC LEGEND OF ARISLAN

Astro Boy 📺
TV series, 104 episodes

(1963-66) ©Mushi Productions/Video Promotions, Inc./NBC Enterprises/Screen Gems

Created, Produced and Directed by: Osamu Tezuka *English adaptation:* Fred Ladd

Although 1962's OTOGI MANGA (Manga Fairytales) CALENDAR is technically the first Japanese-animated series to be broadcast on Japanese TV (beating ASTRO BOY to the airwaves by approximately six months), for all intents and purposes, the start of the "modern anime age" is generally agreed to have begun on 1 January 1963 with the broadcast of this hugely successful, endearingly long-lasting 193-episode (of which 104 episodes made it to America) series. Unfortunately, none of the many one-shot TV specials, theatrical features, or even updated series remakes are, as yet, available in the U.S.; however, many of the TV series episodes as broadcast in English on NBC during the early '60s are available on home video, including a rarely seen "Lost Episode" containing the only voice-track in existence of an episode edited out of the Japanese series lineup by Tezuka himself. (For more information, see Chapter One.) For true die-hard fans of the series, the entire series is available in Japan in a deluxe collector's edition laser disc box set (its price being of the "if you have to ask, you can't afford it" variety), with a similar collector's edition box set available for the 1980-81 "Shin (New) Tetsuwan Atom" color remake series. Released in Japan under the title "Tetsuwan Atom" (lit., "Iron-Arm Atom," sometimes translated as "Mighty Atom") by Nikkatsu Video; select episodes available in North America through The Right Stuf.

Astro Boy 30th Anniversary Vol. 1
In Episode 55, VAMPIRE VALE, in the tiny country of Transmellvania, the famous world explorers Tick and Tock happen upon what seems to be a deserted village... a village with garlic on the doors ... a village that turns out to be "in the vale of Vampires." Can Astro Boy save the day when Tick disappears? In Episode 99, PHOENIX BIRD, on the Islands of Mystery in the Enigmatic Sea, Astro Boy and Astro Girl are enjoying some well-deserved vacation time. While acting "very unscientific for a robot," Astro Girl discovers what appears to be an egg. Stronger than most metals, it resists all attempts at analysis. Still, the larger question of who (or what) created it leads to an incredible discovery. **50 min. B&W**

Astro Boy 30th Anniversary Vol. 2
In Episode 69, FUNNEL TO THE FUTURE, while on a peaceful afternoon drive, Astro Boy, Astro Girl, and Dr. Elefun are swept 70,000 years into the future. The humans who inhabited Earth have been dead for 50,000 years, and only robot-built museums remain. Now, with life or death struggles between the vicious Loki and the defenseless Oriads (Earth's new inhabitants) hanging in the balance, only Astro Boy can turn the tide. In Episode 44, CLEOPATRA'S HEART, on board the 21st Century Limited, Mr. Pompus and Astro Boy are greeted by a mysterious traveler. Before making a hurried escape from the moving train, he leaves both a jewel and a cryptic message. As the Science Institute races to unravel the mystery, the Crimson Brotherhood is only steps behind ... and they will stop at nothing to gain possession of the jewel. **50 min. B&W**

Astro Boy 30th Anniversary Vol. 3
In Episode 23, THE DEADLY FLIES, when people suddenly begin dropping into a comatose state with no rational explanation, Inspector Gumshoe suspects Astro Boy is somehow to blame. Becoming a prime suspect, Astro Boy resolves to clear his good name. After investigating further, he discovers that there are immensely powerful forces at work ... forces that will crush him if he comes too close to the truth. In Episode 37, ASTRO BOY GOES TO SCHOOL, on a class field trip to Futura Park, Astro Girl happens upon a machine that is destroying works of art. It was built by Al McAnic, a man who feels that the world should be useful, not beautiful. And, seeing no need for robots that are anything other than 100% useful, he's going to rebuild all of them, starting with Astro Girl. **50 min. B&W**

Astro Boy 30th Anniversary Vol. 4
In Episode 96, GENERAL ASTRO, Patch, the notorious criminal, has decided that he will exact his revenge on Astro Boy. Using an Iota Ray Gun, he scrambles Astro Boy's brain, and launches him into space. Eventually, Astro Boy returns to Earth in Uglia — a republic in the midst of a civil war. Mistaken for the missing General Astro, he is placed in charge of the resistance forces. In Episode 57, THE VIKINGS, space travel is usually uneventful ... until Long John Floater and his gang of pirates begin plundering ships. Assigned to the Interstellar Police Force, Astro Boy is teamed with Lt. Judy, and he follows the trail of the pirate ship "Lolly" and its gang of pirate Vikings. Can they stop one of the most bloodthirsty gangs to ever sail? **50 min. B&W**

Astro Boy 30th Anniversary Vol. 5

In Episode 75, DOLPHINS IN DISTRESS, with the debut of the underwater city of Casalina only weeks away, Astro Boy is invited on a tour. Soon after, the city is attacked and damaged. Astro Boy goes to investigate, and makes contact with a race of dolphin creatures who want the oceans returned to them. Heel will not abandon his city; nothing will stand in the way of his greatest triumph. In Episode 91, A WONDERFUL CHRISTMAS PRESENT, it's Christmas Eve, 2000 AD. At 9 pm, Dr. Demure's time capsule will open, revealing his will and his greatest inventions. When revealed, the treasure is immediately stolen by Willy and Nilly. The inventions themselves, however, are meant for all of humanity, and only Astro Boy can ensure that they will be brought to the larger world for which they were intended. **50 min. B&W**

Astro Boy Vol. 1

In BIRTH OF ASTRO BOY, in 2,000 AD, Dr. Boynton creates a super-robot in his deceased son's image. He calls the robot Astro Boy. Astro Boy can swim oceans, leap mountains, even fly into space under his own power. Dr. Boynton becomes dissatisfied with the boy robot and disowns him. Then Astro Boy is befriended by Dr. Packadermus J. Elefun who guides him through his adventures. In THE MONSTER MACHINE, when Dr. Muddle builds a radio telescope, he gets more than he bargained for when he makes contact with Ork from Numan Luman. Under Ork's direction, Dr. Muddle builds a machine which teleports Ork to Earth. Ork and his monster machine try to take over the world. Only Astro Boy, with the help of an Ultragun, can stop Ork and his monster machine. **50 min. B&W**

Astro Boy Vol. 2

In THE TERRIBLE TIME GUN, Doctor Tempo, a brilliant but mad scientist, creates atomic time crystals. Doctor Tempo then constructs a time gun which can send its victims back through time. Feeling that he should be the head of the Institute of Science, Doctor Tempo sends Doctor Elefun and Astro Boy back to the time of King Arthur. Astro Boy saves the day while Doctor Elefun finds them a way back to the future. In ONE MILLION MAMMOTH SNAILS, Professor Nutty Fruitcake has developed a unique hobby while living alone in his secluded mountain observatory: he grows giant fruits and vegetables. When the novelty of growing giant watermelons and tangerines wears thin, the Professor takes to breeding snails. The giant snails crawl from their overcrowded mountaintop toward the helpless cities. Astro Boy seems to be the only recourse when the Army, Navy, and Marines fail. **50 min. B&W**

Astro Boy Vol. 3

In SUPER BRAIN, Dr. Numskull Cranium, one of the world's foremost brain surgeons, is murdered by Herringbone Tweed. The doctor has his brain transferred to a super robot to seek revenge on those who planned his death. Only Astro Boy can help bring Herringbone Tweed and his gang to justice while saving the doctor. In MYSTERY OF THE AMLESS DAM, in the small town of Amless, humans accuse robots of being the cause of all their problems. Humans, believing the robots have kidnapped a young boy, demand the robots give up their civil liberties. When the robots refuse, it's up to Astro Boy to set things right. **50 min. B&W**

Astro Boy Vol. 4

In THE MAGIC PUNCH CARD, Dr. Figaro Newton builds the world's first fully automated factory. No longer do robots or humans have to work in factories doing menial labor, as the super factory does it all. However, Dr. Andre Grabitall secretly replaces the control punch card with one of his own, causing the factory to try and destroy everyone around it. In THE GREAT ROCKET ROBBERY, Dr. Goldthumb builds a robot that can see into the future. Future the robot and Astro Boy become friends, until Dr. Goldthumb orders Future to turn against Astro Boy and use his abilities for evil. Sadly, Future predicts his own demise when he decides he must do what is right for humanity. **50 min. B&W**

Astro Boy Vol. 5

In SHIPWRECK IN SPACE, while chasing a gang, Astro Boy mistakenly enters a rocket of the Ponkotsu Gang and is launched into space. Because the rocket breaks up in space they are unable to return to Earth. They head for an emergency space station in search of food. Here they discover a group known as the "Universal Alliance of Food Gluttons" who travel the universe in search of the most delicious foods. In GIFT OF ZEO, a mysterious robot is found sleeping at the construction site of a company notorious for its poor work. The robot, called Zeo, starts to move and to destroy the buildings built by the company. Becoming angry, Hanadaka, the president of the company, attacks Zeo with a destruction machine. Zeo is waiting for the opening of a time capsule that will reveal a culture from one million years ago. **50 min. B&W**

Astro Boy Vol. 6

In MYSTERY OF THE METAL MEN, Astro Boy is blown away by an explosion at a dam construction site. When he vists Dr. Elefun, the doctor says that he has never met him. He is actually in Parallel World, which greatly resembles Astro Boy's own world but where

the people are under the rule of metal men from outer space. Even more surprising is that the leader of the human revolt is none other than Dr. Boynton. Will Astro Boy be able to solve the puzzle and return himself home? In GANGOR, THE MONSTER, in the year 2000, there were robots aplenty. Since human beings no longer worked, there was a wide assortment of robots big and little, fat and thin, tall and short, to perform every conceivable menial task. But nowhere was there a robot like Gangor, the Monster. Created by the arch-criminal Patch, Gangor was actually a gang of robots — 47 robots rolled up into one! By night, and under orders from Patch, they linked together, one behind the other, to form a seemingly endless chain — a mechanical centipede capable of executing the most monstrous crimes. Astro Boy is thrust into a battle at the bottom of the sea that may be his last! **50 min. B&W**

Astro Boy Vol. 7

In BROTHER JETTO, stored away in the warehouse of the Science Academy is Jetto, a robot that was created by Dr. Boynton as a prototype of Astro Boy. However, during a clean-up of the warehouse, the robot is thrown out with the trash. Attempting to return to the Science Academy, Jetto is approached by a scientist engaged in counterfeiting. He is asked by the scientist to give something to Astro Boy. What is inside the box? In DOGMA PALACE, a robot comes to Astro Boy's house from the Supernatural Genghis Khan Empire in search of help. He says that the people there are suffering under the oppression of the emperor. Astro Boy sets off for the empire but is captured by guard robots of the emperor and is rendered powerless. It is then that Astro Boy discovers that the emperor is using bees with poison that make them do what he says in order to keep people under his control. **50 min. B&W**

Astro Boy Vol. 8

In THE MAD BELTWAY, Dr. Elefun prevails against Tobias Toggle's suggestion that air cars be used for public transportation. Dr. Elefun insists that a well-designed beltway would be much more efficient. He agrees to assume full responsibility, then hires as his chief engineer the young but famous Cal E. Brate. Trouble dogs the project and cows the young engineer. When a sabotaged accident leads to his sister Maria being lost, Cal resolves to forge ahead with vigor. Actually, Maria is being held prisoner by the terrible Toggle. Will Astro Boy be able to save Maria and the Beltway from disaster? In MISSION TO THE MIDDLE OF THE WORLD, the Valyx, a rather unique earth-digging vehicle developed by Professor Prober, suddenly appears: ten years and half a world away from its initial plunge. But strange markings have appeared on its surface. Astro Boy, his sister Astro Girl, and a stowaway reporter, Reed Daley, are the ones who take the Valyx back into the Earth to investigate. Many miles down they discover a tribe of Deros, people who originally came from the lost continent of Atlantis. What will Astro Boy do when he discovers the evil intentions of the Atlanteans? **50 min. B&W**

Astro Boy Vol. 9

In THE HOOLIGAN WHODUNIT, Dr. Elefun is surprised to receive a package from his old friend, Dr. Gamma in Tacittown, filled with disconnected parts of a robot. The broken voice box keeps repeating an intriguing message about "Horace" and "Mr. Aurora." Astro Boy and Mr. Pompus decide that Horace must be Horace Hooligan, leader of the gang that has been terrorizing robots all over the world. So they set out for the South Pole where Mr. Aurora is located to see what they can find out. Can Astro Boy save the robots of the world from destruction? In RETURN OF CLEOPATRA, that fiend of the Nile, the evil genius Rasburton, had once before confronted Astro Boy, then fled when the brave little robot thwarted Rasburton's scheme to recreate an Egyptian dynasty. Now he returns with a regal queen whom he calls the new Cleopatra. She is the ancient beauty reborn, he insists, and with the aid of strong-arm tactics, he installs her as Queen of the Nile. Astro Boy, sensing trouble, arrives to investigate. But he is surprised and ambushed by a colossal robot that stuns him and leaves him to perish in the desert. Has Astro Boy finally met his match? **50 min. B&W**

Astro Boy Vol. 10

In INCA GOLD FEVER, Astro Boy goes with Dr. Elefun and Dr. Tonderu, an archaeologist, to investigate Inca ruins. There they meet up with Kapack, an old man who wants to restore the Inca empire. Kapack has used telepathy to amass the secret treasure needed for his goal. Becoming greedy for wealth, Dr. Tonderu creates a device for increasing telepathic powers. Is he really aiding Kapack in his quest for power? In HULLABALOO LAND, no amusement park in the world could compare with the one called "Hullabaloo Land." Here was a child's dream world: everything from Hansel and Gretel's tiny cottage to King Arthur's castle! "Hullabaloo Land" was the creation of Dr. Magico, a mechanical wizard. What no child ever suspected was that kindly old Dr. Magico was actually a power-mad scientist plotting to take over the world! Astro Boy and his guardian, Doctor Elefun, follow a hunch and decide one day to visit Dr. Magico in his castle. Astro Boy discovers the wizard's secret workshop — only to be discovered himself by Dr. Magico and his robot dragon, Firesnout! Astro Boy's escape, his fight with the dragon, and his pursuit of the evil wizard are exploits that could only happen in the bizarre setting of "Hullabaloo Land." **50 min. B&W**

Astro Boy Vol. 11
In SILVER COMET, Tommy Speed is ready to enter the World Champion Motor Car Race when his supersonic car, the Silver Comet, is smashed by thugs. Dr. Elefun rebuilds the car, but it's up to Astro Boy to protect Tommy from the many traps during the race. In THE ROBOT OLYMPICS, at the World Robot Athletic Meet, President Yabure wants his robot, Demon 1, to win. He sets all kinds of traps for Astro Boy, who gets help from Luna, a pretty female robot. But even with her help, can Astro Boy defeat Demon 1 in their final match? **50 min. B&W**

Astro Boy Vol. 12
In THE THREE ROBOTIERS, Un, Deux, and Trois are three daring robots created by Dr. Bonbon. Because of their bravery, they go with Astro Boy to stop the Space Pirates, who have taken over an asteroid and are robbing transport rockets. Can Astro Boy keep the Robotiers together long enough to stop the pirates? In ANGEL OF THE ALPS, the famous Professor Muse has taken his granddaughter, Angelica, to the peace and quiet of the Alps. Dr. Elefun sends Astro Boy to convince him to return and share his inventions with the world. But the evil Mr. Vile is also after Professor Muse, and not for the good of the world! **50 min. B&W**

Astro Boy: The Lost Episode
NOTE: Episode 34, THE BEAST FROM 20 FATHOMS, was created during the 1963 season by a handpicked team of animators. Osamu Tezuka, however, was unsatisfied, and ordered the episode destroyed. Before this occurred, a copy had been sent to NBC for English dubbing. To this day, it does not exist anywhere in Japan. Synopsis: When jewel thieves meet an untimely end near Lake Foggybottom, the authorities become suspicious. Astro Boy, exploring the bottom of the lake, discovers a mass of empty turtle shells — whatever is down there is a meat eater! The lake is ordered drained ... and a mysterious voice orders the water replaced ... and hypnotizes the workers! In Episode 52, THE SNOW LION, an unearthly snow is falling all over the world, and mankind's machines are failing. This snow seeks out all sources of energy (including robots). Only Astro Boy seems unaffected as he has been fitted with an unusually large energy cell. Astro Boy discovers that this is not really snow at all, but the first step in a Rigellian invasion! And the aliens have also brought along Rex, a lion composed of the same energy-absorbing material. His target: Astro Boy! **50 min. B&W**

Domestic Home Video:
Astro Boy Vol. 1
RS 10010 ▲ $19.95 ▲ VHS ▲ DUB ▲ Mono ▲ CP ▲ 06/01/89
Astro Boy Vol. 2
RS 10020 ▲ $19.95 ▲ VHS ▲ DUB ▲ Mono ▲ CP ▲ 09/01/89
Astro Boy Vol. 3
RS 10030 ▲ $19.95 ▲ VHS ▲ DUB ▲ Mono ▲ CP ▲ 03/01/90
Astro Boy Vol. 4
RS 10040 ▲ $19.95 ▲ VHS ▲ DUB ▲ Mono ▲ CP ▲ 09/01/90
Astro Boy Vol. 5
RS 10050 ▲ $19.95 ▲ VHS ▲ DUB ▲ Mono ▲ CP ▲ 03/01/91
Astro Boy Vol. 6
RS 10060 ▲ $19.95 ▲ VHS ▲ DUB ▲ Mono ▲ CP ▲ 09/01/91
Astro Boy Vol. 7
RS 10070 ▲ $19.95 ▲ VHS ▲ DUB ▲ Mono ▲ CP ▲ 09/01/91
Astro Boy Vol. 8
RS 10080 ▲ $19.95 ▲ VHS ▲ DUB ▲ Mono ▲ CP ▲ 11/01/91
Astro Boy Vol. 9
RS 10090 ▲ $19.95 ▲ VHS ▲ DUB ▲ Mono ▲ CP ▲ 11/01/91
Astro Boy Vol. 10
RS 10100 ▲ $19.95 ▲ VHS ▲ DUB ▲ Mono ▲ CP ▲ 11/01/91
Astro Boy Vol. 11
RS 10110 ▲ $19.95 ▲ VHS ▲ DUB ▲ Mono ▲ CP ▲ 03/01/92
Astro Boy Vol. 12
RS 10120 ▲ $19.95 ▲ VHS ▲ DUB ▲ Mono ▲ CP ▲ 03/01/92
Astro Boy 30th Anniversary Vol. 1
RS 3001 ▲ $14.95 ▲ VHS ▲ DUB ▲ Mono ▲ CP ▲ 07/01/93
Astro Boy 30th Anniversary Vol. 2
RS 3002 ▲ $14.95 ▲ VHS ▲ DUB ▲ Mono ▲ CP ▲ 07/01/93
Astro Boy 30th Anniversary Vol. 3
RS 3003 ▲ $14.95 ▲ VHS ▲ DUB ▲ Mono ▲ CP ▲ 07/01/93
Astro Boy 30th Anniversary Vol. 4
RS 3004 ▲ $14.95 ▲ VHS ▲ DUB ▲ Mono ▲ CP ▲ 07/01/93
Astro Boy 30th Anniversary Vol. 5
RS 3005 ▲ $14.95 ▲ VHS ▲ DUB ▲ Mono ▲ CP ▲ 07/01/93

Astro Boy: The Lost Episode
RS 3006 ▲ $14.95 ▲ VHS ▲ DUB ▲ Mono ▲ CP ▲ 05/02/95
LUM 9508 ▲ $39.95 ▲ LD ▲ DUB ▲ Mono ▲ 05/02/95
Astro Boy Vol. 1
4 episodes: The Birth of Astro Boy, One Million Mammoth Snails, The Monster Machine, and The Terrible Time Gun.
ID 2194RI ▲ $34.95 ▲ LD ▲ DUB ▲ Digital HiFi Mono ▲ 04/15/93
Astro Boy Vol. 2
4 episodes: Cleopatra's Heart, Vampire Vale, Funnel To The Future, and Phoenix Bird.
ID 2807RI ▲ $39.95 ▲ LD ▲ DUB ▲ Digital HiFi Mono ▲ 08/30/94

Babel II

OAV series, 4 volumes
(1992) ©Mitsuteru Yokoyama/Hikara Productions/Sohbi Planning/Teeup

Based on Characters by: Mitsuteru Yokoyama *Director:* Yoshihisa Matsumoto *Script:* Bin Namiki *Music:* David Tolley

Four-volume OAV series based on the classic science fiction manga (as serialized in publisher Akita Shôten's WEEKLY SHÔNEN CHAMPION manga anthology) and 1973 TV series of the same name by creator Mitsuteru Yokoyama, the talent behind such '60s "giant robot" classics as TETSUJIN 28 (Iron Man 28, a.k.a. "Gigantor") and GIANT ROBO (a live-action version of which was broadcast in English under the title "Johnny Sokko and his Giant Robot"). In this 1992 remake, a mild-mannered student is transformed into the eponymous title character, a supernatural psychic warrior obliged to battle an army of zombies led by a ruthless enemy named "Magnus." Interestingly, Babel II literally *screams* his enemies into submission (shades of *X-Men*'s Banshee), which goes a long ways toward explaining why footage from this particular anime video was used in Michael Jackson's "Scream" video. Released in Japan under the title "Babel Nisei" (Babel the Second) by Sôbi Entertainment; available in North America through Streamline Pictures.

Babel II Part 1: *The Awakening*
Uncertain as to why he keeps hearing voices which no one else can hear, Koichi soon finds himself drawn to a mysterious rendezvous with Juju, a beautiful disciple of a powerful cult leader. Koichi is asked to join the cult because she believes he possesses latent psychic powers which could benefit her master. His refusal starts a chain reaction which reveals Koichi to be the reincarnation of Babel II- the Chosen One called upon to defend mankind from the forces of evil. **30 min.**

Babel II Part 2: *First Blood*
Learning the origin of his remarkable powers, Babel proceeds to do battle with a cult of telekinetic assassins. He is joined in his fight by a trio of powerful alien warriors as well as a team of special agents working for the U.N. Against overwhelming odds, Babel takes on an army of reconstructed psychic zombies and ruthless espers. The final showdown, in a remote desert tower, forms the backdrop for a cataclysmic battle that tests Babel's strength and resolve. **30 min.**

Babel II Part 3: *Crossroads*
A New York City neighborhood scheduled for demolition is the next site for Babel's ongoing war against evil. Seeking revenge against Babel and his alien allies for defeating her master, Juju devises a foolproof plan guaranteed to destroy her unsuspecting enemy. Her scheme calls for Babel to drain his energy battling an endless stream of psychic zombies. Once Babel has been worn down, Juju will come in for the kill. A bizarre twist of fate brings these two espers to a crossroad which will change them both forever. **30 min.**

Babel II Part 4: *Final Conflict*
There was never any doubt that this day would come - the final conflict from which there is no escape. With the aid of his stalwart allies, Babel faces this ultimate challenge with courage and resolve. If he loses now, mankind will be at the mercy of his arch-enemies. One by one, Babel confronts his powerful foes. Each new battle drains his strength, but with no chance to stop to recharge his psychic reservoir, he quickly realizes that it will take a miracle just to survive the day. The concluding episode in the series. **30 min.**

Domestic Home Video:
Babel II Part 1
SPV 91003 ▲ $9.95 ▲ VHS ▲ DUB ▲ Mono ▲ 07/11/95
Babel II Part 2
SPV 91053 ▲ $9.95 ▲ VHS ▲ DUB ▲ Mono ▲ 07/11/95
Babel II Part 3
SPV 91103 ▲ $9.95 ▲ VHS ▲ DUB ▲ Mono ▲ 07/11/95
Babel II Part 4
SPV 91143 ▲ $9.95 ▲ VHS ▲ DUB ▲ Mono ▲ 07/11/95
Babel II Perfect Collection: *Episodes 1-4*
Episodes 1-4 on one videotape. (120 min.)
SPV 91333 ▲ $19.95 ▲ VHS ▲ DUB ▲ Stereo ▲ CC ▲ 05/28/96

Baoh

(1989) ©Toho/Shueisha

Based on characters by: Hirohiko Araki *Screenplay:* Kenji Terada *Director:* Hiroyuki Yokoyama

Based on the manga series of the same name (published in English by Viz Comics) by Hirohiko "Jo Jo no Myô na Bôken (Jo Jo's Bizarre Adventures)" Araki, as serialized in publisher Shueisha's weekly SHŪKAN SHŌNEN JUMP manga anthology. The story of a genetically altered young man and his psychic girl sidekick on the run from the top secret research lab which created both their powers, this one-shot OAV condensation of the two compiled-volume manga series features gore and guts aplenty, mainly because Baoh (the young man) is a living biological weapon (something like the Guyver... only blue!). Some feel the whacked-out surrealism of the comic loses something in translation to the screen, while others feel it's more than faithful to its manga roots. Released in Japan under the title "Baô Raihôsha" (Baoh the Visitor) by Toho; available in North America through AnimEigo. **50 min.**

Domestic Home Video:
ANI ET095-003 ▲ $19.95 ▲ VHS ▲ DUB ▲ Stereo ▲ 05/24/95
ANI AT095-003 ▲ $24.95 ▲ VHS ▲ SUB ▲ Stereo ▲ 05/24/95
ANI AD095-005 ▲ $44.95 ▲ LD ▲ DUB/SUB ▲ Stereo ▲ 05/24/95

Barefoot Gen

(1983) ©Keiji Nakazawa

Created, Written and Produced by: Keiji Nakazawa *Director:* Masaki Mori *Animation Director:* Kazuo Tomizawa *Art Director:* Kazuo Kojika

A devastating document of the aftermath of the atomic bombing of Hiroshima, drawn from Keiji Nakazawa's true-life experiences in Hiroshima's ruins, BAREFOOT GEN is a semi-autobiographical account of six-year-old Gen and his family's struggle to survive against overwhelming odds. Simple, cartoony animation style only highlights the graphically horrifying scenes of death and destruction, portrayed with such straightforward honesty that it's often too painful to watch. Winner of an award for raising global consciousness of A-bomb survivors. Based on Nakazawa's manga of the same name and released in Japan under the title "Hadashi no Gen" (Barefoot Gen) by Japan Home Video; available in North America through Streamline Pictures. Followed in 1986 by a high-quality 90-minute OAV sequel (as animated by Studio Madhouse) not yet available in the U.S which documents Gen's continuing story. **85 min.**

Domestic Home Video:
SPV 91423 ▲ $29.95 ▲ VHS ▲ DUB ▲ Stereo ▲ CC ▲ 07/11/95

Battle Angel

(1993) ©Yukito Kishiro/Business Jump/Shueisha/KSS Inc./MOVIC

Created by: Kishiro Yukito *Supervisor:* Taro Rin *Director:* Hiroshi Fukutomi *Screenplay:* Akinori Endo *Character Design:* Nobuteru Yuki

Based on the manga of the same name by creator Yukito Kishiro, as originally serialized in publisher Shueisha's BUSINESS JUMP, an office worker-targeted manga anthology. When cybernetic doctor Ido finds the remains of a petite cyborg in a junk heap located beneath the elite, manmade floating city, he takes her home, fits her with a new, indestructible body, and names her "Gally." The reborn Gally's memories of her past life only emerge when she is fighting, so she decides to take on Doc Ido's hobby of bounty hunting. Savage, high speed battles, and unique art design make this dark future particularly eye-catching, and the cyberpunk-flavored story has a sharp-edged sadness that's not easy to forget. Features character designs by RECORD OF LODOSS WAR and ANGEL COP's Nobuteru Yuki. (Incidentally, although the title of the U.S. video release comes from the U.S. published-manga of the same name from Viz Comics, only the title remains consistent: character names are as given in the original Japanese manga, although in a pleasingly ironic twist, later stories in Kishiro's manga series as published in BUSINESS JUMP make reference to "Alita"—the name given Gally by Viz Comics series rewriter Fred Burke, who also came up with the name "Tiphares" for the floating city of Zalem.) Released in Japan under the title "Gunmu" (Gun Dream) by KSS/Nihon Soft System; available in North America through A.D. Vision. This videocassette contains the complete animated films *GUNNM-RUSTY ANGEL* and *GUNNM-TEARS SIGN*. **70 min.**

Domestic Home Video:
ADV BA/001 ▲ $34.95 ▲ VHS ▲ SUB ▲ HiFi Surround ▲ 09/22/93
ADV BA/001D ▲ $19.95 ▲ VHS ▲ DUB ▲ HiFi Surround ▲ 12/03/96
ADV BA/001L ▲ $39.95 ▲ LD-CAV ▲ SUB ▲ Surround ▲ 10/27/95

Battle Royal High School

(1987) ©Tokuma Japan Communications Co., Ltd.

Director: Ichiro Itano

Based on the manga "Majinden" (Magic-God Legend) by creator Shinichi Kuruma, as serialized in publisher Tokuma's weekly SHŪKAN SHŌNEN CAPTAIN manga magazine. An other-dimensional invasion takes over a high school, but if some hard-hittin' kids are tuff enuff, they might be able to push back those slimy monsters kickin' 'n' screamin' back to the hell from which they came. With slick '80s animation featuring unusally adult-looking character designs (for an OAV based on a manga series for young adults, anyway) and high-powered, not-for-the-squeamish martial arts combat with drippy monsters, in terms of over-the-top outrageous action, BATTLE ROYAL tips its hat to the wrestling term from which it takes its name. (If you're a fan of the type of "horror humor" as elevated to an art by John Carpenter, odds are you'll find the shock of this vid's nudity and gore ameliorated somewhat.) In addition to directorial duties, Itano also gets screenplay credit (but did you know he's also the man who put the thrust into MACROSS' missiles back in 1982? It's true). Released in Japan under the title "Shinma Jinden (True-Magic God-Legend) Battle Royal High School" by Tokuma Japan Communications; available in North America through AnimEigo. **60 min.**

Domestic Home Video:
ANI ET096-006 ▲ $19.95 ▲ VHS ▲ DUB ▲ HiFi Stereo ▲ 08/20/96
ANI AT096-001 ▲ $24.95 ▲ VHS ▲ SUB ▲ HiFi Stereo ▲ 08/20/96
ANI AD096-009 ▲ $39.95 ▲ LD ▲ HYBRID ▲ HiFi Stereo ▲ 09/03/96

Battle Skipper

OAV series, 3 volumes

(1995) ©Tomy/Victor Entertainment/Artmic

Screenplay: Hidemi Kamata *Character Design:* Takashi Kobayashi *Music:* Takeo Miratsu *Director:* Takashi Watanabe *Original Story:* Tomy

Backed by Japanese toymaker Tomy in memory of a long, symbiotic relationship between anime videos and anime video toys, BATTLE SKIPPER gives us a team of five squealing, teenaged girls as they take a break from classes to battle evil in custom-built powered armor. Sweet as cotton candy; just about as nutritionally filling. Released in Japan under the title "Bishôjo Yûgeki-Tai (Beautiful-Girl Play-Attack Squadron) Battle Skipper" by Victor Entertainment; available in North America through U.S. Manga Corps.

Battle Skipper 1
Without regard for property or school regulations, the members of the Debutante Club - led by their ruthless leader, Sayaka Kitaoji, the richest girl in the world - will unleash their colossal robotic combat suits (Battle Skippers) to take over the St. Ignacio School For Girls - and then the world! The only hope lies with the five valiant members of the Etiquette Club - and their secret squad of prototype combat suits! **30 min.**

Battle Skipper 2
The Debutantes are determined to salvage their reputation after the humiliating defeat at the hands of the Etiquette Club. As always, Sayaka has a plan. Meanwhile, Saori finds herself in serious trouble—only to be rescued by the handsome and mysterious Brother Gilbert. Only who is Brother Gilbert? Is he destined to be Saori's first love—or does he plan to exploit her for his own nefarious purposes? **30 min.**

Battle Skipper 3
Sayaka's master plan is unfolding- and it spells trouble for the Etiquette Club. First, she'll kidnap the president of the Etiquette Club, and lure the rest of the club into a trap. Then she'll be free to invade the clubhouse and steal the secrets of the Battle Skipper combat suits! Can this be the end of the Exstars? **30 min.**

Domestic Home Video:
Battle Skipper 1
USM 1504 ▲ $12.95 ▲ VHS ▲ DUB ▲ Stereo ▲ 07/02/96
Battle Skipper 2
USM 1505 ▲ $12.95 ▲ VHS ▲ DUB ▲ Stereo ▲ 09/03/96
Battle Skipper 3
USM 1506 ▲ $12.95 ▲ VHS ▲ DUB ▲ Stereo ▲ 11/05/96

 Violence   Profanity   Nudity   Sexual Situations   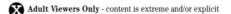 Adult Viewers Only - content is extreme and/or explicit

Be Forever Yamato *See* YAMATO

Big Wars

(1993) ©Yoshio Aramaki/Tokuma Japan Communications Co. Ltd.

Original story: Yoshio Aramaki *Director:* Toshifumi Takizawa *Screenplay:* Kazumi Koide *Character Design:* Mic Mikuriya *Mecha Design:* Kow Yokoyama *Animation Director:* Keizou Shimizu *Music:* Michiaki Kato

A sophisticated, adult-oriented OAV of the 25th century Martian battleground between humanity and the beautiful, humanoid "Gods" who claim divine authority to stop our expansion into space. *Noir* art direction and realistic character designs in the style of a GOLGO 13 or WICKED CITY (see separate entries) give BIG WARS the feel of a World War II movie complete with espionage, propaganda, and partisan attacks, even as the carrier sorties upon the vast seas of sand recall the great naval battles of the Pacific. Released in Japan under the title "Big Wars: Kami Utsu Naki Kôya ni" (On the Plains Where the Attack on God Ran Out) by Tokuma Japan Communications; available in North America through U.S. Manga Corps. **75 min.**

Domestic Home Video:
USM 1372 ▲ $29.95 ▲ VHS ▲ SUB ▲ Stereo ▲ 05/07/96

Black Magic M-66

(1987) ©Bandai Visual/Movic/Masamune Shirow/Seishinsha

Animation Director: Takayuki Sawaura *Mecha Director:* Toru Yoshida *Music:* Yoshihiro Katayama *Character Design and Direction:* Hiroyuki Kitakubo *Original Story, Screenplay and Direction:* Masamune Shirow

Terminator-like story features a military robot running amok in hot pursuit of its test target—its creator's granddaughter. Detailed military hardware and intense combat sequences spice up the cat-and-mouse chase between the M-66 robot, the wailing granddaughter and an intrepid journalist who's been caught in the middle. Manga creator Masamune (GHOST IN THE SHELL, APPLESEED) Shirow's hands-on presence (direction, screenplay) in this video's production shows, and his style has never been adapted better. Released in Japan under the title "Black Magic M- (Mario) 66" by Bandai Visual/ Movic; available in North America through Manga Entertainment. **48 min.**

Domestic Home Video:
MGV 633893 ▲ $14.95 ▲ VHS ▲ DUB ▲ HiFi Stereo ▲ 03/21/95
USR VD6 ▲ $19.95 ▲ VHS ▲ SUB ▲ Stereo ▲ 12/01/91 ▲ Out of Print

Blade of Kamui *See* DAGGER OF KAMUI

Blue Seed

TV series, 26 episodes

(1995) ©Yuzo Takada/Takeshobo • BS Project

Original Story & Character Design: Yuzo Takada *Script Direction:* Masaharu Amiya *Character Design:* Kazuchika Kise, Takayuki Goto *Music:* Kenji Kawai *Director:* Jun Kamiya

A secret Japanese agency is dedicated to fighting the Aragami, an ancient plant-like parasite race out of myth who have waited centuries for the chance to again rule the Earth. Humanity's secret weapon is a teenaged girl named Momiji, next in line to inherit a family destiny of human sacrifice to keep legendary monsters (with traditional Japanese folklore touches) from invading the human world. Most of the series focuses on the super-scientific government team fighting monsters, but Momiji's plight as a possible human sacrifice gives the old aliens vs. monsters concept a special *frisson*. Based on an original story by Yuzo Takada (3x3 EYES), also writer/artist of the manga adapatation. Animation is startlingly good for television due to the series' original plan as an OAV series, with excellent, fast-paced direction and engagingly original designs for the Aragami monsters. Opening and ending themes are high-energy pop, sung by top-o'-the-Japanese-charts voice-actor and singer Megumi Hayashibara. Character designs by Takayuki Goto (PLEASE SAVE MY EARTH) and Kazuchika Kise. 1995 TV series followed a year later in 1996 by a three-volume OAV series by the same director. Released in Japan under the title "Blue Seed" by King Record; available in North America through A.D. Vision.

Blue Seed Vol. 1: *Episodes 1 and 2*

Episode 1: PRINCESS KUSHINADA and Episode 2: IT'S CRUEL! IT'S MYSTERIOUS! IT'S MY DESTINY! Joining the TAC in their battle is Momiji Fujimiya, a young Japanese girl who carries an unborn Aragami, a "blue seed," inside her chest, and Mamoru Kusanagi, a cat-eyed servant of the Aragami with superhuman powers who rebels against the will of his masters to protect Momiji. All Japan is the battleground as the TAC squares off against mankind's oldest enemies, whose ability to impregnate any living creature with a controlling seed means they can attack anywhere, anytime. **60 min.**

Blue Seed Vol. 2: *Episodes 3 and 4*

Episode 3: IT'S SPRING! IT'S THE CAPITAL! I'LL DO MY BEST! and Episode 4: MORE BAD LUCK? WHY DOES THIS ALWAYS HAPPEN TO ME? After she is accidentally implanted with a "blue seed," the unborn form of the Aragami, teenager Momiji Fujiyama finds herself the recipient of bizarre psychic powers. Destined to be sacrificed to the Aragami, will Momiji find protection in the mutated human, Mamoru, and the badly outgunned and outnumbered TAC? **60 min.**

Blue Seed Vol. 3: *Episodes 5 and 6*

Episode 5: SURPRISE! SHE'S THE MOTHER OF SCIENCE! and Episode 6: COMPLICATED AND HARD TO UNDERSTAND! BEING A MAN PUTS YOU IN SUCH A DIFFICULT POSITION! As the strain of the continuing war against the Aragami begins to take its toll, the TAC finds itself under increasing pressure from within as well as without. When Yaegashi's inexperience with weapons almost costs Kome her life, Yaegashi must live with the result. Later, as a giant jellyfish creature attacks Tokyo, Matsudaira must deal with her feelings of inadequacy when she forgets her son's birthday. **60 min.**

Blue Seed Vol. 4: *Episodes 7 and 8*

Episode 7: I'M FIRED UP! I'LL DO IT! BECAUSE I'M THE KUSHINADA! and Episode 8: WHAT? HOW STRANGE! A RIVAL APPEARS! Six-year old Yukiko is kidnapped by the Aragami to force her father to release data from the Kushinada Project. Incensed that an innocent has been put in danger because of her, Momiji makes it her personal crusade to rescue Yukiko. As a result of her popularity after rescuing Yukiko, Momiji is nominated to perform for the Kanto Pop-idol Scout Caravan. However, the contest's climactic singing duel, which pits Momiji against Sakura Yamazaki, a magic-using young lady with her eye on Maoru, is interrupted by the attack of a ginko tree Aragami. **60 min.**

Blue Seed Vol. 5: *Episodes 9 and 10*

Episode 9: ARE YOU SERIOUS? IS THIS A DREAM? AN EXCITING DATE! and Episode 10: INNOCENCE! LOVE! MY FIRST DATE! A new breed of Aragami has appeared in Tokyo. Taking the form of hunting dogs, these Hell Hounds are stronger, faster and meaner than all the Aragami that have come before. Add their mysterious master and his giant fire-breathing toad and the TAC's resources and Kusanagi's abilities will be stretched to the breaking point. **60 min.**

Blue Seed Vol. 6: *Episodes 11 and 12*

Episode 11: IRRITATING! JEALOUS? UNBELIEVABLE! and Episode 12: DO YOU FEEL IT? I CAN'T IGNORE IT! A FOREBODING OF CATASTROPHE! It's an entomologist's dream come true when the world of the TAC is invaded by a host of insectoid Aragami. The fun begins with little black spiders in control of Momji's classmates at school. No sooner is the spider invasion squashed when a giant, skyscraper-scaling centipede appears to terrorize downtown office workers. **60 min.**

Domestic Home Video:
Blue Seed Vol. 1
ADV BS/001D ▲ $24.95 ▲ VHS ▲ DUB ▲ HiFi Surround ▲ 02/15/96
ADV BS/001S ▲ $29.95 ▲ VHS ▲ SUB ▲ HiFi Surround ▲ 02/15/96
Blue Seed Vol. 2
ADV BS/002D ▲ $24.95 ▲ VHS ▲ DUB ▲ HiFi Surround ▲ 04/23/96
ADV BS/002S ▲ $29.95 ▲ VHS ▲ SUB ▲ HiFi Surround ▲ 04/23/96
Blue Seed Vol. 3
ADV BS/003D ▲ $24.95 ▲ VHS ▲ DUB ▲ HiFi Surround ▲ 06/18/96
ADV BS/003S ▲ $29.95 ▲ VHS ▲ SUB ▲ HiFi Surround ▲ 06/18/96
Blue Seed Vol. 4
ADV BS/004D ▲ $24.95 ▲ VHS ▲ DUB ▲ HiFi Surround ▲ 08/27/96
ADV BS/004S ▲ $29.95 ▲ VHS ▲ SUB ▲ HiFi Surround ▲ 08/27/96
Blue Seed Vol. 5
ADV BS-005D ▲ $24.95 ▲ VHS ▲ DUB ▲ HiFi Surround ▲ 10/08/96
ADV BS-005S ▲ $29.95 ▲ VHS ▲ SUB ▲ HiFi Surround ▲ 10/08/96
Blue Seed Vol. 6
ADV BS/006D ▲ $24.95 ▲ VHS ▲ DUB ▲ HiFi Surround ▲ 12/03/96
ADV BS/006S ▲ $29.95 ▲ VHS ▲ SUB ▲ HiFi Surround ▲ 12/03/96
Blue Seed Collection Vol. 1 LD: *Episodes 1-4*
ADV CLVBS/001 ▲ $59.95 ▲ LD ▲ M/A ▲ HiFi Surround ▲ 07/30/96
Blue Seed Collection 2 LD: Episodes 5-8
ADV CLVBS/002 ▲ $59.95 ▲ LD ▲ M/A ▲ HiFi Surround ▲ 12/03/96

Blue Sonnet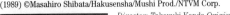

OAV series, 5 episodes

(1989) ©Masahiro Shibata/Hakusensha/Mushi Prod./NTVM Corp.

Director: Takeyuki Kanda *Original Story:* Masahiro Shibata *Character Design:* Shoichi Nakayama *Art Director:* Naoshi Yokose *Music Director:* Susumu Aketagawa

Based on the manga of the same name by creator Masahiro Shibata, as serialized in specialized *shôjo* manga or "girls' comics" monthly manga anthology HANA TO YUME (Flowers and Dreams)…the same magazine which first serialized creator Saki Hiwatari's PLEASE SAVE MY EARTH (see entry). Conjuring much of the energetic spirit and structure of '70s anime action shows, BLUE SONNET is a five-episode, two-volume OAV series featuring the ultimate weapon, a teenaged girl code-named "Blue Sonnet," who was rescued from the slums of an American inner city and surgically rebuilt as a combat cyborg by the Talon organization, a super-scientific cadre bent on a new world order under their command. The story concerns another teenaged and outwardly normal Japanese girl who becomes a target of Talon due to their knowledge of her secret psychic powers, and how her interaction with Sonnet may lead to them unravelling Talon's plans together. Unusual and appealing character designs by Shoichi Nakayama, and direction by Takeyuki Kanda (ROUND VERNIAN VIFAM). Released in Japan under the title "Akai Kiba (Red Fang) Blue Sonnet" by Walkers Company/Polydor; available in North America through U.S. Manga Corps.

Blue Sonnet Vol. 1: *Episodes 1-3*
Sonnet is dispatched to Japan to investigate a powerful esper known only as the "Red Fang." New dangers and clues are exposed: The Red Fang, System RX 606, a forgotten past, a mysterious stranger… Will Sonnet and Lan solve the mystery, or is Dr. Merikus leading them toward a sinister rendezvous? **90 min.**

Blue Sonnet Vol. 2: *Episodes 4 and 5*
With the capture of Lan Komatsuzaki, Talon's plans to conquer the world seem more of a reality than ever before. But just as Lan has begun to learn the secrets behind her origin and the source of her incredible powers, she has been fitted with a collar that supresses those very powers! Locked deep inside the most secure stronghold in Japan, Lan is quickly running out of time. Talon's plans for her are nothing short of satanic: turn Lan's body into a factory for producing an army of super-espers through the processes of artificial insemination and cloning. Meanwhile, Sonnet and Red Fang finally come face-to-face in a battle to the death. **60 min.**

Domestic Home Video:

Blue Sonnet Vol. 1
USM 1077 ▲ $29.95 ▲ VHS ▲ SUB ▲ Stereo ▲ 09/07/94
ID 2885CT ▲ $34.95 ▲ LD ▲ SUB ▲ Stereo ▲ 09/06/95

Blue Sonnet Vol. 2
USM 1229 ▲ $29.95 ▲ VHS ▲ SUB ▲ Stereo ▲ 01/04/95
ID 2891CT ▲ $34.95 ▲ LD ▲ SUB ▲ Stereo ▲ 12/20/95

Bounty Dog  OAV

(1994) ©Zero G Room/Star Child/Toho Ltd./Movic Inc.

Original Story: Zero G Room *Screenplay:* Mayori Sekijima *Assistant Director:* Shin Matsuo *Animation Director & Character Design:* Hirotoshi Sano *Mecha Design:* Atsushi Takeuchi *Art Director:* Tadashi Kudo *Music Director:* Sho Goto *Director:* Hiroshi Negishi

Moody, two-volume OAV outer-space adventure featuring a young man who belatedly finds out that his deceased girlfriend was the spirit of the an alien force identified with the bright side of the moon (meanwhile, her "dark side" twin, the so-called "Sleeper," is about to awaken). Definitely an entry in the "looks beautiful, but what does it mean?" category (reportedly, the video was in pre-production for over a year); fortunately, there's usually enough going on that you don't have to think about the story. Touches of hard SF technology such as a lunar mass driver portray a future society of lunar colonists with a high degree of realism. Nice mecha design work reminiscent of SOL BIANCA (see entry), with sharp-looking, high-contrast animation featuring character designs and animation direction by the busy Hirotoshi Sano (character design for SPACE KNIGHT TEKKAMAN BLADE II, mechanical direction for MOBILE FIGHTER G GUNDAM and THE VISION OF ESCAFLOWNE, mecha concepts for MOBILE SUIT GUNDAM 0083: STARDUST MEMORY). (Additionally, Masamune Shirow himself is said to have contributed to "mechanic design.") As a clever art direction motif, almost all of this video is "filmed" in interesting sepia, ochre or red-wash monochrome palettes. Released in

Japan under the title "Bounty Dog" by King Record/Toho Video; available in North America through Manga Entertainment. **60 min.**

Domestic Home Video:
MGV 635521 ▲ $19.95 ▲ VHS ▲ DUB ▲ HiFi Stereo ▲ 03/19/96

Bubblegum Crisis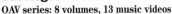

OAV series: 8 volumes, 13 music videos

(1987-91) ©Artmic/Youmex

Planning and Original Story: Toshimichi Suzuki *Directors:* Katsuhito Akiyama (Eps. 1-3), Hiroki Hayashi (Ep. 4), Masami Obari (Eps. 5&6), Fumihiko Takayama (Ep. 7), Hiroaki Goda (Ep. 8) *Screenplay:* Kenichi Matsuzaki, Hideki Kakinuma, Shinji Aramaki, Katsuhito

Akiyama, Emu Arii, Hidetoshi Yoshida *Character Design:* Kenichi Sonoda, Satoshi Urushibara *Music:* Kaoji Makaino

Near-future cyberpunk with a driving rock score, featuring the superhero-like exploits of the Knight Sabers—a mercenary band of four women who use their high-tech "hardsuits" to fight against bio-engineered androids called "Boomers." BUBBLEGUM CRISIS (as in the type that gets bigger and bigger until it blows up in your face) wears its Hollywood influences proudly on its sleeve—the Knight Sabers' leader, Priss, fronts a band straight out of *Blade Runner* called "Priss and the Replicants," while the series' trademark theme, "Konya wa Hurricane" (Tonight, a Hurricane), is straight out of *Streets of Fire*—yet in Japan the BGC series nevertheless helped to mark the end of the experimental early days of the OAV format and the beginning of a trend towards tried-and-true anime formulas and an insular appeal to a hardcore audience (think Hollywood sequelitis). With its slick '80s animation (it doesn't get any more '80s than this), strong female protagonists, mecha action and evil corporatate opposition, BGC has a sure appeal to American superhero fans, although many female anime fans today question any presupposed "feminist" message (high-heels on hardsuits?). Character designer Kenichi Sonoda (GUNSMITH CATS) established himself with one of anime's Top Ten Most Recognizable Styles with the series; mecha designs by Masami Obari (who would later go on to fame as a character designer/director of the FATAL FURY series, not to mention the animated TOSHINDEN) really shine through in "Moonlight Rambler" and "Red Eyes" (Sonoda and his Artmic cohorts did most of the early hardsuit mecha designs in other volumes). Of interest is the fact that "Revenge Road" features direction by Hiroki Hayashi, creator/director of TENCHI MUYÔ!. A made-in-America comic adaptation with new original stories is published in North America by Dark Horse Comics. Released in Japan under the title "Bubblegum Crisis" by Toshiba EMI; available in North America through AnimEigo.

Bubblegum Crisis Episode 1
In the world of Mega-Tokyo, an all-female team of super-suited beauties known as the "Knight Sabers" battle a megalithic corporation and its evil henchmen, the bio-tech menaces, artificial lifeforms called "Boomers." Originally intended for work in space, the Boomers, like Labors, have been used and abused by the wrong people, and the Knight Sabers vigilante group is formed to put a halt to their rampages. Like a superhero team, each member of the four-woman team has a distinct personality—each one, possessed of a special skill essential to the team's success, even hard-rockin' singer Priss, leader of her band, The Replicants. **53 min.**

Bubblegum Crisis Episode 2: *Born To Kill*
The private war between the Knight Sabers and GENOM heats up when GENOM recovers the "Black Box" that controls the U.S.S.D. satellite weapons system from the wreckage of Aqua City. The sinister GENOM executive in charge of the project incorporates the Black Box into his pet project, the Super Boomer android, and sets his Boomer assassins on the trail of anyone who stands in his way. **30 min.**

Bubblegum Crisis Episode 3: *Blow Up*
GENOM's new plan for the "Urban Renewal" of MegaTokyo involves the use of combat Boomer androids to terrorize the population and induce them to sell their land cheaply. Meanwhile, Mason, the sinister GENOM executive, is determined to discover their secret identities and destroy them. When GENOM accidentally kills the mother of a young boy who has been befriended by Priss, the Knight Sabers launch an attack on GENOM's huge, monolithic headquarters. **30 min.**

Bubblegum Crisis Episode 4: *Revenge Road*
A mysterious black car, the "Griffon," is hunting down the rebellious bikers known as Outriders. When Priss tangles with the Griffon on her new bike, she ends up with more than a few lumps and a score to settle. Enlisting the aid of Nene, the Knight Sabers' mole inside AD Police, she begins her own private investigation. They soon narrow down the list of suspects to one man, Gibson, the victim of an Outrider attack. **40 min.**

 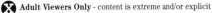

Bubblegum Crisis Episode 5: *Moonlight Rambler*

A group of young women make a panicked escape from an orbiting industrial complex, crashing a stolen space shuttle on the outskirts of MegaTokyo. Priss finds a new friend, but what secret is she hiding? Could it have anything to do with the recent rash of "vampire" murders? Or is it the result of skullduggery at GENOM? Who is the mysterious Largo, who seems to know altogether too much about the Knight Sabers? And just where is the D.D., a semi-intelligent battlesuit with an atomic deadman switch? 45 min.

Bubblegum Crisis Episode 6: *Red Eyes*

The mysterious Largo infiltrates GENOM and uses lookalike Boomers to frame the Knight Sabers. Helping him is Anri, the 33-S "Sexaroid" Boomer who, after the death of Sylvie in "Moonlight Rambler," is the last surviving space station fugitive. Priss, heartbroken because she could not prevent Sylvie's death, resigns from the team. When Largo's imposters reappear, the three remaining Knight Sabers are seriously outclassed. Meanwhile, a chance encounter with Leon and a near-miss by an orbital beam weapon puts Priss on Largo's trail. Largo faces Quincy, the elusive chairman of GENOM, and demands that he hand over the Overmind Control System. Seeking to atone for Sylvie's death by rescuing Anri, Priss takes on Largo alone... a big mistake! 45 min.

Bubblegum Crisis Episode 7: *Double Vision*

A GENOM executive inks a pact with the Gulf & Bradley Corporation to produce a sophisticated new combat Boomer. McLaren, G&B's Boomer expert, is looking forward to sampling the pleasures of MegaTokyo while working on the project. The festivities are rudely interrupted by a powerful crab-like Mecha. McLaren is the only survivor of the attack. Meanwhile, in MegaTokyo, the big news is the upcoming concert by Vision, a very famous and very mysterious rock star. Vision's concert is just a cover. She's really here to avenge the murder of her little sister, Irene, who was murdered by a Boomer in "Born To Kill." Assisted by the faithful Kou, she attacks GENOM's research center in her Mecha, but her reluctance to kill innocent bystanders dooms the attempt to failure. McLaren, more than a little unnerved by the attack, arranges for some protection - the Knight Sabers! 49 min.

Bubblegum Crisis Episode 8: *Scoop Chase*

When would-be VidReporter Lisa Vanette tries to film the Knight Sabers in action, her favorite camera ends up under Priss' heel. Lisa vows to get even by discovering their true identities. It doesn't hurt to be the Chief of AD Police's favorite niece. An unfortunate Nene finds herself saddled with the job of escorting Lisa around town. Priss proves to be more difficult to mislead than Nene anticipates, and almost discovers the Knight Sabers' secret training facility at Raven's garage. Lisa isn't Nene's only problem. Once again, her latest combat simulation is well below par, and the rest of the Knight Sabers won't let her forget it. Lisa refuses to give up her quest, and eventually, persistence pays off. She obtains a photograph that proves Nene is a Knight Saber. Sylia, hoping to protect their identities, pays Lisa a visit. Meanwhile, Dr. Yoshida, a demented GENOM scientist, has secretly built a new type of Boomer. He decides to test them by having them destroy AD Police H.Q. By hacking into the building's central computer, one of the Boomers turns it into an automated death-trap. 50 min.

Hurricane Live 2032—*The Music of Bubblegum Crisis*

(1988) Five music videos created using footage from the animated science-fiction series, with direction and storyboards credited to BGC Vols. 1-3 director Katsuhito Akiyama. Released in Japan under the title "Hurricane Live 2032" by Toshiba EMI. 25 min.

Hurricane Live 2033—*Tinsel City Rhapsody*

(1990) Seven music videos set against footage from the animated science-fiction series. Includes live-action sequences of the Japanese voice-actors from their special "Tinsel City Rhapsody" concerts. Again, direction and storyboards are credited to BGC Vols. 1-3 director Katsuhito Akiyama. Released in Japan under the title "Hurricane Live 2033" by Toshiba EMI. 30 min.

Domestic Home Video:

Bubblegum Crisis Episode 1
ANI ET094-002 ▲ $19.95 ▲ VHS ▲ DUB ▲ Stereo ▲ 10/26/94
ANI AT091-001 ▲ $24.95 ▲ VHS ▲ SUB ▲ Stereo

Bubblegum Crisis Episode 2
ANI ET094-003 ▲ $19.95 ▲ VHS ▲ DUB ▲ Stereo ▲ 10/26/94
ANI AT091-002 ▲ $24.95 ▲ VHS ▲ SUB ▲ Stereo

Bubblegum Crisis Episode 3
ANI ET094-004 ▲ $19.95 ▲ VHS ▲ DUB ▲ Stereo ▲ 12/28/94
ANI AT091-003 ▲ $24.95 ▲ VHS ▲ SUB ▲ Stereo

Bubblegum Crisis Episode 4
ANI ET094-005 ▲ $19.95 ▲ VHS ▲ DUB ▲ Stereo ▲ 12/28/94
ANI AT091-004 ▲ $24.95 ▲ VHS ▲ SUB ▲ Stereo

Bubblegum Crisis Episode 5
ANI ET094-006 ▲ $19.95 ▲ VHS ▲ DUB ▲ Stereo ▲ 03/20/95
ANI AT091-005 ▲ $24.95 ▲ VHS ▲ SUB ▲ Stereo

Bubblegum Crisis Episode 6
ANI ET094-007 ▲ $19.95 ▲ VHS ▲ DUB ▲ Stereo ▲ 03/20/95
ANI AT091-006 ▲ $24.95 ▲ VHS ▲ SUB ▲ Stereo

Bubblegum Crisis Episode 7
ANI ET094-008 ▲ $19.95 ▲ VHS ▲ DUB ▲ Stereo ▲ 05/24/95
ANI AT091-007 ▲ $24.95 ▲ VHS ▲ SUB ▲ Stereo

Bubblegum Crisis Episode 8
ANI ET094-009 ▲ $19.95 ▲ VHS ▲ DUB ▲ Stereo ▲ 05/24/95
ANI AT091-008 ▲ $24.95 ▲ VHS ▲ SUB ▲ Stereo

Bubblegum Crisis Collector Suite
Subtitled volumes 1 - 8 in a collector's slipcase
ANI AS095-011 ▲ $190.00 ▲ VHS ▲ SUB ▲ 07/26/95

Bubblegum Crisis: Hurricane Live 2032
ANI AT092-011 ▲ $19.95 ▲ VHS ▲ SUB ▲ HiFi Mono

Bubblegum Crisis: Hurricane Live 2033
ANI AT092-012 ▲ $19.95 ▲ VHS ▲ SUB ▲ HiFi Mono

Bubblegum Crisis Vol. 1
Episodes 1-3 (111 min.)
ANI AD092-002 ▲ $39.95 ▲ LD ▲ SUB ▲ Stereo ▲ 12/02/92

Bubblegum Crisis Vol. 2
Episode 4, Hurricane Live 2032 and 2033 (95 min.)
ANI AD092-003 ▲ $39.95 ▲ LD ▲ SUB ▲ Stereo ▲ 12/30/92

Bubblegum Crisis Vol. 3
Episodes 5 and 6 (95 min.)
ANI AD092-004 ▲ $39.95 ▲ LD ▲ SUB ▲ Stereo ▲ 02/03/93

Bubblegum Crisis Vol. 4
Episodes 7 and 8 (95 min.)
ANI AD092-005 ▲ $39.95 ▲ LD ▲ SUB ▲ Stereo ▲ 03/03/93

Bubblegum Crisis Universe LD Set
Laserdiscs 1-4, plus AD Police and Bubblegum Crash LDs
ANI AS095-003 ▲ $235.00 ▲ LD ▲ SUB ▲ Stereo ▲ 02/22/95
▲ Out of Print

Bubblegum Crash

OAV series, 3 episodes

(1991) ©Artmic Inc.

Planning and Original Story: Toshimichi Suzuki *Screenplay:* Hiroshi Ishiodori (Vol. 1), Emu Arii (Vols. 2&3) *Director:* Hiroshi Ishiodori (Vols. 1&3), Hiroyuki Fukushima (Vol. 2) *Character Design:* Kenichi Sonoda *Animation Director:* Noboru Sugimitsu (Vols. 1&2), Yasuyuki Noda (Vol. 3) *Art Director:* Yumiko Ogata *Music:* Takehito Nakazawa (Vols. 1&3), Michihiko Ota (Vol. 2)

Excepting the always-exceptional character designs by Kenichi Sonoda, this sequel series seems a pale shadow of the original BUBBLEGUM CRISIS series (see above). The Knight Sabers move on with their lives, most notably Linna, who moves from aerobics instructor to stock broker. The Japanese voice-actor for Priss, one of the series' main draws as the lead singer for her band "The Replicants," changed from Kinuko Omori's husky rock-'n'-roll singer to the sweeter-sounding Ryoko Tachikawa (ironic in that in the story, Priss finally gets her big singing break). The Knight Sabers' hardsuits, redesigned along sleeker lines, somehow look even less functional than the originals. Worth seeing for fans of BGC, but an overall disappointment at best. Released in Japan under the title "Bubblegum Crash" by Polydor; available in North America through AnimEigo.

Bubblegum Crash Vol. 1: *Illegal Army*

An armored mercenary force commits a series of daring bank robberies that AD Police seem unable to prevent. The robberies are but a small part of a much larger design, masterminded by a mysterious "Voice." Meanwhile, the Knight Sabers are ... breaking up? Priss is getting her big singing break, Linna is making a fortune in the stock market, Nene is still stuck in the AD Police, and Sylia ... Sylia seems to have vanished! 45 min.

Bubblegum Crash Vol. 2: *Geo Climbers*

Only two of the original team that created the Boomers remain alive. Dr. Haynes seeks to realize Dr. Stingray's dream, and creates new A.I. software that gives Boomers human reasoning abilities. Dr. Yuri seeks power, and will stop at nothing to get it. Using his Boomer assassins, Yuri murders Haynes and his staff, and steals ADAMA, a prototype Boomer that uses the new A.I. technology. His plans go awry when Adama escapes into the depths of MegaTokyo. Realizing that Adama is the key to her father's legacy, Sylia and the Knight Sabers attempt to find him. When Priss finally tracks him down, all seems well - until the Hit-Boomers arrive. 45 min.

Bubblegum Crash Vol. 3: *Meltdown*

The mysterious "Voice" is infecting Boomers with his purloined A.I. technology, recruiting an army that shares his desire for a new world order, ruled by chaos and fear, with no

place for puny humans. The resulting commotion will keep the Knight Sabers busy while the real plot unfolds. The "Voice" has grander designs, and intends to kill five birds with one stone: the four Knight Sabers, and MegaTokyo's Nuclear Fusion Reactor. **45 min.**

Domestic Home Video:
Bubblegum Crash Vol. 1
ANI ET095-008 ▲ $19.95 ▲ VHS ▲ DUB ▲ Stereo ▲ 09/04/95
ANI AT092-001 ▲ $24.95 ▲ VHS ▲ SUB ▲ Stereo
ANI AD096-006 ▲ $39.95 ▲ LD ▲ HYBRID ▲ Stereo ▲ 06/28/96
Bubblegum Crash Vol. 2
ANI ET095-009 ▲ $19.95 ▲ VHS ▲ DUB ▲ Stereo ▲ 09/04/95
ANI AT092-002 ▲ $24.95 ▲ VHS ▲ SUB ▲ Stereo
ANI AD096-007 ▲ $39.95 ▲ LD ▲ HYBRID ▲ Stereo ▲ 06/28/96
Bubblegum Crash Vol. 3
ANI ET095-010 ▲ $19.95 ▲ VHS ▲ DUB ▲ Stereo ▲ 09/04/95
ANI AT092-003 ▲ $24.95 ▲ VHS ▲ SUB ▲ Stereo
ANI AD096-008 ▲ $39.95 ▲ LD ▲ HYBRID ▲ Stereo ▲ 06/28/96
Bubblegum Crash
Episodes 1, 2 and 3 — 2 discs, 3 sides. (139 min.)
ANI AD094-002 ▲ $49.95 ▲ LD ▲ SUB ▲ Stereo ▲ 04/20/94
▲ Out of Print

Burn Up!

(1991) ©NCS/MRC/AIC

Original Story: Yasunori Ide, Jun Kanzaki *Director:* Yasunori Ide *Writer:* Jun Kanzaki *Character Design:* Kenjin Miyazaki *Art Director:* Kenji Kamiyama *Music:* Kenji Kawai

Based on the manga of the same name, as serialized in publisher Gakken's Comic Nora manga anthology. "Sci-fi police action story" set in near-future Tokyo in which three burnin' hot babes with badges—wild 'n' crazy Maki, by-the-book Reimi, and pert 'n' bubbly Yuka—stumble across a Mafia white slavery ring. If you liked *Charlie's Angels*, you're sure to like this one. Followed by a sequel five years later (see below). Released in Japan under the title "Burn Up" by A.I.C.; available in North America through A.D. Vision (contains supplementary material and footage not found in the Japanese import release). **50 min.**

Domestic Home Video:
ADV BU/001 ▲ $29.95 ▲ VHS ▲ SUB ▲ HiFi Surround ▲ 01/26/94
ADV BU/002 ▲ $19.95 ▲ VHS ▲ DUB ▲ HiFi Surround ▲ 10/17/95

Burn Up W

(1996) ©AIC/MRC

Original Story: AIC, Zero G Room *Screenplay:* Katsuhiko Kochiba, Sumio Uetake *Character Design & Animation Director:* Toshinari Yamashita *Music:* Hiroyuki Nanba *Director:* Hiroshi Negishi

Cheerfully described by certain waggish anime fans as standing for "[W]orthless" or "[W]hy," BURN UP W depicts the adventures of Team Warrior, a group of tightly uniformed young ladies and one man who are called in when the going gets too tough for the regular police. Okay animation, but not what you'd call stunning; busty broads with guns save the day. In an interesting side-note, many of the animation staff worked on TENCHI MUYÔ!, lending BURN UP W a similar style. Released in Japan under the title "Burn Up W" by Media Ring; available in North America through A.D. Vision.

Burn-Up W: File 1: *Skin Dive*
In the near future, high-tech crime is running rampant! But a special SWAT unit, "Warrior" is ready to hit the streets. In SKIN DIVE, a group of terrorists takes over a luxury hotel and it's up to Warrior to get the hostages out. If that involves granting a few unreasonable demands, that's a small price to pay, right? That's what Rio keeps telling herself as she prepares to make the world's highest nude bungee jump. First of a 4-part series from the makers of TENCHI MUYÔ!. **35 min.**

Burn-Up W: File 2: *Search For the Virtual Idol*
When popular female idol Maria disappears, it's up to Warrior Team to locate her... but this is no ordinary kidnapping, as Maria is only a program in the TC computer net! Yet, can an AI program develop a life of its own, and if so, could that life be a life of crime? When the Virtual Drug Cartel, a killer android and a crazed scientists lurking in the basement of the TC Police building all become involved with the program on the run, virtually anything can happen. **35 min.**

Domestic Home Video:
Burn-Up W: File 1
ADV BW-001D ▲ $19.95 ▲ VHS ▲ DUB ▲ HiFi Surround ▲ 06/25/96
ADV BW-001S ▲ $24.95 ▲ VHS ▲ SUB ▲ HiFi Surround ▲ 06/25/96
ADV CAVBW/001 ▲ $39.95 ▲ LD-CAV ▲ HYBRID ▲ HiFi Surround ▲ 07/30/96
Burn-Up W: File 2
ADV BW/002D ▲ $19.95 ▲ VHS ▲ DUB ▲ HiFi Surround ▲ 09/24/96
ADV BW/002S ▲ $24.95 ▲ VHS ▲ SUB ▲ HiFi Surround ▲ 09/24/96

Captain Harlock [TV]

TV series, 42 episodes

(1978-79) ©Toei/Ziv International

Based on the manga of the same name by creator Leiji Matsumoto (STAR BLAZERS). Select episodes from the 42-episode SPACE PIRATE CAPTAIN HARLOCK (see entry in Chapter 1) TV series. Space pirate Captain Harlock, a nihilistic freedom fighter who never met a glass of red wine he didn't like, roams the Sea of Stars in search of both Mazone to kill (the Mazone are a race of plant-based humanoid females) and "a place," as he puts it, "to die." Note that although the TV series predates the Captain Harlock origin story ARCADIA OF MY YOUTH (see entry), in the chronology of the "Leijiverse"—which includes not only this series and ARCADIA, but GALAXY EXPRESS and SSX—the stories in this videotape release take place in the far, far future. The four episodes on tape were dubbed by Ziv International in the early '80s as promotional samples for marketing the series to American TV syndicators. There was no sale, and no other episodes were dubbed. For some unfathomable reason, the alien Mazone race gets a name change to "Zeton." Broadcast in Japan as "Uchû Kaizoku (Space Pirate) Captain Harlock"; released in North America through Malibu Graphics.

Captain Harlock Collector's Video Vol. 1
In ABOVE THE LAKE, the Space Pirate falls into the clutches of Commander Kirita while visiting Mayu on her birthday. In FLYING FROM THE UNKNOWN, Harlock and Dr. Daiu uncover an alien threat, but their warnings are ignored by the Earth. In A WOMAN WHO BURNS LIKE PAPER, Professor Daiu is attacked by a woman who self-destructs. **75 min.**

Captain Harlock Vol.1
2 episodes: ABOVE THE LAKE and FLYING FROM THE UNKNOWN. **55 min.**

Captain Harlock Vol. 2
2 episodes: A WOMAN WHO BURNS LIKE PAPER and ZETON THREAT. **55 min.**

Domestic Home Video:
Captain Harlock Collector's Video Vol. 1
MAL 03 ▲ $29.95 ▲ VHS ▲ DUB ▲ Mono ▲ 1991 ▲ Out of Print
Captain Harlock Vol. 1
MAL 01 ▲ $19.95 ▲ VHS ▲ DUB ▲ Mono ▲ 1990 ▲ Out of Print
Captain Harlock Vol. 2
MAL 02 ▲ $19.95 ▲ VHS ▲ DUB ▲ Mono ▲ 1990 ▲ Out of Print

Casshan: Robot Hunter

OAV series, 4 episodes

(1993) ©Tatsunoko Production Co. Ltd/Harmony Gold USA Inc.

Character Design & Animation Director: Yasuomi Umetsu *Script:* Hiroyuki Fukushima *Music:* Michiru Oshima *Director:* Hiroyuki Fukujima

Slick OAV remake of the classic 1973-74 TV show. In both series, Casshan is a man who willingly forsakes his humanity to become a super-powered robot and to fight against the global subjugation of humanity at the hands of a robot army (whose leader, we learn, was created by Casshan's own father). Superhuman in power but not in emotion, Casshan is tortured by his lost humanity, but staunchly sticks to his mission out of a strong sense of duty (an absolute must when it comes to anime heroes) and in the hopes of redeeming his father's name. Even if you're unfamiliar with the series, Casshan is immediately recognizable for his distinctive, American superhero-like white jumpsuit, as well as for his robot dog companion "Friender" (it's a long, sad story; don't ask). All four OAVs feature character design and animation direction by Yasuomi Umetsu (ROBOT CARNIVAL), with screenplay by director Fukushima. Released in Japan as "Casshan" (the 1973-74 series was released as "Jinzô Ningen (New-Made Man) Casshan") by Nihon Columbia; available in North America through Streamline Pictures.

Casshan: Robot Hunter Part 1: *Return From The Myth*
It is three years since the forces of mankind have been defeated by an army of seemingly unstoppable androids led by the mechanical despot known as Black King. The battle

becomes personal as Casshan must rescue Luna, his true love, before she is killed by Black King. **30 min.**

Casshan: Robot Hunter Part 2: *Journey To The Past*

News of a new super-weapon capable of destroying Black King's army has caused renewed fighting between the human resistance forces and Black King's robot occupation troops. Black King escalates his battle against Casshan in a calculated attempt to drain him of his powers and make him vulnerable to attack. Ironically, Casshan is forced to reveal a dark secret to Luna in an attempt to save her from uselessly sacrificing her life by fighting at his side. **30 min.**

Casshan: Robot Hunter Part 3: *Blitz On The Bridge*

An attack by Black King's forces against a seemingly unimportant civilian target sets Casshan on a remarkable journey of self-discovery. It all comes down to an explosive climax, as resistance fighters planning to sabotage Black King's invasion of a remote, peaceful village must contend not only with an army of androids but also with a confused Casshan, weakened from constant battle. **30 min.**

Casshan: Robot Hunter Part 4: *The Reviver*

With its secret weapon rendered inoperable, the human race is faced with a battle it cannot win ... unless Casshan can defeat an entire army on his own. Not willing to surrender, Casshan stages a heroic attack against the Black King's own defenses. With the odds for his survival decidedly not in his favor, Casshan battles his way to a deadly confrontation with Black King himself. A final dark secret forces Casshan to make the ultimate sacrifice. **30 min.**

Domestic Home Video:

Casshan: Robot Hunter Part 1
SPV 91383 ▲ $9.95 ▲ VHS ▲ DUB ▲ Mono ▲ 07/11/95
Casshan: Robot Hunter Part 2
SPV 91393 ▲ $9.95 ▲ VHS▲ DUB ▲ Mono ▲ 07/11/95
Casshan: Robot Hunter Part 3
SPV 91403 ▲ $9.95 ▲ VHS ▲ DUB ▲ Mono ▲ 07/11/95
Casshan: Robot Hunter Part 4
SPV 91413 ▲ $9.95 ▲ VHS ▲ DUB ▲ Mono ▲ 07/11/95
Casshan: Robot Hunter Perfect Collection: *Episodes 1-4*
SPV 91183 ▲ $19.95 ▲ VHS ▲ DUB ▲ Stereo ▲ CC ▲ 05/28/96

Castle of Cagliostro, The *See* LUPIN III

Cat Girl Nuku Nuku   [OAV] (C)

OAV series, 6 episodes

(1992-93) ©Movic/King Records/Yuzo Takada/Futabasha.

Created by: Yuzo Takada *Directors:* Hidetoshi Shigematsu, Yutaka Takahashi *Production:* Animate Film *Character Design:* Yuji Moriyama

Based on the manga of the same name by creator Yuzo Takada (3x3 EYES, BLUE SEED), as published in weekly SHÔKAN MANGA ACTION ZÔKAN GO manga magazine. To make a friend for his young son, a scientist creates an android protector in the shape of a young human girl and implants in it the brain of an accidentally run-over cat. Comedy ensues as a custody battle between the scientist and his estranged wife pulls the boy back and forth, and the super-powered Nuku Nuku foils the angry wife's multimillion-dollar efforts to kidnap her precious son with wacky mecha handled by goofy henchmen. Cute, fluffy comedy with just about anything an anime fan could ask for, including a performance by fan favorite Megumi "Girl-type Ranma" Hayashibara herself in the lead role. Note that up until Vol. 3 in this four-volume OAV series, creator Takada himself handles screenplay and some direction duties, while as of Vol. 4, PROJECT A-KO/MAISON IKKOKU's Yuji Moriyama takes over (Moriyama also handles character design duties for all four volumes). In case you're wondering, the "All-Purpose" in the title comes directly from the Japanese—"Bannô Bunka"—the obligatory catchphrase for "gadget" kitchen appliances sold on Japanese TV, such as America's own "Salad Spinner" or even "Ginzu Knives." (Who doesn't remember "It slices, it dices"...?) Released in Japan under the title "Bannô Bunka Neko Musume" (All-Purpose Cultural Cat Girl) by King Record; available in North America through A.D. Vision.

Cat Girl Nuku Nuku Episodes 1 and 2

As bodyguard for Ryunosuke, can even Nuku Nuku keep her young charge out of the insidious clutches of the ruthless Akiko Mishima, president of Mishima Heavy Industries, financier of the NK-1124 project, Kyusaku's ex-wife and Ryunosuke's mother? The greatest custody battle of all time erupts in a conflagration across Japan as Akiko unleashes the full force of M.H.I.'s military products division, manned by her elite team of Office-Lady Warriors, in her bid to win back Ryunosuke. **60 min.**

Cat Girl Nuku Nuku Episodes 3 and 4

Nuku Nuku may be super-powered and indestructible, but she has her hands full controlling the damage when inventor Kyusaku and megalomaniac Akiko attempt to reconcile and move back in together. As if that weren't enough, Nuku Nuku must face an even cuter android replacement who wants her job and her body as well. **60 min.**

Cat Girl Nuku Nuku Episodes 5 and 6

When Nuku Nuku breaks Ryunosuke's bike, she takes on a job waitressing at a new family restaurant owned by Ryu's money-hungry mom, Akiko Mishima. What nobody knows is that an overheated Arisa and Kyouko are about to spice up the menu with their own special recipe for trouble. Next, when a new Mishima Weapons satellite malfunctions, Akiko finds herself the target of an automated extermination program. **60 min.**

Domestic Home Video:

Cat Girl Nuku Nuku Vol. 1 (Eps. 1 & 2)
ADV CN/001 ▲ $29.95 ▲ VHS ▲ SUB ▲ HiFi Surround ▲ 04/07/95
Cat Girl Nuku Nuku Vol. 2 (Eps. 3 & 4)
ADV CN/002 ▲ $29.95 ▲ VHS ▲ SUB ▲ HiFi Surround ▲ 05/25/95
Cat Girl Nuku Nuku Vol. 3 (Eps. 5 & 6)
ADV CN/003 ▲ $29.95 ▲ VHS ▲ SUB ▲ HiFi Surround ▲ 06/22/95

Chikyû E... *See* TOWARD THE TERRA

Chô Jikû Yôsai Macross *See* MACROSS

Chô Jikû Seiki Orguss *See* ORGUSS

Chô Jû Kishin Dancougar *See* DANCOUGAR

Chôjin Densetsu Urotsuki Dôji *See* UROTSUKI DÔJI:

LEGEND OF THE OVERFIEND:

Chôjin Locke *See* LOCKE THE SUPERMAN

Countdown   [OAV] ⊗ () ⊚

OAV series, 4 episodes

(1995) ©Hiroyuki Utatane/Fujimi Shuppan/Akane Shinsa/Pink Pineapple

Author: Hiroyuki Utatane *Director:* Shoichi Masuo *Character Design:* Sanae Chikanaga

Two short erotic stories based on adult manga artist Hiroyuki Utatane's comics of the same name (published in English by Eros Comix). Utatane's treats sex with style and wit; the result is kinky, watchable, and, well, sexy, despite the misleadingly lurid copy on the sleeve of the English-subtitled domestic release. Followed by a sequel ("Countdown Continued") a year later. Released in Japan under the title "Yûwaku" (Countdown) by Pink Pineapple; available in North America through SoftCel Pictures, a division of A.D. Vision.

Countdown

2 episodes. ALIMONY HUNTER: An encounter on the subway leads to an extremely unusual free-for-all in which not everybody turns out to be what they appear, and in which all concerned get what's coming to them in the end. SEEK: A heroic macho-adventurer of the chain-mail wearing type learns the joys of being on the receiving end of another kind of chain when he rescues a lovely young lady with a knack for subduing knavish knights. **35 min.** *(Edited version 30 min.)*

Countdown Continued

Two more erotic shorts based on the hit manga. In Part One, a young bride-to-be has a last-minute fling... with another woman. In Part Two, a samurai policewoman and her perverted giant robot must take on a giant walking statue controlled by a sex-crazed megalomaniac. **35 min.** *(Edited version 30 min.)*

Domestic Home Video:

Countdown
ADV CD/001U ▲ $29.95 ▲ VHS ▲ SUB ▲ HiFi Surround ▲ UNCUT ▲ 12/21/95
ADV CD/001G ▲ $29.95 ▲ VHS ▲ SUB ▲ HiFi Surround ▲ EDITED ▲ 12/21/95
Countdown Continued
ADV CD/002U ▲ $29.95 ▲ VHS ▲ SUB ▲ HiFi Surround ▲ UNCUT ▲ 05/28/96
ADV CD/002G ▲ $29.95 ▲ VHS ▲ SUB ▲ HiFi Surround ▲ EDITED ▲ 05/28/96

Crimson Wolf

(1993) ©Toshiba EMI

Based on a graphic novel by: Masahiko Takasho, Kenji Okamura *Director:* Shoichi Masuo *Script:* Shoichi Masuo, Yasuhito Kikuchi, Isamu Imakake.

Based on the manga of the same name by Masahiko Takasho and Kenji Okamura (of "Leo" fame, published in the U.S. by Viz Comics as "Lycanthrope Leo"). Bloody tale of an army of darkness rising from the tomb of Gengis Khan which can be defeated only by three people who bear the mark of the Crimson Wolf. Lack of cute girls and/or robots make this one definitely not your typical otaku fodder. Director Masuo also handles the script. Released in Japan under the title "Hon Ran" (lit., "Crimson Wolf") by Toshiba EMI; available in North America through Streamline Pictures. **60 min.**

Domestic Home Video:
SPV 91373 ▲ $29.95 ▲ VHS ▲ DUB ▲ Mono ▲ CC ▲ 04/14/95

Crying Freeman
OAV series, 5 episodes

(1988-93) ©Toei Video Co. Ltd.

Based on graphic novels by: Kazuo Koike and Ryoichi Ikegami *Directors:* Daisuke Nishio (Ep. 1), Nobutaka Nishizawa (Ep. 2), Johei Matsuura (Ep. 3), Shigeyasu Yamauchi (Ep. 4), Takaaki Yamashita (Ep. 5) *Music:* Hiroaki Yoshino *Screenplay:* Higashi Shimizu (Eps. 1,3,4), Tatsunosuke Ohno (Ep. 2), Ryunosuke Ono (Ep. 5)

A Japanese man is kidnapped and trained as an assassin by a secret society of Chinese mobsters, eventually rising to lead their organization. His codename: Crying Freeman, because of the sorrow he feels for each life he takes. The frankly adult style and hard-edged, sex 'n' violence crime drama of the five FREEMAN OAVs stylistically resemble Hong Kong action films—unsurprisingly, the original manga's been adapted into live-action by French director Christophe Gans, starring martial artist Mark Dacascos as "Freeman" and *Gas, Food, Lodging*'s Julie Condra Douglass as his beautiful Japanese lover, "Emu." Based on the manga—so closely the storyboards are nearly perfect replicas—by Kazuo Koike and Ryoichi Ikegami (published in English by Viz Comics). Ikegami's smoked-glass-&-chrome art style is not helped by the generally lackluster animation quality, while the steamy sexual byplay and the sicko perverted sadism of Freeman's opponents definitely makes this one an adults-only title. Released in Japan under the title "Crying Freeman" by Toei Video; available in North America through Streamline Pictures/Orion Home Video.

Crying Freeman Episode 1: *Portrait of a Killer*
Emu Hino witnesses Yo kill a Yakuza boss. He is subsequently ordered to eliminate her. In an ironic turn of events, victim and assassin form an immediate attraction and mutual bond. Together they vow to face whatever fate has in store for them... but with both the police and organized crime out to destroy them, what can Yo and Emu do? **50 min.**

Crying Freeman Episode 2: *Shades of Death, Part 1*
Camora, a rival criminal syndicate, using every means at its disposal, challenges Freeman's position of leadership in the 108 Dragons. Its methods include assassination, and humiliation at the hands of Baya San - the powerful granddaughter of the former leaders of the 108 Dragons. Eventually, Freeman must engage in deadly hand-to-hand combat with Kitche, a cunning female assassin. **50 min.**

Crying Freeman Episode 3: *Shades of Death, Part 2*
Emu Hino, the artist who loves Freeman, is accepted by the Dragons as his wife, Fu Ching Ran (Tiger Orchid). But to show that she is fit for such a dangerous life, Fu must prove that she is a Tiger in spirit as well as name. African Tusk, a new terrorist gang, tries to muscle in on the international crime scene by launching a deadly surprise attack against the 108 Dragons. Freeman follows an elusive trail to Africa, where he personally challenges the murderous leaders of the Tusk, Jigon and Shikebaro. In a parallel storyline, the 108 Dragons receive the Muramasa, a priceless but accursed ancient samurai sword. To prevent the curse from striking Freeman, Emu travels to the Chinese criminal hellhole of Gauronsai. Her nearly impossible mission is to tame the Muramasa's demon spirit - or die trying. **50 min.**

Crying Freeman Episode 4: *A Taste of Revenge*
Naitai, a powerful and driven fanatic, schemes to use the 108 Dragons' influence to spread his Great Bear God religion throughout the world. Naitai forms an unlikely alliance with two of Freeman's past enemies, Nitta (a crooked cop) and Kimie (a defrocked underworld femme fatale). The plan is to replace Freeman with a perfect double, a brainwashed

---

cultist who is under their control. Their success depends on the support of Oshu Togoku, the almost superhuman world wrestling champion. Burning with jealousy against Freeman's legendary strength and martial-arts skills, Oshu struggles with his personal code of honor and his selfish compulsion to be thought of as the best. **50 min.**

Crying Freeman Episode 5: *Abduction in Chinatown*
The daughter and grandchild of an aging Chinatown crime lord are missing. Working with the crime lord's other daughter, a Pentagon computer expert, Freeman constructs an elaborate sting which seems to backfire - placing him in enemy hands. The lone Freeman is now forced to deal with the K.O. - a crime cartel made up of ex-military personnel which specializes in high profile kidnappings. Nina Heaven, the leader of this band of renegades, has an ulterior motive for not immediately murdering Freeman. Fascinated with his legendary skill as both lover and killer, the love-starved sadist gives Freeman a choice: live as her sex slave or face death at the hands of her trained army of killers. **50 min.**

Domestic Home Video:
Crying Freeman Episode 1
SPV 90663 ▲ $19.95 ▲ VHS ▲ DUB ▲ Mono ▲ CC ▲ 01/15/94
Crying Freeman Episode 2
SPV 90733 ▲ $19.95 ▲ VHS ▲ DUB ▲ Mono ▲ CC ▲ 06/01/94
Crying Freeman Episode 3
SPV 90803 ▲ $19.95 ▲ VHS ▲ DUB ▲ Mono ▲ CC ▲ 07/10/94
Crying Freeman Episode 4
SPV 90863 ▲ $19.95 ▲ VHS ▲ DUB ▲ Mono ▲ CC ▲ 11/20/94
Crying Freeman Episode 5
SPV 90963 ▲ $19.95 ▲ VHS ▲ DUB ▲ Mono ▲ CC ▲ 02/10/95

Crystal Triangle

(1987) ©MOVIC/Sony Video Software International Corp.

Original Story: Seiji Okuda *Screenplay:* Junki Takegami *Character Design:* Toyo'o Ashida, Kazuko Tadano, Mandori Rukurabu *Art Director:* Masazumi Matsumia *Animation Director:* Kazuko Tadano

Reported OAV prequel to a video game of the same name for the original "NES" Nintendo Entertainment System. Heavily inspired by *Raiders of the Lost Ark*, main character Dr. Kamishiro is an Indiana Jones-like archaeologist with seeming mystical powers. Together with his assistants—including a weapons master and a Japanese priestess—Dr. Kamishiro is searching for the "Message from God," which involves deciphering clues from hidden writing on ancient relics—the "Crystal Triangles" of the title. But to get to God's words, they have to survive attacks by the CIA, the KGB (whose agent is the reputed grandson of Rasputin!) and monks who turn out to be monsters in disguise. Eventually, we find out the actual "Message" consists of details on how to survive the visit to the rogue star Nemesis, which apparently also wiped out the dinosaurs (this theory of stellar destruction of the human race also is echoed in the 1984 live-action film *Night of the Comet*). Nifty aerial combat sequences near the end of the film, and a smattering of heavily accented English and Russian dialogue. Character designs by FIST OF THE NORTH STAR director Toyo'o Ashida and Kazuko Tadano (DANCOUGAR, SAILOR MOON). Released in Japan under the title "Kindan no Mokujiroku: Crystal Triangle" (Forbidden Revelation: Crystal Triangle) by Sony Music; available in North America through Central Park Media. **86 min.**

Domestic Home Video:
USM 1029 ▲ $29.95 ▲ VHS ▲ SUB ▲ Stereo ▲ 07/15/92
ID 2205CT ▲ $34.95 ▲ LD ▲ SUB ▲ Stereo ▲ 03/12/93 ▲ Out of Print

Curse of the Undead - Yoma

(1989) ©Toho Co. Ltd./MPS

Original Story: Kei Kusunoki, Shueisha *Character Design:* Matsuri Okuda *Director:* Takashi Anno *Screenplay:* Noboru Aikawa

As with many releases from this U.S. release label, unnecessarily lurid and misleading box copy do a poor job of preparing the viewer for what's really inside: in this case, a stylish, engrossing, supernaturally flavored thriller of a young ninja living in medieval Japan, traveling the warn-torn countryside of "Sengoku" or "Warring States" period Japan, only to discover that the comrade for whom he's searching has become a powerful undead spirit. Animation is fluid and beautiful; frequent bursts of blood and gore are effectively handled for a fascinating, dreamline effect. Striking character designs by Matsuri Okuda; based on an original story by OGRE SLAYER's Kei Kusunoki (see entry), sometimes described as the "most attractive woman working in manga today." Released in Japan as two separate volumes under the simple

---

title "Yôma" (Bewitching Beast) by Toho; available in North America in a double-length feature through A.D. Vision. **85 min.**

Domestic Home Video:
ADV CY/001 ▲ $29.95 ▲ VHS ▲ SUB ▲ HiFi Surround ▲ 05/08/95

Cutey Honey
OAV series, 8 episodes
(1994-95) ©Go Nagai/Dynamic Planning Inc./Toei Video Co. Ltd.

Based on the characters by: Go Nagai *Original Screenplay:* Isao Shiyuza *Director:* Yasuchika Nagaoka

OAV remake of the 1973-74 TV series of the same name from Go "PTA's Favorite Target" Nagai. "Cutey Honey" is the name of a statuesque, red-haired android created by a kindly scientist to resemble his own deceased daughter, albeit with the addition of a super device implanted in her, um, chest (breasts have always been one of Nagai's favorite parts of the female anatomy; that is, if the infamous "breast missiles" of characters such as "Venus" and "Aphrodite-A"in previous Nagai series are any indication). This "airborne element solidifier," we're told, can create most anything from thin air—

something which comes in handy, seeing as changing costumes (or even bodies) has always been an important part of Honey's *oeuvre* (the spinning, mid-air, "nudie transformation sequence" that's *de riguer* these days in any "magical girl" show worth its magic wand is Nagai's own invention, dating back to the '73-74 series, and was apparently quite the *cause célèbre* in its day). 1994's NEW CUTEY HONEY is an excellent video for admirers of the female form; seen through the eyes of young boy Chokei, Honey is an innocent, Wonder Woman-like beauty, rather than a busty sex object. A catchy remix of the CUTEY HONEY theme song and Chokei's squabbling family (including his super-powered, rocket-punchin' Grandpa) livens up the mix. An update of the TV series, entitled CUTEY HONEY FLASH, is in production for the 1997 Japanese TV season. Released in Japan under the title "Shin (New) Cutey Honey" by Toei; available in North America through A.D. Vision.

Cutey Honey Vol. 1: *Episodes 1 and 2*
The legendary battle android returns from a decade-long absence to discover that the evil forces of crime master Dolmeck are laying siege to an entire city. **65 min.**

Cutey Honey Vol. 2: *Episodes 3 and 4*
After joining Mayor Light and the demented Danbel family in their crusade to run Dolmeck's army of shape-changing street trash out of town, Cutey Honey finally makes a major dent in the Lord of Darkness' plans by locating the source of his mutation inducing drugs. Includes bonus production portfolio and answering machine messages. **65 min.**

Cutey Honey Vol. 3: *Episodes 5 and 6*
Whether she's up against mad bombers, acid-spewing terrorists, female assassins or time-tripping samurai, Honey's never been hotter, and, of course, the irrepressible Grandpa Denbai and his psychopathic offspring are all back as well! Former sidekick Chokei's grown up a bit, although now he's got a love interest of his own ... it's just too bad that she's on the wrong side of the law. **60 min.**

Cutey Honey Vol. 4: *Episodes 7 and 8*
The evil forces of Panther Zora are on the march. Standing in their way is the amazon android of a dozen combat bodies, New Cutry Honey! Toss in the slightly psychotic Hayami family as Cutey's backup, and you'll see that the armies of darkness had best march softly. **60 min.**

Domestic Home Video:
Cutey Honey Vol. 1
ADV C/001 ▲ $34.95 ▲ VHS ▲ SUB ▲ HiFi Surround ▲ 09/02/94
Cutey Honey Vol. 2
ADV C/002 ▲ $34.95 ▲ VHS ▲ SUB ▲ HiFi Surround ▲ 11/15/94
Cutey Honey Vol. 3
ADV C/003 ▲ $29.95 ▲ VHS ▲ SUB ▲ HiFi Surround ▲ 11/28/95
Cutey Honey Vol. 4
ADV C/004 ▲ $29.95 ▲ VHS ▲ SUB ▲ HiFi Surround ▲ 01/16/96

Cyber City Oedo 808
OAV series, 3 volumes
(1990) ©Madhouse/Japan Home Video

Director: Yoshiaki Kawajiri *Original Idea:* Juzo Mutsuki *Character Design:* Yoshiaki Kawajiri, Hiroshi Hamazaki, Masame Kosone *Music Director:* Yasunori Honda

Convicts are given a chance to reduce their life sentences in exchange for their services doing dirty work in a three-volume futuristic OAV sci-fi drama reminiscent of *Escape From New York* (or *Escape From L.A.*, as you prefer). The cons wear computer-controlled collars-of-obedience which will blow their heads off if they don't report in within a certain time period, which adds a decided "time pressure" to the proceedings. Character designs are by director Kawajiri (WICKED CITY) and Hiroshi Hamazaki. ("Oedo," by the way, is a variant for "Edo," a name for samurai-era Tokyo.) Released in Japan under the title "Cyber City Oedo 808" by Japan Home Video; available in North America from U.S. Manga Corps.

Cyber City Oedo 808: Data One
Terrorists have taken control of the city's tallest space-scraper. Not only does the building hold the primary nodes for the city's computer grid, but 50,000 people are still trapped inside! In principle, the job is simple: break into the most secure building in the city, find and eliminate the terrorists, and rescue the hostages. There's no time to waste, because the collars have a 24-hour limit, and the clock is ticking! **48 min.**

Cyber City Oedo 808: Data Two
A member of the Cyber Police has turned traitor and sold confidential police data to a mysterious customer who could destroy the Cyber Police forever. But before that can happen, the heroes have 24 hours to uncover the plot. The trail leads to a black market dealing in stolen body parts. Goggles is reunited with his ex-partner-in-crime, and they find come face-to-face with MOLCOS, the military's ultimate killing machine. **52 min.**

Cyber City Oedo 808: Data Three
The Vampire Case. One by one, genetics researchers are turning up dead — all with fang wounds on their necks. The most recent victim used his own blood to scrawl a cryptic message on the wall and left notes for a very unusual retro-virus on his computer. The trail leads Benten to a cryogenic suspension facility tethered at the top of a space elevator. But the frozen death of cryogenic sleep may not have any meaning to one of the undead ... and vampires can be very hungry when they wake up. **49 min.**

Domestic Home Video:
Cyber City Oedo 808: Data One
USM 1295 ▲ $19.95 ▲ VHS ▲ DUB ▲ Stereo ▲ 10/03/95
USM 1174 ▲ $29.95 ▲ VHS ▲ SUB ▲ Stereo ▲ 05/02/95
ID 2900CT ▲ $34.95 ▲ LD ▲ HYBRID ▲ Stereo ▲ 05/21/96
Cyber City Oedo 808: Data Two
USM 1296 ▲ $19.95 ▲ VHS ▲ DUB ▲ Stereo ▲ 10/03/95
USM 1175 ▲ $29.95 ▲ VHS ▲ SUB ▲ Stereo ▲ 08/08/95
ID 2901CT ▲ $34.95 ▲ LD ▲ HYBRID ▲ Stereo ▲ 05/21/96
Cyber City Oedo 808: Data Three
USM 1297 ▲ $19.95 ▲ VHS ▲ DUB ▲ Stereo ▲ 10/03/95
USM 1176 ▲ $29.95 ▲ VHS ▲ SUB ▲ Stereo ▲ 11/07/95
ID 2902CT ▲ $34.95 ▲ LD ▲ HYBRID ▲ Stereo ▲ 08/14/96
Cyber City Oedo 808 3-Pack Brick
USM 1352 ▲ $49.95 ▲ VHS ▲ DUB ▲ Stereo ▲ 10/03/95

Cybernetics Guardian
(1989) ©Soshin Pictures Enterprise Company/A.I.C.

Director: Koichi Ohata *Screenplay:* Mutsumi Sanjo *Character Design:* Atsushi Yamagata *Music:* Norimasa Yamanaka

Known in Japan more by its original release title, "Cyguard," CYBERNETICS GUARDIAN deals with urban blight in a *Robocop*-like way—by creating man-machine monsters to deal with crime. Futuristic cityscapes, unique and impressive mecha designs by director Koichi Ohata (GENOCYBER) and especially clean and well-drawn character designs by Atsushi Yamagata make this a visual treat; the background dealing with the issue of how to handle the slums of the future gets a little convoluted with the addition of a secret cult and too many political machinations. Thankfully, it's all settled in one big, cleansing, gladitorial robot battle. Released in Japan under the title "Seijûki (Holy-Beast Machine) Cyguard" by Sôshin Eizô; available in North America through U.S. Manga Corps. **45 min.**

Domestic Home Video:
USM 1442 ▲ $19.95 ▲ VHS ▲ DUB ▲ Stereo ▲ 02/04/97
USM 1330 ▲ $29.95 ▲ VHS ▲ SUB ▲ Stereo ▲ 02/06/96

 Made for Television Broadcast  Made for Home Video Release Made for Theatrical Release

Cyborg 009: Legend of the Super Galaxy

(1980) ©Toei Co., Ltd.

Director: Masayuki Akihiro

Feature-length film produced in commemoration of creator Shotaro Ishinomori's 25th year as a manga artist; based on his original manga of the same name. In the 26-episode 1968 TV series, we first met Professor Gilmore and the nine cyborgs he commands, each with a different super power (precognition, super strength, fire-breathing, etc.), all of whom use their powers to fight the forces of evil (ironically, it was an evil organization named "Black Ghost" which gave Professor Gilmore the wherewithal to retro-fit his cyborgs in the first place). In this latter-day theatrical feature, the tragic death of Cyborg 004—a man with weapons hidden all over his body—is depicted to shocking effect. Back in the '60s, thought of by some as the so-called "Golden Age" age of anime, CYBORG 009 was one of the most important shows on television, watched by children for the "neat robot gadgets" and by adults for the often surprising level of dramatic tension. To this day, the super ability of Cyborg 009, Joe Shimamura, can be seen on Japanese television programs and in comics; whenever you hear someone make an obvious "klick" with their jaw, they're paying tribute to 009's ability to accelerate to super sonic speeds with his "kasoku sôchi" or "acceleration unit." Released in Japan under the title "Cyborg 009 Gekijô Ban (Theatrical Version): Chô Ginga Densetsu (Super Galaxy Legend)" by Toei Video; available in North America through Best Film & Video. **130 min.**

Domestic Home Video:
BFV 967 ▲ $19.95 ▲ VHS ▲ DUB ▲ Mono

Dagger of Kamui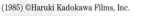

(1985) ©Haruki Kadokawa Films, Inc.

Director: Taro Rin

Based on an original story by Sampei Shirato and the subsequent 1969 TV series "Ninpû Kamui Gaiden." In this 1985 theatrical remake, viewers will encounter a 19th-century, globe-spanning adventure set during the closing years of Japan's feudal samurai government and the days of the American Wild West. A foundling, Jiro, is trained as a ninja to be the puppet of a sinister warrior-priest who molds him into a tool for recovering a treasure that could keep the Shogun in power. In director Taro Rin (HARMAGEDON, GALAXY EXPRESS 999)'s hands, the Japanese countryside of wind-blown woods, burning sulfur springs and snow-swept fields comes alive with elemental power. KAMUI is for those who love the ninja as portrayed in legend: the dark, romantic master of supernatural fighting arts, and can be considered a stylistic predecessor to 1993's NINJA SCROLL (see entry). Released in Japan under the title "Ninpû Kamui no Ken" (Ninja Wind Dagger of Kamui) by Kadokawa Shôten; available in North America through AnimEigo. Also released as THE BLADE OF KAMUI (a severely edited version), whose box erroneously describes it as taking place "on a faraway planet," by Best Film & Video. **133 min.**

Domestic Home Video:
The Dagger of Kamui
ANI AT093-008 ▲ $39.95 ▲ VHS ▲ SUB ▲ HiFi Stereo ▲ 10/06/93
ANI AD095-001 ▲ $59.95 ▲ LD ▲ CLV/CAV ▲ SUB ▲ 03/22/95
The Blade of Kamui
BFV 961 ▲ $19.95 ▲ VHS ▲ DUB ▲ Mono

Dallos

(1983) ©Pierrot Project Co. Ltd

Director: Mamoru Oshii *Screenplay:* Hisaishi Toriumi

Many anime fans know (if only through fan-sponsored quiz shows and the like at dedicated anime conventions) that the very first of the direct-to-video "OAVs" or "original animation videos" which changed the focus of the anime industry was DALLOS. What few fans know is, not only is DALLOS from the director of GHOST IN THE SHELL, it's also a four-volume (1983-84) OAV series. By removing the schedules, decency constraints and budgets of TV production, OAVs offer greater creative freedom for animators. On the business end, though, that freedom is balanced against the often formulaic micro-marketing approach to hardcore fans. As a science fiction story, DALLOS (only the first volume of which is available in the U.S.) is unlikely to win any awards; as a part of anime

history, it'll live forever. Released in Japan under the title "Dallos"; available in North America through Best Film and Video. **85 min.**

Domestic Home Video:
BFV 962 ▲ $19.95 ▲ VHS ▲ DUB ▲ Mono ▲ 11/15/95

Dancougar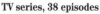

TV series, 38 episodes

(1985) ©Ashi Productions Co., Ltd./IDO International Co., Ltd.

Original Story: Keisuke Fujikawa *Directors:* Nobuyoshi Habara, Seiji Okuda *Character Design:* Indori-Goya *Art Director:* Torao Arai *Mecha Design:* Hisashi Hirai, Masami Obari *Music:* Takeshi Ike, Osamu Totsuka

Domestic home video release of the Japanese TV series. The story of an elite team of warriors who can harness the power of beasts, the five robots which combine to form one giant robot are likely to be reminiscent of the components of the Megazord in MIGHTY MORPHIN POWER RANGERS, or of the U.S.-broadcast VOLTRON. Followed in Japan by several OAVs—1985's 90-minute "Ushinawareta Monotachi e no Requiem" (Requiem for Victims), compiled from 60 minutes of footage from the TV series, with 30 minute of new footage; 1985's "Jûsenki-Tai Songs" (Songs from the Beast-Machine Team), including both songs from the series as well as new songs; 1987's "God Bless Dancougar," an 80-minute concert video starring the series' main characters; as well as "Hakunetsu no Shûshô" (White-Heat Final Chapter), a 1989-90 four-volume OAV sequel series. Released in Japan under the title "Chô Jû Kishin (Super Bestial God-Machine) Dancougar" by Bandai Visual; available in North America through Software Sculptors.

Dancougar Vol. 1: Meet The Almighty
Episode 1: EMPIRE'S DESIRE, Episode 2: I AM BEAST MECHA! HEAR ME ROAR!, Episode 3: SHAPIRO REBORN, Episode 4: TARGET: JAMMING SYSTEM, and Episode 5: THE MAN WHO CAME LAST. Led by the traitor Shapiro Keats, the Earth faces the threat of invasion by the alien forces of Emperor Muge. Our only hope lies in a secret robot unit called the Cyber-Beast Force and Earth's ultimate secret weapon - Super Beastial Machine God Dancougar! **120 min.**

Dancougar Vol. 2: The Battle Escalates
Episode 6: MAIDEN IN THE BATTLEFIELD, Episode 7: A KIND OF HERO, Episode 8: TRAPPED MEMORIES, Episode 9: HELL BEAST IN AMAZON, and Episode 10: LEGEND OF THE KNIGHT. Emperor Muge continues his relentless assault on planet Earth, but now there's a human defense system— The Cyber Beast Force! The Force: Shinobu, commander of the ultrasleek Eagle Fighter; Sara, pilot of the fearsome Land Cougar; Masato, operator of the ferocious Land Tiger; and Ryo, driver of the colossal Mammoth. Finally able to transform themselves into colossal robots and match the Emperor weapon for weapon, Earth's only chance for survival lies in the courage and cunning of its heroes and their Super Beastial Machine God Dancougar. **120 min.**

Dancougar Vol. 3: Survival of the Fiercest
Episode 11: SUPPORTING FIRE FROM THE ENEMY, Episode 12: DON'T WAKE UP MEGALOSAURS, Episode 13: BETRAY TOWN, Episode 14: STREET FIGHT, and Episode 15: GOD BLESS THE MACHINE, ACT 1. Now capable of "humanoid" transformations, the Cyber Beast Force is called into action as the Empire unleashes its newest weapon—a death-spewing monster of unearthly proportions. The only good news for the CBF is the savage infighting between two of the Empire's most formidable commanders: Death Gaia and the Earthling turncoat Shapiro Keats! **120 min.**

Domestic Home Video:
Dancougar Vol. 1: *Episodes 1-5*
SSVS 9601 ▲ $19.95 ▲ VHS ▲ SUB ▲ HiFi Stereo ▲ 07/02/96
Dancougar Vol. 2: *Episodes 6-10*
SSVS 9602 ▲ $19.95 ▲ VHS ▲ SUB ▲ HiFi Stereo ▲ 09/03/96
Dancougar Vol. 3: *Episodes 11-15*
SSVS 9603 ▲ $19.95 ▲ VHS ▲ SUB ▲ HiFi Stereo ▲ 11/05/96

Dangaio

OAV series, 3 episodes

(1987-89) ©A.I.C./Emotion/Artmic

Character Design and Director: Toshihiro Hirano *Screenplay:* Noboru Aikawa, Toshihiro Hirano, Koichi Ohata *Art Directors:* Masumi Higuchi, Hideaki Anno, Kazuhiro Arai *Mecha Design:* Shoji Kawamori, Koichi Ohata, Yasushi Ishizu, Masami Obari *Music:* Michiaki Watanabe, Yasunori Honda

A tribute to giant robot shows from the 70's where a quartet of super-powered teenagers from different

planets are trapped in a galactic power struggle and use their giant robot to fight their way out and later defend the decided underdog of the conflict. The third episode of the series, in which thwarted thug Gil Berg returns to smite the heroes, sports a memorably downbeat ending. Toshiro Hirano (ICZER-ONE) directs and handles character design, while designers Masami Obari (FATAL FURY), Koichi Ohata (MD GEIST) and Shoji Kawamori (MACROSS) create the pretty darn cool-looking giant robots and ships of the series. Hideaki Anno (GUNBUSTER, NEON GENESIS EVANGELION) is credited with art direction. Seen in North America with two spellings for the title— "Dangaio" is the U.S. Renditions three-volume subtitled version, while "Dangaioh" (long "o" at the end) is Manga Entertainment's English version, which is compressed compilation-style, meaning all three volumes have been compressed together to form a single story on one tape. The first expository episode is told in flashback with what was the original introduction to Episode 2. Released in Japan under the title "Haja Taisei (Great Planet Evil-Destroyer) Dangaiô" by Bandai Visual; currently available in North America through Manga Entertainment.

Dangaio Part 1
Professor Tarsan, a capitalistic space scientist, claims that he created the four youths and he plans to sell them as the ultimate mecha warriors to the evil "Bunker Pirates." Equipped with their psionic abilities and their Danfighters, the four escape and set out on a voyage that will lead them to a deadly encounter with the pirates which forces them to form the ultimate mechanical robot - Dangaio! **45 min.**

Dangaio Part 2: *Spiral Knuckles in Tears*
The Dangaio team is training for the next Bunker attack. Their training is put to the test when three assassins arrive on their snowbound base world. During the battle, Lamba must confront horrifying revelations about their terrifying past. Once again the four psychics and Prof. Tarsan unleash the power of Dangaio in a battle for survival. **45 min.**

Dangaio Part 3: *The Demonic Vengeance of Gil Berg*
In the final episode, Roll Kran returns to his homeworld Latecia and finds his people in rebellion against the Bunker Pirates. Much to his surprise, his return home is met with hostility by his old friends in the resistance who blame him for Latecia's military occupation. Roll must defend his world and the Dangaio team from the insane onslaught of the Bunker forces led by the resurrected Gil Berg. **45 min.**

Domestic Home Video:
Dangaio Part 1
USR VD2 ▲ $34.95 ▲ VHS ▲ SUB ▲ Stereo ▲ 02/01/90 ▲ Out of Print
Dangaio Part 2
USR VD7 ▲ $34.95 ▲ VHS ▲ SUB ▲ Stereo ▲ 07/01/92 ▲ Out of Print
Dangaio Part 3
USR VD8 ▲ $34.95 ▲ VHS ▲ SUB ▲ Stereo ▲ 07/01/92 ▲ Out of Print
Dangaioh: Hyper Combat Unit
MGV 636239 ▲ $19.95 ▲ VHS ▲ DUB ▲ HiFi Stereo ▲ 03/19/96

Dangard Ace   [TV]
TV series, 26 episodes
(1977-78) ©Toei Animation Co. Ltd./Jim Terry Productions

Created by: Leiji Matsumoto and Dan Kobayashi *Music:* Shunsuke Kikuchi

The first two episodes from the 1977-78 TV series "Wakusei Robo Danguard A (Ace)," as broadcast in the U.S. as part of the "Force Five" TV series. (The original Japanese series contained 56 episodes, but only 26 were incorporated into the American "Force Five" version). Unusual "giant robot" entry as created by Leiji Matsumoto, the artist who dominated anime in the late '70s and early '80s with such series as "Uchû Kaizoku (Space Pirate) Captain Harlock" and GALAXY EXPRESS 999 (see entry). Note that DANGUARD ACE is unconnected to the so-called "Leijiverse" of loose continuity and character-swapping other that many of his creations share. TV series not yet available on home video in Japan; released in North America by Parade Video.

2 episodes: in ENTER CAPTAIN MASK, Winstar and the crew at the World Space Institute meet Captain Mask who has escaped from Commisar Krell's Slave Station. In DOWN FROM MACH 2, Captain Mask assumes his duties as instructor on Dangard Ace and the future pilots learn just how tough he's going to be. **46 min.**

Domestic Home Video:
PRV 6610 ▲ $12.95 ▲ VHS ▲ DUB ▲ Mono ▲ 02/01/93

Dark Warrior   [OAV] ✦
OAV series, 2 episodes
(1991) ©Sho Takeshima/Kadokawa Publishing/Daiei Co., Ltd.

Director: Masahisa Ishida *Screenplay:* Yu Yamamoto *Character Design:* Kenichi Onuki *Created by:* Sho Takejima

Based on the novel of the same name by author Sho Takejima, whose life was struck short the year of this two-volume OAV release due to a tragic motorcycle accident. DARK WARRIOR unites several themes from popular action movies: Silicon Valley computer scientists, A.I. technology, a government agency that can control your destiny at will, and an alien takeover of the human race. In the best tradition of Philip K. Dick, a brilliant 20-year-old scientist named Joe working at a top Silicon Valley company discovers his life has been a lie and that he's a top-secret clone with super-powers created in a special project entitled "System God-Blood," leading to gore aplenty as he fights the agents that have come to claim him. Animation is low-end for an OAV, but the story is compelling in the same way action-movies are. Takes place in Silicon Valley and Salinas, California. Released in Japan under the title "Makyû Senjô" (Magic-Labyrinth Battlefield) by Daiei/ Tokuma Japan Communications; available in North America through A.D. Vision.

Dark Warrior: *First Strike*
When computer genius Joe Takami hacks into the Pentagon's computer in search of information on a mysterious girl, he uncovers evidence of a secret government experiment. Now it seems that everyone, including his best friend and his personal computer, is turning against him— and a ruthless team of ninjas has marked him for death! Joe must depend on the unsuspected powers that lie buried within his past, and evade the government assassins before they terminate the human genetic experiment named Joe Takami. **60 min.**

Dark Warrior Part 2: *Jihad*
After discovering that he is a clone created at the command of David Rockford, CEO of America's largest electronics company, Joe Takagami sets out on a path for revenge. Pursued by an army of superhuman Battle Beings, along the way he meets Aya Lee Rose, a young girl with very special powers. Together they face the combined might of Rockford Electronics. **60 min.**

Domestic Home Video:
Dark Warrior
ADV DW/001 ▲ $29.95 ▲ VHS ▲ SUB ▲ HiFi Surround ▲ 06/25/96
Dark Warrior Part 2
ADV DW/002 ▲ $29.95 ▲ VHS ▲ SUB ▲ HiFi Surround ▲ 10/15/96

Deluxe Ariel   [OAV] ✦
OAV series, 2 episodes
(1991) ©Yuichi Sasamoto/Ariel Project

Character Design: Masahisa Suzuki *Director:* Junichi Watanabe *Screenplay:* Junichi Watanabe, Muneo Kubo *Original Story:* Yuichi Sasamoto *Music:* Kohei Tanaka

The follow-up 2-part OAV series to ARIEL (see entry). (The acronym "ARIEL," by the way, stands for [A]ll- [A]round [I]ntercept and [E]scort [L]ady.) Released in Japan as "Deluxe Ariel" by Pony Canyon; available in North America through U.S. Manga Corps.

Deluxe Ariel 1
Those incompetent aliens are still plotting to conquer Earth! The only obstacle in their path is the giant, feminine robot Ariel. But the young pilots have lives of their own. When Kazumi receives a mysterious love letter from a secret admirer, should she cancel her first date, just to save Earth? **45 min.**

Deluxe Ariel 2
Things have not gone well for the invaders. Their budget has been slashed and their technology is falling apart, but now their star drive has failed and their immense starship is about to crash into Tokyo! And unless something is done really soon, the impact will start a chain reaction that will extinguish all life on Earth! **45 min.**

Domestic Home Video:
Deluxe Ariel 1
USM 1434 ▲ $29.95 ▲ VHS ▲ SUB ▲ Stereo ▲ 06/04/96
Deluxe Ariel 2
USM 1435 ▲ $29.95 ▲ VHS ▲ SUB ▲ Stereo ▲ 09/03/96

Demon Beast Invasion

OAV series, 6 volumes

(1990-94) ©T. Maeda/Daiei Co. Ltd.

Director: Jun Fukuda (1,2,5,6), Juki Yoma (3,4) *Script:* Joji Maki (1,2), Wataru Amano (3-6) *Art Director:* Naoto Yokose (1,2), Kengo Inagaki (3,4), Geki Katsumata (5,6) *Character Design:* Mari Muzuta (1,2), Hisashi Ezura (3,4), Toshikazu Usami (5,6) *Music Director:* Teruo Takahama *Original Author:* Toshio Maeda

One hundred million years ago, an ecological disaster drove them from their homeworld. Now the Demon Beasts have returned, and they're ready to clean up the old homestead! Unable to survive in Earth's new environment, they seek out human women to mate with ... to create a new breed of Demon Beast who will clear the way for the return of the rest of its brood. Hardcore demon-sex in the style of LEGEND OF THE OVERFIEND: UROTSUKI DÔJI, but not as well animated. Alien invasion. With cops. Whatever. Released in Japan as "Yôjû Kyôshitsu" (Demon-Beast Classroom) by Daiei/Tokuma Japan Communications; available in North America through Anime 18.

Demon Beast Invasion 1

The Demon Beasts are on the run from Kasu and Muneto, agents of the Interplanetary Mutual Observation Agency. Vowing to stop the creatures from stealing the Earth, they race to track down their latest suspect. But when Muneto's old friends, Tsutomu and Kayo, are caught up in this covert war, can he keep his mind on the case long enough to find the killer alien? **48 min.**

Demon Beast Invasion 2

Devastated by the loss of both Tsutomu and Kasu, Kayo and Muneto struggle to come to terms with their feelings. The mating of Kayo and the possessed Tsutomu has yielded a horrifying child that grows within its mother. Forcing its own birth prematurely, it moves to create an army of mindless fighters from the ranks of Kayo's own friends. As the Demon Beast brood floats silently in orbit awaiting their vanguard's success, the Demon Child vows to murder Muneto to avenge its father's death! As time runs out, the forces of IMO Agency renew their counter-strike, and Muneto gains a new partner. **45 min.**

Demon Beast Invasion 3

The invasion is over, but the nightmare lives on as the demon-spawn plots a deadly family reunion. But this time the Interplanetary Mutual Observation Agency dispatches a trio of female warriors to finish the job. They're cold, efficient, deadly, beautiful... and completely out of their league. They'll need Muneto and Kayo to unleash the power that defeated the Demon Beast last time. **45 min.**

Demon Beast Invasion 4

This time, both Kayo and Muneto are targets! When the Demon Beast appears at Muneto's family temple, Muneto's father orders the two lovers to go to the same area where Kayo's cousin, Miyuki, lives. Not only is the Demon Beast still after Kayo, but Miyuki harbors an ancient force within her soul— and it wants Muneto! The ensuing battle may be more than even Kayo and Muneto can handle! **45 min.**

Demon Beast Invasion 5

The Demon Beast has multiplied and is taking over gang members' bodies in Hong Kong. The Mutual Observation Agency is on the case, but the only sure way to cure someone who gives birth to the Demon Beast is to kill them! Will Muneto be gaining a new ally, or another enemy? **45 min.**

Demon Beast Invasion 6

The Demon Beast is dead—blown apart outside of Hong Kong. The invasion is finally over... or is it? Something is killing Muneto's classmates during a school trip, and Kayo senses the presence of the Demon Beast. Is there a link to the island legend of a love between a young girl and a monster? **45 min.**

Domestic Home Video:

Demon Beast Invasion 1
A18 1311 ▲ $29.95 ▲ VHS ▲ SUB ▲ Stereo ▲ 08/08/95
Demon Beast Invasion 2
A18 1312 ▲ $29.95 ▲ VHS ▲ SUB ▲ Stereo ▲ 12/05/95
Demon Beast Invasion 3
A18 1313 ▲ $29.95 ▲ VHS ▲ SUB ▲ Stereo ▲ 02/06/96
Demon Beast Invasion 4
A18 1314 ▲ $29.95 ▲ VHS ▲ SUB ▲ Stereo ▲ 04/02/96
Demon Beast Invasion 5
A18 1315 ▲ $29.95 ▲ VHS ▲ SUB ▲ Stereo ▲ 07/02/96
Demon Beast Invasion 6
A18 1316 ▲ $29.95 ▲ VHS ▲ SUB ▲ Stereo ▲ 09/03/96

Demon City Shinjuku

(1988) ©Hideyuki Kikuchi, Asahi Sonorama, Video Art, Japan Home Video.

Original Story: Hideyuki Kikuchi *Character Design & Director:* Yoshiaki Kawajiri *Script:* Kaori Okamura *Setting:* Masao Maruyama *Animation Director:* Naoyuki Onda *Art Director:* Yuji Ikeda

From the director of WICKED CITY and NINJA SCROLL; based on an original story by WICKED CITY's Hideyuki Kikuchi. DEMON CITY SHINJUKU has the same fabulous visual style as WICKED CITY, but the story is more on the simplistic side: An evil sorcerer named Levi Rah has cordoned off Tokyo's high-rise-filled Shinjuku district via a mystically summoned earthquake in order to summon the forces of darkness. In order to save a kidnapped dignitary, a young man, accompanied the dignitary's daughter, must fight his way through this nightmare ghost city and its deadly supernatural creatures to reclaim his father's mystical sword and defeat the Rah. Gorgeous animation, fascinating monsters, but a rather abrupt ending. Director Kawajiri also handles the clean character designs. Worth seeing for the nifty visuals alone. Released in Japan under the title "Makai Toshi Shinjuku" (Demon City Shinjuku) by Japan Home Video; available in North America through U.S. Manga Corps. **82 min.**

Domestic Home Video:

USM 1351 ▲ $19.95 ▲ VHS ▲ DUB ▲ Stereo ▲ 09/05/95
USM 1107 ▲ $29.95 ▲ VHS ▲ SUB ▲ Stereo ▲ 01/27/94
ID 2869CT ▲ $39.95 ▲ LD-CLV/CAV ▲ SUB ▲ Stereo ▲ 11/30/94

Detonator Orgun

OAV series, 3 volumes

(1991) ©Darts/Artmic

Director: Masami Obari *Script & Original Story:* Hideki Kakinuma *Music:* Susumu Hirasawa *Character Design:* Michitaka Kikuchi *Production Design:* Hideki Kakinuma, Kimitoshi Yamane, Junichi Akutsu

Completely original 1991 three-volume OAV series (no "based on the manga by"; no "based on the TV of the same name") in which a glittering, antiseptic future is threatened by an invasion from outer space. A bored young man, Tomoru Shindo, stirs himself from his video game fantasies and takes on the mantle of hero when a suit of alien armor arrives on Earth and seeks him out to be the planet's protector. From the director of FATAL FURY, with character designs by Michitaka (SILENT MÖBIUS) Kikuchi. Mecha designs by Kimitoshi Yamane (THE VISION OF ESCAFLOWNE, 08TH MS TEAM, MOBILE SUIT G-GUNDAM). Released in Japan under the title "Detonator Orgun" by Polydor; available in North America through U.S. Manga Corps.

Detonator Orgun Part 1

As he struggles to grasp what is happening, Michi, a young Earth Defense Forces intelligence researcher along with Izack, a super computer, race to unlock the secrets of a suit of alien armor. But the armor seems to have an agenda all of its own! A force of hostile aliens arrives and dispatches a killing machine in Tomoru's city. Its mission: destroy the renegade soldier, Orgun. But what it finds is a confused Tomoru, who now has to fight an enemy straight out of his worst nightmares! **57 min.**

Detonator Orgun Part 2

Tomoru's connection to the renegade soldier Orgun still isn't clear and he wants to keep it that way. Every memory Michi draws from his subconscious frightens him more and more, and he begins to rebel against his new role as the only human able to resist the coming Evoluder invasion. Meanwhile, Orgun's presence has drawn two more aliens to Earth: one a deadly enemy, the other a possible ally. As the psychic Kumi Jefferson begins to make contact with the aliens' leader, and Tomoru tries to escape his destiny, City Number 5 is once again under fire as Orgun is hunted by this latest threat. With the EDF forces powerless to stop it, the city shakes under his assault. Meanwhile, Michi finds her own dreams being invaded by the aliens. **49 min.**

Detonator Orgun Part 3

With the Evoluder battle planet only three months away, things look completely hopeless for the embattled Earth forces ... until Tomoru finally unlocks the secret behind the advanced technology of Orgun's weapons systems. For the first time, the Earth Defense Force will pose a real threat to their enemies, but is there enough time to prepare for the final battle? As Earth's armies scramble to build their new hardware, psychic Kumi

Jefferson's connection with the invaders' leader deepens. With the fate of Earth hanging in the balance, a last minute appeal from her may be the key to turning the battle to the EDF's advantage. **53 min.**

Domestic Home Video:
Detonator Orgun Part 1
USM 1088 ▲ $29.95 ▲ VHS ▲ SUB ▲ Stereo ▲ 06/01/94
ID 2878CT ▲ $34.95 ▲ LD ▲ SUB ▲ Stereo ▲ 05/24/95

Detonator Orgun Part 2
USM 1089 ▲ $29.95 ▲ VHS ▲ SUB ▲ Stereo ▲ 12/07/94
ID 2890CT ▲ $34.95 ▲ LD ▲ SUB ▲ HiFi Stereo ▲ 12/20/95

Detonator Orgun Part 3
USM 1090 ▲ $29.95 ▲ VHS ▲ SUB ▲ Stereo ▲ 03/07/95
ID 2894CT ▲ $34.95 ▲ LD ▲ SUB ▲ HiFi Stereo ▲ 03/06/96

Devil Hunter Yohko
OAV series, 6 volumes

(1990-95) ©N.C.S./Toho Co. Ltd./Madhouse

Original Story: Juzo Mutsuki *Character Design:* Takeshi Miyao *Script:* Yoshihiro Tomita *Screenplay:* Hisaya Takabayashi (Part 2), Katsuhisa Yamada (Part 3) *Directors:* Tetsuro Aoki (Part 1), Hisashi Abe (Parts 2&3), Harou Itsuki (4-ever), Junichi Sakata (Part 5), Akiyuki Shinbo (Part 6) *Art Directors:* Hidetoshi Kaneko (Part 5), Masumi Nishikawa (Part 5) *Character Design:* Yuzo Sato (Part 5), Takeshi Miyao (Parts 5&6), Yoshimitsu Ohashi (Part 6) *Music:* Hiroya Watanabe

Comedy-drama of teenage cutie fighting netherworld demons. Teenage Yohko is your typical Japanese high school girl on the outside, but she's also the 108th generational heir to a legacy of devil hunters. Since her mother flubbed the job of staying chaste until she could assume the family mantle, the burden of protecting the world from things that go bump in the night now falls on Yohko. With the help of her ninja Granny, Yohko learns to swing an exorcist's sword. SAILOR MOON-like in visuals and story (no, really!), with more sexual content and Hong Kong action flick-like improbable martial arts. That the series has more than a little in common with the live-action film *Buffy the Vampire Slayer* is no discredit—those who loved the campiness of *Buffy* are certain to find in YOHKO its anime twin. According to some reports, the OAV series was produced in tandem with a TV game of the same name, which may give a hint to the series' pacing and action. Released in Japan as "Mamono Hunter Yôko" by Toho; available in North America through A.D. Vision.

Devil Hunter Yohko
Grandma says Yohko is the only one who can stop our world from being invaded by an army of demons, and that they'll do anything they can to get rid of her first. So it looks like she'll be taking over the family business, even if it's not the most glamorous occupation. She just hopes that this bit about her having to stay "physically pure" isn't going to put a crimp in her social life. I mean, she is in high school, after all. **45 min.**

Devil Hunter Yohko 2 & 3
In PART 2, a local shrine is destroyed and 16-year-old Yohko is stuck with the task of shoving the vengeful spirits back into their graves. Even confronting killer construction equipment, woman-eating trees and possessed puppy dogs, however, pales in comparison to the task of training her new apprentice, Azusa; and to complicate matters even further, Yohko's pal Chigako has her own agenda for exploiting her friend's new talents. Yohko's skills are put to the ultimate test when she finds herself kidnapped to a strange alternate dimension in PART 3, where she must battle Harpy, Griffon and Dragonewt in deadly mortal combat. At stake: the life of Biryu, the handsome son of Ryu-O, the Dragon King. Aiding Yohko are the mysterious sorceress Yanagi and Biryu's servant, Obaba; but unbeknownst to our intrepid heroine, her so-called "allies" have plans of their own for Biryu's future... **60 min.**

Devil Hunter Yohko 4-Ever: *The Music Collection*
For those who didn't get enough of that buxom teenage exorcist in the red silk dress in her first three OAV adventures, there's a music video collection as well. This is a compilation of original animation, live-action, and the hottest animated clips from *Devil Hunter Yohko Parts 1, 2* and *3*, all combined with a soundtrack designed to drive Yohko-holics into a frenzy. **30 min.**

Devil Hunter Yohko 5
She's cheated death before, but bouncy teenage exorcist Yohko Mano steps beyond the veil into the greatest mystery of all. The question is, will her passed-on condition prove permanent? The action begins as all hell literally breaks loose when the master of the shadow demons possesses the body of Yohko's new boyfriend, then uses the body of another friend to open the door to the demon plane. By the time Yohko and Grandma realize what's going on, it's way too late and the last two generations of devil hunters find

themselves hopelessly outmatched. Yohko doesn't even know the meaning of the word "hopeless," however, and she'll find some way to stop the forces of evil, even if it literally kills her! **50 min.**

Devil Hunter Yohko 6
A new girl who looks just like Yohko shows up at school. It's bad enough when this impersonator beats Yohko to the punch in putting the moves on a sexy new teacher, but when the Yohko clone starts fighting demons as well, with a young assistant who looks suspiciously like Yohko's own Azusa, things are really getting out of hand! Can Yohko beat her toughest opponent ever? And what does Grandma's secret past have to do with the origin of the new Anti-Devil Hunter? **45 min.**

Domestic Home Video:
Devil Hunter Yohko
ADV Y/001 ▲ $29.95 ▲ VHS ▲ SUB ▲ HiFi Surround ▲ 12/10/92
ADV Y/001L ▲ $34.95 ▲ LD ▲ SUB ▲ HiFi Surround ▲ 04/13/94

Devil Hunter Yohko: *Special Edition*
Dubbed version with extra footage not on subtitled version. (50 min.)
ADV Y/001D ▲ $19.95 ▲ VHS ▲ DUB ▲ HiFi Surround ▲ 01/16/96

Devil Hunter Yohko 2 & 3
ADV Y/023 ▲ $34.95 ▲ VHS ▲ SUB ▲ HiFi Surround ▲ 11/02/94

Devil Hunter Yohko 4-Ever
ADV Y/004 ▲ $19.95 ▲ VHS ▲ SUB ▲ HiFi Surround ▲ 11/02/94

Devil Hunter Yohko 4 & 5
Devil Hunter Yohko 4-Ever and Devil Hunter Yohko 5 together on one tape. (75 min.)
ADV Y/045 ▲ $34.95 ▲ VHS ▲ SUB ▲ HiFi Surround ▲ 11/15/95

Devil Hunter Yohko 5
ADV Y/005 ▲ $29.95 ▲ VHS ▲ SUB ▲ HiFi Surround ▲ 06/22/95

Devil Hunter Yohko 6
ADV Y/006 ▲ $29.95 ▲ VHS ▲ SUB ▲ HiFi Surround ▲ 11/21/95

Devilman
OAV Series, 2 volumes

(1987-90) ©Dynamic Planning/Kodansha/Bandai Visual

Original Work and Supervisor: Go Nagai *Director:* Tsutomu Iida *Script:* Go Nagai, Tsutomu Iida *Character Design:* Kazuo Komatsubara *Music:* Kenji Kawai

Two-volume OAV remake of the famous 1972-73 TV series, which in turn is based on the infamous original manga of the same name by creator Go Nagai (ABASHIRI FAMILY, CUTEY HONEY). The human race is threatened by an invasion of demons, and to fight them, a young man named Akira allows himself to be possessed by a demon in order to fight the hellish menace on its own terms. His war with them destroys property and lives as the demons often strike at his human friends and loved ones. Violent and gory, DEVILMAN is only one of the reasons creator Nagai's earned the unofficial nickname "PTA's Favorite Target," for just like a naughty little boy always trying to see how much he can get away with, it's difficult even for a woman in this reasonably enlightened age to take the bare boobies, scatalogical humor, and spurting blood he loves to pack into his manga and anime series *too* seriously. (For more information, author Fred Schodt's MANGA! MANGA! THE WORLD OF JAPANESE COMICS has an excellent look at some of Nagai's early manga work, especially the series that set the heads of the Japanese PTA on fire back in those days.) OAV remake released in Japan under the title "Devilman" by Kodansha/King Record; available in North America through U.S. Renditions and Manga Entertainment.

Devilman Vol. 1: *The Birth*
First Akira's parents go missing, then his pet rabbit is viciously slaughtered and finally his best friend, Ryo Asuka, reveals a terrifying secret - something that guarantees that Akira's life can never be the same again. Ryo's dead archaeologist father left him a dark and sinister legacy, knowledge of which may only condemn Ryo in the same way it condemned his father - to an eternal sentence of suffering and torment. However, Ryo understands that his legacy also has the power to salvage the human race from torturous damnation at the hands of demons. But whoever kills a demon must become a demon - and only one who is pure of heart can possess the body of a demon... only one like Akira. **55 min.**

Devilman Vol. 2: *Demon Bird*
Akira is confronted by more deadly horror as obscene and twisted creatures struggle to take control of the world. Miki, his girlfriend, is brutally attacked by the fiendish water-demon Gelmar whilst Devilman takes on Jinmen, who carries the tortured souls of his victims in his gruesome shell. The

 Made for Television Broadcast Made for Home Video Release  Made for Theatrical Release

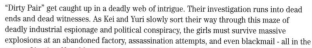

combination of human and demon makes Akira a formidable force... until he meets the talons of Siren, the invincible Demon Bird. **55 min.**

Domestic Home Video:
Devilman Vol. 1
MGV 634791 ▲ $14.95 ▲ VHS ▲ DUB ▲ HiFi Stereo ▲ 05/23/95
USR DIE03 ▲ $19.95 ▲ VHS ▲ SUB ▲ HiFi Stereo ▲ 08/25/93
Devilman Vol. 2
MGV 634793 ▲ $14.95 ▲ VHS ▲ DUB ▲ HiFi Stereo ▲ 05/23/95
USR DIE05 ▲ $19.95 ▲ VHS ▲ SUB ▲ HiFi Stereo ▲ 11/03/93

Dirty Pair   OAV 🎆 🌙
OAV series, 3 volumes
(1985/87/90) ©1986 Haruka Takachiho/Studio Nue/Sunrise Inc./NTV

Created by: Haruka Takachiho *Mecha Design:* Studio Nue, Kazutaka Miyatake, Yasushi Ishizu *Character Design:* Tsukasa Dokite *Screenplay:* Kazunori Ito (Nolandia), Fuyushi Itsutake (Flight 005), Hiroyuki Hoshiyama (Eden) *Music:* Yoshihiro Kunimoto (Nolandia), Toru Okada (Flight 005), Kenzo Shiguma (Eden) *Art Director:* Ariaki Okada (Flight 005), Mitsuharu Miyama (Eden) *Director:* Mashahara Okuwaki (Nolandia), Toshihumi Takizawa (Flight 005), Koichi Mashita (Eden)

The essential babes-in-bikinis-with-guns franchise, the "Dirty Pair" were created by Studio Nue head Haruka Takachiho as the stars of his first novel (illustrated by "Mobile Suit Gundam"'s Yoshikazu Yasuhiko), and their animated adaptation quickly proved to be a giant hit. Kei and Yuri are "trouble consultants," code-named the "Lovely Angels," agents for the WWWA, a government organization of the future that seems to operate like a galaxy-wide FBI. Lovely and lethal as two James Bond girls (in equally unrealistic action attire), these two troubleshooters typically tend to cause more trouble and chaos than they were originally called in to solve—none of it *really* being their fault, anymore than widespread property destruction is *any* action hero's fault. A OAV sequel series not yet available in the U.S., "Dirty Pair Flash," involves a different (some might say alternate) future, in which Kei and Yuri sport toned-down I.Q.s and, in the grand tradition of CUTEY HONEY (see entry), make spinning, mid-air "nudie transformations" into their outfits. Five issues of an English-translated DIRTY PAIR comic, using actual cel art from five of the original TV episodes, have also been released by Viz Comics. References to DIRTY PAIR strike far and wide in fandom; most notably the infamous anime in-jokes inserted by anime fan Rick Sternbach into the *Star Trek: The Next Generation* TV show, such as where a Ferengi commander begins to intone (supposedly in Ferengese) a secret code which begins: "Ke-i, Yu-ri...." A made-in-America manga version with original stories is also available from Dark Horse Comics. Released in Japan under the titles "Dirty Pair no Dai-Shôbu: Nolandia no Nazo (The Dirty Pair's Great Victory: The Mystery of Nolandia)," "Dirty Pair: Bôryaku 005 Ben (Conspiracy of Flight 005)," and "Dirty Pair: Gekijô Hen (The Movie)" by Bandai Visual; available in North America through Streamline Pictures.

Dirty Pair: *Affair on Nolandia*
(1985) Kei and Yuri, find themelves trapped in a bizarre arboreal wonderland on the planet Ukbar, where a routine investigation reveals a deadly caper of galactic conquest. As the mystery unfolds, the two special agents tangle with a pair of villains who will stop at nothing in their quest to attain ultimate power. The girls are forced to deal with unexpected psychic attacks, brutal murders, sabotage and wild, improbable mind games as they cope with their formidable adversaries. The finale, a classic chase sequence, zooms by with ferocious vitality and exciting, non-stop action. **57 min.**

Dirty Pair: *Project Eden*
(1987) In 2141 A.D., galactic travel is possible only through the use of warp engines made of the rare, extremely valuable metal vizorium, which comes from the planet Agerna. Agerna is involved in a power struggle between two rival nations for control of this precious natural resource. The leaders of Edia and Uldas both lay claim to the vizorium, and the rivalry has created a booming black market for the metal. When a major vizorium refinery is destroyed, the stage is set for all out war. This brings Kei and Yuri, "The Dirty Pair," onto the scene. These top agents of WWWA stumble upon a deranged biochemical genius, Professor Wattsmann, who believes life is lurking inside the atomic structure of vizorium. If he has his way, he will bring this new lifeform into existence. This geological Dr. Frankenstein meets his match in the Dirty Pair, and before the final credits roll, the girls treat Agerna to their own personal brand of "planetary makeover." **80 min.**

Dirty Pair: *Flight 005 Conspiracy*
(1990) The WWWA is called to investigate a mysterious explosion which destroyed Dubahl Spaceliner Flight 005, as well as to look into the disappearance of the world's key scientist involved in production of liquid ignite. Kei and Yuri - the agency's hottest investigators - are assigned to both cases. Shuttling between the planets Dahl, Dubahl, and Zahl, the

"Dirty Pair" get caught up in a deadly web of intrigue. Their investigation runs into dead ends and dead witnesses. As Kei and Yuri slowly sort their way through this maze of deadly industrial espionage and political conspiracy, the girls must survive massive explosions at an abandoned factory, assassination attempts, and even blackmail - all in the name of justice. Not able to trust anyone, the Dirty Pair must rely on their own skills and intuition in order to get to the bottom of this ruthless crime. A departure from the usual high-spirited antics which have defined the Dirty Pair, *Flight 005 Conspiracy* is a complex thriller which unfolds in true dramatic fashion. **60 min.**

Domestic Home Video:
Dirty Pair: *Affair on Nolandia*
SPV 90403 ▲ $19.95 ▲ VHS ▲ DUB ▲ Mono ▲ CC ▲ 03/15/93
ID 2978SE ▲ $39.95 ▲ LD ▲ DUB ▲ 12/04/96
Dirty Pair: *Project Eden*
SPV 90813 ▲ $19.95 ▲ VHS ▲ DUB ▲ Mono ▲ CC ▲ 04/15/94
Dirty Pair: *Flight 005 Conspiracy*
SPV 90883 ▲ $19.95 ▲ VHS ▲ DUB ▲ Mono ▲ CC ▲ 06/01/94

Dog Soldier: Shadows of the Past   OAV 🎆 🌙
(1989) ©Movic/Sony Music Entertainment (Japan) Inc.

Director: Hiroyuki Ebata *Based on the comic by:* Tetsuya Saruwatari *Screenplay:* Sho Aikawa *Character Design:* Masateru Kudo *Art Director:* Takuji Jizomoto *Animation Producers:* Motomu Sakamoto, Nagateru Katou

Based on the manga of the same name by Tetsuya Saruwatari. Modern day action-adventure starring a young Japanese-American commando who dresses in *Rambo: First Blood II* mode, sent to retrieve a putative AIDS virus from a criminal syndicate linked to his past. Released in Japan under the title "Dog Soldier" by Sony Music; available in North America through U.S. Manga Corps. **45 min.**

Domestic Home Video:
USM 1470 ▲ $14.95 ▲ VHS ▲ DUB ▲ Stereo ▲ 06/18/96
USM 1032 ▲ $34.95 ▲ VHS ▲ SUB ▲ Stereo ▲ 05/20/92
ID 2207CT ▲ $29.95 ▲ LD ▲ SUB ▲ Stereo ▲ 02/17/93

Dôkyûsei: Natsu no Owari ni *See* END OF SUMMER

Dominion Tank Police   OAV 🎆 🌙
OAV series, 4 acts
(1989) ©Masamune Shirow/Hakusensha/Agent 21/Toshiba Video Softwares, Inc.

Original Story: Masamune Shirow *Screenplay:* Koichi Mashimo (Acts I&II), Dai Kono (Acts III&IV) *Directors:* Koichi Mashimo (Acts I&II), Taka'aki Ishiyama (Acts III&IV) *Character Design and Director of Animation:* Hiroki Takagi *Art Director:* Mitsuharu Miyamae (Acts I&II), Osamu Honda (Acts III&IV)

Based on the manga of the same name by Masamune "APPLESEED" Shirow (published in English by Dark Horse Comics). In a future where the level of pollution in the atmosphere is so bad that no one goes out of the house without checking their rad and contam levels, the cops need armored tanks to help fight their war on crime. Bubbly ace tank-cop Leona and her pet tank Bonaparte will either save the city or destroy it trying. Shirow goes for the gusto in a tale with over-the-top cops, guns and *Police Academy*-style hijinks. Look for very America comic-style characters the "cat-girls" Vols. 3-4 of the four-volume OAV series are directed by KISHIN CORPS' Taka'aki Ishiyama. Followed in Japan (not yet available in the U.S.) by a 1993-94 sequel OAV series under the title "Tokusô Sensha-Tai (Special-Assignment TankTeam) Dominion," which is based on the comic of the same name running in COMIC GAIA manga magazine. Released in Japan under the title "Dominion" by Toshiba EMI; available in North America through U.S. Manga Corps. **Also see *New Dominion Tank Police* entry.**

Dominion Tank Police Act I
The space-age law and order patrol welcomes its newest member, Leona, during a round of "grenade golf" which puts the "terror" back into their interrogation of a suspect. However, these extreme tactics are necessary against the notorious Buaku gang. This gang stoops so low as to terrorize a hospital in order to steal the urine samples of people unaffected by the toxic atmosphere. They only escape the fearsome Tank Police by virtue of a

deadly striptease performed by the feline crime sisters. **40 min.**

Dominion Tank Police Act II

The ruthless Buaku gang is still at large, and still committed to stealing that ever so precious commodity... urine of "healthy" people. The elite squad hounds Buaku and the wicked "Cat" sisters as they try once again to rob the "hospital for healthy people" of its valuable collection of human excretions. As the Tank Police pours after them, Buaku unleashes his new secret weapon (with phallic potential) that he's sure will stop the tanks in their tracks. **40 min.**

Dominion Tank Police Act III

Leona Ozaki, the newest member of the Tank Police, is assimilating well to their none-too-gentle style of handling criminal suspects. It's a good thing, too, because she is about to experience the "hospitality" of the vicious Buaku gang firsthand. This time, the gang is not out to steal the urine of "healthy" people. Rather, they're after an 80-year-old nude painting of Buaku himself - the last known artwork created while the world was still environmentally healthy. What is the secret behind this mysterious painting? How will Leona escape the deadly trap Buaku has set for her? **40 min.**

Dominion Tank Police Act IV

We have followed the acts of the deadly Buaku gang and seen the Tank Police - crime busters extraordinaire - repeatedly match the fierceness (if not the ruthlessness) of Buaku and the machine gun-happy, cleavage-bearing Cat sisters. We have watched Buaku change his villainous focus from urine to fine art, risking life and limb to remove a nude painting of himself from a heavily guarded auction warehouse. Finally, we learn the truth about Buaku's origins. Could there be something noble in the half-human, half-cyborg blood of this renowned gang leader? Will Leona, the newest member of the Tank Police, be able to breathe again without Buaku's help? How can she possibly thwart the intrusion of the Red Commandos while trying to handle Buaku on her own? **40 min.**

Domestic Home Video:

Dominion Tank Police Act I
USM 1037 ▲ $19.95 ▲ VHS ▲ SUB ▲ Stereo

Dominion Tank Police Act II
USM 1016 ▲ $19.95 ▲ VHS ▲ SUB ▲ Stereo

Dominion Tank Police Act III
USM 1017 ▲ $19.95 ▲ VHS ▲ SUB ▲ Stereo

Dominion Tank Police Act IV
USM 1018 ▲ $19.95 ▲ VHS ▲ SUB ▲ Stereo

Dominion Tank Police Part 1
Dominion Tank Police Acts I and II together on one tape.
USM 1069 ▲ $29.95 ▲ VHS ▲ DUB ▲ Stereo ▲ 05/24/93

Dominion Tank Police Part 2
Dominion Tank Police Acts III and IV together on one tape.
USM 1070 ▲ $29.95 ▲ VHS ▲ DUB ▲ Stereo ▲ 05/24/93

Dominion Tank Police Acts I-IV
Dominion Tank Police Acts I-IV in a 2-disc laserdisc set.
ID 8582CT ▲ $69.95 ▲ LD ▲ SUB ▲ Mono ▲ 07/05/91

Doomed Megalopolis

OAV series, 4 episodes

(1991) ©Toei Co. Ltd.

Supervising Director: Taro Rin *Original Story:* Hiroshi Aramata *Original Scenario:* Akinori Endo *Music:* Kazz Toyama

Based on the novel "Capital City" by Hiroshi Aramata, and adapted for animation by screenwriter Akinori Endo (3x3 EYES). A sorcerer attempts to resurrect the guardian spirit of Tokyo in order to increase his power on Earth and wreak havoc in the city. Sorcery, nightmare visions, incest, subways and the Great Kanto Earthquake of 1923 all fit into this complex and deeply creepy four-volume OAV story. Evokes true horror in both atmosphere and plot, accompanied by nicely spooky music. Character designs by Studio Gainax's Yoshiyuki Sadamoto. Released in Japan under the title "Teito Monogatari" by Toei Video; available in North America through Streamline Pictures.

Doomed Megalopolis Vol. 1: *The Haunting of Tokyo*

Tokyo is under siege as occult forces lay claim to the burial site of Taira No Masakado, a founder of the centuries-old city. Driven by a lust for power, the necromancer Kato hopes to free the soul of this ancient warrior and in doing so gain ultimate control of this budding metropolis as it boldly moves into the 20th Century. Standing in the way of Kato's quest for power are an aging priest, an innocent virgin and a group of untested heroes. But, they soon learn that the sadistic Kato is not an easy enemy to defeat. **50 min.**

Doomed Megalopolis Vol. 2: *The Fall of Tokyo*

Realizing that he cannot resurrect the spirit of Masakado through the traditional occult means, the powerful necromancer, Kato, subjects an innocent victim to the ultimate physical debasement as he psychically forces his seed into her unwilling body. Standing against him is a group of honorable men from varied walks of life who have come together to keep the unspeakable from happening. These men, driven to the brink of madness by Kato's evil, must do all that they can to keep the balance between good and evil in check. The final conflict results in a massive earthquake which rips Tokyo apart. Set in the early 1920s, this second installment of the mind-boggling mini-series by the master animator, Taro Rin, is filled with powerful images and a sophisticated storyline which transforms this story into an epic saga of horror and black magic. **50 min.**

Doomed Megalopolis Vol. 3: *The Gods of Tokyo*

Following the devastating earthquake of 1923, plans are made to rebuild Tokyo into a modern metropolis. A key element of this plan is the building of a subway system. Kato schemes to use this subterranean construction to awaken a supernatural dragon which lies beneath Tokyo. Through the resulting mayhem, Kato hopes to gain control of the soul of Tokyo's guardian spirit, the ancient warrior Masakado. The project is plagued by a series of hideous murders. Anxious to discover the cause of these presumably supernatural deaths, Prof. Terada calls upon a psychic, Kuroda, for help. Together they face Kato's forces. Meanwhile, Masakado has begun to fight back. Keiko, a Shinto priestess, puts up a spiritual barrier to keep Kato from sacrificing a young girl to the dragon. But as Keiko soon learns, Kato's power is not so easily defeated. **47 min.**

Doomed Megalopolis Vol. 4: *The Battle for Tokyo*

The evil Kato is bent upon revenge. Masakado, the city's guardian spirit, and Keiko, the temple maiden who serves as Masakado's agent, have proven that they can defend the burgeoning metropolis against the powerful necromancer. Astronomers throughout the world are baffled when the Moon starts moving toward the Earth. Keiko knows that Kato is responsible for the impending cataclysm, together with the accursed Tatsumiya family. Thus the final battle lines are drawn. The ensuing battle is of such cosmic proportions, that both the temple maiden and the sorcerer become the personification of deities - she the Goddess of Mercy and he the Spirit of the Dead. **47 min.**

Domestic Home Video:

Doomed Megalopolis Vol. 1
SPV 90603 ▲ $19.95 ▲ VHS ▲ DUB ▲ Mono ▲ CC ▲ 06/22/93

Doomed Megalopolis Vol. 2
SPV 90653 ▲ $19.95 ▲ VHS ▲ DUB ▲ Mono ▲ CC ▲ 08/15/93

Doomed Megalopolis Vol. 3
SPV 90713 ▲ $19.95 ▲ VHS ▲ DUB ▲ Mono ▲ CC ▲ 12/01/93

Doomed Megalopolis Vol. 4
SPV 90743 ▲ $19.95 ▲ VHS ▲ DUB ▲ Mono ▲ CC ▲ 01/15/94

Dragon Ball

(1986) ©Akira Toriyama/Toei

Based on the Manga by: Akira Toriyama *Director:* Minoru Okazaki

TV and movie series based on the explosively popular manga of the same name by creator Akira Toriyama (DR. SLUMP). The animated DRAGON BALL is one of the most loved animation series ever released in Japan, producing hundreds of TV episodes and two short animated features a year since the beginning of its ten-year run. A quest story with a band of adventurers searching for seven mystical dragon balls in order to make a wish for anything at all from the Eternal Dragon, DRAGON BALL quickly advanced from an updated parody of the "Monkey King" legend (the hero, "Goku," shares the name of the Monkey King, and his followers are humorous renditions of the Monkey King's traditional companions) to a martial arts face-off of galactic proportions, featuring aliens, gods, superhumans and brain-numbing cosmology. DRAGON BALL merchandise—from posters, toys and video games to food, clothing and more—is ubiquitous in Asian markets all over the world. The TV series, as seen on U.S. TV, required some careful editing to pass U.S. broadcast standards—the producers chose to handle the problem of young Goku's childish nudity in some scenes by deft digital retouching. (Presto! Underpants!) Though the initial DRAGON BALL series achieved poor ratings in the U.S. during its one-season run, the follow-up series DRAGON BALL Z has since zoomed to the top of the charts in syndication markets across the country. Released in Japan under the title "Dragon Ball" by Toei Video; available in North America through Kidmark/Funimation Productions.

Dragon Ball Pilot Episode: *Curse of the Blood Rubies*
If all seven dragon balls are brought together, a dragon will appear and grant one wish. The cursed king is having his minions collect balls so he can wish away his unending hunger. Bulma has one ball and is collecting more to make her own wish. Raised in the wilderness, young Goku learns the importance of his dragon ball when he meets Bulma. When his ball is stolen, he joins Bulma in her search. After many hair-raising adventures, they make it to the palace where the king has collected six balls. **48 min.**

Dragon Ball Vol. 1: *Secret of the Dragon Ball*
Episodes 1 & 2: SECRET OF THE DRAGON BALL and THE EMPEROR'S QUEST. **45 min.**

Dragon Ball Vol. 2: *The Nimbus Cloud of Roshi*
Episodes 3 & 4: THE NIMBUS CLOUD OF ROSHI and OOLONG THE TERRIBLE. **45 min.**

Domestic Home Video:
Dragon Ball: *Curse of the Blood Rubies*
VMM 6344 ▲ $12.99 ▲ VHS ▲ DUB ▲ CC ▲ 09/24/96
Dragon Ball Vol. 1
VMM 6345 ▲ $12.99 ▲ VHS ▲ DUB ▲ CC ▲ 09/24/96
Dragon Ball Vol. 2
VMM 6346 ▲ $12.99 ▲ VHS ▲ DUB ▲ CC ▲ 09/24/96

Dragon Century
OAV series, 2 episodes

(1985) ©Kubo Shoten/A.I.C.

Character Design & Animation Director: Hiroyuki Kitazume, Hiroyuki Etsutomo *Original Work*: Ryu Kihei *Director*: Kiyoshi Fukimoto *Art Direction*: Tetsuo Anzai, Tetsuhito Shimono *Music*: Michiaki Kato

Notable as one of character designer Hiroyuki "MOLDIVER" Kitazume's early OAV projects. In Episode 1: AD 1990-RIKO, an angry young girl named Riko rescues a baby dragon from the military forces that killed her mother. Riko raises the dragon to be her tool of revenge against society, but when demons invade the world, she changes her mind and joins the dragon in fighting demons. In Episode 2: DEMON CHAPTER, the scene is nearly three hundred years later. In this far off age, another young girl teams up with an old dragon to fight in the Ryuto (Dragon Martial Arts) tournament for vengeance. Available in North America through U.S. Renditions. **60 min.**

Domestic Home Video:
USR 032 ▲ $24.95 ▲ VHS ▲ SUB ▲ HiFi Stereo ▲ 10/01/96

Dragon Half
OAV series, 2 episodes

(1993) ©Ryusuke Mita/Kadokawa Shôten/Victor Entertainment, Inc.

Planning: Toshio Azami *Script Director*: Shinya Sadamitsu *Original Creator*: Ryusuke Mita *Character Design*: Masahiro Koyama *Art Director*: Takahiro Kishida and Masahiro Koyama *Visual Art Director*: Yusuke Takeda

Based on the manga of the same name by Ryusuke Mita, as serialized in weekly SHŪKAN DRAGON MAGAZINE manga anthology. Goofy comedy featuring a half-human, half-dragon (she's got little wings and a tail), firebreathing teenybopper named Mink who falls in love with a handsome pop star/dragon slayer named Dick Saucer. Hilariously silly superdeformed hijinks set in ye olde medieval times. Main character "Mink" is voiced by Kotono Mitsuishi ("Usagi," SAILOR MOON). Released in Japan under the title "Dragon Half" by Victor Entertainment; available in North America through A.D. Vision. **55 min.**

Domestic Home Video:
ADV DH/001 ▲ $29.95 ▲ VHS ▲ SUB ▲ HiFi Surround ▲ 08/14/95

Dragon Knight
OAV series, 2 volumes

(1991/95) ©Polystar Co. Ltd./élf/All Products

Based on "Dragon Knight" by: élf RPG *Original Concept*: Yoshinori Nakamura *Original Story*: Masato Hiruta *Script*: Akira Hatta (2) *Character Design*: Ako Sahara (2), Akira Kano (2) *Animation Director*: Yuma Nakamura (2) *Director*: Jun Fukada (1), Kaoru Toyo'oka (2)

OAV series based on the adult-oriented personal computer game of the same name, the object of which was to defeat monsters in order to be rewarded by "naughty pictures" of pretty girls. In video form, DRAGON KNIGHT largely skips the monsters and goes right to the girls sans any pretense at story, something which no doubt interests soft-core fans, but proves disappointing to those looking forward to the cool monsters from the game. Released in Japan under the title "Dragon Knight" by Polystar/Polydor; available in North America through A.D. Vision.

Dragon Knight
The morally impaired Takeru must rescue the multiple damsels in distress imprisoned in an enchanted castle by an army of demons, pausing only for a quick snapshot as the young lasses struggle to cover their lithesome charms. Is it not possible to believe that even this rogue might still discover the true meaning of love, risking all his ill-gotten gains to save the life of the one woman who has become his friend? Includes bonus production art portfolio. **40 min.**

Dragon Knight 2: *Another Knight on the Town*
Swinging swordsman Takeru finds himself saddled with a young boy who turns out not to be a boy at all. With evil wizards, elven witches and horned demons against him, and with a teenage pickpocket and a bold female swordslinger at his back, this outing looks to be even wilder than the first one. **50 min.**

Domestic Home Video:
Dragon Knight
ADV DK/001 ▲ $34.95 ▲ VHS ▲ SUB ▲ HiFi Surround ▲ 06/01/94
Dragon Knight 2
ADV DK/002 ▲ $34.95 ▲ VHS ▲ SUB ▲ HiFi Surround ▲ 09/05/95

Dragon Pink
OAV series, 3 episodes

(1994-95) ©Itoyoko/Pink Pineapple

Created by: Itoyoko *Directors*: Wataru Fujii (1), Hitoshi Takai (2,3) *Produced by*: Pink Pineapple *Animation*: A.I.C.

Sword 'n' sorcery three-volume OAV sex series with a young cat-girl named "Pink" as the love-slave of her heroic sword-swinging patron. Lots of oversexed monsters and lizard girls. Story is unremarkable, but animation is pretty to look at, and Pink's characterization calls up that the image of a soap opera where the master must declare his real love for the slave instead of the fine lady up the hill. Creator "Itoyoko" is well-known in Japanese otakky circles both for his work as a creator of adult-oriented games for the personal computer as well as for the creation of small-scale production figure models known as "garage kits." Released in Japan under the title "Dragon Pink" by Pink Pineapple; available in North America from SoftCel Pictures/A.D. Vision.

Dragon Pink 1
Santa the swordsman thinks her tail is really cute, and the fact that Pink's a little fuzzy around the edges certainly hasn't caused him to pussyfoot around when it comes to trying to get the cat out of her pajamas! Of course, neither Pink nor Santa will have any kind of life at all unless they can team up with the sultry elfin sorceress Pias and warrior Bobo to defeat the assorted evil beings that lurk in the heart of Tajif Forest. Includes bonus video production portfolio. **35 min.** *(Edited version 30 min.)*

Dragon Pink 2
Pink's associates, Santa the Swordsman, Pierce the Elf, and Bobo the Barbarian are still using her for monster bait, and even using her jewelry for food and lodging. When the jewelry runs out, guess who's left behind as a security deposit? Can Santa, Bobo and Pierce trace a monster to its lair and steal its treasure horde in time to get Pink out of hock? **35 min.** *(Edited version 30 min.)*

Dragon Pink 3
Once again Pink and her fellow rag-tag adventurers find themselves coming up on hard times, and now poor Santa's too pooped to perform. That's bad news for anyone who makes a living with his sword and even worse news for Pink when she and Santa are trapped by the nefarious Nymphomania! Meanwhile, Bobo and Pierce get stuck in a similarly sticky situation, but they are bailed out by an unexpected new source for Pierce's magic. **35 min.** *(Edited version 30 min.)*

Domestic Home Video:

Dragon Pink 1
ADV DP/001U ▲ $29.95 ▲ VHS ▲ SUB ▲ Uncut ▲ Surr ▲ 09/10/94
ADV DP/001G ▲ $29.95 ▲ VHS ▲ SUB ▲ Edited ▲ Surr ▲ 11/21/95

Dragon Pink 2
ADV DP/002U ▲ $29.95 ▲ VHS ▲ SUB ▲ Uncut ▲ Surr ▲ 11/14/95
ADV DP/002G ▲ $29.95 ▲ VHS ▲ SUB ▲ Edited ▲ Surr ▲ 11/14/95

Dragon Pink 3
ADV DP/003U ▲ $29.95 ▲ VHS ▲ SUB ▲ Uncut ▲ Surr ▲ 11/28/95
ADV DP/003G ▲ $29.95 ▲ VHS ▲ SUB ▲ Edited ▲ Surr ▲ 11/28/95

El-Hazard, The Magnificent World
OAV series, 4 volumes
(1995) ©A.I.C./Pioneer LDC Inc.

Director: Hiroki Hayashi *Screenplay:* Ryoei Tsukimura *Character Design, Supervising Animation Director:* Kazuto Nakazawa *Design:* Koji Watanabe *Art Director:* Nobuhito Sue *Music:* Seiko Nagaoka *Direction:* Akihiko Nishiyama (1), Shigeru Kimiya (2,5), Akihiko Nishiyama (3-5), Haruo Nakayama (6) *Animation Director:* Yuji Ikeda (5), Kazunobu Hoshi (6), Koji Watanabe (7)

Alternate universe hijinks by TENCHI MUYÔ! co-creator Hiroki Hayashi and scriptwriter Ryoei Tsukimura gives the time-honored *Prisoner of Zenda* plotline a new spin, making a dimensionally transferred young boy the uncanny doppelganger of that world's princess. Witty plot and characters, with attractive design work. Loads of laffs; heavy on the sexual innuendo, but still suitable for most pre-teen audiences. Released in Japan under the title "Shinpi no Sekai (World of Mysteries) El Hazard" by Pioneer LDC; available in North America through Pioneer LDCA.

El-Hazard Vol. 1: *The First Night*
It all begins with the discovery of mysterious ruins beneath the school. Meet Makoto Mizuhara, an ordinary Japanese high school student. Katsuhiko Jinnai, a not-so-ordinary high school student, has somehow gotten it into his head that Makoto is his destined rival, and hatches plot after plot against him. Makoto's never given Jinnai any reason to believe this, but that doesn't stop Jinnai from luring Makoto to the school late one night for his own nefarious reasons. Once at the schoolyard, Makoto is summoned by a mysterious woman who shows him the way to El-Hazard, The Magnificent World. Pulled this way and that by the threads of destiny, Makoto and several others venture into this incredible new land. What amazing adventures lie in store? 2 episodes: THE WAR ZONE and EL-HAZARD. **50 min.**

El-Hazard Vol. 2: *The Second and Third Nights*
The Second Night, THE WORLD OF BEAUTIFUL GIRLS: A mysterious power transports Makoto and the others to this magnificent other world. Because Makoto resembles the missing Princess Fatora, he is persuaded to impersonate her. The group heads to Mt. Muldoon, where three priestesses capable of releasing the seal on a weapon capable of topping the Bugrom invasion, the "Eye of God," reside. What the group doesn't know is that Jinnai, now part of the Bugrom invasion, is waiting for them and dead set on stopping their progress. The Third Night, THE WORLD OF HOT SPRINGS: Makoto & Company must chase the fleeing duo to the site of the annual Purification Ceremony. From there they end up in a vast desert where the Spring of Arliman is located, and meet one of the three priestesses: Miz. Later, with the arrival of Shayla-Shayla, the group takes a dip in the hot spring. Meanwhile, Jinnai decides to go after the forbidden weapon of El-Hazard. **60 min.**

El-Hazard Vol. 3: *The Fourth and Fifth Nights*

The Fourth Night, THE WORLD OF THE DEMON GOD: Three high priestesses of El-Hazard must reach a forbidden island before Jinnai and his Bugrom soldiers discover the ancient Demon God. Whoever awakens the slumbering god will attain ultimate power. As the two groups battle on the island, Ifurita awakens, and Makoto is astonished to discover it's the mysterious woman who transported him to El-Hazard! The Fifth Night, THE WORLD OF THUNDER: Jinnai begins a campaign of devastation as new master of Ifurita. To The Eye of God, their doomsday weapon. As priestess Shayla discovers she's smitten with Makoto, his special abilities are revealed in another encounter with Ifurita. **60 min.**

El Hazard Vol. 4: *The Sixth and Seventh Nights*
The Sixth Night, THE WORLD OF GLEAMING NIGHT: the allied countries are gradually destroyed by Ifurita and the Bugrom troops, but Rune Venus receives even worse news —

the Phantom tribe occupies the "stairs to heaven" leading to "The God's Eye." El Hazard is in danger of being devastated! The Seventh Night, THE WORLD OF ENDLESS ADVENTURES: Jinnai succeeds in abducting Princess Fatora from the Phantom tribe and plans to use her as a human shield. Makoto, Mr. Fujisawa and the three priestesses are waylaid by Ifurita and the Bugrom troops on their way to help Fatora. Within the fortress, Jinnai orders Ifurita to kill Makoto. The conclusion of the series. **75 min.**

Domestic Home Video:
El-Hazard Vol. 1
PI VA-1261D ▲ $24.95 ▲ VHS ▲ DUB ▲ HiFi Stereo ▲ CC ▲ 07/25/95
PI VA-1261S ▲ $29.95 ▲ VHS ▲ SUB ▲ HiFi Stereo ▲ 07/25/95
PI LA-1261A ▲ $39.95 ▲ LD-CAV ▲ M/A ▲ HiFi Stereo ▲ CC ▲ 07/25/95

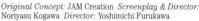

El-Hazard Vol. 2
PI VA-1262D ▲ $24.95 ▲ VHS ▲ DUB ▲ HiFi Stereo ▲ CC ▲ 10/24/95
PI VA-1262S ▲ $29.95 ▲ VHS ▲ SUB ▲ HiFi Stereo ▲ 10/24/95
PI LA-1262A ▲ $39.95 ▲ LD-CAV ▲ M/A ▲ HiFi Stereo ▲ CC ▲ 10/24/95

El-Hazard Vol. 3
PI VA-1264D ▲ $24.95 ▲ VHS ▲ DUB ▲ HiFi Stereo ▲ CC ▲ 12/19/95
PI VA-1264S ▲ $29.95 ▲ VHS ▲ SUB ▲ HiFi Stereo ▲ 12/19/95
PI LA-1264A ▲ $39.95 ▲ LD-CAV ▲ M/A ▲ HiFi Stereo ▲ CC ▲ 12/19/95

El-Hazard Vol. 4
PI VA-1266D ▲ $24.95 ▲ VHS ▲ DUB ▲ HiFi Stereo ▲ CC ▲ 06/04/96
PI VA-1266S ▲ $29.95 ▲ VHS ▲ SUB ▲ HiFi Stereo ▲ 06/04/96
PI LA-1266A ▲ $44.95 ▲ LD-CAV ▲ M/A ▲ HiFi Stereo ▲ CC ▲ 06/04/96

Ellcia
OAV series, 4 volumes
(1992-93) ©JVC/JAM Creation/J.C. Staff

Original Concept: JAM Creation *Screenplay & Director:* Noriyasu Kogawa *Director:* Yoshimichi Furukawa

Four-volume fantasy-adventure OAV series. "Ellcia," they say, is the name of a ship of god recorded in holy books since the dawn of time. In search of it, a young girl named Aela and her merry band of kiddie pirates travel the countryside. If you can stay awake past the first half hour, you're doing better than most. Released in Japan under the title "Gensô Jodan (Illusionary Tale) Ellcia" by CIC/Victor Entertainment; available in North America through A.D. Vision.

Ellcia Vol. 1: *The Legend Begins*
When Nabosu, the King of Megaronia, finds himself in possession of the awesome power of an ancient race, he sets upon a course of conquest. Seeking further remnants of the ancient technology, he plunders the four holy islands of God until at last his brutal tide sweeps across the island of Eija. Slaughtering the King and Queen and taking their son, Elluri, as a hostage to insure the allegiance of the Eijian people, Nabosu now rules the world. However, in the very ruins of the technology that has brought Nabosu to power lie the seeds of his downfall. In an ancient manuscript are the words that confirm the truth of the prophecies of the Eijian Holy Book. Prophecies which warn that one day the land shall be conquered, but that vengeance will come swiftly in the form of a chosen one, who will rally the people and, with the fiercest ship on the seas, vanquish the blasphemous invaders, wiping Megaronia from the very face of the world. Her name is Eira, and this is her story. **50 min.**

Domestic Home Video:
Ellcia Vol. 1
ADV EL/001D ▲ $24.95 ▲ VHS ▲ DUB ▲ HiFi Surround ▲ 11/12/96
ADV EL/001S ▲ $29.95 ▲ VHS ▲ SUB ▲ HiFi Surround ▲ 11/12/96

The Elven Bride
OAV series, 2 volumes
(1995) ©Kazuma G-Version/Mediax/Pink Pineapple

Original Creator: Kazuma G-Version *Director:* Hiroshi Yamakawa *Animation Production:* A.I.C.

Two-volume OAV softcore sex fantasy, based on an original story by Kazuma G-Version. "Meet-cute" comedy (as they say in Hollywood) detailing the story of how Kenji (human male) met Milfa (elven female) and their subsequent romantic difficulties. Premise is not without its charm, but as soon as Kenji and Milfa start having difficulties consumating their union because of human-elf physiological differences, the channel changes suddenly from HBO to Playboy. Released in Japan under the title "Elf no Waka Okusama" (A Young Elven Bride) by Pink Pineapple; available in North America through A.D. Vision.

The Elven Bride

When young elf maiden Milfa and the very human Kenji decide to marry, no one in the village is happy with the situation. Thanks to some unforseen anatomical differences, neither are Milfa and Kenji. As if things weren't bad enough, a two-headed dragon attacks the village while Kenji is away in the land of the harpies on a quest for the ultimate marital aid. **30 min.**

The Elven Bride 2: *The Elf Examination*

Still experiencing bedroom difficulties with her human husband, newlywed elf Milfa, decides that a visit to the gynecologist is in order. Unfortunately, the only doctor who can help is not only a lecher, he's an incubus! However, with a little help from Michiko, a sexy succubus, Kenji just might be in time to save his elven spouse. **30 min.**

Domestic Home Video:

The Elven Bride
ADV EB/001 ▲ $29.95 ▲ VHS ▲ SUB ▲ HiFi Surround ▲ 04/30/96
The Elven Bride 2
ADV EB/002 ▲ $29.95 ▲ VHS ▲ SUB ▲ HiFi Surround ▲ 05/28/96

End of Summer

OAV series, 2 volumes

(1994) ©élf/Pink Pineapple/Cinema Paradise/Hero

Created by: Masato Hiruda *Character Concepts:* Masaki Takei *Screenplay:* Yuhiro Tomita *Character Design:* Ryunosuke Otonashi *Director:* Kinji Yoshimoto

Two-volume OAV series from the director of PLASTIC LITTLE; based on the adult-oriented personal computer game "Dôkyûsei." END OF SUMMER details the crossover loves of several high school students. In the game, you (a teenage male, of course) attempt to "make" as many of the girls as you can. The video series is sweet in that you also have to be a nice guy about it. Funny, sexy and not without charm. The second video's animation quality drops markedly, and loses some of the first volume's gentle atmosphere in favor of silly hijinks. Released in Japan under the title "Dôkyûsei: Natsu no Owari ni" (Classmates: End of Summer) by Pink Pineapple; available in North America through A.D. Vision. Followed by a sequel, "Kakyûsei" (see below).

End of Summer

The course of true love seldom runs true, and cast like mines in Wataru's path are four other young women: juvenile and infatuated Miho, tomboyish athlete Misa, Kurumi, the somewhat naive girlfriend of Wataru's best friend Kazuya, and caustic Satomi, who works in the restaurant where Wataru hangs out. Includes production art portfolio. **55 min.**

End of Summer 2

Picking up where *End of Summer* left off, the story continues young hero Wataru's last summer before college, and his continuing attempts at making it with Mai, the girl of his dreams. In addition to his relationships with Mai and Satomi, Wataru must also figure out what to do about his best friend's ex-girlfriend, Kurumi, who comes to him for advice and ends up getting much more personally involved. Will Wataru finally get it together with Mai, or will he be distracted again? **55 min.**

Domestic Home Video:

End of Summer
ADV E/001 ▲ $29.95 ▲ VHS ▲ SUB ▲ HiFi Surround ▲ 07/06/94
End of Summer 2
ADV E/002 ▲ $29.95 ▲ VHS ▲ SUB ▲ HiFi Surround ▲ 12/21/95

Explorer Woman Ray

(1989) ©Takeshi Okazaki/A.I.C./Animate Film/Toshiba Video Softwares, Inc.

Based on the comic by: Takeshi Okazaki *Screenplay:* Masayori Sekijima *Director:* Hiroki Hayashi *Character Design:* Hiroyuki Ochi *Art Director:* Junichi Higashi

Two-volume OAV series (released in the U.S. as one, 60-minute volume), based on the comic of the same name by Takeshi Okazaki as serialized in COMIC NORA, but featuring a completely original story. Borrowing strongly from Lucas/Spielberg's *Indiana Jones* films, EXPLORER WOMAN RAY nonetheless manages to put a unique anime spin on a classic tale of archaeological rivalry in a way that's daring and fun. From the director of TENCHI MUYÔ!. Released in Japan under the title "Explorer Woman Ray" by Toshiba Eizô Soft; available in North America through U.S. Manga Corps. **60 min.**

Domestic Home Video:

USM 1026 ▲ $19.95 ▲ VHS ▲ SUB ▲ Mono ▲ 04/29/93
ID 2228CT ▲ $34.95 ▲ LD ▲ SUB ▲ HiFi Mono ▲ 07/27/93

F³: Frantic, Frustrated & Female

OAV series, 3 volumes

(1994-95) ©Wan Yan A Gu Da/Pink Pineapple.

Created by: Wan Yan A Gu Da (Fujimi Publishing) *Director:* Masakazu Akan *Character Design & Animation Director:* Koji Hamaguchi *Planning:* Kinya Watanabe

She's gotta have it and her best girl friend wants to make sure she gets it. Although based on one of the bestselling "etchi" or softcore manga titles in Japan, F3 may have been better left as a comic book—other personal computer-based anime videos (such as the superior "Dôkyûsei," which is released in the U.S. as END OF SUMMER) have proven that it's possible to still make enjoyable and original anime despite the limitations imposed by video game plotlines, but F3 seems little more than an excuse for masturbatory excess (Meg Ryan did it much better anyway). Released in Japan under the perfectly wonderful title "Nageki no Kenkô Yûryôji" (The Lament of an Otherwise Perfectly Healthy Girl) by Pink Pineapple; available in North America through A.D. Vision.

F3: Frantic, Frustrated & Female

Hiroe's bound and determined to get rid of her three "F's." No helping hands are refused, even when they belong to the local mad scientist and his unbelievable inventions. Hiroe may take quite a licking before she reaches her ultimate goal, but rest assured that she'll finally get what she wants in the end. The shocking bare facts of one young woman's quest to find a solution for a problem she can't even discuss in polite company are exposed as never before. Includes bonus video production portfolio. **35 min.**

F3 Part 2

The lusty Hiroe is back in the sequel to F3. This time she's the focus of a chopper chick who puts the moves on Hiroe at a local pool, and shows up later at her house with a couple of cuddly playmates. Hiroe's more than willing, and as the gals get into some four-way heavy breathing, they are joined by Hiroe's sister and even her mom! **35 min.**

F3 Part 3

She's still frantic, frustrated and female, but now she's literally burning up with desire! You won't believe what happens when a very male demon takes up residence in Hiroe Ogawa's luscious female body. Mayaka and company quickly realize that they're going to need professional help to get the Hell out of Hiroe, but the professional turns out to have a few kinks of her own. **35 min.**

Domestic Home Video:

F3
ADV F/001 ▲ $29.95 ▲ VHS ▲ SUB ▲ HiFi Surround ▲ 08/28/94
F3 Part 2
ADV F/002 ▲ $29.95 ▲ VHS ▲ SUB ▲ HiFi Surround ▲ 01/30/96
F3 Part 3
ADV F/003 ▲ $29.95 ▲ VHS ▲ SUB ▲ HiFi Surround ▲ 03/26/96

Fantasia *See* F3

Farewell to Space Battleship Yamato *See* YAMATO

Fatal Fury

2 TV specials

(1992/93) ©SNK/Fuji TV/NAS

Original Concept: SNK/NEO•GEO "Fatal Fury" *Directors:* Hiroshi Fukutomi (1), Kazuhiro Furuhashi (2) *Music:* Toshiro Masuda/SNK Sound Team (1), Toshihiko Sahashi (2) *Character Design, Executive Animation Director:* Masami Obari

Based on the video game series by SNK for the Neo•Geo game system, both the FATAL FURY games and anime videos detail the adventures of the most powerful fighters in the world as they are drawn together by blood, honor, greed, love, revenge or simply the desire to prove that they are the best—modern day gladiators traveling the world facing danger, braving adventure and spreading their legend. The video series in particular zeroes in on the characters' background and personalities, especially street-fightin' hero Terry Bogard, creating a martial arts world as pure as a Bruce Lee movie. The characters' motivations are simple, but the formula works.

The animation of modern-day ninja girl Mai Shiranui gave an all-new meaning to "bouncy" anime girls. Released in Japan under the title "Battle Fighters Garô Densetsu (Legend of the Hungry Wolf)" by King Record; available in North America through Viz Video.

Fatal Fury: *Legend of the Hungry Wolf*

When world-class martial artist Jeff Bogard is brutally murdered before his sons' eyes by a former family friend, young Terry and Andy Bogard must devote their spirits, their talents, their very lives to bare-knuckled street-fighting techniques. If they get good enough, fast enough, furious enough, they stand a chance of avenging their father's death. As the time of the King of Fighters tournament approaches, only one son will be chosen to learn the legendary Hakkyokuseiken technique. Will it be older brother Terry, a loner by nature, whose freedom-loving spirit finds great joy in his own hard-earned street fighting skills? Or will it be tough little brother Andy, silver-haired and beautiful, whose special attacks include "Flying Wing Fist" and "Super Explosive Rending Bullet"? In the blood soaked and honor bound world of martial arts, a martial artist's technique isn't just a means to an end... it's a way of life. **50 min.**

Fatal Fury 2: *The New Battle*

Flushed with victory after defeating Geese Howard, the man responsible for the brutal murder of his father, Terry "Hungry Wolf" Bogard spars one stormy night with deadly German nobleman Wolfgang Krauser. Krauser leaves Terry with his life but not much else, and the bruised and embittered street fighter must gather up what's left of his pride and start down the lonely road to recovery. Meanwhile, silver-haired Andy sets out to find his missing brother while red-haired Mai Shiranui, daughter of martial arts master Hanzo Shiranui, sets her sights on Andy. A scrappy young street punk named Tony may be able to give Terry back his will to live, but what good is passion when honor is gone? **70 min.**

Domestic Home Video:

Fatal Fury
VV FF-001 ▲ $19.95 ▲ VHS ▲ DUB ▲ HiFi Stereo ▲ 03/01/95

Fatal Fury 2
VV FF-002 ▲ $19.95 ▲ VHS ▲ DUB ▲ HiFi Stereo ▲ 05/10/95

Fatal Fury Box Set
Fatal Fury, Fatal Fury 2, and Fatal Fury Motion Picture in a collector's set. (220 min.)
VV FFB-001 ▲ $54.95 ▲ VHS ▲ DUB ▲ HiFi Stereo ▲ 11/01/96

Fatal Fury: The Motion Picture

(1994) ©SNK/Fuji TV/Shochiku/Asatsu International

Original Concept: SNK/NEO•GEO "Fatal Fury" *Director, Character Design, and Executive Animation Director:* Masami Obari *Music:* Toshihiko Sahashi

The 1994 full-length theatrical feature, introduces what should be, by now, a familiar element to anime: the *Indiana Jones*-style archaeological quest. Prideful young Laocorn Gaudeamus, descendant of an ancient family, has scoured archaeological sites around the world for the legendary "Armor of Mars" lost by his ancestors during the Crusades. With the help of his three associates — Jamin, Panni, and Hauer — Laocorn plans to use the immense, almost godlike powers of the armor to take vengeance on those who persecuted his family all those many years ago. To prevent her brother from acquiring it, Laocorn's beautiful, estranged twin sister Sulia enlists the aid of the only man in the world powerful enough to challenge him ... bare-knuckled street fighter and martial arts legend, Terry "Hungry Wolf" Bogard. Unless Terry and his own associates — Andy, Joe Higashi, and Mai Shiranui — can stop him, Laocorn will don the final piece of armor and become invincible. Power corrupts, and absolute power corrupts absolutely. What will become of Laocorn? **100 min.**

Domestic Home Video:
VV FF-003 ▲ $19.95 ▲ VHS ▲ DUB ▲ HiFi Stereo ▲ 11/07/95

Final Yamato *See* YAMATO

Fire Tripper *See* RUMIK WORLD

First Loves

OAV series, 4 episodes
(1995) ©Pink Pineapple

Screenplay: Yu Yamamoto *Character Design & Animation Director:* Yuji Takahashi *Storyboards:* Kan Fukumoto, Hiroshi Yoshida

Four-volume softcore OAV sequel to END OF SUMMER ("Dôkyûsei") recasting the series' familiar "classmates" in a younger mode. In Japan, the original "Dôkyûsei" PC video game series was released as two different games, making "Kakyûsei" (released on video as FIRST LOVES) the third in the series. U.S. video release contains two OAVs per volume. Released in Japan under the title "Kakyûsei" (Under-Classmates) by Pink Pineapple; available in North America through A.D. Vision.

First Loves
2 episodes. The problem with love is that everyone has to have a first time, but poor Kakeru's trying to hit so many moving targets that he may never score. When beautiful young Urara appears, however, Kakeru's sure he's found the girl he's been searching for, but first he's got to overcome two obstacles: The first is Hiromi, who's just broken up with Kakeru's rival Doda and is looking for a guy, any guy, to pick up on the rebound. The second is Mika, Kakeru's sister, who in typical sister fashion thinks her brother is a drooling dolt. **35 min.**

First Loves 2
2 episodes. Kakeru's girlfriend has left for the United States and he's feeling blue. But with the arrival of the pretty redhead Rei, things are definitely looking up. There's only one problem - Doda, the star of the boys' tennis team, wants her also! **35 min.**

Domestic Home Video:
First Loves
ADV FL/001 ▲ $29.95 ▲ VHS ▲ SUB ▲ HiFi Surround ▲ 05/07/96
First Loves 2
ADV FL/002 ▲ $29.95 ▲ VHS ▲ SUB ▲ HiFi Surround ▲ 06/04/96

Fist of the North Star

(1986) ©Toei Animation Co. Ltd.

Based on graphic novels by: Buronson & Tetsuo Hara *Music:* Katsuhisa Hattori *Director:* Toyo'o Ashida

Based on the manga of the same name by Buronson and Tetsuo Hara and then-animated TV series (1984-87). The meek shall inherit the Earth...but only if they live long enough. In this post-apocalyptic hell, the biker gangs and most powerful martial artists have taken over. Only the strongest and most skillful can hope to overcome this blight upon the world. Fortunately for the weak and downtrodden, there is one who will champion their cause. He is the Fist of the North Star, and this is the legend of the savior of the end of the century. Attempting to retell the massive story as told in the manga and TV series, this full-length theatrical feature suffers from a lack of cohesion due to necessary edits for length. Additionally, much to the frustration of the series' fans, the original version of the film as rumored to have been screened in Japanese theaters back in 1986 (with all the exceptionally detailed blood and gore intact) is nowhere to be found; subsequent prints have all been struck from the digitized master, meaning the worst of the violence has been digitized out. (We're told, however, that if you look carefully, there exists a single film trailer recorded on the Japanese rental version of the import film that either forgets or neglects to add the digitizing, allowing fans to savor one scene, at least, of the mayhem they crave.) Perhaps as a result of the fierce loyalty the series inspires in its fans, domestic versions of the FIST OF THE NORTH STAR manga and anime series have never been well received; the response of one fan we know to translations he deems unacceptable (the infamous "Two-Finger Grasp of Nil Space" comes to mind) has been to tear copies of the English-translated comic in half and hurl it across the room, while other fans—prompted by lines such as "I... have... a... splitting... headache" and "This may feel strange at first, but you'll get used to it"—have sometimes been known to break out in fits of *Mystery Science Theater 3000*-style interactive heckling. Released in Japan under the title "Seikimatsu Kyûseishu Densetsu Hokuto no Ken: Gekijô Ban" (Fin de Siécle Savior Legend Fist of the North Star: Theatrical Version) by Toei Video; available in North America through Streamline Pictures. **110 min.**

Domestic Home Video:
SPV 90263 ▲ $19.95 ▲ VHS ▲ DUB ▲ Mono ▲ CC ▲ 09/15/92
ID 2973SE ▲ $39.95 ▲ LD ▲ DUB ▲ 11/13/96

Fuma Conspiracy *See* Lupin III

Gaiking

TV series, 26 episodes

(1976-77) ©Toei Animation Co. Ltd./Jim Terry Productions

Music: Shunsuke Kikuchi

Based on an original story of the same name, as serialized in various Japanese publications, as well as on the 44-episode animated television series broadcast in Japan during 1976-77. Details the adventures of Sanshiro Tsuwabuki, a young Japanese baseball player who joins an elite team of specialized warriors committed to piloting giant robots against the evil hordes of the "Black Horror." Broadcast in the U.S. as part of the FORCE FIVE series (the other four series were DANGARD ACE, GRANDIZER, STARZINGER, and GETTA ROBO G), to date only two episodes of GAIKING as seen on "Force Five" are available on home video. Original series released in Japan under the title "Ôzora Maryû (Great Skies Demon-Dragon) Gaiking" by Toei Video; available in North America through Parade Video. This videotape contains the first two episodes of the series. In ARIES JOINS THE TEAM, Darius and his Black Horror Corps plan to save Zela from being swallowed by the Black Hole. Aries Astronopoulos, a baseball player, is recruited to pilot Gaiking, the giant robot. The crew of the Great Space Dragon is introduced. In RIGHT DOWN THE MIDDLE, Aries learns to pilot Gaiking and use its weapons. But he may be quitting... until he meets the Garwings. **46 min.**

Domestic Home Video:
PRV 6614 ▲ $12.95 ▲ VHS ▲ DUB ▲ Mono ▲ 02/01/93

Galaxy Express 999

(1979) ©Leiji Matsumoto/Toei Animation Co., Ltd.

Director: Taro Rin.

Based on the epic manga series of the same name by Leiji "STAR BLAZERS" Matsumoto. Classic bildungsroman story of a young boy's transition to manhood as he journeys on the far-future space train *Galaxy Express 999* seeking revenge for his mother's murder. GE 999's romantic, humanistic ethic—and especially its treatment of the theme of replacing the flesh with advanced electronics and machinery—is a counterpoint in mood to the cyberpunk ethic that would appear in 1980s science fiction such as "Neuromancer," and this theme is developed even further in 1981's ADIEU GALAXY EXPRESS, the second GE 999 movie, wherein young Tetsuro's journey comes full circle and the horrifying secret behind the Machine Empire is revealed. Both films sport cameo appearances by Matsumoto's panverse of characters, including the infamous space pirates Captain Harlock and Emeraldas; however, until recently, only the first film was available domestically, in a severely edited form from Roger Corman's New World Pictures, which aired on HBO in a severly edited form in the 1980s. Released in Japan under the titles "Ginga Tetsudô 999" (Galaxy Express 999) and "Sayonara Ginga Tetsudô 999: Andromeda Shûchaku Eki" (Adieu Galaxy Express 999: Final Station Andromeda) by Toei Video; available uncut and unedited in North America through Viz Video. ADIEU is scheduled for domestic release in the first half of 1997 by the same distributor. **120 min.**

Domestic Home Video:
VV GE-001 ▲ $24.95 ▲ VHS ▲ DUB ▲ Digital HiFi Stereo ▲ 09/17/96
VV GES-001 ▲ $29.95 ▲ VHS ▲ SUB ▲ Digital HiFi Stereo ▲ 09/17/96

Galaxy Fraulein Yuna

OAV series, 2 volumes

(1995) ©Reds/Hudson/Toho/Starchild/Movic

Original Story & Character Design: Mika Akitaka *Director:* Yorifusa Yamaguchi *Supervision:* Katsumi Shimazaki *Mecha Design:* Kunihiro Abe, Hajime Katoki

Two-volume OAV sci-fi comedy based on the video game of the same name, with original story and character designs by game designer Mika Akitaka, better known for his aerodynamically spiky mecha designs for the likes of "Gundam Double Zeta" and "Gundam 0083," and as originator of those oh-so-cute "mobile suit girls"—girls dressed in "robot" outfits made to resemble actual mecha in "Mobile Suit Gundam" (art books have been published filled with drawings of these cuties in chrome). Suprise, surprise—YUNA looks not unlike one of said MS girls. Featuring mecha designs by mecha-design wonder boy Hajime Katoki ("Gundam 0083," "Victory Gundam"). Released in Japan as "Ginga Ojôsama Densetsu Yuna" by King Record/Toho; available in North America through A.D. Vision.

Galaxy Fraulein Yuna

Cosmic cooking contests, house-destroying wake-up calls, and kidnapped puppies are all in a day's work for Yuna and her sidekick Yuri, the incredible eating machine. But is the new girl at school really what she seems? And what about those two around the corner? Yuna better watch out! The aliens have arrived and they're after her! **35 min.**

Galaxy Fraulein Yuna 2

After watching a person she believes to be Yuna destroy large portions of the city, Galactic Investigator Misaki takes Yuna in to stand trial on charges of treason. Much to the dismay of a bemused Yuna, she is found guilty and sentenced to die by being thrown into a black hole. Or will Taro-chan, the kidnapped puppy, prove to be the loose thread that will unravel Fraulein D's nefarious plans? **35 min.**

Domestic Home Video:
Galaxy Fraulein Yuna
ADV GY/001 ▲ $29.95 ▲ VHS ▲ SUB ▲ HiFi Surround ▲ 05/21/96
Galaxy Fraulein Yuna 2
ADV GY/002 ▲ $29.95 ▲ VHS ▲ SUB ▲ HiFi Surround ▲ 09/03/96

Gall Force

Theatrical feature and 2 OAV sequels

(1986-88) ©MOVIC, Sony Video Software International Corp.

Original Story: Hideki Kakinuma *Screenplay:* Sukehiro Tomita (1), Hideki Kakinuma (2&3) *Director:* Katsuhito Akiyama *Character Design:* Kenichi Sonoda *Art Director:* Junichi Azuma *Music:* Ichizo Seo *Mecha Design:* Rei Yumeno (3)

Sci-fi action-drama of an all-female race fighting a desperate war against an inhuman enemy, possibly leading to the creation of the human race, featuring character designs by Kenichi Sonoda (BUBBLEGUM CRISIS, GUNSMITH CATS). An animated movie inspired by a serialized manga story "Star Front Gall Force," done with figure models and minature sets, á la THUNDERBIRDS, which ran in the Japanese modeling magazine MODEL GRAPHIX, the first GALL FORCE of them all, ETERNAL STORY, spawned a successful set of OAVs based on the characters established in the first film, or their later-generation heirs and/or doppelgängers. In addition to the first three videos in the first GALL FORCE series, also available on home video are the one-volume "mini OAV series" RHEA GALL FORCE; the three-volume GALL FORCE EARTH CHAPTER series; the NEW ERA series; as well as three "novelty" videos, one available in the U.S. and two not: TEN LITTLE GALL FORCE, a comedic, "super deformed" look at the series' familiar characters; "Gall Force Chikyû Shô (Earth Chapter): Visual Collection," a compilation-style video featuring six original songs sung by the series' Japanese voice-actors, set to footage from the EARTH series; and finally, "Gall Force Fightin' Spirits Special Lady's Live," a 35-minute live-action "in concert" special featuring eight songs as, again, sung by the series' Japanese voice-actors. (The GALL FORCE series has also recently inspired a remake, GALL FORCE: THE REVOLUTION, which has yet to make it to home video in the U.S.) Released in Japan under the titles "Gall Force," "Rhea Gall Force," "Gall Force Chikyû Shô," "Gall Force Shin Seiki Hen," "Ten Little Gall Force," and "Gall Force Chikyû Shô: Visual Collection" by Polydor; all videos (except for TEN LITTLE GALL FORCE, which is available through AnimEigo) available as noted in North America through U.S. Manga Corps.

Gall Force: *Eternal Story*

Somewhere deep in space, an ancient war rages between the all-female Solnoid race and the bio-mechanical Paranoid civilization. The titanic space battles between the monstrous Paranoids and the feminine Solnoids erupt into a hair-raising roller coaster ride as the

Solnoid crew flee their alien enemies to a distant star system untouched by the war. Ordered to their newly created homeworld, Chaos, in the 9th Star System, the seven surviving crew members of the Solnoid cruiser *Starleaf* are cut off from the rest of their fleet. As they battle their way to Chaos, the young women find themselves pawns in the plans of the high commands of both sides. What they learn when they reach the new world will shake their loyalty to its very foundations. **86 min.**

Gall Force 2: *Destruction*

Now, others take up the fight - and it's about to get a lot tougher! Ace pilot Lufy, survivor of the ill-fated *Starleaf*, rejoins the Solnoid army just as it is learned that both the Paranoid and Solnoid home planets have been destroyed. Now it seems no planet is safe, and the next world targeted for destruction is the very planet that has been selected for a bold experiment that could end the fighting forever. Lufy's new companions are determined not to let this happen... but their breakneck race against time to prevent destruction seems doomed from the start. **50 min.**

Gall Force 3: *Stardust War*

The destruction of the 9th Star System has been averted. With the destruction of DAMIA, the new race on the planet Terra is free to develop in peace. But the Solnoid and the Paranoid are doomed to annihilation. Gathering together their remaining ships and Planet Destroyers, the Solnoid have retreated to a forgotten star system to await their enemies. There, in the light of a dying star, the final battle will be fought... with neither side expecting to escape alive. As both races prepare themselves for Armageddon, Lufy and the last survivors of the Lorelei fleet scramble to avert the inevitable. Finding a new ally and a new purpose, they prepare to attempt one last, desperate gamble. If they succeed, both races may still have a future. Fail, and all will be reduced to stardust. **60 min.**

Domestic Home Video:
Gall Force: Eternal Story
USM 1467 ▲ $19.95 ▲ VHS ▲ DUB ▲ 11/05/96
USM 1033 ▲ $29.95 ▲ VHS ▲ SUB ▲ Mono ▲ 10/14/92
ID 8584CT ▲ $29.95 ▲ LD ▲ SUB ▲ HiFi Mono ▲ 07/05/91

Gall Force 2
USM 1034 ▲ $29.95 ▲ VHS ▲ SUB ▲ Stereo ▲ 10/06/93
ID 2865CT ▲ $34.95 ▲ LD ▲ SUB ▲ HiFi Mono ▲ 11/08/94

Gall Force 3
USM 1035 ▲ $29.95 ▲ VHS ▲ SUB ▲ Stereo ▲ 07/06/94
ID 2877CT ▲ $34.95 ▲ LD ▲ SUB ▲ HiFi Stereo ▲ 05/10/95

Gall Force: Earth Chapter   `OAV`

OAV series, 3 volumes

(1989-90) ©Artmic

Director: Katsuhito Akiyama *Screenplay:* Yuichi Tomioka (1), Hideki Kakinuma (2&3) *Original Story:* Hideki Kakinuma *Music:* Kaoru Mizutani *Character Design:* Kenichi Sonoda

In 2085, Earth is a ruined wasteland ruled by the lethal war machines that were the only winners in mankind's final, apocalyptic war. When humanity fled the planet to regroup on Mars, only a handful of warriors were left behind. Now, Sandy Newman and her comrades fight for their lives every day.

Gall Force: Earth Chapter 1

If they could only reach one of the unlaunched nuclear missiles, the MME citadel - the main stronghold of the cyberoid war machines - could be destroyed. Searching for the missiles, Sandy's team discovers a secret underground retreat where the Geo Chris religious sect has been quietly worshipping their "Tree of Revival" - rumored to have the power to restore life to the shattered planet. As the opposing forces come together in a devastating showdown, Sandy is driven to the breaking point. This may be humanity's last chance as Gorn plans to annihilate the human race! **48 min.**

Gall Force: Earth Chapter 2

Mankind, banished to Mars, races desperately against time to build a super-weapon - an immense, plasma cannon - which could operate from deep space and destroy an entire continent in a single blast. And the MME citadel, located right in the middle of Australia, would be the perfect target. Meanwhile on Earth, Sandy Newman and her comrades are staging a desperate fight from their hidden Australian bases. As their troops and supplies dwindle, their only hope lies in reinforcements from Mars - reinforcements which may never arrive. At the same time, computer leader Gorn's plans for the destruction of humanity are dangerously near completion. All that is needed is one last key element. These plans are based on the work of Dr. Newman who perished in the apocalypse that destroyed Earth. But his daughter, Sandy, survived and Gorn issues the supreme order: Get Sandy Newman! **50 min.**

Gall Force: Earth Chapter 3

Although Sandy Newman and her comrades have fought valiantly against the MME war machines, their supplies and ammunition are nearly exhausted. Across Earth, the soldiers of the resistance grimly prepare for their final battle - a battle they cannot win. But on Mars, General McKenzie is planning a massive return to Earth. The invasion will use every technique at their disposal: massive space fleets, asteroid bombardment, orbital troop carriers, and high speed re-entry vehicles. This is the ultimate war between man and computer. Fought across two planets, from orbit to ground, and across the devastated landscape of Earth, it's a battle of utter annihilation. But the crucial contest may come deep inside the half-mile tall MME citadel as Sandy Newman comes face-to-face with the

computer leader Gorn. As always, Gorn is one step ahead of its human opponents, and unless Sandy can accomplish a miracle, humanity is doomed. **58 min.**

Domestic Home Video:
Gall Force: Earth Chapter 1
USM 1085 ▲ $29.95 ▲ VHS ▲ SUB ▲ Stereo ▲ 12/07/94
ID 2889CT ▲ $34.95 ▲ LD ▲ SUB ▲ HiFi Stereo ▲ 12/06/95

Gall Force: Earth Chapter 2
USM 1086 ▲ $29.95 ▲ VHS ▲ SUB ▲ Stereo ▲ 02/05/95
ID 2895CT ▲ $34.95 ▲ LD ▲ SUB ▲ HiFi Stereo ▲ 03/06/96

Gall Force: Earth Chapter 3
USM 1087 ▲ $29.95 ▲ VHS ▲ SUB ▲ Stereo ▲ 06/06/95
ID 2896CT ▲ $34.95 ▲ LD ▲ SUB ▲ HiFi Stereo ▲ 03/27/96

Gall Force: New Era   `OAV`

OAV series, 2 volumes

(1992-93) ©Artmic

Animation Directors: Hideaki Oba, Yoshitaka Fujiimoto *Original Story and Screenplay:* Hideki Kakinuma *Music:* Takehito Nakazawa *Character Design:* Kenichi Sonoda *Production Designers:* Hideki Kakinuma, Kimitoshi Yamane

Generations ago, humanity's war against the Cyberoid war machines left our planet a desolate wasteland. Now, dozens of "ecropolis" cities are scattered across the landscape. Life is a hyper-modern utopia inside these artificial habitats. But someone has a different idea of Utopia. "Yumans" are genetically engineered and "improved" humans. Although some yumans coexist peacefully with normal humans, some believe that their genetic superiority has destined them to rule.

Gall Force: New Era 1

Fifty years ago, the yuman tyrant Genova attempted a coup to seize power for the yumans. In the end, the bloody rebellion failed, further damaging Earth's fragile ecology. Now Genova's descendant, Nova, is ready to try again. This time the yumans have a powerful ally — a being that once came close to completely destroying the human race. Our only hope lies in the android Catty. A creation of the Solnoids, the long-dead ancestors of humanity, Catty understands the eternal cycles of destruction which plague our race. Only Catty can gather the seeds of mankind's salvation — but time is running out. For Earth and humanity, this will be the last battle — ever. **50 min.**

Gall Force: New Era 2

Mankind is dead, destroyed by the evil computer intelligence Gorn. The only survivors are six young women, shot into deep space by the android Catty. The creation of an ancient alien race, only she understands the terrible cycles of war and destruction that devastate our race. And only she foresaw the coming disaster. Now, as the Earth smolders, a single escape pod races away, bound for an unknown destination. But Gorn is close behind, with a powerful pursuit ship and a squadron of fighters. Through brain surgery and cybernetic implants, Gorn now inhabits the body of Nova, its human tool. But Gorn is not limited to a single body or single location. Like a computer virus, Gorn can transmit itself into any computer. Meanwhile, six young women wait desperately around their radio, hoping to learn that somewhere, other people have survived the disaster. No one realizes that their radio may lead to their doom. Soon, no place in the solar system, not even their own ship, will be safe. And then the annihilation of humanity will be complete! **49 min.**

Domestic Home Video:
Gall Force: New Era 1
USM 1083 ▲ $29.95 ▲ VHS ▲ SUB ▲ Stereo ▲ 09/05/95
ID 2897CT ▲ $34.95 ▲ LD ▲ SUB ▲ HiFi Stereo ▲ 03/27/96

Gall Force: New Era 2
USM 1084 ▲ $29.95 ▲ VHS ▲ SUB ▲ Stereo ▲ 12/05/95
ID 2898CT ▲ $34.95 ▲ LD ▲ SUB ▲ HiFi Stereo ▲ 05/01/96

Garaga   `MOVIE`

(1989) ©Satomi Mikuriya/AVN/ASMIK

Director and Screenplay: Hidemi Kubo *Character Design:* Moriyasu Taniguchi *Original Story:* Satomi Mikuriya *Music:* Tatsumi Yano

Based on the unfinished manga by Satomi Mikuriya. In the year 2755, a spacecraft malfunction forces a crew of explorers onto an alien planet for psychic adventures, thus the Japanese-supplied preface to the series title, "Hyper Psychic Geo." Not particularly original story wins points for persistance; once you've reached the 90-minute point in this hour and a half theatrical feature, you'll be wondering why you've stuck with it

that long. Released in Japan under the title "Garaga" by Asmic; available in North America through U.S. Manga Corps. **100 min.**

Domestic Home Video:
USM 1332 ▲ $29.95 ▲ VHS ▲ SUB ▲ Stereo ▲ 01/09/96

Genesis Survivor Gaiarth

OAV series, 3 volumes

(1992-93) ©Artmic

Character Design: Hiroyuki Kitazume *Animation Directors:* Jun Okuda (1), Seiji Tanda (1), Makoto Bessho (2&3), Keiichi Sato (3), Eisaku Inoue (3), Tomokazu Tokoro (3) *Mecha Director:* Hiroyuki Ochi (1), Noire Kuwabara (2) *Directors:* Hiroyuki Kitazume (1&2), Shinji Aramaki (1&2), Hideaki Oba (3)

That this three-volume OAV series is better known in some circles for the persistence in which its U.S. manufacturer clings to the Japanese-supplied misspelling of "Survivor" than for its other virtues is a sad irony, for even if the story breaks no new ground—young, mostly untried warrior pitted against evil cyber-warlord in a futuristic world; can you say *Star Wars*?—it's nevertheless an intriguing blend of sci-fi elements, 100% anime mecha gimcracks and fantasy themes which combine to create the kind of fast-paced sci-fi fantasy to which many OAVs aspire, but which few achieve. (Spell-casting robots? Cool.) Released in Japan under the title "Sôsei Kishi Gaiarth" (Genesis Survivor Gaiarth) by Toshiba EMI; available in North America through AnimEigo.

Genesis Survivor Gaiarth Stage 1
Gaiarth - the world of Ital del Labard, a young man raised by an aging Warroid, Sahari, the leader of a band of Junk-hunters, and Zaxon, an amnesiac Warroid who may be a link to the fabled past. Gaiarth - a world in which an old and terrible evil has reawakened, threatening to bring about the end of the world - again! **51 min.**

Genesis Survivor Gaiarth Stage 2
After defeating the Beast-Master (in Stage 1), Ital, Zaxon and Sahari travel to Metro City, where a gigantic Kampfdraken has reportedly awakened. Our heroes confidently engage the monster, only to discover that it's more than they bargained for. When the Draken is finally defeated, they discover that it is guarding a treasure, an egg containing a mysterious Elf, a synthetic human named Sakuya - the same Sakuya that the Beast-Master was searching for. But when Sakuya awakens, the mysterious General is able to set his terrible plan into motion. **46 min.**

Genesis Survivor Gaiarth Stage 3
After the defeat of the Kampfdraken (in Stage 2), a mysterious Elf named Sakuya awoke from a century-long slumber, only to be captured by the diabolical General, who plans to use her to dominate the world - or destroy it in the attempt. Can Ital, Sahari, Fayk, and Zaxon the Warroid rescue Sakuya, defeat the General, and save Gaiarth from a fate worse than Armageddon? **45 min.**

Domestic Home Video:
Genesis Survivor Gaiarth Stage 1
ANI ET095-016 ▲ $19.95 ▲ VHS ▲ DUB ▲ Stereo ▲ 03/12/96
ANI AT093-001 ▲ $34.95 ▲ VHS ▲ SUB ▲ Stereo
ANI AD095-009 ▲ $39.95 ▲ LD ▲ HYBRID ▲ Stereo ▲ 03/26/96
Genesis Survivor Gaiarth Stage 2
ANI ET095-017 ▲ $19.95 ▲ VHS ▲ DUB ▲ Stereo ▲ 05/15/96
ANI AT093-003 ▲ $34.95 ▲ VHS ▲ SUB ▲ Stereo ▲ 07/07/93
ANI AD096-010 ▲ $39.95 ▲ LD ▲ HYBRID ▲ Stereo ▲ 05/15/96
Genesis Survivor Gaiarth Stage 3
ANI ET095-018 ▲ $19.95 ▲ VHS ▲ DUB ▲ Stereo ▲ 05/15/96
ANI AT093-010 ▲ $34.95 ▲ VHS ▲ SUB ▲ Stereo ▲ 04/20/94
ANI AD095-011 ▲ $39.95 ▲ LD ▲ HYBRID ▲ Stereo ▲ 05/15/96

Genma Taishi *See* HARMAGEDDON

Genocyber

OAV series, 5 episodes

(1993) ©Artmic/Plex

Director: Koichi Ohata *Script:* Noboru Aikawa(1&2), Emu Arii (1), Koichi Ohata (2) *Original Story:* Artmic *Music:* Takehito Nakazawa, Hiroaki Kagoshima *Character Design:* Atsushi Yamagata *Production Design:* Kimitoshi Yamane, Shinji Aramaki, Koichi Ohata, Yoshio Harada, Hitoshi Fukuchi

The first OAV in anime history to go on sale in the U.S. before it was released in Japan, the five-part

GENOCYBER series presents a corporation experimenting with that which they should not tamper with: two sisters—one a cyborg, the other, a powerful psychic—who, if they could be fused into a single creature, might prove to be the most powerful creature the world has ever seen...the "Genocyber." Once released, however, the power of the Genocyber is more than either of them can handle, and there's definitely going to be a price to pay. Frequently defying its limited budget with creative insight and excellent design work, GENOCYBER is flamboyant, violent mecha action from the creator of M.D. GEIST, loosely based on the comic by Tony Takezaki, as serialized in HOBBY JAPAN magazine (published in English by Viz Comics), adapted by Noboru Aikawa and Emu Arii. Also features production designs by Kimitoshi Yamane (THE VISION OF ESCAFLOWNE). Released in Japan under the title "Genocyber" by Bandai Visual; available in North America through U.S. Manga Corps.

Genocyber Part 1: *Birth of Genocyber*
Their scientist father never considered how deeply each girl hates the other nor how far his employers would go to ensure the project's success. Now as the battle for possession of Genocyber erupts, the cyber-punk world of the future explodes with violence as not even death can be taken for granted. **46 min.**

Genocyber Parts 2 & 3: *Vajranoid Showdown*
The destruction of Hong Kong was only the beginning. Now, emerging from the ashes, the Genocyber's rage is unleashed against its creators. Wandering into a small nation's war of aggression, Elaine is embroiled in the Kyuryu Group's latest weapons test: The Vajranoid, a biomechanical monstrosity designated to be the ultimate fighter pilot. Capable of merging with almost any piece of machinery, the Vajranoid is the only one who can sense the dangerous power within this innocent-looking girl's cybernetic body. **50 min.**

Genocyber, Parts 4 & 5: *The Legend of Ark de Grande*
The Endtimes are here. After a nearly 100-year battle with the forces of the Kyuryu Group, Genocyber has succeeded in its defeat ... at the cost of all human civilization. But, on the eve of its final battle with the last remnants of Kyuryu's forces, it mysteriously vanishes from the surface of the Earth. Some 300 years later, mankind has only barely recovered from the destruction. In the city of Ark de Grande, mankind's pre-apocalyptic civilization has been re-created. As two young lovers arrive to start a new life, they are swept up in the plots rippling through the city. As one is unwittingly linked with the growing rebel movement, the other is mistaken for a heavenly messenger by a cult devoted to the legend of Genocyber. As tensions build, one final enemy from the old world floats in the darkness above the Earth, waiting ... For 300 years Genocyber has slept, but now the time for its rebirth is almost at hand. **60 min.**

Domestic Home Video:
Genocyber Part 1
USM 1091 ▲ $29.95 ▲ VHS ▲ SUB ▲ Stereo ▲ 03/02/94
ID 2870CT ▲ $34.95 ▲ LD ▲ SUB ▲ HiFi Stereo ▲ 03/01/95
Genocyber Parts 2 & 3
USM 1101 ▲ $29.95 ▲ VHS ▲ SUB ▲ Stereo ▲ 10/05/94
ID 2880CT ▲ $34.95 ▲ LD ▲ SUB ▲ HiFi Stereo ▲ 06/20/95
Genocyber Parts 4 & 5
USM 1228 ▲ $29.95 ▲ VHS ▲ SUB ▲ Stereo ▲ 01/04/95

Gensô Jodan Ellcia *See* ELLCIA

Ghost in the Shell

(1995) ©Masamune Shirow/Kodansha Ltd./Bandai Visual Co., Ltd./Manga Entertainment

Director: Mamoru Oshii *Screenplay:* Kazunori Ito *Animation Director:* Toshihiko Nishikubo *Key Animation Supervisors:* Kazuchika Kise, Hiroyuki Okiura *Character Design:* Hiroyuki Okiura *Mecha Design:* Shoji Kawamori, Atsushi Takeuchi *Art Director:* Hiromasa Ogura *Music:* Kenji Kawai

A big-budget theatrical feature noteworthy for being one-third financed and co-produced by a Western company, GHOST became the first anime video to reach #1 on *Billboard*'s sales charts in the U.S. Based on the action/intrigue manga by Masamune Shirow (APPLESEED, DOMINION), GHOST is the story of a cyborg intelligence officer hunting a bodiless super-hacker with links to her own government. In animation, GHOST is remade in the director's image, with Oshii trademarks such as Biblical epigrams, drifting, dream-like observations of city life, and realist, if slightly spooky character designs (departing radically from Shirow's typical cute-sexiness). Raises interesting questions about the point of human identity in a world of *Neuromancer*-inspired mind-computer transfer. Sophisticated computer graphics give GHOST a *Virtuosity*-like atmosphere of cyber-reality, while beautiful art direction by Hiromasa

Ogura (NINJA SCROLL, PATLABOR 2, THE WINGS OF HONNEAMISE) creates a near-photographic Hong Kong-like 21st century "Newport City." While not quite the masterpiece of Oshii's 1993 PATLABOR 2, the director's quietly creepy sensiblity adds an unexpected dimension to the film, his theological bent elevating Shirow's oft-juvenile technological preoccupations to a more spiritual level. Released in Japan under the title "Kôkaku Kidô-Tai" by Kodansha/Bandai Visual; available in North America through Manga Video and Pioneer Animation. *CAV laserdisc (115 min.) includes "The Making of" featurette.* **85 min.**

Domestic Home Video:
MGV 635529 ▲ $19.95 ▲ VHS ▲ DUB ▲ HiFi Stereo ▲ 06/18/96
MGV 635571 ▲ $29.95 ▲ VHS ▲ SUB ▲ HiFi Stereo ▲ 07/30/96
PI 34990 ▲ $34.95 ▲ LD ▲ M/A ▲ HiFi Stereo ▲ 11/19/96
PI 35008 ▲ $49.95 ▲ LD-CAV ▲ M/A ▲ HiFi Stereo ▲ 12/10/96

Giant Robo
OAV series, 6 episodes

(1992-95) ©Hikari Productions/Amuse Video/Plex/Atlantis

Director: Yasuhiro Imagawa *Original Story:* Mitsuteru Yokoyama *Animation Direction:* Kazuyoshi Katayama *Art Directors:* Hiromasa Ogura, Masanori Kikuchi, Yusuke Takeda, Dai Ota *Music:* Masamichi Amano

Director Imagawa's dream project, this retro remake adapts original "G Robo" creator Mitsuteru (GIGANTOR) Yokoyama's eponymous King Tut-influenced mecha character into an original story, seamlessly blending in other Yokoyama manga characters from totally separate series into an idealized world of giant robots, evil syndicates, and plans to take over the world with a perfect energy source. Art style is stunning, animation powerfully dynamic; the only drawback is, other, currently Japan-only projects (such as G GUNDAM, and THE VIOLINIST OF HAMLIN) keep distracting Imagawa's attention from finishing the series. Released in Japan (six OAVs to date, with a seventh expected as a finale) under the title "Giant Robo" by Bandai Visual; formerly available in North America through U.S. Renditions, and currently through Manga Video.

Giant Robo Episode 1: *The Black Attache Case*
The Experts of Justice desperately try to save Dr. Shizuma from the hands of Big Fire. Dr. Shizuma created the "Shizuma Drive," a power source which has replaced all forms of energy on Earth. Big Fire assigns Lord Alberto, one of the mysterious Magnificent Ten, to capture Shizuma and the third of three prototype Shizuma Drives that will usher in Earth's greatest age of darkness! Can a young boy, Daisaku, and Giant Robo stop them? **45 min.**

Giant Robo Episode 2: *The Tragedy of Bashtarlle*
The Experts of Justice and Dr. Shizuma narrowly escape the clutches of the renegades known to the world as Big Fire, only to be trapped by the terrible Ivan. Giant Robo, unable to penetrate a spectacular force field, witnesses the Experts of Justice in conflict with Ivan who explains the power of the Shizuma Drive over the city of Bashtarlle. Will Lord Alberto's plan to destroy Robo's power source finish the Experts of Justice? **45 min.**

Giant Robo Episode 3: *Magnetic Web Strategy*
When an energy sucking orb advances toward the last power source on Earth (the Shanghai oil refinery), all the Experts of Justice except Tetsugyu, Daisaku and Robo are ordered to gather there. Disobeying orders, the three arrive in Shanghai. One by one the Magnetic Web Devices fail because of sabotage. All hope seems lost when Robo and Daisuku charge after the Orb and are defeated. Even Robo's tremendous strength is no match for the menacing eyeball. Will Robo and the Experts survive their greatest challenge yet and save the Earth from total destruction? **45 min.**

Giant Robo Episode 4: *The Twilight of the Superhero*
Even Giant Robo's punch has no effect on the menacing Eye of Folger. When Magnetic Web Devices are sabotaged, Taiso and Alberto battle for the ultimate destiny of Earth. Elsewhere, members of Big Fire attack the Greta Garbo and Ginrei must protect Daisaku, even if it means sacrificing her life. She makes a startling discovery when she comes face to face with her father. Will the efforts of Issei and Youshi be enough to protect everyone against the mysterious Koenshaku? **45 min.**

Giant Robo Episode 5: *The Truth of Bashtarlle*
Inside the fiery Greta Garbo, Daisaku plummets into the icy depths of the Himalayan mountains. Ginrei and Tetsugyu desperately search for their fallen comrade who has been sucked into the darkness of the snowy mountains. As Daisaku lies unconscious, he dreams of his past and the origins of Giant Robo. When Ginrei and Tetsugyu finally track down their friend, Tetsugyu must fight his greatest battle ever. **45 min.**

Giant Robo Episode 6: *Conflict in the Snow Mountains*
With the Bashtarlle phenomenon weighing heavily on their minds — Big Fire and the Magnificent Ten attempt to follow through with their initial scheme, "Operation Earth Stand Still." Using their newest weapon, "The Big Balloon" — a device that absorbs energy, Big Fire hope to annihilate the Earth. Giant Robo and comrades, Daisaku and Ginrei, team up once again to protect the sample and to stop the detonation of "The Big Balloon." The drama heightens as Daisaku fights to rescue Ginrei and save the world.

Domestic Home Video:
Giant Robo Vol. 1: *Episode 1*
USR VD20 ▲ $24.95 ▲ VHS ▲ SUB ▲ HiFi Stereo ▲ 01/15/93 ▲ Out of Print
PI 33653 ▲ $34.95 ▲ LD ▲ M/A ▲ Stereo ▲ CC ▲ 03/23/94
Giant Robo Vol. 1: *Episode 2*
PI 33899 ▲ $34.95 ▲ LD ▲ M/A ▲ Stereo ▲ CC ▲ 06/29/94
Giant Robo Vol. 1: *Episodes 1 & 2*
MGV 633897 ▲ $19.95 ▲ VHS ▲ DUB ▲ HiFi Stereo ▲ 04/18/95
Giant Robo Vol. 2: *Episode 3*
MGV 634795 ▲ $14.95 ▲ VHS ▲ DUB ▲ HiFi Stereo ▲ 06/20/95
PI 33903 ▲ $34.95 ▲ LD ▲ M/A ▲ HiFi Stereo ▲ CC ▲ 11/16/94
Giant Robo Vol. 3: *Episode 4*
MGV 634803 ▲ $14.95 ▲ VHS ▲ DUB ▲ HiFi Stereo ▲ 08/22/95
PI 34334 ▲ $34.95 ▲ LD ▲ M/A ▲ HiFi Stereo ▲ CC ▲ 01/11/95
Giant Robo Vol. 4: *Episode 5*
MGV 634809 ▲ $14.95 ▲ VHS ▲ DUB ▲ HiFi Stereo ▲ 10/24/95
Giant Robo Vol. 5: *Episode 6*
MGV 635531 ▲ $14.95 ▲ VHS ▲ DUB ▲ HiFi Stereo ▲ 05/21/96

Gigantor
TV series, 52 episodes

(1963-65) ©TCJ Animation Center/Delphi Associates Inc.

American Adaptation by: Fred Ladd & Al Singer *Animation Production by:* TCJ Animation Center

Mitsuteru Yokoyama's robot creation Tetsujin 28-go ("Ironman no. 28") was retitled "Gigantor" for its U.S. release (which was sung mantra-like, over in over in the catchy new American theme song), but much of its original brio survived the crossing of the waters from Japan to the U.S.; one of the building blocks of a genre now recognized as a staple of Japanese animation, GIGANTOR is a kind of apotheosis of the "giant robot" genre, featuring a mighty super-robot built by a kindly scientist and operated by his young son in the service of the Japanese police. The black and white animation is '50s sci-fi at its crude but energetic best, directed with all the gleeful energy of a superhero comic. Although a new full-color version with slicker animation (but lacking the spirit of the original) was produced in 1980-81, it was not shown in the U.S. until the early '90s (and even then, only on cable). Yet another remake—1992-93's "Tetsujin 28 FX," was never brought over at all, possibly in recognition of the fact that the new series had strayed even farther than the first sequel when it came to "dumbing down" what had been a (pardon the expression) riveting storyline for a presumed juvenile audience. 96 episodes released in Japan under the title "Tetsujin 28-go" by Sega Enterprises (only 52 episodes made it to America); available in North America through Scott Wheeler Productions and The Right Stuf.

Gigantor Vol. 1: *Episodes 1 - 3*
In Episode 1, STRUGGLE AT THE SOUTH POLE, upon a request from the United Nations, Jimmy Sparks and Gigantor hurry to the South Pole, where several Antarctic bases have been attacked by unknown enemies. Arriving in the Antarctic, the evil Dr. Katzmeow sprays Gigantor with scalding water which immediately envelops him in ice, and gives Jimmy 24 hours to surrender. In Episode 2, BATTLE AT THE BOTTOM OF THE WORLD, Dr. Katzmeow captures Gigantor and proceeds to fashion his own robot, Flip Q. UN forces are attacked by unidentified submarines, and a fierce battle ensues between Gigantor and Flip Q. In Episode 3, STING OF THE SPIDER, Reeny, daughter of the famous Dr. Emeritus, takes his invention, the Super-Elex, to Jimmy and his friends. Bob Brilliant demonstrates that the device generates 100,000 volts and cautions that the Spider will try everything to steal it. **75 min. B&W**

Gigantor Vol. 2: *Episodes 4 - 6*
In Episode 4, RETURN OF THE SPIDER, Jimmy and his friends receive a message from Dick Strong that Captain Spider has escaped from Snake Island. He has returned to Polyvania and imprisoned the King, Queen, and also Dr. Emeritus. In Episode 5, SPIDER'S REVENGE, when we last saw Spider, he had led a military coup to become dictator of Polyvania, and he has the Super-Elex! Spider is intent on ruling the world through the power of the Super-Elex, and is willing to do anything to prevent Dr. Emeritus from creating a duplicate. Spider's

VOLUME 3
3 Full Episodes

Scott Wheeler Productions

desperation mounts as his plans to eliminate Dr. Emeritus fail. Finally, he can wait no longer. He launches an attack on the United States. Can Gigantor stop Spider and his Super-Elex powered Ray Gun? In Episode 6, SECRET VALLEY, Jimmy and the gang's plane is shot down enroute to Australia, and find themselves attacked by savages. Dick Strong discovers that the attacks are part of the evil Von QBall's plan to protect his secret base and mask his plans for conquering the world. Gigantor struggles against Von QBall's arsenal, including a bouncing robot, electrical bees, and a flying buzz saw! **75 min. B&W**

Gigantor Vol. 3: *Episodes 7 - 9*
In Episode 7, THE DIAMOND SMUGGLERS, Jimmy and Inspector Blooper travel to India. They soon are investigating disappearing policemen and mysterious rockets. Posing as "holy men" Jimmy, Blooper, and Inspector Currycomb journey to the Himalayas to see the rockets for themselves. Gigantor destroys one of the rockets, and our heroes assume the diamond smugglers have been scared off for good. But are they jumping to conclusions? In Episode 8, DANGEROUS DR. DIAMOND, from his underground sanctuary, Dr. Diamond retaliates against the police by unleashing a herd of sacred white cattle robots. Gigantor bests the bulls in an exciting battle, but Dr. Diamond is still confident of success. A giant rubber rocket is launched, and Gigantor's blows merely bounce off. When the rocket sprays a freeze gas, Gigantor falls and is captured. Can Jimmy help Gigantor? Also Episode 9: FORCE OF TERROR. **75 min. B&W**

Gigantor Retrospective 30 Vol. 1
In WORLD IN DANGER, the spectacular theft of 70 million dollars is just the beginning of Dr. Nefarious' plan. Now fully bankrolled, he's going to unleash terror on a vast scale and when the dust settles, he'll wind up controlling the planet. The forces of good must undertake a desperate search to find and stop Nefarious before he can succeed with his mad scheme! In BADGE OF DANGER, UFOs are attacking the city and even Gigantor is unable to stop them. Using a mysterious ray, Gigantor has been stopped — and it's up to Bob Brilliant to build something that will tip the scales. Fearing Bob Brilliant might come up with something that would enable Gigantor to beat him, Bob is abducted by the evil Ugablob — the person responsible for the attack on the city! **50 min. B&W**

Gigantor Retrospective 30 Vol. 2
In THE SMOKE ROBOTS, Dr. Birdbrane has developed a new spacecraft — a ship that can easily make the jump between planets. Dubble Trubble, an evil gang leader, has decided that he wants these plans for his own. He sends a highly unusual robot to do his bidding — a robot who has the power to disappear into smoke! Can Gigantor and Jimmy solve the mystery before it's too late? In THE FREEZING RAY, the unthinkable has happened: the evil Ugablob has stolen both Jimmy Sparks' control box and the mighty Gigantor himself! Jimmy and Inspector Blooper then discover that Bob Brilliant is also missing, and head to Ugablob's hideout. Forced to make an emergency landing by a Freezing Ray, they discover that Ugablob is trying once again to take over the world, but this time Gigantor will be used as a tool of evil! **50 min. B&W**

Gigantor Retrospective 30 Vol. 3
In THE MAGIC MULTIPLIER, it's Ugablob again, and this time he's kidnapped Professor Dimdome's daughter. He'll exchange her if the professor will give him the secret of the Multiplier Projector — a fantastic device that causes people to see multiple images of the real person. The professor reluctantly agrees, and it's up to Jimmy and Gigantor to prevent this powerful weapon from falling into evil hands. In THE SUBMARINE BASE, Professor Brainy has been captured. The Evil Swami Fami wants the formula for the Professor's new super rocket fuel, and will stop at nothing to get it. When Gigantor arrives to stop the evil Swami, he too is captured! Even Jimmy Sparks is taken prisoner, and it seems there is nothing to stop Swami Fami from taking over the world! **50 min. B&W**

Gigantor Retrospective 30 Vol. 4
In TREASURE MOUNTAIN, Professor Digadig has been lost deep in the Andes mountains, and Jimmy and the rest of the team have been dispatched to help locate him. Legend has it that a giant robot roams freely in these Peruvian mountain ranges — perhaps even a match for the great Gigantor! Can our heroes stop the evil plans of Pizaro and recover the lost golden treasure of the Incas? In THE MYSTERY MISSILE, no defense system is truly failsafe, as Bob Brilliant proves. A submarine mistakenly fires a nuclear-tipped missile at what is thought to be an attack by a mysterious (presumed hostile) flying object. Realizing the launch was an error, the submarine crew tries to destroy their missile but finds they cannot. It's up to Gigantor to save Earth from nuclear Armageddon! **50 min. B&W**

Gigantor Retrospective 30 Vol. 5
In THE GIANT COBRA, the Kingdom of Morabia is under attack! The evil prince Abdul Ben Hothead is using an incredibly powerful Cobra robot. The Cobra robot and Gigantor battle, discovering that they are fairly evenly matched. Realizing that this opponent will

not be easily defeated, it's up to Bob Brilliant to save the day and somehow give Gigantor the edge! In THE GREAT HUNT, in the dense tropical jungles, the countries of Bongo Bongo and Ping Pang are at war. While on a safari in Bongo Bongo, Bob Brilliant and the rest of the team are suddenly alerted to an emergency: a vital serum is needed from the distant country of Munchabone. **50 min. B&W**

Domestic Home Video:
Gigantor Vol. 1
RS 40010 ▲ $29.95 ▲ VHS ▲ DUB ▲ Mono
Gigantor Vol. 2
RS 40020 ▲ $29.95 ▲ VHS ▲ DUB ▲ Mono
Gigantor Vol. 3
RS 40030 ▲ $29.95 ▲ VHS ▲ DUB ▲ Mono
Gigantor Retrospective 30 Vol. 1
RS 4301 ▲ $19.95 ▲ VHS ▲ DUB ▲ Mono ▲ CP ▲ 03/16/94
Gigantor Retrospective 30 Vol. 2
RS 4302 ▲ $19.95 ▲ VHS ▲ DUB ▲ Mono ▲ CP ▲ 03/16/94
Gigantor Retrospective 30 Vol. 3
RS 4303 ▲ $19.95 ▲ VHS ▲ DUB ▲ Mono ▲ CP ▲ 03/16/94
Gigantor Retrospective 30 Vol. 4
RS 4304 ▲ $19.95 ▲ VHS ▲ DUB ▲ Mono ▲ CP ▲ 03/16/94
Gigantor Retrospective 30 Vol. 5
RS 4305 ▲ $19.95 ▲ VHS ▲ DUB ▲ Mono ▲ CP ▲ 03/16/94
Gigantor 30th Anniversary Vol. 1
Episodes 1 - 4. (120 min.)
LUM 9408 ▲ $39.95 ▲ LD ▲ DUB ▲ HiFi ▲ 10/26/94 ▲ Out of Print
Gigantor 30th Anniversary Vol. 2
Episodes 5 - 8. (120 min.)
LUM 9504 ▲ $39.95 ▲ LD ▲ DUB ▲ HiFi ▲ 05/09/95

Ginga Ojôsama Densetsu Yuna *See* GALAXY FRAULEIN YUNA
Ginga Tetsudô no Yoru *See* NIGHT ON THE GALACTIC R.R.
Ginga Tetsudô 999 *See* GALAXY EXPRESS

The Girl From Phantasia

(1993) ©King Records, Japan

Director: Jun Kamiya *Original Story:* Akane Nagano *Character Design and Art Direction:* Kazuya Kise *Music:* Toshiyuke Watanabe

Based on the manga of the same name by Akane Nagano, as serialized in COMIC GAMMA manga magazine and from the director of BLUE SEED, with character design and art direction by Kazuya Kise, another BLUE SEED staffer. Young girl comes out of a magic carpet connecting two worlds and makes life a living hell for young boy; shades of both Clive Barker's "Weaveworld" and Rumiko Takahashi's URUSEI YATSURA. Nothing new under this sun, but as a bonus, none of the pandering lechery the salacious U.S. box copy prepares us to expect, either. Released in Japan under the title "Fantasia" by King Record; available in North America through A.D. Vision. Includes bonus art portfolio. **40 min.**

Domestic Home Video:
ADV PH/001 ▲ $29.95 ▲ VHS ▲ SUB ▲ HiFi Surround ▲ 02/14/94

Godmars

(1982) ©Hikari Production/TMS Inc.

Director: Hideyuki Motohashi

Bearing little else in common with the manga of the same name by creator Mitsuteru Yokoyama (GIGANTOR, GIANT ROBO, BABEL II), this full-length theatrical feature (inspired by the not-yet-available-in-the-U.S. 1981-82 TV series) is an otherwise completely original story of mankind's exploration of space and those who stand to profit from that exploration not going any further. Meat and potatoes sci-fi in a giant robot vein from a master of the genre. Released in Japan under the title "Rokushin Gattai Godmars Gekijô Ban" (Six-God Combining Godmars: Theatrical Version) by VAP; available in North America through The Right Stuf. **93 min.**

Domestic Home Video:
RS 9002 ▲ $24.95 ▲ VHS ▲ SUB ▲ Mono ▲ CP ▲ 10/05/94

Golden Boy

(1995) ©Tatsuya Egawa/Shueisha • KSS

Original Creator: Tatsuya Egawa *Director, Storyboards & Production Design:* Hiroyuki Kitakubo *Character Design & Animation:* Toshihiro Kawamoto *Music:* Joyo Katayanagi

Sophisticated fun from the director of ROUJIN-Z and the original manga by creator Tatsuya Egawa ("Be Free," "Magical Tarurûto-kun"). A young man realizes he can learn more about life outside the university classroom, so he hops on his bike for what he calls "tanoshii o-benkyô" (fun learning) in the larger school of life. Kintaro (a seeming pervert on the surface) gets into one scrape after another, but the moment he's gone, the people whose lives he's touched almost immediately realize the difference he's made for the better. In the manga, Kintaro's not above voyeurism and toilet seat sniffing; he's not much classier in the anime version, but heartfelt character designs (remarkably close to Egawa's manga originals) and a basically pure heart make the character more likeable (and sexy, in a weird kind of way) than you might otherwise think. Released in Japan under the title "Golden Boy" by KSS/TBS; available in North America through A.D. Vision. **30 min.**

Domestic Home Video:
ADV GB/001D ▲ $19.95 ▲ VHS ▲ DUB ▲ HiFi Surround ▲ 07/30/96
ADV GB/001S ▲ $24.95 ▲ VHS ▲ SUB ▲ HiFi Surround ▲ 07/30/96
ADV GB/001L ▲ $39.95 ▲ LD-CAV ▲ HYBRID ▲ HiFi Surround ▲ 08/27/96

GoShogun: The Time Étranger

(1985) ©Tokuma Shôten/Ashi Productions

Original Story & Screenplay: Takeshi Shudo *Director:* Kunihiko Yuyama *Character Design & Animation Director:* Hideyuki Motohashi

Based on the 1981-82 mecha TV series GOSHOGUN. ÉTRANGER is a fascinating example of the potential of an OAV sequel to a TV show to go in an interesting new direction, rather than simply remaking the original with more modern animation, as is often the case. ÉTRANGER takes only the main characters from the original show and creates an intriguing, *Jacob's Ladder*-like scenario where the heroine, Remy Shimada, dying in her hospital bed of a metabolic disorder, fights for life simultaneously on three fronts: in her present, in the recalled past of her childhood, and with her old friends in an otherwordly, Arab-esque city where they are under a sentence of death from a murderous populace. A good example of the mid-'80s trend of going beyond action-packed plots to experimenting with characters' psychology. Released in Japan under the title "Sengoku Machine GoShogun: Toki no Ihôjin" (Warring-States Machine Goshogun: The Time Stranger) by Tokuma Shôten/Tokuma Japan Communications; available in North America through U.S. Manga Corps. **90 min.**

Domestic Home Video:
USM 1310 ▲ $29.95 ▲ VHS ▲ SUB ▲ Stereo ▲ 07/11/95

Grandizer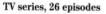

TV series, 26 episodes

(1975-77) ©Toei Animation Co. Ltd./Jim Terry Productions

Created by: Go Nagai *Music:* Shunsuke Kikuchi

Third entry in creator Go Nagai's "Mazinger" series; broadcast in the U.S. as part of the "Force Five" series (the other four series were DANGARD ACE, GAIKING, STARZINGER, and GETTA ROBO G). To date, only two TV episodes of GRANDIZER as seen on "Force Five" are available on home video. 74 episodes released in Japan under the title "UFO Robo Grandizer" by Toei Video (only 26 episodes were used in the "Force Five" version); available in North America through Parade Video. 2 episodes. In ROBOT BACK TO ACTION, Lance arrives at the institute and immediately shows his cockiness. Although he may have been able to pick himself off the ground after falling from a horse at Panhandle's Triple Triangle Ranch, he needs Orion's help against the Vegans. In BEWARE THE RED MOON, Bellicose gives orders to attack Earth. Panhandle takes a plane ride. Lance learns Johnny's true identity. **46 min.**

Domestic Home Video:
PRV 6613 ▲ $12.95 ▲ VHS ▲ DUB ▲ Mono ▲ 02/01/93

Grave of the Fireflies

(1988) ©Akiyuki Nosaka/Shinchosha Co.

Original Story: Akiyuki Nosaka *Written and Directed by:* Isao Takahata *Character Design:* Yoshifumi Kondo *Art Director:* Nizo Yamamoto

Based on the novel by Akiyuki Nosaka, detailing the semi-autobiographical story of his own experiences in the ruins of post WW II Japan. Longtime Hayao Miyazaki producer Isao Takahata adapts this utterly heartwrenching story of two starving orphans struggling to survive on the uncaring streets of a nation devastated by the firebombings and other atocities of war. It is frankly impossible to watch this production without being drained emotionally. In Japan it ran as the first showing in a double-feature with Miyazaki's MY NEIGHBOR TOTORO, the cheerful tone of which is desperately needed after viewing this bleak, brilliant masterwork. Released in Japan under the title "Grave of the Fireflies" by Bandai Visual; available in North America through Central Park Media. **90 min.**

Domestic Home Video:
CPM 1053 ▲ $29.95 ▲ VHS ▲ SUB ▲ HiFi Stereo ▲ 06/02/93
ID 2231CT ▲ $39.95 ▲ LD ▲ SUB ▲ HiFi Surr ▲ W/S ▲ 08/10/93

Great Conquest: The Romance of 3 Kingdoms

(1992) ©Shinano Kikaku

Story: Takamasa Yoshinari *Character Design and Animation Director:* Koichi Tsunoda *Music:* Seiji Yokayama *Director:* Mashahara Okuwaki *Narrated by:* Pat Morita

The true story of Liu Pei, the father of historical China, circa 169 A.D. Adapted from the well-known historical epic. Set in what was to become Imperial China, the story follows the key characters who would come together to forge a new nation out of the flames of chaos and the unrelenting sufferings of the oppressed. English narration by Pat Morita. Released in Japan under the title "Sangokushi" (Romance of the Three Kingdoms) by Toei Video; available in North America through Streamline Pictures. **118 min.**

Domestic Home Video:
SPV 90893 ▲ $19.95 ▲ VHS ▲ DUB ▲ Mono ▲ CC ▲ 02/10/95

Green Legend Ran

OAV series, 3 episodes

(1992) ©Pioneer LDC, Inc.

Series Director: Satoshi Saga *Screenplay:* Yu Yamamoto *Directors:* Satoshi Saga (#1)/Kengo Inagaki (#2)/Junichi Watanabe (#3) *Character Design:* Yoshimitsu Ohashi *Art Director:* Ken Arai *Music:* Yoichiro Yoshikawa.

Man no longer owns a wasted and depleted future Earth after it's visited by the aliens known as the Rodo, who— in echoes of *Dune*—rule through a bloated, mutated caste of human "bishops" having dominion over what little water remains within the enclaves of the "Holy Greens" scattered amongst the seas of sand. A young boy named Ran embarks on a journey of adventure when he joins a rebel movement, and encounters the visions of a mysterious girl who may hold the key to the human future. Three-episode OAV series; both the VHS and LD domestic box sets include the impressive premium of a 20-page booklet and 3 sets of postcards. Screenplay by Yu Yamamoto, one of the staff writers for the original "Mobile Suit Gundam" TV series. Released in Japan under the title "Green Legend Ran" by Pioneer LDC; available in North America through Pioneer LDCA.

Green Legend Ran Episode 1: Departure
A hot-blooded young boy, Ran, is a survivor who tries to join the anti-Rodo group Hazzard. When his love, young Aira is captured by Hazzard, Ran departs to rescue her. **50 min.**

Green Legend Ran Episode 2: Green 5
Ran travels the vast sea of sand in search of Hazzard's gigantic ship "Red Centipede." He is rescued from near death by Jeke, who helps him join Hazzard. Rodoist troops attack the Hazzards, capture Aira, and take her away to Rodo's central holy shrine, Green 5. **50 min.**

Green Legend Ran Episode 3: Holy Green
The five Bishops from the Holy Greens assemble to test whether Aira is a true selected Silver Maiden. Ran goes into the Holy Green to rescue Aira and Jeke learns the secret of Rodo. **51 min.**

      Made for Television Broadcast    Made for Home Video Release   Made for Theatrical Release

Domestic Home Video:
PI LA-1130D ▲ $39.95 ▲ VHS ▲ DUB ▲ Stereo ▲ 10/26/94
PI LA-1130S ▲ $59.95 ▲ VHS ▲ SUB ▲ Stereo ▲ Box Set ▲ 10/26/94
PI LA-1130A ▲ $99.95 ▲ LD-CAV ▲ M/A ▲ Box Set ▲ 10/26/94

Gunbuster, Aim for the Top!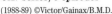

OAV series, 6 episodes

(1988-89) ©Victor/Gainax/B.M.D.

Character Design: Haruhiko Mikimoto *Mecha Design:* Kazuki Miyatake, Koichi Ohata *Story:* Toshio Okada *Music:* Kohei Tanaka *Director:* Hideaki Anno *Animation Directors:* Yuji Moriyama, Toshiyuki Kubo'oka, Yoshiyuki Sadamoto

This enduringly popular six-episode OAV series begins largely as a parody, combining the sport/schoolgirl rivalry of the 1970s TV show "Aim for the Ace!" with *Top Gun*, as the teenaged high school girl Noriko struggles to become a giant robot pilot. The narrative gradually tilts towards drama, as the emotional Noriko has to fight her first battles against an implacable, uncommunicative alien enemy bent on the destruction of all human life. By the end, massive fleets square off with super-beam weapons and black hole bombs, and the series' realistic depiction of the relativistic effects of near-light speed travel adds an additional dramatic note. The final episode, animated in black-and-white, conveys the victory-or-death ethos of a heroic old war movie, and yet despite the final dramatic turn, the series is loaded with in-jokes and creative whimsy, such as the Gunbuster robot's hilarious "Buster Shield," which looks suspiciously like the cape from a giant robot of a previous generation. From Studio Gainax (NEON GENESIS EVANGELION, THE WINGS OF HONNEAMISE), with character designs by Haruhiko "MACROSS" Mikimoto and mecha designs by Kazuki Miyatake and GENOCYBER's Koichi Ohata. Animation direction is by Yuji Moriyama (PROJECT A-KO), Toshiyuki Kubo'oka and Yoshiyuki Sadamoto. Released in Japan under the title "Top o Nerae!" ("Aim For the Top!," with the additional title "GunBuster" listed in most publicity materials) by Bandai Visual/Victor Entertainment; formerly available through U.S. Renditions, currently through Manga Video.

Gunbuster Episode 1
Noriko is struggling at the Space High School for Girls. Surprisingly, she is selected to join Kazumi Amano and advance to the Earth Space Force. Noriko is challenged by a school rival who is out to prove that she was picked only because of her father. **27 min.**

Gunbuster Episode 2
The pair arrive in space and Kazumi is challenged by the pilot "genius" Jung-Freud. Noriko and Kazumi are sent to investigate an alien object which has entered the solar system. Noriko is brought face to face with her greatest nightmare. **28 min.**

Gunbuster Episode 3
As the *Exelion* and the Earth Fleet prepare to engage the enemy forces, Noriko discovers romance in the form of male pilot Smith Toren. Kazumi and Noriko's relationship becomes strained as Kazumi loses confidence in Noriko's abilities. Noriko is once again faced with the uncompromising reality of war in her first battle. **30 min.**

Gunbuster Episode 4
Noriko tries to cope with the loss of a friend as the final phases of her training are completed and she is given command of the Earth Space Force's top-secret ultimate fighting machine: the monolithic GunBuster. With an impending alien attack, uncertain feelings, and the Earth's survival at stake, Noriko faces her greatest challenge. **30 min.**

Gunbuster Episode 5

Ten years have passed on Earth and Noriko and Kazumi graduate from the Space Academy. The alien forces are preparing a massive attack on Earth. Ota devises a revolutionary plan as Kazumi and Noriko once again fight for Earth's survival in the ultimate fighting machine: GunBuster. **30 min.**

Gunbuster Episode 6
The year is 2048 A.D. (15 years after episode 5), the alien forces are regrouping for a final assault. Earth Space Force has devised the ultimate weapon, The Black Hole Bomb, to destroy the alien menace once and for all. Courage and bravery propel Noriko, Kazumi, and their comrade Jung-Freud into a battle of epic proportions where Earth's survival hangs in the balance. *EPISODE 6 is Black & White, letterboxed.* **30 min.**

Domestic Home Video:
Gunbuster Vol. 1: *Episodes 1 and 2*
MGV 636235 ▲ $19.95 ▲ VHS ▲ SUB ▲ HiFi Stereo ▲ 08/20/96
USR VD1 ▲ $34.95 ▲ VHS ▲ SUB ▲ HiFi Stereo ▲ 02/01/90 ▲ Out of Print
Gunbuster Vol. 2: *Episodes 3 and 4*
MGV 636237 ▲ $19.95 ▲ VHS ▲ SUB ▲ HiFi Stereo ▲ 09/24/96
USR VD3 ▲ $34.95 ▲ VHS ▲ SUB ▲ HiFi Stereo ▲ 08/01/91 ▲ Out of Print
Gunbuster Vol. 3: *Episodes 5 and 6*
MGV 638305 ▲ $19.95 ▲ VHS ▲ SUB ▲ HiFi Stereo ▲ 10/22/96
USR VD5 ▲ $34.95 ▲ VHS ▲ SUB ▲ HiFi Stereo ▲ W/S ▲ 12/01/91 ▲ Out of Print

Gunmu See BATTLE ANGEL

Gunsmith Cats

(1995-96) ©Kenichi Sonoda/Kodansha/VAP/TBS

Based on the manga by Kenichi Sonoda *Director:* Takeshi Mori *Character Design:* Kenichi Sonoda *Screenplay:* Atsuji Kaneko

Based on the manga of the same name, as serialized in publisher Kodansha's monthly AFTERNOON manga anthology by Kenichi Sonoda, creator of RIDING BEAN and character designer of BUBBLEGUM CRISIS and GALL FORCE. GUNSMITH CATS is more guns- 'n' bullets action in the RIDING BEAN vein (and similarly set in the American city of Chicago). This time, two young ladies—a proprietor of a gunshop named "Gunsmith Cats" (thus the series name) and an underaged demolitions expert—are bounty-hunters for hire in the windy city. Look for lots of *Blues Brothers*-like car chases with the main character's favorite, a Shelby GT-500. Somewhat limited OAV animation, but kinetic action compensates; the addition of actual gun effects to the soundtrack adds additional realism. Authentic U.S. bluesy soundtrack recorded in Chicago. Released in Japan under the title "Gunsmith Cats" by VAP/TBS; available in North America through A.D. Vision.

Gunsmith Cats Chapter 1
In the first adventure the Feds make Rally an offer she literally can't refuse. Forced to infiltrate a gun-running operation, the Cats are left stranded under a hot tin roof when a double-cross leaves them with no recourse but to literally blow the opposition away! **30 min.**

Gunsmith Cats Chapter 2: *Swing High!*
When gun runner James Washington claims his life is in danger and makes a desperate plea for help, the girls are disinclined to listen to him. However, when Washington and a whole host of agents are gunned down inside an ATF safehouse mere minutes after the girls leave, Rally is forced to go looking for the killer. Then, when May is kidnapped by a psychotic Russian, it's up to Rally and her Shelby GT-500 to run them down! **30 min.**

Domestic Home Video:
Gunsmith Cats Chapter 1
ADV GS/001D ▲ $19.95 ▲ VHS ▲ DUB ▲ HiFi Surround ▲ 02/20/96
ADV GS/001S ▲ $24.95 ▲ VHS ▲ SUB ▲ HiFi Surround ▲ 02/20/96
ADV GS/001L ▲ $39.95 ▲ LD-CAV ▲ HYBRID ▲ HiFi Surround ▲ 02/20/96
Gunsmith Cats Chapter 1: *Special Edition*
Includes a bonus 40-minute :Making of Gunsmith Cats" featurette. (70 min.)
ADV GS/001E ▲ $34.95 ▲ VHS ▲ SUB ▲ HiFi Surround ▲ 02/20/96
Gunsmith Cats Chapter 2
ADV GS/002D ▲ $19.95 ▲ VHS ▲ DUB ▲ HiFi Surround ▲ 07/09/96
ADV GS/002S ▲ $24.95 ▲ VHS ▲ SUB ▲ HiFi Surround ▲ 07/09/96
ADV GS/002L ▲ $39.95 ▲ LD-CAV ▲ HYBRID ▲ HiFi Surround ▲ 08/27/96

Guy

OAV series, 2 episodes

(1988-92) ©Media Station.

Director: Yorihisa Uchida *Music:* Nobuhiko Kashihara (1), Kishio Yamanaka (2) *Character Design:* Yakihiro Makino (1), Yorihisa Uchida (2) *Monster Design:* Masami Obari *Mecha Design:* Yukio Tomimatsu (1), Eichi Akiyama (2), Eiko Murata (2)

Outer space adventure with a decidedly adult overtone. Guy is a hard-boiled detective sort of guy with a curvaceous sidekick named Raina. While Guy shoots the baddies, putative partner Raina often gets molested. '80s OAV animation is good, but not outstanding for the era. In North America, both volumes are available on a single tape under the title "Double Target." Character designs are by Yakihiro Makino and Yorihisa Uchida, with "monster designs" by Masami Obari (DETONATOR ORGUN, BUBBLEGUM CRISIS). Listen for a cameo vocal role by A.D. Vision General Manager Matt Greenfield. Released in Japan under the title "Guy: Yôma Kakusei" (Disillusionment of the Demon) by Media Station; available in North America through A.D. Vision.

Guy: *Awakening of the Devil*
When Guy and Raina discover a seemingly abandoned spaceship, what looks to be a simple salvage operation turns into a nightmare odyssey to the prison planet Geo, where the sadistic warden Helga has built an illegal empire based on white slavery. The sinister Dr. Vail is also a resident of this forgotten penal colony, where he has developed a horrifying new devolutionary process that turns hapless inmates into inhuman monsters. **40 min.** *(Edited version is 35 min.)*

Guy II: *Second Target*
After destroying an entire gambling casino (along with the entire space station it was located on), Guy and Raina decide to look into more spiritual matters... such as stealing a giant Goddess of Gold from the floating fortress of a sinister cult. Nothing's ever as easy as it seems, however, and when Raina ends up a prisoner of the Telekinetic Tyrants who rule the planet Frezon, there's only one Guy who can save her. **40 min.**

Domestic Home Video:
Guy
ADV G/001U ▲ $29.95 ▲ VHS ▲ SUB ▲ HiFi Surround ▲ Uncut
ADV G/001G ▲ $29.95 ▲ VHS ▲ SUB ▲ HiFi Surround ▲ Edited
Guy II
ADV G/002 ▲ $29.95 ▲ VHS ▲ SUB ▲ HiFi Surround
Guy: *Double Target*
Both Guy episodes on one videotape. (70 min.)
ADV G/DUBU ▲ $39.95 ▲ VHS ▲ DUB ▲ HiFi Sur ▲ Uncut ▲ 6/15/94
ADV G/DUBG ▲ $39.95 ▲ VHS ▲ DUB ▲ HiFi Sur ▲ Edited ▲ 6/15/94
ADV G/003 ▲ $39.95 ▲ VHS ▲ SUB ▲ HiFi Surr ▲ Uncut ▲ 6/15/94
ADV G/004 ▲ $39.95 ▲ VHS ▲ SUB ▲ HiFi Surr ▲ Edited ▲ 6/15/94

The Guyver
OAV series, 12 episodes

(1987-90) ©Takaya Productions/K.S.S./Bandai/MOVIC/Tokuma Shôten

Original Story: Yoshiki Takaya *Direction:* Koichi Ishiguro *Character Design:* Hide Omori *Animation Direction:* Sumio Watanabe, Atsuo Tobe *Direction:* Masahiro Otani (4-6), Naoto Hashimoto (4-6) *Art Direction:* Junichi Higashi (1-3), Masuo Nakayama (4-6) *Screenplay:* Atsushi Sanjo *Music Director:* Jun Watanabe

Superheroes plus gore! A Japanese schoolboy's body is taken over by an invincible organic battlesuit of alien origin called a "Guyver" when he accidentally runs across the suit's activation unit. Unfortunately, the evil organization "Chronos" wants the unit back, and sends legions of mutated monsters to find him. Chronos' plan to overtake the world with mutated "Zoanoid" monsters has overtones of the *X-Files*. Basis for two live-action movies, the first a semi-parody starring Mark Hamill, the second dark and brooding, hewing closely to the original manga's atmosphere. Six-volume OAV series based on the manga of the same name by Yoshiki Takaya, as serialized in weekly SHŪKAN SHŌNEN CAPTAIN manga anthology (published in English by Viz Comics). Character designs are by ROBOT CARNIVAL's Hidetoshi Omori. The animation quality drops severely in later volumes of the series, but the story is good enough to hold interest, and the catchy theme song doesn't hurt. Released in Japan under the title "Kyôshoku Sôkô (Bio-Booster Guyver) Guyver" by Bandai Visual; formerly available in North America through Dark Image Entertainment, currently through Manga Entertainment.

The Guyver Episode 1: *Genesis of the Guyver*
The 3 Guyver units are stolen from the enigmatic Chronos Corporation in Japan. A high school student named Sho Fukamachi accidentally discovers Guyver 1 and triggers the control metal. He becomes the Guyver and battles biomorphic Zoanoids controlled by Chronos. **30 min.**

The Guyver Episode 2: *The Battle of the Two Guyvers*
Lisker, an agent of Chronos headquarters, unwittingly joins with Guyver 2. He abducts Sho and his friend Tetsuro in an attempt to locate the other missing units. Sho summons the Guyver and the two are thrust into a deadly battle for survival. **30 min.**

The Guyver Episode 3: *Mysterious Shadow-Guyver III*
Commander Guou arrives from Chronos headquarters to lead the recovery of the Guyver units. Meanwhile, Chronos Japan creates the Zoanoid "Zerububuse" in a final desperate attempt to eliminate the Guyver. To bait the trap for Sho, Mizuki is kidnapped and Sho once again must become the Guyver and face the challenge of Zerububuse as well as the mysterious shadow, Guyver III. **30 min.**

The Guyver Episode 4: *Attack of the Hyper-Zoanoid Team Five*
Commander Guou takes full control of Chronos Japan and deploys his Hyper-Zoanoids

against Sho. Together with Tetsuro, Sho tries to expose Chronos but the media won't believe their story. In order to force out the Guyver, the Hyper-Zoanoids attack Sho's school! **30 min.**

The Guyver Episode 5: *The Death of the Guyver*
Chronos Japan transforms Makishima into Enzyme, a powerful Zoanoid created to eliminate the Guyver. To force a confrontation with Sho, Commander Guou again kidnaps Mizuki and Sho. They are taken to the mountains and forced to watch as Sho and Enzyme battle in a fight to the death! **30 min.**

The Guyver Episode 6: *Terminal Battle! The Fall of Chronos Japan*
Tetsuro and Mizuki are held hostage at Chronos headquarters. Meanwhile, Guyver III's identity is revealed as he initiates his plan to destroy Chronos. Will Guyver regenerate in time to save Tetsuro and Mizuki? **30 min.**

The Guyver Episode 7: *Prelude To the Chase*
Agito (Guyver III) meets with the Chronos scientist Dr. Balcus. Later, Sho grieves about his father's death while his friends Tetsuro and Mizuki are kidnapped by Chronos. Again the trap is set to capture the Guyver. **30 min.**

The Guyver Episode 8: *The Lost Unit's Challenge*
Sho heads for Mt. Minakami in search of friends. During the journey he confronts the "Lost Unit" (a monstrous Guyver) and other villainous Zoanoids. **30 min.**

The Guyver Episode 9: *Shocking Transformation, The Tragedy of Enzyme II*
Sho discovers that his father is alive and attempts a daring rescue to save him and Mizuki. Balcus, knowing what Sho will do, has set a trap to capture the Guyver. **30 min.**

The Guyver Episode 10: *Can We Escape? Haunted Takeshiro Village*
The tragic clash with Enzyme II has affected Sho's ability to transform into the Guyver. When everyone tries to escape Mount Minikami by going through Takeshiro village, they fall into Balcus' ambush. **30 min.**

The Guyver Episode 11: *Masaki Murakami: Transforming Beast Master*
Murakami reveals the origin and purpose of the Guyvers and Zoanoids. To rescue Guyver III from several Enzyme II creatures, Murakami must expose his most guarded secret. **30 min.**

The Guyver Episode 12: *Aptom's Attack: Reactive Guyver*
Sho must transform into the Guyver to save Mizuki from Aptom. However, his inability to bio-boost may cost them their lives. **30 min.**

Domestic Home Video:
The Guyver Data 1
MGV 635535 ▲ $12.95 ▲ VHS ▲ DUB ▲ HiFi Stereo ▲ 02/27/96
The Guyver Data 2
MGV 635537 ▲ $12.95 ▲ VHS ▲ DUB ▲ HiFi Stereo ▲ 03/19/96
The Guyver Data 3
MGV 635539 ▲ $12.95 ▲ VHS ▲ DUB ▲ HiFi Stereo ▲ 04/16/96
The Guyver Data 4
MGV 635541 ▲ $12.95 ▲ VHS ▲ DUB ▲ HiFi Stereo ▲ 05/21/96
The Guyver Data 5
MGV 635543 ▲ $12.95 ▲ VHS ▲ DUB ▲ HiFi Stereo ▲ 06/18/96
The Guyver Data 6
MGV 635545 ▲ $12.95 ▲ VHS ▲ DUB ▲ HiFi Stereo ▲ 07/30/96
The Guyver Data 7
MGV 638293 ▲ $12.95 ▲ VHS ▲ DUB ▲ HiFi Stereo ▲ 08/20/96
The Guyver Data 8
MGV 638295 ▲ $12.95 ▲ VHS ▲ DUB ▲ HiFi Stereo ▲ 09/24/96
The Guyver Data 9
MGV 638297 ▲ $12.95 ▲ VHS ▲ DUB ▲ HiFi Stereo ▲ 10/22/96
The Guyver Data 10
MGV 638299 ▲ $12.95 ▲ VHS ▲ DUB ▲ HiFi Stereo ▲ 11/26/96
The Guyver Vol. 1: *Episodes 1 and 2*
USR VD9 ▲ $24.95 ▲ VHS ▲ DUB ▲ HiFi Stereo ▲ 08/01/92
▲ Out of Print
The Guyver Vol. 2: *Episodes 3 and 4*
USR VD12 ▲ $24.95 ▲ VHS ▲ DUB ▲ HiFi Stereo ▲ 01/01/93
▲ Out of Print
The Guyver Vol. 3: *Episodes 5 and 6*
USR VD17 ▲ $24.95 ▲ VHS ▲ DUB ▲ HiFi Stereo ▲ 04/12/93 ▲ Out of Print
The Guyver Vol. 4: *Episodes 7 and 8*
USR VD21 ▲ $24.95 ▲ VHS ▲ DUB ▲ HiFi Stereo ▲ 04/26/94 ▲ Out of Print
The Guyver Vol. 5: *Episodes 9 and 10*
USR VD25 ▲ $24.95 ▲ VHS ▲ DUB ▲ HiFi Stereo ▲ 07/11/94 ▲ Out of Print
The Guyver Vol. 6: *Episodes 11 and 12*
USR 030 ▲ $24.95 ▲ VHS ▲ DUB ▲ HiFi Stereo ▲ 01/18/95 ▲ Out of Print

The Guyver: Out of Control

(1986) ©Takaya Productions

Original Story: Yoshiki Takaya *Direction:* Hiroshi Watanabe *Character Design:* Indori Goya *Animation Direction:* Hiromi Matsushita *Art Direction:* Torao Arai *Screenplay:* Monta Ibu *Music Director:* Shoji Nanba

One-shot video totally different in style from the multi-volume OAV series which would follow it three years later; altogether a cheezy and lackluster adaptation. Screenplay by Monta Ibu, with character designs by Indori Goya. Released in Japan under the title "Kyôshoku Sôkô (Bio-Booster) Guyver" by Bandai Visual; available in North America through U.S. Renditions. Sho Fukamachi, a young school boy, discovers a mysterious metal object. A blinding flash, and Sho finds that he has accidentally fused with the Guyver, an alien bio-armor of unlimited power. To save the life of his girlfriend, Mizuki Segawa, Sho must battle the Chronos corporation and their biomorphic creatures, the Zoanoids. **55 min.**

Domestic Home Video:
USR DIE04 ▲ $19.95 ▲ VHS ▲SUB ▲ HiFi Stereo ▲ 08/01/93 ▲ Out of Print

---

Hadashi no Gen *See* BAREFOOT GEN
Hades Project Zeorymer *See* ZEORYMER
Haja Taisei Dangaiô *See* DANGAIO

The Hakkenden: Legend of the Dog Warriors

OAV series, 13 episodes

(1990-93) ©AIC/Pioneer LDC Inc.

Director: Takashi Anno (1-6), Yukio Okamoto (7-13) *Character Design:* Hiroyuki Ochi, Atsushi Yamagata, Atsushi Okuda *Screenplay:* Noboru Aikawa (1-3,5-7), Takeshi Narumi (4), Hidemi Kamata (8-13) *Direction:* Yukio Okamoto (2,5), Takeshi Aoki (3,6,12), Takashi Nakamura (4), Satoru Utsunomiya (8,9), Shinya Ohira (10,11), Kenji Kamiyama (6-8,12), Yusuke Takeda (9,10), Masaru Ota (11), Hiroshi Kato (13) *Art Direction:* Yoichi Nango (1), Takeshi Waki (2), Tatsuya Kushida (4), *Animation Directors:* Hiroyuki Ochi (3,11), Takashi Nakamura (4), Atsushi Okuda (1-6,11,13), Fumiko Ikehata (5), Hideyuki Motohashi, Atsushi Yamagata (6,12), Masaaki Yuasa (10), Tatsuya Sotomaru (11), Noboru Furuse (11), Nobuyuki Kitajima (12) *Music:* Takashi Kudo

Character designs and animation direction by ARMITAGE III's director/character designer Hiroyuki Ochi and a screenplay by Noboru Aikawa enhance this classy retelling of the classic Japanese novel, which in itself is loosely based on the Chinese legend "The Water Margin." Don't let the fact that the quality of animation drops from incredibly detailed to god-awfully amateurish and then back up again detour you, as terrific heart-rending drama and enough samurai action to satisfy any Kurosawa fan make this one a modern-day must-see. Released in Japan under the title "The Hakkenden" by Sôshin Eizô/Asmic; available in North America through Pioneer LDCA.

The Hakkenden Episode 1: *The Kaleidoscope*
The year is 1457 and Princess Fuse is forced into matrimony with her dog, Yatsufusa. Under siege from an invading army, and facing starvation, Lord Yoshizane makes a desperate promise to the dog. Ultimately, the princess and the dog are killed by the man who came to rescue them. At the moment of Fuse's death, eight spirit beads from her necklace disperse and the legend of the dog warriors begins. **30 min.**

The Hakkenden Episode 2: *Dark Music of the Gods*
A child is born named Shino Inukuka. Coming of age, he is entrusted by his father with a legendary sword, the Murasame. Devastated by his father's tragic death, Shino somehow comes into possession of a small bead, on which the Chinese character "KO" appears, symbolizing filial devotion. **30 min.**

The Hakkenden Episode 3: *The Futility Dance*
Sosuke is ordered by Kamezasa to kill Shino. The two warriors, however, make a pledge of brotherhood. Hamaji learns that her hand in marriage has been promised to the jindai, Higami Kyuroku, and decides to kill herself, but is saved at the last minute by Samojiro Aboshi, who later sets upon Hamaji himself. Hamaji's subsequent rescuer turns out to be her long lost brother, Dosetsu Inuyama. **30 min.**

The Hakkenden Episode 4: *Horyu Tower*
Into Otsuka village comes the arrival of evil itself, personified by the jindai and his retainer. Only Sosuke can stand up to them, though he is ultimately arrested and blamed for the murders of his step-parents. Meanwhile, Shino arrives in Koga and is granted an audience with the Shogun. The

legendary Murasame sword that he offers up, however, is revealed to be a fake and Shino becomes a hunted criminal. But the man released from captivity in the castle dungeon and assigned to capture Shino turns out to be none other than the fourth dog warrior, Genpachi Inukai. **30 min.**

The Hakkenden Episode 5:
Demon's Melody
One day, in the town of Gyotoku, an innkeeper named Kobungo Inuta rescues Shino and Genpachi, who had been adrift since falling into the river from Hiryu Tower. Kobungo's brother-in-law Fusahachi, however, recognizes the two as fugitives, and alerts the authorities. During the heat of an intense battle, Fusahachi mistakenly kills his wife, Nui, and in his moment of shock, he is struck down by Kobungo. But all that remains are the carcasses of two dogs... **30 min.**

The Hakkenden Episode 6: *The Cicada Spirit Cry*
Leaving Gyotoku, the three warriors take Nui's infant son Daihachi and set off for Otsuka village. Back in Otsuka, Sosuke faces a death sentence after being charged with the murders of his stepmother and father. After getting wind of this, Shino and Genpachi go to his rescue. Under cover of night, the two sneak onto the killing ground and hide themselves. Just as Sosuke is to have his crucifixion carried out, they pounce. **30 min.**

The Hakkenden *Digest*
A compilation episode which summarizes the first six episodes of the series. In addition, a bonus music clip of the ending theme song, "Blue Skies" is included. **30 min.**

The Hakkenden Episode 7: *Spirits*
Six of the eight Dog Warriors have assembled. Chudai, Shino, Sosuke, Genpachi, Kobungo and Dosetsu learn that they are destined to work for the Satome clan. Although the young warriors are confused, their destinies are leading them to the war. **30 min.**

The Hakkenden Episode 8: *Taigyuro Hall*
Kobungo kills an intruder in self defense while traveling through a small village. When he is arrested as a suspect, he meets a dog warrior in disguise. **30 min.**

The Hakkenden Episode Episode 9: *The Legend of the Ghost Cat*
Genpachi puts his life in jeopardy as he pays a visit to the dojo of a famous swordsman. When the swordsman's son Daikaku harbors Genpachi at his mountain hideaway, Genpachi saves him from a legendary Ghost Cat. **30 min.**

The Hakkenden Episode 10:
Hamaji's Resurrection
Hamaji's spirit reappears and talks Sosuke into thinking about killing Shino. In the meantime, Shino is caught in a bear trap while wandering about on a mountain. **30 min.**

The Hakkenden Episode 11: *Dog Warriors in the Netherworld*
On the way to see Yoshizane, the seven dog warriors encounter an old foe— one that may have the secret of the eighth dog warrior. **30 min.**

The Hakkenden Episode 12: *Aspirations of Paradise*
The eight dog warriors finally gather under the Satomi flag. They plan a strategy to attack Hikita's castle and rescue Princess Hamaji, who is being held captive as a human shield by Aboshi and Hikita. **30 min.**

The Hakkenden Episode 13: *Taking Leave of a Sullied World*
Hikita's troops manage to escape the downed castle and occupy the Satomi's castle instead. The dog warriors must now devise a plan to rescue their brothers and the Princess from the Satomi castle. The fate that the dog warriors are born to gradually leads them into a living hell. The grand finale to the series. **30 min.**

Domestic Home Video:
The Hakkenden Vol. 1: *Episodes 1 & 2*
PI VA-1191D ▲ $24.95 ▲ VHS ▲ DUB ▲ HiFi Stereo ▲ CC ▲ 07/25/95
PI VA-1191S ▲ $29.95 ▲ VHS ▲ SUB ▲ HiFi Stereo ▲ 07/25/95
PI LA-1191A ▲ $39.95 ▲ LD-CAV ▲ M/A ▲ HiFi Stereo ▲ CC ▲ 07/25/95
The Hakkenden Vol. 2: *Episodes 3 & 4*
PI VA-1192D ▲ $24.95 ▲ VHS ▲ DUB ▲ HiFi Stereo ▲ CC ▲ 09/26/95
PI VA-1192S ▲ $29.95 ▲ VHS ▲ SUB ▲ HiFi Stereo ▲ 09/26/95
PI LA-1192A ▲ $39.95 ▲ LD-CAV ▲ M/A ▲ HiFi Stereo ▲ CC ▲ 09/26/95
The Hakkenden Vol. 3: *Episodes 5 & 6*
PI VA-1193D ▲ $24.95 ▲ VHS ▲ DUB ▲ HiFi Stereo ▲ CC ▲ 11/28/95
PI VA-1193S ▲ $29.95 ▲ VHS ▲ SUB ▲ HiFi Stereo ▲ 11/28/95
PI LA-1193A ▲ $39.95 ▲ LD-CAV ▲ M/A ▲ HiFi Stereo ▲ CC ▲ 11/28/95
The Hakkenden Vol. 4: *Episode 7 & Digest*
PI VA-1194D ▲ $24.95 ▲ VHS ▲ DUB ▲ HiFi Stereo ▲ CC ▲ 01/30/96
PI VA-1194S ▲ $29.95 ▲ VHS ▲ SUB ▲ HiFi Stereo ▲ 01/30/96
PI LA-1194A ▲ $39.95 ▲ LD-CAV ▲ M/A ▲ HiFi Stereo ▲ CC ▲ 01/30/96
The Hakkenden Vol. 5: *Episodes 8 & 9*
PI VA-1195D ▲ $24.95 ▲ VHS ▲ DUB ▲ HiFi Stereo ▲ CC ▲ 04/16/96
PI VA-1195S ▲ $29.95 ▲ VHS ▲ SUB ▲ HiFi Stereo ▲ 04/16/96
PI LA-1195A ▲ $39.95 ▲ LD-CAV ▲ M/A ▲ HiFi Stereo ▲ CC ▲ 04/16/96

The Hakkenden Vol. 6: *Episodes 10 & 11*
PI VA-1197D ▲ $24.95 ▲ VHS ▲ DUB ▲ HiFi Stereo ▲ CC ▲ 06/04/96
PI VA-1197S ▲ $29.95 ▲ VHS ▲ SUB ▲ HiFi Stereo ▲ 06/04/96
PI LA-1197A ▲ $39.95 ▲ LD-CAV ▲ M/A ▲ HiFi Stereo ▲ CC ▲ 06/04/96

The Hakkenden Vol. 7: *Episodes 12 & 13*
PI VA-1199D ▲ $24.95 ▲ VHS ▲ DUB ▲ HiFi Stereo ▲ CC ▲ 08/06/96
PI VA-1199S ▲ $29.95 ▲ VHS ▲ SUB ▲ HiFi Stereo ▲ 08/06/96
PI LA-1199A ▲ $39.95 ▲ LD-CAV ▲ M/A ▲ HiFi Stereo ▲ CC ▲ 08/06/96

Hanappe Bazooka

(1992) ©Kazuo Koide/Go Nagai/Dynamic Planning, Inc./Nippon Crown

Original Creator: Kazuo Koike/Go Nagai *Director:* Yoyu Ikegami *Art & Character Design:* Fujio Oda *Animation by:* Studio Signal

Based on the manga of the same name by "Lone Wolf and Cub" writer Kazuo Koike and artist Go Nagai, as serialized in publisher Shûeisha's weekly SHÛKAN YOUNG JUMP manga anthology. Nagai's outrageous sense of humor is in full flower here, 'cause when high school loser Hanappe isn't beating off, he's getting beat up. But then one day, two demons arrive from the great beyond only wanting to give him ultimate power; too bad there's no truth in demonic advertising. All the dysfunctional families, scatological humor, and lewd sexual hijinks we've come to expect from the creator of DEVILMAN and CUTEY HONEY. (As a bonus, characters from other Nagai series make cameo appearances.) Released in Japan under the title "Hanappe Bazooka" by Nihon Crown; available in North America through A.D. Vision. Followed by a currently import-only "Making Of" video in 1992, featuring live-action interviews with the main cast (including RANMA 1/2's Kappei "Boy-type Ranma" Yamaguchi and Kikuko "Kasumi" Inoue) and even a sing-along "karaoke corner." 55 min.

Domestic Home Video:
ADV HB/001 ▲ $29.95 ▲ VHS ▲ SUB ▲ HiFi Surround ▲ 03/26/96

Harmagedon

(1983) ©Kadokawa Shôten Publishing Co. Ltd.

Original Story by: Kazumasa Hirai and Shotaro Ishimori *Director:* Taro Rin *Character Design:* Katsuhiro Otomo *Art Director:* Takamura Mukuo

Full-length theatrical feature based on the manga by Kazumasa Hirai and CYBORG 009'S Shotaro Ishimori. Breakthrough work for character designer Katsuhiro Otomo (who'd later go on to direct AKIRA) in which a telepathic princess and her cyborg guardian from another planet assemble a band of psychics to prevent demons from destroying the world. Stunning visuals. Released in Japan under the title "Genma Taisen" (Great Occult-Demon War) by Kadokawa Shôten; available in the U.S. through U.S. Manga Corps. 132 min.

Domestic Home Video:
USM 1468 ▲ $19.95 ▲ VHS ▲ DUB ▲ Stereo ▲ 11/05/96
USM 1038 ▲ $29.95 ▲ VHS ▲ SUB ▲ Stereo ▲ 07/07/93
ID 2232CT ▲ $49.95 ▲ LD-CLV/CAV ▲ SUB ▲ Stereo ▲ 08/10/93

Hello Kitty

OAV series, 20 episodes

(1994) ©Sanrio, Ltd.

Directors: Tameo Ogawa (Cinderella), Yasuo Ishikawa (Heidi, Snow White, Mom, Sisters, Santa), Masami Hata (Sleeping Princess, Dream Thief, Prince, Christmas Eve) *Animation Director:* Kanji Akabori *Art:* Yukio Abe, Yoko Nagashima *Music:* Ryo Kitagama (Cinderella), Senji Nanba (Heidi), Toyomi Kajima (Sleeping Princess)

Sanrio godhead Hello Kitty comes to animated life in this multi-volume (20 OAVs and one 1991 theatrical feature, at last count!) series. Together with her twin sister Mimi, Kitty and Co. embark on a variety of fairytale and family-oriented adventures. In the original Japanese version, top 'o the charts Japanese pop star Megumi Hayashibara ("girl-type Ranma," RANMA 1/2; "Momoko," BLUE SEED; "Lina Inverse," SLAYERS) stars in the title role. USELESS TRIVIA QUESTIONS: (1) How do you tell Kitty and twin sister Mimi apart? (2) How much does Kitty weigh? Answers below.*

Hello Kitty: Cinderella

2 episodes: CINDERELLA: Kitty plays Cinderella as her animal friends help her prepare for the prince's ball. HEIDI: Kitty plays Heidi as she teaches her grumpy old grandfather how to enjoy life again. 52 min.

Hello Kitty: Snow White

2 episodes. SNOW WHITE: Kitty plays Snow White as she is taken in by seven kindly dwarves after she flees the evil queen. THE SLEEPING PRINCESS: Kitty and Mimi receive a mysterious invitation and make a mystical journey to the beautiful Dream Castle, where they discover that the princess needs their help. 52 min.

Hello Kitty: Mom Loves Me After All

2 episodes. MOM LOVES ME AFTER ALL: When her mom takes care of a baby for a few days, Kitty feels neglected and runs away to her grandparents' house. There she learns how her parents met and that love can conquer anything. THE WONDERFUL SISTERS: Mimi has a huge crush on a boy at school, but is too shy to talk to him. Twin sister Kitty tries to help by impersonating Mimi, but it only makes matters worse. 52 min.

Hello Kitty: The Dream Thief

2 episodes. THE DREAM THIEF: A mischievous creature named Puffin is eating little kids' dreams up. Kitty and Mimi cook up a plan to catch the prankster before he eats up all the good dreams and is left with just nightmares. THE PRINCE IN HIS DREAM CASTLE: Kitty travels back in time to help a handsome prince escape his castle during a terrible battle. Her friends say it was a dream, but Kitty suspects it may have really happened. 52 min.

Hello Kitty: Santa's Missing Hat

2 episodes. SANTA'S MISSING HAT: Kitty and Mimi are shocked to hear some of their friends don't believe in Santa Claus. When a Santa cap blows off a display, the two chase after it and end up lost in the woods. Then they see someone approaching on the path... THE CHRISTMAS EVE GIFT: Keroppi and his friends help Twinkle the little star shine brightly to guide Santa on Christmas Eve. 55 min.

*(1) Kitty wears her bow on the left side; Mimi wears hers on the right; (2) The same as three shiny red apples. (That's shiny red, not waxy green, mind you.)

Domestic Home Video:

Hello Kitty: Cinderella
FHE 27573 ▲ $12.95 ▲ VHS-EP ▲ DUB ▲ HiFi ▲ CC ▲ 03/21/95
Hello Kitty: The Dream Thief
FHE 27608 ▲ $12.95 ▲ VHS-EP ▲ DUB ▲ HiFi ▲ CC
Hello Kitty: Mom Loves Me After All
FHE 27607 ▲ $12.95 ▲ VHS-EP ▲ DUB ▲ HiFi ▲ CC
Hello Kitty: Santa's Missing Hat
FHE 27613 ▲ $12.95 ▲ VHS-EP ▲ DUB ▲ HiFi ▲ CC
Hello Kitty: Snow White
FHE 27574 ▲ $12.95 ▲ VHS-EP ▲ DUB ▲ HiFi ▲ CC ▲ 03/21/95

Here is Greenwood

(1991-93) ©Yukie Nasu/Hakusensha Inc./Victor Entertainment, Inc./Pierrot Project

Based on the manga by: Yukie Nasu *Directed and Written by:* Tomimitsu Mochizuki *Character Design and Animation Director:* Masako Goto *Music:* Shigeru Nagata

Clever, fresh OAV series detailing the travails of Kazuya, a haplessly normal fellow who, in going to an exclusive prep school to forget an unrequited love (his older brother's wife!), finds himself assigned to the dorm of the damned, Greenwood—an inmate-run asylum for the strangest students on campus. Greenwood's style is redolent of its origins as a *bishônen* ("pretty-boy") manga by Yukie Nasu, with androgynous characters and bisexual overtures by both men and women—although there's plenty of traditional boy-girl romantic feelings present as well. Good-hearted hijinks by the director of RANMA 1/2, with character designs and eye-pleasing animation direction by Masako Goto (KIMAGURE ORANGE ROAD). Released in Japan under the title of "Here is Greenwood" by Victor Entertainment; available in North America through Software Sculptors.

Here is Greenwood Vol. 1: *Episodes 1 and 2*

Episode 1: THOU SHALT LOVE THY DAILY LIFE, and Episode 2: NAGISA HYPER-RHAPSODY. Meet Kazuya Hasukawa: he's just a regular teenager who wants to live a normal, peaceful life. But when his first love marries his older brother and moves into their house, Kazuya decides that he has to move out to preserve his sanity! Things go from

bad to worse when he discovers he's been assigned to the strangest dorm on campus—an asylum call Greenwood—where weirdos, outcasts, and lunatics at the prestigious Ryokuto Academy reside. **60 min.**

Here is Greenwood Vol. 2: *Episodes 3 and 4*
Episode 3: THE MAKING OF HERE IS DEVILWOOD, and Episode 4: THE PHANTOM OF GREENWOOD. As Ryokuto Academy prepares for its annual school festival, the residents at Greenwood are planning the unthinkable—they're making a movie. If they are voted as the winning group, they'll win enough cash to throw the biggest party the dorm has ever seen. Once the school festivities are over, terror strikes Greenwood! Mitsuru is being haunted by a teenage ghost named Misako, whom at first, everyone but Mitsuru welcomes. And before she passes on to the next world, her only wish is to possess Shinobu's body and kiss Mitsuru! **60 min.**

Here is Greenwood Vol. 3: *Episodes 5 and 6*
Episodes 5 and 6: SECOND LOVE... ALWAYS BE WITH YOU, ACTS 1 & 2. Greenwood is in turmoil when a mysterious girl suddenly appears late one night. Mistaken for a gang leader, she's on the run from a rival gang of girl-thugs and begs Mitsuru to let her stay at the dorm. Acting as the new dorm president, Kazuya decides to help the endangered girl with whom he soon falls in love. The problem: Miya has been involved with another boy for the last ten years! Will Kazuya once again come between a relationship, or has he found true love? **60 min.**

Domestic Home Video:
Here is Greenwood Vol. 1
SSVD 9613 ▲ $24.95 ▲ VHS ▲ DUB ▲ Stereo ▲ 12/13/96
SSVS 9610 ▲ $24.95 ▲ VHS ▲ SUB ▲ Stereo ▲ 10/01/96
SSLD VILF-13 ▲ $39.95 ▲ LD ▲ M/A ▲ Stereo ▲ 12/03/96
Here is Greenwood Vol. 2
SSVD 9614 ▲ $24.95 ▲ VHS ▲ DUB ▲ Stereo ▲ 12/13/96
SSVS 9611 ▲ $24.95 ▲ VHS ▲ SUB ▲ Stereo ▲ 10/01/96
SSLD 9661 ▲ $39.95 ▲ LD ▲ M/A ▲ Stereo ▲ 12/03/96
Here is Greenwood Vol. 3
SSVD 9615 ▲ $24.95 ▲ VHS ▲ DUB ▲ Stereo ▲ 01/07/97
SSVS 9612 ▲ $24.95 ▲ VHS ▲ SUB ▲ Stereo ▲ 12/03/96
SSLD VILF-26 ▲ $39.95 ▲ LD ▲ M/A ▲ Stereo ▲ 12/03/96

The Heroic Legend of Arislan   [OAV] 🗡 🄍
OAV series, 4 episodes
(1991-93) ©Yoshiki Tanaka/Kadokawa Shôten/MOVIC/Sony Music Entertainment

Created by: Haruki Kadokawa/Hiroshi Inagaki/Yutaka Takahasi *Original Writer:* Yoshiki Tanaka *Director:* Mamoru Hamatsu *Screenplay:* Tomoya Miyashita, Kaori Takada (3&4) *Character Design:* Sachiko Kamimura *Chief Animator:* Kazuchika Kise (1), Masao Nakada (2) *Music:* Norihiro Tsuru

Based on the original novel of the same name by Yoshiki Tanaka ("Legend of the Galactic Heroes"). Four-video (two screened as theatrical features, two released as OAVs) heroic fantasy tale in which a young prince battles to regain his kingdom from a usurping warlord. Like Tanaka's "Galactic Heroes," ambitious story is epic in scale, but starts to drag like a network mini-series unless attention is kept focused. Character designs by Sachiko Kamimura (VENUS WARS), with animation direction by Kazuchika Kise (BLUE SEED). Released in Japan under the title "Arslan Senki" (Arslan Chronicles) by Kadokawa Shôten/Sony Music; available in North America through Central Park Media.

The Heroic Legend of Arislan Part 1
Returning to the prince's palace, Daryoon and Prince Arislan stop at the cottage of the reclusive artist, Lord Narsus. Prince Arislan knows that the Lord is, despite his love for wine, extremely wise, and therefore a valuable ally. He convinces both the Lord Narsus and the archer Elam, to join them in their quest. Meanwhile, Gieve encounters Pharangese, the beautiful servant of the Goddess Misra. Pharangese's mission is to protect Prince Arislan, chosen by the Goddess Misra herself to rule the kingdom. Gieve resolves to join her in protecting the Prince, but how can these six overcome an army of 300,000 enemy soldiers? **59 min.**

The Heroic Legend of Arislan Part 2
A mysterious fog has been lying over the kingdom of Palse for weeks, hindering its army's attempt to defeat the Lusitanian army in battle. To help defend his kingdom, Prince Arislan has formed his own troop of renegade warriors including the exiled Daryoon, legendary artist Lord Narsus, Goddess Misra's devoted servant Pharangese, and traveling

minstrel Gieve. How can this group possibly survive a confrontation with 300,000 trained Lusitanian soldiers? Among them is Silvermask, a mysterious figure who wears a rigid steel mask covering his face and claims that he is the rightful heir to the throne. The Palse must also defend themselves against forces arriving by sea. Prince Arislan is certain his kingdom could benefit from an alliance with these forces, but as part of the alliance agreement a battle to determine the heir to the crown must be fought. Will Daryoon be the victor or his opponent - a ferocious, 12-foot-tall beast? **59 min.**

The Heroic Legend of Arislan Parts 3&4
Betrayed from within and overwhelmed by sorcery, Palse's army was burned alive when it was invaded by the religious fanatics of Lusitania. With the aid of five exceptional warriors, Prince Arislan managed to escape to the farthest corner of his realm. Even as the Lusitanians revel in Palse's wealth, they must not lose sight of their next problem: eliminate the fanatic priest, Jon Bodan. The mysterious Lord Silvermask, architect of their victory, is chosen for this mission which will bring him in contact with the dark powers of sorcery. And it is this sorcery that will provide Silvermask with the key to his deepest desires. Having rallied over 100,000 troops, Prince Arislan is ready to wage the war of liberation. He'll need the most devious strategies to defeat an army that would rather die than surrender. But even that won't be enough when Arislan finds himself alone and face-to-face with Lusitania's most fanatic troops. **60 min.**

Domestic Home Video:
The Heroic Legend of Arislan Part 1
USM 1110 ▲ $19.95 ▲ VHS ▲ DUB ▲ Stereo ▲ 01/05/94
USM 1081 ▲ $29.95 ▲ VHS ▲ SUB ▲ Stereo ▲ 01/05/94
ID 2867CT ▲ $34.95 ▲ LD ▲ SUB ▲ Stereo ▲ W/S ▲ 11/30/94
The Heroic Legend of Arislan Part 2
USM 1132 ▲ $19.95 ▲ VHS ▲ DUB ▲ Stereo ▲ 03/02/94
USM 1082 ▲ $29.95 ▲ VHS ▲ SUB ▲ Stereo ▲ 03/02/94
ID 2872CT ▲ $34.95 ▲ LD ▲ M/A ▲ Stereo ▲ W/S ▲ 03/07/95
The Heroic Legend of Arislan Pts 3&4
USM 1444 ▲ $19.95 ▲ VHS ▲ DUB ▲ Stereo ▲ 10/08/96
USM 1097 ▲ $29.95 ▲ VHS ▲ SUB ▲ Stereo ▲ 02/01/95
ID 2893CT ▲ $34.95 ▲ LD ▲ M/A ▲ Stereo ▲ W/S ▲ 02/15/96

Homeroom Affairs   [OAV] ❌ 🄍 🄢

(1994) ©Ichiro Arima/Hakusensha Publishing/Jam Creation/J.C. Staff

Director: Osamu Sekita *Screenplay:* Hiroyuki Kawasaki *Music:* Hiroyuki Takei *Character Design:* Minoru Yamazawa *Art Direction:* Akira Furuya

Based on the manga of the same name by Ichiro Arima, as serialized in publisher Hakusensha's YOUNG ANIMAL MAGAZINE. A new teacher at an elite all-girl high school in Tokyo runs into trouble with a precocious 18-year-old coed who seems to have decided to make him her own. A lighthearted sex comedy with a playful edge, sexy without nastiness. Released in Japan under the title "Tanin no Kankei" (Human Relations) by Tokuma Japan Communications; available in North America through Star Anime Enterprises.

Homeroom Affairs Part 1:
Part 1, I'LL TEACH YOU A LESSON YOU'LL NEVER FORGET: Tokiro Ehara lands a teaching job at an elite all-girl high school in Tokyo, and discovers just how advanced his pretty pupils are — especially Miyako, an 18-year-old coed with a mind all her own. Miyako's father asks Tokiro to watch over his daughter, but Tokiro soon begins to wonder, who's teaching whom? **43 min.**

Homeroom Affairs Part 2
Part 2, I WAS BORN RECKLESS: Miyako and her teacher Tokiro have been living together for two months now, but Tokiro continues to resist the 18-year-old's advances. Then Miyako's ex arrives on the scene. **43 min.**

Domestic Home Video:
Homeroom Affairs Part 1:
SAE 001 ▲ $24.95 ▲ VHS ▲ SUB ▲ HiFi Mono ▲ 10/26/94
Homeroom Affairs Part 2
SAE 002 ▲ $24.95 ▲ VHS ▲ SUB ▲ HiFi Mono ▲ 12/19/94

Honran *See* CRIMSON WOLF
Hotaru no Haka *See* GRAVE OF THE FIREFLIES

The Humanoid

(1986) ©Hiro Media/Kaname Productions/Toshiba-EMI Ltd.

Screenplay: Koichi Minade/Kaname Productions *Director:* Shinichi Masaki *Character and Mecha Design:* Shohei Obara *Animation Director:* Osamu Kamijo *Art Director:* Hagemu Katsumata

Dr. Watson's crowning achievement is Antoinette, a chrome-bodied android, whose altruistic programming seems to give her a heart of flesh. She commands a strikingly beautiful form and vast knowledge. Yet, she is as a child confronted by a world which seems to elude her intuitive grasp. The planetary governor Proud is not at all taken by Antoinette's charm. His only interest lies in the remains of an ancient high-tech society which could yield him the ultimate weapon! And when Proud discovers who possesses the final piece to unleashing this great power, Antoinette, Dr. Watson and his visiting transport crew find themselves fighting for their lives. Animates the female metal android "gynoid" look of world-famous Japanese illustrator Hajime Soriyama. Eccentric scientist endeavors to give his beautiful creation a normal life. "If you liked *Galaxina*" (as they say in those ads), "you'll love THE HUMANOID." Released in Japan under the title "The Humanoid" by Toshiba EMI; available in North America through Central Park Media. **45 min.**

Domestic Home Video:
USM 1466 ▲ $14.95 ▲ VHS ▲ DUB ▲ Stereo ▲ 06/18/96
USM 1023 ▲ $34.95 ▲ VHS ▲ SUB ▲ Stereo ▲ 03/18/92
ID 2233CT ▲ $29.95 ▲ LD ▲ SUB ▲ HiFi Stereo ▲ 03/05/93

Hyper Doll
OAV series, 2 volumes

(1995) ©Shinpei Ito/Tokuma Shôten/Pioneer LDC, Inc.

Original Author: Shinpei Ito *Director:* Makoto Moriwaki *Screenplay:* Ryo Motohira *Character Design & Animation Director:* Satoru Nakamura *Art Director:* Kazuhiro Arai *Music:* Takayuki Negishi

Two scantily dressed androids save the Earth from oh-so-scarily ridiculous monsters in this four-volume OAV superhero parody, which includes the title characters singing silly Pink Lady-like '70s pop tunes. So forgettable, you'll have an easier time remembering where you left your car keys than figuring out why you turned on the TV. Released in Japan under the title "Rakushô! (Easy Win!) Hyper-Doll" by Pioneer LDC; available in North America through Pioneer LDCA.

Hyper Doll Act 1
One day, when the dolls were lounging by the pool, they encountered "Kurage-man" (a jellyfish-like creature). Akai managed to get rid of Kurage-man, but a new enemy landed on Earth-"Inago-man" (a locust-like creature). Tokyo's in chaos, and Mew and Mica join forces to protect Earth. **40 min.**

Hyper Doll Act 2
Mew and Mica go to see fireworks with their high school classmates, but the real fireworks begin when the worm monster Mimizu-man goes after Akai and Shoko! It's the Hyper Dolls to the rescue. **40 min.**

Domestic Home Video:
Hyper Doll Act 1
PI VA-1299D ▲ $19.95 ▲ VHS ▲ DUB ▲ HiFi Stereo ▲ 04/16/96
PI VA-1299S ▲ $24.95 ▲ VHS ▲ SUB ▲ HiFi Stereo ▲ 04/16/96
PI LA-1299A ▲ $34.95 ▲ LD-CAV ▲ M/A ▲ HiFi Stereo ▲ 04/02/96
Hyper Doll Act 2
PI VA-1300D ▲ $19.95 ▲ VHS ▲ DUB ▲ HiFi Stereo ▲ 06/18/96
PI VA-1300S ▲ $24.95 ▲ VHS ▲ SUB ▲ HiFi Stereo ▲ 06/18/96
PI LA-1300A ▲ $34.95 ▲ LD-CAV ▲ M/A ▲ HiFi Stereo ▲ 06/18/96

Iczer-One
OAV series, 3 episodes

(1985-87) ©Kubo Shoten/A.I.C.

Screenplay, Character Design and Direction: Toshihiro Hirano *Original Story:* Rei Aran *Mecha Design:* Hiroaki Motoigi, Shinji Aramaki *Animation Directors:* Narumi Kakinouchi, Masami Obari, Hiroaki Ogami *Art Direction:* Yasushi Nakamura, Kazuhiro Arai *Music:* Michiaki Watanabe

A three-volume action drama built upon the basic concept of a satire on Japanese live-action "tokusatsu" or "special effects" shows, and an early star of the then-nascent OAV

format, ICZER-ONE became famous as much for its gruesome violence as for Hirano's all-female cast of spandex-and-short-skirted heroines and villainesses. High school student Nagisa Kano is pushed kicking, screaming and bawling to Earth's defense when she is forced by Iczer-One, a benevolent alien, to unite with her in order to fight off the invading tentacles of the sinister Cthuwulf, a race of malevolent, H.P. Lovecraft-inspired brain-sucking monsters. Gross, but funny, with some genuinely scary moments. Features screenplay and character designs by director Hirano (HADES PROJECT ZEORYMER, VAMPIRE PRINCESS MIYU), mecha designs by Shinji Aramaki (GAIARTH), and monster designs by Junichi Watanabe (ANGEL OF DARKNESS). Released in Japan under the title "Tatakae! (Fight!) Iczer-1" by Kubo Shôten/Toshiba EMI; available in North America through U.S. Renditions.

Iczer-One Act 1
Nagisa and Iczer-One meet when the Cthuwulf attack. The aliens send their bio-mechanical Voids and trap Iczer-One and Nagisa in dimensional subspace. Later, Commander Cobalt launches an attack against Nagisa's city using the Dilos-Theta mecha. Iczer-One must convince Nagisa to join her and challenge Cobalt with their mecha, Iczer-Robo! **30 min.**

Iczer-One Act 2
A Cthuwulf fortress arrives on Earth. Nagisa befriends a young girl while Iczer-One investigates the alien fortress. Iczer-One becomes trapped in subspace and Nagisa is forced to protect the young girl from parasitic monsters. Iczer-One escapes only to face the challenge of a new enemy, her "sister" Iczer-Two. **30 min.**

Iczer-One Act 3
Nagisa and Iczer-One battle against Iczer-Two's mecha, Iczer-Sigma. Later, the leader of the Cthuwulf, Big Gold, orders Nagisa's capture and conversion into Iczer-Two's partner. Iczer-One must try to save humanity and defeat her sister and Big Gold in a final battle for humanity's survival. **48 min.**

Domestic Home Video:
Iczer-One Vol. 1: *Acts 1 and 2*
USR VD13 ▲ $14.95 ▲ VHS ▲ DUB ▲ HiFi Stereo ▲ 01/01/93
Iczer-One Vol. 2: *Act 3*
USR VD14 ▲ $14.95 ▲ VHS ▲ DUB ▲ HiFi Stereo ▲ 01/01/93
The Complete Iczer-One
Iczer-One Acts 1 through 3 in a subtitled format. (100 min.)
USR 031 ▲ $24.95 ▲ VHS ▲ SUB ▲ HiFi Stereo ▲ 10/01/96

Iczer 3
OAV series, 3 volumes

(1990) ©Artmic/A.I.C./Kubo Shoten

Director, Original Story & Character Design: Toshihiro Hirano *Script:* Emu Arii, Toshihiro Hirano *Music:* Takashi Kudo

The successful ICZER series continues with the saga of android Iczer-One's "younger sister," Iczer 3 (voiced by a Japanese pro wrestler, Cutey Suzuki) and her fight against the villainous Neos-Gold, descendant of the original video's menace, Big Gold. Again, screenplay and character designs are by director Hirano. Released in Japan as a six-volume series under the title "Bôken! (Adventure!) Iczer-3" by Polydor; available in North America through U.S. Manga Corps.

Iczer 3 Vol. 1
Years ago, Iczer 1 defeated the evil forces of Big Gold, saving Earth from her monstrous army. But the battle was far from over; Big Gold left many of her progeny still at large in the galaxy. Iczer 1, now protector of the Cthuwulf, has finally tracked down and destroyed all but the mightiest of Big Gold's children - Neos Gold. At a stalemate, Neos Gold and Iczer 1 withdraw to heal their wounds and regroup for what will have to be their final battle. But Neos Gold doesn't play fair, and invades Earth to force Iczer 1 to war. Earth's fate suddenly falls into the hands of Iczer 1's younger sister, Iczer 3, who is sent by the Cthuwulf to defend the planet until Iczer 1 can regain her strength. And now, with the aid of a single Earth battle cruiser and the descendant of Iczer 1's original partner, Iczer 3 is thrust into battle with some of the most bizarre adversaries imaginable. But don't count her out - what she lacks in experience, she makes up for in all-out enthusiasm! **60 min.**

Iczer 3 Vol. 2
Enthusiasm is one of Iczer 3's best assets. Unfortunately, it was that same enthusiasm which nearly got Nagisa, her slightly unwilling battle partner, killed and caused the Iczerio, power source for the mighty Iczer Robo, to fall into Neos Gold's clutches. Now, without two of her best allies and the trust of her new Earth comrades, Iczer 3 must prepare for battle alone. While Iczer 3 leaves the ship to fight Neos herself, Neos is busily experimenting with her newly captured power source and creates a new opponent made especially to battle the diminutive warrior.

TV Made for Television Broadcast   **OAV** Made for Home Video Release   **MOVIE** Made for Theatrical Release

In the midst of a battle with the beast woman Bigro and her deadly pet, Iczer 3 encounters Atros, an exact copy of herself! Now Iczer 3 must face an opponent with all her power and knowledge. Can Nagisa be the deciding factor in defeating this new menace? And what else is Neos cooking up for both of them to face? **60 min.**

Iczer 3 Vol. 3

As the crew of the *Queen Fuji* finally reaches Neos' base and Iczer 1 arrives to help, Iczer 3 has her hands full dealing with Atros, Golem, and the newly-revived Iczer 2. With a team like this fighting for her, how can Neos possibly lose? But Neos hasn't counted on Atros' wavering loyalty, or how intensely jealous Golem has become of Neos' latest creations. While Iczer 2 helps finish Atros' job, Atros is becoming more and more confused as to where her loyalties lie. And now, as Nagisa and her friends prepare for the final desperate assault on Neos' fortress, Iczer 1 is forced into a rematch she never wanted. But count on Neos to have a few dirty tricks left to play on our heroes. The Earth's fate is in the hands of these three mighty warriors and there's no telling how it will end up! The saga of the Iczers concludes in an epic struggle of violence and sacrifice, as Neos reveals her new, terrifying form to us while the world edges closer to absolute destruction. **60 min.**

Domestic Home Video:
Iczer 3 Vol. 1
USM 1092 ▲ $29.95 ▲ VHS ▲ SUB ▲ Stereo ▲ 05/04/94
ID 2879CT ▲ $34.95 ▲ LD ▲ SUB ▲ Digital HiFi Stereo ▲ 06/13/95
Iczer 3 Vol. 2
USM 1093 ▲ $29.95 ▲ VHS ▲ SUB ▲ Stereo ▲ 08/03/94
ID 2887CT ▲ $34.95 ▲ LD ▲ SUB ▲ Digital HiFi Stereo ▲ 11/22/95
Iczer 3 Vol. 3
USM 1094 ▲ $29.95 ▲ VHS ▲ SUB ▲ Stereo ▲ 01/04/95
ID 2892CT ▲ $34.95 ▲ LD ▲ SUB ▲ Digital HiFi Stereo ▲ 01/16/96

Iczelion [OAV] 💥 🌙

(1994) ©Hirano Toshihiro Jimusho/KSS Inc.

Original Story and Director: Toshihiro Hirano *Character Design:* Toshihiro Hirano, Masanori Nishii *Design Works:* Yasuhiro Moriki *Mecha Design:* Takashi Hashimoto *Animation Directors:* Masanori Nishii, Takafumi Nishii

Called his "life work" by some, Hirano (who returns yet again for direction, script, and character designs) gives his consistently popular concept yet another update by introducing four human girls instead of one and replacing the spandex look with powered armor. Nagisa Kai is a normal girl until fate intervenes and makes her the combat partner of the intelligent alien battlesuit Iczelion. Now, together with three other young women, Nagisa must save the planet Earth from conquest and total subjugation at the hands/tentacles of an insidious army of invading aliens. Fused with alien 'bots, or "Iczels," the girls form fighting units called "Iczelions" through by-now expected nudie transformation scenes and fight off an evil inorganic lifeform. This two-part OAV was released in Japan under the title "Iczer Gal: Iczelion" by KSS; available in North America through A.D. Vision. **60 min.**

Domestic Home Video:
ADV IZ/001 ▲ $34.95 ▲ VHS ▲ SUB ▲ HiFi Surround ▲ 08/21/95

Injû Seisen Twin Angels *See* TWIN DOLLS

IRIA: Zeiram the Animation [OAV] 💥
OAV series, 6 episodes

(1994) ©Crowd/Bandai Visual/Mitsubishi Corporation/Banpresto

Original Work: Keita Amemiya *Director:* Tetsuro Amino *Script:* Tetsuro Amino (Ep.1,3), Naruhisa Arakawa (Ep.2), Hajime Matsumoto (Ep.4) *Visual Concept:* Keita Amemiya *Original Character Designs:* Masakazu Katsura *Character Design:* Ryunosuke Otonashi *Music:* Yoichiro Yoshikawa

Six-episode animated adaptation of Keita Amemiya's live-action sci-fi monster movie *Zeiram,* featuring the tough-edged bounty hunting chick Iria vs. the mushroom-capped demon-from-hell villain Zeiram. The animation shows Iria in a younger incarnation than the original film, introducing her home planet, a bounty-hunting older brother, and "Bob," who shows up in the live-action movie as a disembodied computerized voice (and in this video, we see how he got that way). Character designs by Masakazu "Denei Shôjo (Video Girl Ai)" Katsura gives the titular Iria a decidedly bouncy appearance not atypical for the average anime femme, but definitely odd coming off the tough-as-nails, husky-voiced Sigourney Weaver-esque live-action version. Otherwise, this is a slickly produced video, if much more generic than the dark-toned film by which it was inspired. By the director of

"Macross 7." Released in Japan under the title "Iria: Zeiram, the Animation" by Bandai Visual; available in North America through U.S. Manga Corps.

IRIA: Zeiram the Animation Vol. 1: *Episodes 1 and 2*
He is feared in every corner of the galaxy. He exists only to kill. His name is Zeiram. The Starship Karma has been hijacked. Iria, an apprentice bounty hunter, accompanies her brother and his boss on a mission to rescue a V.I.P. and a mysterious cargo. Things turn deadly when it is discovered that the cargo is Zeiram. A mysterious corporation attempted to import the monster for use as a new bio-weapon—and now it's loose. Only Iria and her streetwise sidekick, Kei, can halt the monster's rampage. The animated prequel to the live-action film *Zeiram!* **60 min.**

IRIA: Zeiram the Animation Vol. 2: *Episodes 3 and 4*
Iria's on the run from a major conspiracy, and someone's out to silence her before she can learn the truth. All she knows is that she holds the key to exposing the Tedan Tippedai Corporation and their link to the monster, Zeiram. But Iria is not alone. A mysterious client has hired another bounty hunter to keep her alive at all costs. **60 min.**

IRIA: Zeiram the Animation Vol. 3: *Episodes 5 and 6*
All hell breaks loose in the explosive finale to the series. Iria faces Zeiram for their final battle - predator against predator - and discovers the awful truth behind her brother's disappearance and her own connection to the monster as well. She has a dangerous plan to discover Zeiram's Achilles Heel - if he has one - but will she be able to escape the trap the authorities have set? **60 min.**

Domestic Home Video:
IRIA: Zeiram the Animation Vol. 1
USM 1439 ▲ $19.95 ▲ VHS ▲ DUB ▲ Stereo ▲ 11/05/96
USM 1369 ▲ $29.95 ▲ VHS ▲ SUB ▲ Stereo ▲ 03/05/96
IRIA: Zeiram the Animation Vol. 2
USM 1440 ▲ $19.95 ▲ VHS ▲ DUB ▲ Stereo ▲ 11/05/96
USM 1370 ▲ $29.95 ▲ VHS ▲ SUB ▲ Stereo ▲ 05/07/96
IRIA: Zeiram the Animation Vol. 3
USM 1441 ▲ $19.95 ▲ VHS ▲ DUB ▲ Stereo ▲ 11/05/96
USM 1371 ▲ $29.95 ▲ VHS ▲ SUB ▲ Stereo ▲ 07/02/96

Judge [OAV] 💥 🌙

(1991) ©Fujihiko Hosono/Futabasha

Director: Hiroshi Negishi *Original Story:* Fujihiko Hosono *Music:* Toshiro Imaizumi *Chief Animator:* Shin Matsuo *Art Designer:* Chisato Sunakawa *Art Director:* Tetsunori Oyama

Based on the story of the same name by Fujihiko Hosono ("Crusher Joe"). Visually fascinating supernatural tale of a nerdish salaryman named Oma who leads a double life as a "Judge of Darkness," bringing harsh otherworldly justice to evildoers who are unlikely to be punished by human law. Oma sentences humanity under the "Laws of Darkness," contained in a mystic book made entirely from human skin. The first episode features a ruthless executive who has embezzled, lied and killed on his climb to the top; the Judge disposes of him by grisly means, starting with a nail driven through his tongue and finishing with suffocation. A second episode features Oma's boss Kawamata being charged with ordering the death of his longtime friend and coworker. The stakes are raised when a "metaphysical attorney" appears and offers to defend Kawamata; a pitched mystical battle ensues, followed by the convening of the "Court of Ten Kings," presided over by the lords of hell. Striking, starkly lit animation with great dramatic use of shadows, and impressive effects for the spiritual battles; the Ten Kings are especially impressive, rich in detail and bathed in a shifting colored light. The metaphysical angle should appeal to fans of Neil Gaiman's "The Sandman." Released in Japan under the title "Yami no Shihôkan: Judge" (Judicial Official of Darkness: Judge) by Sony Music; available in North America through U.S. Manga Corps. **50 min.**

Domestic Home Video:
USM 1448 ▲ $14.95 ▲ VHS ▲ DUB ▲ Stereo ▲ 10/08/96
USM 1078 ▲ $29.95 ▲ VHS ▲ SUB ▲ Stereo ▲ 11/02/94

Junk Boy [OAV] 🌙

(1987) ©Yasuyuki Kunitomo/Futabasha Co./Victor Entertainment, Inc.

Director: Yuusaka Saotome *Written by:* Tatsuhiko Urahata, Hiroyuki Fukushima *Character Design & Chief Animator:* Hiroshi Hamasaki *Music:* Takashi Kudo

Based on the manga of the same name by Yasuyuki Kunitomo, as serialized in publisher Futabasha's weekly MANGA ACTION anthology (home of LUPIN III). A young man named Ryohei with an above-average interest in sex gets his dream job being "boy Friday" at a men's magazine, assigned to duties such as evaluating sexy photos of naked girls, assisting on photo shoots with naked girls), making investigative visits to Turkish baths (being soaped down by naked girls!). In the course of all this, he meets his dream girl (not naked, at least not at first), a tough-as-nails investigative reporter. Initially she's not interested, and he's forced to woo her, for once putting her pleasure above his. Sweet, funny and inventively sexy, Ryohei's dream sequences (with—all together now—naked girls!) are truly hilarious—cartoony symbols for sex includes bananas and fireworks. Released in Japan under the title "Junk Boy" by Victor Entertainment; available in North America through Manga Entertainment. **45 min.**

Domestic Home Video:
MGV 635547 ▲ $19.95 ▲ VHS ▲ DUB ▲ HiFi Stereo ▲ 09/24/96

Kabuto

(1992) ©Buichi Terasawa/NEP/KSS Inc.

Original Story, Screenplay and Direction: Buichi Terasawa *Director of Animation:* Hisashi Harai *Art Director:* Takeshi Waki

One-shot OAV based on the manga of the same name (as serialized in weekly SHŪKAN FRESH JUMP manga anthology) by director Terasawa, also credited for original story, screenplay, and even rock 'n' roll song lyrics. Main character Kabuto is a super-powered martial artist in medieval Japan who must fight an evil sorceress and her troll-like, mechanical genius henchman to save a beautiful princess, which is, of course, Terasawa's oeuvre to the core. Steampunk elements in the troll-like henchman's mechanical creations, including a steam-spouting armored warrior and a flying traditional Japanese castle. Released in Japan under the the title "Karasu Tengu Kabuto: Ôgon no Me no Kemono" (Raven Tengu Kabuto: The Golden-Eyed Beast) by NHK Enterprises/Visual Book; available in North America through U.S. Renditions. A 1991-92 TV series of the same name is also available, although it has yet to be brought over to the U.S. **45 min.**

Domestic Home Video:
USR DIE01 ▲ $19.95 ▲ VHS ▲ SUB ▲ HiFi Stereo ▲ 04/01/93

Kakyûsei *See* FIRST LOVES
Kamui no Ken *See* DAGGER OF KAMUI
Karasu Tengu Kabuto *See* KABUTO
Kaze no Na wa Amnesia *See* A WIND NAMED AMNESIA
Kaze no Tani no Nausicäa *See* WARRIORS OF THE WIND

Kekko Kamen

OAV series, 2 volumes

(1991-92) ©Go Nagai/Dynamic Planning

Based on the characters by: Go Nagai *Directors:* Hideji Iuchi, Kinji Yoshimoto

Based on the manga of the same name by creator Go Nagai (CUTEY HONEY), as serialized in weekly SHŪKAN SHŌNEN JUMP manga anthology. Kekkô Kamen is a superhero who superficially bears a startling resemblance to Marvel Comics' Daredevil—she has no particular powers other than martial arts ability, and fights with a billy club—except that her "costume" is to appear buck nekkid except for a red mask, boots and gloves. Her signature tagline being "Everybody knows my body, but nobody knows my face!," she beats up the bad guys with a combination of fighting and, um…flashing. It's too funny to be dirty, even with Nazi-uniformed teachers who are fond of punishing tardiness and the like with chain-'em-in-the-dungeon-type torture. A lack of ingenuity shows on the animators' part; rather than finding exotic camera angles to shield the heroine's holiest of holies from the prying eye, they simply give her a featureless Barbie™ crotch. Believe it or not, a live-action version of this story has also been produced. Released in Japan under the title "Kekkô Kamen" ("Quite Something" Mask) by Nihon Columbia; available in North America through A.D. Vision.

Kekko Kamen Vol. 1
At the academy Miami Takahashi attends, higher education has sunk to the lowest levels of depravity, with Nazi hall monitors, teachers who wear masks to hide their identities, and special detention sessions in the torture chamber beneath the gym! And now that the deranged principal has taken a personal interest in Miami, she's been voted the "Least Likely To Survive." Enter Kekko Kamen, the most outrageous superheroine ever. This first volume details the Denuded Dynamo's first encounters with the overzealous Punishment Teacher and the incredibly macho Superstud. Includes bonus production portfolio. **55 min.**

Kekko Kamen Vol. 2
Now the naked crusader must not only rescue everybody's favorite victim, Miami Takahashi, from the beautiful tentacles of an electrically-charged exchange student from hell; she's also got to stop an incredibly sleazy samurai from taking naughty pictures of every girl on campus! **50 min.**

Domestic Home Video:
Kekko Kamen Vol. 1
ADV KK/001 ▲ $29.95 ▲ VHS ▲ SUB ▲ HiFi Surround ▲ 01/24/95
Kekko Kamen Vol. 2
ADV KK/002 ▲ $29.95 ▲ VHS ▲ SUB ▲ HiFi Surround ▲ 03/10/95

Keroppi

OAV series, 15 episodes

(1994) ©Sanrio Co., Ltd.

Director: Masami Hata *Animation Director:* Kanji Akabori *Art:* Junko Ina *Graphic Creation:* Yukio Abe *Music:* Katsuyoshi Kobayashi, Takeshi Ike

Released in Japan under its full title, "Kero Kero Keroppi" ("kero kero" being Japanese onomatopoeia for the croaking of a frog), KEROPPI follows in the tradition established by HELLO KITTY in retelling familiar fairytales and enacting gentle morality lessons with his posse of fly-eating homefrogs. Yet another member of the far-reaching Sanrio pantheon, in Japan, the KEROPPI series has produced fifteen separate OAVs to date. Released in North America by Family Home Entertainment.

Keroppi: Let's Play Baseball
2 episodes. LET'S PLAY BASEBALL: The baseball field has been taken over by some big, mean bullies. Keroppi and his friends muster their courage and challenge them to a game-the winner getting to use the field. One problem: Keroppi and friends have never played baseball before. LET'S BE FRIENDS: Everyone thinks Wink the Snake is mean and dangerous because he has a poison fang. But Keroppi can see that underneath the slimy skin beats the heart of a new friend. **52 min.**

Keroppi: Robin Hood
2 episodes. ROBIN HOOD: Keroppi as Robin Hood thwarts the plan of the greedy sheriff to capture him and his band of merry men. THE ADVENTURES OF GULLIVER: When Keroppi as Gulliver is shipwrecked on a distant island, he meets some very strange new people, proves his courage, falls in love, and finally finds his way back home. **52 min.**

Domestic Home Video:
Keroppi: Let's Play Baseball
FHE 27576 ▲ $12.95 ▲ VHS-EP ▲ DUB ▲ HiFi ▲ CC ▲ 03/21/95
Keroppi: Robin Hood
FHE 27575 ▲ $12.95 ▲ VHS-EP ▲ DUB ▲ HiFi ▲ CC ▲ 03/21/95

Kidô Keisatsu Patlabor *See* PATLABOR

Kimagure Orange Road

OAV series, 9 episodes

(1988-89) ©Toho/Studio Pierrot

Based on characters created by: Izumi Matsumoto *Character Design:* Akemi Takada *Music:* Sagisu *Screenplay:* Kenji Terada, Isao Shizuya *Art Director:* Satoshi Miura *Directors:* Naoyuki Yoshinaga, Takeshi Mori, Koichiro Nakamura

Based on the manga of the same name by creator Izumi Matsumoto, as serialized in weekly SHŪKAN SHŌNEN JUMP manga anthology. Cross-format high school love-triangle comedy—TV, OAV, theatrical—series with occasional psychic hijinks. A young man named Kyosuke can't make up his mind between two young women, mysterious and exciting Madoka, or her cute and earnest best friend Hikaru. That he also possesses a strange ability to teleport (and that the rest of his family also has weird powers) is beside the point, but does lead into a lot of strange situations. Naturally, the lynchpin of all successful series in the love-comedy genre is the ability to prolong romantic resolution for as long as possible—*without* losing the interest of the audience, which is no mean trick—and in that respect, KOR has always been one of the all-time champs, despite the release in 1996 of a theatrical feature which may or may not let you know which girl Kyosuke ends up with. Titled "Soshite, Ano Natsu no Hajimari" (And Then, the Start of that Summer), Kyosuke flashes forward three years into his own,

TV Made for Television Broadcast **OAV** Made for Home Video Release **MOVIE** Made for Theatrical Release

college-age future after he's injured in a traffic accident...an accident which takes place, in terms of story chronology, at the *end* of the 1987-88 TV series. In addition to fan-pleasing character designs by Akemi Takada (PATLABOR), KOR also features an extensive body of jazz-pop style background music, instrumentals, and vocals, all of which are naturally available on CD. (Naturally.) To date, only the OAV series and the 1988 movie "I Want to Return to That Day" are available in North America, although the TV series and more recent film are both available on home video in Japan. Released in Japan under the title "Kimagure (Capricious) Orange Road" by VAP/ Toho; available in North America through AnimEigo.

Kimagure Orange Road Vol. 1:
OAVs 1 and 2
In I WAS A CAT; I WAS A FISH, Kyosuke has an accident with a family heirloom and swaps souls with the family goldfish and cat. In HURRICANE! AKANE THE SHAPECHANGING GIRL, Kyosuke's cousin Akane pays a visit, complete with her shape-changing powers. **50 min.**

Kimagure Orange Road Vol. 2: *OAVs 3 & 4*
Hikaru loves Kyosuke and everybody knows it. Madoka thinks she loves Kyosuke, but nobody knows it. Kyosuke can't decide whom he loves! In WHITE LOVERS, a ski-trip to the Japan Alps goes awry when an avalanche traps Kyosuke and Madoka in a cave. Normally, Kyosuke wouldn't mind being alone with Madoka, except... they aren't quite alone. In HAWAIIAN SUSPENSE, Hikaru is mistaken for an heiress and kidnapped! Madoka and Kyosuke make it worse by bungling a rescue attempt. Can Kyosuke get them out of a jam without revealing his psychic powers? **50 min.**

Kimagure Orange Road Vol. 3: *OAVs 5 & 6*
In Part 1, SPRING IS FOR IDOLS, Kyosuke gets jealous when Hayakawa, a famous pop singer and ladies' man, comes to town to host a song contest - and Madoka spends all her time practicing. A head-on encounter with Hayakawa doesn't improve matters when it results in Kyosuke and Hayakawa swapping bodies. Hayakawa doesn't quite know what's going on, but decides to make the best of the situation - by putting the moves on Madoka and Hikaru! How on Earth is Kyosuke going to protect the family secret this time? In Part 2, BIRTH OF A STAR, Kyosuke must convince Hayakawa not to spill the beans, and make sure that Madoka gets to the stage on time. It's a good thing he has a knack for teleportation! **50 min.**

I was a Cat; I was a Fish
Hurricane! Akane the Shapechanging Girl

Kimagure Orange Road Vol. 4: *OAVs 7 & 8*
When Kyosuke's cousin Akane comes back for a return visit, it's guaranteed to be AN UNEXPECTED SITUATION. This time around, Akane traps Kyosuke into pretending to be her boyfriend in front of her friends. He'd better pray Madoka and Hikaru don't see him. Next, in MESSAGE IN ROUGE, Madoka's father returns to give a concert, but when Madoka finds out he's being unfaithful to her mother, she runs away from home. Will Kyosuke and Hikaru be able to find her? **50 min.**

Kimagure Orange Road Vol. 5: *I Want to Return to That Day*
A special OAV also known as "The Kimagure Orange Road Movie." A brisk day in early spring. Kyosuke and Madoka walk together on the grounds of a University, toward the signboard that will tell them if they have passed the entrance examinations. A chance comment overheard and Kyosuke's thoughts range back... to the previous summer, when he was struggling to prepare for the all-important examinations, amid the myriad distractions of youth... to the previous summer, when Madoka and he finally admitted their feelings for each other... to the previous summer, when he tried not to break Hikaru's heart. **70 min.**

Stage of Love = Heart on Fire!
Spring is for Idols
Birth of a Star

Domestic Home Video:
Kimagure Orange Road Vol. 1
ANI AT092-006 ▲ $24.95 ▲ VHS ▲ SUB ▲ HiFi Stereo
Kimagure Orange Road Vol. 2
ANI AT092-007 ▲ $24.95 ▲ VHS ▲ SUB ▲ HiFi Stereo
Kimagure Orange Road Vol. 3
ANI AT092-008 ▲ $24.95 ▲ VHS ▲ SUB ▲ HiFi Stereo
Kimagure Orange Road Vol. 4
ANI AT092-009 ▲ $24.95 ▲ VHS ▲ SUB ▲ HiFi Stereo
Kimagure Orange Road Vol. 5
ANI AT092-010 ▲ $24.95 ▲ VHS ▲ SUB ▲ HiFi Stereo
ANI AD093-003 ▲ $39.95 ▲ LD-CLV/CAV ▲ SUB ▲ HiFi Stereo

Kimagure Orange Road Collector's Suite
Volumes 1-5 in a special pre-pack.
ANI AS095-010 ▲ $119.95 ▲ VHS ▲ SUB ▲ HiFi Stereo ▲ 07/26/95
Kimagure Orange Road Laserdisc Vol. 1
OAVs 1-4 (100 min.)
ANI AD093-001 ▲ $39.95 ▲ LD ▲ SUB ▲ HiFi Stereo ▲ 07/07/93
Kimagure Orange Road Laserdisc Vol. 2
OAVs 5-8 (104 min.)
ANI AD093-002 ▲ $39.95 ▲ LD ▲ SUB ▲ HiFi Stereo ▲ 09/29/93
Kimagure Orange Road Whimsical Highways Set
OAVs 1-8 in a laserdisc set (204 min.)
ANI AS094-015 ▲ $109.95 ▲ LD ▲ SUB ▲ HiFi Stereo ▲ 12/28/94 ▲
Out of Print

The Kimagure Orange Road Movie "I Want to Return to That Day"

Kimba The Lion Prince [TV]
TV series, 52 episodes
(1966) ©Mushi Productions/Suzuki Associates International, Inc.

Created and produced by Osamu Tezuka *Directed by* Eiichi Yamamoto *Music:* Paul J. Zaza

The 1966 TV series "Jungle Taitei (Jungle Emperor)" was created and produced by the legendary Osamu Tezuka. The version syndicated in this country, KIMBA THE WHITE LION (see entry in Chapter 1), was immensely popular, and remains so to this day among anime fans. The original 1966 Americanized version has never been released on home video in America, but recently a newly translated version has appeared—not the 1966 NBC version. These four new 2-episode videos titled KIMBA THE LION PRINCE have new voices, new music, many new character names, and new credits indicating a 1993 Canadian production. This new version uses the original Mushi Productions animation—and to that extent it conforms to Tezuka's story—but the rewritten script is closer to Disney's LION KING, especially by making Kimba's tyrannical lion foe his wicked uncle. It's debatable whether the new dialogue, voices, and songs are as witty as the original Fred Ladd production, but there's no doubt that the new music lacks the richness of Isao Tomita's original orchestrated score. For those who want to see the original Mushi animation, these tapes will be welcome. For those looking to recover their memories of the music, dialogue, and characterizations of the 1966 syndicated version... well, it's better than nothing. Released by United American Video.

Kimba The Lion Prince: *Legend of the Claw*

2 episodes. In LEGEND OF THE CLAW, the series premise is set up, as Kimba's pregnant mother is kidnapped by hunters and put on a ship. Kimba is born on board, but jumps ship and swims to shore. In a series of flashbacks, we discover what happened to his father back in Africa, and how Kimba makes his way home to assume his mantle as King. In WIND IN THE DESERT, Kimba is captured by hunters, but his human friend Jonathan helps him escape and return to the jungle. Kimba learns that sometimes one must stand and fight against evil. **45 min.**

Kimba The Lion Prince: *River Battle*
2 episodes. In RIVER BATTLE, after battling a giant python, Kimba earns the respect of the jungle animals but still must prove that he is a strong and wise ruler like his legendary father, Panja. In HUMAN FRIEND, when human hunters enter the jungle, the animals fear for their lives. However, Kimba's human friend Jonathan shows that people can do more than shoot guns. **45 min.**

Kimba The Lion Prince: *Jungle Thief*
2 episodes. In JUNGLE THIEF, there is a drought in the jungle and all the animals turn to Kimba to solve the problem. To make matters worse, someone is stealing the emergency food supplies! In A FRIEND INDEED, Kimba has a new enemy in the jungle... Bongo the leopard cub. The two battle as they learn more about each other on the way to a lasting friendship. **45 min.**

Kimba The Lion Prince: *Insect Invasion*
2 episodes. In INSECT INVASION, swarms of hungry insects invade the jungle and threaten to eat all the animals' food. Kimba is brave, but how can he stop millions of flying insects? In TROUBLEMAKER, Kimba's evil uncle, King BooBoo, is plotting to turn the jungle animals against each other. With the help of his new friend Lea, a beautiful lioness cub, Kimba sets a trap to catch BooBoo and the hyenas and restore peace to the jungle. **45 min.**

Domestic Home Video:
Kimba The Lion Prince: *Legend of the Claw*
UAV 3533 ▲ $12.95 ▲ VHS ▲ DUB ▲ Mono ▲ 01/01/96
Kimba The Lion Prince: *River Battle*
UAV 3534 ▲ $12.95 ▲ VHS ▲ DUB ▲ Mono ▲ 01/01/96
Kimba The Lion Prince: *Jungle Thief*
UAV 3535 ▲ $12.95 ▲ VHS ▲ DUB ▲ Mono ▲ 01/01/96
Kimba The Lion Prince: *Insect Invasion*
UAV 3536 ▲ $12.95 ▲ VHS ▲ DUB ▲ Mono ▲ 01/01/96

Kindan no Mokujiroku
See CRYSTAL TRIANGLE

Kishin Corps
OAV series, 7 episodes

(1993) ©Masaki Yamada/Chuokoronsha/Pioneer LDC Inc.

Based on a novel by: Masaki Yamada *Director:* Taka'aki Ishiyama *Character Design:* Masayuki Goto *Mecha Director:* Takeshi Yamazaki, Koji Watanabe *Art Director:* Mitsuki Nakamura *Music:* Kaoru Wada

OAV series based on the novel by Masaki Yamada, adapted for a somewhat younger audience. In an alternate 1941, an alien invasion changes the entire course of World War II. Each side is building giant robots based on captured alien technology. An international brigade called the "Kishin Heidan" or "Kishin Corps" opposes the unholy alliance that forms between the Axis powers and the inhuman invaders. Stylish retro-look is comparable to (but definitely different than) the approach of contempory production GIANT ROBO, including Masayuki Goto's '60s-style character designs and the kind of giant, steel-plated, steam-shovel, riveted robots they might have been built during WWII if they'd only had the technology. Earth-shaking mecha direction by Takeshi Yamazaki and Koji Watanabe. Excellent Wagnerian full-symphony music by Kaoru Wada (SILENT MÖBIUS). Released in Japan under the title "Kishin Heidan" (Machine-God Corps) by Pioneer LDC; available in North America through Pioneer LDCA.

Kishin Corps Vol. 1: *Episode 1*
Episode 1, MISSION CALL FOR KISHIN THUNDER: October 1941: a Manchurian railway train is boarded by a division of the Kanto army for inspection. The division, led by Colonel Shinkai, is after a scientist named Takamura and his "black lunch box." Suddenly, the sky is lit by a mysterious glow. Mysterious aliens descend from the sky and begin firing indiscriminately upon the Kanto army and innocent passengers. Professor Takamura's son, Taishi, who safeguards the "black lunch box" escapes from the train during the confusion. But he is soon trapped. Just as he believes it's all over, a third force appears. "Kishin Corps, Attack!" **60 min.**

Kishin Corps Vol. 2: *Episodes 2 and 3*
In Episode 2, SURPRISE ATTACK!, it's December 1941, and the Kanto army, having stolen the module, heads for their secret base on Fortress Island. The Kishin Corps wait for the aliens to appear to commence their raid with Kishin Dragon in the sea and Kishin Wind in the sky. In Episode 3, THE BATTLE, the Kanto army has escaped and is transporting the module on a camouflaged train. The Kishin Corps begin firing on the Kanto army train as they race side-by-side. But suddenly another train appears, headed right for the Kishin Express! **60 min.**

Kishin Corps Vol. 3: *Episodes 4 and 5*
In Episode 4, KISHIN vs. PANZER KNIGHT PART 1, it's July 1943. Shinkai, having transferred his division to Europe, arranges an alliance with the Nazis and the aliens through a young Nazi strategist called Hans. Meanwhile, the Kishin Corps prepare Albert, the scientist who has developed a new defense bomb, for his escape to the United States. But just as they are flying off on the Fugaku, the Nazis begin attacking. And an even more formidable enemy appears! In Episode 5, KISHIN vs. PANZER KNIGHT PART 2, the module is unexpectedly stolen. Taishi in search of the stolen module meets the thief at his hiding place. It is none other than his long lost friends from the Urajina banks! Meanwhile, the Kanto army also comes to the hiding place for the module and suddenly the whole city is in trouble with aliens and the Panzer Knight appearing. Kishin Thunder is immediately dispatched! **60 min.**

Kishin Corps Vol. 4: *Episodes 6 and 7*
Episode 6, STORMING THE BASE OF THE ALIEN FOE: April 1945. The Kishin Corps completes Kishin Four, but the module itself is now in the hands of Shinkai. The Aliens and the Nazis have begun mass production of the Panzer Knight on their base on Rügen Island. Shinkai has also joined forces. At the same time, the United States completes the atomic bomb and decides to use it on Rügen Island. The Kishin Corps must attack and

destroy the Alien Base before the atomic bomb is dropped! Episode 7: YOUTH TO THE RESCUE: The final battle has begun. The Nazis' Super Cannon blasts the Kishin Express. It is engulfed in flames but continues to plunge towards the Alien Base. Kishin Thunder, Dragon and Wind fight Panzer Knight as Taishi looks for the module for his Kishin Four. The B-29 carrying the "Glamour Girl" is approaching fast! Will the Kishin Four and the Kishin Corps destroy Panzer Knight and the Aliens in time? **60 min.**

Domestic Home Video:
Kishin Corps Vol. 1
PI VA-1171D ▲ $24.95 ▲ VHS ▲ DUB ▲ HiFi Surr ▲ CC ▲ 11/30/94
PI VA-1171S ▲ $29.95 ▲ VHS ▲ SUB ▲ HiFi Surround ▲ 11/30/94
PI LA-1171A ▲ $39.95 ▲ LD-CAV ▲ M/A ▲ HiFi Stereo ▲ 11/30/94
Kishin Corps Vol. 2
PI VA-1172D ▲ $24.95 ▲ VHS ▲ DUB ▲ HiFi Surr ▲ CC ▲ 02/21/95
PI VA-1172S ▲ $29.95 ▲ VHS ▲ SUB ▲ HiFi Surround ▲ 02/21/95
PI LA-1172A ▲ $39.95 ▲ LD-CAV ▲ M/A ▲ Stereo ▲ CC ▲ 02/21/95
Kishin Corps Vol. 3
PI VA-1174D ▲ $24.95 ▲ VHS ▲ DUB ▲ HiFi Surr ▲ CC ▲ 03/28/95
PI VA-1174S ▲ $29.95 ▲ VHS ▲ SUB ▲ HiFi Surround ▲ 03/28/95
PI LA-1174A ▲ $39.95 ▲ LD-CAV ▲ M/A ▲ Surr ▲ CC ▲ 03/28/95
Kishin Corps Vol. 4
PI VA-1176D ▲ $24.95 ▲ VHS ▲ DUB ▲ HiFi Surr ▲ CC ▲ 05/23/95
PI VA-1176S ▲ $29.95 ▲ VHS ▲ SUB ▲ HiFi Surround ▲ 05/23/95
PI LA-1176A ▲ $39.95 ▲ LD-CAV ▲ M/A ▲ Surr ▲ CC ▲ 05/23/95
Kishin Corps Box Set
Vols 1-4 in a special boxed set.
PI VB-001 ▲ $97.95 ▲ VHS ▲ DUB ▲ HiFi Surr ▲ CC ▲ 04/01/96

Kishin Heidan *See* KISHIN CORPS

Kizuna
OAV series, 2 episodes

(1994-95) ©Daiei

Director: Rin Hiro *Scenario:* Miyo'o Morita *Character Design and Animation Director:* Ayako Mihashi *Music:* Fujio Takano

Based on the manga by Kazuma Kodaka, as serialized in BE BOY manga magazine. Two-volume animated example of the "shônen ai" or "boys' love" (i.e., gay) sub-genre of anime produced in Japan almost entirely by women for women, although not without its appeal to gay audiences here in the U.S. KIZUNA is the story of a young man injured in a traffic accident when a car attempts to run down his lover, the son of a mob boss. The grateful boyfriend then promises to take care of his injured friend for the rest of his life. Gay love is depicted here romantically yet frankly; this is the first "shônen ai" video title we know of to be released domestically, and hopefully it won't be the last. Released in Japan as "Kizuna" (Bonds) by Daiei; available in North America through CQC Pictures.

Kizuna Part I
As Ran undergoes rehabilitation after his tragic accident, he and Enjoji decide to move in together. In less than two years, Ran has recovered enough to attend college, and get a part-time job as a teaching assistant. Professor Sakata turns out to be the worst kind of pervert who tries to force himself on Ran. Sakata tries to get rid of Enjoji, not realizing his Yakuza background.

Kizuna Part II
Enjoji's rival half-brother Sagano has a crush on Ran, and enrolls in college to be near him. Sagano's father, the Yakuza boss, sends a bodyguard to keep an eye on him, not realizing how this will further complicate the entangled gay relationship.

Domestic Home Video:
Kizuna Part I
CQC 01 ▲ $29.95 ▲ VHS ▲ SUB ▲ 12/01/96
Kizuna Part 2
CQC 02 ▲ $29.95 ▲ VHS ▲ SUB ▲ 12/01/96

Kôkaku Kidô-Tai *See* GHOST IN THE SHELL
Koko wa Greenwood *See* HERE IS GREENWOOD
Kumo-Kai no Meikyû Zeguy *See* ZEGUY
Kyôfu no Bio-Ningen: Saishû Kyôshi *See* ULTIMATE TEACHER
Kyôshoku Sôkô Guyver *See* BIO-BOOSTER GUYVER
Kyûketsu-Hime Miyu *See* VAMPIRE PRINCESS MIYU

La Blue Girl

OAV series, 6 volumes

(1992-94) ©T. Maeda/Daiei Co. Ltd.

Director: Raizo Kitakawa (1), Kan Fukumoto (2,3,5,6), Rin'o Yanagikaze (4,6) *Script:* Megumi Ichiyanagi *Character Design:* Kinji Yoshimoto (1), Rin Shin (2-6) *Art Director:* Bibimba Miyake (1), Taro Taki (2-6) *Music Director:* Teruo Takahama *Original Author:* Toshio Maeda

Six-volume OAV sexploits of the teenaged Miko, descendant of a ninja clan which possesses a secret signet case with the power to control oversexed demons. Unfortunately, the clan's ancestral enemies snatch the signet case back, leaving Miko at the mercy of a procession of tentacular demons. In Japan, the full pornographic details of the sex scenes were hidden behind an electronically digitized screen (a standard practice for live-action porn). The digitizing effect was removed for the North American release, the result being oddly featureless genitalia. Released in Japan under the title "Injû Gakuen (Lustful-Beast Academy) La Blue Girl" by Daiei Pictures; available in North America through Anime 18.

La Blue Girl Vol. 1
Miko Mido, a ninja-in-training, is suddenly entrusted with the family business: making sure the sex-starved Shikima stay out of humanity's hair. But when the rival Suzuka clan steals the signet case that symbolizes this demonic deal, Miko and her sister Miyu become targets of the most dangerous race of perverts ever to walk the Earth. What's a girl to do? Fight back, with every bit of battle skill and sexual sorcery she can muster. But is she strong enough to save Miyu from the clutches of the Shikima in the bowels of the underworld itself? **45 min.**

La Blue Girl 2
The struggle for power over the world of the Shikima boils over as Miko, the Suzuka Clan, and even the renegade Shikima race to gain control over the Mido family's signet case. When the Mido girls and their faithful (though slightly frustrated) ninja sidekick Nin-Nin return to the underworld to investigate Miyu's odd sense of deja-vu, they're caught up in the crossfire as the Suzuka clan attacks! Before you know it, it's a veritable sexual endurance test to see who can get the case. But just when things are looking up for our much put-upon heroine, she's in for a few shocks! Who's this woman that Miyu claims is their mother? And if she is, then where's dear old dad? **45 min.**

La Blue Girl 3
Miko becomes a traveling warrior! To avenge a ruined village, Miko must hunt down Kamiri— Master of the Miruko Sez Craft, and Kugutsumen— Man of a Thousand Faces, a renegade of the Suzuka clan. In addition, she must retrieve the enchanted sword, Zipang. The control of ninja clans—and the life of her father—hang in the balance! **45 min.**

La Blue Girl 4
With the narrow escape from Kamiri and Kugutsumen's fiendish trap still fresh in their minds, Miko and Yaku continue their search. However, their opponents get the drop on them and soon the girls are fighting for their lives. But as Kamiri succumbs to the power of the magic sword, Kugutsumen manages to take control of Miko for his most diabolical plan yet—to have her murder her new friend! Is Miko strong enough to break his hold on her before she kills Yaku? **45 min.**

La Blue Girl 5
A new girl has transferred into Miko's school, Fubuki Kai. She's pretty and popular, but she's also a ninja—maybe as good as Miko! Fubuki has plans to conquer the underworld, but first she needs to find out how Miko gains entry to the underworld... Will Fubuki be able to get Miko to give up the secret? **45 min.**

La Blue Girl 6
Our half-demon heroine returns to the human world, leaving Fubuki and Nin-Nin behind in the underworld, and now the bio-mechanical monstrosities from Miko's nightmares have kidnapped her classmates! Her mother and father are in danger— all part of a plot to invade the underworld from an even more bizarre realm! **60 min.**

Domestic Home Video:
La Blue Girl 1
A18 1457 ▲ $29.95 ▲ VHS ▲ DUB ▲ Stereo ▲ 08/06/96
A18 1317 ▲ $29.95 ▲ VHS ▲ SUB ▲ Stereo ▲ 06/06/95
La Blue Girl 2
A18 1458 ▲ $29.95 ▲ VHS ▲ DUB ▲ Stereo ▲ 08/06/96
A18 1318 ▲ $29.95 ▲ VHS ▲ SUB ▲ Stereo ▲ 10/03/95
La Blue Girl 3
A18 1459 ▲ $29.95 ▲ VHS ▲ DUB ▲ Stereo ▲ 08/06/96
A18 1319 ▲ $29.95 ▲ VHS ▲ SUB ▲ Stereo ▲ 01/09/96

La Blue Girl 4
A18 1460 ▲ $29.95 ▲ VHS ▲ DUB ▲ Stereo ▲ 08/06/96
A18 1320 ▲ $29.95 ▲ VHS ▲ SUB ▲ Stereo ▲ 03/05/96
La Blue Girl 5
A18 1461 ▲ $29.95 ▲ VHS ▲ DUB ▲ Stereo ▲ 08/06/96
A18 1321 ▲ $29.95 ▲ VHS ▲ SUB ▲ Stereo ▲ 05/07/96
La Blue Girl 6
A18 1462 ▲ $29.95 ▲ VHS ▲ DUB ▲ Stereo ▲ 08/06/96
A18 1322 ▲ $29.95 ▲ VHS ▲ SUB ▲ Stereo ▲ 08/06/96
La Blue Girl Collector's Set
Tapes 1-6 (285 min.)
A18 1463 ▲ $129.95 ▲ VHS ▲ DUB ▲ Stereo ▲ 08/06/96
A18 1530 ▲ $129.95 ▲ VHS ▲ SUB ▲ Stereo ▲ 08/06/96

Laughing Target *See* RUMIK WORLD

Legend of Lemnear

(1989) ©Sôshin Pictures Enterprise Co./A.I.C.

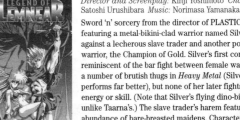

Director and Screenplay: Kinji Yoshimoto *Character Design:* Satoshi Urushibara *Music:* Norimasa Yamanaka

Sword 'n' sorcery from the director of PLASTIC LITTLE featuring a metal-bikini-clad warrior named Silver pitted against a lecherous slave trader and another power-mad warrior, the Champion of Gold. Silver's first combat scene is reminiscent of the bar fight between female warrior Taarna and a number of brutish thugs in *Heavy Metal* (Silver actually performs far better), but none of her later fights show the same energy or skill. (Note that Silver's flying dino-bird is also not unlike Taarna's.) The slave trader's harem features an abundance of bare-breasted maidens. Character designs by PLASTIC LITTLE's Satoshi Urushibara. Released in Japan under the title "Kyokuguro no Tsubasa: Valkisus" (Pitch-Black Wings of Valkisus) by Sôshin Pictures; available in North America through U.S. Manga Corps. **45 min.**

Domestic Home Video:
USM 1331 ▲ $29.95 ▲ VHS ▲ SUB ▲ Stereo ▲ 01/09/96

Legend of Lyon: Flare I & II

(1986/90) ©Media Station

Character Design: Yorihisa Uchida *Directors:* Yakihiro Makino, Yorihisa Uchida

A medieval-style planet's princess Flare is the center of attention in an invasion by aliens looking for ripe females to rape. The typical tentacles come into play in an odd combination of D&D-type fantasy and demon porn. Flare has powers which she typically forgets to use until after all her friends have been assaulted first. Described in the words of one U.S. reviewer as "UROTSUKI DÔJI'S drooling idiot cousin." Released in Japan under the title "Lyon Densetsu (Legend of Lyon): Flare" by Media Station; available in North America on a single tape through A.D. Vision.

Legend of Lyon: *Flare*
A monstrous army of alien invaders attacks the peaceful castle of Lyon with lust and carnage on their slimy little brains, and only the combined forces of Swordsman Neris and the psychic heroine Flare stand between Lyon and the sadistic Glode and his alien horde. **30 min.**

Legend of Lyon: *Flare 2*
The abandoned castle of Lyon becomes host to a malevolent force that consumes all who trespass in the surrounding forest, and when both Lady Neris and her brother Eon disappear, it's up to Flare to find out what new evil lurks in the heart of Lyon. **30 min.**

Domestic Home Video:
ADV L/001 ▲ $29.95 ▲ VHS ▲ SUB ▲ HiFi Surround ▲ 10/12/94

 Violence   Profanity   Nudity   Sexual Situations   Adult Viewers Only - content is extreme and/or explicit

Legend of the Forest

(1987) ©Tezuka Productions

OAV

Director: Osamu Tezuka *Music:* Peter I. Tchaikovsky
Experimental mini-epic from Osamu Tezuka, set to Tchaikovsky's 4th Symphony, dealing with the environmental theme of deforestation. No dialogue; the animation style(s) is a virtual survey of American cartoon history, progressing from a black & white Winsor McCay look through a Fleischer and Warners style, all the way up to a lush full-color Disney treatment. A visually stunning and beautifully conceived film that pays visual homage to every major stylistic influence in Hollywood through the years. Released in Japan under the title "Mori no Densetsu" (Legend of the Forest) by NHK Enterprises/ Visual Book; available in North America through The Right Stuf, who donate a portion of each home video sale to a charity to benefit environmental awareness. Right Stuf release includes a full-color booklet on Tezuka's life and works. Laserdisc version also contains "Astro Boy: The Lost Episode." **30 min. Color/B&W**

Domestic Home Video:
RS 9003 ▲ $12.95 ▲ VHS ▲ ND ▲ Stereo ▲ CP, W/S ▲ 07/01/94
LUM 9508 ▲ $39.95 ▲ LD ▲ ND ▲ Stereo ▲ W/S ▲ 10/04/95

Legend of the Gold of Babylon See LUPIN III

Lensman

(1984) ©E.E. "Doc" Smith/MK Company

MOVIE

Original Concept: E.E. "Doc" Smith *Written by:* Soki Yoshikawa *Directors:* Yoshiaki Kawajiri and Kazuyuki Hirokawa *Character Design:* Yoshiaki Kawajiri, Kazuo Tomizawa *Producer:* Hiroshi Suto

Full-length theatrical adaptation of E.E. "Doc" Smith's classic *Lensman* sci-fi novels, incorporating what were at the time state-of-the-art computer graphics. All things considered, the film still holds up remarkably well, and if you get the chance to view the film in its original Japanese, grab it, 'cause the casting is delightful ("RENZUMAN—!"). In Japan of 1984-85, the story begun in the theatrical feature continued in a 25-episode GALACTIC PATROL: LENSMAN TV series; unfortunately, it has yet to be released domestically. Character designs by Kazuo Tomizawa and Yoshiaki Kawajiri (WICKED CITY) add an oddly appropriate touch to these pulp sci-fi icons. Released in Japan as "SF Shin Seiki (Science Fiction New Century) Lensman" by Pony Canyon; available in North America through Streamline Pictures. **107 min.**

Domestic Home Video:
BFV 955 ▲ $19.95 ▲ VHS ▲ DUB ▲ Mono ▲ 08/15/93 ▲ Out of Print
SPV 90015 ▲ $29.95 ▲ VHS ▲ DUB ▲ Mono ▲ 12/15/91
LUM 9266 ▲ $39.95 ▲ LD ▲ DUB ▲ Mono ▲ 03/15/93 ▲ Out of Print

Leo the Lion

TV series, 26 episodes

(1966) ©Mushi Productions/Sonic International

TV

Created and produced by: Osamu Tezuka

When NBC told Osamu Tezuka that they did not want the title character of KIMBA THE WHITE LION to grow to adulthood in that series, Tezuka was forced to make this sequel TV series that charts the progress of the adult Leo/ Kimba, his mate, and two sons. It has much the same charm as KIMBA, and Tezuka was left to develop it as he saw fit, without interference from the American syndicators. Originally broadcast in Japan as "Jungle Taitei Susume Leo! (Jungle Emperor Go Leo!)" in 1966, the show did not make it to American TV screens until 1984 on the Christian Broadcasting Network. Eight episodes are available on home video in North America through Palm Beach Entertainment.

Leo the Lion Vol. 1: *The First Adventure*
Young Chris is left alone in the jungle when his grandfather is kidnapped by thugs. He is befriended by Leo, who shows Chris his secret jungle kingdom. Chris, Leo and Leah then set out to find the kidnapped man. **25 min.**

Leo the Lion Vol. 2: *Map of Danger*
Leo sends his jungle friends on a mission to locate all the dangers of the jungle. In their travels, the animals encounter some unfriendly lions and other dangerous spots, shown on a map called the "Map of Danger." **25 min.**

Leo the Lion Vol. 3: *The Blue Lion*
Leo sets out to find a cure for his wife Leah's illness. On the way, he encounters Zamba the Blue Lion. Zamba attacks Leo's friends in the jungle. When Leo comes to their rescue, he discovers the reason for the Blue Lion's cruelty. **25 min.**

Leo the Lion Vol. 4: *Leo Becomes a Father*
There's excitement in the jungle as Leo and Leah become parents. Their two cubs, Rune and Rukyo, are born on a sunny day in the jungle and it doesn't take long before they get into trouble. **25 min.**

Leo the Lion Vol. 5: *The Mighty Gorilla*
Rukyo makes friends with "Dwimog," the mightiest of all gorillas. All is well until the mandrills challenge the giant gorilla to a fight. With the help of Leo, the mighty gorilla battles the mandrills to see who will rule the Golden Valley. **25 min.**

Leo the Lion Vol. 6: *The Golden Bow*
A strange friendship grows when Leo meets the chief of one of the tribes with whom he shares the jungle. Leo and the wise chief form a team to conquer a new and dangerous enemy, with the help of a magical golden bow. **25 min.**

Leo the Lion Vol. 7: *The Case of the Moonlight Stone*
British agent Sterling Bond enlists Leo to help him search for the famous "Moonlight Stone." Leo helps Bond, and together they fight off spies who plan to use the stone for evil purposes. **25 min.**

Leo the Lion Vol. 8: *The Sabertooth Tiger*
Leo and his son Rune take a trip back in time when an unexpected snow storm hits the jungle. They make friends with an elephant and meet a giant sabertooth tiger. **25 min.**

Domestic Home Video:
Leo the Lion Vol. 1
PBE 8501 ▲ $6.95 ▲ VHS ▲ DUB ▲ Mono ▲ 07/01/94
Leo the Lion Vol. 2
PBE 8502 ▲ $6.95 ▲ VHS ▲ DUB ▲ Mono ▲ 07/01/94
Leo the Lion Vol. 3
PBE 8503 ▲ $6.95 ▲ VHS ▲ DUB ▲ Mono ▲ 07/01/94
Leo the Lion Vol. 4
PBE 8504 ▲ $6.95 ▲ VHS ▲ DUB ▲ Mono ▲ 07/01/94
Leo the Lion Vol. 5
PBE 8505 ▲ $6.95 ▲ VHS ▲ DUB ▲ Mono ▲ 07/01/94
Leo the Lion Vol. 6
PBE 8506 ▲ $6.95 ▲ VHS ▲ DUB ▲ Mono ▲ 07/01/94
Leo the Lion Vol. 7
PBE 8507 ▲ $6.95 ▲ VHS ▲ DUB ▲ Mono ▲ 07/01/94
Leo the Lion Vol. 8
PBE 8508 ▲ $6.95 ▲ VHS ▲ DUB ▲ Mono ▲ 07/01/94

Lily-C.A.T.

(1987) ©Victor Music Co. Ltd.

OAV

Director: Hisayuki Toriumi *Monster Design:* Yoshitaka Amano *Character Design:* Yasuomi Umetsu *Mecha Design:* Yasuhiro Moriki *Animation Director:* Toshiyasu Okada *Screenplay:* Hiroyuki Hoshiyama *Music:* Akira Inoue

2264 A.D.: The starship *Saldes* is sent into deep space to explore a newly discovered planet. The journey will take twenty years. The *Saldes'* crew of thirteen, mixing experienced space jockeys with eager but naive scientists, are prepared for anything - except an unseen alien invader with an insatiable appetite. Monster designs by VAMPIRE HUNTER D's Yoshitaka Amano and character designs by ROBOT CARNIVAL's Yasuomi Umetsu add class but can't help much with plot in this absolutely blatant *Alien* rip-off space drama. Released in Japan under the title "Lily C.A.T." by Victor Entertainment; available in North America through Streamline Pictures. **67 min.**

Domestic Home Video:
SPV 90873 ▲ $19.95 ▲ VHS ▲ DUB ▲ Mono ▲ CC ▲ 07/01/94

Locke the Superman

MOVIE ★★★★

(1984) ©Nippon Animation Co. Ltd./Shochiku Co. Ltd.

Director: Hiroshi Fukutomi

From the director of BATTLE ANGEL and FATAL FURY: LEGEND OF THE HUNGRY WOLF comes this full-length theatrical retelling of the popular sci-fi action manga of the same name by Saki Hijiri. The intergalactic wars have begun. The federal army is no match for Lady Chan's legion of robotic soldiers. Defeat is at hand. Now living the peaceful life of a civilian, super-powered psychic Locke is asked to come out of retirement in answer to the new menace to the Earth. As with LENSMAN, the combination of traditional animation techniques with what had been at the time state-of-the-art computer graphics add a contemporary touch. Released in Japan under the title "Chôjin (Super-Person) Locke" by Toshiba EMI; available in North America through Best Film and Video. Followed in Japan by a multi-episode OAV series, some episodes of which feature direction by STAR BLAZERS and ROBOTECH's Noboru Ishiguro. **120 min.**

Domestic Home Video:
BFV 966 ▲ $19.95 ▲ VHS ▲ DUB ▲ Mono

Lodoss Jima Senki *See* RECORD OF LODOSS WAR

Luna Varga

OAV (())

OAV series, 4 episodes

(1991) ©Toru Akitsu/Kadokawa Shoten/NEXTART

Director: Shigenori Kageyama *Screenplay:* Aki Tomato, Yumiko Tsukamoto *Original Story:* Toru Akitsu

Princess Luna finds herself fused with a dragon (she sits on his forehead; when not in use, he shrinks down to a vestigial tail) in this sword-swingin' action/comedy. The dragon Varga is an obvious spiritual descendant of Godzilla, even wielding a *very* slightly altered version of the big lizard's battle roar. Character designs by Yuji Moriyama (PROJECT A-KO, MAISON IKKOKU) in addition to opening credits sung by Masato Shimon, one of the classic old tyme singers of anime themes for series such as "Science Ninja Team Gatchaman" and "Yûsha Raideen" (a.k.a. "Raideen the Brave"), add a familiar touch. Released in Japan under the title "Majû Senshi (Magic-Beast Warrior) Luna Varga" by Kadokawa Shôten/Nexstar; available in North America through A.D. Vision.

Luna Varga Vol. 1: *Episodes 1 and 2*
Luna has inadvertently invoked the ancient spell that summoned Varga, a 200-foot-tall mythical beast. In doing so, Luna finds herself stuck on her dragon's forehead... permanently. The bad news is that it's her rear end attached to the dragon. The good news is that Varga can shrink himself down to a vestigial tail that only ruins the cut of Luna's dress. **60 min.**

Luna Varga Vol. 2 : *Episodes 3 and 4*
The sinister Dark Lord has a secret weapon up his inhuman sleeve and Luna's walked right into it! Demons and creatures made of living rock are bad news, but can even the mighty Varga stand up against the villainous Dark Varga? The conclusion of the series. **60 min.**

Domestic Home Video:
Luna Varga Vol. 1
ADV LV/001 ▲ $29.95 ▲ VHS ▲ SUB ▲ HiFi Surround ▲ 02/20/96
Luna Varga Vol. 2
ADV LV/002 ▲ $29.95 ▲ VHS ▲ SUB ▲ HiFi Surround ▲ 04/23/96

Lupin III

TV

(1977-80) ©Monkey Punch/TMS

Based on Characters by: Monkey Punch *Produced by:* Tokyo Movie Shinsha *Script and Direction:* Hayao Miyazaki *Music:* Yuji Ono *Art Director:* Noburo Tatsuke

The original *Mad Magazine*-inspired manga by Kazuhiko Kato (who draws under the pen name of "Monkey Punch") featured a hero who was supposedly the grandson of the fictitious thief Arsene Lupin from the stories of French author Maurice LeBlanc. However, Monkey Punch's "Lupin III" was no gentleman, but lusty, greedy and ruthless,

in stories that were wild, funny and anarchic—a funky criminal mood comparable to that of *Pulp Fiction.* This style was in a large part carried over to Lupin's early anime adaptations—the 1969 pilot film and first 1971-72 TV series (23 episodes), which brimmed with adult attitude and real-world detail. One of the rare anime TV shows whose major characters are all adults, Lupin sported grown-up sponsors such as Nissan, and ads for whiskey and cigarettes run during its broadcast, rather than the typical toys and anime-related merchandise. In succeeding incarnations, the tone turned more to action-comedy—not what Monkey Punch had in mind, but a formula that contributed to the marked success of the series since. All incarnations of the series feature Lupin III's eternal cast of five main characters: Lupin's partners—the sardonic gunman Jigen and taciturn swordsman Goemon, Lupin's part-time lover, the grifting, balloon-breasted Fujiko (her name is meant to evoke Mt. Fuji, and you can guess what that implies), and Lupin's full-time pursuer, the indestructible, trenchcoated, Inspector Clouseau-like Zenigata. The two episodes available from Streamline Pictures are from the end of the second Lupin series (1977-80, 155 episodes), and are the only two directed by Hayao Miyazaki (under the pseudonym Teruki Tsutomu). Due to legal considerations from the estate of Maurice LeBlanc, these video releases from Streamline Pictures appear under the alias "The Wolf."

Lupin III: *Albatross: Wings of Death*
In this episode, originally broadcast in 1980, Wolf (Lupin III) learns that the world's most eccentric entrepreneur, Dr. Lonebach, has a nuclear device and plans to blackmail the world from his one-plane "air force" - a retro-fitted 1929 Dornier luxury airship - culled from his personal airplane museum. What makes matters worse is that Fujiko Mine - Wolf's sometimes girlfriend/partner - has been kidnapped by this wealthy madman. It's up to Wolf and his capable sidekicks to knock the wind out of this terrorist's deadly sails and put a stop to this potentially fatal fiasco. Wolf's only problem is finding an antique plane that doesn't fall apart before he can get close enough for a dogfight. **30 min.**

Lupin III: *Aloha, Lupin!*
A powerful flying robot, stolen from a top-secret Japanese military arsenal, is committing robberies all over Tokyo and, thanks to a timely "public service announcement" by Lupin III, all indications point to this loveable rogue as the most likely suspect. Inspector Zenigata vows to finally capture Lupin and put an end to his nefarious career. But as the plot winds toward an inevitable showdown, fans will recognize that both thief and detective are acting strangely out of character. A cute and daring robot jockey, a wild sky ride and some dynamic fireworks help make this one of the most spectacular pieces of TV animation ever filmed. Originally broadcast as the final episode of the second *Lupin III* TV series (1977-80), Tokyo Movie Shinsha gave Japan's top theatrical animation director Hayao Miyazaki carte blanche in order to let the series go out with a bang. The result is the essence of the wit and cleverness of *Lupin III* distilled into one superb short effort. **30 min.**

Domestic Home Video:
Lupin III: *Albatross: Wings of Death*
SPV 90503 ▲ $14.95 ▲ VHS ▲ DUB ▲ Mono ▲ 12/15/93
Lupin III: *Aloha, Lupin!*
SPV 90513 ▲ $14.95 ▲ VHS ▲ DUB ▲ Mono ▲ 03/15/94
Lupin III's Greatest Capers
Albatross Wings of Death and Aloha Lupin (50 min.)
SPV 91153 ▲ $19.95 ▲ VHS ▲ DUB ▲ Mono ▲ CC ▲ 02/21/95

Lupin III: The Mystery of Mamo

MOVIE ★★★★ (())

(1978) ©Monkey Punch/TMS

Based on characters by: Monkey Punch *Director:* Soji Yoshikawa *Script:* Atsushi Yamatoya, Soji Yoshikawa *Layouts:* Tsutomu Shibayama *Animation Directors:* Yoshio Kabashima, Yuza Aoki *Music:* Yuji Ono

This is the first "Lupin" theatrical feature, and probably the closest of all the "Lupin" films to the mood of the original manga, and notable especially for its villain: an immortality-obsessed, godhead-claiming, reclusive tycoon, supposedly modeled on Howard Hughes, but looking like a dead ringer for Paul Williams in *The Phantom of the Paradise.* With its halter-tops, disco basslines, and "cameos" by Henry Kissinger and Jimmy Carter, MAMO has the firm funky reek of the '70s, and its plot, like the Bond film *You Only Live Twice,* begins with Lupin's "presumed death." The film has been dubbed in English twice; the first, done by its distributor, Toho, played American art theaters several times during the 1980s and gained much fan affection for the energy and verve the unknown English voice-actors brought to the roles.

Streamline Pictures re-dubbed the film in the 1990s under the title "The Mystery of Mamo." Currently released in Japan under the title "Lupin Sansei: Lupin vs. Fukusei Ningen" (Lupin III: Lupin vs. the Clone People) by Toho; available in North America through Streamline Pictures. **102 min.**

Domestic Home Video:
SPV 90943 ▲ $29.95 ▲ VHS ▲ DUB ▲ Mono ▲ CC ▲ 04/14/95

Lupin III: The Castle of Cagliostro

(1979) ©Monkey Punch/TMS

Based on the comics by: Monkey Punch *Script:* Hayao Miyazaki, Haruya Yamazaki *Director:* Hayao Miyazaki *Music:* Yuji Ono *Art Director:* Shichiro Kobayashi *Animation Director:* Yasuo Otsuka

Master animator Hayao Miyazaki (MY NEIGHBOR TOTORO) tries his hand at the "Lupin III" franchise, creating the second and what is probably the most famous of the "Lupin" films. After robbing a casino in Monte Carlo, Lupin discovers his carful of cash is all funny money. Clues point him to the postage-stamp nation of Cagliostro. His hurt pride impels him to travel there, but upon arriving Lupin instead becomes entangled with the young Princess Clarisse, a girl soon to be forced into marriage with the little nation's sinister ruler, Count Cagliostro. As seen by Miyazaki, Lupin is something of a knight-in-shining armor hero rather than the bodice-ripping rogue, and he romantically vows to both rescue Clarisse and rob the Count, in grand *Raiders of the Lost Ark*-style. Seen by some as the greatest Lupin film due to Miyazaki's genius, by others (creator Monkey Punch included) as the film that deviates the most from his original vision of the character. Either way, CASTLE OF CAGLIOSTRO is one of finest pure adventure films in anime; a practically perfect tightrope-walk between comedy and suspense, yet also evocative and moody in its use of the fairyland beauty and heirloom evil of its setting—the fantastic Cagliostro Castle. Released in Japan under the title "Lupin Sansei: Cagliostro no Shiro" (Lupin III: Cagliostro's Castle) by Toho; available in North America through Streamline Pictures, although 1997 will bring a new release through Manga Video. **100 min.**

Domestic Home Video:
SPV 90283 ▲ $29.95 ▲ VHS ▲ DUB ▲ Mono ▲ 10/15/92
BFV 960 ▲ $19.95 ▲ VHS-EP ▲ DUB ▲ Mono ▲ 08/15/93 ▲ Out of Print

Lupin III: Legend of the Gold of Babylon

(1985) ©YTV/Monkey Punch/NTV

Based on the characters by: Monkey Punch *Screenplay:* Yoshio Urasawa, Chiku Owaya *Music:* Yuji Ono *Directors:* Kiyoshi Suzuki, Shigetsugu Yoshida

The third "Lupin" theatrical feature is very much in the goofy-looking style of the latter part of the third TV series during which it was made. A New York bag lady named Rosetta who babbles about Babylon and its lost gold, and an ancient artifact in her possession, prompts Lupin and Co. to go on a global hunt, pursued both by Zenigata and a rapacious New York gangster. Funny, and sometimes exciting and tough, BABYLON also has what is perhaps long-time LUPIN III composer Yuji Ono's consistently best soundtrack, whose tracks compare favorably to Kitaro and David Sanborn. Released in Japan under the title "Babylon no Ôgon Densetsu" (Legend of the Babylon Gold) by Toho; available in North America through AnimEigo. Note that the North American release titles vary due to legal considerations from the estate of Maurice LeBlanc, and as the result, AnimEigo's releases are entitled "Rupan." **100 min.**

Domestic Home Video:
Rupan III: Legend of the Gold of Babylon
ANI AT095-002 ▲ $24.95 ▲ VHS ▲ SUB ▲ HiFi Stereo ▲ 03/29/95
ANI AD095-004 ▲ $39.95 ▲ LD ▲ SUB ▲ HiFi Stereo ▲ 03/29/95

Lupin III: The Fuma Conspiracy

(1987) ©Toho Co. Ltd./Tokyo Movie Shinsha

Based on the Characters by: Monkey Punch *Screenplay:* Makoto Naito *Animation Director:* Kazuhide Tomonaga *Art Director:* Shichiro Kobayashi *Music:* Kiyoshi Miyaura *Director:* Masayuki Ozeki

The fourth "Lupin" theatrical feature. Borrowing many plot elements from CAGLIOSTRO, and returning to the look of that film and the first TV series, the unusual premise of FUMA had Lupin faking his death to go into retirement, a despondent Zenigata sequestered in a Buddhist monastery, and the still-taciturn Goemon nevertheless meeting a nice girl and

preparing to settle down. Nevertheless, the bride is kidnapped at the wedding by a modern-day ninja clan, and Lupin gets drawn into helping his old friend. Very well-paced, action-packed, and clear and sharp in its art direction, evoking the beauty of rustic Japan. Released in Japan under the title "Lupin III: Fûma Ichizoku no Imbô" (Plot of the Fuma Clan) by Toho; available in North America through AnimEigo. Note that the North American release titles vary due to legal considerations from the estate of Maurice LeBlanc, and as the result, AnimEigo's releases are entitled "Rupan." **73 min.**

Domestic Home Video:
Rupan III: The Fuma Conspiracy
ANI ET095-001 ▲ $19.95 ▲ VHS ▲ DUB ▲ HiFi Stereo ▲ 04/26/95
ANI AT095-001 ▲ $24.95 ▲ VHS ▲ SUB ▲ HiFi Stereo ▲ 02/22/95
ANI AD095-002 ▲ $39.95 ▲ LD-CLV/CAV ▲ SUB ▲ HiFi Stereo ▲ 03/22/95

Macron 1 [TV]

(1986) ©Saban/Tamerline Publishing/Orbis

Seen on U.S. TV in the 1980s, this was another fusion of different anime TV shows (in this case, GOSHOGUN and SRUNGLE) on the ROBOTECH or CAPTAIN HARLOCK AND THE QUEEN OF A THOUSAND YEARS model, in order to make a minimum number of episodes for daily American syndication of shows that aired weekly in their original Japanese runs. As with CAPTAIN HARLOCK AND THE QUEEN OF A THOUSAND YEARS, this was accomplished in part with such devices as using video editing to make characters from one show appear to converse with those from the other through a monitor screen. The two "different groups" of characters in MACRON 1 were then said to exist, one on Earth, the other in an a parallel universe. Both fought against "Dark Star and the tyrannical armies of GRIP." Another unusual feature of MACRON 1 was its use of '80s Top 40 singles as replacement music for that of the original series. See also GOSHOGUN, THE TIME ÉTRANGER (above), which was the experimental OAV sequel to the original Japanese show. Released in Japan under the titles "Sengoku Majin Go Shôgun" (Demon-God [or "machine," in an alternate reading] of the War-Torn Land") and "Aku Dai-Sakusen: Srungle" (Great Military Operation in Subspace: Srungle) by Tokuma Japan Communications and Pony Canyon, respectively; available in North America (four volumes only) through Celebrity Home Entertainment.

Macron 1 Vol. 1: *Dark Discovery in A New World*
4 episodes. The year is 2545. A teleportation experiment goes haywire and rockets Major David Chance into an alternate universe. The resulting vacuum sucks the evil Dark Star and half his forces into our universe. Now the sinister armies of GRIP want control of both universes. The good forces in each world must team up to battle these tyrannical legions. Together they form Macron 1, united in the fight for the future. **115 min.**

Macron 1 Vol. 2: *Fighting For Truth & Justice*
4 episodes. Discovering a new universe means unleashing a relentless new enemy: Dark Star and the tyrannical armies of GRIP! To save themselves from sure destruction, the people of Earth must fight back with the best they've got and that means Macron 1, the mightiest cosmic crime-fighting team ever to probe the cold depths of space. **115 min.**

Macron 1 Vol. 3: *Flight of the Battle Robots*
4 episodes. Macron 1! Two teams strong, they're the peace keepers of the 41st century. Their enemy? The fanatic forces of GRIP and their dread leader Dark Star. In an ongoing contest of wits and nerves, they battle each other with an amazing arsenal of futuristic weaponry. **120 min.**

Macron 1 Vol. 4: *Dark Star's Revenge*
4 episodes. Dark Star, the evil genius from an alternative universe, launches his latest ploys to control Earth in the year 2525. Doing battle against him are the key forces for good: Macron 1. This team of freedom fighters battles on Earth and in a parallel world to defeat this threat to two universes. **120 min.**

Domestic Home Video:
Macron 1 Vol. 1
CEL 3037 ▲ $39.95 ▲ VHS ▲ DUB ▲ HiFi Mono
Macron 1 Vol. 2
CEL 3041 ▲ $39.95 ▲ VHS ▲ DUB ▲ HiFi Mono
Macron 1 Vol. 3
CEL 3044 ▲ $39.95 ▲ VHS ▲ DUB ▲ HiFi Mono
Macron 1 Vol. 4
CEL 3118 ▲ $39.95 ▲ VHS ▲ DUB ▲ HiFi Mono

Macross II, "Lovers Again"
OAV series, 6 episodes
(1992) ©Big West/Macross II Project English version by L.A. Hero

Direction: Kenichi Yatagai *Character Design:* Haruhiko Mikimoto *Mecha Design:* Koichi Ohata, Junichi Akutsu, Jun Okuda *Art Direction:* Hidenori Nakahata *Music Direction:* Yasunori Honda

Thought to be a sequel at the time of its initial release, most (including its Japanese producers!) now think of this six-episode OAV series as an "alternate future" of the MACROSS universe. The menaces of the original MACROSS, the Zentraedi, have been assimilated into human society, but a new alien threat, a renegade Zentraedi splinter race called the Marduk, arrives to shake things up. The Zentraedi were defeated by Lynn Minmay's song of peace and love, awakening emotions their race had long buried; the Marduk, on the other hand, have their own singers (called "emulators"), who sing their warriors into a battle frenzy. A young reporter named Hibiki Kanzaki, Marduk emulator Ishtar, and U.N. Spacy's ace female pilot Sylvie Gena get caught up in the clash between cultures. The animation quality drops rather severly in the later volumes, but the overall design work is still eye-catching. Those allergic to idol singers should beware of several vocal numbers. Character designs by Haruhiko Mikimoto of MACROSS fame, with mecha designs by Koichi Ohata (GENOCYBER), Junichi Akutsu and Jun Okuda. Opening credits are by Masami Obari (FATAL FURY). Released in Japan under the title "Chô Jikû Yôsai (Superdimensional Fortress) Macross II: Lovers Again" by Bandai Visual; available in North America through U.S. Renditions.

Macross II Episode 1: *Contact*
Hibiki Kanzaki of SNN news network is after a story about Valkyrie ace Silvie Gena. Events in his life quickly change as an invading alien force enters the solar system. Armed with the legendary Minmay Song Attack, the Earth forces are sent to stop the intruders. Hibiki is assigned to cover the battle and encounters a mysterious and exotic alien woman, Ishtar. **23 min.**

Macross II Episode 2: *Ishtar*
Hibiki returns with the beautiful Micron Ishtar. Hibiki wants to teach her about human culture, but the alien warrior Feff plans to rescue her from Earth. Both Feff and Silvie follow Hibiki and Ishtar to Culture Park Plaza, the site of Earth's greatest monuments as well as the *SDF-1 Macross*. Ishtar is strangely drawn to the old ship, but Feff attacks before she can discover the secret of *Macross*. **23 min.**

Macross II Episode 3: *Festival*
Ishtar seeks to discover the truth about the legendary *Super Dimensional Fortress, Macross.* She and Hibiki visit the ancient battle fortress but are unknowingly followed by U.N. Spacy Valkyrie ace Silvie Gena. Later, Hibiki and Ishtar visit the annual U.N. Spacy moonbase festival to enjoy the airshow as well as the performance of singer Wendy Ryder. Who could have known the alien Marduk and their Zentraedi warriors would attack in another attempt to recover Ishtar? **23 min.**

Macross II Episode 4: *Marduk Disorder*
Hibiki is tortured and held captive by the aliens. Ishtar undergoes "purification" in the sacred shrine of Alus Nova. Silvie attempts a daring rescue of Hibiki, and Feff tries to save Ishtar before the "culturally contaminated" Marduk ship is destroyed by order of the Marduk Lord Emperor, Ingues. **23 min.**

Macross II Episode 5: *Station Break*
The U.N. Spacy, commanded by Captain Balzae, deploys the Macross Cannon against the invading Marduk forces. During the epic battle Hibiki is imprisoned for revealing the truth about the Marduk invasion to the public. **23 min.**

Macross II Episode 6: *Sing Along*
Silvie persuades Exxegran to let her use the *Macross* in a desperate assault against the Marduk flagship. Ishtar returns to Earth and tries to discover the truth behind the power of Alus. Can Silvie, Hibiki, and Ishtar stop the insane Marduk Emperor Ingues? **23 min.**

Domestic Home Video:
Macross II Vol. 1: *Episodes 1&2*
USR VD11 ▲ $24.95 ▲ VHS ▲ DUB ▲ HiFi Stereo ▲ 08/01/92
▲ Out of Print
Macross II Vol. 2: *Episodes 3&4*
USR VD16 ▲ $24.95 ▲ VHS ▲ DUB ▲ HiFi Stereo ▲ 01/01/93
▲ Out of Print
Macross II Vol. 3: *Episodes 5&6*
USR VD26 ▲ $24.95 ▲ VHS ▲ DUB ▲ HiFi Stereo ▲ 01/25/94
▲ Out of Print

Macross II: The Movie
(1992) ©Big West/Macross II Project

Director: Kenichi Yatagai *Character Design:* Haruhiko Mikimoto *Mecha Design:* Koichi Ohata, Junichi Akutsu, Jun Okuda *Art & Music Direction:* Yasunori Honda

A 120-minute compilation video which edits all six OAV episodes into one theatrical feature that saw limited U.S. distribution in the early '90s. Eighty years have passed on Earth since the events chronicled in MACROSS-DO YOU REMEMBER LOVE? The descendants of the Zentraedi/Meltrandi conflict have established a new society with the people of Earth. When alien invaders identified as renegade Zentraedi threaten this uneasy alliance, the *Superdimensional Fortress Macross* must resurrect itself after generations of inactivity to fight the enemy forces. Hibiki Kanzaki, an investigative reporter for Scramble News Network (SNN), is caught up in the battle when he inadvertently allies himself with Ishtar, an enigmatic Zentraedi princess. **120 min.**

Domestic Home Video:
MGV 634811 ▲ $19.95 ▲ VHS ▲ DUB ▲ HiFi Stereo ▲ 10/24/95
MGV 636241 ▲ $29.95 ▲ VHS ▲ SUB ▲ HiFi Stereo ▲ 03/19/96

Macross Plus
OAV series, 4 volumes
(1994-95) ©Big West/Macross Plus Project/Hero Co. Ltd.

Original Story: Studio Nue/Shoji Kawamori *Director & Mecha Design:* Shoji Kawamori *Co-Director:* Shinichiro Watanabe *Character Design:* Masayuki *Screenplay:* Keiko Nobomuto *Animation Director:* Yuji Moriyama *Art Director:* Katsufumi Hariu *Music:* Yoko Kanno

Fast-forward the MACROSS universe forty years to a new colony planet of Earth called Eden. Two childhood friends/Valkyrie test pilots become rivals over competing designs from two different companies. While they're at it, they also become rivals over the love of the same woman, their mutual old friend Myung, who is now manager to Sharon Apple, a completely computer-generated superstar singer. (Well, almost completely.) Director Kawamori and co-director Shinichiro Watanabe traveled to the U.S. and actually flew in jet planes over U.S. testing grounds to gather information for animating the aerial combat scenes; the results are breathtaking as are Sharon Apple's computer-generated concert sequences. (Although taking place on a colony world, Eden, audiences may notice many "location shots" in the story based on actual parts of California, which the director toured for his research.) MACROSS PLUS includes impressive speculation on future aviation technology, and in its 21st-century society's willing embrace of artificial, computer-generated dreams, can be seen as a creepy satire of the "virtual idol" technology emerging in Japan and elsewhere. As with some recent high-budget mecha productions such as GUNDAM 0083, MACROSS PLUS has a dedicated mecha director; in this case, Ichiro Itano (ANGEL COP), the man who put the thrust in the original MACROSS TV series' missiles. Features mecha designs by director Kawamori, the original creator of the Valkyrie, with character designs by DOOMED MEGALOPOLIS' Masayuki, who gives the MACROSS world an entirely new look. As an additional grace note, the soundtrack features sweeping orchestral music by Yoko Kanno (PLEASE SAVE MY EARTH, THE VISION OF ECAFLOWNE), as performed by the Israel Philharmonic Orchestra, not to mention Sharon Apple's techno vocals (performed by Gabriela Robin). As with MACROSS II, the individual OAV episodes of MACROSS PLUS have also been edited into one theatrical feature, and although the film (released with a bilingual English/Japanese soundtrack) has

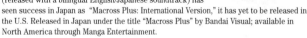

seen success in Japan as "Macross Plus: International Version," it has yet to be released in the U.S. Released in Japan under the title "Macross Plus" by Bandai Visual; available in North America through Manga Entertainment.

Macross Plus Part 1
In 2040 A.D. on the colonial planet Eden, the Ministry of Defense is testing and developing transforming aircraft, a new advanced defense to counter alien attacks. Isamu Dyson is an extrovert jet fighter maverick assigned as a new test pilot on Project Super Nova. Competition heats up when he discovers that his old rival Guld is test pilot for the competing project. The arrival of Myung, a mutual ex-girlfriend, adds more tension to the conflict. **40 min.**

Macross Plus Part 2

Computer-generated mega-pop star Sharon Apple has packed in the masses again for another of her bestselling concerts. Amongst the fans are Isamu Dyson, the maverick pilot, and Yang, who is about to pull off one of the biggest computer hacking stunts ever in front of millions. When Isamu returns to New Edwards Test Center he is up against his old rival Guld for air supremacy as well as fighting for the affections of Myung, the discontented producer of Sharon Apple. A computer transmitted message alarms the pilots that Myung is in danger and both rush to her rescue. Guld emerges a hero and Isamu is jealous. Sparks fly and rivalry turns violent as they meet in aerial combat. **40 min.**

Macross Plus Part 3

The dangerous rivalry between hotshot renegade Isamu Dyson and ice-cool Zentraedi half-breed Guld Bowman reaches the boiling point amid the pressure of the Super Nova test program. Former singer Myung Lone, now the manager of the computer-generated virtual idol Sharon Apple, is torn between her feelings for the two men as her memories of days gone by on planet Eden are shattered by harsh reality. After an investigation into the so-called "accident" that left Dyson hospitalized in Part 2, the U.N. Government in charge of the test program unveils its hidden agenda and cancels both Dyson and Bowman's experimental star fighters in favor of a new artificially intelligent aircraft. Myung leaves them behind, heading for Earth and an uncertain future, while Dyson, with the help of a hacker genius Yang, hijacks the YF-19 fighter and heads after her. Only one other plane can catch him — the rival YF-21. Bowman climbs aboard and the chase is on. Meanwhile on Earth, on the eve of her greatest concert, the computerized Sharon Apple has become self-aware for the very first time ... and the consequences could be murder. **45 min.**

Macross Plus Part 4

Angered by the news that the Stealth Valkyrie trials have been abruptly stopped, Isamu and Yang head toward Earth to get even with the pilot-less Valkyrie, "Ghost X-9." Guld, hearing the same news goes after them for a final battle. The two fighters clash amidst interceptor missiles being fired from Earth. During this fight to the death, Guld recalls the fateful event that had been sealed in his memory. Meanwhile in Macross City, Sharon Apple absorbs Myung's thoughts and twists them in a terrifying fashion. She now has full control over the city as well as the minds of its citizens. Sharon sends the "Ghost X-9" after Isamu and Guld. **45 min.**

Domestic Home Video:

Macross Plus Part 1
MGV 633881 ▲ $14.95 ▲ VHS ▲ DUB ▲ HiFi Stereo ▲ 02/28/94
MGV 634267 ▲ $24.95 ▲ VHS ▲ SUB ▲ HiFi Stereo ▲ 02/28/94
PI 34413 ▲ $34.95 ▲ LD ▲ M/A ▲ Stereo ▲ CC ▲ 04/25/95

Macross Plus Part 2
MGV 633883 ▲ $14.95 ▲ VHS ▲ DUB ▲ HiFi Stereo ▲ 05/23/95
MGV 634865 ▲ $24.95 ▲ VHS ▲ SUB ▲ HiFi Stereo ▲ 05/23/95
PI 34635 ▲ $34.95 ▲ LD ▲ M/A ▲ Stereo ▲ CC

Macross Plus Part 3
MGV 633885 ▲ $14.95 ▲ VHS ▲ DUB ▲ HiFi Surr ▲ 08/22/95
MGV 635353 ▲ $24.95 ▲ VHS ▲ SUB ▲ HiFi Stereo ▲ 08/22/95
PI 34983 ▲ $29.95 ▲ LD ▲ M/A ▲ Stereo ▲ CC ▲ 11/26/96

Macross Plus Part 4
MGV 634807 ▲ $14.95 ▲ VHS ▲ DUB ▲ HiFi Stereo ▲ 04/16/96
MGV 635355 ▲ $24.95 ▲ VHS ▲ SUB ▲ HiFi Stereo ▲ 04/16/96
PI 34980 ▲ $29.95 ▲ LD ▲ M/A ▲ Stereo ▲ CC ▲ 12/10/96

Macross, Super Dimensional Fortress

MOVIE

(1984) ©Big West

Director: Noboru Ishiguro

Retells the original 1982-83 MACROSS TV series that became the first part of ROBOTECH in compact theatrical form, and is considered by many to be one of anime's landmark films. The MACROSS movie of necessity sacrifices much of the original series' character and story development, and in its compression of many tragedies, creates a somewhat claustrophobic and depressing mood lying behind its spectacular portrayal of space warfare that utilized the early talents of such future giants as Shoji Kawamori (MACROSS PLUS) and Hideaki Anno (NEON GENESIS EVANGELION). Released in Japan under the title "Chô Jikû Yôsai Macross: Ai•Oboete Imasu ka?" (Superdimensional Fortress Macross: Do You Remember Love?) by Victor Entertainment; available in North America through Best Film & Video. **115 min.**

Domestic Home Video:

BFV 965 ▲ $19.95 ▲ VHS ▲ DUB ▲ Mono

Mad Bull 34

OAV

(1990-92) ©Kazuo Koike, Noriyoshi Inoue/Shueisha Inc./Pony Canyon Inc./Magic Bus

Original Work: Kazuo Koike, Noriyoshi Inoue *Screenplay:* Toshiaki Imaizumi *Art Director:* Nobutaka Ike *Music Director:* Katsunori Shimizu *Director:* Satoshi Dezaki

The original manga by Kazuo Koike of "Lone Wolf and Cub" fame is a grotesque display of *Dolomite*-like graphic sex and violence; its buff, bulging characters sweat, drool and bleed their way through each installment. But, to be fair, the same could be said at times for Koike's later CRYING FREEMAN; it's just that being set in an exotic playground of international gangsters, it's nothing personal for an American reader. MAD BULL is different; it's set in New York City, and was written in the mid-1980s, when the city's violence was at an all-time high and the subject of international media attention. So perhaps it's not surprising then that Koike eschewed NYC's status as the center of world culture to instead portray it as an exciting land of rape and honey, where a corrupt, hulking, shotgun-toting cop, Mad Bull, sidelines as a pimp and rarely, if ever takes in a suspect alive. And, again, to be fair, MAD BULL had the same theory as a lot of American-made ninja films: that is, the other guy's country is a great place to find exotic, willing women and men willing to deal out a horrible death. The problem for the four-volume anime OAV version of MAD BULL is that if you want to pull off this kind of material at all, you really need a good artist; Noriyoshi Inoue was the man for the manga, blowing out each dirty page with crack-pipe gusto. The low, low-budget anime (you won't believe these prices) fails in the adaptation, and the English (literally!) adaptation isn't helped by its British dub voice-actors who in their accented efforts forget that New Yorkers usually insert a "the" into phrases such as "in hospital" or "at university." As you may have already guessed, MAD BULL is no *Hill Street Blues* or even a *NYPD Blue*; it's more like a momentary lapse of licensing judgment from a company that brought the English-speaking world MACROSS PLUS, PATLABOR 2, and THE WINGS OF HONNEAMISE. Maybe it's appropriate that the only distinguished part of MAD BULL is its end—the original jazz theme by Donald Ross Skinner and Markus Williams is really quite good. Released in Japan under the title "Mad Bull 34" by Shueisha/Pony Canyon; available in North America through Manga Entertainment.

Mad Bull Part 1: *Scandal*

Meet New York cop John "Sleepy" Estes, aka Mad Bull, and his partner Eddy Diazaburo Ban, a new 18-year old recruit. Together they patrol New York's dangerous 34th precinct, battling gangsters, corrupt cops, armed robbers, drug barons, and cop killers— fighting to maintain law and order. Eddy Ban struggles to deal with his partner's methods of law enforcement and to face the myriad of violent crimes they are called upon to deal with on a daily basis. **60 min.**

Mad Bull Part 2: *The Manhattan Connection*

When an attractive new female detective—who happens to be an old friend of Mad Bull—is transferred to the 34th Precinct, Mad Bull and his partner Diazaburo find themselves pulled into one of the most dangerous cases of their career. A major new player is moving into Manhattan's 34th Precinct, bringing the plague of drugs onto the streets once more, and a desire for vengeance against the cop who put him in a wheel chair! **60 min.**

Mad Bull Part 3: *City of Vice*

An accused rapist and murderer is released from police custody due to lack of evidence. An eager news reporter gets in over her head while trying to break the case, and her life is soon threatened - along with the lives of Mad Bull and his partner. The corruption and conspiracy surrounding the accused - head of a notorious crime syndicate - reaches all the way to the top of the local government, leaving Mad Bull to attempt to solve the case with no back up. **60 min.**

Mad Bull Part 4: *Cop Killer*

Two policemen are found lying in a pool of blood, horribly murdered by an incredibly strong and vicious assailant. This is the grisly introduction to one of the worst series of killings that New York City has ever seen, and it may spell the end for the NYPD! Mad Bull and his partner are thrown in at the deep end when the killer turns out to have a grudge against Mad Bull—and the means to exact revenge. **50 min.**

Domestic Home Video:

Mad Bull Part 1
MGV 635319 ▲ $19.95 ▲ VHS ▲ DUB ▲ HiFi Stereo ▲ 03/19/96

Mad Bull Part 2
MGV 635549 ▲ $19.95 ▲ VHS ▲ DUB ▲ HiFi Stereo ▲ 05/21/96

Mad Bull Part 3
MGV 635551 ▲ $19.95 ▲ VHS ▲ DUB ▲ HiFi Stereo ▲ 07/30/96

Mad Bull Part 4
MGV 636247 ▲ $19.95 ▲ VHS ▲ DUB ▲ HiFi Stereo ▲ 09/24/96

Madox-01: Metal Skin Panic

(1987) ©FujiSankei Communications, International

Story and Direction: Nobuyuki Aramaki *Character Design:* Hideki Tamura *Mecha Design:* Nobuyuki Aramaki, Kimitoshi Yamane

Accidentally trapped in an experimental secret military battle suit he doesn't quite know how to operate, Sujimoto Koji, the teenaged hero of this one-shot OAV, still tries to make his way across town to meet his girlfriend on time. All he has to do is survive traffic, the police and the fanatic tank battalion commander hellbent on destroying the suit. Great, fast-paced action; plenty of mecha for those who need a shot of grinding gears to make it through the day. Features character designs by Hideki Tamura, with mecha designs by Nobuyuki Aramaki and Kimitoshi Yamane. Released in Japan under the title "Metal Skin Panic: Madox-01" by Pony Canyon; available in North America through AnimEigo. **50 min.**

Domestic Home Video:
ANI ET095-011 ▲ $19.95 ▲ VHS ▲ DUB ▲ 12/27/95
ANI AT089-001 ▲ $24.95 ▲ VHS ▲ SUB ▲ HiFi Stereo ▲ 04/15/90
ANI AD093-004 ▲ $39.95 ▲ LD ▲ SUB ▲ HiFi Stereo ▲ 07/18/93

Magical Princess Gigi

(1987) ©Harmony Gold U.S.A. Inc.

Directed by: Hiroshi Watanabe *Story by:* Carl Macek and Takeshi Studio

Theatrical version of the 1982-83 and then 1991-92 TV series "Mahô no Princess Minky Momo," in which the eponymous Minky, sent by a loving Mum and Dad to help the people of Earth gain happiness, fails her first mission and is replaced by a second Minky when Minky No. 1 is run over by a dumptruck. (What, you think we'd make something like that up?) Released in Japan under the title "Mahô no Princess (Magical Princess) Minky Momo" by Bandai Visual; available in North America through Celebrity Home Entertainment. **80 min.**

Domestic Home Video:
CEL 3111 ▲ $14.95 ▲ VHS ▲ DUB ▲ HiFi Mono ▲ 04/01/90

Magical Twilight

OAV series, 3 volumes

(1994/95) ©Yuki/Pink Pineapple.

Based on characters by: Yuki (Akane Shinshaken) *Director:* Toshiaki Kobayaski (1,2), Toshiaki Komura (3) *Character Design:* Jun'ichi Mihara *Animation:* A.I.C.

Not since peanut butter met chocolate has there been a combo as eagerly anticipated by male hetero anime fans as this one: the "mahô no shôjo" or "magical girls" genre gets the "etchi" or softcore anime treatment in a plot about as likely as the power guy "just dropping in to check the meter." (Cue '70s porn music.) Magical witches have to go to Earth to pass their certification exam, and *somehow*, this ends up involving a competition between two girls to have sex with a young man. Released in Japan under the title "Magical Twilight" by Pink Pineapple; available in North America through SoftCel Pictures, a division of A.D. Vision.

Magical Twilight
Tachibana Tsukasa's about to take his final exams for the third time, but he's plagued by nightmares of his own impending death. Now three apprentice witches have shown up on his doorstep, all determined to pass their own final exams... and Tsukasa's the test subject! Witch number one is Chipple, a sweet and charming white witch whose task is to make Tsukasa like her. Witch number two is Irene, a sultry siren who's convinced that the way to Tsukasa's heart is through the perils of the flesh. Worst of all is Liv, the apprentice black witch, whose assignment is to murder Tsukasa - making him suffer first! **35 min.**

Magical Twilight 2
A trip to a popular hot springs resort turns into a complete fiasco when Irene and Chipple derail Japan's famous Bullet Train in a "minor" dispute over who's going to take a dip in the hot tub with Chipple's human stud, Tsukasa. Then they wreak total havoc on the unsuspecting health spa. But while Chipple and Irene are getting all steamed up, the lovely owner of the resort starts a steam bath of her own, and her special guest is Tsukasa. **35 min.**

Magical Twilight 3
Studly young Tsukasa and winsome witch Chipple are still spending a few stolen moments at the hot springs resort to which Tsukasa won a trip. Unfortunately, it's not much of a vacation for poor Tsukasa when he has to spend all his time guarding his manhood against the advances of several young babes, especially now that the sexy resort owner's equally seductive young daughter has decided to join the game of musical hot tubs. At least over-sexed Irene seems to have found a young mortal who can handle her legendary appetite. **35 min.**

Domestic Home Video:
Magical Twilight
ADV M/001 ▲ $29.95 ▲ VHS ▲ SUB ▲ HiFi Surr ▲ 09/23/94
Magical Twilight 2
ADV M/002U ▲ $29.95 ▲ VHS ▲ SUB ▲ Uncut ▲ HiFi Surr ▲ 11/21/95
ADV M/002G ▲ $29.95 ▲ VHS ▲ SUB ▲ Edited ▲ HiFi Surr ▲ 11/21/95
Magical Twilight 3
ADV M/003U ▲ $29.95 ▲ VHS ▲ SUB ▲ Uncut ▲ HiFi Surr ▲ 01/30/96
ADV M/003G ▲ $29.95 ▲ VHS ▲ SUB ▲ Edited ▲ HiFi Surr ▲ 01/30/96

Magma Taishi *See* AMBASSADOR MAGMA
Mahô no Princess Minky Momo *See* MAGICAL PRINCESS GIGI

Maison Ikkoku

TV series, 96 episodes

(1986-88) ©Rumiko Takahashi/Shogakukan, Inc./Kitty/Fuji TV

Based on the comics by: Rumiko Takahashi *Music:* Takao Sugiyama *Character Design:* Yuji Moriyama *Chief Director:* Kazuo Yamazaki

Based on the manga of the same name by the Queen of Romantic Comedy, Rumiko Takahashi (RANMA 1/2, URUSEI YATSURA). Maison Ikkoku is the name of a run-down apartment building housing the strangest assortment of tenants this side of NBC's *Seinfeld* or MTV's *The Real World*. When a beautiful new manager arrives on its broken-down doorstep, Yusaku Godai, a penniless would-be college student, falls in love at first sight, and the rest of the series' 96 episodes details the story of their on-again, off-again romance. In Japan, the series extends beyond the initial TV series to include several OAVs and one theatrical feature: "Maison Ikkoku Bangai Hen: Ikkoku Jima Nanpa Shimatsu Ki" (Maison Ikkoku Side-Story: Castaways of Ikkoku Island), filmed in the style of a "lost episode" in which the shipwreck of smarmy tennis coach Mitaka's cruiser and subsequent hijinks of the Maison Ikkoku gang on a southern island are detailed; "Maison Ikkoku: Prelude," currently available in Japan on laser disc only, in which previous footage from the TV series is given a new voice-over and background music to tell the story of Manager Kyoko thinking back with mingled happiness and sadness to the days before she moved into Maison Ikkoku; "Maison Ikkoku: Utsuri Yuku Kisetsu no Naka de" (Within the Changing Seasons), a 90-minute compilation video taken from the TV series; and finally, "Maison Ikkoku: Kanketsu Hen" (Final Chapter), the 1988 theatrical feature in which the final days before the climactic end of Godai and Manager Kyoko's romance are chronicled (don't see it until you've finished watching the TV series). To date, only the TV series is available on domestic home video, but plans are in the works for future release of the other videos in the series. Released in Japan under the title "Maison Ikkoku" by Kitty/Five Ace/Pony Canyon; available in North America through Viz Video.

Maison Ikkoku Vol. 1: *Welcome to Maison Ikkoku*
2 episodes. SORRY TO KEEP YOU WAITING! I'M KYOKO OTONASHI: Yusaku Godai is a *ronin*—that is, a student trying his best to study for his college entrance exams—but his rowdy housemates and their loud all-night parties (usually in *his* room) are wearing the guy down. Poor Godai is on the verge of moving out in frustration when a beautiful new building manager shows up on the doorstep of his rickety old boarding house. Suddenly, moving is the farthest thing from his mind... LOVE IS IN THE AIR! WHICH ONE DOES KYOKO LOVE BEST?: Is it that time already? The holiday season has arrived, and while new manager Kyoko Otonashi busies herself with fixing up the rundown boarding house, the thoroughly smitten Godai tries to muster up his courage to give Kyoko a gift to show his affection. But it seems that fate is determined to prevent this shy student from carrying out his plan for a romantic holiday gesture. **52 min.**

Maison Ikkoku Vol. 2: *Ronin Blues*
2 episodes. HEARTS ON FIRE IN THE DARK! ALL ALONE WITH KYOKO: While poor Godai desperately tries to study for his upcoming college entrance exams, his unsympathetic housemates are hell-bent on distracting him. But then, just when his patience is about to crack for good, a power outage in Maison Ikkoku sends him to the attic with Manager Kyoko to find the problem. Alone together in the dark... could there *be*

another situation more distracting? KYOKO'S HEART GOES PITTY-PAT! GODAI IS PUT TO THE TEST: Now the long-dreaded exams have finally arrived, and while Akemi, Ichinose and Yotsuya place bets on which college exam Godai will fail next, Kyoko does her best to encourage him to keep on trying. Unfortunately, this simple gesture of kindness doesn't escape the attention of the meddling members of the household. **52 min.**

Maison Ikkoku Vol. 3: *Spring Wasabi*
2 episodes. KYOKO'S CLIMBING THE WALLS! GODAI'S HEADED FOR THE HILLS! With his exam results looming over the horizon, a panicked Godai can't bring himself to face either the ridicule of his housemates or the prospect of Kyoko's sympathy, and disappears from Maison Ikkoku, taking refuge at his buddy Sakamoto's place while waiting for the axe to fall. Meanwhile, just as a concerned Kyoko is about to turn the town upside down to find him, Godai's grandmother makes a surprise appearance at the boarding house to see her grandson's test results firsthand. SHOCKING SPRINGTIME! KYOKO'S SECRET: Springtime has arrived, school is starting, and Godai's future is finally beginning to look brighter. But even such a springtime can have its sadness, as Godai and the other tenants of Maison Ikkoku finally discover what it is that's been making Kyoko so melancholy, especially now that the cherry blossoms are in bloom. **52 min.**

Maison Ikkoku Vol. 4: *Soichiro's Shadow*
2 episodes. GODAI'S AGONY! THE ONE KYOKO LOVES: A request to home-tutor Ikuko from Kyoko's father-in-law seems a heaven-sent opportunity to both earn some pocket money as well as score some brownie points with Ikuko's beautiful young aunt, Manager Kyoko. But with thoughts of Soichiro weighing so heavily on her heart these days, Kyoko may not be ready to accept his affections. GODAI'S UNSPEAKABLE DECLARATION! IF YOU'RE GOING TO DO IT, <u>DO</u> IT!: Godai's going to need every ounce of courage he can muster (and every ounce of alcohol his buddy Sakamoto can pour) if he's going to finally come right out and tell Kyoko how he feels about her, whether she's ready to hear it or not. But does the entire neighborhood have to hear it, too!? **52 min.**

Maison Ikkoku Vol. 5: *Playing Doubles*
2 eoisodes. THE MYSTERIOUS TENNIS COACH IS THE RIVAL OF LOVE: It's going to be a while before Kyoko gets over Godai's drunken confessions of love, but in the meantime, life at Maison Ikkoku goes on. Godai, determined to improve his income and his prospects, gets a part-time job at a local liquor store, and Kyoko—prodded by well-meaning neighbors—takes up tennis lessons at the local country club. A little sun, a little fun, and a handsome tennis coach... it sounds like a recipe that would cheer *any* woman up. Which, of course, is exactly what Godai's worried about. Can Godai hold his own against a man with an income, a car and a smile like a toothpaste ad? LOVE PANIC ON THE BEACH! THE COMPETITION'S A DOG-HATER: After commiserating with a particularly miserable Kentaro about the tragedy of a wasted summer, Godai decides to liven up both of their lives with a day trip to the beach. Three definitely *isn't* a crowd when Kyoko agrees to come as well, but *five* certainly is —Kyoko's neice Ikuko inviting herself along and handsome tennis coach Mitaka offering to drive the group in his car. It's hard to compete with a man who has ecerything, but even coach Mitaka has a weakness... and it looks just like a particularly shaggy creature that just happened to come along for the ride. **52 min.**

Domestic Home Video:
Maison Ikkoku Vol. 1
VV MI-001 ▲ $24.95 ▲ VHS ▲ DUB ▲ HiFi Stereo ▲ 05/14/96
VV MIS-01 ▲ $29.95 ▲ VHS ▲ SUB ▲ HiFi Stereo ▲ 10/04/96
Maison Ikkoku Vol. 2
VV MI-002 ▲ $24.95 ▲ VHS ▲ DUB ▲ HiFi Stereo ▲ 07/02/96
VV MIS-02 ▲ $29.95 ▲ VHS ▲ SUB ▲ HiFi Stereo ▲ 11/15/96
Maison Ikkoku Vol. 3
VV MI-003 ▲ $24.95 ▲ VHS ▲ DUB ▲ HiFi Stereo ▲ 08/30/96
Maison Ikkoku Vol. 4
VV MI-004 ▲ $24.95 ▲ VHS ▲ DUB ▲ HiFi Stereo ▲ 11/08/96
Maison Ikkoku Vol. 5
VV MI-005 ▲ $24.95 ▲ VHS ▲ DUB ▲ HiFi Stereo ▲ 12/06/96

Majû Senshi Luna Varga *See* LUNA VARGA
Makai Toshi Shinjuku *See* DEMON CITY SHINJUKU
Mamono Hunter Yôko *See* DEVIL HUNTER YOHKO

Maps

OAV series, 4 episodes

(1994-95) ©Yuichi Hasegawa/Gakken/KSS/TMS

Author: Yuichi Hasegawa *Screenplay:* Masaki Tsuji *Chief Animator:* Hideyuki Motohashi *Director:* Susumu Nishizawa *Art Director:* Yukihiro Shibuya *Art Director:* Yukihiro Shibuya *Character Design:* Masahiko Ohkura *Music:* Masahiro Kawasaki

Based on the manga of the same name by Yuichi Hasegawa, as serialized in publisher Gakken's COMIC NORA manga anthology. Rollicking space adventure featuring a galaxy-hopping quest for a legendary treasure. Skimpily dressed space privateer Lipumura comes

to Earth in search of the "Mapman," an Earthling descendant of the "Nomad Star Tribe" who holds to the key to one crucial part of a star map genetically encoded in his body. Lipumura is also a cyborg of sorts—the half-organic, half-mechanical "brain" of her ship, which itself looks like a giant, angel-shaped chromium hood ornament. The downside of this situation is, when the angelic ship is attacked (and there's more than one bone-rattling space battle between ships in this series), damage registers on Lipumura as bloody physical wounds. MAPS shares a certain stylistic similarity to GIANT ROBO in that both feature healthy amounts of serious drama, Earth-shattering spectacle and coming-of-age story, livened up by imaginative and outrageous design work. Among realistic science fiction elements such as detailed space stations and orbital elevators, you also get silly aliens that look like mollusks, parrots and toothy watermelons. Slick, luscious animation, some nudity and violence, rousing action, and swell, sweeping sci-fi music. Preceeded in Japan (not yet available in the U.S.) by "Maps: Densetsu no Samayoeru Seijintachi" (Legendary Space Wanderers), a 53-minute, 1987 one-shot based on the same manga. Released in Japan under the title "Maps" by KSS; available in North America through A.D. Vision.

Maps 1 & 2
When Gen Tokishima and his girlfriend Hoshimi step out after seeing a sci-fi movie, they're confronted by half-naked Space Hunter Lipumira and her sixty-story-tall spaceship. They are told that as a result of thousands of years of genetic programming, Gen is the only being in the universe who can locate the long-lost crystal Maps that show the way to a p•õceless artifact hidden millennia ago by a mysterious race of aliens! Immediately, a second hunter's ship arrives and begins destroying the city in search of Gen. This convinces the two to join Lipumira on an interstellar quest for the ultimate treasure. The odds are impossible, and every hunter in the universe will be out to get them, but the prize is wealth and knowledge beyond imagination. **60 min.**

Maps 3 & 4
The universe is already a dangerous place, and when every Hunter in the galaxy is after you it can be downright deadly. For hundreds of years Hunters have searched in vain for the Flowing Light, a priceless artifact hidden by an ancient race, but the beautiful Hunter Lipumira had found the key in the form of Gen. Having located the first set of maps, Gen, Lipumira and Hoshimi are the focus of a galaxy-wide manhunt, with the ultimate treasure as the prize. But first Lipumira must confront a dark shadow from her past and Gen will find himself face to face with the most unusual alien of all. **60 min.**

Domestic Home Video:
Maps 1 & 2
ADV MA/001 ▲ $29.95 ▲ VHS ▲ SUB ▲ HiFi Surround ▲ 09/15/95
Maps 3 & 4
ADV MA/002 ▲ $29.95 ▲ VHS ▲ SUB ▲ HiFi Surround ▲ 10/24/95

Maris the Chôjo *See* RUMIK WORLD

MD Geist

(1986) ©Nippon Columbia Co./Hiro Media/Production Wave

Director: Hayato Ikeda *Original Story, Assistant Director & Mecha Design:* Koichi Ohata *Screenplay:* Riku Sanjo *Animation Director:* Hiroshi Negishi *Character Design:* Tsuneo Ninomiya *Art Director:* Yoshinori Takao

Using advance bio-technology, one race has the perfect soldier with the advent of the MDS. "MD" stands for "most dangerous," as in "most dangerous soldier." MD Geist, the second and deadliest of the Most Dangerous Soldiers, finds his way back to his homeworld Jerra after awakening from a forced sleep on an orbiting satellite, and he joins a biker gang to get revenge on the officers who sealed him away for years in orbit. But now he must choose: help those who marooned him in space, or stand back and let his homeworld be ravaged by the "Death Program." Both original story and assistant director/mecha design credit go to GENOCYBER's Koichi Ohata, while animation direction goes to BOUNTY DOG's Hiroshi Negishi. Followed by a sequel a decade later. Released in Japan by Nihon Columbia; available in North America through U.S. Manga Corps. **45 min.**

Domestic Home Video:
USM 1260 ▲ $19.95 ▲ VHS ▲ DUB ▲ Stereo ▲ 03/07/95 ▲ Out of Print
USM 1507 ▲ $19.95 ▲ VHS ▲ DUB ▲ Stereo ▲ Director's Cut ▲ 08/06/96
USM 1024 ▲ $29.95 ▲ VHS ▲ SUB ▲ Stereo ▲ 08/05/92
ID 2235CT ▲ $34.95 ▲ LD ▲ SUB ▲ HiFi Stereo ▲ 07/27/93

MD Geist II: Death Force

(1996) ©Central Park Media/Koichi Ohata/Riku Sanjo/Nippon Columbia Co., Ltd.

Director: Koichi Ohata *Original Script:* Riku Sanjo *Music:* Yoshiaki Ouchi

Sequel to 1986's MD GEIST. The Death Force has been unleashed and the murderous robots are slaughtering every living thing on the planet. As the surviving remnants of humanity hatch a dangerous plan to destroy the Death Force, Geist goes head-to-head with the prototype Most Dangerous Soldier. Like BURN UP W or GHOST IN THE SHELL (see entries), MD GEIST II, in what seems to be a trend for the future, was co-financed by the American company which released it. Release in North America by U.S. Manga Corps. **45 min.**

Domestic Home Video:
USM 1508 ▲ $19.95 ▲ VHS ▲ DUB ▲ HiFi Stereo ▲ 08/06/96

Megami Paradise

(1995) ©Megami Takada/Kensetsu Iinkai/Media Works/King Records/MOVIC

Created by: Akihiro Yoshizane, Miyasumi, Media Works *Director:* Katsuhiko Nishijima *Screenplay:* Mayori Sekijima

Based on the video game and then manga (as serialized in DENGEKI PC ENGINE magazine) of the same name. Two-volume OAV series in which the raison d'etre is to showcase as many young girls as possible in wispy Amazon outfits indulging in Paradise Island-like actitivies such as fighting, spellcasting, falling down in trance, playing lutes, swinging swords, and the like. The plot's no more substantial than the girls' outfits, but if the amount of dramatic narrative in, say, a typical "Playboy Showcase" video is enough to suit your tastes, you'll have no complaints with this. Released in Japan under the title "Megami (Goddess) Paradise" by King Record; available in North America through A.D. Vision.

Megami Paradise: *Assemble! Shrine Maidens to the Mother Goddess*
Enter a world where every girl is literally a goddess! Shielded from the corruption of the outside universe by the purifying Astrostar, the Megami Paradise has long been desired by the evil followers of the Dark Goddesses. Now, as the retiring Mother Megami prepares for her final ritual of purification before the selection of a new Mother Goddess, the forces of darkness make their move. Can Lilith, her companions Rurubell, Stasia, and Julliana defeat the Dark Goddesses' fearsome champion, or will the Megami Paradise be destroyed forever? **30 min.**

Megami Paradise 2: *Paradise Lost?*
Attack of Yamimama!
The forces of the Dark Goddess kidnap Lilith and Astrostar as Lilith prepares to ascend to the position of Mother Goddess. Stasia and Juliana race to the fortress of the Dark Goddess to rescue Lilith before she is sacrificed. Will their combined power be enough to stop the Dark Goddess and rescue their friend, or is the Megami Paradise doomed? **35 min.**

Domestic Home Video:
Megami Paradise
ADV MP/001 ▲ $29.95 ▲ VHS ▲ SUB ▲ HiFi Surround ▲ 04/30/96
Megami Paradise 2
ADV MP/002 ▲ $29.95 ▲ VHS ▲ SUB ▲ HiFi Surround ▲ 06/11/96

Megazone 23

(1985) ©Idol/Artmic

Original Author & Director: Noboru Ishiguro *Music:* Shiro Sagisu *Script:* Hiroyuki Hoshiyama *Producer:* Toru Miura *Animation by:* Idol Co., Ltd.

The high-water mark of the early years of the OAV format, MEGAZONE 23 was not only the bestselling anime video of 1985, but No. 2 in overall video sales in Japan that year, second only to USA for Africa's "We Are the World." Originally conceived as a TV show sequel to the series "Kikō Sōseiki Mospeada" ("Genesis Climber Mospeada," the original 1983-84 series that became the third part of ROBOTECH), MEGAZONE 23 ended up borrowing the transforming motorcycle concept from "Mospeada," and, in having to modify what was to have been thirteen episodes' worth of plot into one 80-minute OAV, had a bittersweet, inconclusive ending, but otherwise has no real resemblance.

MEGAZONE's backdrop is 1980s Tokyo; its hero, a young biker, Shogo, witnesses the brutal murder, by what appear to be government agents, of a test-driver friend who "borrowed" a prototype motorcycle. Escaping with the prototype and pursued over succeeding days, Shogo finds that the bike indeed has a secret, but it's utterly trivial compared to the truth about his and everybody's life that is gradually revealed by his dangerous encounters with the "men in black." Although MEGAZONE 23 is an exciting, SF action drama, the quality that truly made it memorable was how it managed to capture the feeling of what it was like to be young and alive in its place and time. Its sequels, unreleased here, bore little relationship to the spirit of the original. Released in Japan under the title "Megazone 23" by Victor Entertainment; available in North America as "Megazone 23, Part 1" through Streamline Pictures. **80 min.**

Domestic Home Video:
SPV 90913 ▲ $29.95 ▲ VHS ▲ DUB ▲ Mono ▲ CC ▲ 07/20/95

Meiô Keikaku Zeorymer *See* HADES PROJECT ZEORYMER
Meitantei Holmes *See* SHERLOCK HOUND
Mermaid Forest *See* RUMIK WORLD

Mermaid's Scar

(1993) ©Rumiko Takahashi/Shogakukan, Inc.

Based on the Comics by: Rumiko Takahashi (published by Viz Comics) *Character Design and Animation Director:* Kumiko Takahashi *Art Director:* Hidetoshi Kaneko *Music:* Norihiro Tsuri *Director:* Morio Asaka

Based on the manga of the same name (published in English by Viz Comics) by RANMA 1/2 and MAISON IKKOKU creator Rumiko Takahashi. The animation production team changes from that of the preceding MERMAID FOREST (see RUMIK WORLD below), but the underlying story's essentially the same: a young man, Yuta, travels the land in search of others like himself after eating the mermaid flesh which has cursed him with immortality. In MERMAID'S SCAR, Yuta and his immortal companion Mana meet a precocious little boy who may be more than he seems. Note that scenes of extreme violence may frighten younger viewers. Features character designs and animation direction by "Tokyo Babylon"'s Kumiko Takahashi, with exceptionally haunting music by Norihiro Tsuri. Released in Japan under the title "Ningyo no Kizu" (Mermaid's Scar) by Victor Entertainment; available in North America through Viz Video. **50 min.**

Domestic Home Video:
VV MS-001 ▲ $19.95 ▲ VHS ▲ DUB ▲ HiFi Stereo

Metal Fighters Miku
TV series, 13 episodes

(1994) ©JVC/TV Tokyo/Enoki Films

Original Story: Daisaku Ogawa *Director:* Akiuki Shinbo *Production:* J.C. Staff

Home video version of the Japanese TV series in which girl wrestlers of the future use powered armor to take their opponents down to the mat. Entering this highly competitive sport is The Pretty Four. Miku, Ginko, Sayaka and Nana, face the likes of the monstrous Crushers and the deadly Lady Ninjas. Silly, yet enjoyable fun; yet another of a generation of shows initially planned as OAVs ending up as TV series (i.e., BLUE SEED), meaning higher budgets and subsequently higher-quality animation. Probably only the second time ever for girls' pro wrestling to be animated. (Only in Japan....) Broadcast in Japan under the title "Metal Fighters Miku"; available in North America through Software Sculptors.

Metal Fighters Miku Vol. 1: *Episodes 1 - 3*
Episode 1, MIKU ENTERS THE RING; Episode 2, MIKU STARTS TRAINING; and Episode 3, MIKU GETS SPECIAL TRAINING. When The Pretty Four enter a grand championship elimination tournament, they find that they need help to prepare. Help comes in the form of drunken Metal Fighter coach Eiichi Suo. What Suo lacks in appearances he more than makes up for in skill. And soon, Miku and the other girls are on the way to Neo-Wrestling stardom. **90 min.**

Metal Fighters Miku Vol. 2: *Episodes 4 and 5*
Episode 4: MIKU UNDER SUSPICION: THE PRETTY FOUR vs. THE MASKERS, and Episode 5: MIKU TURNS CHICKEN: THE PRETTY FOUR vs. THE BEAUTIES OF NATURE. With the arrival of a new girl to join the ranks of the TWP, it looks as though Miku's found both a doting fan and a new friend. But when mysterious accidents begin striking everyone on the team except Miku herself, she's soon under suspicion by everyone around her. Coach Suo's solution? A battle royale between the Pretty Four themselves! Because, as he says, someone so weak who has to resort to cheating could never win in a fair fight. Later on, the Pretty Four go on the road for their next match. When Miku sprains her shoulder in an accident, it looks as though the Star of Beauty may fall in her next battle. But when SWWP's Beauties of Nature cut down everyone in their path, Miku is once again all that stands between defeat and victory. **60 min.**

Metal Fighters Miku Vol. 3: *Episodes 6 and 7*
Episode 6: MIKU FALLS HEAD OVER HEELS: THE MOONLIGHT JEWELS vs. THE AMAZONS and Episode 7: MIKU TELLS ALL: THE PRETTY FOUR vs. THE STAR WOLVES. With Ginko still in the hospital recovering from the last match, Miku and the other girls get some well-deserved time to themselves. But Shibano and his son Naoya are still hard at work trying to destroy the TWP, and now they've come up with their most devious plot yet: if you can't destroy them from without, set the Pretty Four to destroy themselves! This cunning plan takes the form of a two-pronged strike on the girls' morale, with Naoya playing the doting new boyfriend for an unsuspecting Miku while offering Ginko a chance at stardom in the American Neo Pro-Wrestling leagues. As Miku begins to doubt whether she wants to continue living her rough and tumble life, a sorely tempted Ginko considers a decision that will break the team apart forever. But when Ginko is told to prove herself to the recruiter by beating the next team singlehanded, she's setting herself up for another crushing defeat. **60 min.**

Metal Fighters Miku Vol. 4: *Episodes 8 and 9*
Episode 8: MIKU BECOMES A SINGING STAR, and Episode 9: MIKU ENTERS THE FINALS. The Pretty Four leave the semifinals behind in a blaze of victory! But now, Miku and the rest of the girls must prepare for their greatest challenge yet— and their training and skills will be completely useless! The Pretty Four must step into the ring and sing! And now, as the girls try to prepare for their final match against the Moonlight Jewels, can they focus on anything but trying to get the edge on Sapphire's killer team? Will the Pretty Four triumph and face Aquamarine in the championship, or will Shibano and his minions pull off one last dirty trick to rob them of their victory? **60 min.**

Metal Fighters Miku Vol. 5: *Episodes 10 and 11*
Episode 10: MIKU GOES TO WAR, and Episode 11: MIKU FLIES IN THE SKY. Since the last match was declared invalid, Miku prepares for a one-on-one rematch against Sapphire. But despite Yohko's insistence that Sapphire can beat Miku without resorting to dirty tricks, Shibano plays his trump card—and he's not bothering with subtlety—this time it's all out war! **60 min.**

Metal Fighters Miku Vol. 6: *Episodes 12 and 13*
Episode 12: MIKU DROPS OUT, and Episode 13: MIKU BECOMES A STAR. Miku is slated to face the great Aquamarine, the JWMF Champion and Queen of the Neo-Pro Wrestling world, in a one-on-one battle royale, but Miku's starting to have second thoughts. Concludes the series. **60 min.**

Domestic Home Video:
Metal Fighters Miku Vol. 1
SSVS 1001 ▲ $24.95 ▲ VHS ▲ SUB ▲ Stereo ▲ 09/05/95
Metal Fighters Miku Vol. 2
SSVS 1002 ▲ $24.95 ▲ VHS ▲ SUB ▲ Stereo ▲ 12/05/95
Metal Fighters Miku Vol. 3
SSVS 1003 ▲ $24.95 ▲ VHS ▲ SUB ▲ Stereo ▲ 12/05/95
Metal Fighters Miku Vol. 4
SSVS 1004 ▲ $19.95 ▲ VHS ▲ SUB ▲ Stereo ▲ 02/06/96
Metal Fighters Miku Vol. 5
SSVS 1005 ▲ $19.95 ▲ VHS ▲ SUB ▲ Stereo ▲ 04/02/96
Metal Fighters Miku Vol. 6
SSVS 1006 ▲ $19.95 ▲ VHS ▲ SUB ▲ Stereo ▲ 06/04/96

Metal Skin Panic: Madox-01 *See* MADOX-01

Mighty Space Miners
(1994) ©KSS Inc. English version by A.D. Vision Inc.

Author: Horceman Lunchfield *Screenplay:* Ritsuko Hayasaka, Tsutomu Iida *Character Design:* Toshihiro Kawamoto *Director:* Umanosuke Iida

Based on a story by Horceman Lunchfield, as adapted by scriptwriters Ritsuko Hayasaka and Tsutomu Iida. A disaster on a deep-space asteroid mine leaves colonists struggling to survive in the harsh reality of space. Told from the point of view of a young boy, this film documents the surviving colonists' desperate battle to survive in a hostile environment in which every moment carries the possibility of instant death by fire, cold, radiation or explosive decompression. Hard sci-fi concepts with a softer anime edge thanks to character designs by Toshihiro Kawamoto. Released in Japan under the title "Oira Uchû no Tankôfu" ("We're Space Miners") by KSS; available in North America through A.D. Vision. **60 min.**

Domestic Home Video:
ADV MS/001D ▲ $24.95 ▲ VHS ▲ DUB ▲ HiFi Surr ▲ 11/21/95
ADV MS/001S ▲ $29.95 ▲ VHS ▲ SUB ▲ HiFi Surr ▲ 11/21/95

Miyuki-chan in Wonderland
(1995) ©CLAMP/Sony Music Entertainment/Kadokawa Shôten Publishing Co., Ltd./Movic

Director: Masao Maruyama *Original creators:* CLAMP *Production:* Masahiro Otake/MAD HOUSE/Animate Film

Based on the manga of the same name, as serialized in publisher Kadokawa Shôten's COMIC GENKI manga magazine. Obviously, there's an element of Rev. Charles Lutwidge Dodgson (a.k.a. Lewis Carroll)'s "Alice in Wonderland" here, but even more prevalent are the influences from the adult-oriented personal computer games of which screenwriter Nanase Okawa cheerfully admits being a big fan. With unmistakable design work by Clamp, the four-woman team behind such hits as TOKYO BABYLON, RG VEDA, and the as-yet import only "Magic Knight RayEarth," MIYUKI-CHAN is an adult wonderland where every little thing seems designed to make a girl's clothes fall off. Released in Japan under the title "Fushigi no Kuni no Miyuki-chan" (Miyuki-chan in Wonderland) by Sony Music Entertainment; available in North America through A.D. Vision. **35 min.**

Domestic Home Video:
ADV MW/001 ▲ $29.95 ▲ VHS ▲ SUB ▲ HiFi Surround ▲ 08/27/96

Mobile Police Patlabor *See* PATLABOR

Moldiver
OAV series, 6 episodes
(1993) ©AIC/Pioneer LDC Inc.

Original Concept, Director, Character Design: Hiroyuki Kitazume *Series Director:* Hirohide Fujiwara *Director:* Yasunori Urata (4), Taro Mozaiku (5) *Concept Design:* Masaharu Kawamori, Kazuki Miyatake *Design:* Takashi Watabe *Screenplay:* Manabu Nakamura (1,4), Ryoei Tsukimura (2,3,5) *Art Director:* Masumi Nishikawa *Animation Director:* Yasutaka Kono (4) *Music:* Kei Wakakusa

Six-volume OAV superhero parody wherein young girl "borrows" younger geeky brother's "supersuit" and takes it out for a joyride, initially using it for personal convenience but eventually turning it to the suppression of evil in the form of an insane inventor and his bevy of beautiful hench-girls (look for cameos in the form of Hollywood beauties such as Vivian Leigh, Elizabeth Taylor, and even "it girl" redux Brooke Shields). Descends at times into "the heartbreak of psoriasis"-type teen romantic angst, but any series that straps an idol singer to a rocket and threatens to shoot her into space has gotta be doing something right. "Gundam ZZ" character designer Kitazume gets credit for original story, design, and direction. Released in Japan under the title "Moldiver" by Pioneer LDC; available in North America through Pioneer LDCA. Followed by a currently import-only 12-minute "Making Of" video called "Secret of Moldiver: Himitsu Dai-Hyakka" (Secret Encyclopedia), which includes detailed character profiles, a look at the Moldiver transformation concept, and more.

📺 Made for Television Broadcast   [OAV] Made for Home Video Release   [MOVIE] Made for Theatrical Release

Moldiver #1: *Metamorforce*

Tokyo 2045: The year the Mysterious Superhuman appears - identity: Moldiver. One day in the future, Mirai Ozora discovers the true identity of this strange superhero. This astounding mystery is merely her brother Hiroshi. Hiroshi, discoverer of the supersuit; when worn, enables the wearer with the absolute infinite power; power to twist the laws of physics and repel all forces of the outer world. Such is the power of the entity known as Moldiver. Mirai Ozora: young, energetic and also gorgeous, Mirai is also a very helpful girl. She becomes the Moldiver too! Another ordinary day in 21st century Tokyo. **30 min.**

Moldiver #2: *Overzone*

Hiroshi Ozora is off to Florida for a business trip. His brother Nozomu tags along so they may both attend a concert by everyone's favorite international idol, Amy Lean. Mirai remains in Japan for part-time work to pay off her numerous bills. However, when she finds that her admired Mr. Misaki is in Florida with her love rival Mao, duty must be set aside. A very piqued Mirai changes into Moldiver and soars off to Florida. Meanwhile, at the concert, the Space Shuttle is hijacked by Machinegal in yet another of his evil plans. **30 min.**

Moldiver #3: *Longing*

"I have something to give you ..." Is your admired Mr. Misaki asking you on a date? An ecstatic Mirai goes to the meeting place of the Hachiko dog monument. However, due to a misunderstanding, they miss each other. The two can't meet because of many small disasters. Frustrated, Mirai searches high and low with Metamorforce. There, the Machinegal dolls gather after tracking her Mol reaction and a tremendous battle ensues over Tokyo, causing even greater inconvenience. Can Mirai really meet with Mr. Misaki? **30 min.**

Moldiver #4: *Destruction*

Professor Amagi directs the Yamato salvage for ZIC's "Battleship Yamato's Centennial Celebration." But Professor Amagi's actual motive is to continue his grandfather's unfinished study: The Ultra Dimension System, which sank with the *Yamato* 100 years before. However, a small stowaway, Nozomu, unexpectedly appears there. Nozomu covertly discovers the secret of The Moltron, and with his precocious intelligence, starts the system, causing a mysterious power to overtake the *Yamato* and Moldiver! **30 min.**

Moldiver #5: *Intruder*

With Hiroshi's efforts, the Mol-unit is successfully divided into #1 and #2. "I have to hand it over to Mr. Misaki!" says an impatient Mirai, but the rocket that Misaki will board is in the midst of going to a launch site at Mount Fuji. Hurriedly Mirai transforms into Moldiver II and pursues him, coming face to face with Machinegal's Superdolls who plan to stop the project from going forward. A battle ensues, and the Superdolls, using Mol theory prove to be powerful indeed. A mysterious new "Intruder" also appears, promising to be the most powerful adversary yet. **30 min.**

Moldiver #6: *Verity*

The dimension-bound Sakigake continues to speed up in preparation for launch, however Moldiver II appears, trying to stop the proceedings. With her opponent's efficiency superior to both Moldiver I and Moldiver II's, Mirai is truly in her biggest pinch! The Sakigake is launched into space where there is yet another obstacle. The Sakigake and its mission are threatened. Then Isabelle challenges Mirai to defend her dignity. Can Mirai keep her word to her beloved Misaki and save the Sakigake? Her appeal brings a miracle from the Mol-unit! The final episode of the OAV series. **30 min.**

Domestic Home Video:

Moldiver #1
PI VA-1007D ▲ $19.95 ▲ VHS ▲ DUB ▲ Stereo ▲ CC ▲ 09/14/94
PI VA-1007S ▲ $24.95 ▲ VHS ▲ SUB ▲ HiFi Stereo ▲ 09/14/94
PI LA-1139A ▲ $34.95 ▲ LD-CAV ▲ M/A ▲ Stereo ▲ CC ▲ 05/11/94

Moldiver #2
PI VA-1008D ▲ $19.95 ▲ VHS ▲ DUB ▲ Stereo ▲ CC ▲ 09/14/94
PI VA-1008S ▲ $24.95 ▲ VHS ▲ SUB ▲ HiFi Stereo ▲ 09/14/94
PI LA-1140A ▲ $34.95 ▲ LD-CAV ▲ M/A ▲ Stereo ▲ CC ▲ 06/29/94

Moldiver #3
PI VA-1009D ▲ $19.95 ▲ VHS ▲ DUB ▲ Stereo ▲ CC ▲ 09/14/94
PI VA-1009S ▲ $24.95 ▲ VHS ▲ SUB ▲ HiFi Stereo ▲ 09/14/94
PI LA-1141A ▲ $34.95 ▲ LD-CAV ▲ M/A ▲ Stereo ▲ CC ▲ 07/24/94

Moldiver #4
PI VA-1010D ▲ $19.95 ▲ VHS ▲ DUB ▲ Stereo ▲ CC ▲ 09/14/94
PI VA-1010S ▲ $24.95 ▲ VHS ▲ SUB ▲ HiFi Stereo ▲ 09/14/94
PI LA-1142A ▲ $34.95 ▲ LD-CAV ▲ M/A ▲ Stereo ▲ CC ▲ 08/24/94

Moldiver #5
PI VA-1011D ▲ $19.95 ▲ VHS ▲ DUB ▲ Stereo ▲ CC ▲ 09/28/94
PI VA-1011S ▲ $24.95 ▲ VHS ▲ SUB ▲ HiFi Stereo ▲ 09/28/94
PI LA-1143A ▲ $34.95 ▲ LD-CAV ▲ M/A ▲ Stereo ▲ CC ▲ 09/28/94

Moldiver #6
PI VA-1012D ▲ $19.95 ▲ VHS ▲ DUB ▲ Stereo ▲ CC ▲ 10/26/94
PI VA-1012S ▲ $24.95 ▲ VHS ▲ SUB ▲ HiFi Stereo ▲ 10/26/94
PI LA-1144A ▲ $34.95 ▲ LD-CAV ▲ M/A ▲ Stereo ▲ CC ▲ 10/26/94

Mori no Densetsu *See* LEGEND OF THE FOREST

My My Mai ▢OAV◯

OAV series, 4 parts

(1993) ©Masakazu Yamaguchi/Akita Shôten/Apple

Director: Osamu Sekita *Character Design:* Yumi Nakayama *Music:* Koichi Ohta, Koji Tajima

Based on the manga by Masakazu Yamaguchi, as serialized in weekly SHÛKAN SHÔNEN CHAMPION manga anthology. Softcore sex romp starring the innocently sexy Mai, who runs a sort of detective/ consultancy agency, dealing with cases such as finding a missing surgeon needed to treat a terminally ill girl, or treating a rock star's paralyzing fear of the media. Mai's approach to problems is typically a combination of amateur psychology and the apparently therapeutic effect of the sight of her nearly naked body on her clients. Goofily naughty, the weirdness factor runs high, such as in a grotesque-looking, big-headed, Frankenstein lookalike grandma (an obvious parody of a drag queen) that Mai turns to for advice, or in a doctor with a Jekyll-and-Hyde dual personality manifested as goggle-eyed, unpleasant, cartoony freakishness whenever his wig of long, glossy *bishônen* or "pretty boy" tresses falls off. (He's bald, see? No one said it was *subtle*.) Though Mai seems to run afoul of her share of drooling perverts, and she's featured frequently in her scanties, her innocence is maintained throughout the first volume, at least. Released in Japan under the title "Sono Ki ni Sasete yo" (C'mon, Get Me in the Mood) by Apple/Sôbi Entertainment; available in North America through U.S. Manga Corps.

My My Mai Vol. 1: *Parts 1 and 2*

Mai is a super counselor with blazing sex appeal. She'll be happy to solve anyone's problems or troubles with a lot of devotion and motherly love—but male clients are preferred. In PART 1, Mai is consulted by the family of a dying girl, and must locate the mysterious Dr. Shinobi. But time is running out, and Mai has no idea what the good doctor looks like or where to find him! In PART 2, Mai must cure a famous rock star of his phobias—using her own, special brand of shock therapy! **45 min.**

My My Mai Vol. 2: *Parts 3 and 4*

In PART 3, Kazumi's near death, and Mai and Dr. Shinobi haven't shown up yet! A mysterious stranger, Yua, arrives and diagnoses the problem as demonic possession! Will Yua be able to exorcise the demon by herself, or will Mai arrive and save the day? In PART 4, Mai and company take some time off and head for a summer resort—which turns out to be haunted! Will Mai be able to solve the mystery and exorcise the "non-paying residents" once and for all? **45 min.**

Domestic Home Video:

My My Mai Vol. 1
USM 1511 ▲ $19.95 ▲ VHS ▲ DUB ▲ Stereo ▲ 10/08/96

My My Mai Vol. 2
USM 1512 ▲ $19.95 ▲ VHS ▲ DUB ▲ Stereo ▲ 12/03/96

My Neighbor Totoro ▢MOVIE◯

(1988) ©Nibariki/Tokuma Shôten

Original Story, Script, Producer and Director: Hayao Miyazaki *Music:* Joe Hisaishi *Animation Director:* Yoshiharu Sato

Beloved director and now, thanks to the recent international distribution deal with Disney, possibly the most powerful filmmaker in Japan, Miyazaki's original story of friendly forest spirits befriending two young girls living in the Japanese countryside evokes nostalgia in Japanese viewers for a simpler life. It's impossible not to be charmed by TOTORO; the film has also proven quite successful on video in the United States, with sales in the hundreds of thousands, and lauded as a "Pick of the Year" by *At the Movies*' Siskel & Ebert. From the director of CASTLE OF CAGLIOSTRO; music by Joe Hisaishi. Released in Japan under the title "Tonari no Totoro" (My Neighbor Totoro) by Tokuma Shôten/Tokuma Japan Communications; available in North America through Fox Home Video. **86 min.**

Domestic Home Video:
CFX 4276 ▲ $19.95 ▲ VHS ▲ DUB ▲ Stereo ▲ 07/21/94
CFX 4276-80 ▲ $29.95 ▲ LD ▲ DUB ▲ HiFi Stereo ▲ 07/12/94

My Youth in Arcadia *See* ARCADIA OF MY YOUTH
Mystery of Mamo *See* LUPIN III

 Violence   Profanity   Nudity   Sexual Situations    Adult Viewers Only - content is extreme and/or explicit

Nadia
TV series, 39 episodes
(1990-91) ©NHK/Sogovision/Toho

Animation Director: Hideaki Anno *Character Design:* Yoshiyuki Sadamoto *Art Designer:* Mahiro Maeda *Music:* Shiro Saezu *Animation Design and Production:* Gainax

The Paris International Exposition of 1889 provides the opening backdrop for this intriguing, Jules Verne-inspired fantasy TV series of a circus-acrobat waif named Nadia and her inventor friend Jean as they quest to discover Nadia's mysterious origins, and the secrets of her jewel, the Blue Water. Similar in plot and tone to Hayao Miyazaki's film "Laputa" (the story was initially planned as a project for Miyazaki), NADIA also adds a villainous trio in deliberate takeoff on the classic characters established in the Japanese comedy TV series "Time Bokan," an armload of anime in-jokes and references, and references to multiple Verne works. The plot construction is crafted so that every four episodes of the 39 total form a sort of "mini-feature." Produced by Studio Gainax (THE WINGS OF HONNEAMISE, GUNBUSTER), with character designs by Yoshiyuki Sadamoto, and art direction by Mahiro Maeda. Note that although the series has twice been released since 1992 by Streamline/Orion (once under the title "Nadia" and then under the name "The Secret of Blue Water," which was Gainax's own English name for the series), only eight episodes are currently available in the U.S. Released in Japan under the title "Fushigi no Kuni no Nadia" (Nadia of the Mysterious Seas) by NHK Enterprises/Visual Book; available in North America through Streamline Pictures/Orion Home Video. Followed in Japan (none of which are available domestically) by the six-volume "Fushigi no Kuni no Nadia: Nautilus Story," a condensed retelling of the original 39-episode TV series; a 1991 theatrical feature; a two-OAV volume music video series; and variety video with clips from the series, music, and interviews with the production staff.

Nadia Episode 1: *The Girl on the Eiffel Tower*
As the story begins, Jean-Coq Raltigue, a young inventor, is on his way to Paris to enter the first International Flying Competition. On a whim, Jean meets up with Nadia, a young orphan girl who works as a circus acrobat. Jean soon discovers that Nadia is pursued by Grandis Granva and her two henchmen Hanson and Sanson, who will stop at nothing to get her mysterious amulet. **25 min.**

Nadia Episode 2: *The Little Fugitives*
In an attempt to distance themselves from Grandis, Jean takes Nadia to his home in Le Havre. Along the way, they must out-maneuver "The Gratan" - Grandis' armored vehicle and face bigotry from Jean's socially unenlightened aunt. The high point of the episode is a thrilling escape in Jean's newest invention "Etoile de la Mer #7" - a two-seat airplane destined to make an unexpected maiden voyage. **25 min.**

Nadia Episode 3: *The Mysterious Sea Monsters*
Jean and Nadia make an emergency landing in the mid-Atlantic. As luck would have it, they are rescued by the U.S. battleship *Abraham*, on a top secret mission to investigate rumors of sea monsters which have terrorized the Atlantic sea lanes and are blamed for sinking many commercial and military vessels. But they soon learn that the battleship's real mission is to hunt down and destroy the "sea beast" on sight. Nadia's pleas for restraint fall on deaf ears as the battleship prepares to fire on two massive "sea monsters." **25 min.**

Nadia Episode 4: *The Nautilus to the Rescue*
Jean, Nadia and King are again stranded at sea following an unprovoked attack on the *Abraham* by a mysterious submarine. They are rescued by Captain Nemo and the crew of the *Nautilus* at the prompting of Electra - Nemo's First Officer. Jean is fascinated by the technology they encounter on Nemo's vessel. Nadia is not so quick to befriend these puzzling submariners. But before they can learn much about Nemo and his awesome vessel, the *Nautilus* is attacked by the same submarine which rammed the U.S.S. *Abraham*. **25 min.**

Nadia Episode 5: *Mari's Island*

With a newly repaired flying machine, courtesy of Captain Nemo, the young adventurers continue their search for Nadia's true home. They are shot down over an island by a mysterious attacker. Grandis, Hanson and Sanson are marooned on this same island. As they make their way toward the downed aircraft, they are captured by hooded soldiers. Jean and Nadia learn that the island is under the control of ruthless invaders who have enslaved the native population. Fleeing for their lives with their

newfound friend, a young orphaned girl named Mari, their only chance of survival is to find shelter and means of escape from this unsuspected deathtrap. **25 min.**

Nadia Episode 6: *Gargoyle's Fortress*
Mari and King have been captured by invading troops. Jean and Nadia devise a plan to rescue them. The daring journey takes them into a strange, technologically advanced fortress. Working as forced laborers, Grandis and her henchmen attempt to escape, but are captured. As Jean and Nadia emerge from the complex, they note the arrival of Gargoyle, leader of the masked troops. Jean is wounded and unable to keep up with the accomplished acrobat. The nimble Nadia sets herself up as a decoy in the hopes of allowing Jean a chance to escape. **25 min.**

Nadia Episode 7: *The Tower of Babel*
Nadia has been captured and brought before Gargoyle. True to his promise to rescue Nadia, Jean begins his single-handed assault upon Gargoyle's fortress, but he runs into Grandis and company - recent escapees from the Gargoyle's dismal dungeon. While Gargoyle attempts to sway Nadia to the doctrine of his cult of Neo-Atlanteans, Jean and the others make their way toward a showdown with these would-be world conquerors. Single-minded of purpose, Gargoyle shows off his powerful new weapon of destruction, the crystal-powered "Tower of Babel." **25 min.**

Nadia Episode 8: *Operation: Rescue!*
Gargoyle forces Nadia to reveal to him that Jean is now in possession of the powerful gemstone - "The Blue Water." A massive search is initiated to capture the young adventurer and seize the stone. Amidst the resulting confusion, Jean, who has now linked up with Grandis and her henchmen, proposes that they rescue Nadia, Mari and King. Their hasty plan calls for a risky diversion, but Gargoyle sees through their trick. The action comes at breakneck speed in the exciting finale to the second story arc of this epic serial, which marks the return of Captain Nemo and the *Nautilus*. **25 min.**

Domestic Home Video:
Nadia Episode 1
SPV 90019 ▲ $9.95 ▲ VHS ▲ DUB ▲ Mono ▲ 03/01/92 ▲ Out of Print
Nadia Episode 2
SPV 90022 ▲ $9.95 ▲ VHS ▲ DUB ▲ Mono ▲ 04/01/92 ▲ Out of Print
Nadia Episode 3
SPV 90243 ▲ $9.95 ▲ VHS ▲ DUB ▲ Mono ▲ 07/01/92 ▲ Out of Print
Nadia Episode 4
SPV 90253 ▲ $9.95 ▲ VHS ▲ DUB ▲ Mono ▲ 08/01/92 ▲ Out of Print
Nadia Episode 5
SPV 90293 ▲ $9.95 ▲ VHS ▲ DUB ▲ Mono ▲ 10/01/92 ▲ Out of Print
Nadia Episode 6
SPV 90313 ▲ $9.95 ▲ VHS ▲ DUB ▲ Mono ▲ 03/22/93 ▲ Out of Print
Nadia Episode 7
SPV 90483 ▲ $9.95 ▲ VHS ▲ DUB ▲ Mono ▲ 06/06/93 ▲ Out of Print
Nadia Episode 8
SPV 90583 ▲ $9.95 ▲ VHS ▲ DUB ▲ Mono ▲ 08/19/93 ▲ Out of Print
The Secret of Blue Water Vol. 1: *Episodes 1-4*
SPV 91193 ▲ $14.95 ▲ VHS-EP ▲ DUB ▲ Stereo ▲ CC ▲ 01/30/96
The Secret of Blue Water Vol. 2: *Episodes 5-8*
SPV 91223 ▲ $14.95 ▲ VHS-EP ▲ DUB ▲ Stereo ▲ CC ▲ 01/30/96
Nadia Vol. 1
Episodes 1-4 (100 min.)
LUM 9350 ▲ $39.95 ▲ LD-CLV/CAV ▲ M/A ▲ Stereo ▲ 05/27/94

Nageki no Kenkô Yûryô Ji *See* F3
Nausicäa *See* WARRIORS OF THE WIND

Neo-Tokyo
(1987) ©Haruki Kadokawa Films Inc.

Written and Directed by: Taro Rin/Yoshiaki Kawajiri/Katsuhiro Otomo *Music:* Mickey Yoshino

Three short films in an anthology or "omnibus" format. Taro Rin's LABYRINTH is a dark urban tale which pays homage to "Through The Looking Glass." A young girl, Sachi, and her cat fall through a mirror and end up in the alleyway behind their house. An ominous clown leads them along surreal streets where invisible children play and streetcars are filled with glowing skeletal commuters. In Yoshiaki Kawajiri's RUNNING MAN, driver Zach Hugh has been the reigning champion of the Death Race for ten years. In the 21st Century, race car drivers are psionically plugged into their vehicles. After so much adrenalin Zach's nerves are getting a little frayed. In Katsuhiro Otomo's THE ORDER TO STOP CONSTRUCTION, a young bureaucrat must shut down a building project deep in the

Amazon jungle. As the only living person on site, his biggest problem is getting the robot crew to obey his commands in a grim sci-fi comedy. Note that the original title was apparently changed by U.S. releaser Streamline in order to create an association between it and the highly successful AKIRA (see above); however, aside from the fact that AKIRA's Otomo also contributed to this project, there is no connection to his previous film. Released in Japan under the title "Meikyû Monogatari" (Labyrinth Tales) by Kadokawa Shôten/Toho; available in North America through Streamline Pictures. **50 min.**

Domestic Home Video:
SPV 90723 ▲ $24.95 ▲ VHS ▲ DUB ▲ Mono ▲ 12/03/93 ▲ Out of Print

Neon Genesis Evangelion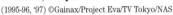
TV series, 26 episodes
(1995-96, '97) ©Gainax/Project Eva/TV Tokyo/NAS

Planning & Original Story: GAINAX *Character Design:* Yoshiyuki Sadamoto *Mecha Design:* Ikuto Yamashita, Hideaki Anno *Art Director:* Hiroshi Kato *Music:* Shiro Sagisu *Director:* Hideaki Anno

Credited with helping to revive the current anime industry in Japan, EVANGELION is the first smash-hit anime TV show since SAILOR MOON in the early '90s, and marked the return of Studio Gainax to anime after a four-year hiatus. EVANGELION begins with the oldest premise in the giant-robot book: a son called to pilot the robot that his father built—but quickly shows its real interest to be the dysfunctional relationships between its three different generations of main characters. These work for NERV, a secret, super-technological organization based in the artificial city Tokyo-3 in the year 2015, whose research into artificial evolution and resistance against the invading, ultra-powerful entities known as the Angels are somehow connected. With a background motif of Kabbalistic mysticism and hidden conspiracy, EVANGELION offers an *X-Files*-like investigatory feel as well as fantastic scenes of combat between the Angels and the "Eva" biomechanical robots of NERV. Becoming more and more emotionally intense in later episodes, the clever and intricate design work, otaku in-jokes and bouncy "fan service" expected from Gainax are in EVANGELION interleaved with bizarre, brutal, surrealistic and shocking scenes which caused much controversy and even calls for a boycott against the show. Public outrage over the ambiguous, mocking conclusion of the series—combined with the factor of EVANGELION's vast popularity—led to the announcement from Gainax that a double-feature EVA "movie" would be released in the spring of 1997. The first film will be a feature-length edit of the first 24 episodes, the second, an all-new version of the final two which will provide, according to Anno, "the same ending, but from a different perspective." The two movies will be released together under the title EVANGELION: "Death" and EVANGELION: "Rebirth." Released in Japan under the title "Shin Seiki (New Century) Evangelion" by King Record; available in North America through A.D. Vision.

Neon Genesis Evangelion 1: *Episodes 1 and 2*
In the year 2015, the awesome alien war machines, the Angels, return to Tokyo as the remnants of the human race cower in subterranean cities. Only the humanoid fighting machine Evangelion, piloted by teenager Shinji Ikari, stands in their way. Can Shinji find the courage and strength to not only fight, but survive, or risk losing everything? Meanwhile, NERV, mankind's special agency, tries to penetrate the mystery of the Angels. Why was Earth attacked? And why were the only Evangelion-qualified pilots born exactly nine months after the giant meteor impact that massacred half the human race? **60 min.**

Neon Genesis Evangelion 2: *Episodes 3 and 4*
After saving Tokyo-3 from total destruction, young Shinji Ikari finds himself attending his first day of classes at a new school. Just as he's getting accustomed to the classroom, another Angel attacks and he must once again merge with the giant living machine known as Evangelion. **60 min.**

Domestic Home Video:
Neon Genesis Evangelion - Genesis 0:1
ADV EV/001D ▲ $24.95 ▲ VHS ▲ DUB ▲ HiFi Surround ▲ 08/20/96
ADV EV/001S ▲ $29.95 ▲ VHS ▲ SUB ▲ HiFi Surround ▲ 08/20/96
Neon Genesis Evangelion - Genesis 0:2
ADV EV/002D ▲ $24.95 ▲ VHS ▲ DUB ▲ HiFi Surround ▲ 11/12/96
ADV EV/002S ▲ $29.95 ▲ VHS ▲ SUB ▲ HiFi Surround ▲ 11/12/96

New Angel
OAV series, 4 volumes
(1994-95) ©Studio Angel/U-Jin/Pink Pineapple

Original Writer: U-Jin *Director:* Kaoru Toyo'oka *Screenplay:* Koji Sakakibara *Character Design:* Rin Shin *Chief Animator:* Masato Ijuin

Based on the manga "Angel" by softcore sex artist U-Jin (U-JIN BRAND), Keisuke is a young man who keeps running into adventures of the hormonal kind, such as a sexy ghost, three girls competing for his attention, and parentally approved cohabitation with the pantiless girl-next-door. Above-average animation for a video of this kind; plenty of extended sex scenes with glossy girls for those who look for that sort of thing. Released in Japan under the title "Shin (New) Angel" by Pink Pineapple; available in North America through SoftCel Pictures, a division of A.D. Vision.

New Angel
When high school nerds Keisuke and Shinoyama spot a gorgeous new girl at school, they try to find out who she is... but, strangely, she doesn't seem to exist at all. When our heroes learn the rumors about the school being haunted by a mysterious spirit, they begin to put the facts together. Entranced by the blithe spirit, Keisuke goes to a medium. **50 min.**

New Angel 2
Keisuke, that lucky stiff who scored with a ghost in the erotic fantasy *New Angel*, goes back to school in this steamy sequel. It's not all fun and games, however, as Keisuke must deal with an obnoxious new rival, a lecherous photographer, and a girl who keeps trying to jump off the roof of the building. Can Keisuke bring her down and keep her from being "over-exposed" on film? **50 min.**

New Angel 3
Hijinks ensue when nerdy Ogiwara invites both Keisuke and the luscious Shizuka to a weekend in the mountains. Naomi is Ogiwara's incredibly sexy young maid, an uninhibited miss who loves to play tennis with no underwear. Between the amorous Naomi, the unstable Keisuke, and the combative Shizuka, poor Ogiwara really has his hands full. **35 min.**

New Angel 4
Keisuke's wildest fantasy becomes reality when both his and Shizuka's parents unexpectedly leave the country. It looks like New Angel 4 may turn out to be Keisuke's lucky number, especially when Shizuka arrives with a suitcase that's been accidentally packed with her mom's lingerie. **35 min.**

Domestic Home Video:
New Angel
ADV NA/001U ▲ $29.95 ▲ VHS ▲ SUB ▲ HiFi ▲ Uncut ▲ 10/20/95
ADV NA/001G ▲ $29.95 ▲ VHS ▲ SUB ▲ HiFi ▲ Edited ▲ 10/20/95
New Angel 2
ADV NA/002U ▲ $29.95 ▲ VHS ▲ SUB ▲ HiFi ▲ Uncut ▲ 11/21/95
ADV NA/002G ▲ $29.95 ▲ VHS ▲ SUB ▲ HiFi ▲ Edited ▲ 11/21/95
New Angel 3
ADV NA/003U ▲ $29.95 ▲ VHS ▲ SUB ▲ HiFi ▲ Uncut ▲ 01/30/96
ADV NA/003G ▲ $29.95 ▲ VHS ▲ SUB ▲ HiFi ▲ Edited ▲ 01/30/96
New Angel 4
ADV NA/004U ▲ $29.95 ▲ VHS ▲ SUB ▲ HiFi ▲ Uncut ▲ 03/19/96
ADV NA/004G ▲ $29.95 ▲ VHS ▲ SUB ▲ HiFi ▲ Edited ▲ 03/19/96

New Cutey Honey See CUTEY HONEY

New Dominion Tank Police
OAV series, 6 episodes
(1993-94) ©Masamune Shirow/Seishinsha/Plex

Original Story: Masamune Shirow *Director & Character Design:* Noboru Furuse *Screenplay:* Hiroshi Yamaguchi, Mitsuo Mutsuki, Nemuruanzu *Art Director:* Noboru Yoshida *Mecha Design:* Akira Ogura, Kengo Inagaki *Music:* Yoichiro Yoshikawa

Semi-comedic tale of cops in tanks taking on crime in a future choked with pollution and corruption. Based on the manga by Masamune Shirow (APPLESEED, GHOST IN THE SHELL). Character design by director Furuse. Screenplay by Hiroshi Yamaguchi, Mitsuo Mutsuki and Nemuruanzu. Released in Japan under the title "Tokusô Sensha-Tai (Special Assignment Tank Team) Dominion" by Bandai Visual/Sanctuary; available in North America through Manga Entertainment. See also DOMINION TANK POLICE entry.

New Dominion Tank Police Vol. 1: *Episodes 1 and 2*
Episode 1, LAUNCH TANK POLICE: Ignoring the mayor's direct orders to tone down their law enforcing tactics, Leona and the Tank Police blast their way into the middle of a mysterious terrorist attack involving the chief of police. Episode 2, CHARLES BRENTEN, MASTER DETECTIVE: Leona's friend and former co-worker is murdered. Bent on revenge, Leona quits her job to track down the killer, and finds herself captured by the terrorists responsible for her friend's death. **60 min.**

New Dominion Tank Police Vol. 2: *Episodes 3 and 4*
Episode 3, LIMIT THE TUBE WAY: A Dai Nippon Giken truck is out of control, destroying everything in its path. Its cargo: enough Liberium W23 to obliterate a city. Headquarters attempts to shut down its automatic pilot, but unknown terrorists have taken control of the truck via satellite. Episode 4, THE CHASE: Under cover of the biochemical smog engulfing Newport City, the Cat Sisters manage to steal Bonaparte on behalf of a mysterious gang. The gang plans to eliminate the Cat Sisters after retrieving secrets hidden within Bonaparte. **60 min.**

New Dominion Tank Police Vol. 3: *Episodes 5 and 6*
Episode 5, CONFLICT CITY: Leona and Brenten find out that the mayor of Newport City has been assaulted. When they arrive at the mayor's house, they find a high-maneuver combat robot—the property of the Dai Nippon Giken Corporation. Episode 6, END THE DREAMING: With the news that the mayor is still alive, the two military research corporations plan an all-out assault on Newport City Hospital. The Tank Police surround the building and wait in anticipation for a surprise attack by Coldsman's combat robot. **60 min.**

Domestic Home Video:
New Dominion Tank Police Vol. 1
MGV 633895 ▲ $14.95 ▲ VHS ▲ DUB ▲ HiFi Stereo ▲ 04/18/95
New Dominion Tank Police Vol. 2
MGV 634799 ▲ $14.95 ▲ VHS ▲ DUB ▲ HiFi Stereo ▲ 07/25/95
New Dominion Tank Police Vol. 3
MGV 634805 ▲ $14.95 ▲ VHS ▲ DUB ▲ HiFi Stereo ▲ 09/26/95

Night on the Galactic Railroad
(1985) ©Asahi Group/Herald Group/TAC

Original Story: Kenji Miyazawa *Screenplay:* Mijoru Betsuyaku *Character Design:* Takao Kodama *Animation:* Marisuke Eguchi *Art Director:* Mihoko Magori *Music:* Haruomi Hosono *Director:* Gisaburo Sugii

One of the most unusual anime films ever made, GALACTIC RAILROAD is a visionary-symbolic tale in the tradition of Bunyan's "Pilgrim's Progress" or Dante's "Paradiso," and is based on the incomplete 1927 novel of the same name by Japanese author Kenji Miyazawa. A young boy, Giovanni (portrayed, as are most of the characters in this anime version of the story, as a cat) living a hard life of small-town poverty, finds himself transported with his only friend, Campanella, onto a magical train which traverses the constellations of the Milky Way. The journey is full of symbolic landscapes and intimations of death, salvation, and the migration of the spirit that draw upon both Miyazawa's scientific and religious background, as a naturalist, devout Nichiren Buddhist, and student of Christianity. A decade later, Sugii would direct both the STREET FIGHTER II anime movie and TV series, but the viewer should be warned that GALACTIC RAILROAD (which, further, has no connection to the similarly titled GALAXY EXPRESS) is not very much like them—like the films of Mamoru Oshii (PATLABOR 2, GHOST IN THE SHELL), it has in its beautiful art direction a most deliberate pace. Released in North America by Central Park Media. **115 min.**

CPM 1334 ▲ $29.95 ▲ VHS ▲ SUB ▲ Stereo ▲ 04/02/96

Ningyo no Kizu *See* MERMAID'S SCAR
Ningyo no Mori *See* RUMIK WORLD: MERMAID'S FOREST

Ninja Scroll
(1993) ©Yoshiaki Kawajiri/Madhouse/JVC/Toho Co. Ltd./Movic Inc.

Story, Screenplay & Director: Yoshiaki Kawajiri *Character Design & Animation Director:* Yutaka Minowa *Art Director:* Hiromasa Ogura *Sound Director:* Yasunori Honda

Written and directed by the director of WICKED CITY. Gorgeous animation combines with graphic sexuality and violence (often, in the same scene) to create a slick, stylishly noir thriller. Shades of Carpenter in director Kawajiri's use of atmosphere and lighting to create palpable on-screen menace. Winner of the 1993 Yubari City International Adventure Fantastic Film Festival award. Released in Japan

under the title "Jubei Ninpucho" by Nihon Victor/Kadokawa Shōten/Victor Entertainment/Toho; available in North America through Manga Entertainment. **94 min.**

Domestic Home Video:
MGV 634813 ▲ $19.95 ▲ VHS ▲ DUB ▲ HiFi Stereo ▲ 06/20/95
MGV 635427 ▲ $24.95 ▲ VHS ▲ SUB ▲ HiFi Stereo ▲ 06/20/95
MGV 636447 ▲ $19.95 ▲ VHS ▲ SPAN ▲ HiFi Stereo ▲ 10/24/95

Ninpû Kamui Gaiden *See* DAGGER OF KAMUI
No Need For Tenchi! *See* TENCHI MUYÔ!
O-Tenki Onêsan *See* WEATHER REPORT GIRL

Odin: Photon Space Sailer Starlight
(1985) ©West Cape Corp.

Original Story: Yoshinobu Nishizaki *Screenplay:* Kazuo Kasahara, Toshio Masuda, Eiichi Yamamoto *Directors:* Toshio Masuda, Tekashi Shirado, Eiichi Yamamoto *Art Directors:* Geki Katsumata, Tadano Tsuji *Music:* Hiroshi Miyagawa

Based on an original story by Yoshinobu Nishizaki (STAR BLAZERS). Numbingly long (140 minutes!) prologue to a plot that never gets off the ground, the only wind in this film's sails comes courtesy of a great early number by Japanese heavy metal rock band Loudness. Nishizaki had reportedly been hoping to use the proceeds from this film to fund a raft of other projects—including a long-rumored YAMATO sequel known as "Dessler's War"—but financially the film was a failure, and to date "Dessler's War" remains nothing more than a title. In addition to asking audiences to accept a spaceship which runs on solar-powered sails (hey, if they can buy a WW II battleship, not to mention a galaxy choo-choo…), ODIN sends its poor starlight soldiers out into the great unknown armed with nothing more than a laser communications cannon. (Jordy would be proud to see how they reconfigured it, though.) Released in Japan under the title "Odin: Kôshi Hansen (Photon Sailer) Starlight" by Toei Video; available in North America through Central Park Media. **93 min.**

Domestic Home Video:
USM 1074 ▲ $19.95 ▲ VHS ▲ DUB ▲ Stereo
USM 1050 ▲ $29.95 ▲ VHS ▲ SUB ▲ Stereo
ID 2236CT ▲ $49.95 ▲ LD ▲ SUB ▲ Stereo ▲ 2 discs ▲ 10/12/93

Ogre Slayer
(1995, '96) ©Kei Kusunoki/Shogakukan, Inc./KSS/TBS

Based on the Original Manga Series By: Kei Kusunoki (Serialized in *Manga Vizion*) *Director:* Yoshio Kato *Animation Director and Character Design:* Masayuki Goto

Based on the manga by Kei Kusunoki (published in English by Viz Comics). Grisly yet psychologically fascinating horror tale exlporing the mythology behind the "oni" or "ogres" of traditional Japanese folklore. The "Ogre Slayer" of the title is an ogre himself, born in the shape of a young man, and fated to kill his own kind. Carrying a special ogre-killing sword, he cuts a swath of destruction through the beastly ogre brood in hopes of becoming human once all other ogres are eradicated from the world. A grim-faced young man dressed in a Japanese schoolboy's uniform, the Ogre Slayer is like an update of the archetypal samurai hero, stoically pitting himself against an overwhelming adversary. In this case, that would be the ogres, which appear as huge, toothy, bestial giants. The violence here is shocking in its level of grisy detail: a human girl gives graphic birth to ogre children, heads are pulled off, blood splashes in fountains, monstrous ogres munch tiny babies with lip-smacking relish. Though not for weak of stomach, this production has a great moody atmosphere, rich in Japanese mythology, and a challenging exploration of humanity's relation to the creatures they themselves create. A disturbing, grainy video effect (call it "Ogre-Cam") is used for seeing through the ogres' point of view. Animation direction and character designs by Masayuki Goto. Released in Japan under the title "Onikirimaru" by Shogakukan/KSS/TBS; available in North America through Viz Video.

Ogre Slayer
From the fading warmth of his mother's cooling corpse, an ogre in the form of a young human boy is born. His ancestry? Pure ogre. His destiny? To kill his own kind. He bears not an ogre's horn, but an ogre-killing sword. Believing that he will become human once all his kind are extinct, he travels the land, sword in hand, daring to dream. He has no human name. Mankind refers only to his sword, "Onikiriimaru," otherwise known as … Ogre Slayer. **60 min.**

Ogre Slayer 2: *Grim Fairy Tale*
2 episodes: A desperate mother prays for a child at a temple with a terrible curse. Alas, any child conceived with the aid of prayers made at this site is destined to die by the age

of five, when the ogre that lives at the temple appears to claim it! In the second grisly episode, the clock is turned back to the era of Japan's Meiji Restoration. In that time, there lived an elusive ogre who could hide its presence even from Ogre Slayer. **60 min.**

Domestic Home Video:
Ogre Slayer
VV OS-001 ▲ $24.95 ▲ VHS ▲ DUB ▲ HiFi Stereo ▲ 10/03/95
Ogre Slayer 2
VV OS-002 ▲ $24.95 ▲ VHS ▲ DUB ▲ HiFi Stereo ▲ 03/05/96

Oh My Goddess! `OAV`
OAV series, 5 episodes
(1993-94) ©Kosuke Fujishima/Kodansha/TBS/SS Films.

Based on Kosuke Fujishima's "Oh My Goddess!" comics. Directed by: Hiroaki Goda Character Design & Animation Director: Hidenori Matsubara Art Direction & Layout: Hiroshi Kato Music Director: Tomoaki Yamada

A modern-day incarnation of one of the Fates of Norse mythology, the young goddess Belldandy comes down to Earth to grant the wish of a college-age man in a five-part OAV series based on the manga by Kosuke Fujishima, as serialized in publisher Kodansha's monthly AFTERNOON manga anthology (published in English by Dark Horse Comics). When Keiichi wishes simply that Belldandy stay with him as his girlfriend forever, the first of many unforeseen consequences is that he gets booted out of his all-male dorm; Belldandy's younger sister Skuld and older sister Urd, completing the "Goddess Trio," are bound to drop in to meddle, complain, and generally look cute. OH MY GODDESS, leavened with comedy, a strictly teasing sexiness, and Fujishima's love of cars, bikes and gadgets, is essentially a sweet tale of a naive, innocent love between two adolescents struggling to prevail against a world of complications and a universe of larger designs. Originally planned as a four-volume OAV series, but extended to five volumes in answer to the demand of the series' Japanese fans. Released in Japan under the title "Aa, Megami-sama" (Oh My Goddess) by Kodansha/TBS Video/KSS/Nihon Soft System; available in North America through AnimEigo.

Oh My Goddess! Episode 1: *Moonlight & Cherry Blossoms*
College freshman Morisato Keiichi gets more than he bargained for when the mysterious Ultimate Force that enforces all Wish Contracts comes into play, and he and Belldandy are now inseparable. **29 min.**

Oh My Goddess! Episode 2: *Midsummer Night's Dream*
Five months later, Keiichi still hasn't the nerve to put the moves on Belldandy, and her big sister Urd is not amused. Urd counsels a trip to the seashore, where every attempt by Keiichi to advance a base or two with Belldandy goes hilariously askew. Then Urd brings out her ultimate weapon - the love potion! **29 min.**

Oh My Goddess! Episode 3: *Burning Hearts on the Road*
Skuld pays her big sister Belldandy a visit to convince her to return to heaven. Meanwhile, Keiichi gets stuck representing the Auto Club in the University Drag Race, only to find out that his *sempai*, Tamiya, has a secret bet laid down on the outcome. He's also got an angry little Skuld gunning for him! **29 min.**

Oh My Goddess! Episode 4: *Evergreen Holy Night*
System Bugs are escaping from the Heavens, upsetting the balance of the Earthly Plane. Skuld the Heavenly Hacker gets on the case, and soon discovers that whenever Belldandy and Keiichi get close, a Bug Exhaust Port is formed. Until the problem is solved, Belldandy and Keiichi can't be together. Then Belldandy gets a Notice of Recall from the Lord. She has to go back to the Heavens, or else! **29 min.**

Oh My Goddess! Episode 5: *For the Love of Goddess*
In two days, Belldandy has to relocate home to Heaven. As the clock ticks down, Belldandy must begin to erase herself from Keiichi's life and memory. Meanwhile, Urd and Skuld, hoping to avert the recall, plot to solve the Bug problem. And Keiichi! He's working himself to the bone so he can buy a ring for Belldandy. A ring that will fulfill a promise... a promise he doesn't remember making! **40 min.**

Domestic Home Video:
Oh My Goddess! Episode 1
ANI ET096-001 ▲ $14.95 ▲ VHS ▲ DUB ▲ HiFi Stereo ▲ 05/29/96
ANI AT094-002 ▲ $19.95 ▲ VHS ▲ SUB ▲ HiFi Stereo ▲ 06/29/94
Oh My Goddess! Episode 2
ANI ET096-002 ▲ $14.95 ▲ VHS ▲ DUB ▲ HiFi Stereo ▲ 06/28/96
ANI AT094-003 ▲ $19.95 ▲ VHS ▲ SUB ▲ HiFi Stereo ▲ 06/29/94

Oh My Goddess! Episode 3
ANI ET096-003 ▲ $14.95 ▲ VHS ▲ DUB ▲ HiFi Stereo ▲ 06/28/96
ANI AT094-004 ▲ $19.95 ▲ VHS ▲ SUB ▲ HiFi Stereo ▲ 06/29/94
Oh My Goddess! Episode 4
ANI ET096-004 ▲ $14.95 ▲ VHS ▲ DUB ▲ HiFi Stereo ▲ 08/28/96
ANI AT094-009 ▲ $19.95 ▲ VHS ▲ SUB ▲ HiFi Stereo ▲ 09/09/94
Oh My Goddess! Episode 5
ANI ET096-005 ▲ $14.95 ▲ VHS ▲ DUB ▲ HiFi Stereo ▲ 09/25/96
ANI AT094-010 ▲ $19.95 ▲ VHS ▲ SUB ▲ HiFi Stereo ▲ 09/09/94
Oh My Goddess! Collector's Suite
Volumes 1 - 5 in a collector's slipcase
ANI AS095-009 ▲ $95.00 ▲ VHS ▲ SUB ▲ HiFi Stereo ▲ 07/26/95
Oh My Goddess! Vol. 1: *Episodes 1-3*
ANI AD094-003 ▲ $39.95 ▲ LD-CLV/CAV ▲ SUB ▲ HiFi Stereo ▲ 06/29/94
Oh My Goddess! Vol. 2: *Episodes 4&5*
ANI AD094-004 ▲ $39.95 ▲ LD-CLV/CAV ▲ SUB ▲ HiFi Stereo ▲ 08/31/94
Oh My Goddess! Completely Divine LD Set
Laserdisc Vols 1 and 2.
ANI AS095-002 ▲ $69.95 ▲ LD-CLV/CAV ▲ SUB ▲ HiFi Stereo ▲ 01/28/95 ▲ Out of Print
Oh My Goddess! Hybrid LD #1: *Episodes 1 & 2*
ANI AD096-001 ▲ $39.95 ▲ LD ▲ HYBRID ▲ HiFi Stereo ▲ 06/28/96
Oh My Goddess! Hybrid LD #2: *Episodes 3&4*
ANI AD096-002 ▲ $39.95 ▲ LD ▲ HYBRID ▲ HiFi Stereo ▲ 09/11/96
Oh My Goddess! Hybrid LD #3: *Episode 5*
ANI AD096-003 ▲ $39.95 ▲ LD ▲ HYBRID ▲ HiFi Stereo ▲ 09/25/96

Oira Uchû no Tankôfu *See* MIGHTY SPACE MINERS

One-Pound Gospel `OAV`
(1988) ©Rumiko Takahashi/Shogakukan Inc.

Based on the Comics by: Rumiko Takahashi Director: Osamu Dezaki Character Design: Katsumi Aoshima Animation Director: Shojuro Yamauchi

Based on the manga by Rumiko Takahashi (RANMA 1/2, MAISON IKKOKU, URUSEI YATSURA), as serialized in publisher Shogakukan's weekly YOUNG SUNDAY manga anthology (published in English by Viz Comics). From the director of THE PROFESSIONAL: GOLGO 13 comes this unlikely tale of an overeating boxer and the soft-hearted nun who tries to keep him out of Jenny Craig and in his weight class. Released in Japan under the title "Ichi-Pound no Fukuin" (One-Pound Gospel) by Victor Entertainment; available in North America through Viz Video. **55 min.**

Domestic Home Video:
VV OP-001 ▲ $29.95 ▲ VHS ▲ SUB ▲ HiFi Stereo ▲ 07/12/95

Oneamisu no Tsubasa: Oritsuin Uchû-Gun
See WINGS OF HONNEAMISE
Onikirimaru *See* OGRE SLAYER
Orange Road *See* KIMAGURE ORANGE ROAD

Orguss, Superdimensional Century `TV`
TV series, 35 episodes
(1983-84) ©T.M.S./Big West

Original Story: Studio Nue Direction: Noboru Ishiguro, Yasuyoshi Mikamoto Character Design: Haruhiko Mikimoto Art Direction: Yoshiyuki Yamamoto Music: Kentaro Haneda

Rumored for years among fans to be the sequel to "Superdimensional Fortress Macross" (i.e., the first part of ROBOTECH) due to a similar title and like-minded character designs by MACROSS designer Haruhiko Mikimoto, ORGUSS features a patchwork world created by the accidental detonation of a "dimensional bomb." From there, it's a series-long journey to find a way to repair the shattered Earth, and put all the weird new races and cultures back where they belong. Released in Japan under the title "Chô Jikû Seiki (Superdimensional Century) Orguss" by Taki Corporation; available in North America through U.S. Renditions.

Orguss Episode 1: *Space/Time Collapse*

In the year 2062 A.D., Earth's two superpowers are battling over the Orbital Elevator. Lt. Kei Katsuragi is part of a fighter envoy dispatched to destroy the elevator. Kei activates the super dimensional space/time oscillation bomb and is thrust through time into a strange new world. **27 min.**

Orguss Episode 2: *Lonely Wolf*

On the new Earth, Kei has been discovered by the Emaan, a band of gypsies who trade in high technology, and finds himself a highly valued pawn in the struggle between the Emaan and militaristic Chiram. **27 min.**

Orguss Episode 3: *Pretty Machine*

The appearance of Kei has strained the relationship between the Emaan and Chiram. At Chiram headquarters, a mysterious soldier receives orders about the capture of the "differentiated idioblast." Meanwhile, at a small village, Kei acquires a new companion in the form of a small girl named Mome. **27 min.**

Orguss Episode 4: *Caravan*

The Emaan set up a marketplace in the village of Tran but are attacked when two Chiram soldiers identify Kei as the "idioblast." Kei must defend the village from the attacking Chiram with the just-completed Orguss. **27 min.**

Orguss Episode 5: *Lovers*

A young man steals the Orguss to rescue his girlfriend from a Chiram prison camp. Kei takes the Orguss into combat against the Chiram to liberate the prisoners. **27 min.**

Orguss Episode 6: *Vanishing Point*

The Emaan are in desperate need of new supplies when Jabby discovers a secret vineyard. While gathering the new crop, Jabby recounts his origin to Kei. Suddenly, the Chiram attack and Jabby warns the Emaan about an imminent dimensional shift! **27 min.**

Orguss Episode 7: *I Love You*

Weary of endless Chiram aggression, the Emaan flee toward the Straits of Gibraltar and their homeland. Kei must contend with Slay's jealousy, Mimsy's uncertainty, Mome's advances, and an attack from the Chiram Navy! **27 min.**

Orguss Episode 8: *Runaway*

The Chiram navy continues to pursue the *Glomar*. Meanwhile, Kei tries to tell Mimsy about his feelings, but must again face her indecision and Slay's bitterness. As usual, the Chiram disrupt the personal turmoil in another senseless attack! **27 min.**

Orguss Episode 9: *Revolution*

The Emaan stop in France to sell some goods. Kei and Mimsy get embroiled in the French revolution and must help "Joan of Arc" capture the menacing Smash Cannon before it destroys the underground! **27 min.**

Orguss Episode 10: *Barbarians*

The Emaan are challenged by the vicious Mozuku tribe as they journey toward the homeland. Slay risks his life to fend off the attack and win Mimsy's love. **27 min.**

Orguss Episode 11: *Dummy*

The Emaan develop an idioblast sensor jammer that shields Kei from the enemy, but the Chiram attack and the Orguss is seemingly destroyed. Distraught over Kei's "death," Mimsy flees the *Glomar* and finds herself in a perilous situation. **27 min.**

Orguss Episode 12: *Chiram Girl*

Slay and others are weary of the constant danger from the Chiram and order Kei to leave. Later, a mysterious Chiram commander (Olson) sends his ace pilot Athena to challenge Kei in combat. **27 min.**

Orguss Episode 13: *Caspian Crater*

Slay volunteers for a dangerous mission to spread the jamming field that is protecting Kei from the Chiram. Meanwhile, Olson discovers Kei is the target of Chiram aggresson and orders his forces to retreat. **27 min.**

Orguss Episode 14: *Operation D*

The Chiram have created a device called the D-system to destroy the robotic MU and restore order to the world. Believing that the idioblast is now expendable, the Chiram try to have Kei killed. Will Olson risk his command to save his friend? **27 min.**

Orguss Episode 15: *The Idioblast*

Kei and Olson are finally reunited and Kei learns more about how the world was changed after he detonated the super dimension bomb. The Emaan reach the homeland and Kei makes a shocking discovery. **27 min.**

Orguss Episode 16: *The Factory*

Kei is captured by Shaya's family and subjected to mind altering brainwashing techniques. Will Shaya risk everything to challenge her family and save Kei's life or will he become the mindless puppet of the House of Tove?! **27 min.**

Orguss Episode 17: *Seventeen*

Mimsy is nearing the age where she will not be able to have children and becomes very sick. Meanwhile, Slay makes the ultimate sacrifice to save Kei and restore order to the patchwork world. **27 min.**

Domestic Home Video:

Orguss Vol. 1: *Episodes 1-3*
USR VD10 ▲ $19.95 ▲ VHS ▲ DUB ▲ Stereo ▲ 08/01/92 ▲ Out of Print

Orguss Vol. 2: *Episodes 4 & 5*
USR VD15 ▲ $19.95 ▲ VHS ▲ DUB ▲ Stereo ▲ 01/01/93 ▲ Out of Print

Orguss Vol. 3: *Episodes 6 & 7*
USR VD18 ▲ $19.95 ▲ VHS ▲ DUB ▲ Stereo ▲ 05/01/93 ▲ Out of Print

Orguss Vol. 4: *Episodes 8 & 9*
USR VD19 ▲ $19.95 ▲ VHS ▲ DUB ▲ Stereo ▲ 05/01/93 ▲ Out of Print

Orguss Vol. 5: *Episodes 10 & 11*
USR VD22 ▲ $19.95 ▲ VHS ▲ DUB ▲ Stereo ▲ 11/01/93 ▲ Out of Print

Orguss Vol. 6: *Episodes 12 & 13*
USR VD23 ▲ $19.95 ▲ VHS ▲ DUB ▲ Stereo ▲ 11/01/93 ▲ Out of Print

Orguss Vol. 7: *Episodes 14 & 15*
USR VD24 ▲ $19.95 ▲ VHS ▲ DUB ▲ Stereo ▲ 01/31/94 ▲ Out of Print

Orguss Vol. 8: *Episodes 16 & 17*
USR VD27 ▲ $19.95 ▲ VHS ▲ DUB ▲ Stereo ▲ 11/01/94 ▲ Out of Print

Orguss 02

OAV series, 6 episodes

(1993-95) ©Big West/Orguss 02 Project

Original Story & Directed by: Fumihiko Takayama *Character Design:* Haruhiko Mikimoto *Screenplay:* Mayori Sekijima, Hiroshi Yamaguchi, Yuji Kishino *Art Director:* Shichiro Kobayashi *Music:* Torsten Rasch

200 years after the events of the 1983-84 ORGUSS TV series (see entry), various factions are uncovering the massive robots left behind by the previous cast's battles. Two opposing military factions scramble to recover artifacts from an interdimensional war that threatened to destroy the planet, while a handful of soldiers and civilians and the only remaining beings from the other dimension are all that can hope to stop the two countries from waging a new war that will destroy all that remains. Although power designer Haruhiko "Macross" Mikimoto is credited in the U.S. release for character designs, "character concepts created by" might be more accurate, as Japanese sources identify another designer in that capacity. Torsten Rasch's music is some of the most unique in recent years, though his most experimental piece was deleted from the English release. Released in Japan under the title "Chô Jikû Seiki (Superdimentional Century) Orguss-02" by Bandai Visual; available in North America through Manga Entertainment.

Orguss 02 Vol. 1: *Episodes 1 and 2*

Two armies race to unearth the massive machines of war, the Decimators. As more of these vast robots are reactivated the world moves closer to all-out war. One victim is Lean, a young mechanic working on a routine excavation of a submerged Decimator. Routine that is, until an ambush by the hostile Zafrins forces Lean to pilot the armor in order to survive. The ensuing battle changes Lean's life irretrievably as he sets out on a risky mission to infiltrate a secret Zafrin base and eliminate their Decimators. **55 min.**

Orguss 02 Vol. 2: *Episodes 3 and 4*

In Episode 3, FUGITIVES, war is finally declared between the nations of Revillia and Zafrin while Lean, a young Revillian officer, is trapped behind enemy lines. With him is a mysterious young girl rescued from a secret base - a young girl that everyone seems desperate to capture. In Episode 4, SEARCHER, the Zafrin army unveils the largest and most powerful Decimator the world has ever seen! Lean finally reaches safety, only to be betrayed by a close friend. **60 min.**

Orguss 02 Vol. 3: *Episodes 5 and 6*

Episode 5, DESTROYER: Lean and the mysterious girl fall into the hands of a stranger who needs their help. The secret of the Decimators is revealed, and the ancient stranger reveals his plans to return the world to peace. Episode 6, THOSE WHO WISH FOR TOMORROW: As the Prince of Revillia leaves a path of destruction and a trail of death across the country, Lean and his friends battle desperately to stop him! They cannot bring peace to the world until the last, greatest Decimator is destroyed forever. **60 min.**

Domestic Home Video:

Orguss 02 Vol. 1: *Episodes 1 and 2*
MGV 633889 ▲ $14.95 ▲ VHS ▲ DUB ▲ HiFi Stereo ▲ 03/21/95

Orguss 02 Vol. 2: *Episodes 3 and 4*
MGV 633891 ▲ $14.95 ▲ VHS ▲ DUB ▲ HiFi Stereo ▲ 06/20/95

Orguss 02 Vol. 3: *Episodes 5 and 6*
MGV 634815 ▲ $14.95 ▲ VHS ▲ DUB ▲ HiFi Stereo ▲ 09/26/95

  Made for Television Broadcast    Made for Home Video Release   Made for Theatrical Release

Otaku no Video

(1991) ©Gainax

Director: Takeshi Mori. *Character Designer:* Kenichi Sonoda
Actually two videos released separately in that same year,
"Otaku no Video 1982" and "More Otaku no Video 1985," this is
a unique document in anime: Studio Gainax (NEON GENESIS
EVANGELION)'s confession of their feelings as obsessed fans,
or "otaku"—part satire, part autobiography, and part wish-
fulfillment. OTAKU NO VIDEO's structure cuts back and forth
between anime and live-action. The anime portion, with
character designs by Kenichi Sonoda (BUBBLEGUM CRISIS,
GUNSMITH CATS), tells the story of Kubo, a clean-cut young
university student who gets gradually sucked into the otaku
lifestyle, and, subsequently rejected by society, vows to become
"Otaking," and attempts to "otakunize" the human race through
building a mighty corporation that will sell "otaku culture" to
the world. The live-action portions contain mocking, purported
interviews with "real otaku" whose identities are concealed in
the style of a tabloid-TV "true crime" show. Fascinating, blunt, and hilarious, loaded with
in-jokes (the English release comes with dense-packed liner notes); any fan who can't see
his/her own face in this video isn't looking hard enough. The approximate translation of the
title is "your video." Released in Japan under the titles "1982 Otaku no Video" and
"1985 Tsuki (More) • Otaku no Video" by Toshiba EMI; available in North America through
AnimEigo. **100 min.**

Domestic Home Video:
ANI AT093-002 ▲ $39.95 ▲ VHS ▲ SUB ▲ HiFi Stereo ▲ 04/12/93

Outlanders

(1986) ©Johji Manabe/Hakusensha/Tatsunoko Production/Victor

Based on the comic by: Johji Manabe *Director:* Katsuhisa
Yamada *Art Director:* Yusaku Saotome *Character Design &
Animation Director:* Hiroshi Hamazaki *Music:* Megumi
Wakakusa

Based on the manga of the same name by creator Johji
"Caravan Kidd" Manabe (published in English by Dark Horse
Comics). Alien Princess Kahm, on her way to subjugate Earth
for her daddy's empire of Santovasku, falls in love with a
human named Tetsuya instead and takes him home to meet the
family. Her Emperor father is less than pleased by the prospect
of an Earth "primate" for a son-in-law, and eventually, the
situation escalates into clashing space fleets. A lighthearted,
innuendo-filled "meet cute." Released in Japan under the title
"Outlanders" by Victor Entertainment; available in North
America through U.S. Renditions. **50 min.**

Domestic Home Video:
USR DIE07 ▲ $19.95 ▲ VHS ▲ DUB ▲ HiFi Stereo ▲ 09/01/93

Ôzora Maryû Gaiking *See* GAIKING

Patlabor

OAV series, 7 episodes

(1988-93) ©Headgear/Emotion/TFC

Director & storyboard: Mamoru Oshii
Screenplay: Kazunori Ito *Concept:* Masami
Yuki *Character Design:* Akemi Takada
Mecha Design: Yutaka Izubuchi *Music:* Kenji
Kawai

The PATLABOR series is a creator-owned
joint project of the five-member group
known as Headgear, consisting of a concept
and character designs by Masami Yuki
("Tetsuwan Birdy," "Assemble Insert");
additional character designs by Akemi Takada (KIMAGURE ORANGE ROAD, "Creamy
Mami"); mecha designer Yutaka Izubuchi ("Gundam 0080: War in the Pocket," RECORD
OF LODOSS WAR); writer Kazunori Ito (MAISON IKKOKU, GAMERA: GUARDIAN OF
THE UNIVERSE), and director Oshii (URUSEI YATSURA: BEAUTIFUL DREAMER,
GHOST IN THE SHELL). In 1999, Tokyo's advanced robots called "Labors" are used for a
multitude of tasks, from construction to forestry, but when the new technology is abused
by careless workers or ambitious criminals, it's up to Tokyo's Mobile Police unit SVII and
their patrol labors, or "Patlabors," to keep them under control. PATLABOR's cast, ranging
from young adult to middle-aged, is unusually old for anime, and the writing is often quite
interesting, swinging in mood freely between action, comedy, social comment, and
relationship issues; the two movies, however, are generally quite serious in tone. The 1988

and 1990-92 OAV series are released in North America by U.S. Manga Corps; the 1989 TV
series is expected to follow in 1997 from USMC. Note that although the 1990-92 OAV
series has already been released, its storyline is a continuation of the as yet-unreleased TV
series. The two PATLABOR feature films are released by Manga Entertainment.

Patlabor Episode 1: *Second Unit, Move Out!*
What are the members of the newly-established Second Unit to do? They've been ordered
to apprehend a terrorist Labor - and their new Labors are stuck in traffic! **30 min.**

Patlabor Episode 2: *Longshot*
The Mayor of New York comes to Tokyo to inspect Project Babylon, but can the SV2 stop
an environmental terrorist group trying to foil the land development project? **30 min.**

Patlabor Episode 3: *The 450 Million-Year-Old Trap*
The second unit is asked to investigate a series of strange occurreneces around Tokyo
Bay. Could they be the work of an actual sea monster? **30 min.**

Patlabor Episode 4: *The Tragedy of L*
Captain Goto sends the team back for training after a delicate hostage situation gets out
of hand. Could the training camp be haunted? **30 min.**

Patlabor Episode 5: *The SV2's Longest Day, Part 1*
A rogue element of Japan's military seizes Tokyo. Can the SV2 restore order? **30 min.**

Patlabor Episode 6: *The SV2's Longest Day, Part 2*
The police have a warrant for Goto's arrest due to his previous affiliation with the
terrorists. Can SV2 stop Kai before he plays his nuclear trump card? **30 min.**

Patlabor Episode 7: *Go North, SV2!*
A prototype Labor has been stolen by communists, but then it's
stolen from them! Why is the manufacturer so tight-lipped
about the new design? **30 min.**

Domestic Home Video:
Patlabor Original Series Vol. 1: *Episodes 1-3*
USM 1500 ▲ $24.95 ▲ VHS ▲ SUB ▲ Stereo ▲ 09/09/96
Patlabor Original Series Vol. 2: *Episodes 4 & 5*
USM 1501 ▲ $24.95 ▲ VHS ▲ SUB ▲ Stereo ▲ 10/08/96
Patlabor Original Series Vol. 3: *Episodes 6 & 7*
USM 1502 ▲ $24.95 ▲ VHS ▲ SUB ▲ Stereo ▲ 10/08/96
Patlabor Original Series Box Set
Tape volumes 1 - 3 in a collector's case. (210 min.)
USM 1503 ▲ $69.95 ▲ VHS ▲ SUB ▲ Stereo ▲ 10/08/96

Patlabor, The Movie 1

(1989) ©Headgear/Emotion/TFC

Director: Mamoru Oshii *Concept:* Masami Yuki *Script:*
Kazunori Ito *Character Design:* Akemi Takada *Mecha Design:*
Yutaka Izubuchi *Animation Production:* Studio Deen

The technology-hating Unabomber suspect revealed himself as
a genius mathematician. What are the limits of terrorism in a
time when only one person might fully understand an emerging
science, yet never be understood himself? That's the question
Oshii asks in a discourse on society and the development that
sustains it, in this day-after-tomorrow action-mystery that can
be compared to the works of Michael Crichton. Art direction by
Hiromasa Ogura (THE WINGS OF HONNEAMISE, NINJA
SCROLL, GHOST IN THE SHELL) gives a sophisticated, moody
look to this feature set in a summer Tokyo (compare with
PATLABOR 2, below). Released in Japan under the title "Kidô
Keisatsu Patlabor: Gekijô Ban" (Mobile Police Patlabor: The
Movie) by Tohoku Shinsha/Bandai Visual; available in North America through Manga
Entertainment. **100 min.**

Domestic Home Video:
MGV 634801 ▲ $19.95 ▲ VHS ▲ DUB ▲ HiFi Stereo ▲ 07/25/95
MGV 635485 ▲ $24.95 ▲ VHS ▲ SUB ▲ HiFi Stereo ▲ 07/25/95
MGV 636449 ▲ $19.95 ▲ VHS ▲ SPAN ▲ HiFi Stereo ▲ 10/24/95

Patlabor, The Movie 2

(1993) ©Headgear/Emotion/TFC

Directed by: Mamoru Oshii *Concept:* Masami Yuki *Script:* Kazunori Ito *Character
Design:* Akemi Takada, Masami Yuki *Mecha Design:* Yutaka Izubuchi, Masaharu
Kawamori, Hajime Katori *Animation:* Kazuchika Kise *Art:* Hiromasa Ogura *Music:* Kenji
Kawai

Features special guest mecha design by Shoji Kawamori and Hajime Katoki. In the spring
of 1995, the ruthless attack of the Aum Shinri Kyo cult would shatter Japan's sense of
itself as an island apart from the unrest of the world. Yet such sudden urban terror and its
consequences for a nation drifting into dreams and nightmares was joltingly forseen in an
anime film made just two years before, PATLABOR 2—director Mamoru Oshii's
masterpiece, and standing in the narrow circle of the very best anime films ever made.

 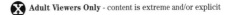

Fantastic yet believable, it is precisely PATLABOR 2's speculations on Japan's distorted place in the world that should make the film of interest to viewers in Japan's most important ally, the United States. In both its emphasis on the defense consequences of politics and its accurate portrayal of modern, Gulf War-era military hardware and tactics, PATLABOR 2 is comparable to the works of Tom Clancy. More than all this, PATLABOR 2 is also a brilliant, beautiful film visually, with realistic character designs by Takada, and the dream-like landscape of the narrative, set in a winter Tokyo, from the master's hand of art director Hiromasa Ogura (THE WINGS OF HONNEAMISE, NINJA SCROLL, GHOST IN THE SHELL). Released in Japan under the title "Kidô Keisatsu (Mobile Police) Patlabor 2: The Movie" by Bandai Visual/Tohoku Shinsha; available in North America through Manga Entertainment. **108 min.**

Domestic Home Video:
MGV 635555 ▲ $19.95 ▲ VHS ▲ DUB ▲ HiFi Stereo ▲ 11/21/95
MGV 635575 ▲ $24.95 ▲ VHS ▲ SUB ▲ HiFi Stereo ▲ 11/21/95

Pekkle   [OAV]

(1994) ©Sanrio Co., Ltd.

Director: Akira Shimizu *Script:* Mitsukuni Kumagai *Art:* Toshikazu Ishiwatari *Sound Director:* Yasunori Honda

More Sanrio character fun, this time not with a cat or a frog, but a duck named Pekkle. If you find yourself attracted to the character, you'd best go out and buy yourself that Pekkle lunchbox now because, as with all Sanrio characters, a funny li'l duck like Pekkle's longevity is only as long as his merchandise keeps selling. (Whatever happened to the endearingly gluttonous Zashikibuta, anyway?) Released in North America by Family Home Entertainment.

Pekkle: Aladdin and His Magic Lamp
2 episodes. In ALADDIN AND HIS MAGIC LAMP, A sweet princess will be forced to marry someone she doesn't love unless Aladdin (Pekkle) can build her father a new palace overnight. In THE ADVENTURES OF SINBAD, Pekkle and his crew fight a scary monster and a double-crossing sailor to rescue a shipwrecked princess and her treasure from a faraway island. **50 min.**

Domestic Home Video:
FHE 27610 ▲ $12.95 ▲ VHS-EP ▲ DUB ▲ HiFi ▲ CC

Phantom Quest Corp.   [OAV] (◖)

OAV series, 4 episodes

(1994) ©Madhouse/Pioneer LDC Inc.

Concept: Rika Mutsuki *Screenplay:* Mami Watanabe(1,3), Tetsu Kimura (3,4), Tatsuhiko Urahata(2,4) *Director:* Koichi Chiaki (1), Morio Asaka (2,4), Takuji Endo (3) *Opening Direction:* Yoshiaki Kawajiri *Character Design:* Hitoshi Ueda *Music:* Junichi Kanezaki

Ghostbusters-like files of an exorcist detective agency named the "Phantom Quest Corporation," headed by busty, flame-haired, frivolous C.E.O. Ayaka Kisaragi, who in the best Bond-girl tradition, sports fun gadgets such as a lipstick capable of transforming into a lightsaber-like sword. The stories are hilariously campy and take on standard horror schticks such as vampires and ghosts, given a humorous spin, such as an anemic, cowardly vampire who runs a tea room for young ladies. Backing up Ayaka is a young man who also works a boy-Friday and keeps her financial books, and a Columbo-esque police Inspector. A lighthearted good time, offering more than a few belly laughs, a series highlight features a drunken Ayaka belting out a slurred karaoke song over a loudspeaker while riding in a taxicab. Directed by Koichi Chiaki (TOKYO BABYLON), with opening credits directed by WICKED CITY's Yoshiaki Kawajiri. Note that the original Japanese title, "Yûgenkaisha," is a complicated pun based on the substitution of sound-alike characters meaning "ghost" and "monster" in place of the more mundane ones used for "limited-responsibility corporation." (In fact, the series is said to have begun with the word-processor mishap which created the pun in the first place.) Released in Japan under the title "Yûgenkaisha" by Pioneer LDC; available in North America through Pioneer LDCA.

Phantom Quest Episode 1: *Kiss of Fire*
The Transylvanian ambassador hires this trio of psychics when Dracula's casket is found empty, and recent murders are believed to have been committed by the resurrected vampire. Owner Ayaka Kisaragi is handed the case by her police inspector friend, Karino. According to Suimei the fortune teller, the next target will be Makiko. **30 min.**

Phantom Quest Episode 2: *End of the World*
One night a drunken Ayaka is belting out a karaoke ballad during a taxi ride when she senses danger. She grabs the steering wheel and escapes disaster, but causes a multi-car pile-up in the process. Visiting the taxi driver in the hospital the next day, Ayaka and Mamoru learn he has died. Remembering Suimei's prediction, Ayaka is convinced someone has made a pact with the devil and caused his death. **30 min.**

Phantom Quest Episode 3: *Love Me Tender*
The "Curse of the Sahara" is spooking workers in the ancient Sahara exhibit at the museum. Ayaka is upset because the client, Mr. Nakasugi, calls exorcism foolish. Suimei reads her crystal ball and concludes that spirits are present. Meanwhile, Mr. Nakasugi tries to get his hands on Natsuki Ogawa, and an explorer appears. **30 min.**

Phantom Quest Episode 4: *Lover Come Back to Me*
President Ayaka Kisaragi has been chasing a werewolf around in the middle of the night. A man named Mukyo, together with a group of monks, quickly terminates the werewolf. Mukyo, leader of a Buddhist Group, Hadja, declares that from now on they will perform all exorcisms in the city. As time goes on, Phantom Quest Corp finds itself being squeezed out of more and more assignments. Then one day, Karino disappears. **30 min.**

Domestic Home Video:
Phantom Quest Corp. Vol. 1: *Episodes 1 & 2*
PI VA-1271D ▲ $24.95 ▲ VHS ▲ DUB ▲ Stereo ▲ CC ▲ 04/25/95
PI VA-1271S ▲ $29.95 ▲ VHS ▲ SUB ▲ Stereo ▲ 04/25/95
PI LA-1271A ▲ $39.95 ▲ LD-CAV ▲ M/A ▲ Stereo ▲ CC ▲ 04/25/95
Phantom Quest Corp. Vol. 2: *Episodes 3 & 4*
PI VA-1273D ▲ $24.95 ▲ VHS ▲ DUB ▲ Stereo ▲ CC ▲ 05/23/95
PI VA-1273S ▲ $29.95 ▲ VHS ▲ SUB ▲ Stereo ▲ 05/23/95
PI LA-1273A ▲ $39.95 ▲ LD-CAV ▲ M/A ▲ Stereo ▲ CC ▲ 05/23/95

Phoenix 2772   [MOVIE ★★★★]

(1980) ©Toho/Tezuka Productions

Based on the epic manga by Osamu Tezuka. In the future, the people of Earth are born in laboratories, raised by robots, and ruled by a tyrannical government. Into this bleak world, Godah is born, a sensitive boy who will soon hold the future of the world in his hands. While training to become a spaceship pilot, Godah learns of the Legend of the Phoenix, a mystical space Firebird with magical blood. Whoever controls the Firebird will have immortality and everlasting power. When an evil scientist orders Godah to retrieve the Firebird, the young hero is determined to capture and use its powers to rejuvenate a dying Earth. Released in Japan under the title "Hi no Tori 2772: Ai no Cosmo Zone" (Firebird 2772: Cosmo Zone of Love) by Kadokawa Shôten/Tohoku Shinsha; available in North America through Best Film & Video. **121 min.**

Domestic Home Video:
BFV 968 ▲ $19.95 ▲ VHS ▲ DUB ▲ Mono ▲ 11/15/95

Planet Busters   [MOVIE ★★★★]

(1984) ©Idol Co. Ltd./Harmony Gold USA Inc.

Director: Shinya Sadamitsu *Art Director:* Geki Katsumata *Animation Director:* Shinya Sadamitsu *Character Design:* Koretak Kanda *Mecha Design:* Makoto Kobayashi *Music:* Randy Miller

Follows the film festival-like exploits of a young girl on a hoverbike, and the end of an alien planet. Makes as much linear sense as an episode of *Aeon Flux*, but nifty animation redeems the experience. The action takes place on the remote, barren planet Pandora, homeworld of Dongamaharu - the self-described creator of the universe. It is here that four unlikely heroes form a fellowship to search for "The Planetbuster" - the big D's ultimate secret weapon. Look for the sight gag in which an Inorganic's mighty cannon ball rolls through a ruined city and topples a set of enormous bowling pins! Features mecha design by GIANT ROBO's Makoto Koyabashi. Released in Japan (on LD only, which includes a bonus "Making Of" video) under the title "Birth" by Michael Hummingbird/Bandai Visual; available in North America through Streamline Pictures. **80 min.**

Domestic Home Video:
SPV 90017 ▲ $9.95 ▲ VHS ▲ DUB ▲ Mono ▲ 03/01/92 ▲ Out Of Print

---

    Made for Television Broadcast   [OAV] Made for Home Video Release   [MOVIE ★★★★] Made for Theatrical Release

Plastic Little

The Adventures of Captain Tita
(1994) ©Kinji Yoshimoto/Satoshi Urushibara/MOVIC/Sony Music Entertainment (Japan)

Director: Kinji Yoshimoto *Character Design:* Satoshi Urushibara

Adventure tale featuring a doe-eyed adolescent ship's captain and her faithful crew versus an entire military armada on an alien planet in order to save a similarly doe-eyed acquaintance from evil thugs. Bee-YOO-tiful animation; mind-numbingly stupid story, sci-fi trappings punctuated by frequent scenes focusing on female breasts taken to an almost medical level of detail ("Tita"…get it?). Roundly booed at a Japanese con showing by Japanese female fans. Character designs by Satoshi Urushibara (LEGEND OF LEMNEAR), also designer for video games such as "Der Langrisser." Released in Japan under the title "Plastic Little" by Sony Music Entertainment; available in North America through A.D. Vision. **55 min.**

Domestic Home Video:
ADV PL/001D ▲ $29.95 ▲ VHS ▲ DUB ▲ HiFi Surround ▲ 01/27/97
ADV PL/001 ▲ $34.95 ▲ VHS ▲ SUB ▲ HiFi Surround ▲ 07/20/94

Please Save My Earth

OAV series, 3 volumes
(1994) ©Saki Hiwatari/Hakusensha/Victor Entertainment

Based on the manga by: Saki Hiwatari *Director:* Kazuo Yamazaki *Animation Director and Character Design:* Takayuki Goto *Music:* Hajime Mizoguchi

Adaptation of Saki Hiwatari's twenty-one volume "shôjo manga" or "girls' manga" series (although of interest to fans of both genders) featuring the lives and loves of seven alien scientists reincarnated on Earth trying to cope with the loves and hates carried over from their previous lives. The series conclusion suffers somewhat from extreme compression of material, though the overall story still packs the core emotional wallop of the manga series. Interesting depictions of psychic powers, gorgeously animated, with exceptional music by Yoko Kanno (MACROSS PLUS). Released in Japan under the title "Boku no Chikyû o Mamotte" (Please Save My Earth) by Victor Entertainment; available in North America through Viz Video.

Please Save My Earth Part 1
A tale of love, loss, and reincarnation. Ever since she was a little girl, plants and animals have seemed to love Alice—a young high school student. One day, Alice's classmates tell her about a strange and recurring dream they've been having in which a team of scientists on the moon are collecting data about Earth: people, politics, wildlife, resources, you name it. Nothing more than a sci-fi fairy tale, thinks Alice.. Until she has the same dream. **65 min.**

Please Save My Earth Part 2: *Memories of the Moon*
Alice continues to be haunted by the "Lunar" dreams. Rin now joins Alice and her friends as they gather to discuss these strange dreams. That Rin is in love with Alice is no secret, but what hold does he have over Haru Kasama, a gentle-eyed boy with a heart condition and strange powers? Is history doomed to repeat itself, even when that history carries over from a previous life? **60 min.**

Please Save My Earth Part 3: *The Moments Mem'ry*
Who is Rin Kobayashi? To neighbor Alice Sakaguchi, he's an eight-year-old child with an oddly adult way about him. To his loving parents, he's a young son, his whole life before him, yet burdened by a terrible sadness. To a warm and wonderful woman named Mokuren, he's a love of a lifetime... and a lifetime... who must endure pain, lonliness, and even madness for the chance to love her once more. The present, the future, and the past all come together in the final volume of the series voted by Japanese fans as the best OAV release of 1994. **60 min.**

Domestic Home Video:
Please Save My Earth Vol. 1
VV PS-001 ▲ $24.95 ▲ VHS ▲ DUB ▲ Stereo ▲ 04/09/96
Please Save My Earth Vol. 2
VV PS-002 ▲ $24.95 ▲ VHS ▲ DUB ▲ Stereo ▲ 06/18/96
Please Save My Earth Vol. 3
VV PS-003 ▲ $24.95 ▲ VHS ▲ DUB ▲ Stereo ▲ 08/06/96

Pochacco

(1994) ©Sanrio Co., Ltd.

Directors: Masami Hata, Akira Shimizu, Seiichi Mitsuoka *Script:* Kyoko Kuribayashi *Art Director:* Toshikazu Ishiwatari *Sound Director:* Yasunori Honda

The final deity of the Sanrio pantheon available in North America on home video is Pochacco, a cuddly widdle puppy with an assortment of animal sidekicks. Like Hello Kitty and Keroppi and Pekkle and an innumerable parade of other characters throughout the years, Pochacco's likeness graces everything from toothbrushes to stationary to dinnerware and tissues. Nothing objectionable here, folks. Available in North American through Family Home Entertainment.

Pochacco: Exciting Birthday
4 episodes. In EXCITING BIRTHDAY, Pochacco's friends seem to have forgotten his birthday party. After he rescues a nestful of eggs, the newly hatched chicks help him celebrate. In THE EXCITEMENT AT THE CARROT PATCH, Pochacco and his friends hunt down a carrot-stealing thief. Also THE BIG ADVENTURE and FIND THE PINK MUSHROOM. **52 min.**

Domestic Home Video:
FHE 27609 ▲ $12.95 ▲ VHS-EP ▲ DUB ▲ HiFi ▲ CC

Princess Minerva

(1995) ©Ko Maisaka/Run Ishida/Red/Toho/Group TAC

Director: Yoshihiro Yamaguchi *Script:* Hideki Sonoda *Art Direction:* Katsuyoshi Kanemura *Designer:* Tokuhiro Matsubara *Music Director:* Fusanobu Fujiyama *Original Author:* Ko Maisaka

Based on the original novels by Ko Masaka as well as the RPG parody video game of the same name, Princess Minerva is the spoiled heir to ye olde fantasy world kingdom of Wisler, who amuses herself by olde-tyme rich girl entertainment such as experimenting with magic and arranging martial arts tournaments to audition bodyguards. The video sends up every convention of the RPG format, with all-in-good fun pokes at the standard RPG characters—the thief, the barbarian, the super-cool swordsman, the magic-user—with even more tongue-in-cheek treatments of video game conventions such as g-string-clad swordswomen and cackling bondage mistresses. Mixed into this, you also get anime parodies, such as Minerva's secret alter ego, a masked CUTEY HONEY parody called "Cutey Kamen" (who even shows up singing like an idol at one point!). Despite the rest of the video's lighthearted tone, a climatic battle with a powerful sorceress named Dynastar captures the appeal of the fantasy RPG as well as any straight-faced story, and eye-pleasing character designs (the CUTEY HONEY influence shows up strongly here, with an emphasis on curves) make PRINCESS MINERVA a charming treat. The video assumes you're already familiar with the backstory behind the characters (from the game), but it hardly matters. Music by Kenji Kawai (RANMA 1/2). Released in Japan under the title "Princess Minerva" by Toho; available in North America through A.D. Vision. **45 min.**

Domestic Home Video:
ADV PM/001 ▲ $29.95 ▲ VHS ▲ SUB ▲ HiFi Surr ▲ 08/25/95

The Professional: Golgo 13

(1983) ©Saito Productions/Tokyo Movie Shinsha

Based on the graphic novels by: Takao Saito *Writer:* Hideyoshi Nagasaka *Music:* Toshiyuki Omori *Director:* Osamu Dezaki

Based on the manga "Golgo 13" by Takao Saito (as serialized in Shogakukan's monthly Big Comic manga anthology), featuring the adventures of a cold-eyed killer and his unbelievable marksmanship. One of the many collaborations ("Aim for the Ace!," "Space Adventure Cobra," "Black Jack") between Dezaki and animation director/character designer Akio Sugino, GOLGO 13 is the only anime adaptation ever made of the 100-plus volume manga series, although a slick new update is currently in production in Japan, timed to release around the same time as a new "Golgo 13" CD-ROM. The unusual art direction simulates 1960s live-action avant-garde camera and editing techniques such as image multiplication and split-screen, and the realist character designs and noir atmosphere strongly prefigures the style of Yoshiaki Kawajiri (NEO-TOKYO, WICKED CITY, NINJA SCROLL). A much-underrated classic, deserving of a closer look. Released in Japan under the title "Golgo 13" by Pony Canyon; available in North America through Streamline Pictures/Orion Home Video. **94 min.**

Domestic Home Video:
SPV 90703 ▲ $19.95 ▲ VHS ▲ DUB ▲ Mono ▲ CC ▲ 08/15/93

 Violence Profanity Nudity Sexual Situations **Adult Viewers Only** - content is extreme and/or explicit

Project A-Ko

OAV series, 4 episodes

(1986-90) ©Soeishinsha/Final-Nishijima/Pony Canyon

Director: Katsuhiko Nishijima (1), Yuji Moriyama(2-4) *Character Design & Director of Animation:* Yuji Moriyama *Art Director:* Shinji Kimura (1), Junichi Azuma (2,4), Satoshi Matsudaira (3), Kobayashi Productions *Original Story:* Katsuhijo Nishijima, Kazumi Shirasaka, Yuji Moriyama *Screenplay:* Yuji Moriyama (1), Katsuhiko Nishijima (1), Tomoko Kawasaki (1-4), Takao Koyama (2) *Music Director:* Yasunori Honda

The title is a parody of Jackie Chan's *Project A*, and the video is a parody of every popular anime genre of recent memory at the time of its production; in other words, in-jokes galore. Super schoolgirl A-ko (who gets her power from being the daughter of Superman and Wonder Woman) fights with super-rich daddy's girl B-ko over the friendship of super cutesy schoolgirl C-ko. Notable guest-starring or cameo roles go to Captain Harlock (as an alcoholic transvestite), FIST OF THE NORTH STAR's Kenshiro (a pigtailed schoolgirl—picture it if you can), and Kentucky Fried Chicken's Colonel Sanders (!). Character design and animation direction by Yuji Moriyama, who assumed direction duties for Vols. 2-4. Released in Japan under the title "Project A-Ko" by Sôei Shinsha/Pony Canyon; available in North America through U.S. Manga Corps. Followed by a "Making Of" video titled "Project A-Ko: Secret File" with musical clips as sung by the series' three main voice-actors, as well as by a two-volume OAV sequel titled "A-Ko the Versus" (see below) which, despite the return of the main cast, many consider as a separate series.

Project A-Ko

In the prestigious Graviton High School for Girls, Miss Ayumi introduces two new students: A-ko and her ditzy sidekick C-ko. A-ko is a normal seventeen-year-old... except for her superhuman strength. The trouble begins when the spoiled, brilliant B-ko decides she wants C-ko for herself. B-ko goes up against the invincible A-ko with her arsenal of powered robot-suits, including the most powerful of all, "Akagiyama 23." Meanwhile, a monstrous alien spaceship plies its way toward Earth, in search of... ? **86 min.**

Project A-ko 2: *Plot of the Daitokuji Financial Group*

The girls each have big plans for summer vacation. A-ko vows to lose a few pounds, B-ko resolves to get A-ko out of the way, and C-ko makes a shopping list. B-ko starts working on a giant anti-A-ko robot. But her father, head of the powerful Daitokuji Financial Group, programs the robot to attack the alien spacecraft that has landed in Graviton City. Meanwhile, the aliens have asked A-ko and C-ko to help them get back to their planet. C-ko appeals to B-ko, who, eager to please C-ko, agrees to help them repair the ship. **70 min.**

Project A-ko 3: *Cinderella Rhapsody*

A-ko is lost in her dreams of the perfect man. Meanwhile, C-ko gets so bored with A-ko that she throws a tantrum and barely misses getting run over by K, an extremely handsome motorcyclist. A-ko takes a part-time job at the local fast food restaurant and comes face to face with K. It's love at first sight! Her dreams are shattered when B-ko threatens to expose her job to the school officials and at the same time becomes infatuated with K. **50 min.**

Project A-ko 4: *Final*

During an archaeological dig on Earth, a mysterious hexagram symbol found engraved on a wall causes the scientists' guide to flee in panic. Out in space, this same symbol is evident on the flagship of a huge fleet of spaceships heading straight towards Earth! While Miss Ayumi is away, C-ko, angered by A-ko, storms out of the class and stumbles upon her teacher holding a mysterious pendant and reciting a strange prayer. Just as Miss Ayumi's meeting with a possible suitor is about to begin, they are spotted by A-ko and C-ko. A-ko, extremely distraught, barges in on the meeting because the suitor is none other than K. While Miss Ayumi admonishes her behavior, she announces her plan to marry K the very next day. **59 min.**

Domestic Home Video:

Project A-Ko
USM 1068 ▲ $19.95 ▲ VHS ▲ DUB ▲ Stereo ▲ 01/06/93
USM 1015 ▲ $29.95 ▲ VHS ▲ SUB ▲ Stereo ▲ 01/22/92
ID 8583CT ▲ $39.95 ▲ LD ▲ SUB ▲ HiFi Surr ▲ W/S ▲ 07/05/91

Project A-Ko 2
USM 1133 ▲ $19.95 ▲ VHS ▲ DUB ▲ Stereo ▲ 07/27/94
USM 1102 ▲ $29.95 ▲ VHS ▲ SUB ▲ Stereo ▲ 03/02/94
ID 2871CT ▲ $39.95 ▲ LD ▲ M/A ▲ HiFi Mono ▲ 03/07/95

Project A-Ko 3
USM 1134 ▲ $19.95 ▲ VHS ▲ DUB ▲ Stereo ▲ 05/07/94
USM 1103 ▲ $29.95 ▲ VHS ▲ SUB ▲ Stereo ▲ 05/04/94
ID 2875CT ▲ $34.95 ▲ LD ▲ M/A ▲ HiFi Stereo ▲ 04/05/95

Project A-ko 4
USM 1135 ▲ $19.95 ▲ VHS ▲ DUB ▲ Stereo ▲ 12/07/94
USM 1104 ▲ $29.95 ▲ VHS ▲ SUB ▲ Stereo ▲ 07/01/94
ID 2881CT ▲ $34.95 ▲ LD ▲ M/A ▲ HiFi Stereo ▲ 06/13/95

Project A-Ko Versus

OAV series, 2 volumes

(1990) ©Final-Nishijima/NEXTART

Director: Katsuhiko Nishijima *Original Idea:* Katsuhiko Nishijima, Kazumi Shiraishi, Yuji Moriyama *Character Design & Director of Animation:* Hideyuki Motohashi (1), Katsuhiko Nishijima (2) *Screenplay:* Katsuhiko Nishijima (1), Tomoko Kawasaki (1), Yuji Kawahara (2) *Art Director:* Mitsuharu Miyamae (1), Yoji Nakaza (2) *Music Director:* Yasunori Honda

A two-volume fantasy-world OAV foray with the characters from PROJECT A-KO in new roles: A-ko and B-ko are bounty hunters on an alien world; C-ko is the spoiled daughter of a rich industrialist who's been kidnapped by two greedy but inept crooks. The money-hungry duo of A-ko and B-ko give chase, and the rest is your average adventure. Interesting to see, but not fully satisfying for fans of the original series; straight-faced treatment of the subject earns VERSUS no gut-busting laffs like the original. Released in Japan under the title "Project A-Ko the Versus: Battles 1-2" by Nexstar/Pony Canyon; available in North America through U.S. Manga Corps.

Project A-Ko Versus Battle 1: *Grey Side*

C-ko is kidnapped by two pirates from her father's spaceship. Enroute to the rendezvous with her kidnappers' boss, their ship breaks apart in mid-air and C-ko plummets to the planet below. Fortunately, she lands right on top of A-ko, one of the planet's monster-hunters. A-ko arrives at the home she shares with her partner B-ko and, famished, quickly changes for dinner. But before she gets to the table, C-ko has devoured everything in sight. A-ko is incensed but is somewhat appeased when B-ko points out the reward that they could collect for returning C-ko. When C-ko is re-kidnapped, A-ko and B-ko take off in pursuit. Their rescue attempt is foiled by the pirates' boss, Gail, who strikes B-ko down with a single blow. **54 min.**

Project A-Ko Versus Battle 2: *Blue Side*

In pursuit of the 3-headed dragon, A-ko, B-ko and Maruten board the enemy's base and are pounced on by the pirates. While A-ko is battling Liza, B-ko encounters Gail and instead of destroying him is overcome by her attraction to him and ends up joining forces with him. Just as the base is about to be blown up, Gail, B-ko, and C-ko escape but find the military forces of the Kotobuki fleet hot on their trail. C-ko, now possessed by the spirit of master Xena, summons the dragon to destroy the fleet. A-ko and Maruten, having somehow survived, are in pursuit of Gail when they learn that C-ko was adopted and may be from the same race as Xena and Gail. They manage to sneak aboard Gail's ship and a battle between A-ko and Gail ensues. **52 min.**

Domestic Home Video:

Project A-Ko Versus Battle 1
USM 1136 ▲ $19.95 ▲ VHS ▲ DUB ▲ Stereo ▲ 01/18/95
USM 1105 ▲ $29.95 ▲ VHS ▲ SUB ▲ Stereo ▲ 09/07/94
ID 2884CT ▲ $34.95 ▲ LD-CLV/CAV ▲ M/A ▲ Stereo ▲ 09/06/95

Project A-Ko Versus Battle 2
USM 1137 ▲ $29.95 ▲ VHS ▲ DUB ▲ Stereo ▲ 03/22/95
USM 1106 ▲ $29.95 ▲ VHS ▲ SUB ▲ Stereo ▲ 11/02/94
ID 2888CT ▲ $34.95 ▲ LD ▲ SUB ▲ Stereo ▲ 12/06/95

Rakushô! Hyper-Dolls *See* HYPER-DOLLS

Ranma 1/2 TV Series

TV series (First Season), 18 episodes

(1989-90) ©Rumiko Takahashi/Shogakukan Inc./Kitty/Fuji TV

Based on the Comics By: Rumiko Takahashi (Published by Viz Comics) *Director:* Tsutomu Shibayama *Series Director:* Tomomitsu Mochizuki *Music:* Eiji Mori *Character Design:* Atsuko Nakajima

Based on the manga of the same name by Rumiko Takahashi (MAISON IKKOKU, URUSEI YATSURA), as serialized in publisher Shogakukan's weekly SHÛKAN SHÔNEN SUNDAY manga anthology. On an impromtu training trip to China, a pair of martial artists fall into mystical springs that transform their victims into whoever—or whatever—drowned there hundreds of years ago, be it a panda, a pig, a duck, or a beautiful, bosomy young girl. The last is the fate of the title character, a boy martial artist who becomes a female (thus the title, as in half-boy, half-girl). A wildly successful, long-running manga series in Japan (which only recently ended), the RANMA 1/2 series has spawned a long-running TV series with OAV and movie followups, and is basically a "Taming of the Shrew"-like love story where the potty-mouthed, teenaged Ranma often plays both parts. The plot is equal parts martial arts absurdity (marital arts food delivery, martial arts figure skating, "Cat-Fu"), gender and species-bending hijinks (frequent magical transformations regulated by hot and cold water), and crazed romance, as both of Ranma's incarnations have a dizzying array of suitors. Features character designs by Atsuko Nakajima (YOU'RE UNDER ARREST!). The North American video release of the TV series is broken up into "seasons": the first 18 episodes are known simply as "Ranma 1/2"; the next 22 episodes of

the second TV series (released in Japan as "Nettô Hen") are titled "Ranma 1/2: Anything-Goes Martial Arts"; while the current batch (as of this writing) fall under the heading of "Ranma 1/2: Hard Battle." All in all, 161 half-hour TV episodes, 12 half-hour OAVs, two full-length theatrical features (see below), and two "music videos"—released under the title "Ranma 1/2: Nettô Uta Gassen" (Hard Song Battle), featuring various songs by the cast—are available on home video, and of them all, only the "Hot Song" videos have yet to be or aren't already in release domestically. Released in Japan under the title "Ranma (Nibun no Ichi) 1/ 2" Kitty/Shogakukan/Pony Canyon; available in North

America through Viz Video.

Ranma 1/2 Episode 1: *The Strange Strangers From China*
A feisty red-haired girl and a giant panda show up on the Tendos' doorstep. After the details of the tragic training exercise in China are revealed, older sisters Kasumi and Nabiki waste no time in nominating Akane for bridal duty. **26 min.**

Ranma 1/2 Episode 2: *School Is No Place For Horsing Around*
Akane is given the duty of escorting her fiancé to his new school, Furinkan High. Ranma learns there's more to Akane than he thought when he meets her many suitors. **26 min.**

Ranma 1/2 Episode 3: *A Sudden Storm of Love ... Hey, Wait A Minute!*
Poetry-spouting high school swordsman Kuno discovers a new object of affection... the lovely, bosomy, red-haired wench he knows only as the "pig-tailed girl." Naturally, Ranma doesn't react too well to Kuno's come-ons, and a battle is arranged between the two. If (female) Ranma wins, Kuno will allow her to date his glorious self. If Kuno wins, Ranma still gets to date Kuno! **26 min.**

Ranma 1/2 Episode 4: *Ranma and... Ranma? If It's Not One Thing, It's Another*
Ranma is still reeling from Kuno's declaration of love for the robustly healthy "pig tailed girl." Meanwhile, the ever-resourceful Nabiki has discovered a new source of income... selling "French postcards" of female Ranma to a lovesick Kuno! Will Ranma be flattered by Kuno's interest in him/her? Or will he find a whole new use for that wooden sword Kuno's always waving around? **26 min.**

Ranma 1/2 Episode 5: *Love Me To The Bone! The Compound Fracture of Akane's Heart*
Kendo master Kuno continues his assault upon male Ranma for alleged lechery against his darling female Ranma, whom he knows only as the "pig-tailed girl." An angry Akane hears one wisecrack too many and sends Ranma limping to kindly chiropractor Dr. Tofu. Akane takes a phone call from someone Dr. Tofu "really likes" and who's already on her way over. **26 min.**

Ranma 1/2 Episode 6: *Akane's Lost Love ... These Things Happen, You Know*
Dr. Tofu's patients know it's time to run for cover when his mystery sweetheart stops by. Being treated by the good doctor is not such a good idea when she's around, as he's prone to forgetting who he's talking to and to running around town with his skeleton "Betty" on his back. When Genma counsels Ranma to be nicer to his intended, Ranma grudgingly admits that Akane may not be so unattractive after all. **26 min.**

Ranma 1/2 Episode 7: *Enter Ryoga, The Eternal Lost Boy*
We meet a brand-new character: Ryoga Hibiki, a boy with a pathological bump of misdirection. For Ryoga, life is lonely and travel is torture, as it can take him days or even weeks just to find his way around the block. When Ryoga comes to Furinkan High (after several false starts) in order to settle a score with Ranma, will this mysterious new rival be able to make it to school on time? **26 min.**

Ranma 1/2 Episode 8: *School is a Battlefield! Ranma vs. Ryoga*
The fight at Furinkan High between Ryoga and Ranma continues. Nabiki, never one to miss a money-making opportunity, acts as a bookmaker and takes bets from gawking students. Akane tries to reason with the two combatants and ends up being caught in the middle. **26 min.**

Ranma 1/2 Episode 9: *True Confessions! A Girl's Hair is Her Life!*
Newly coiffed Akane learns that the gender-bending Ranma isn't always a jerk. Newly humbled Ranma learns that a few measly pieces of bread aren't going to solve his

---

problems with the pathologically misdirected Ryoga. And newly aquaphobic Ryoga learns to stay out of the rain... or else. **26 min.**

Ranma 1/2 Episode 10: *P-P-P-Chan! He's Good For Nothin'*
A not completely unsympathetic Ranma is obliged to listen to Ryoga's tale of woe. A small black pig by the unlikely name of "P-Chan" steals Akane's heart. And the wacky Chinese guide from the legendary "Training Grounds of Cursed Springs" makes a long-awaited appearance. **26 min.**

Ranma 1/2 Episode 11: *Dead-On! Enter The Delinquent Juvenile Gymnast*
Ranma's reluctant fiancée Akane is elected champion gymnast of her team for an upcoming match against a black-clad girl from another school. Why is there such a strong resemblance between this girl and a certain poetry-spouting swordsman? **26 min.**

Ranma 1/2 Episode 12: *A Woman's Love is War! The Martial Arts Rhythmic Gymnastics Challenge*
A training accident forces Akane to withdraw from the upcoming match. Could it be that the champion fighting to decide who'll go steady with Ranma is ... Ranma? **26 min.**

Ranma 1/2 Episode 13: *A Tear in a Girl-Delinquent's Eye? The End of The Martial Arts Rhythmic Gymnastics Challenge*
The conclusion to the martial arts rhythmic gymnastics tournament. Kodachi's still got a lot of dirty tricks up her sleeve, not the least of which includes handcuffing a very angry P-Chan to female Ranma. Remember, if Kodachi wins, Ranma's honor-bound to break off his engagement with Akane. If Ranma wins, Kodachi must give up her "Ranma Dream" forever. Can Ranma dodge Kodachi long enough to break the chains of love? **26 min.**

Ranma 1/2 Episode 14: *Pelvic Fortune-Telling! Ranma is the No. 1 Bride in Japan*
Dr. Tofu's mother comes bearing gifts... in this case, photos of a prospective daughter-in-law! Worried, Akane tells his mother that she's his intended. For a slight fee, Nabiki does the same. When Dr. Tofu's no-nonsense mama decides the best bride for her boy's got the biggest child-bearing hips, who do you think will be the one to measure up as the winner... Akane, Nabiki or Ranma? **26 min.**

Ranma 1/2 Episode 15: *Enter Shampoo, The Gung-Ho Girl! I Put My Life in Your Hands*
Ranma discovers that turning into a girl isn't entirely bad. For example, he can indulge his sweet tooth for elaborate desserts that he'd be too embarrassed to order as a guy. But there's a price for being a girl, especially when Shampoo, the cutie from China, is around. According to the custom of her Amazon tribe, those defeated by a man must wed that man, while those defeated by a woman must kill that woman! Guess which one Ranma was when he first met Shampoo? **26 min.**

Ranma 1/2 Episode 16: *Shampoo's Revenge! The Shiatsu Technique That Steals Heart and Soul*
Shampoo's decided that she's going to wash that Ranma right out of Akane's hair with a secret memory-erasing shampoo formula. Oddly enough, Akane seems to recognize everyone in her family, at school, even Dr. Tofu... everyone but Ranma. Shampoo offers Ranma an antidote, but there's one catch: Ranma must grant Shampoo one wish. Will the price of restoring Akane's memory be too high, even for Ranma? **26 min.**

Ranma 1/2 Episode 17: *I Love You Ranma! Please Don't Say Goodbye*
Akane still can't remember Ranma. Shampoo's more than willing to give Ranma the special shampoo formula that will restore Akane's memory, but in return, Ranma has to grant Shampoo one favor ("But don't go asking me to marry you or kill Akane or nothing, okay?"). Now that Ranma's agreed to "almost" kill female Ranma, will he be able to persuade his rival, Ryoga, to help him help Akane? **26 min.**

Ranma 1/2 Episode 18: *I am A Man! Ranma's Going Back To China*
Ranma and Genma come to blows when the younger Saotome announces he's returning to China. Join Ranma and Genma in a look back at their adventures thus far, including the fateful fall into the accursed springs at Jusenkyo, Ranma's first meeting with Akane, Kuno's pursuit of the mysterious "pigtailed girl," Kodachi's martial arts rhythmic gymnastics vendetta against female Ranma, Ryoga's own Jusenkyo plunge, and more. Final volume in the first TV series. **26 min.**

Domestic Home Video:
Ranma 1/2 TV Series Vol. 1: *Episodes 1 and 2*
VV RT-001 ▲ $29.95 ▲ VHS ▲ DUB ▲ HiFi Stereo ▲ 11/15/93
Ranma 1/2 TV Series Vol. 2: *Episodes 3 and 4*
VV RT-002 ▲ $29.95 ▲ VHS ▲ DUB ▲ HiFi Stereo ▲ 01/25/94
Ranma 1/2 TV Series Vol. 3: *Episodes 5 and 6*
VV RT-003 ▲ $29.95 ▲ VHS ▲ DUB ▲ HiFi Stereo ▲ 02/15/94
Ranma 1/2 TV Series Vol. 4: *Episodes 7 and 8*
VV RT-004 ▲ $29.95 ▲ VHS ▲ DUB ▲ HiFi Stereo ▲ 04/09/94
Ranma 1/2 TV Series Vol. 5: *Episodes 9 and 10*
VV RT-005 ▲ $29.95 ▲ VHS ▲ DUB ▲ HiFi Stereo ▲ 05/13/94
Ranma 1/2 TV Series Vol. 6: *Episodes 11 and 12*
VV RT-006 ▲ $29.95 ▲ VHS ▲ DUB ▲ HiFi Stereo ▲ 08/22/94

 Violence   Profanity   Nudity   Sexual Situations   **Adult Viewers Only** - content is extreme and/or explicit

Ranma 1/2 TV Series Vol. 7: *Episodes 13 and 14*
VV RT-007 ▲ $29.95 ▲ VHS ▲ DUB ▲ HiFi Stereo ▲ 10/12/94

Ranma 1/2 TV Series Vol. 8: *Episodes 15 and 16*
VV RT-008 ▲ $29.95 ▲ VHS ▲ DUB ▲ HiFi Stereo ▲ 01/18/95

Ranma 1/2 TV Series Vol. 9: *Episodes 17 and 18*
VV RT-009 ▲ $29.95 ▲ VHS ▲ DUB ▲ HiFi Stereo ▲ 02/15/95

Ranma 1/2 Collector's Ed. Vol. 1: *Episodes 1-3*
VV RS-001 ▲ $34.95 ▲ VHS ▲ SUB ▲ HiFi Mono ▲ 07/15/94

Ranma 1/2 Collector's Ed. Vol. 2: *Episodes 4-6*
VV RS-002 ▲ $34.95 ▲ VHS ▲ SUB ▲ HiFi Mono ▲ 01/11/95

Ranma 1/2 Collector's Ed. Vol. 3: *Episodes 7-9*
VV RS-003 ▲ $34.95 ▲ VHS ▲ SUB ▲ HiFi Mono ▲ 04/15/95

Ranma 1/2 Collector's Ed. Vol. 4: *Episodes 10-12*
VV RS-004 ▲ $34.95 ▲ VHS ▲ SUB ▲ HiFi Mono ▲ 06/13/95

Ranma 1/2 Collector's Ed. Vol. 5: *Episodes 13-15*
VV RS-005 ▲ $34.95 ▲ VHS ▲ SUB ▲ HiFi Stereo ▲ 08/15/95

Ranma 1/2 Collector's Ed. Vol. 6: *Episodes 16-18*
VV RS-006 ▲ $24.95 ▲ VHS ▲ SUB ▲ HiFi Stereo ▲ 11/07/95

Ranma 1/2 Anything-Goes Martial Arts

TV series (Second Season), 22 episodes

(1990-91) ©Rumiko Takahashi/Shogakukan Inc./Kitty/Fuji TV

Based on the Comics By: Rumiko Takahashi (Published by Viz Comics) *Director:* Tsutomu Shibayama *Series Director:* Tomomitsu Mochizuki *Music:* Eiji Mori *Character Design:* Atsuko Nakajima

Ranma 1/2 ATG: *Darling Charlotte*
Episode 1, DARLING CHARLOTTE: An encounter at the rink with the "Golden Pair" of high school skating means trouble for Ranma and Akane. Azusa falls for a certain widdle bwack piggy. Problem: Akane isn't about to give up her pet without a fight. Solution: An anything-goes martial arts figure-skating match... the "Charlotte Cup!" Episode 2, CLOSE CALL! THE DANCE OF DEATH...ON ICE: Mikado Sanzenin is a ladykiller, and Ranma vows to stop him from presuming *way* too much with the "pigtailed girl." But to settle his score, first he and Akane have to win the "Charlotte Cup" ...and Ranma still hasn't learned to skate! **52 min.**

Ranma 1/2 ATG: *It's Fast or It's Free*
Episode 3, IT'S FAST OR IT'S FREE: A stranger shows up claiming to be Ranma's long-lost dad. It seems Genma, lost and starving, traded baby Ranma to the stranger for some fish! The stranger has come to reclaim Ranma, wed him to his own daughter, and have them carry on the Daikoku School of Martial Arts Restaurant Takeout. Also includes the continuation of the Martial Arts Figure-Skating Competition. Episode 4, CLASH OF THE DELIVERY GIRLS! THE MARTIAL ARTS TAKEOUT RACE: Now, in order to keep Ranma as the Anything-Goes Martial Arts heir, Akane has to win in the Martial Arts Restaurant Takeout Race against Kaori, Ranma's newest would-be fiancée and champion of the Daikoku School of Martial Arts Restaurant Takeout. **52 min.**

Ranma 1/2 ATG: *Cat-Fu Fighting*
Episode 5, CAT-FU FIGHTING: Poetry-spouting Tatewaki Kuno is willing to do whatever it takes to find Ranma's weak spot. But Ranma is special, so his weak spot has to be something extraordinary. But who would have thought that it would be something so ... so ... Also featuring the debut of a brand-new martial arts match! Episode 6, THIS OLD GAL'S THE LEADER OF THE AMAZON TRIBE!: The beauteous Chinese Amazon Shampoo has come back to Japan, and she means to make a reluctant Ranma marry her! Shampoo's brought her great-grandmother with her, and this old dame's got over a hundred years of Amazon history on her side...or is it two hundred? **52 min.**

Ranma 1/2 ATG: *Chestnuts Roasting on an Open Fire*
Episode 7, CHESTNUTS ROASTING ON AN OPEN FIRE: Ranma can't shake the curse of Shampoo's great-grandmother, the "Full-Body Cat Tongue." Even lukewarm water seems boiling, and if Ranma's gonna turn back into a guy, he needs that hot water. The Phoenix Pill can reverse the curse, but to get it, Ranma's gotta take a part-time job slinging ramen at the infamous Cat Cafe. We also meet Shampoo's erstwhile Chinese sweetheart, the myopic Mousse. Episode 8, ENTER MOUSSE! THE FIST OF THE WHITE SWAN: The hopelessly lovesick (and nearsighted) Mousse has come all the way from China to try to win back Shampoo's heart. He challenges Ranma to a fight, but even Ranma may have trouble with Mousse and his arsenal of hidden weapons. **52 min.**

Ranma 1/2 ATG: *Cold Competition*
Episode 9, COOL RUNNINGS! THE RACE OF THE SNOWMAN: Ranma tries a new cure in a "Martial Arts Snowman-Carry Race" sponsored by the infamous Cat Cafe. If he wins, he gets a ski-tour with Shampoo and the much-needed Phoenix Pill. Episode 10, DANGER AT

THE TENDO DOJO: Ranma is looking forward to the final result of his date with Shampoo: never to be a girl again! Meanwhile, Akane is back home fighting off a challenger to the Tendo dojo singlehandedly. **52 min.**

Ranma 1/2 ATG: *The Breaking Point*
Episode 11, RANMA TRAINS ON MT. TERROR: Ranma discovers that Ranma is mixing it up with Cologne. Did Cologne mean it when she said she'd teach him a new technique to defeat Ranma? Episode 12, THE BREAKING POINT!? RYOGA'S GREAT REVENGE: Ryoga makes great progress with his *bakusai tenketsu*, a martial arts technique based on the assumption that every living thing has one certain spot — a "breaking point," if you will — which, when touched in just the right way, causes the victim to shatter into a thousand pieces! **52 min.**

Ranma 1/2 ATG: *Fowl Play*
Episode 13, THE ABDUCTION OF AKANE: A mysterious masked man takes Akane hostage! Or ... does he!? Ranma follows the trail to the circus, where he becomes the target for a knife-throwing trick performed by some dopey duck. Episode 14, RANMA vs. MOUSSE! TO LOSE IS TO WIN: If Ranma doesn't answer the summons to the circus, Akane's going to get a healthy dose of *Yahzu-Nii-Chuan*, cursed water from the "Spring of Drowned Duck"! Yep, that's right, the latest person to take the Jusenkyo plunge is Mousse, and he's not above a little, uh, fowl play to get his revenge. **52 min.**

Ranma 1/2 ATG: *The Evil Wakes*
Episode 15, THE EVIL WAKES: A string of bad omens all make sense when a sleeping demon once again rears its ugly head: Happosai, the martial arts master who trained both Ranma and Akane's fathers! Episode 16, ASSAULT ON THE GIRLS' LOCKER ROOM: Ryoga Hibiki has a map to a magical Japanese "Spring of Drowned Man" just like the one in China, which of course leads Ranma and Ryoga to mount an assault on the place where the magical spring is supposed to be: *THE GIRLS' LOCKER ROOM IN FURINKAN HIGH SCHOOL!* **52 min.**

Ranma 1/2 ATG: *Goodbye Girl-Type*
Episode 17, KUNO'S HOUSE OF GADGETS! GUESTS CHECK IN, BUT THEY DON'T CHECK OUT: According to Shampoo's great-grandmother Cologne, when the three *Nan-nii-chuan* or "Spring of Drowned Man" urns — red, blue, and gold — are brought together in a certain place at a certain time, the waters of Japan's *Nan-nii-chuan* will rise once more, putting an end to the Jusenkyo curse. The first urn was found beneath the girls' locker room at Furinkan High School. The second urn, it seems, is located somewhere on the grounds of Castle Kuno. Episode 18, GOODBYE GIRL-TYPE: Ranma & Co. have acquired the second urn. If they can convince Happosai to return it to them, all they'll have to do is find the third one. The hard part is yet to come: Namely, finding the proper location where the three urns must be assembled before the waters of Japan's *Nan-niichuan* can rise again. **52 min.**

Domestic Home Video:

Ranma 1/2 ATG: *Darling Charlotte*
VV RA-001 ▲ $24.95 ▲ VHS ▲ DUB ▲ HiFi Stereo ▲ 03/15/95
VV RAS-01 ▲ $29.95 ▲ VHS ▲ SUB ▲ HiFi Stereo ▲ 07/02/96

Ranma 1/2 ATG: *It's Fast or It's Free*
VV RA-002 ▲ $24.95 ▲ VHS ▲ DUB ▲ HiFi Stereo ▲ 04/12/95
VV RAS-02 ▲ $29.95 ▲ VHS ▲ SUB ▲ HiFi Stereo ▲ 07/16/96

Ranma 1/2 ATG: *Cat-Fu Fighting*
VV RA-003 ▲ $24.95 ▲ VHS ▲ DUB ▲ HiFi Stereo ▲ 05/10/95
VV RAS-03 ▲ $29.95 ▲ VHS ▲ SUB ▲ HiFi Stereo ▲ 08/06/96

Ranma 1/2 ATG: *Chestnuts Roasting on an Open Fire*
VV RA-004 ▲ $24.95 ▲ VHS ▲ DUB ▲ HiFi Stereo ▲ 06/13/95
VV RAS-04 ▲ $29.95 ▲ VHS ▲ SUB ▲ HiFi Stereo ▲ 09/13/96

Ranma 1/2 ATG: *Cold Competition*
VV RA-005 ▲ $24.95 ▲ VHS ▲ DUB ▲ HiFi Stereo ▲ 08/08/95
VV RAS-05 ▲ $29.95 ▲ VHS ▲ SUB ▲ HiFi Stereo ▲ 10/11/96

Ranma 1/2 ATG: *The Breaking Point*
VV RA-006 ▲ $24.95 ▲ VHS ▲ DUB ▲ HiFi Stereo ▲ 09/05/95
VV RAS-06 ▲ $29.95 ▲ VHS ▲ SUB ▲ HiFi Stereo ▲ 11/15/96

Ranma 1/2 ATG: *Fowl Play*
VV RA-007 ▲ $24.95 ▲ VHS ▲ DUB ▲ HiFi Stereo ▲ 10/03/95
VV RAS-07 ▲ $29.95 ▲ VHS ▲ SUB ▲ HiFi Stereo ▲ 12/06/96

Ranma 1/2 ATG: *The Evil Wakes*
VV RA-008 ▲ $24.95 ▲ VHS ▲ DUB ▲ HiFi Stereo ▲ 11/07/95

Ranma 1/2 ATG: *Goodbye Girl-Type*
VV RA-009 ▲ $24.95 ▲ VHS ▲ DUB ▲ HiFi Stereo ▲ 12/19/95

Ranma 1/2 Hard Battle

TV series (Third Season)

(1991-92) ©Rumiko Takahashi/Shogakukan/Kitty/Fuji TV

Based on the comics by: Rumiko Takahashi (published by Viz Comics) *Series Director:* Tomomitsu Mochizuki *Director:* Tsutomu Shibayama *Character Design:* Atsuko Nakajima *Music:* Eiji Mori

Ranma 1/2 Hard Battle: *Ukyo Can Cook*

2 episodes. RANMA GAINS YET ANOTHER SUITOR: Say hello to Furinkan High School's newest transfer student, *UKYO KUONJI,* warrior and *okonomiyaki* chef par excellence. Lots of people have their reasons for despising the younger Saotome, but Ukyo's grudge against Ranma goes all the way back to their childhood, when Ranma's father Genma leveraged his son's future in exchange for an *okonomiyaki or* "Japanese pizza" cart. With a father like that, who needs enemies!? RYOGA AND AKANE: 2-GETHER 4-EVER: Ukyo's angry because Ranma betrayed a promise in favor of some quick eats and an even faster getaway; Ryoga's angry because Ranma's gained yet *ANOTHER* fiancée; and Akane's cranky because Ranma's acting like a complete jerk (what else is new?). The only *LOGICAL* solution is for Ukyo to set up a romantic date for Akane and Ryoga, so that she and her darling "Ran-chan" can be alone. But, as Ryoga's about to find out, perhaps a boating trip on a cold, cold lake wasn't exactly the *BEST* of ideas.... **52 min.**

Ranma 1/2 Hard Battle: *Dim Sum Darling*

2 episodes. SNEEZE ME, SQUEEZE ME, PLEASE ME: No matter how many times Ranma's told her to take a hike, Shampoo still hasn't given up on the only man who's ever defeated her in combat. A new recipe which produces a posthypnotic suggestion-like willingness to please seems the perfect plan...until Shampoo accidentally *"a-choo's!"* during a crucial moment. The good news is, whenever he hears a sneeze, Ranma is now compelled to throw himself into the arms of whoever's close by. The bad news is, Akane's coming down with the sniffles.... RUB-A-DUB-DUB! THERE'S A PERVERT IN THE TUB: If they can find the scroll Master Happosai has stashed at the girls' side of a Japanese-style hot springs resort, maybe Soun and Genma can use his own *Happo-Daikarin* or "Happosai Bomb" technique against him. Given the unique nature of his "problem," Ranma would seem the ideal candidate to infiltrate the girls' side and recover that scroll. Just a hint of that hot springs water, though, and Ranma'll be exposed for the guy he is! Genma may have a solution, but then again, whoever heard of polar bears in Japan!? **52 min.**

Ranma 1/2 Hard Battle: *Dharma Chameleon*

2 episodes. I LOVE YOU! MY DEAR, DEAR UKYO: When Ukyo Kuonji came to Tokyo, she thought she'd left her problems behind her. But now they've caught up with her: coquettish camouflager *TSUBASA KURENAI,* equally adept at soda machine, tree, and mailbox disguise. THE WITCH WHO LOVED ME: A JAPANESE GHOST STORY: Soun's been elected Chairman of the Town Assembly—on the condition that he apprehend the pesky underwear thief who's been troubling the locals—and so, together with Genma and Ranma, the three must prevent the theft of a legendary bra from a curséd antique shop. What a surprise when they find out Happosai's latest loot is occupied by a scaly seductress with love on her mind...! **52 min.**

Ranma 1/2 Hard Battle: *Once Upon A Time in Jusenkyo*

2 episodes. TRANSFORM! AKANE THE MUSCLEMAN: It's easy to forget sometimes that Akane's a martial artist too. After she eats some magic super noodles that make her super strong, however, Akane can't *wait* to enter a local Japanese badminton tournament and beat Shampoo and Ranma at their own game. But it looks like those super noodles may have some super disturbing side-effects.... THE KILLER FROM JUSENKYO: Like earthquakes, hurricanes, and other dangerous phenomena, the cursed training grounds of Jusenkyo, China are a natural disaster area which demand respect—*or else*! When Ranma, Genma, Shampoo, Ryoga and Mousse are targeted for punishment by a secret society for abusing their transformations, a powerful swordsman is sent after them. But this swordsman's got a little Jusenkyo secret of his own.... **52 min.**

Ranma 1/2 Hard Battle: *Pretty Womanhood*

2 episodes. AM I...PRETTY? RANMA'S DECLARATION OF WOMANHOOD: An accidental thwack on the noggin on the way into the carp pond's got Ranma not only *looking* like a girl, but *thinking* like one, too! It's bad enough "she" wants to take up flower-arranging, but now she's also got Akane taking her shopping for lingerie and buying her party dresses. A sudden enthusiasm for cooking, Genma can handle, but when Ranma declares she "abhors violence" and "isn't interested" in carrying on the Dojo, Ranma's poor dad must stage the strangest little "father-daughter" talk in the history of the art. FINAL FACEDOWN! HAPPOSAI vs. THE INVISIBLE MAN: A long time ago, back during their training days, Soun and Genma stumbled exhausted and half-starved into the remote dojo of a certain Master Chingensai. There, they learned his "Super Secret Special Attack," a martial arts technique they're now hoping to use against the so-called "most evil master in Japan," their own *dear* Master Happosai. However, before they can use the technique against him, first they must learn to stop running away from home.... **52 min.**

Domestic Home Video:

Ranma 1/2 Hard Battle: *Ukyo Can Cook*
VV HB-001 ▲ $24.95 ▲ VHS ▲ DUB ▲ HiFi Stereo ▲ 05/07/96

Ranma 1/2 Hard Battle: *Dim Sum Darling*
VV HB-002 ▲ $24.95 ▲ VHS ▲ DUB ▲ HiFi Stereo ▲ 07/02/96

Ranma 1/2 Hard Battle: *Dharma Chameleon*
VV HB-003 ▲ $24.95 ▲ VHS ▲ DUB ▲ HiFi Stereo ▲ 08/05/96

Ranma 1/2 Hard Battle: *Once Upon A Time in Jusenkyo*
VV HB-004 ▲ $24.95 ▲ VHS ▲ DUB ▲ HiFi Stereo ▲ 09/27/96

Ranma 1/2 Hard Battle: *Pretty Womanhood*
VV HB-005 ▲ $24.95 ▲ VHS ▲ DUB ▲ HiFi Stereo ▲ 11/29/96

Ranma 1/2: Big Trouble in Nekonron, China

(1991) ©Rumiko Takahashi/Shogakukan Inc./Kitty/Fuji TV A Viz Video Production

Based on the Comics By: Rumiko Takahashi (Published by Viz Comics) *Director:* Shuji Iuchi *Character Design:* Atsuko Nakajima *Original Screenplay:* Shuji Iuchi

Details the hijinks ensuing from the arrival of a scroll-carrying girl from faraway lands on the doorstep of the Tendo Dojo with pet elephant in tow; subsequent kidnapping of Akane by Prince Kirin (don't ask) prompts Ranma & the rest of the gang to mount an impromptu rescue mission to China. Happosai, the lecherous martial arts master who trained both Ranma and Akane's fathers, has a particular chance to shine in this 75-minute theatrical feature. Released in Japan under the title "Ranma 1/2: Nekonron Dai-Kessen! Okite-Yaburi no Gekitô Hen!" (Big Battle at Nekonron! The No-Rules All-Out Battle) by Five Ace/Pony Canyon; available in North America through Viz Video. **74 min.**

Domestic Home Video:
VV RM-001 ▲ $34.95 ▲ VHS ▲ DUB ▲ HiFi Stereo ▲ 04/06/94
VV RMS-001 ▲ $34.95 ▲ VHS ▲ SUB ▲ HiFi Stereo ▲ 04/09/96

Ranma 1/2: Nihao My Concubine

(1992) ©Rumiko Takahashi/Shogakukan Inc./Kitty/Fuji TV

Based on the Comics By: Rumiko Takahashi (Published by Viz Comics) *Director:* Ko Suzuki *Character Design:* Atsuko Nakajima *Original Screenplay:* Ryota Yamaguchi

Ranma and father Genma join the Tendos for a cruise on Upperclassman Kuno's luxury yacht, but disaster strikes in the form of a sudden squall and the gang's shipwrecked on a strange island. When the girls in the group start disappearing one by one, the decision as to which male will be sent after them is only obvious. Sometimes referred to affectionately by its fans under the title "Silicon Beach," a longer running time isn't the only thing that's expanded in this second theatrical feature—the cup sizes of all the girls (excepting, perhaps, Shampoo's Great-Grandma Cologne) are now filled to overflowing, thanks to newly pumped up designs by Atsuko Nakajima. Released in Japan under the title "Ranma 1/2: Kessen Tôgenkyô! Hanayome o Torimodose!" (Decisive Battle at Togenkyo! Get Back the Brides) by Five Ace/Pony Canyon; available in North America through Viz Video. **60 min.**

Domestic Home Video:
VV RM-002 ▲ $34.95 ▲ VHS ▲ DUB ▲ HiFi Stereo ▲ 09/15/94
VV RMS-002 ▲ $34.95 ▲ VHS ▲ SUB ▲ HiFi Stereo ▲ 05/21/96

Ranma 1/2 OAV Series

OAV series, 8 episodes

©1994 Rumiko Takahashi/Shogakukan Inc./Kitty/Fuji TV A Viz Video Production

Based on the Comics By: Rumiko Takahashi (Published by Viz Comics) *Director:* Junji Nishimura *Character Design:* Atsuko Nakajima *Music:* Akihisa Matsu'ura *Original Screenplay:* Ryota Yamaguchi

Ranma 1/2 OAVs 1&2: *Desperately Seeking Shampoo*

In SHAMPOO'S SUDDEN SWITCH! THE CURSE OF THE CONTRARY JEWEL, Shampoo's great-grandmother gives Cologne a cursed brooch which, when worn right-side up, enhances one's feelings of love. When worn upside-down, even the sweetest love turns into bitter hatred. When adoring Shampoo turns contrary toward Ranma, he must hatch a desperate scheme to get her to say those three little words out loud. In TENDO FAMILY CHRISTMAS SCRAMBLE, Kris Kringle himself visits eldest daughter Kasumi and tells her to throw a Christmas party. The entire cast of the show turns up on the Tendos' doorstep to indulge in holiday-themed mayhem. Nabiki schemes to auction off "seven minutes in heaven" with male Ranma. The female cast sings a special karaoke quintet, and Soun Tendo joins forces with Ranma's future father-in-law to give their two children a gift to last a lifetime. **60 min.**

Ranma 1/2 OAVs 3&4: *Like Water For Ranma*
In AKANE VS. RANMA! I'LL BE THE ONE TO INHERIT MOTHER'S RECIPIES (sic), youngest Tendo daughter Akane discovers a volume of her mother's recipes. The family isn't too excited at having to eat Akane's infamously bad cooking. Add the sudden arrival of Ranma's own mother, Nodoka, unaware of her husband and son's little secret, and Genma must become "Mister Panda," while Ranma becomes "Ran-ko," Akane's charming country cousin. In STORMY WEATHER COMES TO SCHOOL! GROWING UP WITH MISS HINAKO, we meet Hinako Ninomiya, a winsome teacher sent to Furinkan High to "discipline" its notoriously free-spirited students. It isn't long before her ability to absorb the fighting aura of her opponents catches the interest of battle-happy Ranma. The two square off in a competition to determine who rules the roost at Furinkan High. **60 min.**

Ranma 1/2 OAVs 5&6: *Akane and Her Sisters*
An original two-part story not found in the original comics. Everyone knows that there are only two clans who fight in the Anything-Goes style: the Saotomes and the Tendos. That's why it comes as such a shock when two girls show up on the Tendo's doorstep pointing to an old photo of the man they believe to be their father. Only the figure's back is visible, but the legend "Anything-Goes School of Martial Arts" is clearly written. "It could be anyone," Soun pleads as all eyes turn to him. "When you're all grown up," Nabiki reads, "I'll let you take over the Tendo dojo. Signed, your father... Soun Tendo." **60 min.**

Ranma 1/2 OAVs 7&8: *An Akane to Remember*
In REAWAKENING MEMORIES PART 1, a fleeting memory of being rescued by a boy with a horn whistle is triggered when Akane sees a news special about "monster sightings" in a remote area of Japan. To find out if her memory is true, Akane sets out alone and eventually meets the boy in her memory, Shinnosuke, who lives with his grandfather in the deep forest. A reluctant Ranma is dispatched by Akane's father Soun to bring his daughter home again. In REAWAKENING MEMORIES PART 2, Ranma finds Akane and discovers that a mysterious "water of life" may account for the area's enormous creatures. but why is Akane's cooking suddenly tasting good!? Akane learns that all that keeps Shinnosuke alive is the magic water, guarded by a dragon. All of them must join forces to defeat the vicious dragon and get the life-saving magical water. Also includes four bonus *Ranma 1/2* music videos. **65 min.**

Ranma 1/2 OAVs 9&10: *One Grew Over the Kuno's Nest*
In TEAM RANMA VS. THE LEGENDARY PHOENIX, Kuno schemes to employ the power of a legendary Phoenix egg to defeat Ranma. But before he can carry out his plan, the egg hatches and the Phoenix latches onto him like glue! In THE TUNNEL OF LOST LOVE, Ranma and company spend their vacations near a haunted cave. Legend has it that any couple who enters will exit ready to take out personal ads! Featuring all-new bonus music videos. **60 min.**

Ranma 1/2 OAVs 11 & 12: *Faster, Kasumi! Kill! Kill!*
An ogre possesses gentle Kasumi. How long can the devil in Miss Tendo hold the whole household hostage to terror before somebody takes matters into their own hands? Then, an evil doll switches consciousness with Akane. As the eerie doppelgänger menaces Ranma, tiny Akane has to find a way to warn him of the danger he's in.. but how can she when she can't even talk? **65 min.**

Domestic Home Video:
Ranma 1/2 OAVs 1&2:
Desperately Seeking Shampoo
VV RO-001 ▲ $34.95 ▲ VHS ▲ DUB ▲ HiFi Stereo ▲ 12/15/93
LUM 9528 ▲ $39.95 ▲ LD ▲ M/A ▲ HiFi Stereo ▲ CC ▲ 11/07/95

Ranma 1/2 OAVs 3&4: *Like Water For Ranma*
VV RO-002 ▲ $34.95 ▲ VHS ▲ DUB ▲ HiFi Stereo ▲ 06/08/94
LUM 9544 ▲ $39.95 ▲ LD ▲ M/A ▲ HiFi Stereo ▲ CC ▲ 04/30/96

Ranma 1/2 OAVs 5&6: *Akane and Her Sisters*
VV RO-003 ▲ $34.95 ▲ VHS ▲ DUB ▲ HiFi Stereo ▲ 11/09/94

Ranma 1/2 OAVs 7&8: *An Akane To Remember*
VV RO-004 ▲ $29.95 ▲ VHS ▲ DUB ▲ HiFi Stereo ▲ 07/12/95

Ranma 1/2 OAVs 9&10:
One Grew Over The Kuno's Nest
VV RO-005 ▲ $29.95 ▲ VHS ▲ DUB ▲ HiFi Stereo ▲ 03/05/96

Ranma 1/2 OAVs 11&12: *Faster, Kasumi! Kill!*
VV RO-006 ▲ $29.95 ▲ VHS ▲ DUB ▲ HiFi Stereo ▲ 07/02/96

Ranma 1/2 Collector's Edition: The OAVs Vol. 1
OAVs 1-3 in a subtitled version. (90 min.)
VV ROS-001 ▲ $34.95 ▲ VHS ▲ SUB ▲ HiFi Stereo

Ranma 1/2 Collector's Edition: The OAVs Vol. 2
OAVs 4-6 in a subtitled version. (90 min.)
VV ROS-002 ▲ $34.95 ▲ VHS ▲ SUB ▲ HiFi Stereo ▲ 01/16/96

Record of Lodoss War   [OAV]
OAV series, 13 episodes
(1990-91) ©Group SNE/Kadokawa Shôten/Marubeni Corp./Tokyo Broadcasting System

Directors: Shigeto Makino (1), Akinori Nagaoka (2), Katsuhisa Yamada (3) Taiji Ryu (4,7,9-11), Kazunori Mizuno (5), Akio Sakai (6), Hiroshi Kawasaki (8), Akinori Nagaoka (12,13) *Screenplay:* Mami Watanabe (1-8, 10-13), Kenichi Kanemaki (9,11) *Original Story:* Hitoshi Yasuda, Ryo Mizuno *Music:* Mitsuo Hagita *Character Design:* Yutaka Izubuchi, Nobuteru Yuki *Music:* Mitsuo Hagita

Fans of fantasy role-playing games can't ask for a better anime portrayal of a great campaign than RECORD OF LODOSS WAR, a six-volume (thirteen episode) OAV based on the actual gaming sessions of creator Ryo Mizuno and friends. LODOSS details the adventures of a party of six adventurers: Parn, the teenaged fighter son of a disgraced paladin, Deedlit, a flighty, haughty elf attracted to Parn, Ghim, a stolid, haunted dwarven warrior, Slayn, an experienced sorcerer, Etoh, a novice cleric and close friend to Parn, and Woodchuck, a cynical but good-natured thief. The grand journey of this untested band will take them across the length of Lodoss, the accursed island continent, as a "War of Heroes" revives an elemental battle between good and evil. Original story credit goes to Hitoshi Yasuda, Ryo Mizuno, Asami Watanabe, while music is credited to Mitsuo Hagita. Character designs are by Nobuteru Yuki (BATTLE ANGEL) and Yutaka Izubuchi (PATLABOR). Domestic release of Vol. 1 also includes "The Making of Record of Lodoss War" mini-documentary. Released in Japan under the title "Lodoss Jima Senki" (titled "Record of Lodoss War" by its Japanese producer) by Kadokawa Shôten; available in North America through U.S. Manga Corps.

Record of Lodoss War Vol. 1: *Episodes 1-3*
Episode 1: PROLOGUE TO THE LEGEND, Episode 2: BLAZING DEPARTURE and Episode 3: THE BLACK KNIGHT. A party of six are drawn together to battle for the future of Lodoss. Among them: Parn, a young fighter who lacks experience and is driven by his desire to redeem his father's tarnished name; Deedlit, a young and haughty elf who is both attracted to the young fighter and infuriated by his lack of interest; Ghim, a dwarf warrior haunted by a personal failure; Etoh, a young priest; Slayn, a skilled magic user; and Woodchuck, a cynical but good-natured thief. Plus "The Making of Record of Lodoss War" mini-documentary. **80 min.**

Record of Lodoss War Vol. 2: *Episodes 4 and 5*
Episode 4: THE GREY WITCH and Episode 5: THE DESERT KING. The fall of Myce has dragged Parn and his friends into the midst of the invasion of Lodoss, and now they race against time to warn the remaining free kingdoms of the impending peril. The party must do battle with Karla, the mysterious "Grey Witch," as she attempts to kidnap Princess Fianna. After rescuing Fianna, Parn meets a powerful new ally: Kashue, the warrior king of the desert kingdom of Flaim. As Karla's mysterious plans continue to touch everyone in King Fahn's palace, as Kashue is targeted for assassination. As Emperor Beld's forces approach Valis, Parn and his friends seek out the sage Wort to learn about Karla's origins and her real intentions. **55 min.**

Record of Lodoss War Vol. 3: *Episodes 6 and 7*
Episode 6: THE SWORD OF THE DARK EMPEROR and Episode 7: THE WAR OF HEROES. The heroes return to Valis and advise the king that Karla is the last descendant of an ancient kingdom of sorcery. Pleased with Parn's success, King Fahn invites him to serve in his army of Holy Knights. Meanwhile, Ghim leaves his friends behind to pursue his own personal quest. Once out on the battlefield, Parn confronts the Black Knight, Ashram; the man upon whom he swore vengeance at the fall of Myce. And two kings, once friends, face each other in a duel to the death. **55 min.**

Record of Lodoss War Vol. 4: *Episodes 8 and 9*
Episode 8: REQUIEM FOR WARRIORS and Episode 9: THE SCEPTER OF DOMINATION. The War of Heroes has left Lodoss in turmoil, and it is clear that Karla must be stopped at any cost. The heroes encounter the mercenary fighter, Shiris, and her berserker partner, Orson, who are soon valuable allies. At Karla's stronghold, Ghim faces the witch in a duel of wills in an attempt to free Leylia. Meanwhile, the forces of Marmo are in disarray as Ashram prepares to take up the struggle where Beld left off. Urged on by the dark wizard Wagnard, he sets off for Fire Dragon Mountain to obtain the Scepter of Domination. But Wagnard has plans of his own, as he dispatches the elf Pirotess to kidnap Deedlit. **55 min.**

Record of Lodoss War Vol. 5: *Episodes 10 and 11*
Episode 10, THE DEMON DRAGON OF FIRE DRAGON MOUNTAIN: The journey to Fire Dragon Mountain becomes a race between Kashue and Ashram, with the scepter of Domination being the prize. But the scepter is guarded by a formidable obstacle: Shooting Star, one of the last of the ancient dragons of Lodoss. Episode 11, THE WIZARD'S AMBITION: The evil of Kardis the Destroyer stirs beneath the dark island of Marmo, and

Wagnard takes the final steps toward her resurrection. As he plots for his chance at godhood, Kashue and the others prepare for one last assault on Marmo. Since no one is prepared for the powers Wagnard has already gained from Kardis, he succeeds in kidnapping Deedlit. But not even Wagnard can know that Karla is still plotting to prevent any one man from controlling all of Lodoss. **55 min.**

Record of Lodoss War Vol. 6: *Episodes 12 and 13*

Episode 12: FINAL BATTLE! MARMO, THE DARK ISLAND and Episode 13: LODOSS-THE BURNING CONTINENT. As Kashue and the remaining armies of Lodoss cross the southern straits enroute to the dark island to stop the resurrection of Kardis, Parn and his friends arrive just ahead of them. With Deedlit's eternal life about to be sacrificed to Kardis by the now power-mad Wagnard, they have no time to lose! But the island of Marmo holds a frightening trump card: the evil dragon Narse. This remnant of the ancient dragons stands ready to fight the forces of light while Wagnard proceeds with his dark ceremony far beneath the Earth's surface. As Parn and the others rush to stop this dark rite underground, Kashue and his army face the demonic forces of Kardis on the surface. **55 min.**

Domestic Home Video:

Record of Lodoss War Vol. 1
USM 1274 ▲ $19.95 ▲ VHS ▲ DUB ▲ Stereo ▲ 06/04/96
USM 1267 ▲ $29.95 ▲ VHS ▲ SUB ▲ Stereo ▲ 03/07/95

Record of Lodoss War Vol. 2
USM 1275 ▲ $19.95 ▲ VHS ▲ DUB ▲ Stereo ▲ 06/04/96
USM 1268 ▲ $29.95 ▲ VHS ▲ SUB ▲ Stereo ▲ 05/02/95

Record of Lodoss War Vol. 3
USM 1276 ▲ $19.95 ▲ VHS ▲ DUB ▲ Stereo ▲ 06/04/96
USM 1269 ▲ $29.95 ▲ VHS ▲ SUB ▲ Stereo ▲ 07/11/95

Record of Lodoss War Vol. 4
USM 1277 ▲ $19.95 ▲ VHS ▲ DUB ▲ Stereo ▲ 06/04/96
USM 1270 ▲ $29.95 ▲ VHS ▲ SUB ▲ Stereo ▲ 09/05/95

Record of Lodoss War Vol. 5
USM 1278 ▲ $19.95 ▲ VHS ▲ DUB ▲ Stereo ▲ 06/04/96
USM 1271 ▲ $29.95 ▲ VHS ▲ SUB ▲ Stereo ▲ 11/07/95

Record of Lodoss War Vol. 6
USM 1279 ▲ $19.95 ▲ VHS ▲ DUB ▲ Stereo ▲ 06/04/96
USM 1272 ▲ $29.95 ▲ VHS ▲ SUB ▲ Stereo ▲ 11/07/95

Record of Lodoss War Gift Box
Episodes 1-13 (355 min.)
USM 1273 ▲ $129.95 ▲ VHS ▲ SUB ▲ Stereo ▲ 11/07/95

Rei Rei

(1994) ©Toshimitsu Shimizu (Shônen Gahôsha)/Pink Pineapple

Created by: Toshimitsu Shimizu *Director:* Yoshiki Yamamoto *Screenplay:* Mitsuru Mochizuki

Based on the manga by Toshimitsu Shimizu (801 T.T.S. AIRBATS). Two-volume OAV story of a supernatural "missionary of love" named Kaguya, who seems to function as a sort of arbiter in relationships doomed to sexual frustration with the help of her gnome-like butler/sidekick Pipi. From her palace in an undefined netherworld, the provocatively dressed Kaguya senses disturbances between couples (which oddly enough, seem to cloud her view of the moon like a bad case of smog) and sets off for Earth to set things right. In most cases, this involves forcing the originators of the psychic disturbances to graphically face their own desires, such as a boy in love with a lesbian who's temporarily given the body of a well-endowed girl, and a young man who has trouble expressing his emotions who must come to terms with his feelings about being abandoned by his mother. The main goal, of course, is to get these lonely hearts couples together for the joy of sex. For the most part, REI REI is sweet in tone, though some rather Freudian sexual politics are hard at work in some spots, such as the second video's video game world, which is quite funny...until the shy young man manifests the dark side of his id as a gratuitously tentacle-raping demon. Released in Japan under the title "Utsukushiki Sei no Dendôshi: Rei Rei" (Sexy Evangelist: Rei Rei) by Pink Pineapple; available in North America through A.D. Vision. *Edited version is not X-rated.* **60 min.**

Domestic Home Video:

ADV R/001 ▲ $34.95 ▲ VHS ▲ SUB ▲ HiFi Surround ▲ Uncut ▲ 05/14/94
ADV R/002 ▲ $29.95 ▲ VHS ▲ SUB ▲ HiFi Surround ▲ Edited ▲ 05/08/95

RG Veda

OAV series, 2 volumes

(1991,'92) ©Clamp/Shinshôkan/Sony Music Entertainment (Japan) Inc./MOVIC.

Created by: Mitsuhisa Hida, Yutaka Takahashi, Meguma Sugiyama *Original Writer:* Clamp *Director:* Takamasa Ikegami *Screenplay:* Nanase Okawa *Character Design:* Mokona Apapa, Tetsuro Aoki, Kiichi Takaoka, Futoshi Fujikawa *Chief Animators:* Tetsuro Aoki, Kiichi Takaoka *Art Director:* Yoji Nakaza, Masuo Nakayama *Music:* Nick Wood

A fanciful two-volume OAV retelling of the classic Vedic scriptures, the Rig Vedas, based on the manga by Clamp (TOKYO BABYLON, "Magic Knight Rayearth"). Six warriors must band together to overthrow a usurper to the throne of heaven. As usual with Clamp animation, the design work is stunning. Screenplay by Clamp's head writer Nanase Okawa, with character designs by the manga's artist Mokona Apapa. Released in Japan as "RG Veda" by Sony Music; available in North America through U.S. Manga Corps.

RG Veda Part 1

Legend says that a shimmering six-pointed star will rise into the heavens and restore the world to a golden age. The six points are six warriors, each with the power to move the stars and the hearts of all people. But now, there are only five: their leader Yasha; his companion, the child Ashura; the impetuous Ryuoh; the wise Karura; and Sohma, skilled in battle. The devious Taishakuten plots to undermine the courage of the warriors by leading them into a trap. Nobody suspects that the beautiful butterflies that descend into the remains of Yasha's village are really messengers of destruction. **45 min.**

RG Veda Part 2

The warriors' quest leads them into the heart of Taishakuten's castle. As his guards descend on Ashura, the youngest and most powerful warrior, she is mysteriously transported in a blaze of white light to another time dimension. Will she return safely and in time to rescue Yasha, who now lies beneath Taishakuten's sword? For if any of the five are killed, all hope of saving the universe is lost! Time is running out and the sixth point of the star is still unknown to the others. **41 min.**

Domestic Home Video:

RG Veda Part 1
USM 1079 ▲ $29.95 ▲ VHS ▲ SUB ▲ Stereo ▲ 01/05/94
ID 2866CT ▲ $34.95 ▲ LD ▲ SUB ▲ HiFi Stereo ▲ 11/08/94

RG Veda Part 2
USM 1080 ▲ $29.95 ▲ VHS ▲ SUB ▲ Stereo ▲ 04/06/94
ID 2874CT ▲ $34.95 ▲ LD ▲ SUB ▲ HiFi Stereo ▲ 04/05/95

Rhea Gall Force

(1989) ©MOVIC CBS/Sony Group, Inc.

Director: Katsuhito Akiyama *Original Story and Screenplay:* Hideki Kakinuma *Music:* Etsuko Yamakawa *Character Design:* Kenichi Sonoda

The Solnoid race is long dead, annihilated along with their enemies in the final battle at Sigma Narse. But their descendents survive on Earth, and have now inherited the sad destiny predicted so many centuries before. The year is 2085. The third world war between East and West has reduced the cities of Earth to mountains of rubble. The mechanical killing machines created by both sides now ruthlessly hunt down the remnants of humanity. Old hatreds between human factions prevent an effective resistance, and the only hope for survival rests in a desperate plan: evacuate the survivors to Mars base. There they can rebuild and plan the liberation of the home world. Among them, one young woman carries the guilt of her father's hand in the destruction of civilization. Unknown to her, she also carries the key to a possible salvation. As destiny draws new friends and allies to her, a new Gall Force is born to rise up against the coming destruction. **60 min.**

Also see GALL FORCE entry.

Domestic Home Video:

USM 1036 ▲ $29.95 ▲ VHS ▲ SUB ▲ Stereo ▲ 10/05/94
ID 2886CT ▲ $34.95 ▲ LD ▲ SUB ▲ HiFi Stereo ▲ 12/31/95

Riding Bean

(1989) ©Youmex, Inc.

Original Story and Character Design: Kenichi Sonoda
Director: Yasuo Hasegawa

A notorious Chicago getaway driver and his sharpshooter partner are set up to take the fall for a gang of kidnappers trying to skip town. When things go wrong, the action storms the streets of the Windy City, and this is all before the police get involved. Car chases, shootouts and sexual perversity in Chicago make this the perfect adaptation of a Kenichi Sonoda story; an authentic R&B soundtrack by Los Angeles performer Phil Perry clinches the atmosphere. A crowd-pleaser that compares favorably in mood to a *Lethal Weapon* or *48 Hrs.*, Sonoda would later go on to adapt RIDING BEAN's Rally Vincent and Bean Bandit as characters in his manga GUNSMITH CATS, now also an anime (see entry). Story and character designs are by Sonoda (GALL FORCE, BUBBLEGUM CRISIS). Released in Japan under the title "Riding Bean" by Toshiba EMI; available in North America through AnimEigo. **48 min.**

Domestic Home Video:
ANI ET094-001 ▲ $19.95 ▲ VHS ▲ DUB ▲ HiFi Stereo ▲ 03/30/94
ANI AT90-001 ▲ $24.95 ▲ VHS ▲ SUB ▲ HiFi Stereo
ANI AD093-004 ▲ $39.95 ▲ LD ▲ SUB ▲ HiFi Stereo ▲ 07/18/93

Robot Carnival

(1987) ©A.P.P.P. Co. Ltd.

Produced by: Kazufumi Nomura *Music:* Joe Hisaishi/Isaku Fujita/Masahisa Takechi

Nine of Japan's leading animators contributed segments to this compilation, each showcasing robots and independently produced: "Starlight Angel" by Hiroyuki Kitazume (MOLDIVER); the experimental "Cloud" by Mao Lamdo; "Deprive" by Hidetoshi Ohmori; "Franken's Gears" by Koji Morimoto; "Presence" by Yasuomi Umetsu; "A Tale Of Two Robots" by Hiroyuki Kitakubo (ROUJIN-Z); "Nightmare" by Takashi Nakamura. Opening and closing sequences are by Atsuko Fukushima and Katsuhiro Otomo (AKIRA). Each segment is worth seeing, although not all of them ("Clouds" comes to mind) are as easily accessible as others. Released in Japan as "Robot Carnival" by Victor Entertainment; available in North America through Streamline Pictures. **100 min.**

Domestic Home Video:
BFV 958 ▲ $19.95 ▲ VHS ▲ DUB ▲ Mono ▲ 08/15/93 ▲ Out of Print
SPV 90014 ▲ $29.95 ▲ VHS ▲ DUB ▲ Mono ▲ 12/01/91
LUM 9267 ▲ $39.95 ▲ LD ▲ DUB ▲ Mono ▲ 10/18/93 ▲ Out of Print

Robotech

TV series, 85 episodes

(1985) ©Harmony Gold USA/Tatsunoko Prod. Co./ZIV International

Produced by: Carl Macek

Odds are you're already familiar with this U.S.-broadcast mecha series, which amalgamated three separate Japanese TV series from the venerable Tatsunoko Productions (SPEED RACER, TEKNOMAN) into one sprawling storyline, supposedly representing different generations of characters fighting successive waves of alien invaders in the 21st century. The first story arc, a nearly intact "Superdimensional Fortress Macross" (1982-83), provided the base for the other two—"Southern Cross" (1984) and "Mospeada"(1983-84)—which were nearly completely rewritten to fit into the "Macross"-based continuity. ROBOTECH spawned a toy line (domestic releases of the Japanese "Macross" and "Mospeada" toys, some of which have been recently re-released under the "Exo-Squad" line) and many spinoff comics, based in the ROBOTECH universe, which continue to be produced to this day. An 65-episode original sequel, "Robotech II," was to have been produced by Tatsunoko, but the commercial failure of the ROBOTECH toys resulted in only four episodes being made; these were released in one volume as ROBOTECH II: THE SENTINELS. Although the approach taken by the series' U.S. producers remains highly controversial, the show managed to exhibit many of the more daring and creative aspects of Japanese animation to a wide American audience and did a great deal for U.S. recognition of the medium. Released in Japan under the titles "Chô Jikû Yôsai (Superdimensional Fortress) Macross," "Chô Jikû Kidan (Superdimensional Calvary)

Southern Cross," and "Kikô Sôsei (Machine-Armor Genesis) Mospeada" by Hero/Bandai Visual, Taki Corporation, and Hero/Bandai Visual; available in North America as "Robotech" through Family Home Entertainment and in a different, "Perfect Collection" edition by Streamline Pictures, which includes subtitled versions of the original Japanese episodes put together with their corresponding ROBOTECH episodes.

Robotech Vol. 1: *Episodes 1 and 2*

Episode 1: BOOBYTRAP, and Episode 2: COUNTDOWN. In 2099, the entire Earth celebrates the launching of *SDF-1*, a huge alien spaceship which crashed on Macross Island ten years earlier and has been reconstructed. Lt. Commander Fokker is outraged when his young friend Rick Hunter upstages the air show with his daredevil flying - but all this is forgotten when the Zentraedi, savage alien warriors, launch an attack on the ship. As the invaders rain destruction on the Earth, Captain Gloval realizes that despite an untested ship and an inexperienced crew he must take *SDF-1* into battle. Rick Hunter, in the midst of struggling to control a Veritech fighter and survive the onslaught, meets Lynn Minmei, a charming young girl whose life he must now save. **45 min.**

Robotech Vol. 2: *Episodes 3 and 4*

Episode 3: SPACE FOLD and Episode 4: THE LONG WAIT. As the alien attack on Earth continues, Fokker must rescue Rick and Minmei, while Captain Gloval searches for a way to save *SDF-1* from destruction by the merciless Zentraedi. His solution is the space fold maneuver - transporting the ship into deep space and leaving the attackers behind. Unfortunately, the jump also causes Macross Island and its 70,000 residents to be transported into hyperspace. As Captain Gloval discovers that the fold system has vanished, preventing a return to Earth, the crew of *SDF-1* works frantically to retrieve the civilians. Meanwhile, trapped in a remote corner of the vast ship, Rick and Minmei struggle for their own survival. **45 min.**

Robotech Vol. 3: *Episodes 5 and 6*

Episode 5: TRANSFORMATION and Episode 6: BLITZKRIEG. Macross City is reconstructed aboard *SDF-1* and its citizens, including Rick Hunter and Minmei, try to resume their lives. But their attempts are disrupted as Captain Gloval discovers how to transform *SDF-1* into its awesome robotic configuration - just in time to do battle with the approaching Zentraedi armada. The Earthlings repel the enemy, but again must recover from massive damage. Rick has resisted becoming a Veritech combat pilot, but soon he has no choice: the Zentraedi attack again and Rick and the Robotech forces see furious action. Desperate, Gloval attempts a blitzkrieg maneuver against the alien warriors and the battle rages through the rings of Saturn. **45 min.**

Robotech Vol. 4: *Episodes 7 and 8*

Episode 7: BYE-BYE MARS and Episode 8: SWEET SIXTEEN. Breetai, commander of the Zentraedi forces, takes steps to capture *SDF-1*: he sets a trap for the ship and calls for help from the ruthless warlord Khyron. When the Robotech fortress visits Mars to investigate the fate of Sara observation base, gravity mines hold the ship and Khyron attacks. Lisa Hayes, exploring the destroyed base, attempts a daring plan to explode the gravity mines. The plan succeeds, but Lisa avoids death only through Rick Hunter's last minute rescue. Saved for the moment, *SDF-1* orbits Mars. Aboard, Minmei prepares a party for her sixteenth birthday. But the celebration is interrupted when Khyron launches another furious attack on the wounded ship. **45 min.**

Robotech Vol. 5: *Episodes 9 and 10*

Episode 9: MISS MACROSS and Episode 10: BLIND GAME. To boost morale while they struggle with the aliens, Macross City holds a beauty contest and Minmei is named Miss Macross. Watching the broadcast, the Zentraedi are mystified. In their culture the sexes do not mingle or indulge in music, dance or fashion. Seeking to discover more, the Zentraedi commander Breetai dispatches a reconnaissance squad - which is all but destroyed by Rick Hunter. Khyron again attacks *SDF-1* and succeeds in knocking out the ship's radar. As Captain Gloval refuses an ultimatum to surrender, Lisa Hayes mounts a dangerous mission to pilot a radar ship into Zentraedi-controlled space under the protection of Rick Hunter's Vermillion Squad. **45 min.**

Robotech Vol. 6: *Episodes 11 and 12*

Episode 11: FIRST CONTACT and Episode 12: THE BIG ESCAPE. Captured while on their mission, Lisa, Rick and Ben are taken to the Zentraedi flagship and questioned by Dolza, the supreme commander. The giant aliens are mystified by the Earthlings' customs and shocked to observe Rick and Lisa kissing. They are convinced that *SDF-1* holds the secret to protoculture, the substance that allowed their race to develop, and plan to infiltrate the ship with spies. When Lisa, Rick and Ben initiate a plan to escape, they discover that their guard is Max Sterling in disguise. He has come to rescue his friends and, despite a perilous pursuit by the Zentraedi, they succeed in returning to *SDF-1*. **45 min.**

Robotech Vol. 7: *Episodes 13 and 14*

Episode 13: BLUE WIND, and Episode 14: GLOVAL'S REPORT. Completing their escape, Lisa, Rick, Max, and Ben return to *SDF-1* and a hero's welcome. They relate what they have learned of the Zentraedi, and receive promotions. Meanwhile, the alien spies, shrunk down to human size, try to blend in and are amazed by what they observe. In a daring plan, Captain Gloval pilots the battle fortress back towards Earth. The Zentraedi commander Khyron pursues, and is about to destroy the Micronians, when his superior, Azonia, forbids him to proceed. Gloval has counted on this, and safely pilots *SDF-1* back to Earth. After two years in deep space, the Robotech ship is home, and Gloval prepares a full report. **45 min.**

Robotech Vol. 8: *Episodes 15 and 16*
Episode 15: HOMECOMING and Episode 16: BATTLE CRY. Captain Gloval and Commander Lisa Hayes give their report and try to convince the United Earth Government to negotiate a truce with the Zentraedi. Meanwhile, Rick Hunter and Minmei visit Minmei's parents - who are shocked that they are alive. The government has circulated word that *SDF-1*, Macross Island and all its inhabitants have been destroyed by terrorists. Because the government wants to maintain its story - and prevent Earth from learning of the alien attack - it refuses to negotiate with the Zentraedi and won't allow the landing of the 70,000 inhabitants of Macross Island. *SDF-1* must return to space, only to face another furious attack from Khyron and his forces. **45 min.**

Robotech Vol. 9: *Episodes 17 and 18*
Episode 17: PHANTASM and Episode 18: FAREWELL, BIG BROTHER. Rick Hunter, seriously wounded in an incredible aerial dogfight, is in the hospital. While his body fights for life, his delirious mind travels through a phantasmagoric dreamscape where both Lynn Minmei and Lisa Hayes make appearances. While Rick recovers, Roy Fokker's squadron takes on a fierce Zentraedi attack led by Miriya, a beautiful pilot. She challenges Max Sterling and follows him into the ship itself, intent on destroying him. Their battle wreaks havoc on the city, but finally she fails. In the raging battle, Roy is wounded. At first, the wound doesn't seem serious, but later that night, Roy dies. It is up to Lisa Hayes to tell Rick that his "big brother" is gone. **45 min.**

Robotech Vol. 10: *Episodes 19 and 20*
Episode 19: BURSTING POINT, and Episode 20: PARADISE LOST: With the civilian population of *SDF-1* shrinking due to the catastrophes of war, Captain Gloval is desperate to relocate the survivors to Earth. His broadcast appeal is responded to by the North American Ontario quadrant, but before Gloval can land the refugees, Khyron attacks again. In the face of the Zentraedi offensive, Gloval tries a new barrier-shield system. It protects the ship, but with drastic results: a system overload leads to a chain reaction which destroys part of the Veritech squad and a 25-mile area of Earth. The Earth government lays down the law - the battle fortress is dangerous, and must not come near the planet! **45 min.**

Robotech Vol. 11: *Episodes 21 and 22*

Episode 21: A NEW DAWN and Episode 22: BATTLE HYMN. A lull in the war with the Zentraedi invaders allows the citizens of Macross City to celebrate the premiere of Minmei's first film. She co-stars with her cousin Kyle, and the film is a huge hit with everyone except Rick Hunter and Lisa Hayes. Rick still loves Minmei; Lisa still loves Kyle; and neither can stand to see the one they love kissing someone else - even if it is only a movie. Even more upset are the Zentraedi who have never seen a movie before and think that humans have developed a new weapon. As the Zentraedi prepare to respond, dissension once again breaks out in their ranks and the renegade warrior Khyron launches an attack on Macross City just as the humans are gathering for Minmei's concert. **45 min.**

Robotech Vol. 12: *Episodes 23 and 24*
Episode 23: RECKLESS and Episode 24: SHOWDOWN. Khyron's attack takes its toll on Macross City as fierce combat rages in the streets. But almost certain victory for the warlord proves elusive when growing numbers of his troops begin to desert, going off in search of the movie star Minmei. Even stranger still, the deserters turn out to be genetically identical to humans. This convinces Captain Gloval that peace is perhaps possible between the Zentraedi and humans. Lisa volunteers to return to Earth to try to convince her father, Admiral Hayes, and the rest of the reluctant military command to resume peace negotiations. Meanwhile, action on the romantic front heats up when Max Sterling falls for Miriya, a girl who's also a video game wizard. Minmei's cousin Kyle, recovered from his battle wounds, surprises Minmei by proposing marriage in front of a crowd of reporters. **45 min.**

Robotech Vol. 13: *Episodes 25 and 26*
Episode 25: WEDDING BELLS and Episode 26: THE MESSENGER. Max Sterling is waiting in a park to meet his new girlfriend Miriya when suddenly he is attacked. His assailant is none other than Miriya herself - she is out to kill him. Max subdues her, and the girl makes an astonishing confession: she is actually a Zentraedi warrior, their greatest pilot, and she is tired of being humiliated time and again by Max. She demands that he take her life. Instead, he proposes marriage. The wedding is to be a monumental and unique occasion, the first marriage ever between human and alien. Before the ceremony, Captain Gloval addresses the crowd, pleading for peace, but a faction of the Zentraedi launches an attack on the humans. A truce is finally called, and in the peace talks that follow, the alien leaders reveal that one of the humans' greatest weapons is the psychological power of Minmei's singing, which has influenced so many of the Zentraedi warriors to desert from battle. **45 min.**

Robotech Vol. 14: *Episodes 27 and 28*
Episode 27: FORCE OF ARMS and Episode 28: RECONSTRUCTION BLUES. The alien Zentraedi launch an attack on Earth with their entire armed force. Whole cities are obliterated in a matter of moments. The humans counter-attack with two weapons: one psychological, the other military. Minmei's singing with its disorienting effects on the aliens is broadcast to the enemy. Meanwhile, Captain Gloval directs the battle fortress *SDF-1* into a head-on collision with the alien flagship, destroying the entire attacking armada. Planet Earth has been severely damaged. But the humans' will to survive and rebuild is indomitable. Two years later as he surveys the damage from the sky, Rick Hunter is amazed by all the reconstruction and the signs of new life everywhere. With the passage of time, Rick and Lisa Hayes have become closer friends while Kyle and Minmei have drifted further apart. **45 min.**

Robotech Vol. 15: *Episodes 29 and 30*
Episode 29: THE ROBOTECH MASTERS and Episode 30: VIVA MIRIYA. From their home in a remote galaxy, the Robotech Masters have finally managed to locate their lost battle fortress, the *SDF-1*, the same ship used to wipe out the Zentraedi armada. Meanwhile, many of the former Zentraedi warriors left on Earth are growing restless and uneasy. Trained for combat alone, they are lost and confused in a life of peace. Large numbers have begun to ominously leave the cities and assemble in the planet's vast desert wastelands. At the same time, other Zentraedi are working together with Earth's human leaders, making plans in case the Robotech Masters should venture to this galaxy in search of their long-lost battle fortress. **45 min.**

Robotech Vol. 16: *Episodes 31 and 32*

Episode 31: KHYRON'S REVENGE and Episode 32: BROKEN HEART. Khyron continues his relentless attacks on Earth and achieves his aim of controlling the last remaining protoculture chamber. Zentraedi who have shrunken themselves to live on Earth are now lining up to return to their former giant size - and become part of Khyron's army. In a desperate defense against the alien forces, the Veritech warriors take to the sky. But the odds are overwhelming and Minmei and Kyle are captured. Gloating, Khyron takes the two back to his ship and holds them for ransom. The price for their return is the Robotech battle fortress *SDF-1*. With Minmei and Kyle's fates in their hands, Rick Hunter and Lisa Hayes launch an urgent mission to save them. **45 min.**

Robotech Vol. 17: *Episodes 33 and 34*
Episode 33: A RAINY NIGHT and Episode 34: PRIVATE TIME. When Lisa Hayes' relationship with Rick Hunter fizzles, Claudia shares some advice with her. She tells Lisa the story of her courtship with the late Ray Fokker - a stormy affair that blossomed into love. Communication is the most important thing, Claudia counsels, and Lisa should let Rick know how she feels. Minmei has returned from a morale-boosting tour of the frontier, and she's eager to see Rick. He can't turn down her invitation, and keeps Lisa waiting for a picnic they have planned. When he finally arrives, things go well until Lisa smells Minmei's perfume on Rick's scarf and leaves Rick to ponder his conflicting emotions. **45 min.**

Robotech Vol. 18: *Episodes 35 and 36*
Episode 35: SEASON'S GREETINGS and Episode 36: TO THE STARS. While the humans prepare to counterattack the Zentraedi invaders, Admiral Gloval promotes Lisa Hayes to commander of the newly-built *SDF-2*, and she finally finds the courage to tell Rick of her affection for him. Forced to confront his feelings, Rick realizes he loves Lisa and he leaves Minmei as the Earth forces fly into battle. In his frenzy to destroy the Earthlings, Khyron mounts a climactic attack that disables the already weakened *SDF-1*. Using his ship as a brutal weapon, he continues his mission of destruction, steering his ship into a head-on collision that unleashes awesome devastation and decides the fates of Gloval, Lisa, and the populations of *SDF-1* and *SDF-2* - and of Khyron himself. The consequences mark the end of an era in Earth's relations with the aliens. **45 min.**

Robotech Vol. 19: *Episodes 37 and 38*
Episode 37: DANA'S STORY and Episode 38: FALSE START. Fifteen years after the destruction of *SDF-1* and *SDF-2* and the Zentraedi holocaust, Dana, the daughter of Max Sterling and Miriya, is among the first graduates of the United Earth Forces Military Academy. The academy is an oasis of order and optimism on the ravaged planet, but the mood changes when the Robotech Masters arrive from far space in pursuit of their long-lost protoculture factory. Now the pilots are on emergency alert. Dana is bright and spunky, and she manages to get herself thrown in the brig because of her escapades. But she gets out in time to shine when she leads her squad into batle with the Robotech Masters. The aliens are surprised by the Earthlings' bold defense, and the first encounter ends with neither side victorious. **45 min.**

Robotech Vol. 20: *Episodes 39 and 40*
Episode 39: THE SOUTHERN CROSS and Episode 40: VOLUNTEERS. As the Robotech Masters continue their attacks, the Earth goes on alert for war. Dana Sterling is assigned to a defensive position, away from the action. When she sees the main base is in jeopardy, she enters the fight and changes the course of the battle, forcing the bioroids away.

Violence Profanity Nudity Sexual Situations **Adult Viewers Only** - content is extreme and/or explicit
143

Acclaimed as a hero and promoted, Dana volunteers for an even more dangerous mission - reestablishing control of Space Station Liberty. With fellow volunteer Marie Crystal, Dana flies to the orbital station where she wages a furious battle to free the base and comes face-to-face with the giant red bioroid which has been haunting her dreams. The alien invaders fight fiercely to hold on to the vital communication link, testing the abilities of Dana and Marie. **45 min.**

Robotech Vol. 21: *Episodes 41 and 42*

Episode 41: HALF MOON and Episode 42: DANGER ZONE. When Dana and Bowie engage an advance party of Robotech warriors in a fiery skirmish near the ruins of New Macross City, Bowie is captured. The aliens are excavating the crash site of *SDF-1* - backed up by a massive bioroid attack. Dana, circumventing her orders, mounts a dangerous rescue operation while Bowie attempts his own escape. Trying to avoid a battle on Earth, Supreme Commander Leonard sends the Global forces into space to attack the enemy, but the result is a disaster, with many killed and captured. Again, Dana and the 15th Squad must come to the rescue, using an untried plan to disrupt the workings of the huge Robotech fortress. With the fates of the prisoners and possibly all of Earth in the balance, Dana and the 15th roar into battle against the Robotech Masters. **45 min.**

Robotech Vol. 22: *Episodes 43 and 44*

Episode 43: PRELUDE TO BATTLE and Episode 44: THE TRAP. As Dana and the 15th Squad prepare for a reconnaissance mission on the downed alien battle fortress, Bowie Grant is arrested twice by the Global Military Police in an off-limits music club. His desire to play the piano lands him in a cell just when the rest of the squad leaves for its assignment. Bowie is freed in time to join his comrades as they penetrate and explore the ominous alien battleship - secretly observed all the while by the Robotech Masters. Their discoveries include a high tech biomechanical android factory and Musica, a mysterious and beguiling woman who plays a cosmic harp. By the time they realize they are in a trap, the 15th Squad is locked in jeopardy deep within the deadly fortress. **47 min.**

Robotech Vol. 23: *Episodes 45 and 46*

Episode 45: METAL FIRE and Episode 46: STARDUST. Examining a captured bioroid, the Earth Forces struggle to unlock the nature and motives of the Robotech invaders. Risking her position, Dana objects to a plan to kill the opposing pilots - she feels a strange kinship with the aliens. Meanwhile, the Robotech Masters are eager to regain the protoculture matrix before another alien race, the Invid, reaches Earth. They decide to take human prisoners to probe their knowledge and usefulness. Combat rages through the city as the invaders seize Earthlings and the Global Command counterattacks. Dana carries out a desperate mission to destroy the Robotech ship, but when the aliens receive help from their hidden armada, her plans go awry. **48 min.**

Robotech Vol. 24: *Episodes 47 and 48*

Episode 47: OUTSIDERS and Episode 48: DEJA VU. Zor Prime, an enemy bioroid pilot suffering from amnesia, is captured by the Global Forces. They think he is an Earthling forced into service, not realizing that he is a clone of the genius who invented Robotechnology, and that the Robotech Masters have implanted controls in him. As the military police probe and study Zor, the aliens are aware of their every move. Dana's half-alien parentage continues to cause her confusing feelings and strange dreams. Bowie cannot stop thinking about Musica, the alien harpist. But their personal problems are small when compared to the frayed defenses of Earth. A reconnaissance mission from *SDF-3* fights through the alien war fleet and is rescued by the 15th Squad, only to bring word that no aid will be coming. **47 min.**

Robotech Vol. 25: *Episodes 49 and 50*

Episode 49: A NEW RECRUIT and Episode 50: TRIUMVIRATE. The captured alien Zor is made a member of the 15th Squad, which delights Dana, but not all the others. She enjoys training the exceptional new recruit and feels a kinship with him. With their secret control of Zor, the Robotech Masters are able to observe military plans made on Earth. When Commander Leonard, despite opposition from some, throws the Earth forces into a full-blown battle, they take advantage of their knowledge. In a fiery clash, the human forces must struggle against a superior enemy. The 15th Squad is left out of the battle. Instead, they take Zor to the buried wreck of *SDF-1*, where the eerie remains and strange growths stimulate his memory of his mysterious previous life. **48 min.**

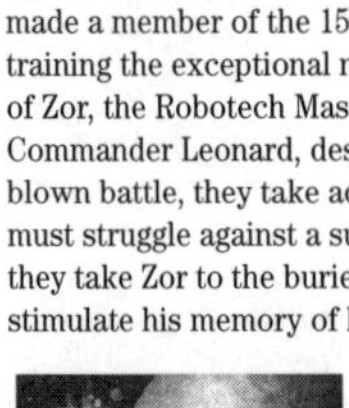

Robotech Vol. 26: *Episodes 51 and 52*

Episode 51: CLONE CHAMBER and Episode 52: LOVE SONG. The Robotech Masters' supply of protoculture is dwindling, causing their bioroids to malfunction and their enemies, the Invids, to draw closer. Still, their remaining forces, aided by intelligence unknowingly supplied by Zor, are formidable. They keep the combat pressure on Air Cavalry One, led by Lieutenant Marie Crystal, which has been sent to rescue the defeated Earth attack fleet. Supreme Commander Leonard plans a second offensive against the aliens and places General Emerson in charge. Emerson opposes Leonard and knows that the mission is perilous, but he assumes his duty and prepares for the struggle. Meanwhile, Military Intelligence searches for the source of the continuing leaks, without success. Marie keeps up her pursuit of Sean, and finally gets what she wants - a date. Unfortunately, things aren't always what they seem, and the evening takes a bewildering turn. **47 min.**

Robotech Vol. 27: *Episodes 53 and 54*

Episode 53: THE HUNTERS and Episode 54: MIND GAME. While playing games with the other members of the 15th Squad, Louie devises a system for targeting weapons with eyesight. He and Dana develop the device for training purposes, but when the military uses it for combat, Louie revolts and tries to destroy his creation. The Earth Defense Fleet, under General Emerson, needs Louie's invention for the titanic struggle against the Robotech Masters. Both sides unleash massive forces and the balance swings back and forth. Zor rallies Dana and the 15th Squad as their attack blasts and penetrates the enemy command ship. But, when victory seems at hand, the alien commanders reactivate their hidden neurosensor in Zor and the brave warrior for Earth again becomes a pawn in their game. **47 min.**

Robotech Vol. 28: *Episodes 55 and 56*

Episode 55: DANA IN WONDERLAND and Episode 56: CRISIS POINT. Pursued all the while, Dana and the 15th Squad range through the Robotech Masters' command ship, discovering many of the secrets of life in this complex alien civilization. The advanced biotechnology allows complete control of the cloned population - but contact with humans and their emotions has an unsettling effect on them. Bowie finds Musica, the alien woman who has haunted his thoughts. He is able to help her unlock the emotions hidden within her and she rebels against the cold-hearted Masters. With Musica's help, Zor also overcomes the mental control of the alien masters and rejoins his human friends. Now the challenge is to escape from the huge ship as the Robotech Masters fight furiously for control. And Zor, now neither programmed clone nor human, must find his own destiny. **47 min.**

Robotech Vol. 29: *Episodes 57 and 58*

Episode 57: DAY DREAMER and Episode 58: FINAL NIGHTMARE. Musica returns to Earth with the 15th Squad and the rest of the attack fleet, but Nova and the military police think that she may be a spy. Bowie and Musica flee to the ruins of *SDF-1*, where the protoculture has been invaded by the Invid "Flower of Life," forerunners of an enemy alien race. With the Invid flowers also depleting the protoculture aboard their command ship, the Robotech Masters are losing control of the clone population. Desperate, they plan an all-out effort to seize Earth's supply. Their attack will be met by an equally furious campaign led by Emerson. Zor regains his memory of the past when he sees the Invid flowers in *SDF-1* - now the true nature of protoculture and the Invid threat can be explained. **48 min.**

Robotech Vol. 30: *Episodes 59 and 60*

Episode 59: THE INVID CONNECTION and Episode 60: CATASTROPHE. The second Robotech War reaches a climax as the Robotech Masters and the Earth Forces meet in total combat. The aliens take brutal steps in a desperate fight for survival, while the humans struggle against their huge armada. As he maneuvers to defend Earth, Emerson is captured. A prisoner exchange to regain Emerson goes awry and the 15th Squad is trapped aboard the alien fortress-ship. Zor reveals his goal - rebellion against the culture which his former self created. Bent on destruction, Zor demolishes the Robotech Masters' power - and their ship. The immediate danger has passed, but the protoculture has been spread over the Earth - making an Invid onslaught inevitable. **48 min.**

Robotech Vol. 31: *Episodes 61 and 62*

Episode 61: THE INVID INVASION and Episode 62: THE LOST CITY. The alien Invids have conquered Earth, turning it into a giant protoculture farming colony essential to their plans to dominate the universe. When the Invid destroy Admiral Hunter's rescuing force, Robotech Commander Scott Bernard finds himself alone on the Earth's surface. As he remembers his fellow freedom fighters and his fiancée Marlene, now dead in battle, Scott vows to destroy the Invid headquarters known as "Reflex Point." Scott joins forces with rebel fighter Rand and they start a dangerous journey toward the very heartland of the Invid empire. They meet little Annie whose boyfriend Ken leads them into a deadly trap in a devastated island city. Suddenly surrounded by overwhelming Invid forces, Scott, Rand and Annie are aided in their battle by a mysterious female cyclone warrior. **45 min.**

Robotech Vol. 32: *Episodes 63 and 64*

Episode 63: LONELY SOLDIER BOY and Episode 64: SURVIVAL. Robotech Commander Scott Bernard, rebel fighter Rand and little Annie reach a desert outpost on the edge of the Invid empire where they are joined by three new freedom fighters: Lunk, who repairs and rearms a Veritech Alpha fighter; the mystery female cyclone warrior Rook Bartley; and Lancer, who as rock star Yellow Dancer fights for freedom undetected by the Invid or their human spies. After battling off both the Invid and outlaw soldiers, the Robotechs elude their pursuers in a mysterious and danger-filled forest. The band then makes a terrifying discovery - the Invid are tracking them by the scent of protoculture given off by their weapons. At first reluctant to use Lunk's hidden Veritech fighter, Scott Bernard pilots the powerful ship against the Invid, striking the first blow for Earth's freedom. **46 min.**

Robotech Vol. 33: *Episodes 65 and 66*

Episode 65: CURTAIN CALL and Episodes 66: HARD TIMES. Using Yellow Dancer's rock concert as a diversion, Commander Scott Bernard leads the freedom fighters in a daring

daylight assault on the Invid stronghold, overcoming its human security force and making off with a sizeable supply of protoculture weapon fuel. Enraged, the Invid throw everything they have into their pursuit of the intrepid Robotech warriors. Later, as the Robotechs prepare to penetrate further into the Invid empire, Rook remembers her betrayal to the feared Red Snake gang by the man she once loved. With Rand protectively trailing her, Rook returns to her home town to challenge the Red Snake leader in the ultimate game of chicken. Then as the Invid attack Scott's Veritech fighter, Rook realizes that she must forget the past - her loyalty is now to her new Robotech family. **45 min.**

Robotech Vol. 34: *Episodes 67 and 68*
Episode 67: PAPER HERO and Episode 68: EULOGY. A battle rages as the Robotech fighters destroy an enemy scout troop and head for a nearby village to help Lunk keep a promise made in battle to a dying comrade. Lunk is afraid he is a coward but is determined to seek out his dead comrade's father and return a mysterious book to him. When the fearful and hostile villagers turn on the freedom fighters, Lunk proves himself a hero as he comes to the Robotechs' rescue - just in time for an Invid attack. Later, near an Invid stronghold, the valiant defenders stumble upon a military outpost under the command of Colonel Jonathan Wolff, one of Admiral Hunter's new brand of Robotech defenders and a hero of the Robotech Wars. But Rand begins to believe that Colonel Wolff is not the hero everyone believes him to be. **44 min.**

Robotech Vol. 35: *Episodes 69 and 70*
Episode 69: THE GENESIS PIT and Episode 70: ENTER MARLENE. The Invid use their advanced biogenetic engineering to make a genesis pit in which to create Earth creatures - from prehistory to modern times - to further their quest for universal domination. Scott, Rand and Annie accidentally fall into the pit and must battle not only Invid troops but flesh-eating dinosaurs as well. After the genesis pit is destroyed, the Invid decide to introduce a human-looking female simul-agent into the ranks of the Robotech warriors. The freedom fighters are on their way to meet up with Admiral Hunter's advance attack force. When they find the force destroyed, Scott goes into a deep depression, certain that nothing and no one can overcome the Invids. But the appearance of the mysterious woman and two usable Veritech fighter planes brings him to his senses and he leads the Robotechs back into battle. **45 min.**

Robotech Vol. 36: *Episodes 71 and 72*
Episode 71: THE SECRET ROUTE and Episode 72: THE FORTRESS. As winter and Invid shock troops close in, the Robotech fighters head for a local village to search out a way through the mountains to the Invid heartland. The village mayor promises a map to anyone with money. Only his beautiful fiancée, Carla, knows the map's horrible secret. Carla has another secret; she was the one responsible for helping Lancer escape the Invid by creating his female rock star disguise. Then the Robotech fighters must stage a daring attack on an abandoned Robotech mountain fortress now used by the Invid as a military base and research laboratory. The group's plans are complicated by the discovery of a massive living computer and the fact that they cannot activate their weapons or vehicles - their protoculture fuel will attract Invid troops. **44 min.**

Robotech Vol. 37: *Episodes 73 and 74*
Episode 73: SANDSTORMS and Episode 74: ANNIE'S WEDDING. Unknown to even herself, Marlene is an Invid simul-agent and the closer the freedom fighters get to the Invid stronghold, the more the girl experiences painful attacks. As Rand searches the desert for some help for the girl, he falls victim to an Invid sandstorm and a nightmare hallucination, gaining further insight into the destructive power of the Invid and their mission on Earth. While the Invid continue their biotechnic experiments, the Robotech defenders find themselves in the midst of battle with their fuel cells down to a desperate point. They escape into a sacred Invid garden but are accused of offending the local tribe's river god. Scott and Lunk find a way to use the river's might to turn back the Invid and become heroes to the tribesmen. Annie says goodbye to her Robotech friends and stays with the tribe. **45 min.**

Robotech Vol. 38: *Episodes 75 and 76*
Episode 75: SEPARATE WAYS and Episode 76: METAMORPHOSIS. Trapped by the Invid in an abandoned subway tunnel in a ruined city, the Robotech friends begin to bicker among themselves. Lunk goes amok and blames Scott for their predicament - everyone but Scott wants to get away from the danger and the fighting. After the band's escape Rand and Rook decide to go off on their own. Annie returns from the sacred garden just as the group splits apart. But driven by a sense of fellowship and a hope for the future, the Robotech freedom fighters rejoin their forces. They decide to rest on a tropical island paradise near an abandoned Robotech base.

However, the Invid Queen transforms her royal children into perfect human replicas to contact the simul-agent Marlene and activate her spy mechanism. If she does not activate properly, they are to destroy Marlene and the rest of the Robotechs. **45 min.**

Robotech Vol. 39: *Episodes 77 and 78*
Episode 77: THE MIDNIGHT SUN and Episode 78: GHOST TOWN. Haunted by her memories of Lancer and confused by the new human emotions growing inside her, the

Invid princess Sera is ordered by her mother, the Regis, into battle against the Robotech defenders. While the bloody fray rages around them, Sera and Marlene gaze at one another across a chasm - each not knowing the other but both feeling their intense kinship. The Invid Queen reaches out to Marlene, calling her back to the hive and the power of the Invid. Later in the vast desert of the American Southwest, the past comes vividly alive as Scott and his crew come face-to-face with a group of aging veterans of Admiral Rick Hunter's earlier wars. Though the young Robotech fighters doubt the ability and heroism of the veterans, they join forces in an attempt to destroy an Invid transmitting tower. **45 min.**

Robotech Vol. 40: *Episodes 79 and 80*
Episode 79: FROSTBITE and Episode 80: BIRTHDAY BLUES. High in the frigid Rocky Mountains and closing in on the Invid headquarters, the Robotech freedom fighters stumble across the remains of the lost city of Denver. The city's generator is still active and warming. Exploring the city's deserted streets and stores, Commander Scott Bernard and Marlene begin to fall in love while Lancer and Lunk try to repair the vehicles and Rook, Rand and Annie replenish the supplies. When the Invid attack, the Robotechs must leave their glimpse of civilization and return to the battle. Afterwards, in a small village, the warriors distract the Invid long enough to give young Annie a surprise birthday party. Though it is only a brief moment of joy, this night will long be remembered by these seven young people who are now much more than a band of warriors - they are now truly a family. **46 min.**

Robotech Vol. 41: *Episodes 81 and 82*
Episode 81: HIRED GUN and Episode 82: THE BIG APPLE. Rook Bartley and her fellow Robotechs come face-to-face with the inhumanity of the Invid in their quest for universal control. Dusty Ayres, once the horribly tortured captive of the Invid, has been taking deadly revenge on his friends who made no attempt to rescue him. When he meets Rook, his faith in humanity begins to be restored. Later, in the remains of New York City, the royal children of the Invid Queen, the Regis, argue over the fate of humankind. Prince Corg is determined to destroy the people of Earth while Princess Sera, feeling human emotions, argues against him. As Corg begins his death-dealing attack, Sera seeks out the simul-agent Ariel, known to the Robotechs as Marlene, for some answers as to why she is feeling compassion for the humans. **45 min.**

Robotech Vol. 42: *Episodes 83, 84 and 85*
Episode 83: REFLEX POINT, Episode 84: DARK FINALE and Episode 85: SYMPHONY OF LIGHT. As the Invid begin the process of transforming all their hibernating population into humanoids, an advance battalion of Admiral Hunter's fighters attack. Marlene finally remembers she is the Invid Ariel and runs away from her Robotech friends. On the dark side of the moon, Admiral Hunter launches his final invasion of Earth. As the battle looms, Ariel begs the Invid Queen to stop the war - reminding her how their own planet was stolen from them. And though Sera finally joins Ariel's pleas, neither the Invid nor Robotech will listen. Prince Corg and Commander Scott Bernard fight in mortal combat and the Invid race out to meet Admiral Hunter's fleet. As the desperate battle now rages in space as well as on Earth, all wonder whether the Earth will be destroyed or will peace ever come again to the planet. **67 min.**

Domestic Home Video:
Robotech Vol. 1
FHE 27465 ▲ $14.95 ▲ VHS ▲ DUB ▲ Mono ▲ CC,NR ▲ 08/18/93
Robotech Vol. 2
FHE 27466 ▲ $14.95 ▲ VHS ▲ DUB ▲ Mono ▲ CC,NR ▲ 08/18/93
Robotech Vol. 3
FHE 27467 ▲ $14.95 ▲ VHS ▲ DUB ▲ Mono ▲ CC,NR ▲ 08/18/93
Robotech Vol. 4
FHE 27468 ▲ $14.95 ▲ VHS ▲ DUB ▲ Mono ▲ CC,NR ▲ 08/18/93
Robotech Vol. 5
FHE 27469 ▲ $14.95 ▲ VHS ▲ DUB ▲ Mono ▲ CC,NR ▲ 08/18/93
Robotech Vol. 6
FHE 27470 ▲ $14.95 ▲ VHS ▲ DUB ▲ Mono ▲ CC,NR ▲ 08/18/93
Robotech Vol. 7
FHE 27471 ▲ $14.95 ▲ VHS ▲ DUB ▲ Mono ▲ CC,NR ▲ 08/18/93
Robotech Vol. 8
FHE 27472 ▲ $14.95 ▲ VHS ▲ DUB ▲ Mono ▲ CC,NR ▲ 08/18/93
Robotech Vol. 9
FHE 27473 ▲ $14.95 ▲ VHS ▲ DUB ▲ Mono ▲ CC,NR ▲ 08/18/93
Robotech Vol. 10
FHE 27474 ▲ $14.95 ▲ VHS ▲ DUB ▲ Mono ▲ CC,NR ▲ 08/18/93
Robotech Vol. 11
FHE 27493 ▲ $14.95 ▲ VHS ▲ DUB ▲ Mono ▲ CC,NR ▲ 01/26/94
Robotech Vol. 12
FHE 27494 ▲ $14.95 ▲ VHS ▲ DUB ▲ Mono ▲ CC,NR ▲ 01/26/94
Robotech Vol. 13
FHE 27495 ▲ $14.95 ▲ VHS ▲ DUB ▲ Mono ▲ CC,NR ▲ 01/26/94

 Violence   Profanity   Nudity   Sexual Situations   Adult Viewers Only - content is extreme and/or explicit

Robotech Vol. 14
FHE 27496 ▲ $14.95 ▲ VHS ▲ DUB ▲ Mono ▲ CC,NR ▲ 01/26/94
Robotech Vol. 15
FHE 27497 ▲ $14.95 ▲ VHS ▲ DUB ▲ Mono ▲ CC,NR ▲ 01/26/94
Robotech Vol. 16
FHE 27498 ▲ $14.95 ▲ VHS ▲ DUB ▲ Mono ▲ CC,NR ▲ 01/26/94
Robotech Vol. 17
FHE 27499 ▲ $14.95 ▲ VHS ▲ DUB ▲ Mono ▲ CC,NR ▲ 01/26/94
Robotech Vol. 18
FHE 27500 ▲ $14.95 ▲ VHS ▲ DUB ▲ Mono ▲ CC,NR ▲ 01/26/94
Robotech Vol. 19
FHE 27501 ▲ $14.95 ▲ VHS ▲ DUB ▲ Mono ▲ CC,NR ▲ 01/26/94
Robotech Vol. 20
FHE 27502 ▲ $14.95 ▲ VHS ▲ DUB ▲ Mono ▲ CC,NR ▲ 01/26/94
Robotech Vol. 21
FHE 27517 ▲ $14.95 ▲ VHS ▲ DUB ▲ Mono ▲ CC,NR ▲ 06/20/94
Robotech Vol. 22
FHE 27518 ▲ $14.95 ▲ VHS ▲ DUB ▲ Mono ▲ CC,NR ▲ 06/20/94
Robotech Vol. 23
FHE 27519 ▲ $14.95 ▲ VHS ▲ DUB ▲ Mono ▲ CC,NR ▲ 06/20/94
Robotech Vol. 24
FHE 27520 ▲ $14.95 ▲ VHS ▲ DUB ▲ Mono ▲ CC,NR ▲ 06/20/94
Robotech Vol. 25
FHE 27521 ▲ $14.95 ▲ VHS ▲ DUB ▲ Mono ▲ CC,NR ▲ 06/20/94
Robotech Vol. 26
FHE 27522 ▲ $14.95 ▲ VHS ▲ DUB ▲ Mono ▲ CC,NR ▲ 06/20/94
Robotech Vol. 27
FHE 27523 ▲ $14.95 ▲ VHS ▲ DUB ▲ Mono ▲ CC,NR ▲ 06/20/94
Robotech Vol. 28
FHE 27524 ▲ $14.95 ▲ VHS ▲ DUB ▲ Mono ▲ CC,NR ▲ 06/20/94
Robotech Vol. 29
FHE 27525 ▲ $14.95 ▲ VHS ▲ DUB ▲ Mono ▲ CC,NR ▲ 06/20/94
Robotech Vol. 30
FHE 27526 ▲ $14.95 ▲ VHS ▲ DUB ▲ Mono ▲ CC,NR ▲ 06/20/94
Robotech Vol. 31
FHE 27578 ▲ $14.95 ▲ VHS ▲ DUB ▲ Mono ▲ CC,NR ▲ 06/20/95
Robotech Vol. 32
FHE 27579 ▲ $14.95 ▲ VHS ▲ DUB ▲ Mono ▲ CC,NR ▲ 06/20/95
Robotech Vol. 33
FHE 27580 ▲ $14.95 ▲ VHS ▲ DUB ▲ Mono ▲ CC,NR ▲ 06/20/95
Robotech Vol. 34
FHE 27581 ▲ $14.95 ▲ VHS ▲ DUB ▲ Mono ▲ CC,NR ▲ 06/20/95
Robotech Vol. 35
FHE 27582 ▲ $14.95 ▲ VHS ▲ DUB ▲ Mono ▲ CC,NR ▲ 06/20/95
Robotech Vol. 36
FHE 27583 ▲ $14.95 ▲ VHS ▲ DUB ▲ Mono ▲ CC,NR ▲ 06/20/95
Robotech Vol. 37
FHE 27584 ▲ $14.95 ▲ VHS ▲ DUB ▲ Mono ▲ CC,NR ▲ 06/20/95
Robotech Vol. 38
FHE 27585 ▲ $14.95 ▲ VHS ▲ DUB ▲ Mono ▲ CC,NR ▲ 06/20/95
Robotech Vol. 39
FHE 27586 ▲ $14.95 ▲ VHS ▲ DUB ▲ Mono ▲ CC,NR ▲ 06/20/95
Robotech Vol. 40
FHE 27587 ▲ $14.95 ▲ VHS ▲ DUB ▲ Mono ▲ CC,NR ▲ 06/20/95
Robotech Vol. 41
FHE 27588 ▲ $14.95 ▲ VHS ▲ DUB ▲ Mono ▲ CC,NR ▲ 06/20/95
Robotech Vol. 42
FHE 27589 ▲ $14.95 ▲ VHS ▲ DUB ▲ Mono ▲ CC,NR ▲ 06/20/95
Robotech Macross Vol. 1: *Episodes 1-4*
FHE LD27465/6 ▲ $34.95 ▲ LD ▲ DUB ▲ Mono ▲ CC ▲ 08/18/93
Robotech Macross Vol. 2: *Episodes 5-8*
FHE LD27467/8 ▲ $34.95 ▲ LD ▲ DUB ▲ Mono ▲ CC ▲ 08/18/93
Robotech Macross Vol. 3: *Episodes 9-12*
FHE LD27469/0 ▲ $34.95 ▲ LD ▲ DUB ▲ Mono ▲ CC ▲ 08/18/93
Robotech Macross Vol. 4: *Episodes 13-16*
FHE LD27471/2 ▲ $34.95 ▲ LD ▲ DUB ▲ Mono ▲ CC ▲ 08/18/93
Robotech Macross Vol. 5: *Episodes 17-20*
FHE LD227473/4 ▲ $34.95 ▲ LD ▲ DUB ▲ Mono ▲ CC ▲ 08/18/93
Robotech Macross Vol. 6: *Episodes 21-24*
FHE LD27493/4 ▲ $34.95 ▲ LD ▲ DUB ▲ Mono ▲ CC ▲ 08/18/93
Robotech Macross Vol. 7: *Episodes 25-28*
FHE LD27495/6 ▲ $34.95 ▲ LD ▲ DUB ▲ Mono ▲ CC ▲ 08/18/93
Robotech Macross Vol. 8: *Episodes 29-32*
FHE LD27497/8 ▲ $34.95 ▲ LD ▲ DUB ▲ Mono ▲ CC ▲ 08/18/93

Robotech Macross Vol. 9: *Episodes 33-36*
FHE LD27499/5 ▲ $34.95 ▲ LD ▲ DUB ▲ Mono ▲ CC ▲ 08/18/93
Robotech Masters Vol. 1: *Episodes 37-40*
FHE LD27501/2 ▲ $34.95 ▲ LD ▲ DUB ▲ Mono ▲ CC ▲ 06/22/94
Robotech Masters Vol. 2: *Episodes 41-44*
FHE LD27517/8 ▲ $34.95 ▲ LD ▲ DUB ▲ Mono ▲ CC ▲ 06/22/94
Robotech Masters Vol. 3: *Episodes 45-48*
FHE LD27519/0 ▲ $34.95 ▲ LD ▲ DUB ▲ Mono ▲ CC ▲ 06/22/94
Robotech Masters Vol. 4: *Episodes 49-52*
FHE LD27521/2 ▲ $34.95 ▲ LD ▲ DUB ▲ Mono ▲ CC ▲ 06/22/94
Robotech Masters Vol. 5: *Episodes 53-56*
FHE LD27523/4 ▲ $34.95 ▲ LD ▲ DUB ▲ Mono ▲ CC ▲ 06/22/94
Robotech Masters Vol. 6: *Episodes 57-60*
FHE LD27525/6 ▲ $34.95 ▲ LD ▲ DUB ▲ Mono ▲ CC ▲ 06/22/94

Robotech Perfect Collection

(1982-1984) ©Tatsunoko Production Co. Ltd. ©1985 Harmony Gold, USA, Inc./Tatsunoko Production Co. Ltd.

A unique presentation of the hit American animated TV series, along with the original episodes of the Japanese programs which comprised it. Each SUPERDIMENSIONAL FORTRESS MACROSS, GENESIS CLIMBER MOSPEADA, and SUPERDIMENSIONAL CAVALRY SOUTHERN CROSS episode is taken from the best available uncut source material and subtitled from scripts provided by the original production company. Each ROBOTECH episode is shown exactly as it originally appeared on American television.

Robotech Perfect Collection- *Macross Vol. 1: Episodes 1 and 2*
Episodes #1 and #2 of *Super-Dimensional Fortress: MACROSS*, broadcast in Japan as *The Macross Special* in October 1982, and episodes #1 and #2 of *Robotech* as originally broadcast on US television in March 1985. **100 min.**

Robotech Perfect Collection- Macross Vol. 2: *Episodes 3 and 4*
Episodes #3 and #4 of *Super-Dimensional Fortress: MACROSS*, as broadcast in Japan in October 1982, and episodes #3 and #4 of *Robotech* as originally broadcast on US television in March 1985. **100 min.**

Robotech Perfect Collection- Macross Vol. 3: *Episodes 5 and 6*
Episodes #5 and #6 of *Super-Dimensional Fortress: MACROSS*, as broadcast in Japan in October and November 1982, and episodes #5 and #6 of *Robotech* as originally broadcast on US television in April 1985. **100 min.**

Robotech Perfect Collection- Macross Vol. 4: *Episodes 7 and 8*
Episodes #7 and #8 of *Super-Dimensional Fortress: MACROSS*, as broadcast in Japan in November 1982, and episodes #7 and #8 of *Robotech* as originally broadcast on US television in April 1985. **100 min.**

Robotech Perfect Collection- Macross Vol. 5: *Episodes 9 and 10*
Episodes #9 and #10 of *Super-Dimensional Fortress: MACROSS*, as broadcast in Japan in December 1982, and episodes #9 and #10 of *Robotech* as originally broadcast on US television in April 1985. **100 min.**

Robotech Perfect Collection- Macross Vol. 6: *Episodes 11 and 12*
Episodes #11 and #12 of *Super-Dimensional Fortress: MACROSS*, as broadcast in Japan in December 1982, and episodes #11 and #12 of *Robotech* as originally broadcast on US television in April 1985. **100 min.**

Robotech Perfect Collection- Macross Vol. 7: *Episodes 13 and 14*
Episodes #13 and #14 of *Super-Dimensional Fortress: MACROSS*, as broadcast in Japan in January 1983, and episodes #13 and #14 of *Robotech* as originally broadcast on US television in April 1985. **100 min.**

Robotech Perfect Collection- Macross Vol. 8: *Episodes 15 and 16*
Episodes #15 and #16 of *Super-Dimensional Fortress: MACROSS*, as broadcast in Japan in January 1983, and episodes #15 and #16 of *Robotech* as originally broadcast on US television in May 1985. **100 min.**

Robotech Perfect Collection- Mospeada Vol. 1: *Episodes 1 and 2*
Episodes 1 and 2 of *Genesis Climber: MOSPEADA* as broadcast in Japan in October 1983. Episodes 61 and 62 of *ROBOTECH* as broadcast on US television in Spring 1985. **100 min.**

Robotech Perfect Collection- Mospeada Vol. 2: *Episodes 3 and 4*
Episodes 3 and 4 of *Genesis Climber: MOSPEADA* as broadcast in Japan in October 1983. Episodes 63 and 64 of *ROBOTECH* as broadcast on US television in Spring 1985. **100 min.**

Robotech Perfect Collection- Mospeada Vol. 3: *Episodes 5 and 6*
Episodes 5 and 6 of *Genesis Climber: MOSPEADA* as broadcast in Japan in October and November 1983. Episodes 65 and 66 of *Robotech* as broadcast on US television in Spring 1985. **100 min.**

  Made for Television Broadcast   Made for Home Video Release   Made for Theatrical Release

Robotech Perfect Collection- Mospeada Vol. 4:
Episodes 7 and 8
Episodes 7 and 8 of *Genesis Climber: MOSPEADA* as broadcast in Japan in November 1983. Episodes 67 and 68 of *Robotech* as broadcast on US television in Spring 1985. **100 min.**

Robotech Perfect Collection- Mospeada Vol. 5:
Episodes 9 and 10
Episodes 9 and 10 of *Genesis Climber: MOSPEADA* as broadcast in Japan in November and December 1983. Episodes 69 and 70 of *Robotech* as broadcast on US television in Spring 1985. **100 min.**

Robotech Perfect Collection- Mospeada Vol. 6: *Episodes 11 and 12*
Episodes 11 and 12 of *Genesis Climber: MOSPEADA* as broadcast in Japan in December 1983. Episodes 71 and 72 of *Robotech* as broadcast on US television in Spring 1985. **100 min.**

Robotech Perfect Collection- Mospeada Vol. 7: *Episodes 13 and 14*
Episodes 13 and 14 of *Genesis Climber: MOSPEADA* as broadcast in Japan in December 1983. Episodes 73 and 74 of *Robotech* as broadcast on US television in Spring 1985. **100 min.**

Robotech Perfect Collection- Southern Cross Vol. 1: *Episodes 1 and 2*
Episodes 1 and 2 of *Super-Dimensional Cavalry: SOUTHERN CROSS* as broadcast in Japan in April 1984. Episodes 37, 38 and 39 of *Robotech* as broadcast on US television in Spring 1985. **125 min.**

Robotech Perfect Collection- Southern Cross Vol. 2: *Episodes 3 and 4*
Episodes 3 and 4 of *Super-Dimensional Cavalry: SOUTHERN CROSS* as broadcast in Japan in April & May1984. Episodes 40 and 41 of *Robotech* as broadcast on US television in Spring 1985. **100 min.**

Robotech Perfect Collection- Southern Cross Vol. 3: *Episodes 5 and 6*
Episodes 5 and 6 of *Super-Dimensional Cavalry: SOUTHERN CROSS* as broadcast in Japan in May 1984. Episodes 42 and 43 of *Robotech* as broadcast on US television in Spring 1985. **100 min.**

Robotech Perfect Collection- Southern Cross Vol. 4: *Episodes 7 and 8*
Episodes 7 and 8 of *Super-Dimensional Cavalry: SOUTHERN CROSS* as broadcast in Japan in May & June 1984. Episodes 44 and 45 of *Robotech* as broadcast on US television in Spring 1985. **100 min.**

Robotech Perfect Collection- Southern Cross Vol. 5: *Episodes 9 and 10*
Episodes 9 and 10 of *Super-Dimensional Cavalry: SOUTHERN CROSS* as broadcast in Japan in June 1984. Episodes 46 and 47 of *Robotech* as broadcast on US television in Spring 1985. **100 min.**

Robotech Perfect Collection- Southern Cross Vol. 6: *Episodes 11 and 12*
Episodes 11 and 12 of *Super-Dimensional Cavalry: SOUTHERN CROSS* as broadcast in Japan in June and July 1984. Episodes 48 and 49 of *Robotech* as broadcast on US television in Spring 1985. **100 min.**

Robotech Perfect Collection- Southern Cross Vol. 7: *Episodes 13 and 14*
Episodes 13 and 14 of *Super-Dimensional Cavalry: SOUTHERN CROSS* as broadcast in Japan in July 1984. Episodes 50 and 51 of *ROBOTECH* as broadcast on US television in Spring 1985. **100 min.**

Domestic Home Video:

Robotech Perfect Collection- Macross Vol. 1
SPV 90373 ▲ $19.95 ▲ VHS ▲ DUB/SUB ▲ Mono ▲ 12/01/92

Robotech Perfect Collection- Macross Vol. 2
SPV 90443 ▲ $19.95 ▲ VHS ▲ DUB/SUB ▲ Mono ▲ 06/01/94

Robotech Perfect Collection- Macross Vol. 3
SPV 90523 ▲ $19.95 ▲ VHS ▲ DUB/SUB ▲ Mono ▲ 06/30/94

Robotech Perfect Collection- Macross Vol. 4
SPV 90553 ▲ $19.95 ▲ VHS ▲ DUB/SUB ▲ Mono ▲ 12/01/94

Robotech Perfect Collection- Macross Vol. 5
SPV 90613 ▲ $19.95 ▲ VHS ▲ DUB/SUB ▲ Mono ▲ 03/10/95

Robotech Perfect Collection- Macross Vol. 6
SPV 90673 ▲ $19.95 ▲ VHS ▲ DUB/SUB ▲ Mono ▲ 07/01/95

Robotech Perfect Collection- Macross Vol. 7
SPV 90753 ▲ $19.95 ▲ VHS ▲ DUB/SUB ▲ Mono ▲ 09/25/95

Robotech Perfect Collection- Macross Vol. 8
SPV 90823 ▲ $19.95 ▲ VHS ▲ DUB/SUB ▲ Mono ▲ 09/24/96

Robotech Perfect Collection- Mospeada Vol. 1
SPV 90393 ▲ $19.95 ▲ VHS ▲ DUB/SUB ▲ Mono ▲ 12/01/92

Robotech Perfect Collection- Mospeada Vol. 2
SPV 90463 ▲ $19.95 ▲ VHS ▲ DUB/SUB ▲ Mono ▲ 06/01/94

Robotech Perfect Collection- Mospeada Vol. 3
SPV 90543 ▲ $19.95 ▲ VHS ▲ DUB/SUB ▲ Mono ▲ 06/30/94

Robotech Perfect Collection- Mospeada Vol. 4
SPV 90573 ▲ $19.95 ▲ VHS ▲ DUB/SUB ▲ Mono ▲ 12/01/94

Robotech Perfect Collection- Mospeada Vol. 5
SPV 90633 ▲ $19.95 ▲ VHS ▲ DUB/SUB ▲ Mono ▲ 03/10/95

Robotech Perfect Collection- Mospeada Vol. 6
SPV 90963 ▲ $19.95 ▲ VHS ▲ DUB/SUB ▲ Mono ▲ 07/01/95

Robotech Perfect Collection- Mospeada Vol. 7
SPV 90773 ▲ $19.95 ▲ VHS ▲ DUB/SUB ▲ Mono ▲ 09/25/95

Robotech Perfect Collection- Southern Cross Vol. 1
SPV 90383 ▲ $19.95 ▲ VHS ▲ DUB/SUB ▲ Mono ▲ 12/01/92

Robotech Perfect Collection- Southern Cross Vol. 2
SPV 90453 ▲ $19.95 ▲ VHS ▲ DUB/SUB ▲ Mono ▲ 06/01/94

Robotech Perfect Collection- Southern Cross Vol. 3
SPV 90533 ▲ $19.95 ▲ VHS ▲ DUB/SUB ▲ Mono ▲ 06/30/94

Robotech Perfect Collection- Southern Cross Vol. 4
SPV 90563 ▲ $19.95 ▲ VHS ▲ DUB/SUB ▲ Mono ▲ 12/01/94

Robotech Perfect Collection- Southern Cross Vol. 5
SPV 90623 ▲ $19.95 ▲ VHS ▲ DUB/SUB ▲ Mono ▲ 03/10/95

Robotech Perfect Collection- Southern Cross Vol. 6
SPV 90683 ▲ $19.95 ▲ VHS ▲ DUB/SUB ▲ Mono ▲ 07/01/95

Robotech Perfect Collection- Southern Cross Vol. 7
SPV 90763 ▲ $19.95 ▲ VHS ▲ DUB/SUB ▲ Mono ▲ 09/25/95

Robotech II: The Sentinels

(1988) ©Harmony Gold USA Inc.

Written & Directed by: Carl Macek *Animation Design and Creation:* Tatsunoko Production Co. Ltd.

Robotech, adapted from three Japanese animated TV series, created a legion of loyal fans following its initial US broadcast in the mid 80's. ROBOTECH II: THE SENTINELS was conceived as a 65-episode follow-up to the original series. But due to the whims of TV programming, ROBOTECH II was never completed. What remains of this production are 4 partially completed episodes. The feature length film is compiled from this animation, with additional "rediscovered" footage. The story fills in many of the mysteries presented in the original series. We follow the crew of the *SDF-3* as they prepare to take off on a voyage to a distant star system, and watch as a hostile alien race, bent on revenge, annihilates the population of the homeworld of the Robotech Masters. **90 min.**

Domestic Home Video:
SPV 90020 ▲ $19.95 ▲ VHS ▲ DUB ▲ Mono ▲ CC ▲ 03/15/92
LUM 9327 ▲ $39.95 ▲ LD-CLV/CAV ▲ DUB ▲ Mono ▲ 12/01/93 ▲ Out of Print

Rokushin Gattai God Mars See GOD MARS

Roots Search

(1986) ©Nippon Columbia Co. Ltd.

Director: Hisashi Sugai *Screenplay:* Mitsuru Shimada *Character Design and Animation Supervisor:* Sanae Kobayashi *Art Director:* Yoshinori Takao

Coming right between (1) *Blade Runner* and (3) *Raiders of the Lost Ark* comes (2) *Alien*, the second of the three most often ripped-off Hollywood films in anime. In this, yet another no-excuses-asked-or-given *Alien* "homage," we get instead of Sigourney the one-woman army the deathless duo of Moira the Esper and Scott, her lover. On the satellite-based Tolmeckius Research Institute, Moira and the rest of the crew find their ship in alarm mode. In fact, an alien has invaded the ship, and is slithering into the minds of the surviving crew members. The alien imparts a deluge of painful remembrances upon its victims, before effecting a fatal blow to end the nightmare. RIP, Ripley. Released in Japan under the title "Roots Search" by Nihon Columbia; available in North America through U.S. Manga Corps. **45 min.**

Domestic Home Video:
USM 1025 ▲ $34.95 ▲ VHS ▲ SUB ▲ Stereo ▲ 12/02/92
ID 2237CT ▲ $34.95 ▲ LD ▲ SUB ▲ HiFi Stereo ▲ 10/12/93

Roujin Z

(1991) ©Tokyo Theatres Co., Inc./The Television Inc./Movie Co., Ltd./TV Asahi/Sony Music Entertainment (Japan) Inc.

Original Story, Screenplay and Mecha design: Katsuhiro Otomo *Original Character Design:* Hisashi Eguchi *Chief Director:* Hiroyuki Kitakubo *Animation Director:* Fumio Iida *Art Director:* Hirishi Sasaki *Music:* Bun Itakura *Mecha Design:* Mitsuo Iso *Art Design:* Satoshi Kon

The subject of aging in society gets an unflinching examination with this tale of a totally automated robot bed gone berserk in the service of an invalid old man. The Z-001 can monitor, bathe, feed, exercise and entertain by linking with Takazawa's brainwaves. However, when it begins providing for his every need, the Z-001 transforms into an unstoppable robot that smashes out of the hospital and battles through police barricades! Truly unique visuals and frenetic pacing as the bed shambles across the countryside absorbing everything in its path, *Tetsuo the Iron Man*-like, to use as fuel for its journey. Story, screenplay and design work by Katushiro Otomo, creator of AKIRA and direction by Hiroyuki Kitakubo (BLACK MAGIC M-66). Released in Japan under the title "Rôjin Z" (Old Man "Z") by Sony Music; available in North America through U.S. Manga Corps. **80 min.**

Domestic Home Video:
USM 1292 ▲ $19.95 ▲ VHS ▲ DUB ▲ Stereo ▲ 04/16/96
USM 1323 ▲ $29.95 ▲ VHS ▲ SUB ▲ Stereo ▲ 04/16/96

Rumik World: Fire Tripper

(1985) ©Rumiko Takahashi/Shogakukan

Original Work and Character Designs: Rumiko Takahashi *Screenplay:* Tomoko Konparu *Character Design:* Katsumi Aoshima *Director:* Osamu Uemura *Art Director:* Torao Arai *Music:* Koiichi Oku

In a departure from the territory of "romantic comedy" which she knows so well, creator Rumiko Takahashi (RANMA 1/2, MAISON IKKOKU) ventures into more serious turf with this collection of animated short stories. In FIRE TRIPPER, the first of the "Rumik World" videos, a gas tank explosion sends a young girl hurling back in time to "Sengoku" or "Warring States" period Japan, where she meets a young warrior who plays a crucial role in her own past, present, and future. Based on the manga of the same name, available in an English-translated "Rumic World" graphic novel from Viz Comics. Released in Japan under the title "Fire Tripper" by Victor Entertainment; available in North America through U.S. Manga Corps. **50 min.**

Domestic Home Video:
USM 1456 ▲ $14.95 ▲ VHS ▲ DUB ▲ Stereo ▲ 09/03/96
USM 1041 ▲ $29.95 ▲ VHS ▲ SUB ▲ Stereo ▲ 02/03/93
ID 2229CT ▲ $29.95 ▲ LD ▲ SUB ▲ HiFi Stereo ▲ 06/08/93

Rumik World: Laughing Target

(1987) ©Rumiko Takahashi/Shogakukan

Original Work: Rumiko Takahashi *Screenplay:* Tomoko Konparu, Hideo Takayashiki *Director:* Toru Matsuzono *Character Design:* Hidekazu Obara *Music:* Kawachi Kuni *Art Director:* Torao Arai

Two young cousins are promised to each other for future marriage in the ancient Japanese tradition. When they are reunited years later, the boy has a new girlfriend, and little interest in tradition, but the spurned girl (who also shows strong signs of demonic possession) has no intentions of giving him up in this supernatural-flavored anime version of *Fatal Attraction*. One creepy scene even pays homage to the classic horror film *Cat People*, while eerie background music adds splendidly to the horrific feel. Released in Japan under the title "Rumik World: Warau Hyôteki" (Laughing Target) by Victor Entertainment; available in North America through U.S. Manga Corps. **50 min.**

Domestic Home Video:
USM 1455 ▲ $14.95 ▲ VHS ▲ DUB ▲ Stereo ▲ 09/03/96
USM 1042 ▲ $29.95 ▲ VHS ▲ SUB ▲ Stereo ▲ 04/07/93
ID 2234CT ▲ $34.95 ▲ LD ▲ SUB ▲ HiFi Stereo ▲ 08/24/93

Rumik World: Maris the Chôjo

(1986) ©Rumiko Takahashi/Shogakukan

Original Work: Rumiko Takahashi *Screenplay:* Hideo Takayashiki, Tomoko Konparu *Director:* Kazuyashi Katayama, Tomoko Konparu *Art Director:* Toran Arai *Character Design:* Rumiko Takahashi, Katsumi Aoshima

In MARIS THE CHÔJO, the only comedy in the "Rumik World" series, we meet Maris the Thanatosian, resident of a planet where the inhabitants are six times stronger than Earth normal. Problem is, everything she wrecks with her super strength, she has to pay for, and with one mishap happening after another, the income never manages to keep up with the outcome. Hilarious characters and fast-moving plot make this one just the thing to unwind to after a long hard day; the "outtake"-style final credits crawl is a fun bonus. Released in Japan under the title "The Chôjo (Supergal)" by Victor Entertainment; available in North America through U.S. Manga Corps. **50 min.**

Domestic Home Video:
USM 1454 ▲ $14.95 ▲ VHS ▲ DUB ▲ Stereo ▲ 09/03/96
USM 1043 ▲ $29.95 ▲ VHS ▲ SUB ▲ Stereo
ID 2238CT ▲ $39.95 ▲ LD ▲ SUB ▲ HiFi Stereo ▲ 11/09/93

Rumik World: Mermaid Forest

(1991) ©Rumiko Takahashi/Shogakukan/Victor Musical Industries Inc.

Original Work: Rumiko Takahashi *Screenplay:* Masaichiro Okubo *Director:* Takaya Mizutani *Character Design:* Sayuri Ichiishi *Music:* Kenji Kawai *Art Director:* Katsuyoshi Kanemura

A young man named Yuta travels Japan in search of others like himself after eating the cursed flesh of a mermaid which, according to legend, turns those who partake of it immortal. He's traveled across this ephemeral world since the sixteenth century when he was cursed with immortality. For all those lonely years, he's been searching for another like him, an immortal woman to share his infinite life. Finally, he seems to have found her: the young girl Mana. Story continues (albeit with a completely different production team) in MERMAID'S SCAR. Released in Japan under the title "Rumik World: Ningyo no Mori" (Mermaid's Forest) by Victor Entertainment; available in North America through U.S. Manga Corps. **56 min.**

Domestic Home Video:
USM 1453 ▲ $14.95 ▲ VHS ▲ DUB ▲ Mono ▲ 09/03/96
USM 1044 ▲ $29.95 ▲ VHS ▲ SUB ▲ Mono ▲ 03/03/93
ID 2230CT ▲ $39.95 ▲ LD ▲ SUB ▲ HiFi Stereo ▲ 07/27/93

Rupan III *See* LUPIN III
Ryû Senki *See* DRAGON CENTURY

Sailor Moon

(1992-94) ©Toei Animation Co. Ltd./DIC Productions

Director: Kazuko Tadano

Faithful adaptation of the smash hit "shôjo manga" or "girls' comics" series by creator Naoko Takeuchi, as serialized in monthly NAKAYOSHI manga anthology. Energetic television series which traces the adventures of a gaggle of leggy schoolgirls who just so happen to have been magical princesses (from the moon, Mars, Venus, etc.) in former lives. Their memories of previous incarnations are activated by a talking cat named Luna (who also supplies them with weapons), and they then devote their lives to defending our world from alien invaders and extradimensional menaces, in addition to their regular preoccupations with schoolwork, food and romance. Main character Sailor Moon is an endearingly ditzy teenager with down-to-earth foibles such as laziness, hatred of studying, and preoccupations with video games and boys; her selfishness eventually gives way to a more heroic stance (though she never quite becomes a selfless paragon of virtue). Each girl transforms to her superhero outfit (a short-skirted version of the traditional "sailor suit" school uniform sported by Japanese girls) by a stock nude transformation sequence, which was gently retouched for the North American broadcast. The show formula is akin to the monster-of-the-week formula employed by the masked team "ranger" or "sentai" series, where a costumed team fights (often assisted by the enigmatic, you-guessed-what-he-wears male hero Tuxedo Mask) an ever-changing variety of mutated baddies controlled by charismatic bosses. Episodic superhero action is elevated by angst-ridden teen romance and female camaraderie; throughout five series and several movies, the "Sailor Senshi" or "Sailor Scouts" remain firm (if frequently squabbling) friends, which is a source of the series' frequent humor. Clever, amusing visual tricks and endearingly cute character designs make up for sometimes-limited TV animation and frequent stock transformations. The U.S.-broadcast version cut off just short of the climax of the second series, but a limited video re-release of selected episodes and a peppy soundtrack album allow fans to relive the magic. Released in Japan under the title "Bishôjo Senshi (Pretty Soldier) Sailor Moon" by Toei Video; available in North America (in limited markets) through The Incredible World of DIC/Toon Time Video/Buena Vista.

Sailor Moon: *A Moon Star is Born*
2 episodes. In A MOON STAR IS BORN, the ditzy schoolgirl Serena is introduced, along with Darien (a.k.a. Tuxedo Mask) and the talking black cat, Luna. In TALK RADIO, callers who contact a mysterious talk show are afflicted with a strange sleeping disease—can the floral brooches they receive from the radio station be the cause? **44 min.**

Sailor Moon: *Scouts Unite!*
2 episodes. In COMPUTER SCHOOL BLUES, Serena suspects Amy, a new girl in school, of being an alien from the Negaverse. But after their teacher mutates into the real alien, Amy turns out to be Sailor Mercury. In AN UNCHARMED LIFE, young girls who buy lucky charms from an alien in disguise suddenly disappear. Sailor Moon helps Raye transform into Sailor Mars. **44 min.**

Sailor Moon: *Evil Eyes*
2 episodes. In CRUISE BLUES, Serena is jealous when Raye wins cruise tickets and invites Amy instead of her. In SHUTTER BUGGED, a photographer who is possessed by the evil Neflite takes Amy and Raye's pictures, and with it, their energy. **44 min.**

Domestic Home Video:
Sailor Moon: *A Moon Star is Born*
DIC 6145 ▲ $12.95 ▲ VHS ▲ DUB ▲ HiFi Stereo ▲ CC
Sailor Moon: *Scouts Unite!*
DIC 6146 ▲ $12.95 ▲ VHS ▲ DUB ▲ HiFi Stereo ▲ CC
Sailor Moon: *Evil Eyes*
DIC 6148 ▲ $12.95 ▲ VHS ▲ DUB ▲ HiFi Stereo ▲ CC

Saishû Kyôshi *See* THE ULTIMATE TEACHER

Samurai Pizza Cats: The Movie

(1991) ©Tatsunoko Production Co. Ltd./Saban International

Music: Shuki Levy
Released in Japan as a 54-episode TV series under the title "Cats Toninden Teyande," SAMURAI PIZZA CATS is a comedy about the characters who congregate around Little Tokyo's Samurai Pizza Cats Pizza Parlor. Starring superhero felines Speedy Cerviche, Guido Anchovi, and Polly Esther (*groan,* *groan,* and *wince*!), the Samurai Pizza Cats are crime fighters dedicated to delivering the best pizza in Little Tokyo while keeping the streets safe from the diabolical schemes of Big Cheese and his henchmen, Bad Bird and Jerry Atrick. Animated in a "super-deformed" style, the "Americanized" version of the series finally made it to U.S. syndication in 1996. This videotape is actually composed of TV episodes, despite the title. Available in North America through Video Treasures. **55 min.**

Domestic Home Video:
VT SB9483 ▲ $9.95 ▲ VHS-EP ▲ DUB

Samurai Shodown: The Motion Picture

(1993) ©SNK Corporation of America

Based on the SNK/Neo•Geo Game: Samurai Shodown
Director: Hiroshi Ishiodori *Scenario:* Nobuaki Kishima
Character Design and Chief Animator: Zazunori Iwakura
One-shot TV special based on the SNK/Neo•Geo Game "Samurai Spirits." The characters from the video game are now holy warriors who need to defeat the evil overlord (altered to a woman in the North America release due to androgynous look). Main character Haohmaru has the biggest fan of spiky hair yet. Instead of red blood, villains leak an opaque white liquid (very unlike the game). A disappointing experience for fans of the game, calling it "Samurai Letdown" is giving it too much credit; you may want to check out the video game instead. Released in Japan as "Samurai Spirits"; released in North America through A.D. Vision. **80 min.**

Domestic Home Video:
ADV SS/001 ▲ $29.95 ▲ VHS ▲ DUB ▲ HiFi Surround ▲ 06/14/95

Sanctuary

(1996) ©Sho Fumimura/Ryoichi Ikegami/Shogakukan/OB Planning/Toho/VAP

Based on the manga by: Sho Fumimura and Ryoichi Ikegami
Director: Takashi Watanabe. *Screenplay:* Kenishi Terada
Animation Direction and Character Design: Hidemi Kubo
Art Director: Hiroshi Kato

Based on the manga of the same name by Sho Fumimura and Ryoichi Ikegami, as serialized in BIG COMIC SUPERIOR manga anthology (published in English by Viz Comics). Two Japanese survivors of the Khmer Rouge return to Japan and vow to find a "sanctuary" of their own, even if they have to build it for themselves. Gripping political intrigue combines with knee-capping violence (one's a politician, one's a yakuza) as the two men, Asami and Hojo, schmooze, swindle, and steal their way through the two-sided coin of real-world Japanese politics and the criminal underworld. Released in Japan under the title "Sanctuary" by Toho Video; available in North America through Viz Video. **70 min.**

Domestic Home Video:
VV SE-001 ▲ $24.95 ▲ VHS ▲ DUB ▲ Stereo ▲ 11/26/96
VV SS-001 ▲ $29.95 ▲ VHS ▲ SUB ▲ Stereo ▲ 11/26/96

Sangokushi *See* GREAT CONQUEST
Scramble Wars *See* SUPER-DEFORMED DOUBLE FEATURE
Secret of Blue Water *See* NADIA
Sei Jûki Cyguard *See* CYBERNETICS GUARDIAN
Seiden: RG Veda *See* RG VEDA
Seijûden Twin Dolls *See* TWIN DOLLS
Seikimatsu Kyûseishu Densetsu Hokuto no Ken
See FIST OF THE NORTH STAR
Sengoku Machine Gôshôgun *See* MACRON 1
Sengoku Machine Goshogun: Toki no Etránger
See GOSHOGUN: THE TIME ETRÁNGER
SF Saiyûki Starzinger *See* SPACEKETEERS
SF Shin Seiki Lensman *See* LENSMAN

Sherlock Hound

TV series, 26 episodes
(1984-85) ©RAI/Tokyo Movie Shinsha

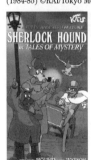

Director: Hayao Miyazaki.
Based on an original idea by Marco Pagott. A co-production between Italy's RAI Broadcasting and Japan's TMS, SHERLOCK HOUND takes for its base the "Sherlock Holmes" stories of Arthur Conan Doyle, adding a new spin by recasting all the characters as anthropomorphic dogs. Charming, high-quality production from the director of MY NEIGHBOR TOTORO. Released in Japan under the title "Meitantei (Famous Detective) Holmes" as a 26-episode TV series; available in North America through Celebrity Home Entertainment. Note that in Japan, two 46-minute theatrical features (1984 and 1986) were released, both consisting merely of two TV episodes. All 26 episodes are available on domestic home video.

Sherlock Hound: *Dr. Watson, I Presume?*
5 episodes. Sherlock and Watson meet on a cruise liner and defeat pirates; Moriarty tries to steal the Crown of Marselene; Moriarty builds a mechanical sea-monster to devour rich cargo ships; Moriarty steals Big Ben's bell, Moriarty tries to win a big airplane race by stealing McBane's secret engine. **120 min.**

Sherlock Hound: *The White Cliffs of Rover*
5 episodes. Sherlock Hound thwarts Professor Moriarty's attempt to steal Sir Focus' gold shipment; Sherlock protects Ellen from the Professor; Moriarty steals the jeweled lobsters; Moriarty robs a bank for gold to cast a statue of himself; Moriarty tries to steal the secret of the Sacred Sword of the Wizards. **120 min.**

Sherlock Hound: *The Dogs of Bowserville*
5 episodes. **120 min.**

Sherlock Hound: *Moriarty Unleashed*
5 episodes. **120 min.**

Sherlock Hound: *Tales of Mystery*
5 episodes. **120 min.**

Domestic Home Video:

Sherlock Hound: *Dr. Watson, I Presume?*
CEL 3164 ▲ $39.95 ▲ VHS ▲ DUB ▲ HiFi

Sherlock Hound: *The White Cliffs of Rover*
CEL 3108 ▲ $39.95 ▲ VHS ▲ DUB ▲ HiFi

Sherlock Hound: *The Dogs of Bowserville*
CEL 3087 ▲ $39.95 ▲ VHS ▲ DUB ▲ HiFi

Sherlock Hound: *Moriarty Unleashed*
CEL 3143 ▲ $39.95 ▲ VHS ▲ DUB ▲ HiFi

Sherlock Hound: *Tales of Mystery*
CEL 3080 ▲ $39.95 ▲ VHS ▲ DUB ▲ HiFi

Shin Angel *See* THE NEW ANGEL
Shin Cutey Honey *See* CUTEY HONEY
Shin Injû Gakuen: Ecstasy Taisen *See* LA BLUE GIRL
Shin Kaitei Gunkan *See* SUPER ATRAGON
Shin Seiki Evangelion *See* NEON GENESIS EVANGELION
Shinpi no Sekai El Hazard *See* EL HAZARD

Shonan Bakusozoku: Bomber Bikers of Shonan

(1986) ©Toei Co. Ltd.

Director: Nobutaka Nishizawa

Although not a particularly distinguished anime in most respects, it is probably the only one ever released in the U.S. to focus on the flamboyant biker gangs of Japan, some of whom, like the video's Shô-Baku, actually do affect a 1950s style and speak in terms of "rumbles" and "bad dudes," swing chains, and sport pompadours. (In other words, this isn't AKIRA—these guys are just out for a good time, a ride down the coast at Kanagawa, and a little corny honor, and about the worst crimes they commit are breaking the speed limit and unbuttoning their school-uniform collars. (Note that although in Japan the series has released more than ten volumes, only one domestic volume has been released to date.) Released in Japan under the title "Shônan Bakusôzoku" (Bomber Bikers of Shônan) by Toei Video; available in North America through AnimEigo. **52 min.**

Domestic Home Video:
ANI AT094-001 ▲ $34.95 ▲ VHS ▲ SUB ▲ HiFi Stereo ▲ 02/02/94

Shuten Doji - The Star Hand Kid

OAV series, 4 volumes

(1989-91) Go Nagai/Dynamic Planning, Inc./Nippon Columbia Co., Ltd.

Director: Junji Nishimura *Script:* Masashi Sogo *Original/Construction:* Go Nagai

Based on the manga of the same name by creator Go Nagai (DEVILMAN), as serialized in publisher Kodansha's weekly SHŪKAN SHŌNEN MAGAZINE manga anthology. Occult tale of a baby delivered by an "oni" (ogres from Japanese folklore) into the hands of a young, childless Japanese couple asked to rear the child and then return it to the ogre in fifteen years' time, at which time the boy (called "Jiro Shutendoji" by his parents) will assume his supernatural inheritance. Calling it a "masterpiece" as do the titles on the box of the domestic release may be an overstatement, as neither animation nor storytelling break any new ground, but a creepy score by Fumitaka Anzai and steady pacing by RANMA 1/2 director Junji Nishimura make for an effective tale…even if the story presupposes a certain familiarity with Japanese folklore on the part of the viewer for purposes of context and dramatic resonance. Released in Japan under the title "Shuten Dôji" (The Star-Hand Kid) by Nihon Columbia; available in North America through A.D. Vision. A brief word in warning: Those who enjoy Nagai's "lighter" fare (i.e., CUTEY HONEY) may want to be sure of what they're in for before viewing this one, due to scenes of sexual violence.

Shuten Doji - The Star Hand Kid 1
Could anything be stranger than finding out you're adopted—and you're actually a time-travelling, space-jumping, intergalactic troll—and your parents raised you as a favor to a priest after a 200-foot-tall troll dropped you off at a local shrine? What if there were other creatures out to get you—and one of them had possessed your teacher and kidnapped your girlfriend—to use as a sacrifice to open an interdimensional barrier and destroy all mankind? **55 min.**

Shuten Doji - The Star Hand Kid 2: *Demon Battle at the Firefly Field*
Time-lashed through time and space in a desperate quest to unlock the mystery of Jiro's origins, Jiro and his companions arrive at the Ankohoku temple just in time for the ultimate battle between good and evil! Jiro and clan take on the awesome might of Iron-Caesar in the Battle of Firefly Field. **55 min.**

Shuten Doji - The Star Hand Kid 3: *Time War*
When Jiro and Miyuki's journey through space is interrupted by a horde of demons intent on killing the Shuten Doji, they become separated in time. While Miyuki is stuck in feudal Japan, Jiro is flung into the far future where mankind has gained the stars. His arrival aboard an interstellar spaceship spells disaster for the hapless crew as, even amid the vastness of space, the Oni continue their relentless pursuit of the Shuten Doji. **50 min.**

Shuten Doji - The Star Hand Kid 4: *Endgame*
Left mentally unstable after Jiro's abduction in Part 2, his foster mother continues to cover the walls of her hospital room with paintings of Oni. Meanwhile, after his narrow escape in Part 3, Jiro returns to the land of his birth where he must defeat the combined might of the Oni. Concludes the series. **50 min.**

Domestic Home Video:

Shuten Doji - The Star Hand Kid 1
ADV SD/001S ▲ $29.95 ▲ VHS ▲ SUB ▲ HiFi Surround ▲ 03/11/96

Shuten Doji - The Star Hand Kid 2:
ADV SD/002S ▲ $29.95 ▲ VHS ▲ SUB ▲ HiFi Surround ▲ 04/09/96

Shuten Doji - The Star Hand Kid 3
ADV SD/003S ▲ $29.95 ▲ VHS ▲ SUB ▲ HiFi Surround ▲ 07/02/96

Shuten Doji - The Star Hand Kid 4
ADV SD/004S ▲ $29.95 ▲ VHS ▲ SUB ▲ HiFi Surround ▲ 12/03/96

Silent Möbius

(1991) ©Kia Asamiya/Kadokawa Publishing Co. Ltd.

Story: Kia Asamiya *Music:* Kaoru Wada *Art Director:* Norihiro Hiraki *Director:* Michitaka Kikuchi

Based on the manga of the same name by creator Kia Asamiya ("Dark Angel," "Compiler"), as serialized in publisher Kodansha's COMIC COMP. In a futuristic Tokyo, an elite team of *X-Files*-like investigators (albeit with fancy dress uniforms) has been formed to protect the world from an otherworldly invasion by "Entities." Six women—a warrior mage, a cyborg, a net-running super-hacker, a priestess, a psychic, and their half-human, half-Entity leader—are all that stand between the human world and the supernatural. Lovely visuals with distinctive, Nagel-esque character designs by director Kikuchi, but hard to follow if not already intimately familiar with the manga (published in English by Viz Comics). Released in Japan as "Silent Möbius" by Kadokawa Shôten; available in North America through Streamline Pictures. Followed in 1992 by a theatrical sequel as well as by a "Making Of" video, neither of which have been released in the U.S. **50 min.**

Domestic Home Video:
SPV 90793 ▲ $24.95 ▲ VHS ▲ DUB ▲ Mono ▲ 12/03/93 ▲ Out of Print

Slayers

TV series, 26 episodes

(1995) ©H. Kanzaka/R. Araizumi/TV Tokyo/SOFTX/Marubeni

Original Story: Hajime Kanazaka, Rui Araizumi *Directors:* Takashi Watanabe (1), Makoto Noriza (2,8), Osamu Yokota (3,9), Masato Sato (4,10,13), Johei Matsu'ura (5,11), Susumu Ishi (6), Yoshiaki Iwasaki (7), Takashi Kobayashi (12)

Home video release of the popular TV, OAV, and movie series (only TV episodes have been released to date, however), based on the manga of the same name by Hajime Kanazaka, as serialized in publisher Fujimi Shôbo's DRAGON MAGAZINE. Sword-swinging comedic fantasy fare with a red-haired sorceress named Lina Inverse accompanied by a blonde male sidekick, who robs from the rich to give to herself. Although first and foremost a slapstick comedy, frequent, heated battles with otherworldly monsters and fantasy RPG overtones add depth. Released in Japan under the title "Slayers" by Toei; available in North America through Software Sculptors.

Slayers Vol. 1: *Episodes 1-4*
Episode 1: ANGRY? LINA'S FURIOUS DRAGON SLAVE!, Episode 2: BAD! MUMMY MEN AREN'T MY TYPE!, Episode 3: CRASH! RED AND WHITE AND SUSPICIOUS ALL OVER!, and Episode 4: DASH! RUN FOR IT! MY MAGIC DOESN'T WORK! **100 min.**

Slayers Vol. 2: *Episodes 5-7*
Episode 5: ESCAPE! NOONSA, THE FLAMING FISH MAN!, Episode 6: FOCUS! REZO'S THE REAL ENEMY!, and Episode 7: GIVE UP! BUT JUST BEFORE WE DO, THE SURE KILL SWORD APPEARS! **75 min.**

Slayers Vol. 3: *Episodes 8-10*
Episode 8: HELP! SHABRANIGDO IS REBORN!, Episode 9: IMPACT! THE EVE OF THE MENACING BATTLE!, and Episode 10: JACKPOT! THE GREAT LIFE OR DEATH GAMBLE! **75 min.**

Slayers Vol. 4: *Episodes 11-13*
Episode 11: KNOCK OUT! THE SEYRUUN FAMILY FEUD!, Episode 12: LOVELY! AMELIA'S MAGIC TRAINING!, and Episode 13: MONEY! CRUSH THOSE BOUNTY HUNTERS! **75 min.**

Domestic Home Video:
Slayers Vol. 1: *Episodes 1-4*
SSVS 9410 ▲ $19.95 ▲ VHS ▲ DUB ▲ Stereo ▲ 06/04/96
SSVS 9403 ▲ $19.95 ▲ VHS ▲ SUB ▲ Stereo ▲ 06/04/96
Slayers Vol. 2: *Episodes 5-7*
SSVS 9411 ▲ $19.95 ▲ VHS ▲ DUB ▲ Stereo ▲ 08/06/96
SSVS 9404 ▲ $19.95 ▲ VHS ▲ SUB ▲ Stereo ▲ 08/06/96
Slayers Vol. 3: *Episodes 8-10*
SSVS 9412 ▲ $19.95 ▲ VHS ▲ DUB ▲ Stereo ▲ 10/01/96
SSVS 9405 ▲ $19.95 ▲ VHS ▲ SUB ▲ Stereo ▲ 10/01/96
Slayers Vol. 4: *Episodes 11-13*
SSVS 9413 ▲ $19.95 ▲ VHS ▲ DUB ▲ Stereo ▲ 12/03/96
SSVS 9406 ▲ $19.95 ▲ VHS ▲ SUB ▲ Stereo ▲ 12/03/96
Slayers Vol. 1: *Episodes 1-2*
SSVS 9651 ▲ $39.95 ▲ LD ▲ M/A ▲ Stereo ▲ 07/02/96
Slayers Vol. 2: *Episodes 3-4*
SSVS 9652 ▲ $39.95 ▲ LD ▲ M/A ▲ Stereo ▲ 07/02/96
Slayers Vol. 3: *Episodes 5-6*
SSVS 9653 ▲ $39.95 ▲ LD ▲ M/A ▲ Stereo ▲ 10/01/96
Slayers Vol. 4: *Episodes 7-8*
SSVS 9654 ▲ $39.95 ▲ LD ▲ M/A ▲ Stereo ▲ 11/01/96

Sohryuden: Legend of the Dragon Kings
OAV series, 12 episodes
(1991-93) ©Yoshiki Tanaka/Kitty Films/Fuji Television/Kodansha

Based on the novel by: Yoshiki Tanaka *Directors:* Shigeru Ueda (1,2), Yoshihiro Yamaguchi (3,4), Renji Kawabata (5), Shinji Sakai (6), Harumi Tamano (7,8,9), Kyosuke Mikuriya (10-12) *Art Direction:* Shichiro Kobayashi, Jiro Kono, Kazuya Fukuda, Takashi Tokushige, Kiyomi Tanaka *Character Design:* Shunji Murata, Kenichi Maeshima *Music Director:* Susumu Aketagawa

Based on the novels by Yoshiki Tanaka ("Legend of the Galactic Heroes," LEGEND OF ARISLAN). The four Ryudo brothers are the *bishônen* or "beautiful boy" teen dreams of Kyôwa School, a private and exclusive institution founded by their grandfather. Ranging in age from 23 to 13, the four brothers live charmed bachelors' lives in a posh mansion, helped out in the housework department by their young cousin Matsuri. But the brothers are also descendants of the legendary Dragon Kings, ancient Chinese rulers of the Earth. Due to this ancestry, the brothers are super-strong, super-fast, possess powers of levitation and, if killed, the ability to summon a huge, fire-like dragon (after which life returns). Gozen, a mysterious, wizened man with sharpened teeth who controls Japan from the shadows (and feeds dead bodies to his fish) wants the Ryudos' secret and tries a variety of ruthless methods to get it. The plot moves at a leisurely TV series pace, but the combination of political machinations, brutal strongarm tactics, Chinese and Japanese history and the brothers' super powers make for a neat suspense/intrigue series, with a relatively realistic animation style. There are sudden spurts of unexpected gore (such as one of Gozen's flunkies committing bloody "seppuku"), and Gozen's dining room is situated above a transparent floor swimming with lethal, giant fish, á la the James Bond movie *The Spy Who Loved Me*. Released in Japan under the title "Sôryûden" (Legend of the Dragon Kings) by Fuji TV/Pony Canyon; available in North America through U.S. Manga Corps.

Sohryuden Vol. 1: *Episodes 1 and 2*
Episode 1: THE FOUR BROTHERS UNDER FIRE, and Episode 2: THE LEGEND OF DRAGON SPRINGS. Kamakura no Gozen, the "old man of Kamakura" has spent his entire life trying to unravel a secret so important, so powerful, that it's worth any price. And somehow, the brothers hold the key to that secret. Until now, the brothers have led a pleasant, peaceful life. But all that is about to change. They weren't bothered when the assault and kidnapping attempts were directed at them ... but when their friends become victims, it's time to get tough. **97 min.**

Sohryuden Vol. 2: *Episodes 3 & 4*
Episode 3: BLACK DRAGON KING REVEALED, and Episode 4: TOKYO BAY RHAPSODY. Until now, Kamakura no Gozen has trusted his underlings to bring the brothers under his control. But now it's time for more desperate action. First he'll kidnap the brothers' only living relatives: their cousin Matsuri and her family. Then he'll force the brothers to stage a rescue attempt in the middle of an army munitions range. Lastly, he's planned one final bit of treachery: an elite combat team with the latest military hardware. **97 min.**

Sohryuden Vol. 3: *Episodes 5 & 6*
Episode 5: THE GRACEFUL AGENT and Episode 6: SKYSCRAPERS AND THE RED DRAGON. The deranged doctor has gained most of his twisted medical knowledge by dissecting living subjects. Now, with his pack of cybernetic Dobermans, the mad doctor is turning a hungry eye towards the unsuspecting brothers. America's biggest business consortium is interested in the brothers as well. **97 min.**

Sohryuden Vol. 4: *Episodes 7 & 8*
Episode 7: REVENGE OF THE FOUR BROTHERS, and Episode 8: RAMPAGE OF THE IRON DRAGON. Dr. Tamozawa has discovered the Ryudo brothers' secret. The mad doctor and his army of surgically created cyborgs will never rest until he has realized his dream of dissecting one of the brothers alive. Meanwhile, all of Tokyo is in an uproar, following the appearance of a gigantic, fire-breathing dragon— and the subsequent destruction left in its wake. **97 min.**

Sohryuden Vol. 5: *Episodes 9 & 10*
Episode 9: STORM OF THE WHITE DRAGON KING and Episode 10: THE BROTHERS' GREAT ESCAPE. The Mulligan Foundation's top agent, Lady L, has kidnapped one of the youngest Ryudo brothers. The researchers of the Foundation hope that, with the proper persuasion, the remaining brothers will agree to become agents of the Foundation — as assassins and saboteurs. **97 min.**

Sohryuden Vol. 6: *Episodes 11 & 12*
Episode 11: THE SOARING BLUE DRAGON KING, and Episode 12: THE FOUR DRAGON KINGS TAKE TO THE SKY. The battle unfolds as the four brothers must unite to fight the evil mastermind who has manipulated their lives for so long. The ultimate battle will pit all four dragons against an invincible and immortal enemy, while the fate of the planet hangs in the balance! **97 min.**

Domestic Home Video:
Sohryuden Vol. 1
USM 1324 ▲ $29.95 ▲ VHS ▲ SUB ▲ Stereo ▲ 08/08/95
Sohryuden Vol. 2
USM 1325 ▲ $29.95 ▲ VHS ▲ SUB ▲ Stereo ▲ 12/05/95
Sohryuden Vol. 3
USM 1326 ▲ $29.95 ▲ VHS ▲ SUB ▲ Stereo ▲ 02/06/96
Sohryuden Vol. 4
USM 1327 ▲ $29.95 ▲ VHS ▲ SUB ▲ Stereo ▲ 04/02/96
Sohryuden Vol. 5
USM 1328 ▲ $29.95 ▲ VHS ▲ SUB ▲ Stereo ▲ 06/04/96
Sohryuden Vol. 6
USM 1329 ▲ $29.95 ▲ VHS ▲ SUB ▲ Stereo ▲ 08/06/96

Sôkô Kishi Votoms *See* ARMORED TROOPER VOTOMS

Sol Bianca
OAV series, 2 volumes
(1990, '91) ©NCS/NEC/Avenue/A.I.C.

Original Concept: Toru Miura *Director:* Katsuhito Akiyama (1), Hiroki Hayashi (2) *Story:* Mayori Sekijima *Character Design:* Naoyuki Onda *Mecha Design:* Atsushi Takeuchi *Art Director:* Shigemi Ikeda *Music:* Toru Hirano (1), Kosei Kenjo (2) *Planning:* Toru Miura (2)

Two-volume OAV series featuring the adventures of a pirate ship manned by armored-suited women as they take on an evil regime in a fast-paced, enjoyable romp. Designs for the spaceship *Sol Bianca* by Atsushi Takeuchi are fascinatingly original, and character designs by Naoyuki Onda lean toward the realistic side, especially in comparison with more recent productions. Some violence (including severed body parts) up the ante when it comes to family viewing. Released in Japan under the title "Sol Bianca" by NEC Avenue/Pony Canyon; available in North America through A.D. Vision.

Sol Bianca
When a young stowaway informs Janny, Feb, April, May and June that the most legendary artifact of all, the fabled "Gnosis," is in the evil clutches of Emperor Batros, the despised dictator of the planet Tres, what choice do they have except to steal it? **60 min.**

Sol Bianca 2

The crew try to corner the interstellar market on pasha, the most valuable substance in the known universe. And then there's also a mysterious stranger who seems much more interested in collecting the *Sol Bianca* and her crew than the pasha. **60 min.**

Domestic Home Video:
Sol Bianca
ADV SB/001 ▲ $29.95 ▲ VHS ▲ SUB ▲ HiFi Surround ▲ 04/28/93
ADV CAVS/001 ▲ $39.95 ▲ LD-CAV ▲ SUB ▲ HiFi Surr ▲ 1/24/95
Sol Bianca 2
ADV SB/002 ▲ $29.95 ▲ VHS ▲ SUB ▲ HiFi Surround ▲ 08/14/95

Sono Ki ni Sasete yo! *See* MY, MY MAI
Sôsei Kishi Gaiarth *See* GENESIS SURVIVOR GAIARTH
Space Battleship Yamato *See* YAMATO
Space Battleship Yamato: The New Voyage *See* YAMATO

Space Warriors Baldios

[MOVIE]

(1981) ©Toei Central Film Co., Ltd.

Sci-fi adventure starring a young man and his robot, the eponymous Baldios. First broadcast in Japan as a 1980-81 television series, an abbreviated storyline and missing episodes prompted Japanese fans to raise the hue and cry for a theatrical sequel to tie up loose ends, thus this full-length, 117-minute film. As evil aliens flee their polluted planet in search of another land to destroy, a lone outcast follows them in his robotic spaceship, Baldios. When they select the Earth as their next target, the courageous pilot vows to stop them. Released in Japan under the title "Uchû Senshi (Space Warrior) Baldios" by Toei Video; available in North America through Best Film and Video (abridged version). Note that the TV series has yet to be released on video in the U.S. **99 min.**

Domestic Home Video:
BFV 963 ▲ $19.95 ▲ VHS ▲ DUB ▲ Mono

Spacekeeteers

[TV]

TV series, 26 episodes

(1978-79) ©Toei Animation Co. Ltd./Jim Terry Productions

Created by: Leiji Matsumoto *Music:* Shunsuke Kikuchi

Based on the manga by Leiji Matsumoto (STAR BLAZERS). Yet another telling of the Monkey King, this take by GALAXY EXPRESS 999's Matsumoto adds a "giant robot" element to a cast of three cyborg warriors charged with protecting a princess through her travels so that she may eventually save the Earth. Broadcast in the U.S. as part of the "Force Five" series (the other four series were DANGARD ACE, GRANDIZER, GAIKING, and GETTA ROBO G), to date only two out of 26 episodes of SPACEKEETEERS as seen on "Force Five" are available on home video. Original 64-episode series released in Japan under the title "SF Saiyûki (The Sci-Fi 'Journey to the West') Starzingers" by Toei Video; available in North America through Parade Video. Followed in Japan a year later by a sequel TV series. In AURORA ACCEPTS THE CHALLENGE, Aurora learns that she is the only one who can save the galaxy from the evil Dekos energy. She leaves on her mission and meets Jesse Dart, a cyborg, who becomes her first Spaceketeer. In THE INVINCIBLE WARRIOR, after Jesse rescues Aurora from the grotesque liquid called "Trakeal," he tells her how he came to be a cyborg. **46 min.**

Domestic Home Video:
PRV 6611 ▲ $12.95 ▲ VHS ▲ DUB ▲ Mono ▲ 02/01/93

Speed Racer

[TV]

TV series, 52 episodes

(1967-68) ©Tatsunoko and Yokino/K. Fujita/Trans-Lux

Produced, directed and created by: Tatsuo Yoshida *Music:* Nobuyoshi Koshibe *Animation and art direction:* Ippei Kuri, Hiroshi Sasagawa *English adaptation:* Peter Fernandez

One of the most famous Japanese-animated series of all time, Speed and his cohorts have recently been popping up across in the U.S. everywhere from reruns of the

Trans-Lux series on MTV to TV spots for Volkswagen reanimated with scrupulous faithfulness to resemble same. (For more information, see Chapter One.) Released in Japan under the title "Maha (Mach) Go Go Go" by Polygram (currently available in Japan on LD only); available in North America through Family Home Entertainment.

Speed Racer Vol. 1: *The Great Plan*
Speed Racer is determined to become a champion race car driver and win the dangerous Sword Mountain Race. Speed wants the prize money to go to his father, Pops Racer, whose new designs will turn Speed's car, the Mach-5, into the fastest race car on any track and the greatest crime-fighting weapon in the world. But someone is out to steal the designs. **50 min.**

Speed Racer Vol. 2: *The Secret Engine*
Speed Racer attempts to stop a mysterious gang led by escaped convict Tongue Blaggard. The gang is after a Model T car owned by kindly Lightfingers Klepto who inherited the car years before when his father was shot down by gangsters. What no one but Blaggard knows is that the Model T's engine is the key to a fantastic treasure. **50 min.**

Speed Racer Vol. 3: *The Fastest Car on Earth*
Can Speed drive a car powered by an engine so fast it takes its drivers into another dimension? Years before Pops had that same engine, the GRX, buried after it caused the deaths of several test drivers. But the devilish and wealthy Oriena and her gang have dug up the GRX and put it into a new race car body to enter the Oriental Grand Prix. Oriena has also invented a formula that speeds up the driver's reflexes to survive the GRX's fantastic speeds - at least long enough to ensure that her car will win. **50 min.**

Speed Racer Vol. 4: *Race Against Time*
Competing in the Sahara Race in Egypt, Speed Racer comes upon Dr. Digger O. Bone, who is being attacked by a death-dealing airplane. Before the doctor dies, he asks Speed to find his daughter Calcia who, along with his assistant Splint Femur, has disappeared while searching for Cleopatra's tomb. When Speed and his girlfriend Trixie locate the treasure-rich tomb, Calcia has been hit on the head by a falling stone and now believes herself to be Cleopatra. **50 min.**

Speed Racer Vol. 5: *Crash in the Jungle*
When Speed's plane is hijacked, Professor Carnivore is kidnapped. After he crashes in the jungle, Trixie, Spridle and Chim Chim search for Speed, but are captured by the evil General Smasher and his crackpot colleague, Dr. Loon, who are also holding Carnivore captive. Unless the professor agrees to

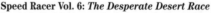

cooperate in a mad scientific experiment to develop an army of giants, Trixie and Spridle will be dropped into a pool of flesh-eating piranhas. **50 min.**

Speed Racer Vol. 6: *The Desperate Desert Race*
Speed is in Sandoland competing in the grueling Desert Race. He runs into trouble when the notorious Black Tiger, driven by competitor Kim Jugger, is sabotaged. Speed's mischievous brother Spridle and pet monkey Chim Chim are blamed. When Speed tries to prove their innocence, he is taken hostage by a rebel army led by Kim's father, General Abdul Noble. But there's a traitor in the army - a one-eyed spy named Ali Ben Schemer who wants Speed and Kim out of the way so that he can overthrow the general. **50 min.**

Speed Racer Vol. 7: *Girl Daredevil*
Circus star Twinkle Banks is forced to perform a deadly tightrope trick above Niagara Falls by the evil Cornpone Brotch, who has kidnapped her father. While the attention is focused on Twinkle, Cornpone and his gangsters search for hidden Indian treasure below. When Speed blows their cover, they steal the mighty Mach-5. Speed and Twinkle locate the hideout where the Mach-5 is stashed and Twinkle's father is held prisoner. **50 min.**

Speed Racer Vol. 8: *The Royal Racer*
Pops Racer is building a mini race car for Prince Jam of the kingdom of Sackaren, where the Baby Grand Prix is to be held. Spridle begs to compete, but he's too young. When the prince is kidnapped, however, Spridle is mistaken for the young monarch and gets his chance to race after all. **50 min.**

Speed Racer Vol. 9: *Challenge of the Masked Racer*
Speed Racer enters the perilous Trans-Country Race. His arch-competitor is the Masked Racer - a mysterious driver who allegedly wins every race because he causes others to crash. Preparing for the big event, Speed winds up in a stormy midnight race against the Masked Racer. After Speed loses control of the Mach-5, his strange rival rescues him and warns him not to attempt the dangerous race. Suspense shifts into high gear when Speed is kidnapped by Wiley's depraved gang. **52 min.**

Speed Racer Vol. 10: *The Fire Race*
Speed Racer enters an event to decide whether Chief Zuma will have to open the borders of his mystical country of Kapetapeck. Speed will be facing the greatest racer of all time,

---

Kabala, who is rumored to be fierce and unscrupulous. Mysterious Racer X and the ominous Kadar, who is out to steal Kapetapeck's treasure, will also compete. When the volcano erupts and creates an 800-mile tunnel, the hazardous Fire Race begins. **52 min.**

Speed Racer Vol. 11: *The Secret Invaders*
Speed Racer tries to stop a gang of ruthless assassins from taking over the country of Avalonia, also the site of the treacherous Twist and Turn Race. The assassins suspect that one of the racers is a secret agent out to thwart their evil plan ... and Speed is their prime target. **52 min.**

Speed Racer Vol. 12: *The Car With A Brain & Junk Car Grand Prix*
In THE CAR WITH A BRAIN, a mad scientist has programmed a monster car to destroy all in its path, and only Speed Racer can save a Scottish county from total obliteration. The evil vehicle's power is so tremendous, even tanks and torpedoes cannot demolish it. In JUNK CAR GRAND PRIX, Speed and Trixie enter a race that turns into a terrifying, cutthroat competition. The wealthy Baron Von Vondervon is holding the race in honor of his long-lost daughter, and the winner will share his fortune. **52 min.**

Domestic Home Video:
Speed Racer Vol. 1
FHE 27483 ▲ $12.95 ▲ VHS-EP ▲ DUB ▲ Mono ▲ CC ▲ 02/16/94
Speed Racer Vol. 2
FHE 27503 ▲ $12.95 ▲ VHS-EP ▲ DUB ▲ Mono ▲ CC ▲ 02/16/94
Speed Racer Vol. 3
FHE 27485 ▲ $12.95 ▲ VHS-EP ▲ DUB ▲ Mono ▲ CC ▲ 02/16/94
Speed Racer Vol. 4
FHE 27504 ▲ $12.95 ▲ VHS-EP ▲ DUB ▲ Mono ▲ CC ▲ 02/16/94
Speed Racer Vol. 5
FHE 27539 ▲ $12.95 ▲ VHS-EP ▲ DUB ▲ Mono ▲ CC ▲ 07/27/94
Speed Racer Vol. 6
FHE 27529 ▲ $12.95 ▲ VHS-EP ▲ DUB ▲ Mono ▲ CC ▲ 07/27/94
Speed Racer Vol. 7
FHE 27530 ▲ $12.95 ▲ VHS-EP ▲ DUB ▲ Mono ▲ CC ▲ 07/27/94
Speed Racer Vol. 8
FHE 27531 ▲ $12.95 ▲ VHS-EP ▲ DUB ▲ Mono ▲ CC ▲ 07/27/94
Speed Racer Vol. 9
FHE 27597 ▲ $12.95 ▲ VHS-EP ▲ DUB ▲ Mono ▲ CC ▲ 07/18/95
Speed Racer Vol. 10
FHE 27598 ▲ $12.95 ▲ VHS-EP ▲ DUB ▲ Mono ▲ CC ▲ 07/18/95
Speed Racer Vol. 11
FHE 27599 ▲ $12.95 ▲ VHS-EP ▲ DUB ▲ Mono ▲ CC ▲ 07/18/95
Speed Racer Vol. 12
FHE 27606 ▲ $12.95 ▲ VHS-EP ▲ DUB ▲ Mono ▲ CC ▲ 07/18/95
Speed Racer: Fastest Car/Race Against Time
FHE LD27504/485 ▲ $34.95 ▲ LD ▲ DUB ▲ HiFi Mono ▲ CC
Speed Racer: The Great Plan/The Secret Engine
FHE LD27483/503 ▲ $34.95 ▲ LD ▲ DUB ▲ HiFi Mono ▲ CC

Speed Racer: The Movie
MOVIE

(1967-68) ©Tatsunoko and Yokino/K. Fujita/Trans-Lux/Speed Racer Enterprises

This theatrical compilation (released as "The Speed Racer Show") features classic episodes of *Speed Racer* and *Colonel Bleep*. First, Speed Racer, Trixie, and all the gang are in a desperate race to save hundreds of lives from the evil clutches of THE CAR HATER. Then Colonel Bleep and his pals Scratch and Squeak are off through outer space after THE TREACHEROUS PIRATE. Next, Speed Racer returns at breakneck speed to battle evil, on and off the track, with THE RACE AGAINST THE MAMMOTH CAR. All this is interspersed with classic animated TV commercials from the 1960s. **80 min.**

Domestic Home Video:
FHE 27505 ▲ $14.95 ▲ VHS ▲ DUB ▲ HiFi Mono ▲ CC ▲ 02/16/94
FHE LD27505 ▲ $34.95 ▲ LD ▲ DUB ▲ HiFi Mono ▲ CC

Spirit of Wonder: Miss China's Ring
OAV

(1992) ©Kenji Tsuruta/Kodansha/Toshiba EMI.

Based on the manga by Kenji Tsuruta *Screenplay:* Michiru Shimada *Director:* Mitsuru Hongo *Character Design/Art Direction:* Yoshiaki Yanagida *Music:* Kohei Tanaka

One-shot OAV based on the manga of the same name by Kenji Tsuruta, as serialized in publisher Kodansha's COMIC AFTERNOON manga anthology (published in English by Dark Horse Comics). Touching, light-hearted love story with a sprinkling of NADIA-like turn of the century super-science. "Miss China," as the locals call her, has a mad scientist called Breckenridge living upstairs. The

mad scientist actually has come up with an incredible invention, and her boyfriend Jim has a plan to use it to give Miss China the most beautiful ring in all the world. Released in Japan under the title "The Spirit of Wonder: China-san no Yû'utsu" (Miss China's Melancholy) by Toshiba EMI; available in North America through AnimEigo. **45 min.**

Domestic Home Video:
ANI ET095-015 ▲ $19.95 ▲ VHS ▲ DUB ▲ HiFi Stereo
ANI AT095-008 ▲ $24.95 ▲ VHS ▲ SUB ▲ HiFi Stereo ▲ 01/31/96
ANI AD095-008 ▲ $39.95 ▲ LD ▲ HYBRID ▲ HiFi Stereo ▲ 02/14/96

Star Blazers
TV

TV series, 77 episodes

(1974-79) ©Office Academy/Sunwagon Productions

Created by: Yoshinobu Nishizaki and Leiji Matsumoto *Director:* Noboru Ishiguro.

The Earth desperately refits an ancient WWII battleship with alien technology to send a hand-picked crew to a distant planet to retrieve necessary materials to save the Earth from slow death by radiation poisoning. On its long journey, this lone vessel battles scores of alien enemies proving time and time again that the spirit of Earth refuses to be crushed, and if the will is there, anything is possible. Original story by Yoshinobu Nishizaki (ODIN) and Leiji Matsumoto (GALAXY EXPRESS), who also did the mecha designs, as well as the manga adaptation. Due to lukewarm ratings, the original 1974-75 TV series was cut short at only 26 episodes (a full year's worth, 52, had been planned), but with shades of Trekdom to come, its fantastic fan base inspired a movie version so popular, it was eventually to prove the foundation of modern-day anime fandom in Japan. Aired in the early '80s on U.S. television under the title "Star Blazers," the first two TV series were favorites at the early anime video rooms of American sci-fi cons, and played a major role in starting anime fandom and the domestic anime industry as it exists today. Thanks to a mammoth effort from New Jersey-based Voyager Entertainment, the entire "Yamato" series is currently available on domestic home video—all three TV series and five movies—and although the more recent "Yamato 2520" OAV series has yet to make it to the U.S., future plans are reportedly in the works. Released in Japan under the title "Uchû Senkan (Space Battleship) Yamato" by Westcape Corporation/Bandai Visual/Nihon Columbia; available in North America through Voyager Entertainment.

Episodes 1-26: The Quest For Iscandar (1974)
Star Blazers Episode 1
It's 2199, and radiation bombs from the planet Gamilon will make Earth uninhabitable in one year's time. Alex Wildstar's heroic self-sacrifice allows Captain Avatar's flagship to escape the battle of Pluto. Queen Starsha of planet Iscandar offers Earth a device which will get rid of the deadly radiation, and plans to build a Wave-Motion Engine capable of making the Quest to Iscandar. **22 min.**

Star Blazers Episode 2
Captain Avatar shows Wildstar, Mark Venture, and Nova (Dr. Sane's nurse) to the spaceship being built inside the wreck of the ancient battleship *Yamato*. A Gamilon fighter-carrier attacks the re-christened *Argo*. Wildstar resents Captain Avatar for surviving the battle that claimed his older brother. **22 min.**

Star Blazers Episode 3
On Pluto, Gamilons Ganz and Bane plan their retaliation for the destruction of the carrier. The Star Force, a crew of young people selected for the mission to Iscandar, receives their baptism of fire when their ship is targeted by the Gamilons' "Ultra Menace Missile." Can they ignite the engines before the missile arrives? The *Argo* is born, emerging from the mushroom cloud. **22 min.**

Star Blazers Episode 4
Gamilon fighter planes approach while the *Argo* is motionless, building energy for the Star Force's first space warp. One of the Black Tiger pilots is damaged, and Wildstar flies out to assist him, narrowly making it back to the ship in time for the instantaneous warp to Mars. **22 min.**

Star Blazers Episode 5
Caught in Jupiter's massive gravity well, the Star Force skirmishes with Gamilon fighters while orbiting Jupiter. The *Argo*'s Wave-Motion Gun builds all the ship's warp-energy into a tachyon-beam that is released from the front of the *Argo*, turning the ship into a gigantic cannon. The Wave-Motion Gun destroys the floating continent on Jupiter, but leaves the *Argo* temporarily powerless, sinking into the gas clouds. **22 min.**

Star Blazers Episode 6
Wildstar, Nova, and IQ-9 land on Titan to search for rare minerals to mine. The Star Blazers skirmish with Gamilon army tanks sent by General Crypt to hunt them down. During the fight, Wildstar finds the frozen wreck of the *Paladin*, the missile frigate

commanded by his brother in the retreat from Pluto, which had crashed on Saturn's largest moon. He finds his brother's pistol in the nick of time, almost as if Alex's spirit is watching over Derek. **22 min.**

Star Blazers Episode 7

Captain Avatar commits the Star Force to attacking the Gamilons' base on Pluto, source of the deadly rain of radioactive planet-bombs. The *Argo* is damaged by Colonel Ganz' new weapon, the Reflex Gun. Venture maneuvers behind Pluto's moon, but the Gamilons bounce the deadly beam off reflector-satellites to strike the *Argo* wherever it moves. The space battleship splashes down onto Pluto's ammonia seas, and sinks beneath the waves. **22 min.**

Star Blazers Episode 8

Captain Avatar wages a war of nerves with the Gamilons, surfacing long enough to draw the Gamilons' fire, so that a team of commandos can find the Reflex Gun. Wildstar, Conroy, Sandor, and IQ-9 infiltrate the base and sabotage the Reflex Gun. When Colonel Ganz fires the gun again, its explosion destroys the Gamilon base, driving the Gamilon fleet into orbit. Leader Desslok banishes Ganz for his failure. **22 min.**

Star Blazers Episode 9

The *Argo* hides in an asteroid field while making desperately needed repairs. Ganz and Bane lead the Gamilon fleet in a frantic search for the Star Force, but Sandor has invented a system to magnetically attract small asteroids, camouflaging the *Argo* while repairs are completed. Battleworthy again, the Star Force sheds its camouflage, creating a revolving ring of rocks, which Sandor angles to intercept incoming fire. Ganz tries a suicidal bid to ram the *Argo*, but Venture uses the rocket-anchor to whip the enemy flagship into an asteroid, eliminating the last Gamilon presence in the Solar System. **22 min.**

Star Blazers Episode 10

The Star Blazers, leaving communication range of Earth, each take turns making their emotional farewells to their loved ones. Nova searches for Wildstar, who avoids his turn to say goodbye to anyone on Earth. Only Captain Avatar knows Wildstar lost his entire family to the war. He seeks the angry young man out, because he too has no one left on Earth to say goodbye to. Wildstar discovers that the captain's only son served aboard Alex's ship and was lost in the battle of Pluto. Together they vow to return to Earth. **22 min.**

Star Blazers Episode 11

The Star Force encounters a minefield the Gamilons placed in their path. The self-propelled mines continually draw closer around the trapped Space Cruiser. Sandor discovers that Star Blazers in spacesuits can manually move the mines away from the ship, allowing the Star Force to escape. Leader Desslok uses the incident to chastise his Generals. **22 min.**

Star Blazers Episode 12

Romance begins to blossom between Wildstar and Nova when the *Argo* becomes enmeshed in another Gamilon trap, a "Space Web." Captain Avatar's radiation sickness becomes more pronounced. Leader Desslok sends his newest invention, an all-consuming cloud of "Ecto-Gas" after the *Argo*, chasing them into a nearby star, the "Sea of Fire." The Star Force uses its Wave-Motion Gun to clear an escape path through the solar flares. **22 min.**

Star Blazers Episode 13

Leader Desslok appoints General Lysis to lead the fight against the Star Force. Wildstar and Conroy disable an enemy fighter and takes its pilot prisoner. The Star Blazers are surprised to find that Gamilons resemble Earthlings, only with green skin. Wildstar, consumed by anger, has to be physically restrained from murdering the prisoner and has a flashback to his parents' death during the Gamilon bombings. Captain Avatar orders the prisoner released, and Wildstar gives him some food at his departure. **22 min.**

Star Blazers Episode 14

Tensions mount as the Star Force must wait for the solar activity to die down at the "Octopus Starstorm." Wildstar and Venture fight, landing most of the crew in K.P. Nova suggests a party to Captain Avatar as a morale booster. Following a Gamilon ship, Wildstar discovers a channel through the closely-packed stars. During the hazardous passage, Wildstar and Venture must pull together to save the ship. **22 min.**

Star Blazers Episode 15

General Lysis takes command of the main Gamilon base at Planet Balin, midway between Earth and Gamilon, displacing General Volgar. The Gamilons chase the Star Force into an energy-draining "Galactic Whirlpool" — a supernova forming into a black hole. The Star Force escapes this graveyard of spaceships with broadcast energy and navigational help sent from afar by Queen Starsha of Iscandar. **22 min.**

Star Blazers Episode 16

Nova and IQ-9 are trapped on the planet of the Bee people — aboriginal insectoid allies of the Gamilons. They become involved in an insurrection against the despotic Queen of Beeland. When Star Force troopers led by Wildstar rescue Nova, IQ-9 realizes the impossibility of his unrequited love for Nova, and the robot agrees when the Bee people call him a monster. **22 min.**

Star Blazers Episode 17

General Volgar invents a method to control the microscopic creatures that inhabit the magma of Planet Balan. He launches his "Balanasaurus" against the Star Force. The monster seems invulnerable, re-forming after being blown apart by the *Argo*'s shock-cannons, but the Wave-Motion Gun destroys it. **22 min.**

Star Blazers Episode 18

The Star Force is halted by Volgar's latest invention, a magnatron satellite which uses magnetic forces to tear ships apart. When Sandor and Wildstar explore the satellite, the engineer's mechanical limbs — cybernetic replacements for limbs lost in the childhood accident that killed his sister — start to malfunction because of the powerful magnetic fields. They remove the cyborg limbs and Sandor detonates their power cells, deactivating the Gamilon satellite. **22 min.**

Star Blazers Episode 19

Dr. Sane prescribes a holodeck session for Homer, but it does not help the homesick communications officer. Even though they are long out of communications range from Earth, messages are inexplicably getting through. A desperate Homer tries to spacewalk home, and discovers the secret satellite the Gamilons set up to destroy the Star Force's morale with bad news from home. **22 min.**

Star Blazers Episode 20

The Star Force reaches the Gamilon's main fleet anchorage base, midway between Earth and Iscandar on the planet Balin. General Lysis tries to crush the *Argo* between the base and the artificial White Dwarf star orbiting the planet, but his plans are interrupted because of General Volgar's jealousy. The Star Force blasts a way clear with its Wave-Motion Gun, and Lysis is called home in disgrace. **22 min.**

Star Blazers Episode 21

Lysis, sentenced to death by a Gamilon court-martial and pardoned by Leader Desslok, sends a challenge to the Star Force for a showdown in the "Rainbow Galaxy" star cluster. Captain Avatar inspires the Star Force with an impassioned speech while Lysis prepares the Gamilons' latest inventions, a teleportation system called Space Matter Instantaneous Transport Equipment, and a gigantic drill-missile specifically designed for use against the Wave-Motion Gun. **22 min.**

Star Blazers Episode 22

The Battle of The Rainbow Galaxy begins when Gamilon fighters suddenly appear out of nowhere and attack the *Argo* at point-blank range. Lysis uses S.M.I.T.E. to send wave after wave of fighters, exhausting the Black Tiger cosmofighters. As the Black Tigers rearm, Lysis S.M.I.T.E.s in a giant missle that drills into the muzzle of the Wave-Motion Gun. Sandor and IQ-9 enter the drill-missile and some desperate re-wiring sends the missile into reverse, starting a chain reaction that destroys the Gamilon carriers. In a final, desperate move, Lysis self-destructs his command ship next to the *Argo*, causing tremendous damage. **22 min.**

Star Blazers Episode 23

The Star Blazers are jubilant as they finally arrive at the Sanzar solar system, home of Planet Iscandar. Captain Avatar's radiation sickness worsens, while romance blossoms between Nova and Wildstar. Deep space missiles envelop the *Argo* in a cloud of magnetic particles, jamming all radio contact. Queen Starsha calls Leader Desslok, berating him for his brutal methods. Desslok insists he is working to save both their peoples' worlds and uses magnetic beams to drag the Star Force down into the massive caverns of Iscandar's twin planet, which a horrified Star Force learns is Gamilon. A bedridden Captain Avatar places Wildstar in command of the Star Force and the *Argo* splashes down into Gamilon's sulfuric acid seas. **22min.**

Star Blazers Episode 24

Gamilon storm generators pour a deadly rain of acid on the Star Force, amid a hail of missiles. Avatar advises Wildstar to submerge the ship in the acid seas. While the acid eats away at the ship's hull, Sandor and IQ-9 find a major tectonic fault. The Wave-Motion Gun triggers a massive eruption of Gamilon's many volcanoes, devastating the planet. Desslok, witnessing the destruction of his world, goes mad. When the Star Force resurfaces, the Gamilon Leader unleashes Armageddon. Amid a storm of missiles, the *Argo* battles its way into the heart of the enemy's fire. After the battle, Wildstar and Nova mournfully survey the devastation and the Star Force departs for Iscandar. **22 min.**

Star Blazers Episode 25

The Star Blazers make planetfall on Iscandar, only to learn Starsha is the last survivor of a pandemic plague. As remotes load the Cosmo DNA aboard the *Argo*, Wildstar meets his long lost brother. Alex Wildstar is overjoyed to be reunited with his brother, his old Captain, and his old friend Sandor. Sparks, who fears the mission is hopeless, kidnaps Nova as part of a mutiny. After the mutiny is put down, the crew bid farewell to Starsha, but Alex elects to stay behind with his love. The Quest for Iscandar complete, the Star Force heads home. **22 min.**

Star Blazers Episode 26

Captain Avatar tells Dr. Sane his hopes to live long enough to see Earth one last time, unaware that Desslok survived the fall of Gamilon. Desslok's flagship rams and boards the *Argo*. The Gamilons advance in a cloud of radioactive gas until Nova activates the Cosmo

DNA. The Gamilons are driven off, but the energy discharge has injured Nova. A heartsick Wildstar carries her to the bridge, when Desslok attacks with his own Wave-Motion cannon, the Desslok Gun. Sandor's reflex-shield reflects Desslok's fire back onto his own ship, which vanishes amid the flames. Avatar reminisces about the journey, and his family and lives long enough to witness Star Force's return. Nova awakens to the bridge crew's jubilation and the *Argo* brings the Cosmo DNA to Earth, which turns green again. **22 min.**

Episodes 27-52: The Comet Empire (1978)
Star Blazers Episode 27
2201 A.D.: The Comet Empire has set its sights on conquering Earth. Leader Desslok arrives on the Comet Empire and allies with Prince Zordar against Earth and the Star Force. The *Argo* is returning from a patrol in the outer solar system when unidentified fighters attack the patrol squadron. A huge power surge starts burning out circuitry as an alien message is beamed to Earth. Returning to Earth with burned out radio, the *Argo* narrowly avoids the new Earth Defense Force flagship, the *Andromeda*, commanded by Captain Gideon. **22 min.**

Star Blazers Episode 28
Wildstar and Nova make up for lost time after his long patrol. Captain Gideon dresses Wildstar down and informs him of the Earth Defense Command's plans to automate much of the *Argo*'s systems and disperse the Star Force as cadre to other ships in the fleet. Sandor shows Wildstar a huge white comet heading for Earth, and the partially translated message from outer space. Amid a massive power blackout that plunges Earth into chaos, Wildstar spots a fighter similar to those that attacked his squadron. **22 min.**

Star Blazers Episode 29
The translated message appears to be a cry for help from Trelaina of the planet Telezart. Wildstar wants to investigate, but the Earth Defense Council rejects the idea. Leader Desslok predicts that the Star Force will go to Trelaina's aid and departs the Comet Empire. General Talan has gathered the far flung Gamilon territorial fleets into a massive armada awaiting their Leader's order to deploy around Telezart. Wildstar and Nova go to the old underground city which sheltered humanity during the Gamilon siege. Because of Starsha's aid in the time of Earth's desperate plight, they feel an obligation to help. Several other Star Force members arrive and agree. **22 min.**

Star Blazers Episode 30
Venture wrestles with his conscience as most of the Star Force crew gather at the *Argo*. General Stone orders the crew to disperse, but they steal their own ship and prepare to launch. Venture shows up at the last minute and pilots the takeoff. The Star Force destroys a defense satellite blocking their way and, as they pass the moonbase they are joined by the Black Tiger cosmofighter squadron. **22 min.**

Star Blazers Episode 31
Captain Gideon is ordered to stop the mutinous Star Force. Wildstar tries to order Nova off the ship, but she insists on staying. The *Andromeda* chases the *Argo* through the asteroid field, but after a tense showdown, Gideon lets them go, muttering, "Captain Avatar taught you well." **22 min.**

Star Blazers Episode 32
The Space Marine garrison on Planet Broomis is under heavy attack. Desslok orders General Naska to watch out for the Star Force. The Star Force defeats Naska's fleet and rescue the surviving Space Marines, led by Sgt. Knox. **22 min.**

Star Blazers Episode 33
The Star Force fights off an attack by stealthed ships. Tensions flare between the Space Marines and the Star Force regulars, culminating in an immense bar-room brawl between Wildstar and Sgt. Knox. Another message arrives from Trelaina, and Venture takes over communications to get a fix on Planet Telezart's location. Back at the Comet Empire, Princess Invidia conspires against Desslok. **22 min.**

Star Blazers Episode 34

The Star Force is caught in a space whirlpool and a time acceleration field, which cause everything to age rapidly as uniforms and the ship itself starts to fall apart. Venture's infatuation with the mysterious Trelaina grows with each message. **22 min.**

Star Blazers Episode 35
Sgt. Knox commandeers a cosmofighter and enters a dogfight which results in the capture of an enemy pilot. Pilot Mazir resists all interrogation, even when Dr. Sane gets him drunk. Mazir escapes, but when his Major denies him permission to return, Mazir kamikazes into the *Argo*. The Star Force then shreds Mazir's squadron. **22 min.**

Star Blazers Episode 36
The Star Force is trapped in a field of energy-siphoning asteroids, while General Torbuck bombards them with missiles. Sandor develops a way to draw power from the asteroids and forms a rotating ring of asteroids to block incoming fire while they break free of the field. Torbuck launches anti-matter missiles at the *Argo*, but the Wave-Motion Gun hurls all their destructive energy back onto Torbuck's ships. **22 min.**

Star Blazers Episode 37
The Star Force passes through a field of "Star Flies" which the crew takes aboard. When Gamilon fighters attack, the *Argo*'s systems begin to fall prey to the metal-eating bacteria in the Star Flies. Desslok recalls his last battle with the Star Force, when he tried to warp out of the way of his own beam reflected back at him, and how the Comet Empire found his body in the wreck drifting in hyperspace and revived him. General Garrot brings up his battle-carrier to finish off the Star Force with energy cannons. **22 min.**

Star Blazers Episode 38

The Star Flies have disabled the guns on Garrot's flagship, forcing his retreat. The Star Force takes refuge in a convenient cocoon-shaped asteroid, unaware that it is a Gamilon trap. Electromagnetic units imprison the *Argo* within the "Tunnel-Satellite." Sandor schemes to blast the *Argo* free by firing the Wave-Motion Gun without its anti-recoil device, which will have to be manually disconnected by Royster. Desslok prepares to immolate the trapped *Argo* with his Desslok Gun, but a call from Princess Invidia delays him long enough for the Star Force to escape. Furious, Desslok returns to the Comet Empire. **22 min.**

Star Blazers Episode 39
The Star Force finally arrives at Telezart, fights its way through a storm of missiles and lands Space Marines on the planet. The Gamilon fleet returns to the Comet Empire where Princess Invidia talks Zordar into letting her handle Desslok. The Space Marines come under heavy attack by Comet Empire tanks led by General Skortch. **22 min.**

Star Blazers Episode 40
Skortch's armored assault is broken by special artillery assembled by Sandor, and the Marines pursue the enemy. Sgt. Knox finishes off Skortch in hand to hand combat. Wildstar, Sandor and IQ-9 penetrate into the cavern which the enemy troops had sealed off, and find the crystalline home of Trelaina. Desslok sees through Invidia's lies, but her guards arrest him. Desslok orders Talan to command the Gamilon fleet in his absence. **22 min.**

Star Blazers Episode 41
Trelaina invites Wildstar, Sandor and Knox into her home and Venture arrives and finally meets Trelaina face to face. Trelaina explains that she was born with great psionic powers that she dare not use ... since the time when, grieving over the loss of a loved one during a battle, she let loose her anguish and power, and slew everyone on the panet. She tells them of the threat of the Comet Empire, a giant war-machine bent on enslaving the universe, that travels within a protective plasma cloud that devours planets for fuel with the gravitic output of a small star. **22 min.**

Star Blazers Episode 42
The Star Force must leave if they are to warn Earth in time. The Comet Empire is on a direct course for Telezart, but Trelaina refuses to leave her homeworld. Venture eventually talks her into departing with the Star Force. Once aboard the *Argo*, she tells Wildstar that she must stay behind and returns to her planet to await the Comet's arrival. **22 min.**

Star Blazers Episode 43
As the Comet Empire approaches Telezart at a speed which will beat the *Argo* back to Earth, Zordar calls Trelaina and offers her asylum. Trelaina refuses and vows to stop Zordar here and now. As the Comet's gravity starts tearing the planet asunder, Trelaina unleashes her powers, converting Telezart into pure energy. Inside the holocaust, Trelaina's last thoughts are for Mark Venture as she fades away. The Comet Empire emerges heavily damaged from the conflagration. Trelaina's sacrifice has bought the Star Force time to warn Earth and prepare its defenses. **22 min.**

Star Blazers Episode 44
The gathering of forces begins as Prince Zordar orders General Bleek's armada to move on Earth. Captain Gideon mobilizes the Earth Defense Fleets to gather at Saturn. Leader Desslok escapes from the Comet Empire and General Talan flies him to the Gamilon fleet. Zordar, learning of Invidia's deception, returns Desslok's flagship. **22 min.**

Star Blazers Episode 45
As the *Argo* approaches Planet Broomis, Sgt. Knox tries to commandeer a cosmofighter to visit the graves of his men. Wildstar orders Knox to scout the planet, and he discovers an enemy base. The Star Force fights it out with the garrison fleet. As the enemy armada approaches, Captain Gideon decides to meet them at Saturn's moon Titan. **22 min.**

Star Blazers Episode 46
General Bleek sends his carriers ahead under the command of General Mannik. Captain Gideon takes advantage of this by detaching the *Argo* to lead Earth's carriers against the enemy carrier fleet. Sandor and IQ-9 scout the enemy carriers. Conroy and Hardy lead Earth's vastly outnumbered cosmofighters in a surprise attack on Mannik's fleet. The *Argo* finishes off the Comet Empire's carriers with point-blank shock cannon fire. **22 min.**

Star Blazers Episode 47
The magna-flame gun on Bleek's dreadnought pounds the EDF ships from long range, so Gideon retreats. Bleek pursues the fleeing Earth ships into Saturn's ice-rings, where the

 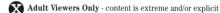

heat of the magna-flame gun vaporizes the ice. The expanding gases buffet Bleek's ships, allowing Gideon's ships to pick them off at will. In that moment of triumph, the Comet Empire warps into Saturn's orbit, devouring many of the EDF ships in its massive gravity well. The damaged *Argo* is hurled free of the battle as the massed wave-motion guns of the EDF fleet fire at the Comet Empire. The comet effect boils away, revealing the citadel within. Before the Earth guns can recharge, the fortress starts revolving, masking the Comet Empire city in a protective tornado of energy, and raining missiles on the Earth fleet. Gideon tells Wildstar to attack the citadel from the bottom, then rams the *Andromeda* into the fortress. **22 min.**

Star Blazers Episode 48
Wildstar is wounded while the Star Force starts repairs on the *Argo*. Zordar blasts the moon into molten slag and demands Earth's unconditional surrender. Wildstar refuses to give in and rallies the Star Force, which departs Titan base and heads for Earth. **22 min.**

Star Blazers Episode 49
Gamilon fighters appear around the *Argo* and Desslok radios Wildstar. The Comet Empire lands in the Pacific Ocean to accept Earth's surrender, as the Gamilon fleet surrounds the Star Force. Desslok SMITEs space mines around the *Argo*, blocking the muzzle of the wave-motion gun. Venture warps the ship out of the way of the Desslok Gun's blast, and rams the Gamilon flagship. Venture is shot as the Star Force storms aboard Desslok's ship and his body drifts away into space. A bleeding Wildstar is cut off from the rest of the Star Force and continues alone. General Talan pleads with Desslok to leave his burning flagship when Wildstar appears, gun in hand. **22 min.**

Star Blazers Episode 50
Nova arrives to see Wildstar and Desslok facing off over drawn pistols. Wildstar collapses from blood loss and Nova shields him with her own body. Desslok, struck by their fierce love for their homeworld and for each other, renounces his revenge, tells Nova of the Comet Empire's weak point, and departs with his fleet. Wildstar awakens to learn of Venture's death and Earth's surrender. Trelaina appears in deep space and transfuses much of her life-energy into Venture's body. As Conroy leads the Black Tigers into Earth's atmosphere, the *Argo* submerges and attacks the Comet Empire from beneath the sea. **22 min.**

Star Blazers Episode 51
The Star Force pursues the Comet Empire out of the atmosphere. The Black Tigers and Space Marines invade the Comet Empire and fight their way toward the main engines. Knox stays behind to blow up the Empire's reactors, leaving the fortress helpless. Wildstar returns to the *Argo* and orders an all-out bombardment. A gigantic superdreadnought rises out of the flaming ruin of the Comet Empire. Prince Zordar fights on. **22 min.**

Star Blazers Episode 52

Zordar unleashes a titanic broadside, reducing the *Argo* to a flaming wreck and killing most of the Star Force. He taunts the survivors, then begins to bombard Earth with his gigantic energy cannon. Wildstar orders the Star Force's evacuation and returns to the *Argo*. Nova, guessing his intention to kamikaze into Zordar's ship, joins him. Before they can begin their suicide run, Trelaina appears, bearing the unconscious Venture. She asks them to give her love to Mark and flies off to confront Zordar, turning to energy as she approaches the giant ship. Zordar flees as Trelaina expends the last of her energy, destroying him and his ship. The battered *Argo* returns to Earth. **22 min.**

Episodes 53-77: The Bolar Wars (1980)

Star Blazers Episode 53
THE SOLAR SYSTEM FACES DESTRUCTION: A Garuman proton missile goes astray during a battle in the Milky Way. Ryusuke Domon's parents are killed as the missile hits their cruise ship. Back at the academy, outstanding cadets are graduated early to augment *Argo*'s crew, but Derek Wildstar assigns a rebellious Domon to the kitchen. Professor Simon concludes that the Sun will go nova in a year, then supernova, destroying the solar system. Wildstar is promoted to Captain of the *Argo* and ordered to search for a new planet for Earth's population to emigrate to. **22 min.**

Star Blazers Episode 54
THE GREAT BATTLE IN THE MILKY WAY: Takeshi Ageha expertly tests *Argo*'s new shuttlecraft, the *Cosmo Hound*, but is pulled from the crew by his string-pulling father. Garuman General Dagon attacks the Earth colony on Alpha Centauri. As solar flares play havoc with Earth machinery, Ageha's mother encourages her son to follow his desires - even if it means he must leave Earth. **22 min.**

Star Blazers Episode 55
ARGO SETS SAIL AT DAYBREAK: IQ-9, fresh from an argument with Sandor, pulls up Nova's skirt. Dagon chases the Earth fleet back toward the solar system, but interceptors destroy a Garuman ship that blunders into Earth's atmosphere. Wildstar gives anyone with doubts a chance to stay home, and Homer elects to stay and search for a girl he met at the airport. The government refuses to acknowledge the crisis, so General Todo dispatches the *Argo* on its own authority. Homer returns and learns his mystery girl is here. **22 min.**

Star Blazers Episode 56
HIT THAT MARS: At a Garuman staff meeting, Leader Desslok threatens Commander Histenberger with death if he fails twice more. The *Argo* crew undergoes 16 hours of grueling training maneuvers near Mars, then destroys three incoming proton missiles. **22 min.**

Star Blazers Episode 57
S.O.S. ROGENDOR: The heavily damaged *Rogendor* is all that remains of Earth's fleet. Capt. Ram requests supplies and a repair port, but General Todo will only grant non-military supplies and 24 hours. Dagon's fleet arrives and demands the *Rogendor*. Argo escorts *Rogendor* out of Earth's territorial space, but before Capt. Ram can warp, Dagon attacks both ships. **22 min.**

Star Blazers Episode 58
FIERCE BATTLE NEAR PLANET 11: Captain Ram thanks *Argo* and Earth for the chance to die a soldier's death before the Garuman fleet destroys the *Rogendor*. Argo counterattacks and Dagon warps away, leaving his fleet to cover his escape. A damaged Garuman ship rams *Argo* and its crew boards. Domon kills an enemy soldier, and later Wildstar holds a funeral for the *Argo* crew killed in the fighting. **22 min.**

Star Blazers Episode 59
THE ROUGH SEAS OF ALPHA: The temperature on Earth begins to rise as *Argo* arrives at the battered colony in Alpha Centauri and half the crew gets shore leave. A bar-room brawl is cut short by a missile attack. **22 min.**

Star Blazers Episode 60
THE LAST PIONEER: An attempt to cool the sun with feedback fails when the relay stations overload and explode. *Argo* arrives at Barnard's Star, where the crew investigates a distress signal, finding a pioneer family dying of fever. *Argo* is attacked by reflex guns - a Gamilon weapon which bounces lasers off battle mirrors. **22 min.**

Star Blazers Episode 61
BATTLE AT BARNARD'S STAR: The crew of the *Cosmo Hound* discovers why *Argo* couldn't locate any reflex satellites - the battle mirrors are mounted on fighters. With the reflection fighters all shot down, *Argo* locates and destroys the Garuman base. Dagon flees. The stubborn pioneer dies. The sole survivor, Tomoko, is pregnant. Wildstar decides to send her and all the female *Argo* crew (except Nova) back to Earth for safety. **22 min.**

Star Blazers Episode 62
DAGON'S NEW FLEET ATTACKS BACK: Admiral Gidel gives General Dagon one last chance - and a new carrier fleet - to destroy the *Argo*. Near a black hole, *Argo* encounters an Earth exploration ship commanded by Captain Dan, who reports seeing a large fleet and requests escort from *Argo*. The request is unfortunately denied, and once *Argo* leaves, a Dagon ship destroys Dan's ship. The Dagon fleet then drives *Argo* toward a group of gravity wells. **22 min.**

Star Blazers Episode 63
ARGO IN DANGER NEAR THE CYNUS: *Argo* pulls free of the "space tornadoes" but is attacked, surprised by enemy fighters appearing by instant teleportation - another Gamilon technology. Dagon brings up his main fleet and orders *Argo* to surrender, but his carriers cannot stand up to the battleship's guns. Dagon tries to push *Argo* into the black hole near Cygnus, but *Argo* breaks free and instead Dagon goes spinning into the black hole. **22 min.**

Star Blazers Episode 64
A PENAL COLONY IN SPACE: Conditions on Earth worsen. General Todo takes charge of the Space Emigration Ministry and assigns space cruisers *Prince of Wales*, *Bismark* and *Arizona* to aid in the effort. *Argo* encounters ships of the Bolar Commonwealth, who heard of *Argo* from Captain Ram. Captain Balsky escorts *Argo* to Planet Berth for repairs and resupply. While *Argo* crew members attend a party given by General Brozof, Domon and Ageha stumble across a concentration camp holding followers of Mother Shalebart. It is obvious that Bolar conquered this planet. The prisoners riot and storm the *Argo*, demanding to go to planet Shalebart. **22 min.**

Star Blazers Episode 65
DREADFUL BOLAR COMMONWEALTH: *Argo*'s crew recaptures all the prisoners, and Premier Bernlaze orders them all executed. Wildstar is outraged and complains to Bernlaze, who orders *Argo* and Earth to become subjects of the Bolar Commonwealth - or its enemies. The *Argo* officers flee to the ship while cosmotigers strafe Balsky and free the prisoners. Bernlaze takes off and destroys the planet with mammoth missiles, killing his own people. **22 min.**

Star Blazers Episode 66
THE SUBSPACE MARINER: GARUMAN WOLF: Gidel sends Captain Frakken after *Argo*. *Argo* cannot detect Frakken's "submarines" and fires blindly at the subspace faults the "submarines" attack from. The bridge is hit and Wildstar is wounded. **22 min.**

Star Blazers Episode 67
ARGO A PRISONER: Dr. Sado operates on Wildstar while Domon takes command. Frakken lures them towards Admiral Gidal's fortress, which captures the *Argo*. Gidal calls Desslok and reports his triumph. When Desslok finds out that Gidel has been fighting *Argo*, he is enraged. Desslok apologizes to Wildstar for his subordinates' unauthorized

TV Made for Television Broadcast   **OAV** Made for Home Video Release   **MOVIE** Made for Theatrical Release

actions, telling him he considers *Argo* and Earth to be eternal friends. Desslok invites them to his new planet. **22 min.**

Star Blazers Episode 68
A FETE DAY FOR DESSLOK: Desslok tells Wildstar and Nova how he liberated Garuman from harsh Bolar rule and was acclaimed leader by its people, ancestral cousins of the Gamilons. He named Garuman's sister world Starsha, and set about taking other planets from Bolar rule. Then they view a massive military parade in honor of the first anniversary of the Garuman Empire. Desslok dedicates the parade to Wildstar's late brother, who also held Starsha's love. **22 min.**

Star Blazers Episode 69
DESSLOK'S EMPIRE AT THE ELEVENTH HOUR: Desslok and Talan visit *Argo*'s bridge and Wildstar tells Desslok of the sun. Desslok offers Garuman's scientific aid as compensation for what his subordinates have done. Sandor approves of Major Frauald's plan to cool down the sun. Wildstar asks Desslok why he doesn't use his power for peace, and Desslok says he must oppose the aggressive Bolar. They are interrupted by an attack from Bolar warp missiles and Desslok orders Frauald's fleet to take off. A mammoth planet-killer missile slips past the defense satellites, but the *Argo* intercepts and Domon destroys it. **22 min.**

Star Blazers Episode 70
THE ANGRY SUN: Frauald's fleet arrives at Earth and is greeted by General Todo. On Garuman/Gamilas, Wildstar and Desslok watch as Frauald's fleet sets up a magnetic field around the sun, and guides proton missiles into it - but the attempt fails and Frauald plummets into the sun. Desslok tells Wildstar of an Earth-like planet his astronomers have discovered, and *Argo* sets off toward the planet Phantom. **22 min.**

Star Blazers Episode 71
ON THE WAY TO PLANET PHANTOM: Earth retreats to underground cities and steps up construction of the Space Arks. Domon and Homer find a derelict ship with starving pilgrims aboard who have been searching for planet Shalabart for 25 years. Sandor repairs their ship as a Bolar fleet under General Hawkins approaches. Wildstar tries to warn them off, but is forced to destroy the fleet. Mother Shalabart appears to the *Argo*'s crew. **22 min.**

Star Blazers Episode 72
PLANET PHANTOM IT IS: *Argo* arrives at Phantom which looks exactly like Earth, even to its flora and fauna. Earth people rejoice and Desslok toasts Wildstar. IQ-9 warns of danger he cannot articulate. Phantoms of dead relatives appear to the *Argo*'s crew. **22 min.**

Star Blazers Episode 73
SHATTERED HOPE: Desslok dispatches Major Helmeyer to help investigate Phantom. A beautiful girl beckons to Ageha. To Helmeyer, Phantom is exactly like Garuman/Gamilas. The Garuman geologist drills for a crust sample and ground ripples. People flee the grass that rises up to engulf the landing ships. Agaha and Domon pursue Ageha's visionary maiden. **22 min.**

Star Blazers Episode 74
FAREWELL PLANET PHANTOM: Phantom is a living planet which emits psycho-hypnotic energy. It asks Ageha to look after Princess Luda, an exile whom it has been guarding. The *Cosmo Hound* retrieves Domon, Ageha and Luda. Lt. General Gustaf destroys Phantom with a proton missile. **22 min.**

Star Blazers Episode 75
BATTLE AT THE SCALAGECK STRAIT: Two months later the *Argo* finds the wreckage of the *Arizona* on the last planet within evacuation range of Earth, apparent victim of a Bolar attack. Gustaf catches up with *Argo* and demands he be turned over to Garuman. Before the battle can erupt, Desslok calls Gustaf and orders him to protect Luda and *Argo* from the Bolar until reinforcements can arrive. Hawkins arrives, demands Luda, and attacks. Gustaf's ship kamikazes into the Bolar fleet and the main Bolar armada attacks. *Argo* destroys it with wave energy cartridges. Agaha prays to Mother Shalabart to save Earth. Luda promises to lead *Argo* to Shalabart. **22 min.**

Star Blazers Episode 76
THE SECRET OF PLANET SHALABART: Luda opens the gateway to planet Shalabart, which lies in another dimension. Desslok's fleet follows *Argo*, and is itself followed by Golsakof's Bolar fleet. Wildstar dismisses suggestions to conquer and occupy Shalabart. The Bolar fleet attacks Desslok and Shalabart, but is destroyed by Desslok's hyper cannon. Luda shows Wildstar the hidden super weapons from Shalabart's past, and gives him a weapon for cooling down stars. Luda then says goodbye and merges with Mother Shalabart. **22 min.**

Star Blazers Episode 77
ARGO, HIT THE SUN: Earth's surface is scorched and the underground cities are starting to roast. *Argo* arrives and prepares to use Shalabart's Hydro-Cosmojin on the sun, but is attacked by Bernlayze's Bolar fleet. Desslok arrives just in time to blow away the Bolar fleet, and then tells Wildstar to concentrate on the sun. Bernlayze's fortress withstands the

attack, however, and fires his black hole gun. Desslok's flagship can withstand the fire, but cannot retaliate. As Domon struggles to prepare the Hydro-Cosmojin, he is strafed by a Bolar fighter. Ageha, guided by Mother Shalabart, kamikazes into the black hole gun, giving Desslok a chance to destroy the Bolar fortress. Domon manages to open the dome over the Hydro-Cosmojin before collapsing from his wounds, and Nova and Wildstar fire the weapon, returning the sun to normal. Domon dies, Shalabart appears bearing Ageha's spirit to comfort Wildstar, Desslok congratulates Wildstar ... and the *Argo* goes home. **44 min.**

Domestic Home Video:
Star Blazers Vol. 1: *Episodes 1 and 2*
VEI 10003 ▲ $19.95 ▲ VHS ▲ DUB ▲ Mono ▲ 06/01/93
Star Blazers Vol. 2: *Episodes 3 and 4*
VEI 10002 ▲ $19.95 ▲ VHS ▲ DUB ▲ Mono ▲ 06/01/93
Star Blazers Vol. 3: *Episodes 5 and 6*
VEI 10003 ▲ $19.95 ▲ VHS ▲ DUB ▲ Mono ▲ 06/01/93
Star Blazers Vol. 4: *Episodes 7 and 8*
VEI 10004 ▲ $19.95 ▲ VHS ▲ DUB ▲ Mono ▲ 06/01/93
Star Blazers Vol. 5: *Episodes 9 and 10*
VEI 10005 ▲ $19.95 ▲ VHS ▲ DUB ▲ Mono ▲ 06/01/93
Star Blazers Vol. 6: *Episodes 11 and 12*
VEI 10006 ▲ $19.95 ▲ VHS ▲ DUB ▲ Mono ▲ 06/01/93
Star Blazers Vol. 7: *Episodes 13 and 14*
VEI 10007 ▲ $19.95 ▲ VHS ▲ DUB ▲ Mono ▲ 06/01/93
Star Blazers Vol. 8: *Episodes 15 and 16*
VEI 10008 ▲ $19.95 ▲ VHS ▲ DUB ▲ Mono ▲ 06/01/93
Star Blazers Vol. 9: *Episodes 17 and 18*
VEI 10009 ▲ $19.95 ▲ VHS ▲ DUB ▲ Mono ▲ 06/01/93
Star Blazers Vol. 10: *Episodes 19 and 20*
VEI 10010 ▲ $19.95 ▲ VHS ▲ DUB ▲ Mono ▲ 06/01/93
Star Blazers Vol. 11: *Episodes 21 and 22*
VEI 10011 ▲ $19.95 ▲ VHS ▲ DUB ▲ Mono ▲ 06/01/93
Star Blazers Vol. 12: *Episodes 23 and 24*
VEI 10012 ▲ $19.95 ▲ VHS ▲ DUB ▲ Mono ▲ 06/01/93
Star Blazers Vol. 13: *Episodes 25 and 26*
VEI 10013 ▲ $19.95 ▲ VHS ▲ DUB ▲ Mono ▲ 06/01/93
Star Blazers Vol. 14: *Episodes 27 and 28*
VEI 10014 ▲ $19.95 ▲ VHS ▲ DUB ▲ Mono ▲ 06/01/93
Star Blazers Vol. 15: *Episodes 29 and 30*
VEI 10015 ▲ $19.95 ▲ VHS ▲ DUB ▲ Mono ▲ 06/01/93
Star Blazers Vol. 16: *Episodes 31 and 32*
VEI 10016 ▲ $19.95 ▲ VHS ▲ DUB ▲ Mono ▲ 06/01/93
Star Blazers Vol. 17: *Episodes 33 and 34*
VEI 10017 ▲ $19.95 ▲ VHS ▲ DUB ▲ Mono ▲ 06/01/93
Star Blazers Vol. 18: *Episodes 35 and 36*
VEI 10018 ▲ $19.95 ▲ VHS ▲ DUB ▲ Mono ▲ 06/01/93
Star Blazers Vol. 19: *Episodes 37 and 38*
VEI 10019 ▲ $19.95 ▲ VHS ▲ DUB ▲ Mono ▲ 06/01/93
Star Blazers Vol. 20: *Episodes 39 and 40*
VEI 10020 ▲ $19.95 ▲ VHS ▲ DUB ▲ Mono ▲ 06/01/93
Star Blazers Vol. 21: *Episodes 41 and 42*
VEI 10021 ▲ $19.95 ▲ VHS ▲ DUB ▲ Mono ▲ 06/01/93
Star Blazers Vol. 22: *Episodes 43 and 44*
VEI 10022 ▲ $19.95 ▲ VHS ▲ DUB ▲ Mono ▲ 06/01/93
Star Blazers Vol. 23: *Episodes 45 and 46*
VEI 10023 ▲ $19.95 ▲ VHS ▲ DUB ▲ Mono ▲ 06/01/93
Star Blazers Vol. 24: *Episodes 47 and 48*
VEI 10024 ▲ $19.95 ▲ VHS ▲ DUB ▲ Mono ▲ 06/01/93
Star Blazers Vol. 25: *Episodes 49 and 50*
VEI 10025 ▲ $19.95 ▲ VHS ▲ DUB ▲ Mono ▲ 06/01/93
Star Blazers Vol. 26: *Episodes 51 and 52*
VEI 10026 ▲ $19.95 ▲ VHS ▲ DUB ▲ Mono ▲ 06/01/93
Star Blazers Vol. 27: *Episodes 53 and 54*
VEI 10027 ▲ $19.95 ▲ VHS ▲ DUB ▲ Mono ▲ 06/01/93
Star Blazers Vol. 28: *Episodes 55 and 56*
VEI 10028 ▲ $19.95 ▲ VHS ▲ DUB ▲ Mono ▲ 06/01/93
Star Blazers Vol. 29: *Episodes 57 and 58*
VEI 10029 ▲ $19.95 ▲ VHS ▲ DUB ▲ Mono ▲ 06/01/93
Star Blazers Vol. 30: *Episodes 59 and 60*
VEI 10030 ▲ $19.95 ▲ VHS ▲ DUB ▲ Mono ▲ 06/01/93
Star Blazers Vol. 31: *Episodes 61 and 62*
VEI 10031 ▲ $19.95 ▲ VHS ▲ DUB ▲ Mono ▲ 06/01/93
Star Blazers Vol. 32: *Episodes 63 and 64*
VEI 10032 ▲ $19.95 ▲ VHS ▲ DUB ▲ Mono ▲ 06/01/93
Star Blazers Vol. 33: *Episodes 65 and 66*
VEI 10033 ▲ $19.95 ▲ VHS ▲ DUB ▲ Mono ▲ 06/01/93

STAR BLAZERS
·SERIES 1·

QUEST FOR ISCANDAR

STAR BLAZERS
SERIES 2

STAR BLAZERS
·SERIES 3·

THE BOLAR WARS

 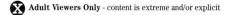

The Complete Anime Guide

Star Blazers Vol. 34: *Episodes 67 and 68*
VEI 10034 ▲ $19.95 ▲ VHS ▲ DUB ▲ Mono ▲ 06/01/93

Star Blazers Vol. 35: *Episodes 69 and 70*
VEI 10035 ▲ $19.95 ▲ VHS ▲ DUB ▲ Mono ▲ 06/01/93

Star Blazers Vol. 36: *Episodes 71 and 72*
VEI 10036 ▲ $19.95 ▲ VHS ▲ DUB ▲ Mono ▲ 06/01/93

Star Blazers Vol. 37: *Episodes 73 and 74*
VEI 10037 ▲ $19.95 ▲ VHS ▲ DUB ▲ Mono ▲ 06/01/93

Star Blazers Vol. 38: *Episodes 75 and 76*
VEI 10038 ▲ $19.95 ▲ VHS ▲ DUB ▲ Mono ▲ 06/01/93

Star Blazers Vol. 39: *Episode 77*
VEI 10039 ▲ $19.95 ▲ VHS ▲ DUB ▲ Mono ▲ 06/01/93

Star Blazers Quest For Iscandar Box Set
Episodes 1-26 in a 6-tape boxed set.
VEI CE1 ▲ $159.95 ▲ VHS ▲ DUB ▲ Mono

Star Blazers Comet Empire Box Set
Episodes 27-52 in a 6-tape boxed set.
VEI CE2 ▲ $159.95 ▲ VHS ▲ DUB ▲ Mono

Star Blazers Bolar Wars Box Set
Episodes 53-77 in a 6-tape boxed set.
VEI CE3 ▲ $159.95 ▲ VHS ▲ DUB ▲ Mono

Starvengers

TV series, 26 episodes

(1975-76) ©Toei Animation Co. Ltd

Music: Shunsuke Kikuchi

Based on the manga by Go Nagai (DEVILMAN). The very first entry in what would eventually become the "transforming robot" genre (reaching an apotheosis of sorts with TRANSFORMERS), "Getta Robo G," the original series upon which "Starvengers" is based, features the adventures of a team of giant robot pilots who, when suitably prompted to do so, can tranform their three "Getter" robots—Dragoon (red in color, specialized in ground-based missions), Raiger (blue in color, specialized in air-based missions), and Poseidon (yellow in color, specialized in water-based missions)—into the great combining robot "Getta Robo." Broadcast in the U.S. as part of the "Force Five" series (the other four series were DANGARD ACE, GRANDIZER, GAIKING, and SPACEKETEERS), to date only two of 26 episodes of STARZINGERS as seen on "Force Five" are available on home video. Original 39-episode series released in Japan under the title "Getta Robo G" by Toei Video; available in North America through Parade Video. In WHO'LL FLY THE POSEIDON, the new, more powerful Starvenger is revealed and the search for a pilot for the Poseidon is underway. The search is successful and Foul Tip gets the job. In DRAGON FORMATION .. SWITCH ON!, the Starvengers combat the Pandemonium Empire as it makes its first attempt to get the star energizer. **46 min.**

Domestic Home Video:
PRV 6612 ▲ $12.95 ▲ VHS-EP ▲ DUB ▲ Mono ▲ 02/01/93

Street Fighter II: The Movie

(1994) ©Capcom Co. Ltd.

Director: Gisaburo Sugii *Screenplay:* Kenichi Imai, Gisaburo Sugii *Music:* Cory Lerios, John D. Andrea

High-quality, full-length (117-minute!) theatrical adaptation of the characters from the video game "Street Fighter II." Unlike the high-spirited campiness of Jean-Claude Van Damme's live-action *Street Fighter* film, the animated movie treats the subject with deadly seriousness, spending lush amounts of screen time detailing one-on-one duels between characters. The direction is distinctly live-action in style, building mood and a sense of atmosphere for each confrontation—particularly effective is an extended, bloody battle between Chun-Li and Balrog (Vega in Japan) in Chun-Li's darkened apartment. Changes for the U.S. domestic release include small edits for gore and a few cels trimmed from a shower scene with the busty Chun-Li; an even more high-profile change is the addition of a thrash soundtrack by groups such as Alice in Chains and Korn instead of the Japanese symphonic soundtrack. Released in Japan as "Street Fighter II: The Movie" by Toei Video; available in America through Sony Music Video. **96 min.**

Domestic Home Video:
SMV 49753 ▲ $14.95 ▲ VHS ▲ DUB ▲ HiFi Stereo ▲ Unrated ▲ CC ▲ 01/16/96
SMV 49756 ▲ $14.95 ▲ VHS ▲ DUB ▲ HiFi Stereo ▲ Edited ▲ CC ▲ 01/16/96
MLV 49861 ▲ $29.95 ▲ LD ▲ DUB ▲ HiFi Stereo ▲ CC ▲ 01/16/96

Suikoden-Demon Century

(1993) ©Hitoshi Yoshioka/Kadokawa Shôten/JVC/J.C. Staff

Created by: Hitoshi Yoshioka *Director:* Hiroshi Negishi *Character Design:* Nobuyuki Tsuru

Based on an original story by Ryohei Fukuoka. Neat one-shot martial arts OAV which loosely draws on the classic legend of "The Water Margin," wherein a group of warriors is reincarnated to fight evil in their time. The characters are all interesting individuals with a slick, fascinating look, and the action is fast and engrossing. One of those rare productions in which you have a hard time deciding which character you think is the coolest. Released in Japan under the title "Yôseiki (Demon Century) Suikoden" by Kadokawa Shôten/CIC/Victor; available in North America through A.D. Vision. **45 min.**

Domestic Home Video:
ADV SU/001D ▲ $29.95 ▲ VHS ▲ DUB ▲ HiFi Surround ▲ 08/06/96
ADV SU/001S ▲ $29.95 ▲ VHS ▲ SUB ▲ HiFi Surround ▲ 08/06/96
ADV CLVSU/001 ▲ $39.95 ▲ LD ▲ M/A ▲ HiFi Stereo ▲ CC ▲ 11/12/96

Sukeban Deka

(1991) ©Shinji Wada/Hakusensha/J.H. Project

Created by: Shinji Wada *Director:* Takeshi Hirota *Character Design:* Nobuteru Yuki *Art Director:* Masahiro Kase *Animation Director:* Hiroshi Nanpa

Based on the manga by Shinji Wada, as serialized in publisher Hakusensha's monthly HANA TO YUME (Flowers and Dreams) "shôjo manga" or "girls' comics" anthology. A live-action TV series (starring a succession of popular teen idols) before it was animated, a gang girl is given the *La Femme Nikita* choice of jail or public service, and decides to turn her lethal yo-yo to the side of light. Although animation is nothing special, it hews closely to the original comics, especially in the second volume, which is when creator Wada joins the production staff as supervising story editor. Character designs are by the high-profile Nobuteru Yuki (RECORD OF LODOSS WAR, BATTLE ANGEL). Released in Japan as "Sukeban Deka" (Girl-Delinquent Cop) by J.H. Project/Pony Canyon; available in North America through A.D. Vision.

Sukeban Deka
The Feds need someone to infiltrate a ruthless crime syndicate that masquerades as an exclusive high school and they think Saki's the girl for the job. Armed with a secret weapon that only looks like a yo-yo, Saki is lethal, and back on the streets. **60 min.**

Sukeban Deka 2
When Saki's friend is kidnapped by Remi Mizuchi, who wants her paintings, Saki is arrested for the crime. But before Saki can convince the authorities of her innocence, her friend is murdered by another of the Mizuchi sisters. **60 min.**

Domestic Home Video:
Sukeban Deka
ADV SK/001D ▲ $24.95 ▲ VHS ▲ DUB ▲ HiFi Surround ▲ 05/21/96
ADV SK/001S ▲ $29.95 ▲ VHS ▲ SUB ▲ HiFi Surround ▲ 05/21/96
ADV SK/001L ▲ $39.95 ▲ LD ▲ M/A ▲ HiFi Surround ▲ 07/30/96
Sukeban Deka 2
ADV SK-002D ▲ $24.95 ▲ VHS ▲ DUB ▲ HiFi Surround ▲ 07/16/96
ADV SK-002S ▲ $29.95 ▲ VHS ▲ SUB ▲ HiFi Surround ▲ 07/16/96

Super Atragon

(1995) ©"Kaitei Gunkan" Production Committee

Original Story: Shunro Oshikawa *Director:* Ichiro Katayama *Script:* Nobuaki Kishima *Character Design:* Yoshikazu Yasuhiko *Mecha Design:* Makoto Kobayashi

Animated revamp of '60s special effects live-action movie, based on the novel by Shunro Oshikawa. In the closing days of World War II, the super scientific battleship *Ragoh* (the mythical, fourth *Yamato*-class ship) squares off against its American opposite number and vanishes into history. Now, a half-century later, the hidden forces behind the battle reveal themselves, as the mysterious race which lives within the hollow Earth invades the surface world and tramples humanity before it. Giving the *Yamato* ("Argo" to STAR BLAZERS devotees) itself a run for its money, the flying, force field-wielding, drill-equipped *Ragoh* is very much the star of the show; it's been redesigned for the new series by Makoto

Kobayashi, the man who gave the eponymous Giant Robo its modernistic makeover. Character designs are by Yoshikazu "Yaz" Yasuhiko of "Mobile Suit Gundam" fame. Released in Japan under the title "Shin Kaitei Gunkan" (The New "Submarine Battleship") by Toho Video/Kadokawa Shôten; available in North America through A.D. Vision. **60 min.**

Domestic Home Video:
ADV SA/001D ▲ $29.95 ▲ VHS ▲ DUB ▲ HiFi Surround ▲ 07/30/96
ADV SA/001S ▲ $29.95 ▲ VHS ▲ SUB ▲ HiFi Surround ▲ 07/30/96
ADV SA/001L ▲ $39.95 ▲ LD ▲ M/A ▲ HiFi Surround ▲ 08/27/96

SuperBook
TV series, 26 episodes
(1982) ©CBN/Tatsunoko Productions

Screenplay: Akiyoshi Sakai *Directors:* Kenjiro Yoshida, Masakazu Higuchi *Character Design:* Akiko Shitamoto *Music:* Masahito Maruyama

The series involves two precocious children—Chris and Joy— and their "R2D2" style talking robot, Gizmo, who wears a cross on his chest. The kids and the robot are transported to biblical times by way of a huge, fourth-dimensional Bible. The children are wide-eyed, "cartoony" characters while the biblical personalities are drawn realistically. Syndicated in 1982 by the Christian Broadcasting Network and cablecast at the same time over the CBN service (now known as Family Channel), the 26-episode SUPERBOOK was the first nationally distributed religious cartoon series since 1960-65's *Davey and Goliath*. Aired on Japanese television as "Anime Oyako Gekijô" (Animated Parent and Child Theatre); available in North America through Tyndale Family Video.

SuperBook Vol. 1: *Adam & Eve*
2 episodes. HOW IT ALL BEGAN: The story of the Earth's early days and its first man and woman. The tempting of Adam and Eve and the consequences of their action. MY BROTHER'S KEEPER: The sons of Adam and Eve, Cain and Abel. One pleases God; the other does not. Cain even commits the first murder. **40 min.**

SuperBook Vol. 2: *Noah & the Ark*
2 episodes. THE FLOOD: Noah was the only righteous man God found on the face of the earth. See God's plan to save Noah's family as he destroys the earth with a great flood. DOUBLE TROUBLE: The story of Isaac and Rebecca's twin sons, Jacob and Esau. The two are rivals from birth until their miraculous reconciliation. **40 min.**

SuperBook Vol. 3: *Moses & the Miracles*
2 episodes. THE MIRACLE ROD: The story of Moses. See how Moses leads the Israelites out of Egypt through God's miraculous power. THOSE AMAZING TRUMPETS: The story of Joshua, who becomes Israel's new leader after Moses dies. Watch as he leads Israel across the Jordan River on dry ground, and see how God gives them Jericho when they faithfully obey him. **40 min.**

SuperBook Vol. 4: *David & Goliath*
2 episodes. THE GIANT KILLER: The story of David. See how this young shepherd boy confronts the giant Goliath and eventually becomes Israel's new king. THE LIONS' DEN: The story of Daniel. This man of great faith and godly convictions finds favor with Babylon's kings, but then finds himself in deep trouble. See how God preserves him in the midst of certain death. **40 min.**

SuperBook Vol. 5: *Abraham & Isaac*
2 episodes. THE TEST: The miracle of Isaac's birth to Abraham and Sarah in their old age. Then the ultimate test of faithfulness as Abraham thinks God may take Isaac from him. HERE COMES THE BRIDE: The story of the search for Isaac's bride Rebecca. **40 min.**

SuperBook Vol. 6: *Joseph & His Dreams*
2 episodes. A DREAM COME TRUE: See how a simple dream gets Joseph in so much trouble. And how his faithfulness in every situation causes God to bless him in the end. SUPERBRAIN: See Solomon, the king who above all things wanted wisdom to govern his people well. See how he became the richest and wisest man who ever lived. **40 min.**

SuperBook Vol. 7: *Samson & Delilah*
2 episodes. MUSCLEMAN: Meet Samson and discover how he loses his strength when he is tricked into revealing the secret of his strength.

PITCHERS OF FIRE: The story of the man chosen by God to save Israel from the Midianites. See how God used Gideon's small army and pitchers of fire to cause such confusion among the enemy that they slew one another. **40 min.**

SuperBook Vol. 8: *Esther & The King*
2 episodes. THE BEAUTY QUEEN: Esther's purpose was for one great act. See how she, as wife of the Perisan King, intervenes to keep her people, the Jews, from destruction. MOTHER'S DAY: The story of a

young girl named Ruth who loves and serves her mother faithfully. See how God rewards her faithfulness. **40 min.**

SuperBook Vol. 9: *Jonah & The Big Fish*
2 episodes. BIG FISH, LITTLE FISH: The story of Jonah, who learns to obey God from the belly of a great fish and takes a trip to Ninevah with a message from God. THE FIRST KING: Saul is anointed as the first king over Israel. See the progression of his life that brought him to the throne. **40 min.**

SuperBook Vol. 10: *Nehemiah & The Wall*
2 episodes. THE WALLS OF JERUSALEM: See the rebuilding of the great walls of Jerusalem and the struggles and victories of Israel as they work to accomplish this task. THE PATIENCE OF JOB: See this great man of God, who is tried in every imaginable manner, only to come out in the end greater and more faithful than before. **40 min.**

SuperBook Vol. 11: *The First Easter*
2 episodes. THE BEST NEWS YET: From Jesus' last days with His disciples and His travail in the garden of Gethsemane to his crucifixion and glorious resurrection. THE MIGHTY CONVERT: See how Paul, who terrorized Christians more than any other, is called by God to be one of the greatest apostles of the New Testament. **40 min.**

SuperBook Vol. 12: *The First Christmas*
2 episodes. THE FIRST CHRISTMAS: Witness the events that lead to the first Christmas and the beginning of God's great plan for the salvation of mankind. MIRACLES OF LOVE: Witness the miracles of Jesus. See him turn water into wine at a wedding; then heal the sick, blind and lame. **40 min.**

SuperBook Vol. 13: *Elijah, True Prophet*
2 episodes. ELIJAH: A TRUE PROPHET: Learn about the mighty prophet Elijah and how God worked powerful miracles through him. See him defeat the prophets of Baal. THE FLAMING CHARIOTS: The story of the prophet Elijah's ascent into heaven on chariots of fire. See how his servant, Elisha, replaced him and became another great prophet, with twice the anointing. **40 min.**

SuperBook Vol. 14: *Abraham and Lot*
2 episodes. WHERE, OH WHERE..?: See Lot's separation from Abraham and how God brings about Lot's rescue after he is abducted by the King of Elam. HOT DOG: Witness the events that lead to the destruction of two wicked cities, Sodom and Gomorrah. See how Lot's constant faithfulness to God saves him and his family. **40 min.**

SuperBook Vol. 15: *Isaac and Rebekah*
2 episodes. LOVE AT FIRST SIGHT: Watch as a caravan is headed for the city of Nahor, at Abraham's command, to seek a suitable wife for his son, Isaac. A TEST OF FAITH AND OBEDIENCE: See how God responds to Abraham's prayers by giving him a son, Isaac. Then see how Abraham responds when God commands him to offer Isaac as a burnt offering. **40 min.**

SuperBook Vol. 16: *Joshua The General*
2 episodes. SNAKES AND A DONKEY: The Israelites have been wandering in the wilderness for forty years, surviving hunger and poisonous snakes. See how they finally enter the promised land, following their new leader, Joshua. WORTH FIGHTING FOR: The Israelites can't seem to conquer the city of Debir, but when Caleb promises to give his daughter as a wife to the man who can accomplish this heroic task, that's all the incentive brave young Othniel needs. **40 min.**

SuperBook Vol. 17: *Deborah & Barak*
2 episodes. STICK IN THE MUD: The story of Deborah and Barak. The Canaanite army is bearing down on Israel. See what happens when the Israelites turn to God to save them. THE GOOD LEFT ARM: Watch as a rebellion breaks and Ehud and the Israelites must fight against King Eglon of Moab for their freedom. **40 min.**

SuperBook Vol. 18: *Samuel: Hearing God's Voice*

2 episodes. JUST REWARDS: See how God replaces two priests who aren't worthy of their occupation with Samuel, a young man who loves God. A WONDERFUL GIFT: The story of Samuel and Saul. Watch as the Israelites' demand to have a king is granted, despite Samuel's warnings and fears. **40 min.**

SuperBook Vol. 19: *David & Jonathan*
2 episodes. FAITHFUL AND TRUE: David closely befriends Saul's son Jonathan, and when Sauls's jealousy and anger toward David grows, Jonathan must help him escape. DAVID THE KING: Saul's anger grows so great that he tries to kill David. See how God saves David and proclaims him king of Israel when Saul dies in battle. **40 min.**

SuperBook Vol. 20: *Hezekiah & Isaiah*
2 episodes. A MATTER OF TIME: The Israelites are being invaded by the mighty Assyrian army. They lift their prayers to God, and he hears them and destroys the Assyrians. THE WICKED QUEEN: An evil queen decides to kill all her rivals for the throne. **40 min.**

SuperBook Vol. 21: *Joseph & His Brothers*
2 episodes. THE HOSTAGE: Joseph's wisdom saves Egypt from a terrible famine. Then

 Violence   Profanity   Nudity   Sexual Situations  Adult Viewers Only - content is extreme and/or explicit

Joseph meets up with his unexpecting brothers when they come to Egypt to buy grain. THE FAMILY REUNION: Joseph discovers his brothers aren't the mean men they used to be, so he reveals who he is and they have a tearful reunion. **40 min.**

SuperBook Vol. 22: *Moses & The Burning Bush*

2 episodes. A GIFT FROM HEAVEN: The Israelites have been enslaved and are being brutally treated. But a young man named Moses sets his sights on changing things. THE BURNING BUSH: A burning bush speaks to Moses in Midian and tells him to return to Egypt and free his people from Pharaoh's slavery. **40 min.**

SuperBook Vol. 23: *Moses & The Plagues*

2 episodes. NO MORE PLAGUES: God sends a series of plagues to Egypt, but Pharaoh won't let the Israelites go until the final plague takes his own son's life. SO YOU WANT TO GO BACK TO EGYPT?: Pharaoh's army traps the Israelites, but God shows his power and devotion by helping Moses lead them through the Red Sea. **40 min.**

SuperBook Vol. 24: *David: Shepherd Boy*

2 episodes. THE MIGHTY LITTLE SHEPHERD: Young David is skilled in the use of musical instruments and weapons. Will he be the next King of Israel? IN ALL HIS GLORY: King Solomon dedicates his magnificent temple to God and demonstrates his God-given wisdom. **40 min.**

Domestic Home Video:

SuperBook Vol. 1
TFV 6807 ▲ $9.99 ▲ VHS ▲ DUB ▲ Mono
SuperBook Vol. 2
TFV 6808 ▲ $9.99 ▲ VHS ▲ DUB ▲ Mono
SuperBook Vol. 3
TFV 6809 ▲ $9.99 ▲ VHS ▲ DUB ▲ Mono
SuperBook Vol. 4
TFV 6810 ▲ $9.99 ▲ VHS ▲ DUB ▲ Mono
SuperBook Vol. 5
TFV 6811 ▲ $9.99 ▲ VHS ▲ DUB ▲ Mono
SuperBook Vol. 6
TFV 6812 ▲ $9.99 ▲ VHS ▲ DUB ▲ Mono
SuperBook Vol. 7
TFV 6813 ▲ $9.99 ▲ VHS ▲ DUB ▲ Mono
SuperBook Vol. 8
TFV 6814 ▲ $9.99 ▲ VHS ▲ DUB ▲ Mono
SuperBook Vol. 9
TFV 6815 ▲ $9.99 ▲ VHS ▲ DUB ▲ Mono
SuperBook Vol. 10
TFV 6816 ▲ $9.99 ▲ VHS ▲ DUB ▲ Mono
SuperBook Vol. 11
TFV 6817 ▲ $9.99 ▲ VHS ▲ DUB ▲ Mono
SuperBook Vol. 12
TFV 6818 ▲ $9.99 ▲ VHS ▲ DUB ▲ Mono
SuperBook Vol. 13
TFV 6825 ▲ $9.99 ▲ VHS ▲ DUB ▲ Mono
SuperBook Vol. 14
TFV 6826 ▲ $9.99 ▲ VHS ▲ DUB ▲ Mono
SuperBook Vol. 15
TFV 6827 ▲ $9.99 ▲ VHS ▲ DUB ▲ Mono
SuperBook Vol. 16
TFV 6828 ▲ $9.99 ▲ VHS ▲ DUB ▲ Mono
SuperBook Vol. 17
TFV 6829 ▲ $9.99 ▲ VHS ▲ DUB ▲ Mono
SuperBook Vol. 18
TFV 6830 ▲ $9.99 ▲ VHS ▲ DUB ▲ Mono
SuperBook Vol. 19
TFV 6833 ▲ $9.99 ▲ VHS ▲ DUB ▲ Mono
SuperBook Vol. 20
TFV 6834 ▲ $9.99 ▲ VHS ▲ DUB ▲ Mono
SuperBook Vol. 21
TFV 6835 ▲ $9.99 ▲ VHS ▲ DUB ▲ Mono
SuperBook Vol. 22
TFV 6836 ▲ $9.99 ▲ VHS ▲ DUB ▲ Mono
SuperBook Vol. 23
TFV 6837 ▲ $9.99 ▲ VHS ▲ DUB ▲ Mono
SuperBook Vol. 24
TFV 6838 ▲ $9.99 ▲ VHS ▲ DUB ▲ Mono

Super-Deformed Double Feature

(1988, '92) ©Artmic/Movic/Sony M.E.

Directors: Kenichi Yatagai, Hiroyuki Fukushima

Includes on one tape 1988's TEN LITTLE GALL FORCE (see GALL FORCE, above) as well as 1992's SCRAMBLE WARS. Both are super-deformed (the squat-bodied, big-headed style of anime and manga caricature) satires of productions by Studio Artmic. TEN LITTLE GALL FORCE purports to be a behind-the-scenes documentary on the making of the GALL FORCE movie; SCRAMBLE WARS features a road rally with characters from GALL FORCE, as well as from BUBBLEGUM CRISIS and GENESIS SURVIVOR GAIARTH, in the spirit of Hanna-Barbera's "Wacky Races." Funniest when you've seen the series they're parodying. Released in Japan under the titles "Ten Little Gall Force" and "Scramble Wars" by Sony Music and Toshiba EMI, respectively; available in North America through AnimEigo. **67 min.**

Domestic Home Video:

ANI AT093-004 ▲ $34.95 ▲ VHS ▲ SUB ▲ HiFi Stereo ▲ 08/04/93

Super Dimensional Fortress Macross *See* MACROSS
Taiho Shichau zo *See* YOU'RE UNDER ARREST

The Tale of Genji

(1987) Asahi Group/Herald/Group TAC

Screenplay: Tomomi Tsutsui *Character Design:* Yasuhiro Nakura *Animation Director:* Yasuo Maeda *Art Director:* Mihoko Magori *Music:* Haruomi Hosono *Director:* Gisaburo Sugii

Adaptation of Lady Shikibu Murasaki's 11th century novel of Heian-era Japan and the lives and loves of court poet and musician Hikaru Genji, who was born the son of an Emperor, but later made a commoner. He was the most handsome man in the nation with abilities in poetry and music that were unparalleled. From the director of NIGHT ON THE GALACTIC RAILROAD. Released in Japan under the title "Murasaki Shikibu: Genji Monogatari" (Shikibu Murasaki: Tale of Genji) by Asahi Shimbunsha; available in North America through Central Park Media. **110 min.**

Domestic Home Video:

CPM 1333 ▲ $29.95 ▲ VHS ▲ SUB ▲ Stereo

Tales of The Wolf *See* LUPIN III
Tanin no Kankei *See* HOMEROOM AFFAIRS
Tatake! Iczer-1 *See* ICZER-1

Techno Police 21C

(1982) ©Toho Co. Ltd.

Director: Takashi Matsumoto

Early one-shot theatrical effort from BUBBLEGUM CRISIS' Toshimichi Suzuki. When criminals run amuck and steal your super-tank, where do you turn? To a hot-headed, jetcar-driving cop and a carload of police androids ("technoids," to be formal). Mecha-philes will no doubt note that this trio of androids—dainty Scanny, blocky Vigoras and handcuff-launching Blader (danger, Will Robinson: they may have changed the names for the US release)—have since been reincarnated in BUBBLEGUM CRISIS' hardsuits, as well as in Hajime Katoki's designs for the fourteen-years-later hit videogame Virtual On. Brought to you by Studio Nue (MACROSS, STAR BLAZERS, DANGAIO) and Artmic (GALL FORCE, BUBBLEGUM CRISIS, MEGAZONE 23) in a rare teamup. Released in Japan under the title "Techno Police 21C" by Toho; available in North America through Best Film &Video. **80 min.**

Domestic Home Video:

BFV 964 ▲ $19.95 ▲ VHS ▲ DUB ▲ Mono

Teito Monogatari *See* DOOMED MEGALOPOLIS

  Made for Television Broadcast   **OAV** Made for Home Video Release   Made for Theatrical Release

Tekkaman The Space Knight

TV series, 13 episodes

(1975) ©William Winckler/Tatsunoko Production Co. Ltd.

Created by: Kenji Yoshida and Ippei Kuri *Written by:* Jinzo Toriumi *Music:* Bob Sakuma

Select episodes from the Tatsunoko "Home of the Heroes" TV series. (For more information, see Chapter One.) 26 episodes released in Japan under the title "Uchû no Kishi Tekkaman" (Tekkaman the Space Knight) by Polydor; available in North America through LDV.

Tekkaman The Space Knight Vol. 1

3 episodes from the TV series. In 2037 A.D., the cruel interstellar Waldarians came blasting their way toward Earth. Dr. Edward Richardson created a space suit of indestructible Tekka alloy, and transformed it into battle armor. He chose young Barry Gallagher to wear this armor as Tekkaman, The Space Knight, a superhero to beat back the Waldarians and their pompous Commander Randrox. **86 min.**

Tekkaman The Space Knight Vol. 2

3 episodes from the TV series. In the year 2037, evil aliens invade the solar system and mysteriously close in on Earth. To combat this threat, Earth's greatest scientist creates an indestructible suit of space armor made from a revolutionary alloy called "Tekka." Selected to don the "Tekka Armor" is young space pilot Barry Gallagher, who, while wearing it, becomes Tekkaman, The Space Knight — the world's greatest superhero! **86 min.**

Domestic Home Video:

Tekkaman The Space Knight Vol. 1
LDV 1017 ▲ $19.95 ▲ VHS ▲ DUB ▲ Mono

Tekkaman The Space Knight Vol. 2
LDV 1018 ▲ $19.95 ▲ VHS ▲ DUB ▲ Mono

Ten Little Gall Force *See* SUPER-DEFORMED DBL. FEATURE

Tenchi Muyô!

OAV series, 13 episodes

(1992-96) ©A.I.C./Pioneer LDC Inc.

Directors: Hiroki Hayashi (1-6), Kenichi Yatagai (7,10-13), Kazuhiro Ozawa (8,9,Mihoshi), Kazuyuki Hirokawa (Pretty Sammy) *Character Design:* Masaki Kajishima (1-13), Yoshitaka Kono (Pretty Sammy) *Design:* Atsushi Takeuchi *Screenplay:* Naoko Hasegawa (1-6), Masaki Kajishima (1-6), Hiroki Hayashi (1-6), Yosuke Kuroda (7-9,12-13,Pretty Sammy), Ryoei Tsukimura (Mihoshi) *Art Directors:* Takeshi Waki (1-13), Chieko Nekazi (Mihoshi), Masaru Sato (Pretty Sammy) *Animation Directors:* Masaki Kajishima (1-5,8-10), Yuji Moriyama (6), Wataru Abe (Mihoshi), Yoshitaka Kono (Pretty Sammy) *Music:* Seiko Nagaoka

Also known as "No Need For Tenchi!" A typical Japanese schoolboy's life is turned upside down as he slowly tumbles to the fact that he's descended from alien royalty, while being firmly thrust into the middle of a subtle and meticulously planned galactic power struggle. Accompanying this situation is a collection of extraordinary females, all vying for his affection: A genetically engineered super powered space pirate, two alien princesses, a Galaxy Police detective, and a seemingly immortal scientific super genius. With power, women, and galactic significance all vying for center stage, TENCHI MUYÔ! is an otaku dream come true. Note that this entry is specific to the original OAV series only; the television series (which reshuffles the original plot details) and the movie rendition (which takes the cast to 1970 to confront a *Back to the Future*-like situation) are generally considered by fans and producers alike as an "alternate" TENCHI universe. Since the last edition of this book, Pioneer has also begun releasing a TENCHI "spin-off" series, PRETTY SAMMY THE MAGICAL GIRL (Mahô Shôjo Pretty Sammy), which strays even farther from established continuity in portraying what one U.S. reviewer described as "a life on Earth Sammy never had." Released in Japan as "Tenchi Muyô!" by Pioneer LDC; available in North America through Pioneer LDCA.

Tenchi Muyô! Episode 1: *Ryoko Resurrected*

Awakened from a deep sleep, Ryoko, the demon, in the form of a beautiful young girl, furious to discover she has been imprisoned for over 700 years, launches an all-out attack on Tenchi. Using her amazing powers, including flying through the air, moving through walls, and hurling massive bolts of electrical power from her hands, she pursues Tenchi in a terrifying midnight chase throughout his school. **30 min.**

Tenchi Muyô! Episode 2: *Here Comes Ayeka!*

Princess Ayeka has sailed far from her home planet Jurai in search for her long lost fiancé. On Earth, she encounters Ryoko instead, her mortal enemy from distant stars. As a blast from Ayeka's main cannon shatters his window, Tenchi finds himself aboard Ryoko's spaceship in flight, only to be captured later by Ayeka! Tenchi doesn't know what to do as the cat-fight between the two girls ends up in a big spaceship crash. **30 min.**

Tenchi Muyô! Episode 3: *Hello Ryo-Ohki!*

Sisters Ayeka and Sasami find themselves without transport back to their mother planet when their spaceship is wrecked in a battle with Ryo-Ohki. With them in addition to Ryoko, there are now three cute girls at Tenchi's house! While Ayeka sinks deeper into her depression because of the unfamiliar life on Earth, Sasami is full of energy. And as for Ryoko... who knows what may be going through her mind... To top it all off, an infant Ryo-Ohki hatches from the spaceship egg! **30 min.**

Tenchi Muyô! Episode 4: *Mihoshi Falls to the Land of Stars*

Tenchi's life with the girls under one roof finally begins to settle down. Now it's fall and the group visits a hot springs resort. While Ryoko tries to seduce Tenchi in her birthday suit, Ayeka goes into a panic when Tenchi sees her stark naked, and Tenchi's father tries hard to take a peek at the ladies' side of the hot springs. One such day, a new character appears before our group: Mihoshi, a female cop with the Galaxy Police. **30 min.**

Tenchi Muyô! Episode 5: *Kagato Attacks!*

Mihoshi, a Galaxy Police Officer joins the group as a new roommate, making Tenchi's life as lively as ever. One day, Kagato, one of the most wanted criminals in the universe, appears before the group. He claims to be Ryoko's creator and he's after Tenchi's sword. Despite Tenchi's and his grandfather's desperate struggle, Kagato kidnaps Ryoko and flees to outer space. **30 min.**

Tenchi Muyô! Episode 6: *We Need Tenchi!*

After losing Tenchi, the girls storm Kagato's spaceship. But Ayeka falls into a trap and into Kagato's hands! In the meantime, Ryoko and Mihoshi find themselves confined in a different dimension where they meet Washu, a scientific genius. To their surprise, she reveals herself as Ryoko's creator. Just as the destruction ray fired at Earth is about to reach its destination, Tenchi is resurrected and reappears! **30 min.**

Tenchi Muyô! Episode 7: *Ryo-Ohki Special: The Night Before The Carnival*

The Kagato incident is over, but Tenchi is at no loss for trouble with five beautiful girls and Ryo-Ohki around him. Ryoko and Ayeka's war for Tenchi's love, Washu's organic experiment on Tenchi, and the case of disappearing carrots caused by a divided and multiplied Ryo-Ohki... An assortment of troubles, everything from small to large! **45 min.**

Tenchi Muyô! Episode 8: *Hello! Baby*

Yet another dependent joins the Tenchi family - it's a baby! Tenchi's aunt arrives with her grandson one day, asking Tenchi & Co. to take care of the baby for a while. Ryoko and Ayeka compete to impress Tenchi and Mihoshi remains good-natured. Everyone works hard, and the incident causes Washu to reveal some of her surprising past. **30 min.**

Tenchi Muyô! Episode 9: *Sasami and Tsunami*

The innkeeper greets Tenchi & Co. happily when they return to the hot spring resort. Then, a ghost is sighted wandering about the inn. Sasami recalls the attack on the royal palace on Planet Jurai by Ryoko, years ago. This caused Tsunami to awaken, and the hidden incident is troubling Sasami deeply now. **30 min.**

Tenchi Muyô! Episode 10: *I Love Tenchi*

One spring day, Tenchi hurts Ryo-Ohki's feelings due to a misunderstanding. The Mass, a strange space creature kept in Washu's lab, picks up Ryo-Ohki's fervent desire to help Tenchi, which causes the situation to head in an unexpected direction. **30 min.**

Tenchi Muyô! Episode 11: *The Advent of the Goddess*

Driven by the will of Queen Tokimi, super-scientist Dr. Clay heads for Earth to capture Washu. Tokimi, a high level dimensional life-form, wishes to meet Washu in person. Dr. Clay has his assassin Zero, an artificial life-form, assume Ryoko's appearance. How would Masaki Family deal with this clone of Ryoko? **30 min.**

Tenchi Muyô! Episode 12: *Zero Ryoko*

Ryoko's imposter Zero is on a deadly mission — to assassinate Tenchi! In addition, Zero has taken Ryoko hostage. Will Tenchi, Ayeka and Washu be able to help? **30 min.**

Tenchi Muyô! Episode 13: *The Royal Family Has Come*

The day has come when Tenchi's family is broken up. Now that the royal family of the planet Jurai has arrived on Earth, the question is: who do they want to bring back to Jurai? Grand finale of the second TENCHI MUYÔ! series. **45 min.**

Tenchi Muyô! Mihoshi Special

Everyone knows Mihoshi, one of the beautiful girls living with Tenchi. She's a bit of a scatterbrain but she's a real Galaxy Policewoman. And, according to her, one of the best!

 Violence   Profanity   Nudity   Sexual Situations  **Adult Viewers Only** - content is extreme and/or explicit

Nobody believes her but maybe they'll acknowledge her abilities after she recounts how she and her partner, Kiyone, solved the galaxy's most notorious case. Tenchi as the Investigator, Ryoko as the space pirate, and Sasami as the Magical Girl Pretty Sammy!? All the TENCHI MUYÔ! characters are cast (against their will?) in her amazing and unbelievable story. **40 min.**

Tenchi & Friends Special: Pretty Sammy The Magical Girl

Sasami Kawai is a 4th grader, a cheerful girl full of energy. One day, she is sent on an errand to an old mansion and meets a strange lady there. The lady identifies herself as Tsunami and claims that she comes from a Magical Kingdom called Juraihelm. She asks Sasami to help make the Earth a better place by using the magical powers she can bestow upon Sasami. Sasami's career as a Magical Girl thus begins. Her mysterious rival — another magical girl called Pixy Misa —, as well as Ryoko and Ayeka who always fight against each other over Sasami's brother Tenchi, her mother who has her head completely in the clouds all the time ... these wacky people only help the already wacky situations go worse, making Sammy's job even more difficult. **45 min.**

Domestic Home Video:

Tenchi Muyô! Episode 1
PI VA-1001D ▲ $19.95 ▲ VHS ▲ DUB ▲ HiFi Stereo ▲ CC ▲ 09/14/94
PI VA-1001S ▲ $24.95 ▲ VHS ▲ SUB ▲ HiFi Stereo ▲ 09/14/94
PI LA-1133A ▲ $34.95 ▲ LD ▲ M/A ▲ HiFi Stereo ▲ CC ▲ 01/12/94

Tenchi Muyô! Episode 2
PI VA-1002D ▲ $19.95 ▲ VHS ▲ DUB ▲ HiFi Stereo ▲ CC ▲ 09/14/94
PI VA-1002S ▲ $24.95 ▲ VHS ▲ SUB ▲ HiFi Stereo ▲ 09/14/94
PI LA-1134A ▲ $34.95 ▲ LD-CAV ▲ M/A ▲ HiFi Stereo ▲ CC ▲ 02/15/94

Tenchi Muyô! Episode 3
PI VA-1003D ▲ $19.95 ▲ VHS ▲ DUB ▲ HiFi Stereo ▲ CC ▲ 09/14/94
PI VA-1003S ▲ $24.95 ▲ VHS ▲ SUB ▲ HiFi Stereo ▲ 09/14/94
PI LA-1135A ▲ $34.95 ▲ LD-CAV ▲ M/A ▲ HiFi Stereo ▲ CC ▲ 02/15/94

Tenchi Muyô! Episode 4
PI VA-1004 ▲ $19.95 ▲ VHS ▲ DUB ▲ HiFi Stereo ▲ CC ▲ 09/14/94
PI VA-1004S ▲ $24.95 ▲ VHS ▲ SUB ▲ HiFi Stereo ▲ 09/14/94
PI LA-1136A ▲ $34.95 ▲ LD-CAV ▲ M/A ▲ HiFi Stereo ▲ CC ▲ 03/12/94

Tenchi Muyô! Episode 5
PI VA-1005D ▲ $19.95 ▲ VHS ▲ DUB ▲ HiFi Stereo ▲ CC ▲ 09/14/94
PI VA-1005S ▲ $24.95 ▲ VHS ▲ SUB ▲ HiFi Stereo ▲ 09/14/94
PI LA-1137A ▲ $34.95 ▲ LD-CAV ▲ M/A ▲ HiFi Stereo ▲ CC ▲ 04/13/94

Tenchi Muyô! Episode 6
PI VA-1006D ▲ $19.95 ▲ VHS ▲ DUB ▲ HiFi Stereo ▲ CC ▲ 09/14/94
PI VA-1006S ▲ $24.95 ▲ VHS ▲ SUB ▲ HiFi Stereo ▲ 09/14/94
PI LA-1138A ▲ $34.95 ▲ LD-CAV ▲ M/A ▲ HiFi Stereo ▲ CC ▲ 05/11/94

Tenchi Muyô! Episode 7
PI VA-1256D ▲ $24.95 ▲ VHS ▲ DUB ▲ HiFi Stereo ▲ CC ▲ 09/14/94
PI VA-1256S ▲ $29.95 ▲ VHS ▲ SUB ▲ HiFi Stereo ▲ 09/14/94
PI LA-1184A ▲ $34.95 ▲ LD-CAV ▲ M/A ▲ HiFi Stereo ▲ CC ▲ 06/29/94

Tenchi Muyô! Episodes 8 & 9
PI VA-1185D ▲ $24.95 ▲ VHS ▲ DUB ▲ HiFi Stereo ▲ CC ▲ 04/25/95
PI VA-1185S ▲ $29.95 ▲ VHS ▲ SUB ▲ HiFi Stereo ▲ 04/25/95
PI LA-1185A ▲ $39.95 ▲ LD-CAV ▲ M/A ▲ HiFi Stereo ▲ CC ▲ 04/25/95

Tenchi Muyô! Episodes 10 & 11
PI VA-1187D ▲ $24.95 ▲ VHS ▲ DUB ▲ HiFi Stereo ▲ CC ▲ 06/27/95
PI VA-1187S ▲ $29.95 ▲ VHS ▲ SUB ▲ HiFi Stereo ▲ 06/27/95
PI LA-1187A ▲ $39.95 ▲ LD-CAV ▲ M/A ▲ HiFi Stereo ▲ CC ▲ 06/27/95

Tenchi Muyô! Episodes 12 & 13
PI VA-1189D ▲ $24.95 ▲ VHS ▲ DUB ▲ HiFi Stereo ▲ CC ▲ 12/19/95
PI VA-1189S ▲ $29.95 ▲ VHS ▲ SUB ▲ HiFi Stereo ▲ 12/19/95
PI LA-1189A ▲ $44.95 ▲ LD ▲ M/A ▲ HiFi Stereo ▲ CC ▲ 12/19/95

Tenchi Muyô! Mihoshi Special
PI VA-1242D ▲ $19.95 ▲ VHS ▲ DUB ▲ HiFi Stereo ▲ CC ▲ 02/28/95
PI VA-1242S ▲ $24.95 ▲ VHS ▲ SUB ▲ HiFi Stereo ▲ 02/28/95
PI LA-1242A ▲ $34.95 ▲ LD-CAV ▲ M/A ▲ Stereo ▲ CC ▲ 02/08/95

Tenchi Muyô! Pretty Sammy The Magical Girl
PI VA-1338D ▲ $19.95 ▲ VHS ▲ DUB ▲ HiFi Stereo ▲ CC ▲ 10/24/95
PI VA-1338S ▲ $24.95 ▲ VHS ▲ SUB ▲ HiFi Stereo ▲ 10/24/95
PI LA-1338A ▲ $34.95 ▲ LD-CAV ▲ M/A ▲ Stereo ▲ CC ▲ 10/24/95

Tenchi Muyô! on Earth TV Series

TV series, 26 episodes

(1995) ©AIC/Pioneer LDC, Inc.

Director: Hiroshi Negishi *Series Construction:* Ryoei Tsukimura *Animation Director & Character Design:* Hiroyuki Horiuchi *Original Character Design:* Masaki Kajishima *Art Director:* Chitose Asakura *Music:* Seiko Nagaoka

A new story line plus some new characters are included in made-for-TV follow-up to the popular OAV series. The domestic release from Pioneer LDCA includes copious goodies, including a collectible "AniMayhem" playing card, as well as a pin-up style 12 x 12 insert.

Tenchi Universe Episode 1: *No Need For Discussions!*
The first episode opens with Tenchi's monologue as he reminisces about "those days." This narration is important, as you will see at the end of this series, so just keep it in mind. **25 min.**

Tenchi Universe Episode 2: *No Need For A Princess!*
The rivalry between Ryoko and Ayeka goes far back to their childhood. You will see this old conflict erupt again during this series. Now you will have a chance to see Ryoko as a little girl for the first time. **25 min.**

Tenchi Universe Episode 3: *No Need For Worries!*
Meet two of the most popular characters, Ryo-ohki and Sasami in the same episode. Like any other pets, our Ryo-ohki has her favorite food; carrots! As for Sasami, you can enjoy watching her both in her space suits and everyday clothes. **25 min.**

Tenchi Universe Episode 4: *No Need For Monsters!*
With her spaceship crippled, Sasami happily joins Mihoshi, Ayeka and Ryoko to live with Tenchi's family. **25 min.**

Domestic Home Video:
Tenchi Universe Collection Vol. 1: *TV Episodes 1-4*
PI VA-1321D ▲ $24.95 ▲ VHS ▲ DUB ▲ HiFi Stereo ▲ 11/26/96
PI VA-1321S ▲ $29.95 ▲ VHS ▲ SUB ▲ HiFi Stereo ▲ 11/26/96
PI LA-1321A ▲ $44.95 ▲ LD ▲ M/A ▲ HiFi Stereo ▲ 11/12/96

Tenchi the Movie: Tenchi Muyô In Love

 MOVIE

(1996) ©AIC/Tenchi Muyô Committee/Pioneer Entertainment (USA) L.P.

Director: Hiroshi Negishi *Screenplay:* Ryoei Tsukimura, Hiroshi Negishi *Character Design & Animation Director:* Hiroyuki Horiuchi *Direction:* Koji Masunari *Animation Directors:* Takahiro Kishida, Kazuya Kuroda, Michiyo Suzuki *Art Director:* Torao Arai *Music:* Christopher Franke

Galaxy Police detectives Mihoshi and Kiyone are on routine patrol near Earth when they find out that the Galaxy Police headquarters has been blown up by a notorious terrorist and escaped prisoner named Kain. Kain possesses a power so strong that he can even warp time and space. Tenchi and friends decide to take a trip twenty-six years into the past, courtesy of Washu's "Time Cause/Effect Controller." The 1970s Tokyo setting gives the film a wonderfully exotic retro background. **95 min.**

Domestic Home Video:
PI VA-1390D ▲ $19.95 ▲ VHS ▲ DUB ▲ HiFi Stereo ▲ 08/27/96
PI VA-1390S ▲ $24.95 ▲ VHS ▲ SUB ▲ HiFi Stereo ▲ 08/27/96
PI LA-1390A ▲ $49.95 ▲ LD-CAV ▲ M/A ▲ HiFi Surround ▲ THX AC-3 ▲ 08/27/96

Tetsujin 28-go *See* GIGANTOR
Tetsuwan Atom *See* ASTRO BOY

They Were 11

MOVIE

(1986) ©Kitty Enterprises Inc./Victor Company of Japan Ltd.

Based on the comic by: Moto Hagio *Screenplay:* Toshiaki Imaizumi, Katsumi Koide *Director:* Tetsu Dezaki, Tsuneo Tominaga *Character Design:* Akio Sugino, Keizo Shimizu *Art Director:* Junichi Azuma

Based on the manga by "shôjo manga" or "girls' comics" pioneer Moto Hagio. THEY WERE 11 is the story of ten students who enter a derelict spaceship for the last segment of their entrance exam into a space academy, only to find that an *eleventh* member of their team has somehow materialized. Trapped aboard the ship for an Outward Bound-like 53-day journey of survival, the eleven examinees are forced to cope with multiple life-threatening menaces to the ship, as well as paranoia within their own ranks about the mysterious "eleventh." Small-scale but riveting drama in the spirit of *Twelve Angry Men* as the characters argue over their various alien races' personal and sexual politics. Believable space hardware and realistic threatment of zero-grav conditions make this a particularly convincing rendition of life in a space-faring future. Memorable character designs by Akio Sugino and Keizo Shimizu enhance a gripping outer space thriller with plenty of "shôjo" touches, as best reflected in the film's extensive characterization. Released in Japan under the title "Jûichi Nin Iru!" (They Were Eleven!) by Sôbi Entertainment; available in North America through U.S. Manga Corps. **91 min.**

TV Made for Television Broadcast **OAV** Made for Home Video Release **MOVIE** Made for Theatrical Release

Domestic Home Video:
USM 1469 ▲ $19.95 ▲ VHS ▲ DUB ▲ Stereo ▲ 12/03/96
USM 1028 ▲ $39.95 ▲ VHS ▲ SUB ▲ Stereo ▲ 01/06/93
ID 2239CT ▲ $34.95 ▲ LD ▲ SUB ▲ HiFi Stereo ▲ 08/17/93 ▲ Out of Print

---

Those Obnoxious Aliens *See* Urusei Yatsura
Tokusô Sensha-Tai Dominion *See* NEW DOMINION

Tokyo Babylon
OAV series, 2 volumes
(1992,'94) ©Clamp/Shinshôkan/MOVIC/Sony Music Entertainment (Japan) Inc.

Original story: Clamp *Screenplay:* Tatsuhiko Urahata (1), Hiroaki Jinno (2) *Music:* Toshiyuki Honda *Director:* Koichi Chigara (1), Kumiko Takahashi (2) *Character Design and Animation Director:* Kumiko Takahashi

Based on the manga of the same name by four-woman manga team Clamp. Like SILENT MÖBIUS (see entry), more *X-Files*-style adventures of a traditional Japanese spiritualist facing supernatural menaces in modern-day Japan. Character design and animation direction is by MERMAID'S SCAR's Kumiko "Not Rumiko" Takahashi, who also directs the second OAV volume. Released in Japan under the title "Tokyo Babylon" by Sony Music; available in North America through U.S. Manga Corps.

Tokyo Babylon Vol. 1
Shinji Nagumo seems to lead a charmed life amidst the inherent dangers of building a skyscraper, but everyone around him has been rather unlucky - fatally so. It's up to Subaru Sumeragi, the most powerful medium in Japan, to piece together the clues before there's another death. Subaru will have to work fast, because the lucky Mr. Nagumo has made many enemies. And one of those enemies is ready to sacrifice everything to create a creature that will end Nagumo's lucky streak - permanently! **52 min.**

Tokyo Babylon Vol. 2
Terror is stalking the subways. Without a motive, the police are helpless against this psychotic killer. With nowhere else to turn, Mirei Hidaka, a psychic "postcognitive" is called in. Using her sense of touch, Mirei can feel the currents of the past and has the ability to witness murders hours or days after they've been committed. But just as the threads are slowly starting to come together, Mirei's own life is in jeopardy! It's now up to Subaru Sumeragi, Japan's most powerful medium, to save the day. **59 min.**

Domestic Home Video:
Tokyo Babylon Vol. 1
USM 1281 ▲ $19.95 ▲ VHS ▲ DUB ▲ Stereo ▲ 04/04/95
USM 1095 ▲ $29.95 ▲ VHS ▲ SUB ▲ Stereo ▲ 04/04/95
ID 2903CT ▲ $34.95 ▲ LD ▲ HYBRID ▲ Stereo ▲ 06/18/96
Tokyo Babylon Vol. 2
USM 1283 ▲ $19.95 ▲ VHS ▲ DUB ▲ Stereo ▲ 07/11/95
USM 1282 ▲ $29.95 ▲ VHS ▲ SUB ▲ Stereo ▲ 07/11/95
ID 2904CT ▲ $34.95 ▲ LD ▲ HYBRID ▲ Stereo ▲ 07/16/96

Tonari no Totoro *See* MY NEIGHBOR TOTORO

Toward the Terra
(1980) ©Toei Animation Co. Ltd.

Original story: Keiko Takemiya *Director:* Hideo Onchi
Full-length theatrical feature based on the manga by "shôjo manga" or "girls' comics" pioneer Keiko Takemiya, as serialized in monthly GEKKAN MANGA SHÔNEN magazine anthology. Director Onchi manages to make the most of a limited budget in this sci-fi tale of humanity's near-extinction due to pollution and the subsequent rise of the great, oppressive supercomputers which try to control every facet of humanity's existence. Released in Japan under the title "Tera e..." (Toward the Terra) by Toei Video; available in North America through The Right Stuf. **112 min.**

Domestic Home Video:
RS 9001 ▲ $29.95 ▲ VHS ▲ SUB ▲ Stereo ▲ CP ▲ 05/15/94
LUM 9502 ▲ $39.95 ▲ LD ▲ SUB ▲ Stereo ▲ 03/08/95

Twilight of the Cockroaches
(1987) ©TYO Productions Inc./Kitty Films Inc.

Written and directed by: Hiroaki Yoshida *Animation Design:* Hiroshi Kurogane *Music:* Morgan Fischer *Starring:* Kaoru Kobayashi and Setsuko Karasumaru

Live-action and animation hybrid about an impending roach holocaust in a Tokyo apartment complex, as told from the insects' point of view, wherein the animated roaches are the heroes and the live-action humans are the villains. (Note that in comparison, the less-funny live-action film *Joe's Apartment* gives viewers the roach action without the genocide allegory.) Released in Japan under the title "Gokiburitachi no Tasogare" (Twilight of the Cockroaches) by TYO Productions, Inc./Kitty Film; available in North America through Streamline Pictures. **102 min.**

Domestic Home Video:
SPV 90273 ▲ $19.95 ▲ VHS ▲ DUB ▲ Mono ▲ 09/01/92
LUM 9201 ▲ $39.95 ▲ LD ▲ DUB ▲ Mono ▲ 02/15/92 ▲ Out of Print

Twin Dolls
OAV series, 2 volumes
(1995) ©Daiei Co. Ltd.

Original Story & Script: Ohji Miyako *Character Design:* Shin Rin *Director:* Kan Fukumoto

They may look like a typical pair of high school girls, but sisters Mai and Ai are professional demon hunters, dedicated to protecting humanity from the severly misnamed "Pleasure Underworld" (seeing that only males seem capable of living to experience "pleasure" twice). Basically, demons want to invade Earth so they can rape every female in sight (after which the females explode, or just die), but the twins stand in their way. Notable for actually animating detailed (if exaggerated!) erect male members instead of the typical amorphous tentacles. Misogynist fantasy reaches new heights with the inclusion of "orbs of orgasm," which, when placed in women's mouths, make them *like* rape. Released in Japan under the title "Injû Seisen (Lustful-Beast Holy War) Twin Angel" by Tokuma Japan Communications; available in North America through Anime 18, a division of A.D. Vision.

Twin Dolls: *Legend of the Heavenly Beasts*
When a jealous classmate makes an oath to beat the Twin Dolls, she is literally possessed by a green-eyed monster! Aided by a horde of scuttling sub-demons, the horned demon quickly builds a harem of Mai and Ai's unsuspecting classmates. **50 min.**

Twin Dolls II: *Return of the Heavenly Beasts*
Before a new demon can take on the nubile Mai and Ai, this over-sexed fiend must first build a harem of sex slaves for himself and his sub-demons. **50 min.**

Domestic Home Video:
Twin Dolls
ADV TD/001 ▲ $34.95 ▲ VHS ▲ SUB ▲ HiFi ▲ Uncut ▲ 04/17/95
ADV TD/003 ▲ $29.95 ▲ VHS ▲ SUB ▲ HiFi ▲ Edited ▲ 01/30/96
Twin Dolls II
ADV TD/002 ▲ $34.95 ▲ VHS ▲ SUB ▲ HiFi Surround ▲ 05/10/95

Uchû no Kishi Tekkaman *See* TEKKAMAN
Uchû Senkan Yamato *See* STAR BLAZERS
Uchû Senshi Baldios *See* SPACE WARRIORS BALDIOS
UFO Robo Grandizer *See* GRANDIZER

U-Jin Brand
(1991) ©Yujin/SEIYO/Animate Film Co. Ltd.

Created by: Hideo Takano *Writer:* U-jin *Director:* Osamu Okada *Chief Animator:* Yumi Nakayama *Music:* Nobuo Ito
Anthology video of three softcore sex tales based on stories by infamous softcore manga artist U-Jin, whose fearless manga depictions of certain restricted-by-law secondary sexual characteristics (how's that for coy) brought down a rain of Japanese PTA rage and subsequent crackdowns on similar adult materials. Two segments are light parodies of the infamous "Rapeman" concept (including the rape, of course), while the other features a songwriter for young "idol" singers who takes advantage of his situation to sleep with teenage

---

 Violence   Profanity   Nudity   Sexual Situations   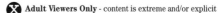 Adult Viewers Only - content is extreme and/or explicit

girls. All the while though, he's dreaming of his schoolgirl love. Non-P.C., but not quite far enough to really call it raunchy, this is porn for beginners. Released in Japan as "Yûjin Brand" by Coconut Boy Project/Nihon Soft System; available in North America through U.S. Manga Corps. **45 min.**

Domestic Home Video:
USM 1075 ▲ $29.95 ▲ VHS ▲ SUB ▲ Stereo ▲ 01/25/94
ID 2869CT ▲ $34.95 ▲ LD ▲ SUB ▲ Stereo ▲ 12/14/94

The Ultimate Teacher

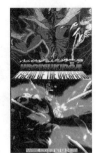

(1988) ©Movic/Sony Music Entertainment (Japan) Inc.

Based on the comic by: Atsuji Yamamoto *Screenplay:* Monta Ibu *Director:* Toyo'o Ashida *Character Design:* Atsuji Yamamoto, Mandoriru Club *Art Director:* Setsuko Ishizu

Based on the manga by Atsuji Yamamoto. The worst school in town gets a new teacher who turns out to be a mutated cockroach! To clean up the gang violence in the school, he goes head to head with the leader: a pretty super-strong schoolgirl. Later in the story, it turns out that the gym shorts she wears instead of panties are the source of her power. A weird combo of *Stand And Deliver*, *The Fly* and *High School High*, from the director of FIST OF THE NORTH STAR. Released in Japan under the title "Kyôfu no Bio-Ningen: Saishû Kyôshi" (The Terrifying Bio-Human: Ultimate Teacher) by Sony Music; available in North America through U.S. Manga Corps. **57 min.**

Domestic Home Video:
USM 1471 ▲ $14.95 ▲ VHS ▲ DUB ▲ Stereo ▲ 06/18/96
USM 1030 ▲ $29.95 ▲ VHS ▲ SUB ▲ Stereo ▲ 11/03/93
ID 2240CT ▲ $34.95 ▲ LD ▲ SUB ▲ HiFi Stereo ▲ 10/20/93

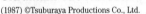

Ultraman: The Adventure Begins

(1987) ©Tsuburaya Productions Co., Ltd.

Original Story and Produced by: Noboru Tsuburaya *Directed by:* Mitsuo Kusakabe *Character Design:* Kazuo Iimura *Music:* Shinsuke Kazato *Co-Production with Hanna-Barbera Voices of:* Michael Lembeck, Chad Everett, Adrienne Barbeau, Stacy Keach Sr.

Animated adventures of the internationally recognized hero, Ultraman, in a co-production of Hanna-Barbera and Tsuburaya Productions. A science patrolman possessed by a powerful alien must defend Earth against giant monsters too destructive for the science patrol to deal with. A new version of the origin story of this long series of live-action, two-fisted, energy slingin', kaijû-crushin' mayhem. Released in Japan as "Ultraman USA" by Bandai Visual; available in North America through Ultra-Action Video, a division of U.S. Renditions. **75 min.**

Domestic Home Video:
USR UAV05 ▲ $14.95 ▲ VHS ▲ DUB ▲ HiFi Stereo ▲ 06/02/93

Urotsuki Dôji

OAV series, 5 episodes

(1989-93) ©Toshio Maeda/JAVN Inc./West Cape Corp.

Original Story: Toshio Maeda *Screenplay:* Goro Sanyo, Noboru Aikawa, Michael Lawrence *Music:* Masamichi Amano *Director:* Hideki Takayama

Sturm and drang with plenty of demonic rape thrown in, UROTSUKI DÔJI made its mark as one of the few anime films other than AKIRA to travel the hip art house movie circuit. A convoluted plot involving three dimensions of beings: humanity, demons, and man-beasts (who function mostly as voyeurs) fighting for possession of the Earth leads the story through discussions on morality while indulging in plenty of gothic gross-out and misogynist tentacle rape. Shockingly graphic, fascinating in small doses, it's like the car wreck from which you can't tear away your horrified eyes; *Hellraiser* fans may find something to relate to here. Released in Japan under the title "Chôjin Densetsu Urotsuki Dôji" (Legend of the Overfiend, Wandering Kid) by Bandai/Westcape Corporation/Nihon Columbia/Jupiter Films; available in North America through Anime 18 (a division of Central Park Media) in both an edited version and an unexpurgated "Perfect Collection."

Urotsukidoji Perfect Collection

According to legend, every 3,000 years the three realms of demons, humans, and man-beasts are united by the Overfiend, whose coming means chaos and destruction!

Determined to prevent the cataclysm, Amano Jyaku and his sister Megumi have tracked the Overfiend to Myojin University in Japan. But other, more sinister demons are bent on beating them to the prize. Two college students, Tatsuo Nagumo and Akemi Ito are unwittingly drawn into the hunt... and after a night of horrific revelations, their lives will be changed forever. The five original OAVs that comprise this series are: *Birth of the Overfiend*, *Curse of the Overfiend*, *Final Inferno*, *Legend of the Demon Womb*, and *Battle at the Shinjuku Skyscrapers*. **250 min.**

Urotsukidoji: Legend of the Overfiend

The first three OAVs of the series edited together into a mini-feature and dubbed in English. **108 min.**

Urotsukidoji II: *Legend of the Demon Womb*

The last two OAVs of the series edited together into a mini-feature and dubbed in English. Infamous for the monstrous Nazi Death Rape Machine sequences. **88 min.**

Domestic Home Video:
Urotsukidoji Perfect Collection (5 tapes/3 discs)
A18 1076 ▲ $99.95 ▲ VHS ▲ SUB ▲ Stereo ▲ 12/01/93
RO 396 ▲ $99.95 ▲ LD ▲ SUB ▲ HiFi Stereo ▲ 09/19/94
Urotsukidoji: Legend of the Overfiend
A18 1072 ▲ $29.95 ▲ VHS ▲ DUB ▲ Stereo ▲ 08/02/93
RO 332 ▲ $49.95 ▲ LD ▲ DUB ▲ HiFi Stereo
Urotsukidoji II: *Legend of the Demon Womb*
A18 1073 ▲ $29.95 ▲ VHS ▲ DUB ▲ Stereo ▲ 11/03/93
RO 333 ▲ $49.95 ▲ LD ▲ DUB ▲ HiFi Stereo

Urotsuki Dôji III: Return of the Overfiend

OAV series, 4 episodes

(1993) ©Toshio Maeda/West Cape Corp.

Based on the comic by: Toshio Maeda *Script:* Noboru Aikawa *Music:* Masamichi Amano *Director:* Hideki Takayama *Character Design:* Rikizo Sekime, Shiro Kasami *Monster Design:* Sumito Ioi *Art Director:* Kenichi Harada

Urotsukidoji III Episode 1

Twenty years after Nagumo, rumored to be the Overfiend, an order called Demon-Beasts has evolved. After only 20 years of sleep, Akemi is about to give birth to the true Overfiend in Osaka Castle. Forcing his own birth decades earlier than planned, the Overfiend warns Amano of the birth of an evil being and orders him to keep this being away from the castle. Under Caesar's rule, Tokyo has become a battleground between Buju and his Demon-Beasts and Caesar's army. **60 min.**

Urotsukidoji III Episode 2

A child has emerged who may be the true Lord of Chaos. Caesar and Faust plot to unite the child, Himi, with their own demonic creation known as Fabrille. This new force will be the one power which could defeat the Overfiend, exacting Caesar's revenge for the untimely death of his daughter, Alecto. Amano recognizes Faust to be the despicable Munhihausen responsible for the emergence of the monstrous Nagumo. **50 min.**

Urotsukidoji III Episode 3

Caesar has taken advantage of the chaos to launch his ultra-titanic nuclear missiles at Osaka, but Amano destroys them one by one. Meanwhile, the Overfiend summons Megumi to Osaka, where he attempts to tap her hidden powers. As her power is released in a burst of energy, it destroys the last of the missiles and sends Fabrille, now in the shape of a giant monster bird, flying back towards Tokyo. As the Demon-Beasts continue their attack on Caesar's Palace, the Overfiend confronts the Lord of Chaos inside Fabrille. As their conversation concludes, Fabrille crashes into the base of Caesar's Palace destroying both the palace and himself. **50 min.**

Urotsukidoji III Episode 4

In his new monstrous form, Caesar pursues his daughter's captors. As Caesar's troops begin to lose ground, it's time to unleash the ultimate weapon: Dieneich the Genocidroid, a powerful android still under assembly. A golden snow begins to fall and drifts into Dieneich's chamber reviving him. Outside, the only sound is Himi's crying. When her crying subsides, she tells Buju that it's time to go to Osaka and meet the Overfiend. She is accompanied by the three Demon-Beasts - all searching for the answer to their own existence. **50 min.**

Urotsukidoji III: The Movie

The four-volume OAV series is condensed into a 120-minute feature film and presented in Japanese with English subtitles. **120 min.**

Domestic Home Video:
Urotsukidoji III Episode 1
A18 1207 ▲ $29.95 ▲ VHS ▲ DUB ▲ Stereo ▲ 09/07/94

Urotsukidoji III Episode 2
A18 1208 ▲ $29.95 ▲ VHS ▲ DUB ▲ Stereo ▲ 10/05/94
Urotsukidoji III Episode 3
A18 1209 ▲ $29.95 ▲ VHS ▲ DUB ▲ Stereo ▲ 11/09/94
Urotsukidoji III Episode 4
A18 1210 ▲ $29.95 ▲ VHS ▲ DUB ▲ Stereo ▲ 11/09/94
Urotsukidoji III: The Movie
A18 1438 ▲ $29.95 ▲ VHS ▲ SUB ▲ Stereo ▲ 06/04/96
Urotsukidoji III 4-Pack Brick
All four volumes of the OAV series. (220 min.)
A18 1211 ▲ $99.95 ▲ VHS ▲ DUB ▲ Stereo ▲ 11/09/94

Urotsuki Dôji IV: Inferno Road   [OAV] ⓧ 🔊 ✳ 🔘 📙
OAV series, 3 episodes

(1995) ©Toshio Maeda/West Cape Corporation

Based on the comic by: Toshio Maeda *Script:*
Nobuaki Kishima *Music:* Masamichi Amano
Character Design: Tetsuya Yanagisawa, Aki Tsunaki
Director: Hideki Takayama (1,2), Shigenori
Kageyama (3)

Urotsukidoji IV Episode 1
It is the early 21st century, and the civilization of
mankind is gone. Powerful, supernatural forces have
sculpted our world into something more... suitable.
Now, flesh-hungry demons and half-demons rule the Earth—raping and slaughtering
thousands. This is the age of the Overfiend. But if Himi can be brought to Osaka, then the
world can be made whole once more. Buju and Himi are interrupted in their quest by a
pair of refugees. Together, they discover a city where innocence masks deadly psionic
powers, and where others serve as slaves, or worse. **45 min.**

Urotsukidoji IV Episode 2
Trapped in the City of Evil once again, Yumi is tortured as an example for the other
slaves—The Masters must be obeyed. But these beings have made a horrifying
discovery—by drinking Himi's living blood, they can become immortal, retaining their
incredible powers forever. Will the half-demon Amano Jyaku be able to rescue Himi from
their sadistic clutches? **45 min.**

Urotsukidoji IV Episode 3
Desperate for the power to destroy Amano Jyaku, Yoenhime turns to the Overfiend's old
nemesis—The Mad Regent Munhihausen! Under the Mad Regent's power, she is reborn as
Munhihausen's newest and deadliest pawn—the demonic Yoenki. Now begins the final
battle for the fate of the Earth, as Yoenki and her monstrous
minions stand against Amano and his allies—and this time, the
winner will reshape the planet to their liking! **45 min.**

Domestic Home Video:
Urotsukidoji IV Episode 1
A18 1513 ▲ $29.95 ▲ VHS ▲ DUB ▲ Stereo ▲ 10/08/96
Urotsukidoji IV Episode 2
A18 1514 ▲ $29.95 ▲ VHS ▲ DUB ▲ Stereo ▲ 10/08/96
Urotsukidoji IV Episode 3
A18 1515 ▲ $29.95 ▲ VHS ▲ DUB ▲ Stereo ▲ 10/08/96
Urotsukidoji IV: Inferno Road 3-Pack
Episodes 1 - 3 (135 min.)
A18 1526 ▲ $79.95 ▲ VHS ▲ DUB ▲ Stereo ▲ 10/08/96

Urusei Yatsura   [TV] 🔊
TV series, 197 episodes

(1981-86) ©Kitty Films

Based on characters created by: Rumiko
Takahashi *Director:* Mamoru Oshii *Planning:*
Shigekazu Ochiai *Character Design:* Akemi
Takada *Art Directors:* Michitaka Nakamura, Tateo
Imamura *Music:* Shinsuke Kazado, Fumitaka Anzai

Based on the manga of the same name by Rumiko
Takahashi (RANMA 1/2, MAISON IKKOKU), as
serialized in publisher Shogakukan's weekly
SHŪKAN SHŌNEN SUNDAY manga anthology (published
in English by Viz Comics). An alien invasion turned
romantic sitcom? You heard right—an unnamed
alien race (who happen to look exactly like
traditional Japanese "oni," or ogres, tiger-striped apparel, horns and all) decide whether or
not to invade a planet by a three-day game of tag between randomly selected opponents.
For Earth, the finger falls on a luckless Japanese lad named Ataru, who must face the
aliens' sprightly princess, the bikini-clad Lum. Even at severe disadvantage (he has to grab
her horns to win, but she can fly, and shoot electrical bolts from her hands), the lecherous
Ataru manages to defeat the bikini-clad alien by pulling off her bikini top, forcing her to

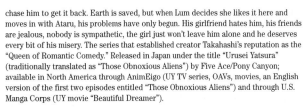

chase him to get it back. Earth is saved, but when Lum decides she likes it here and
moves in with Ataru, his problems have only begun. His girlfriend hates him, his friends
are jealous, nobody is sympathetic, the girl just won't leave him alone and he deserves
every bit of his misery. The series that established creator Takahashi's reputation as the
"Queen of Romantic Comedy." Released in Japan under the title "Urusei Yatsura"
(traditionally translated as "Those Obnoxious Aliens") by Five Ace/Pony Canyon;
available in North America through AnimEigo (UY TV series, OAVs, movies, an English
version of the first two episodes entitled "Those Obnoxious Aliens") and through U.S.
Manga Corps (UY movie "Beautiful Dreamer").

Urusei Yatsura TV Series Vol. 1: *Episodes 1-4*
The series' premise is established when Ataru must win a contest with Lum. Win he does,

but Lum misinterprets his victory cry as a proposal
of marriage - to her! Now Lum's living in his closet,
planning their wedding, and zapping him with high-
voltage electricity if he even looks at another
woman. His girlfriend isn't sure if she's been jilted
or saved from a life of misery, his Lum-crazed
schoolmates are plotting to get him "out of the
way," his parents are loudly wishing he'd never
been born, and to top it all off, a demented
Buddhist monk has been seen lurking around the
neighborhood mumbling something about evil
spirits and curses. Then Lum's relatives start
visiting, and things start to really get weird! **100 min.**

Urusei Yatsura TV Series Vol. 2: *Episodes 5-8*
Ataru runs away from home, and into the arms of Sakura, a Shinto sorceress. Alas, Sakura
has her own agenda; the boys of high school suddenly become accident-prone when
Sakura takes a job as school nurse; Ataru tries to make a secret date with Shinobu and
sneak around on Lum; a midnight mishap with mirrors unleashes an annoying devil, and
Cherry's attempts at exorcism only multiply the problem; Ataru insulates himself from
Lum's electric zaps, resulting in unexpected consequences; Lum starts playing around
with alien voodoo dolls; Oyuki, Princess of Neptune, opens an interdimensional portal
into Ataru's closet to dispose of excess snow; and when Ataru "flies the unfriendly skies,"
a midair mishap grounds the gang in the age of the dinosaurs! **100 min.**

Urusei Yatsura TV Series Vol. 3: *Episodes 9-12*
Princess Kurama is awakened by the kiss of her future husband... but her Prince
Charming is Ataru; making the best of things, Kurama decides to remake Ataru into a
perfect husband, even if it kills him; Megane
plots to discredit Ataru with Lum, and set him
up for the Mother of All Zappings; in a hilarious
parody of the world's first novel, "The Tale of
Genji," we go back to Heian Period Japan,
where pre-incarnations of everyone battle baby-
nappers from the future, and time gets royally
screwed up; Tsubame, Sakura's fiancé and
aspiring black magician, matches wits with
Cherry and turns a nightclub into "Disco
Inferno"; and Kurama's dad agrees to teach
Ataru the secrets of swordsmanship - if Ataru
will teach him about babes! **100 min.**

Urusei Yatsura TV Series Vol. 4: *Episodes 13-16*
During a Hawaiian vacation, someone starts swiping the girls' swimsuits; Cherry and
Sakura take a Hotel's "Full Course From Hell" "Free If You Can Eat It All" challenge;
Mendo Shutaro, the richest boy in Japan, is transferred to Tomobiki High, and causes
chaos when he runs for class president; Lum uses high-tech astrology to decide who is the
best match for her, Ataru or Mendo; Benten and her fellow Chinese Gods of Luck have
their annual End-Of-Winter grudge match against Lum and the Oni; Benten comes back
with a few friends to make Lum's life lousy; a mysterious teacher-for-hire arrives at the
school, and he's going to clean up the class; and if you think Lum, Ataru and Mendo are
bad, the first meeting of their mothers threatens to plunge the galaxy into war! **100 min.**

Urusei Yatsura TV Series Vol. 5: *Episodes 17-20*
Mendo's mysterious camera means more trouble for Ataru; Ataru accidentally trades his
soul for the ability to excel; Ran, Lum's childhood friend, arrives with an avenging agenda;
Ran tries to sucker Lum and steal Ataru; a diary from the future falls into the wrong hands
- Ataru's; an alien baby appears in Mendo's locker; two soporific spirits turn the classroom
into a sleepy battleground; and Cherry's lack of singing ability proves to be a big problem.
100 min.

Urusei Yatsura TV Series Vol. 6: *Episodes 21-24*
Ataru splits not only his personality but his body as well; late night cardplaying leads to
demented daydreams; Ataru's mother recaps the series so far in a half-hour special; The
electric company enlists the gang in a set of public service announcements (for real); a
trip to the ancient capital of Nara pits Ataru against a gang of female Ninja; and Lum's
impatient Dad decides to match Lum with another man! **100 min.**

Urusei Yatsura TV Series Vol. 7: *Episodes 25-28*
Ataru is kidnapped by "kappa" vampires and taken to the bottom of a lake, prompting
Lum to fear he's been drowned; confusion reigns supreme when Ataru and Ten run afoul
of body-switching earmuffs; a strange, green, and very rapidly growing caterpillar eats
everything in its path, then holes up in its cocoon while the gang goes to war over it; and

 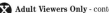

Ten gets a big crush on Sakura, then enlists the aid of Kintaro and his bear in carrying out his assault of love. **100 min.**

Urusei Yatsura TV Series Vol. 8: *Episodes 29-32*

Insanity reigns supreme in Tomobiki Town! An amorous Dracula and his batty "girl-Friday" hit town and redefine the term "nightlife"; Lum travels back in time to re-educate and reform a young lad named Ataru; love blooms when both Ten and Ataru fall for a fair lady florist; and trouble looms for Ataru when an evil rain-spirit dumps all over him. **100 min.**

Urusei Yatsura TV Series Vol. 9: *Episodes 33-36*

Ten loses his powers when his horn disappears, and Ataru wastes no time in taking advantage of the situation; the gang has to recatalog a weird library in order to save the universe; we find out there's one thing worse than a new teacher and Lum as a new student - volleyball; and a sad goblin gets kicked out of his pool and wreaks havoc. **100 min.**

Urusei Yatsura TV Series Vol. 10: *Episodes 37-40*

Ran makes another attempt to steal Ataru from Lum; chaos reigns supreme during self-study period when Rei drops in for a visit; the return of the mysterious "Red Cloak" sets up a night of Disco terror; and Lum tries to thwart Ran's latest scheme by duplicating her darling. **100 min.**

Urusei Yatsura TV Series Vol. 11: *Episodes 41-44*

Lum and Ataru actually go out on a date; a trip to the seaside results in a run-in with a cursed watermelon; a typhoon treads on Tokyo, panicking Ataru's parents; and if you think Lum and Ten are a recipe for chaos, wait until you see them after they get smashed on high-proof pickled plums! **100 min.**

Urusei Yatsura TV Series Vol. 12: *Episodes 45-48*

Ataru takes on every cat in town to save a pretty girl from a cursed fate; in the episode voted "Best Episode" by Japanese viewers, Lum decides to find out if Ataru is really serious about wanting to be rid of her; Benten, Oyuki and the rest of Lum's friends descend upon the High School; and then when the gang starts sneaking from school to get fast-food, the teachers mobilize for all-out war! **100 min.**

Urusei Yatsura TV Series Vol. 13: *Episodes 49-52*

Tabloid TV reporters go on a rampage when Ataru assembles a bird out of old fossils and Lum brings it to life; goblins are galvanized into action as they once again try to find a mate for the lovely Princess Kurama; dentists are delighted when Ten infects the school with a contagious alien toothache; and Mendo is mortified when his younger sister Ryoko arrives and proceeds to put the moves on Ataru. **100 min.**

Urusei Yatsura TV Series Vol. 14: *Episodes 53-56*

The ghost of a large cat stands between Ataru and his dinner; a strange raccoon proves that no good deed goes unpunished; Ataru goes through hell (literally) to get the perfect part-time job; and Lum's year-end party turns into an exercise in demented deduction. **100 min.**

Urusei Yatsura TV Series Vol. 15: *Episodes 57-60*

The *UY* gang run amok in a twisted retelling of the life of Japan's greatest swordsman, Miyamoto Musashi; Onsen-Mark lays down the law in class and ends up getting the silent treatment; Lum's dad decides to live at the Moroboshi house after a family quarrel; and a ski vacation goes rapidly downhill when the guys use every dirty trick they know to obtain "the Kiss of Miss Snow Queen." **100 min.**

Urusei Yatsura TV Series Vol. 16: *Episodes 61-64*

Love becomes ludicrous when Ten gets an unwanted girlfriend in the ST. VALENTINE'S DAY HORROR; gazing into Crystal Eyeballs reveals the future of one's lovelife in LOVE, LOVE, CATCHBALL; Mendo's conniving sister Ryoko arranges for a little mayhem in THE MENDO FAMILY'S MASQUERADE WAR; and when humans start catching Lum's cold, things rapidly degenerate into a SPACE COLD PANIC. **100 min.**

Urusei Yatsura TV Series Vol. 17: *Episodes 65-68*

Ataru, Lum and the Gang go to the beach and meet Ryunosuke for the first time; Shinobu eavesdrops on Ataru and Megane and mistakenly believes that Ataru is going to give up Lum; Ran meets and falls in love with Ryo. Despite Ataru and Lum's efforts, Ran refuses to believe that Ryo is a girl! And it's Ataru's birthday and he wants to be free of Lum (at least for a day)! **100 min.**

Urusei Yatsura TV Series Vol. 18: *Episodes 69-72*

Lum's indescribably bad cooking is the least of the problems facing the gang in FOUND: THE VALLEY OF PEACHES IN THE CAMP-FROM-HELL; those pesky Tengu crows find a near-perfect match for their princess, Kurama, and they set out to fix that one little problem that keeps "him" from being eligible in THE BRIDEGROOM'S NAME IS RYUNOSUKE; a letter in a bottle leads to chaos in A LETTER IN A BOTTLE-SEASIDE SPOOKINESS; and Mendo's deadly rival, the scion of the second-richest family in Japan (they own the other 49.9% of the country) arrives on the scene in THE SENSATIONAL DEBUT OF MIZUNOKOUJI TON! **100 min.**

Domestic Home Video:

Urusei Yatsura TV Series Vol. 1
ANI AT092-101 ▲ $24.95 ▲ VHS ▲ SUB ▲ HiFi Mono

Urusei Yatsura TV Series Vol. 2
ANI AT092-102 ▲ $24.95 ▲ VHS ▲ SUB ▲ HiFi Mono

Urusei Yatsura TV Series Vol. 3
ANI AT092-103 ▲ $24.95 ▲ VHS ▲ SUB ▲ HiFi Mono

Urusei Yatsura TV Series Vol. 4
ANI AT092-104 ▲ $24.95 ▲ VHS ▲ SUB ▲ HiFi Mono

Urusei Yatsura TV Series Vol. 5
ANI AT092-105 ▲ $24.95 ▲ VHS ▲ SUB ▲ HiFi Mono

Urusei Yatsura TV Series Vol. 6
ANI AT092-106 ▲ $24.95 ▲ VHS ▲ SUB ▲ HiFi Mono ▲ 04/12/93

Urusei Yatsura TV Series Vol. 7
ANI AT092-107 ▲ $24.95 ▲ VHS ▲ SUB ▲ HiFi Mono ▲ 05/17/93

Urusei Yatsura TV Series Vol. 8
ANI AT092-108 ▲ $24.95 ▲ VHS ▲ SUB ▲ HiFi Mono

Urusei Yatsura TV Series Vol. 9
ANI AT092-109 ▲ $24.95 ▲ VHS ▲ SUB ▲ HiFi Mono ▲ 09/15/93

Urusei Yatsura TV Series Vol. 10
ANI AT092-110 ▲ $24.95 ▲ VHS ▲ SUB ▲ HiFi Mono ▲ 10/27/93

Urusei Yatsura TV Series Vol. 11
ANI AT092-111 ▲ $24.95 ▲ VHS ▲ SUB ▲ HiFi Mono ▲ 12/29/93

Urusei Yatsura TV Series Vol. 12
ANI AT092-112 ▲ $24.95 ▲ VHS ▲ SUB ▲ HiFi Mono ▲ 02/23/94

Urusei Yatsura TV Series Vol. 13
ANI AT092-113 ▲ $24.95 ▲ VHS ▲ SUB ▲ Mono ▲ 05/25/94

Urusei Yatsura TV Series Vol. 14
ANI AT092-114 ▲ $24.95 ▲ VHS ▲ SUB ▲ HiFi Mono ▲ 05/25/94

Urusei Yatsura TV Series Vol. 15
ANI AT092-115 ▲ $24.95 ▲ VHS ▲ SUB ▲ Mono ▲ 09/28/94

Urusei Yatsura TV Series Vol. 16
ANI AT092-116 ▲ $24.95 ▲ VHS ▲ SUB ▲ Mono ▲ 06/28/95

Urusei Yatsura TV Series Vol. 17
ANI AT092-117 ▲ $24.95 ▲ VHS ▲ SUB ▲ Mono ▲ 12/27/95

Urusei Yatsura TV Series Vol. 18
ANI AT092-118 ▲ $24.95 ▲ VHS ▲ SUB ▲ Mono ▲ 06/28/96

Those Obnoxious Aliens Vol. 1
Episodes 1 and 2 dubbed in English.
ANI ET095-002 ▲ $19.95 ▲ VHS ▲ DUB ▲ Stereo ▲ 03/29/95

Urusei Yatsura OAV Series

[OAV] (⊙)

OAV series, 11 episodes

Tea Party (1986), Memorial Album (1986), Inaba (1987), Raging Sherbet (1988), Nagisa (1988), Household Guard (1989), I Howl (1989), Catch the Heart (1989), Goat and Cheese (1989), Date With A Spirit (1991), Terror (1991) ©Kitty Films.

Urusei Yatsura OAV 1: *Inaba the Dreammaker*

On her way back from the market, Shinobu finds a boy in a bunny suit lying in a trash heap. Inaba the bunny-boy tries to hit on Shinobu, and when the dust settles, Shinobu finds a strange key that dropped out of Inaba's pocket. Lum decides to build a door, and when the key fits, Shinobu, Lum and Ataru go through the door - and literally fall into their own futures. Meanwhile, Inaba's co-workers at Destiny Production Management Bureau feel that he should be the one to fix things. **57 min.**

Urusei Yatsura OAV 2: *Raging Sherbet & I Howl at the Moon*

In RAGING SHERBET, Lum, Benten and Ran decide to take a summer vacation with Oyuki on Neptune. There they learn about the fabulous Sherbet birds, which produce icy treats on demand. In I HOWL AT THE MOON, Ataru learns to think before he eats when he gobbles down some of Lum's homemade treats - and promptly starts turning into a wolf. **53 min.**

Urusei Yatsura OAV 3: *Catch the Heart & Goat and Cheese*

In CATCH THE HEART, a mischievous spirit gives Ran a heart-shaped candy that causes a magical heart to appear over the head of whoever eats it. And whoever catches that heart captures the heart of the person who ate the candy! In GOAT AND CHEESE, Mendo recounts an old story that warns, "Don't take pictures in front of the statue of Great-Grandfather's Goat, or terrible things will happen"! When his father does just that, only Sakura and Onsen-Mark the teacher can ward off the horrifying consequences of an ancient family curse. **50 min.**

  TV Made for Television Broadcast   **OAV** Made for Home Video Release   **MOVIE** Made for Theatrical Release

Urusei Yatsura OAV 4: *Date With A Spirit & Terror of Girly-Eyes Measles*
In DATE WITH A SPIRIT, things get crazy when Ataru tries to hit on a beautiful ghost who has attached herself to Sakura's sorceress fiancé, Tsubame. In TERROR OF GIRLY-EYES MEASLES, Ten gives Ataru an alien disease, the contagious Girl Measles, which makes the victim's eyes turn big and twinkly, and when Ataru's girl-hunting spreads the virus all over Tomobiki Town, chaos ensues! **50 min.**

Urusei Yatsura OAV 5: *Nagisa's Fiancé & The Electric Household Guard*
In NAGISA'S FIANCÉ, Lum, Ataru, Mendo and Shinobu visit an inn which Ryunosuke and her father have opened, but it turns out to be on a haunted desert island. In THE ELECTRIC HOUSEHOLD GUARD, Mendo acquires a new personal Ninja with some very unusual abilities, only to have him fall head-over-heels for his manipulative sister, Ryoko. **50 min.**

Urusei Yatsura OAV 6: *Ryoko's September Tea Party & Memorial Album*
The final *Urusei Yatsura* OAV collection consists of two very unusual offerings, even by *Urusei Yatsura* standards. In RYOKO'S SEPTEMBER TEA PARTY, some of the best scenes of the original TV series are combined with 15 minutes of new animation to reveal the pasts of each of Ryoko's guests. Next, in MEMORIAL ALBUM, I'M THE SHU-CHAN, the Mendo clan's personal satellite narrates the story of the Mendo family, again using a mixture of new animation and scenes from the original series. **90min.**

Domestic Home Video:
Urusei Yatsura OVA 1
ANI AT092-204 ▲ $24.95 ▲ VHS ▲ SUB ▲ Mono
Urusei Yatsura OVA 2
ANI AT092-205 ▲ $24.95 ▲ VHS ▲ SUB ▲ HiFi Stereo
Urusei Yatsura OVA 3
ANI AT092-206 ▲ $24.95 ▲ VHS ▲ SUB ▲ HiFi Mono ▲ 04/29/93
Urusei Yatsura OVA 4
ANI AT092-207 ▲ $24.95 ▲ VHS ▲ SUB ▲ HiFi Mono ▲ 06/03/93
Urusei Yatsura OVA 5
ANI AT092-208 ▲ $24.95 ▲ VHS ▲ SUB ▲ HiFi Mono
Urusei Yatsura OVA 6
ANI AT092-209 ▲ $24.95 ▲ VHS ▲ SUB ▲ HiFi Stereo/Mono

Urusei Yatsura: Only You
(1983) ©Kitty Films

Based on characters by: Rumiko Takahashi *Screenplay and Direction:* Mamoru Oshii *Character Design:* Kazuo Yamazaki *Animation Directors:* Kazuo Yamazaki , Yuji Moriyama *Art Director:* Shichiro Kobayashi

Alien princess Lum is invited to on-again, off-again beau Ataru's wedding…only she's not the bride! Seems some 11 years ago, Ataru played "shadow tag" with a young girl named Elle and won; unfortunately, Elle was another alien princess, and on her planet, if a boy steps on a girl's shadow, they have to be married. Released in Japan under the title "Urusei Yatsura: Only You" by Five Ace/Pony Canyon; available in North America through AnimEigo. **101 min.**

Domestic Home Video:
ANI AT092-201 ▲ $24.95 ▲ VHS ▲ SUB ▲ Mono
ANI AD093-005 ▲ $39.95 ▲ LD ▲ SUB ▲ HiFi Mono ▲ 10/20/93

Urusei Yatsura: Beautiful Dreamer
(1984) Toho Co., Ltd.

Based on characters and situations by: Rumiko Takahashi *Screenplay and Direction:* Mamoru Oshii *Character Design:* Kazuo Yamazaki *Animation Directors:* Kazuo Yamazaki, Yuji Moriyama *Art Director:* Shichiro Kobayashi

Shades of the classic story "The Mandarin and the Butterfly" in this bizarre, 98-minute headtrip which brought the name of director Oshii to the wider world. Is it a dream? Is it reality? Who knows; maybe it's both. Released in Japan under the title "Urusei Yatsura 2: Beautiful Dreamer" by Toho; available in North America through U.S. Manga Corps. **90 min.**

Domestic Home Video:
USM 1472 ▲ $19.95 ▲ VHS ▲ DUB ▲ HiFi Mono ▲ 12/03/96
USM 1039 ▲ $29.95 ▲ VHS ▲ SUB ▲ HiFi Mono ▲ 11/11/92
ID 2241CT ▲ $39.95 ▲ LD ▲ SUB ▲ HiFi Mono ▲ 04/29/93

Urusei Yatsura: Remember My Love

(1985) ©Kitty Films

Based on characters and situations by: Rumiko Takahashi *Director:* Kazuo Yamazaki *Screenplay:* Tomoko Konparu *Character Design:* Akemi Takada *Music:* Micky Yoshino *Art Directors:* Shichiro Kobayashi, Torao Arai *Chief Animation Director:* Yuji Moriyama

When Lum was born, a witchy friend of the family, believing herself snubbed, laid a curse on Lum: that she will never be happy with her true love. In the present, a new amusement park has been built in Tomobiki, and the opening day finds the whole gang sampling its pleasures. At a magic show, however, Ataru gets turned into a pink hippopotamus - for real! Released in Japan under the title "Urusei Yatsura 3: Remember My Love" by Five Ace/Pony Canyon; available in North America through AnimEigo. **93 min.**

Domestic Home Video:
ANI AT092-203 ▲ $24.95 ▲ VHS ▲ SUB ▲ HiFi Mono
ANI AD093-006 ▲ $39.95 ▲ LD ▲ SUB ▲ HiFi Mono ▲ 01/29/94

Urusei Yatsura: Lum the Forever

(1986) ©Kitty Films

Based on characters and situations by: Rumiko Takahashi *Director:* Kazuo Yamazaki *Screenplay:* Toshiki Inoue, Kazuo Yamazaki *Character Design:* Akemi Takada *Music:* Fumi Itakura *Art Director:* Torao Arai *Animation Director:* Tsukasa Dogite

While Lum & Co. are maing a movie, the chopping down of a mystic cherry tree, "Tarozakura," causes dire consequences. Lum loses her horns - and her powers. Released in Japan under the title "Urusei Yatsura 4: Lum the Forever" by Five Ace/Pony Canyon; available in North America through AnimEigo. **94 min.**

Domestic Home Video:
ANI AT092-210 ▲ $24.95 ▲ VHS ▲ SUB ▲ Mono ▲ 11/23/93
ANI AD093-007 ▲ $39.95 ▲ LD ▲ SUB ▲ Mono ▲ 03/30/94

Urusei Yatsura: The Final Chapter

(1988) ©Kitty Films

Based on characters and situations by: Rumiko Takahashi *Director:* Tetsu Dezaki *Screenplay:* Tomoko Konparu *Character Design:* Setsuko Shibunnoichi *Music:* Toshiyuki Omori *Art Director:* Torao Arai *Animation Director:* Yukari Kobayashi

As the title suggests, animates the final story in creator Rumiko Takahashi's epic manga series. Lupa, yet another one of Lum's fiancés, arrives on the scene, and Lum and Ataru have to repeat their game of tag in order to prevent Earth from being destroyed. Released in Japan under the title "Urusei Yatsura: Kanketsu Hen" (Final Chapter) by Five Ace/Pony Canyon; available in North America through AnimEigo. **85 min.**

Domestic Home Video:
ANI AT092-211 ▲ $24.95 ▲ VHS ▲ SUB ▲ Mono ▲ 01/19/94
ANI AD093-008 ▲ $39.95 ▲ LD ▲ SUB ▲ HiFi Mono ▲ 05/25/94

Urusei Yatsura: Always My Darling

(1991) ©Kitty Films

Based on characters and situations by: Rumiko Takahashi *Director:* Katsuhisa Yamada *Screenplay:* Hideo Takayashiki, Tomoko Konparu *Character Design and Animation Director:* Kumiko Takahashi *Art Director:* Shinichi Uehara *Music:* Mitsuru Kotaki

Ataru is abducted by Lupica, another alien princess (that is, aside from Lum) in search of the ultimate love potion. Needless to say, Lum, assisted by her friends Oyuki and Benten, gives chase. Released in Japan under the title "Urusei Yatsura: Itsudatte (Always) My Darling" by Five Ace/Pony Canyon; available in North America through AnimEigo. **77 min.**

Domestic Home Video:
ANI AT092-212 ▲ $24.95 ▲ VHS ▲ SUB ▲ Stereo ▲ 03/30/94
ANI AD093-009 ▲ $39.95 ▲ LD ▲ SUB ▲ Stereo ▲ 07/27/94

 Violence   Profanity   Nudity   Sexual Situations    Adult Viewers Only - content is extreme and/or explicit

Utsukushiki Sei no Dendôshi: Rei-Rei *See* REI-REI

Venus Senki *See* VENUS WARS

Vampire Hunter D

(1985) ©Epic/Sony, Inc./Movic Inc./CBS/Sony Group Inc.

Based on characters by: Hideyuki Kikuchi *Director:* Toyo'o Ashida *Character Design:* Yoshitaka Amano *Music Direction:* Noriyoshi Matsu'ura

Based on characters by Hideyuki Kikuchi (WICKED CITY, DEMON CITY SHINJUKU, A WIND NAMED AMNESIA). In a strange future where vampires and other night creatures hunt and kill at will, a young farm girl becomes a target of the region's vampire lord, who wants the human girl for his bride. To protect herself, she hires a traveling warrior named "D" who's half-vampire himself. There's romance in the strange relationship between D and his human charge, and the music is eerie and haunting in the best tradition of John Carpenter films. Character designs are by Yoshitaka Amano ("Final Fantasy"). Released in Japan under the title "Kyûketsuki (Vampire) Hunter D" by Sony Music; available in North America through Streamline Pictures/Orion Home Video. **80 min.**

Domestic Home Video:
SPV 90023 ▲ $19.95 ▲ VHS ▲ DUB ▲ Mono ▲ CC ▲ 04/15/92
LUM 9306 ▲ $39.95 ▲ LD-CLV/ ▲ M/A ▲ HiFi Stereo ▲ 10/18/93 ▲ Out of Print

Vampire Princess Miyu

OAV series, 4 episodes

(1988) ©Sôeishinsha/Pony Canyon

Director: Toshihiro Hirano *Screenplay:* Noboru Aikawa *Character Design:* Narumi Kakinouchi *Storyboards:* Narumi Kakinouchi (1,2,4), Toshihiro Hirano (3) *Animation Director:* Narumi Kakinouchi (1,2,4), Masahiro Nishii (3) *Art Director:* Yoji Nakaza (1,2), Yoichi Nango (3,4) *Music:* Kenji Kawai

Based on the manga by creator Narumi Kakinouchi. A pragmatic spiritualist finds new reasons to believe in the supernatural when she meets a delicate female vampire and her unearthly servant, both of whom seem dedicated to protecting humanity from invasions by netherworldly demons called the "Shinma." Screenplay by Noboru Aikawa, with character design, storyboards and animation direction by Kakinouchi; music is by RANMA 1/2's Kenji Kawai. Released in Japan under the title "Kyûketsu-Hime (Vampire Princess) Miyu" by Sôeishinsha; available in North America through AnimEigo.

Vampire Princess Miyu Episode 1: *Unearthly Kyoto*
Himiko travels to the ancient capital of Japan to exorcise a slumbering child, only to be confronted with a wave of vampire attacks. Here she meets the mysterious, childlike Miyu and her silent, enigmatic companion. **25 min.**

Vampire Princess Miyu Episode 2: *A Banquet of Marionettes*
Himiko is hired to investigate several mysterious disappearances at a school. At the site of each, a strange doll has been found. Here she again meets Miyu, now apparently a student. Miyu has designs on the body, and perhaps the soul, of the school hero, Kei. But, so it seems, does another... **25 min.**

Vampire Princess Episode 3: *Fragile Armor*
Himiko agrees to help Miyu defeat a ghastly armored monster. In return, Miyu tells the tale of how she met Larva, her silent companion. Later, Himiko learns of the tragic fate of a husband and wife. Meanwhile, a beautiful young man with a ghastly laugh circles and waits. **25 min.**

Vampire Princess Episode 4: *Frozen Time*
Himiko travels to Kamakura, a childhood home. There, she dreams of herself as a child, running in terror from a mysterious mansion. Now the mansion has a new tenant: Miyu. Miyu at last tells all - of her discovery of her true nature after her first meeting with Larva, of the secret concealed by Miyu's parents, and of the night that Darkness and Shinma gathered together. **25 min.**

Domestic Home Video:
Vampire Princess Miyu Vol. 1: *Episodes 1 and 2*
ANI ET096-007 ▲ $19.95 ▲ VHS ▲ DUB ▲ HiFi Stereo ▲ 08/20/96
ANI AT092-004 ▲ $24.95 ▲ VHS ▲ SUB ▲ HiFi Stereo
ANI AD096-010 ▲ $39.95 ▲ LD ▲ HYBRID ▲ HiFi Stereo ▲ 09/03/96
Vampire Princess Miyu Vol. 2: *Episodes 3 and 4*
ANI ET096-008 ▲ $19.95 ▲ VHS ▲ DUB ▲ HiFi Stereo ▲ 09/25/96
ANI AT092-005 ▲ $24.95 ▲ VHS ▲ SUB ▲ HiFi Stereo
ANI AD096-011 ▲ $39.95 ▲ LD ▲ HYBRID ▲ HiFi Stereo ▲ 10/16/96

The Venus Wars

(1989) ©Kugatsusha/Gakken Co. Ltd./Shochiku Co. Ltd./Bandai Co. Ltd.

Original Story, Screenplay and Directed By: Yoshikazu Yasuhiko *Character Design:* Hiroshi Yokoyama, Yoshikazu Yasuhiko *Art Director:* Shichiro Kobayashi

Yoshikazu "Yaz" Yasuhiko ("Arion") directs his own manga story (published in English by Dark Horse Comics). Following the collision of an ice asteroid, massive terraforming has made the planet Venus capable of supporting life. Four generations later, the Venusian city-state of Ishtar launches a strike against the neighbor Aphrodia in an attempted land-grab. Aphrodia's only hope of facing Ishtar's devastating tank battalion is a squadron of specially built battle bikes, and a hotshot motorcycle racer named Hiro Seno is tapped for front-line duty. An Earth journalist (named Susan Somers, but no relation to the actress, other than both being blonde) is caught in the middle of political intrigue between both sides. Character designs by Hiroshi Yokoyama and Yoshikazu Yasuhiko, with especially clever mecha design (love those one-wheeled bikes!) by GIANT ROBO's Makoto Kobayashi. Released in Japan under the title "Venus Senki" (Venus War Chronicles) by Matsutake; available in North America through U.S. Manga Corps. **104 min.**

Domestic Home Video:
USM 1071 ▲ $19.95 ▲ VHS ▲ DUB ▲ Stereo ▲ 09/01/93
USM 1046 ▲ $29.95 ▲ VHS ▲ SUB ▲ Stereo ▲ 09/01/93
ID 2242CT ▲ $34.95 ▲ LD ▲ SUB ▲ HiFi Stereo ▲ W/S ▲ 06/22/93

Violence Jack

(1988) ©Dynamic Planning/Sôeishinsha/Japan Home Video

Original Author: Go Nagai *Directors:* Ichiro Itano (1), Takuya Wada (2), Osamu Kamijo (3), Seiji Okuda (3) *Screenplay:* Noboru Aikawa (1), Takuya Wada (2), Makio Matsushita (3) *Character Design & Animation Director:* Takuya Wada (1,2), Moriyasu Taniguchi (3) *Art Director:* Mitsuharu Miyame (1), Geki Katsumata (2), Torao Arai (3) *Music Director:* Yasunori Honda

Based on the manga of the same name by creator Go Nagai (DEVILMAN). A gigantic earthquake swallows Tokyo whole, sinking large sections into the earth. The buried populace, while trying to dig itself out, reorganizes itself along new lines—one group of men who seem committed to continuing the norms of civilization as they knew it, another group that decides to secede from society into a morality-free, *Road Warrior*-like gang, and a third group consisting solely of women, who fled from the seemingly civilized first group after a night of violent rape. VIOLENCE JACK is a monstrous giant who is discovered in the dig-out operation (somehow still alive after being entombed in tons of earth), and to whom all of the three factions appeal to join them in order to help them defeat their enemies. The art direction summons up a graphic visualization of a destroyed Tokyo, complete with all the stomach-wrenching horrors such an event would entail, such as survivors living in litter-strewn tunnels among skittering cockroaches, scrabbling food from cans, and murdering each other over scraps in the darkness under tons of rock. A difficult video to watch as much for its implications about human nature as well as the right-out gore, the rape scenes are handled graphically, and the violence is of the head-splattering school. There's no glamour to the violence, and the disturbing themes are nearly nightmare-producing. Director Itano hails from ANGEL COP and BATTLE ROYAL HIGH SCHOOL, while character designer and animation director Takuya Wada lists CRYSTAL TRIANGLE on his resume. Released in Japan under the title "Violence Jack" by Pyramid Video; available in North America through Manga Entertainment.

Violence Jack Part 1: *Evil Town*

Evil Town is a buried city, a lightless, vermin-infested hell, suffocating beneath a million tons of masonry and iron, while the survivors struggle against disease and starvation. But no one in this tomb-city is as innocent as they claim, and as an all-out war erupts between the main factions, Violence Jack must decide where his loyalties lie—before the inhabitants of Evil Town wipe each other out! **56 min.**

Violence Jack Part 2: *Hell's Wind*
The once fertile Kanto plain has become a lawless, ruined wasteland. The isolated townships are being wiped out one by one by a brutal army known as Hell's Wind. Jack is caught in the crossfire when he vows to fight for the villagers. But the biker army has some nasty surprises instore, including an arsenal of military weapons. **52 min.**

Violence Jack Part 3: *Slum King*

A huge comet erupts from the depths of space, hurling into the Earth and blasting away the last remnants of civilization. In the wake of this cataclysm, one man has risen to power in the corpse-strewn wasteland that was once Japan. His name is Slum King, and his rule over Kanto is harsh and absolute. Only Violence Jack has the courage to challenge his rule. Enraged at this defiance, Slum King demands the death of his giant enemy, while the arrival of a huge fanged warrior in the nearby village of Trench Town signals the beginning of incredible carnage. **48 min.**

Domestic Home Video:
Violence Jack Part 1
MGV 635557 ▲ $19.95 ▲ VHS ▲ DUB ▲ HiFi Stereo ▲ 09/24/96
CM 6955 ▲ $24.95 ▲ VHS ▲ DUB ▲ HiFi Stereo ▲ Uncut ▲ 11/26/96
CM 6960 ▲ $24.95 ▲ VHS ▲ SUB ▲ HiFiStereo ▲ Uncut ▲ 11/26/96
Violence Jack Part 2
MGV 635559 ▲ $19.95 ▲ VHS ▲ DUB ▲ HiFi Stereo ▲ 10/22/96
CM 6956 ▲ $24.95 ▲ VHS ▲ DUB ▲ HiFi Stereo ▲ Uncut ▲ 01/28/97
CM 6961 ▲ $24.95 ▲ VHS ▲ SUB ▲ HiFiStereo ▲ Uncut ▲ 01/28/97
Violence Jack Part 3
MGV 635561 ▲ $19.95 ▲ VHS ▲ DUB ▲ HiFi Stereo ▲ 11/26/96
CM 6957 ▲ $24.95 ▲ VHS ▲ DUB ▲ HiFi Stereo ▲ Uncut ▲ 02/25/97
CM 6962 ▲ $24.95 ▲ VHS ▲ SUB ▲ HiFiStereo ▲ Uncut ▲ 02/25/97

Waga Seishun no Arcadia *See* ARCADIA OF MY YOUTH
Wakusei Robo Dangard Ace *See* DANGARD ACE

Wanna-Be's

(1986) ©MOVIC/Sony Music Entertainment (Japan) Inc.

Based on the comic by: Toshimichi Suzuki *Screenplay:* Toshimichi Suzuki *Animation Director and Character Design:* Yoshiharu Shimizu *Art Director:* Masazumi Matsumiya

...*All the Marbles*, anime-style. Things are heating up in the world of Japanese female tag-team wrestling. A pair of up-and-coming youngsters rise through the ranks to challenge the undisputed champions. Little do they realize that they may be part of a secret experimental muscle-enhancing drug campaign. WIll it be enough, or does it take more than power to be a champion? The wrasslin' is purty good (some hilarious strength training), but the story takes a serious left turn toward the end as the girls must suddenly fight mutated monsters. (The "villain" wrestlers fought by the Wanna-Be's, the Foxy Ladies, are thinly disguised copies of real-life Japanese female wrestlers.) Character designs in this one-shot OAV are by Kenichi Sonoda (BUBBLEGUM CRISIS, GALL FORCE), while screenplay and original comic are by BUBBLEGUM CRISIS' Toshimichi Suzuki. Released in Japan as "Wanna Be's" by Sony Music; available in North America through U.S. Manga Corps. **45 min.**

Domestic Home Video:
USM 1031 ▲ $34.95 ▲ VHS ▲ SUB ▲ Stereo ▲ 09/09/92
ID 2243CT ▲ $29.95 ▲ LD ▲ SUB ▲ HiFi Mono ▲ 02/17/93

Warriors of the Wind

MOVIE

(1984) ©Tokuma Shoten

Director: Hayao Miyazaki *Music:* Jo Hisaishi

Based on the manga by Miyazaki, as serialized in ANIMAGE magazine (published in English by Viz Comics). Surely it's one of anime's greatest ironies that one of the finest (if not *the* finest) Japanese animated-films ever made is currently available in English solely thru this spindled, folded, and mutilated version. (In addition to slicing out 30 minutes of the film, Nausicäa gets renamed "Zandra"!) In the aftermath of a climactic battle which nearly destroyed the world, a noble princess named Nausicäa extends a slender ray of hope to her people through both her infinite capacity for empathy (she loves even the insects), as well as for what she's learned about an ecosystem slowly coming back from what was assumed to be certain destruction. To U.S. fans, the recent international distribution between Tokuma and Disney is a cause for rejoicing, if for no other reason than English-speaking fans may finally have a chance to see the film as director Miyazaki (MY NEIGHBOR TOTORO) intended, if and when it's re-released. See if you can't find a friend who has it on laser disc instead. Released in Japan under the title "Kaze no Tani no Nausicä" (Nausicäa of the Valley of Wind) by Tokuma Japan Communications; available in North America through Starmaker. **95 min.**

Domestic Home Video:
STM 96007 ▲ $19.95 ▲ VHS ▲ DUB ▲ HiFi Stereo ▲ Out of Print

Weather Report Girl

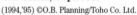

OAV series, 2 episodes
(1994,'95) ©O.B. Planning/Toho Co. Ltd.

Based on the comics by: Tetsu Adachi *Directors:* Kunihiko Yuyama, Takashi Watanabe

Based on the manga by Tetsu Ando, as serialized in publisher Kodansha's weekly SHŪKAN YOUNG MAGAZINE manga anthology. Bottom-ranked TV station ATV is struggling for every ratings point it can get when they score a bona fide hit in the form of a gorgeous new weather girl, who brings good luck (and high ratings!) to every program in which she appears. Kunihiko Yuyama (GOSHOGUN: THE TIME ETRÁNGER, WINDARIA) executive directs. Released in Japan under the title "Otenki Onêsan" (Weather Report Girl) by Toho; available in North America through The Right Stuf.

Weather Report Girl 1: *In For Nasty Weather*
ATV's television ratings are in the toilet. In the midst of the chaos appears replacement weather-girl Keiko Nakadai, whose strategic baring of her voluptuous figure on the air works wonders for the ratings! When regular weathercaster Michiko comes back from vacation, she finds herself suddenly demoted. Michiko vows revenge, but Keiko has no intention of backing down after receiving this once-in-a-lifetime opportunity. **45 min.**

Weather Report Girl 2: *Warm Fronts in Collision*
If you thought Michiko had it in for Keiko, wait until you meet the legendary Kaori Shimamori, best described as Keiko with breeding. She's not going to allow any no-class nobody weathergirl to steal her thunder, and Keiko isn't going to allow an elitist talking head to stand in the way of her success. **45 min.**

Domestic Home Video:
Weather Report Girl 1
CM 6950 ▲ $24.95 ▲ VHS ▲ SUB ▲ HiFi Stereo ▲ 07/02/96
Weather Report Girl 2
CM 6951 ▲ $24.95 ▲ VHS ▲ SUB ▲ HiFi Stereo ▲ 09/03/96

Wicked City

(1987) ©Japan Home Video Co. Ltd.

Director: Yoshiaki Kawajiri *Screenplay:* Kisei Cho *Based on the novel by:* Hideyuki Kikuchi *Music:* Osamu Shoji

Adapted from Hideyuki Kikuchi's novel by screenwriter Kisei Cho, WICKED CITY is (thanks to its director's film noir style) one of the classiest of the "erotic horror" genre which emerged full-blown in the 1980s OAV wave. Two parallel worlds exist side by side—the human world and the "Black World," the residents of which can appear human, or shapeshift into horrible monsters. A treaty has kept the peace between the two worlds for decades, but now it's time for that treaty to be renegotiated. Each world sends an agent to escort a very special delegate to the conference—the human agent is a hard-boiled detective type, the Black World agent is a beautiful woman. The chief hazards they must face to reach the conference are attacks by sexually voracious demons—in one memorable scene, the male human agent has to deal with every man's worst nightmare of a female sex partner with "teeth"—labia dentata, if you prefer. Certain scenes show a John Carpenter influence, most obviously one where the head of a "Black World" denizen sprouts spidery legs á la *The Thing*. Released in Japan as "Yôjû Toshi" (Demon City) by Japan Home Video; available in North America through Streamline Pictures. **90 min.**

Domestic Home Video:
SPV 90923 ▲ $19.95 ▲ VHS ▲ DUB ▲ Mono ▲ CC ▲ 08/12/94

A Wind Named Amnesia

(1993) ©Hideyuki Kikuchi/Asahi Sonorama/Right Stuf Office/Japan Home Video

Original Story: Hideyuki Kikuchi *Director:* Kazuo Yamazaki *Script:* Kazuo Yamazaki, Yoshiaki Kawajiri *Character Design:* Satoru Nakamura *Mecha Design:* Morifumi Naka *Art Director:* Mutsuo Koseki *Music:* Kazz Toyama

Based on a story by DEMON CITY SHINJUKU's Hideyuki Kikuchi, with script by director Yamazaki (LUM THE FOREVER) and WICKED CITY's Yoshiaki Kawajiri. Anime's version of King's *The Stand*, where mankind is destroyed by a toxic cloud that, instead of killing everyone, causes people to forget everything they ever knew. In the resultant barbarous society, the survivors are left to rediscover themselves and relearn how to live while avoiding the last of the killer robots

---

that still roam the land. Released in Japan under the title "Kaze no Na wa Amnesia" (The Name of the Wind is Amnesia) by Japan Home Video; available in North America through U.S. Manga Corps. **80 min.**

Domestic Home Video:
USM 1473 ▲ $19.95 ▲ VHS ▲ DUB ▲ Stereo ▲ 11/05/96
USM 1108 ▲ $29.95 ▲ VHS ▲ SUB ▲ Stereo ▲ 06/01/94
ID 2876CT ▲ $39.95 ▲ LD-CLV/CAV ▲ SUB ▲ HiFi Stereo ▲ 04/18/95

Windaria

(1986) ©Idol Co. Ltd./Harmony Gold USA Inc.

Character Design and Animation: Kanami Productions *Art Director:* Toru Katsumata *Director:* Kunohiko Yuyama

A simple, peaceful world is plunged into a senseless war aggravated by greed and betrayal. Two rival kingdoms vie for fresh water and in the process end up destroying their entire society. As seen through the eyes of an innocent go-between, this tragic story details the depth to which loyalty and everlasting love must be tested, in a futile attempt to save a world from destruction. Spectacular animation filled with powerful images and dramatic storylines, featuring character designs by "The Fantastic Adventure of Leda: Yoko"'s Mutsumi Inomata. Released in Japan under the title "Windaria" by Victor Entertainment; available in North America through Streamline Pictures. **95 min.**

Domestic Home Video:
BFV 956 ▲ $19.95 ▲ VHS ▲ DUB ▲ Stereo ▲ 08/15/93
SPV 90018 ▲ $29.95 ▲ VHS ▲ DUB ▲ Mono ▲ 03/15/92 ▲ Out of Print

The Wings of Honneamise

(1987) ©Bandai Visual

Director & Screenplay: Hiroyuki Yamaga *Character Design:* Yoshiyuki Sadamoto *Animation Directors:* Hideaki Anno, Yuji Moriyama, Fumio Iida, Yoshiyuki Sadamoto *Art Director:* Hiromasa Ogura *Music:* Ryuichi Sakamoto

The premiere work and thus far only original film of Studio Gainax (GUNBUSTER, NADIA, OTAKU NO VIDEO, NEON GENESIS EVANGELION), HONNEAMISE was the most expensive anime movie ever made in its time, and the first anime film ever financed by Japanese toy giant Bandai. Hiroyuki Yamaga, who was only 24 at the time of the film's release, conceived the dramatic premise in HONNEAMISE of replaying, in an exquisitely detailed imaginary world that serves as a kaleidoscopic mirror of our own, the historic moment of man's first journey into space. The main body of the film, however, concerns itself with the road to the rocket for its unlikely astronaut, Shiro, as he discovers and begins to question both the issues of the real world he had sought to avoid, and his own sense of morality. HONNEAMISE's visual approach, of the construction of an epic film model of the world, and its corresponding narrative approach, of searching for meaning and growth within that world, make for a film with many layers and levels of interpretation, including the reflexive one of its creators, Gainax, who, in portraying a society without belief in space travel, also meant to portray a society without belief in the potential of anime (HONNEAMISE was a box-office disaster in its original release). It has been argued, however, that HONNEAMISE made possible the later acceptance of adult efforts in anime by other artists such as Mamoru Oshii, and, ten years later, there are signs of renewed interest in the film in Japan. In the United States, by contrast, HONNEAMISE has always been highly regarded by fans, and receiving praise from such critics as Roger Ebert and *The Washington Post* during its U.S. theatrical run. Released in Japan under the title "Oneamis no Tsubasa: Ôritsu Uchû Gun" (Wings of Honneamise: Royal Space Force) by Bandai Visual; available in North America through Manga Entertainment. Followed in Japan by a "Making Of" video which has yet to be released in English. **125 min.**

Domestic Home Video:
MGV 634797 ▲ $19.95 ▲ VHS ▲ DUB ▲ HiFi Stereo ▲ 06/20/95
MGV 635253 ▲ $24.95 ▲ VHS ▲ SUB ▲ HiFi Stereo ▲ 06/20/95

Yamato: Space Battleship Yamato

(1977)

The 130-minute feature, compiled from the first TV series, which ignited the "Yamato" boom. The *Yamato* has only 365 days to make a 148,000 light year voyage from Earth to the planet Iscandar and return with a neutralizer that will cleanse Earth's irradiated atmosphere. To avoid nuclear fallout, survivors of a surprise attack by the planet Gamilas are living in underground cities - but the radiation is seeping down. In this seminal film we first meet Susumu and Mamoru Kodai, Yuki Mori, Captain Okita, Dr. Sado, Shiro Sanada, IQ-9 and the mysterious Stasha of Iscandar. Released in Japan under the title "Uchû Senkan Yamato: Gekijô Ban (The Movie)" by Nihon Columbia; available in North America through Voyager Entertainment. **135 min.**

Domestic Home Video:
VEI 6003 ▲ $29.95 ▲ VHS ▲ SUB ▲ Mono ▲ 10/15/95

Yamato: Farewell to Space Battleship Yamato: In The Name of Love

(1978)

Details the conflict between the *Yamato* and the Comet Empire, as would later be detailed in the second TV series (unlike the movie, in the TV series, half the cast is left alive, paving the way for further sequels). The crew of the famous space battleship *Yamato* reunites for a last voyage to the stars. An enormous dreadnought, disguised as a comet, is on a rampage of destruction. Although the *Yamato* is outgunned and overwhelmed by this awesome enemy, Commander Kodai's superior military proficiency prevails - but at a terrible cost. Released in Japan under the title "Uchû Senkan Yamato: Ai no Senshitachi (Soldiers of Love) by Nihon Columbia; available in North America through Voyager Entertainment. **120 min.**

Domestic Home Video:
VEI 1003 ▲ $29.95 ▲ VHS ▲ DUB ▲ Mono ▲ 07/15/94
VEI 7003 ▲ $29.95 ▲ VHS ▲ SUB ▲ Mono ▲ 10/15/95

Yamato: Space Battleship Yamato: The New Voyage

(1979) ©Yoshinobu Nishizaki

Director: Yoshinobu Nishizaki

Terror attacks by the Black Star Cluster Empire destroy Gamilas and blast Iscandar out of orbit, hurtling Queen Stasha, her child and Mamoru into the galactic unknown. The refitted *Yamato* is ordered to seek and assist Stasha. Also warping to keep up with the runaway planet are Gamilus leader Dessler and General Medlers, commander of the Dark Empire's fleet. Realizing her allies are still overmatched, Queen Stasha once again intercedes and saves the *Yamato* in a spectacular act of love and sacrifice. Released in Japan as "Uchû Senkan Yamato, Aratanaru Tabidachi: Gekijô Ban" (The New Voyage: The Movie) by Nihon Columbia; available in North America through Voyager Entertainment. **93 min.**

Domestic Home Video:
VEI 2003 ▲ $29.95 ▲ VHS ▲ SUB ▲ Mono ▲ 11/21/94

Yamato: Be Forever Yamato

(1980)

Original theatrical feature inspired by the TV series, featuring a new alien race threatening Earth, and the gallant crew members of the *Yamato* willing to lay down their lives to save their home planet. In 2202, the Dark Empire invades Earth. Kazan, commander of the Black Fleet occupying forces, threatens to destroy human life with a hyperon bomb if the hidden location of space battleship *Yamato* is not revealed. But Kodai and the *Yamato's* old crew escape to *Yamato's* hidden location and set course for the Empire's home base to deactivate the weapon's trigger. They are amazed when Lord Scaldart greets them with the news that they have warped 200 years into the future and are back on Earth, conquered by his ancestors at the beginning of their journey. Refusing to accept defeat, the *Yamato* crew decides to return in time through hyperspace and change history. Released in Japan under the title "Uchû Senkan Yamato Towa ni: Gekijô Ban" (Be Forever: The Movie) by Nihon Columbia; available in North America through Voyager Entertainment. **149 min.**

Domestic Home Video:
VEI 4003 ▲ $29.95 ▲ VHS ▲ SUB ▲ Mono ▲ W/S ▲ 04/28/95

Yamato: Final Yamato
(1983)

Director: Yoshinobu Nishizaki

Nishizaki himself returns to helm what had been, at least until the release of the recent "Yamato 2520" OAV series, the final epic entry in the saga of the "Yamato." Highlights include the return of the presumed-dead Captain Okita (!), as well as the long-anticipated "coming together" of procrastinating lovers Kodai and Yuki (!!). Admiral Okita assumes command of Space Battleship *Yamato* in 2203. With Denguil completely flooded by the water planet Aquarius, General Lugarl plans to warp his fleet to Earth and occupy it. During a climactic battle with the Uruku, Kodai is saved by Lugarl's own son, but the *Yamato* crew seems doomed until Desslar comes to the rescue. Okita orders the crew to abandon *Yamato*, and pilots it to Aquarius. Okita destroys the water planet by fusing energy from Yamato's wave motion gun, forming a hydrogen bomb. The battleship sinks into the same kind of watery grave from which it was originally rescued. Released in Japan under the title "Uchû Senkan Yamato: Kanketsu Hen" (Final Chapter) by Nihon Columbia; available in North America through Voyager Entertainment. **163 min.**

Domestic Home Video:
VEI 5003 ▲ $29.95 ▲ VHS ▲ SUB ▲ Mono ▲ 07/15/95

Yami no Shihôkan Judge *See* JUDGE
Yôjû Kyôshitsu *See* ANGEL OF DARKNESS
Yôjû Toshi *See* WICKED CITY
Yôma *See* CURSE OF THE UNDEAD YOMA
Yôseiki Suikoden *See* SUIKODEN

You're Under Arrest! [OAV]
OAV series, 4 episodes
(1994-95) ©Kosuke Fujishima/Kodansha/Bandai Visual/Marubeni

Based on the manga by creator Kosuke Fujishima (OH MY GODDESS!), as serialized in publisher Kodansha's monthly COMIC AFTERNOON manga anthology (published in English by Dark Horse Comics). Two mismatched female cops (one's demure, and the other's brash) find adventure on the Tokyo Highway Patrol. More *Cagney & Lacey* than *Lethal Weapon*, the series features high-speed chases in customized patrol cars, motorbikes and the like, all in aesthetically pleasing animation. Character designs by Atsuko Nakajima (RANMA 1/2). Released in Japan under the title "Taiho Shichau zo!" (You're Under Arrest) by Bandai Visual; available in North America through AnimEigo.

You're Under Arrest! Episode 1: *And So They Met*
Tokyo Highway Patrol Officers Natsumi and Miyuki get off to a bad start when Miyuki busts Natsumi for reckless moped driving on her way to work. Things get worse when they find out they're going to be partners. Then they run into "The Fox," a mysterious figure who tools around defying every traffic regulation yet invented in an unbelievably customized Morris Minor. **25 min.**

You're Under Arrest! Episode 2: *Tokyo Typhoon Rally*
A fierce typhoon bears down on the city. A mysterious yellow Lancia takes advantage of the deserted streets to indulge in some high-speed harassment. Meanwhile, Natsumi and Miyuki are faced with the challenge of transporting a desperately ill pregnant patient to a specialist hospital during a city-wide blackout. **25 min.**

You're Under Arrest! Episode 3: *Love's Highway Stars*
Matchmaking goes awry when Natsumi and Yoriko become convinced that Ken is about to lose Miyuki to an old high school boyfriend. **25 min.**

You're Under Arrest! Episode 4: *On The Road Again*
Natsumi is offered the chance to go and be a member of the motorcycle patrol, but to do so means breaking up her partnership with Miyuki. **25 min.**

Domestic Home Video:
You're Under Arrest! Episode 1
ANI ET095-004 ▲ $14.95 ▲ VHS ▲ DUB ▲ HiFi Stereo ▲ 09/27/95
ANI AT095-004 ▲ $19.95 ▲ VHS ▲ SUB ▲ HiFi Stereo ▲ 09/27/95
You're Under Arrest! Episode 2
ANI ET095-005 ▲ $14.95 ▲ VHS ▲ DUB ▲ HiFi Stereo ▲ 09/27/95
ANI AT095-005 ▲ $19.95 ▲ VHS ▲ SUB ▲ HiFi Stereo ▲ 09/27/95
You're Under Arrest! Episode 3
ANI ET095-006 ▲ $14.95 ▲ VHS ▲ DUB ▲ HiFi Stereo ▲ 03/27/96
ANI AT095-006 ▲ $19.95 ▲ VHS ▲ SUB ▲ HiFi Stereo ▲ 03/27/96
You're Under Arrest! Episode 4
ANI ET095-007 ▲ $14.95 ▲ VHS ▲ DUB ▲ HiFi Stereo ▲ 04/09/96
ANI AT095-007 ▲ $19.95 ▲ VHS ▲ SUB ▲ HiFi Stereo ▲ 03/27/96
You're Under Arrest! Episodes 1 and 2
ANI AD095-006 ▲ $39.95 ▲ LD ▲ HYBRID ▲ HiFi Stereo ▲ 09/27/95
You're Under Arrest! Episodes 3 and 4
ANI AD095-007 ▲ $39.95 ▲ LD ▲ HYBRID ▲ HiFi Stereo ▲ 04/24/96

Yûgenkaisha *See* PHANTOM QUEST CORP.
Yûjin Brand *See* U-JIN BRAND
Yûwaku *See* COUNTDOWN

Zeguy [OAV]
OAV series, 2 episodes
(1992,'93) ©Shigenori Kageyama

Director, Original Story and Screenplay: Shigenori Kageyama
Music: Soichiro Harada *Production Company:* KSS Inc.

An unsuspecting teenage girl named Miki lands in an abnormal place when she falls through a "cloud road." Without realizing it, she's entered a parallel universe to our own which, with its flying boats, weird creatures, and strange contraptions, is a realm to rival the exotic world of Oz. Soon, Miki is fleeing for her life, as she stumbles onto a plot to control both worlds. Two-volume OAV series. Released in Japan under the title "Kumo-Kai no Meikyû Zeguy" (Labyrinth of the Cloud-World: Zeguy) by KSS/Nihon Soft System; available in North America through U.S. Manga Corps. **79 min.**

Domestic Home Video:
USM 1291 ▲ $29.95 ▲ VHS ▲ SUB ▲ Stereo ▲ 05/02/95

Zenki The Demon Prince [TV]
TV series, 51 episodes
(1995) ©TV Tokyo/Yomiuri Advertising/Kitty Films/Enoki Films

Original Story: Kikuhide Tani, Yoshihiro Kuroiwa
Director: Junichi Nishimura *Production:* Studio Dhin

A magical girl show with a supernatural twist, ZENKI combines SAILOR MOON-style schoolgirls-vs.-monsters magical combat with Japanese mysticism, demons, shrines and magical wards. Ponytailed schoolgirl Chiaki is a descendant of famous exorcist Enno Ozuno, who in centuries past, managed to capture and bind a demon lord named Zenki to his service. When two rogue priests break into the family shrine and steal one of the evil "Seeds of Possession" stored there, Chiaki calls upon Zenki for help against the resulting mutated monster. When first summoned, the demon's power is reduced to that of a child by an extra binding spell, but Chiaki is able to release his full destructive nature through a suitably impressive stock transformation sequence, filling the screen with Chinese characters and burning flames. Zenki's true evil form is only held in check by Chiaki's "Bracelet of Protection," and she frequently has to change him back into a child (shades of RANMA 1/2) to keep his power under control. Along with the mystic monster battles, the main appeal of ZENKI is watching the cute schoolgirl Chiaki beat up on the surly demon lord as well as a seemingly endless parade of creative monsters. Animation direction by Hideyuki Motohashi ("Mars," "Iron Leaguers"). Broadcast in Japan under the title "Kishin Dôji (Demon Prince) Zenki" on TV Tokyo; available in North America through Software Sculptors.

Zenki The Demon Prince Ep. 1: *The Demon Lord Stands Before You!*
Long ago, there was a demon lord whose life had been bound to a mountain-dwelling monk. He was Zenki, the great and powerful. Under the control of the monk, Enno Ozuno, Zenki battled the forces of darkness before they were sealed for all time. Now, 1200 years and 55 generations later, the most powerful of all demon lords is needed once more! **30 min.**

 Violence   Profanity   Nudity   Sexual Situations  Adult Viewers Only - content is extreme and/or explicit

Zenki The Demon Prince Episode 2:
Karma the Malevolent
With the coming of the malevolent god Karma, evil forces are at work in the world, and the one person who can stand against them is a high school girl! Chiaki is the latest descendant of the legendary Enno Ozuno, and heir to the control of the mighty Zenki. **30 min.**

Zenki The Demon Prince Episode 3:
Chiaki in Trouble
When Karma's minions show up at her family's shrine to steal one of the deadly Seeds of Possession (they're like walnuts, only *evil*) sealed inside, Chiaki is thrown into a life or death duel to meet her destiny! She must resurrect the all-powerful demon lord Zenki! Problem: Zenki seems to be a bit less powerful than advertised. In fact, without Chiaki to give him his power, he's downright wimpy. And if Chiaki can figure out how to turn this obnoxious little kid into the mighty demon lord, there's no guarantee Zenki won't be as dangerous as the monsters he's called upon to fight! **30 min.**

Zenki The Demon Prince Episode 4:
The Jar of Desires—Operation: Golden Shikigami-Cho
The race to unleash the Seeds of Possession continues as Gohra arrives in Shikigami-cho for this attempt. This time around, a Seed is in the legendary "Jar of Desires," a valuable piece of pottery which Master Jukai would do almost anything to possess. But when a greedy collector buys the jar before he can, the Seed hiding inside finds a willing host for it to do its mischief. **30 min.**

Zenki The Demon Prince Episode 5:
The Appetite Fiend—How Many Stars Will a Taste of Zenki Rate?
The ever-hungry Zenki is starting to eat Chiaki and her grandma into starvation. Before anyone can stop him, he's off to make a raid on Chiaki's school's cafeteria. But Zenki isn't the only one making a surprise visit to the school, and soon the sinister Guren has the principal under a Seed's control. **30 min.**

Zenki the Demon Prince Episode 6:
Teletemptation—The Little Boy Rings Again
Hiroshi is a quiet boy, whose mother never seems to have enough time for him. While he sits alone and makes prank calls to keep busy, Hiroshi dreams of finding some friends to play with. When Anju discovers his loniness, she grants him the power to make all the friends he's ever wanted. As people all over Shikigami-cho begin to vanish mysteriously, Hiroshi's mother turns to the Enno Shrine for help. **30 min.**

Zenki the Demon Prince Episode 7: *The Obsessed Runner—Dash for the Daybreak Finish Line*
Chiaki's friend Ako finds a new boyfriend—frustrated track star Shunichi. But their budding relationship may be cut short when he falls under Gohra's control. Soon, Shikigami-cho is buzzing with rumors of a fleet-footed devil racing down the streets at night. As Ako becomes suspicious of Shunichi's new "coach," Saki and Jukai sense dark power gathering in the village.**30 min.**

Zenki The Demon Prince Episode 8: *The Mummy Inn—Young Girls Gladly Welcome*
Karma's invasion is not going as well as planned. As the cosmic forces tip in her favor, she sends Guren to attack Chiaki and Zenki. **30 min.**

Zenki The Demon Prince Episode 9:
The Devil in the Basement— Blast Forth Khan! The Spell of Flames
As Chiaki and Zenki vacation at a new resort, it's literally blown to Hell when Zenki smells a Seed of Possession in the hotel. When a mysterious monk appears, the stage is set for a major turning point in the war between Light and Darkness. **30 min.**

Zenki The Demon Prince Episode 10:
March of the Hell Hound— Rage Hard, Fuuta
When Chiaki visits a schoolmate's kennel to see his new puppies, Gohra attacks the Enno shrine himself! **30 min.**

Zenki The Demon Prince Episode 11:
A Voice From the Underworld— Requiem for a Samurai
But when Chiaki's friend is consumed by a Seed of Possession, the battle moves to two fronts. Chiaki and Zenki will have to combat a double possession, because someone else's personality is still linked to the Possession Beast—and this Beast may be more than any of them can handle. **30 min.**

Zenki the Demon Prince Episode 12:
The Witch on the Hill Memories—Lost in the Snow
A pre-holiday snowstorm seems unusually severe, but the storm becomes deadlier when Chiaki and Zenki come face-to-face with a "Snow Woman" out of mythology. **30 min.**

Zenki The Demon Prince Episode 13:
The EMA Struggle Crash—It's a Great Mid-Air Battle
The village's New Year celebration seems to be going well. But when evil Gohra opens his shrine on the outskirts of town, visitors start vanishing mysteriously. It's up to Chiaki and her new ally, Sohma, to save everyone from Gohra's evil threat. **30 min.**

Domestic Home Video:
Zenki The Demon Prince Vol. 1: *Episodes 1-3*
SSVS 1007 ▲ $24.95 ▲ VHS ▲ SUB ▲ Stereo ▲ 09/05/95
Zenki The Demon Prince Vol. 2: *Episodes 4 & 5*
SSVS 1008 ▲ $19.95 ▲ VHS ▲ SUB ▲ Stereo ▲ 11/21/95
Zenki The Demon Prince Vol. 3: *Episodes 6 & 7*
SSVS 1009 ▲ $19.95 ▲ VHS ▲ SUB ▲ Stereo ▲ 01/09/96
Zenki The Demon Prince Vol. 4: *Episodes 8 & 9*
SSVS 1010 ▲ $19.95 ▲ VHS ▲ SUB ▲ Stereo ▲ 03/05/96
Zenki The Demon Prince Vol. 5: *Episodes 10 & 11*
SSVS 1011 ▲ $19.95 ▲ VHS ▲ SUB ▲ Stereo ▲ 05/07/96
Zenki The Demon Prince Vol. 6: *Episodes 12 & 13*
SSVS 1012 ▲ $19.95 ▲ VHS ▲ SUB ▲ Stereo ▲ 07/02/96

Zeorymer, Hades Project [OAV]
OAV series, 4 episodes
(1988-90) ©Morio Chimi/Artmic A.I.C.

Director: Toshihiro Hirano *Script:* Noboru Aikawa *Original Story:* Morio Chimi *Music:* Eiji Kawamura *Character Design:* Michitaka Kikuchi

Script by Noboru Aikawa, based on an original story by Morio Chimi. Grandiose live-action-like robot drama featuring a secret organization with plans for world conquest. Japan's only hope to combat them is the Zeorymer, a godlike robot piloted by a boy who's soon revealed to be the clone of the man who created the Zeorymer in the first place. The boy displays a severe case of split personality while piloting the machine, and other, less savory personality traits as time goes on. The personalities of villains are even more clear-cut, giving an interesting psychological angle to the (pretty darn nifty!) robot battles. Character designs by SILENT MÖBIUS' Michitaka Kikuchi, and great mecha spiky designs. Released in Japan under the title "Meio Keikaku (Hades Project) Zeorymer" by Toshiba EMI; available in North America through U.S. Manga Corps.

Hades Project Zeorymer Vol. 1: *Projects 1 and 2*
PROJECT 1: Teenager Masato Akitsu's world is turned upside down when he discovers that he was only born to pilot the mighty robot warrior Zeorymer. As he struggles to accept the situation, Hau Dragon's Lanstar robot is brought to bear on him. PROJECT 2: As Masato learns more about his true origins, he begins to question who he actually is: a real person or simply a component of Zeorymer. But when he comes face to face with twin warriors Si Aen and Si Tau, the hostile personality triggered by his earlier battle with Lanstar resurfaces stronger than ever. **60 min.**

Hades Project Zeorymer Vol. 2: *Projects 3 and 4*
PROJECT 3: Masato's last battle with Aen and Tau unleashed a frightening new personality. When Miku is kidnapped by Yuratei, Masato is forced to face his greatest challenge all by himself: Rose C'est La Vie of the Moon, one of Hakkeshu's most powerful battle machines. PROJECT 4: As Masato fights to regain his old personality, Yuratei sends the last of the Hakkeshu pilots to destroy him and Zeorymer once and for all. As both sides meet for the final showdown, the world teeters on the knife-edge of nuclear destruction, and the true face of the Hades Project is discovered at last. **60 min.**

Domestic Home Video:
Hades Project Zeorymer Vol. 1
USM 1098 ▲ $29.95 ▲ VHS ▲ SUB ▲ Stereo ▲ 04/06/94
ID 2873CT ▲ $34.95 ▲ LD ▲ SUB ▲ HiFi Mono ▲ 05/10/95
Hades Project Zeorymer Vol. 2
USM 1099 ▲ $29.95 ▲ VHS ▲ SUB ▲ Stereo ▲ 08/03/94
ID 2883CT ▲ $34.95 ▲ LD ▲ SUB ▲ HiFi Stereo ▲ 07/25/95

Zillion [TV]
TV series, 31 episodes
(1987) ©Tatsunoko Production Co. Ltd.

Original Concept and Script: Tsunehisa Ito *Director:* H. Hamasaki *Producer:* Yusaku Saotome *Direction/Design:* Mizuho Nishikubo *Music:* Jun Irie *Animation Production:* Tatsunoko Production Co. Ltd.

In the 24th Century, mankind has entered a new phase of its ongoing development by establishing numerous offworld colonies. One such colony, the planet Maris, now faces annihilation at the hands of a ruthless alien race. The Earthborn colonists' only hope for salvation rests in a mysterious weapon system known as the Zillion Gun...otherwise known in the real-world as the toy series "Lazer Tag." With only three of these alien super guns, an elite team of freedom fighters dubbed the "White Nauts" (called "White Knights" in the English version) wage a life and death battle for their planet. Note that only 5 of the 31 episodes, plus the series' only OAV, 1988's "Burning Night"are available domestically. The 1987 TV series is available in Japan only through a laserdisc box set. Released in Japan as "Akai Kôdan (Red Photon) Zillion" by Vap; available in North America through Streamline Pictures.

Zillion Episode 1: *They Call Me J.J.*
With only three alien "Zillion" super guns, an elite team of freedom fighters, dubbed the White Knights, wage a life and death battle for their planet. Outnumbered and isolated, things couldn't get much worse... **30 min.**

Zillion Episode 2: *Hang Fire*
Three colonists of the planet Maris have been chosen to defend their people against a warrior race known as the Noza. J.J., Champ and Apple, each armed only with their wits

and a Zillion Gun - a powerful firearm energized by a mysterious substance called Zillium - become heroes of a brave new world. It's J.J.'s first mission with the White Knights, and he's learning the ropes the hard way. The Noza ambush a vital energy control center which powers the entire southern hemisphere of Maris. The Knights infiltrate the occupied silos, but are three Zillion Guns enough to take on an entire Nozian army? **30 min.**

Zillion Episode 3: *Split-Second Chance*
The Noza unleash their most lethal weapon - a gigantic plasma energy cannon, which can blow away an entire army with a single blast. But the Noza commander has a larger target in mind - the Marisian capital, Hope City. Can the White Knights find the secret location of the plasma gun and defeat an army of Noza guardian robots within the two hours it takes to recharge the deadly weapon? **30 min.**

Zillion Episode 4: *Target: The White Knights*
It's Sunday on Maris ... a day of relaxation and play for J.J., Champ and Apple - but not for the Noza. Commander Ryxx orders an attack on a vital reactor complex as a ruse to ambush the White Knights. A Noza commando team is sent to destroy the three brave heroes by utilizing a series of ingenious booby traps. Can the Knights survive the onslaught of an elite assassination squad determined to destroy them? **30 min.**

Zillion Episode 5: *Judgement Call*
The Noza invade the Marisian Weapons Research Center in hopes of capturing the Minister of Science - a key figure in the ongoing research concerning the Zillion weapon system. J.J., Champ and Apple attempt a daring rescue, but they are thwarted by Noza at every turn. Can the White Knights liberate the scientists and defeat the enemy invaders before a self-destruct system turns the research center into an inferno? **30 min.**

Zillion Special: *Burning Night*
In the peaceful aftermath of the Noza Wars, the charismatic heroes known as "The White Knights" have shifted their talents from freedom fighting to music making. J.J., Dave, Champ and Apple have re-emerged as the rock & roll group "The White Nuts." But peace on Maris is short-lived, as a new evil threatens the colonial settlers. Apple is kidnapped by the sadistic Odama clan - a family of ruthless killers - based in a heavily fortified mountain retreat. J.J. and company attempt a daring rescue armed only with makeshift Zillion weapons and a limited supply of ammo. This extra-length *Zillion Special* features edge-of-your-seat action, suspense, songs, and surprises. **45 min.**

Domestic Home Video:
Zillion Episode 1
SPV 90003 ▲ $9.95 ▲ VHS ▲ DUB ▲ Stereo ▲ 12/01/90 ▲ Out of Print
Zillion Episode 2
SPV 90004 ▲ $9.95 ▲ VHS ▲ DUB ▲ Stereo ▲ 03/01/91 ▲ Out of Print
Zillion Episode 3
SPV 90005 ▲ $9.95 ▲ VHS ▲ DUB ▲ Stereo ▲ 03/15/91 ▲ Out of Print
Zillion Episode 4
SPV 90006 ▲ $9.95 ▲ VHS ▲ DUB ▲ Stereo ▲ 05/01/91 ▲ Out of Print
Zillion Episode 5
SPV 90007 ▲ $9.95 ▲ VHS ▲ DUB ▲ Stereo ▲ 05/15/91 ▲ Out of Print
Zillion Special
BFV 957 ▲ $19.95 ▲ VHS ▲ DUB ▲ Mono ▲ 08/15/93 ▲ Out of Print
SPV 90013 ▲ $9.95 ▲ VHS ▲ DUB ▲ Mono ▲ 10/01/91 ▲ Out of Print
Zillion: The Beginning: *Episodes 1-3*
Episodes 1-3 (65 min.)
BFV 959 ▲ $19.95 ▲ VHS ▲ DUB ▲ Stereo ▲ 08/15/93 ▲ Out of Print
Zillion Episodes 1-5
ID 2977SE ▲ $49.95 ▲ LD ▲ DUB ▲ HiFi Stereo ▲ 10/22/96

Chapter Four
₳nime Fandom
History and Resources

Fifteen Years Of Japanese Animation Fandom, 1977-1992
By Fred Patten

Organized anime fandom began in North America in 1977, with the formation of the first fan club created expressly to promote Japanese animation to other American fans. This chronology ends in 1992, its fifteenth anniversary year. It is important to remember the events before 1977, to acknowledge how fandom came to start at all; but the "proto-fandom" dates from 1961 through 1976 would have been meaningless without the birth of organized fandom a year later.

Proto-Fandom

1961   **July:** *Panda and the Magic Serpent* (released by Globe Pictures) and *Alakazam the Great* (released by American International Pictures) are the first two Japanese theatrical animated features distributed in America.

August: *Magic Boy* is released by MGM. These three are perceived by the public as "foreign movies" rather than specifically "Japanese movies." Their box-office returns are disappointing.

1963   **September:** *Astro Boy* begins American TV syndication.

1965   **September:** *Eighth Man* begins American TV syndication.

1966   **January:** *Gigantor* begins American TV syndication.

September: *Kimba, The White Lion* and *Prince Planet* begin American TV syndication.

October: *Marine Boy* begins American TV syndication.

1967   **September:** *The Amazing 3* and *Speed Racer* begin American TV syndication.

1968   **January:** Greg Shoemaker begins *The Japanese Fantasy Film Journal*. This fanzine is devoted primarily to live-action cinematic fantasy such as the *Godzilla* movies, but Shoemaker includes articles on Japanese animation when he can get information about it.

late 1960s & early 1970s   Other Japanese theatrical and TV cartoons such as *Princess Knight* (a.k.a. *Choppy and the Princess*), *Puss 'N' Boots*, *Jack and the Witch*, *The Little Norse Prince*, *Gulliver's Travels Beyond the Moon*, and others appear as TV afternoon matinee movies and as 16 mm rental films.

1972   **December:** *Mazinger Z*, the first giant-robot/battle armor TV cartoon, begins in Japan.

December: Graphic Story Bookshop, a mail-order comics-specialty bookshop in Culver City, CA, run by Richard Kyle and Fred Patten, publishes the first illustrated advertisements for imported Japanese manga, in its magazine, *Graphic Story World #8*.

1975   **July:** Earliest-known screening of Japanese TV cartoons for an American fan group; a special program on Japanese sf animation at the Los Angeles Science Fantasy Society, presented by Wendell Washer and Fred Patten.

The Adventures of Little Samurai ***Magic Boy*** (1958) by Taiji Yabushita

Astro Boy artwork ©Mushi Productions
Astro Boy (1963) by Osamu Tezuka.

Kimba The White Lion (1966) by Osamu Tezuka.

Robin Leyden and Osamu Tezuka, 1978.

Battle of The Planets begins syndication

Mattel's *Shogun Warriors*

October: The first commercial VCRs reach the consumer market, enabling the public to make personal video copies of TV programming

1976 **Spring:** Japanese TV cartoons, with English subtitles thanks to Honolulu TV, reach local Japanese-community TV channels in some American major cities. (*Brave Raideen*, the first (?) subtitled giant-robot cartoon to reach the mainland, starts on Channel 47 UHF on March 20.)

Fall: Mark Merlino, a Los Angeles fan, begins taping obscure sf and fantasy movies to show at fannish parties. His videos of Japanese giant-robot cartoons are especially popular.

First Fandom

1977 **February:** The idea of starting a new fan club devoted primarily to Japanese animation is discussed among Los Angeles fans.

April: The LOSCON III convention in Los Angeles includes a test program of anime videos presented by Mark Merlino and Fred Patten. It is a big success.

May: The first monthly meeting of the Cartoon/Fantasy Organization is organized by Robin Leyden, Mark Merlino, Judith Niver, Fred Patten, and Wendell Washer. It draws 16 attendees.

November: The C/FO begins to print a monthly bulletin (one sheet).

1978 **March:** Osamu Tezuka, on a business trip to Los Angeles, is invited to the monthly C/FO meeting. He supplies a special program of his animation never shown in America, and encourages the fans to promote Japanese animation.

May: The English translation of the first volume of Keiji Nakazawa's *Barefoot Gen*, a semi-autobiographical manga novel of a child's personal experience of the 1945 atomic bombing of Hiroshima, is published in Tokyo by Project Gen, for distribution in the U.S. by the New York City-based War Resisters League. This is the first American edition of a translated Japanese manga.

Mid-year: Toei Animation's Hollywood representative, Pico Hozumi, asks the C/FO to help promote Toei's animation in America.

Mid-year: Carl Gafford coins the word "Japanimation," which is picked up by L.A. fandom.

July: The first convention video room is run at Westercon XXXI in Los Angeles by the C/FO, although it mixes anime with TV sf such as *The Prisoner*.

July: The C/FO runs the first anime merchandise dealer's table at the 1978 San Diego Comic-Con. The material is supplied by Toei Animation to test how American fans react to unknown-character cartoon merchandising. The *Space Pirate Captain Harlock* items are especially popular.

September: Toei Animation supplies videos and merchandising for test-marketing at the World Science Fiction Convention in Phoenix. Mark Merlino runs the video room and Fred Patten runs the dealer's table.

September: The first issue of *Animage* (cover-dated July), the first animation-specialty monthly magazine in Japan, reaches America. *Animage* touches off an anime-publication flood, with rival magazines such as *My Anime* and *The Anime* and books such as Tokuma Publishing's "Roman Album" series soon following. Coincidentally, anime toy merchandising evolves from cheap toys to high-quality model kits. These begin arriving in Japanese-community bookshops and toyshops in Los Angeles, San Francisco, New York City and other cities about a month after their release in Japan. Many American fans become hooked by the detailed battle-armor model kits before they learn about the TV anime upon which they are based.

October: *Battle of the Planets* begins American TV syndication; the first Americanized Japanese TV cartoon series since the 1960s, and the first to become known to the public as being Japanese animation.

December: Osamu Tezuka is again the guest speaker at a C/FO meeting.

Expansion and Influences

1979 Early promotion by Wendy Pini for her *ElfQuest* comic book publicizes that one of her artistic inspirations is the animation style of Osamu Tezuka.

February: The C/FO is reorganized to accept annual memberships and publish a directory of members. This enables fans outside Los Angeles to join to get the club's bulletin, and to use the directory to contact other anime fans. William Thomas III in Philadelphia is the first member outside L.A.

February: Marvel Comics begins *Shogun Warriors*, featuring new American superhero adventures starring the Japanese giant robots licensed by Mattel, Inc., for its *Shogun Warriors* toy line. This is the first introduction of giant robots to many American comics fans.

May: Joey Buchanan in Ohio solicits for fans to start a national *Battle of the Planets* Fan Club.

July: *Fanta's Zine*, the first American fanzine devoted to anime, is started by the C/FO.

Summer: Ralph Canino, Jr. in New York, who has penpals in Japan, offers to obtain anime magazines, posters, models, etc. for fellow fans at cost plus postage. This is the first attempt by an American fan to import anime merchandise from Japan on either a social or a business level.

September: *Star Blazers* begins American TV syndication. Its distributor, Westchester Films, is friendly towards fans and is open about the program's Japanese origins.

September: Jim Terry, a TV producer, buys five Toei Animation sf TV cartoon series for a single *Force Five* syndication package. He offers the C/FO advance video copies if the C/FO will help publicize it.

October: *Force Five* episodes are included in a video program shown by Mark Merlino at MileHiCon11 in Denver.

December: The Tatsunoko Fan Club in Japan, selling original cels to its members, agrees to accept American members, with the C/FO serving as its agent.

1980

February: C/FO members in New York City start a chapter there, founded by Joseph Ragus, Sr., and kept going after its second meeting by Jerry Beck.

February: *Fangoria #4* includes "Dawn of the Warrior Robots," the first (?) featured sf media-magazine article on Japanese animation.

May: *Fanfare #3* is the first popular-culture magazine to cover-feature an article on anime, "TV Animation In Japan."

June: Books Nippan, a Los Angeles Japanese-community bookshop (an American subsidiary of Nippan Shuppan Hanbai, a large Japanese book-giftshop chain), becomes the first Japanese-community shop (under manager Mrs. Kim) to import extra quantities of anime merchandise and manga especially for the new Anglo fan market.

July: The C/FO in Los Angeles gets a video-taped greeting from the club's New York City members at one of their meetings. Members in other cities talk about starting local chapters. The club is reorganized to recognize the original group as the Los Angeles chapter, and to create a separate "general C/FO" structure to unite the club.

July: The C/FO gets a 16 mm promotional reel of Toei Animation's sf TV cartoons, and sample complete episodes of some titles, added to the main film program at Westercon XXXIII in Los Angeles.

Summer: Michael Pinto in New York starts the *Star Blazers* Fan Club, the second anime fan club to organize several chapters in different cities. It lasts until late 1985.

July/August: The San Diego Comic-Con is visited by a tour group of around thirty Japanese cartoonists, including Osamu Tezuka, Go Nagai, Monkey Punch, and Yumiko Igarashi. The tour is the idea of Tezuka, who urges the Japanese cartoonists to discover how many fans they have in America. The cartoonists draw sketches for fans and sell their characters' merchandise. Tezuka brings his recently completed *Phoenix 2772* feature for the Comic-Con's movie program. Tokyo Movie Shinsha presents a demonstration of 3-D TV animation. This is also the first (?) convention to include several anime-character costumes in its Masquerade, with a group of six San Diego fans led by Karen Schnaubelt as *Captain Harlock* and *Star Blazers* characters.

August/September: The World Science Fiction convention, in Boston, declines a C/FO-run video room, but appoints three C/FO members to run an official Worldcon video room. Tokyo Movie Shinsha provides a video copy of *Lupin III - The Castle of Cagliostro* for a test-marketing survey.

September: *Force Five* begins American TV syndication.

September: Phil Gilliam in Nashville starts the *Captain Harlock/Galaxy Express 999* Fan Club.

1980 San Diego Comic-Con program.

December: Quinn Kronen in Atlanta starts Animation Adventure, an anime video club.

1981 **January:** The C/FO-Chicago is started by Jim Engel and Doug Rice.

February: The C/FO-Chicago runs an anime video room at the Capricon I convention in Evanston. This is the first (?) American video program to emphasise *Mobile Suit Gundam*.

Spring: Books Nippan's new manager, Yuji Hiramatsu, sets up a special anime/manga department in the store, and begins advertising in anime club bulletins to build up a mail-order trade.

April: "The Gamilion Embassy" is started at the 1981 Balticon in Baltimore, by Colleen Winters, JoLynn Horvath, Robert Fenelon, James Kaposztas, and seven other fans from the Philadelphia/NYC/New Jersey area. Their goal is to travel to fan conventions throughout the Northeast and show anime at open parties in their hotel rooms, to pave the way for official con-run anime rooms as a regular feature at cons. The Embassy is dissolved in 1985, after its goal is considered accomplished.

Mid-year: By this time there are C/FO chapters in Central Texas (Austin), Cleveland, Detroit, Mid-Atlantic (Fairfax, VA) and Orange County, California. From this time, new anime fan clubs appear (and disappear) rapidly, either independent or affiliated with chapter-based clubs such as the *Star Blazers* Fan Club.

October: Susan Horn's *Kimono My House* shop in the San Francisco Bay Area, started in the summer of 1980 to import Japanese kimonos, begins to import anime merchandise as well.

1982 **January:** The Earth Defense Command (EDC) is organized by Derek Wakefield in Texas as another club with "affiliates" in many cities. Originally aggressively devoted to *Star Blazers*, the EDC evolves into a general anime fan club.

July: *Galaxy Express* is released theatrically by New World Pictures (following a two-year postponement of its originally-publicized release in May 1980). This is the first release of a Japanese theatrical animated feature to have an impact on the new anime fandom, with fans requesting theatres in their cities to show it.

July: The 1982 San Diego Comic-Con includes the first appearances by Books Nippan and Pony Toy-Go-Round with major dealers' tables of manga and anime merchandise; a four-day anime video program; and the final appearance at an American fan gathering by Osamu Tezuka. Books Nippan's wares include the first Japanese attempt to enter American comics publishing with *Manga*, a special, glossy 88 page comic book printed in Japan in English. *Manga* is intended to be the first issue of a continuing comic book distributed in America by Books Nippan, but its high price ($8.00) makes it a failure.

September: Carl Macek opens the Carl F. Macek Gallery in Orange, CA, specialising in original animation cels and other movie memorabilia. The shop deals primarily in American animation art, but it is the first American cartoon-art gallery to import and organize a knowledgeable selection of Japanese original animation art.

October: Joshua Quagmire's *Army Surplus Komikz Featuring Cutey Bunny #1* is an independent comic book with "tributes" to many anime characters (seen in background scenes). Quagmire acknowledges editorially that his funny-animal superheroine's name is inspired by Go Nagai's *Cutey Honey*. Quagmire sends copies to several Japanese cartoonists, and prints an encouraging letter from Osamu Tezuka in the fourth issue.

December: James Kaposztas in New Jersey creates the first fan-made comedy anime video, producing an "Anime Music Video" out of violent scenes from *Star Blazers* set to the Beatles' "All You Need Is Love."

Family Home Entertainment begins to release "kiddie cartoon" videos of anime, including *Force Five* episodes and an unsold *Space Pirate Captain Harlock* TV pilot.

1983 **January:** *Trelaina*, the first anime-fandom Amateur Press Association (a fanzine exchange club) is started by Brian Cirulnick in New York for the discussion through fanzines of *Star Blazers* and general anime topics. (The APA has changed officers and renamed itself *Sasha*, and is still active today.)

February: *I Saw It*, Keiji Nakazawa's personal manga account of the 1945 atomic bombing of Hiroshima, published in American comic-book format, is released to the comics-shop market by Leonard Rifas' San Francisco-based Educomics.

February: Books Nippan sets up the Books Nippan Fan Club to sell anime merchandise by mail-order throughout America. It offers its own T-shirts and a discount to members.

February: *Space Fanzine Yamato* is published by Steve Harrison, Ardith Carlton and Jerry Fellows in Michigan as "the ultimate information source" on *Space Battleship Yamato/Star Blazers*. This is the first American fan effort to produce a "Roman Album"-style complete information guide to a particular anime title.

March: Michael Pinto, Brian Cirulnick and Robert Fenelon set up a "*Star Blazers* Room" (video room) at the 1983 Lunacon in the New York City area. This starts an annual anime video room tradition that is still being run by Fenelon at the Lunacon. By this time, anime video programs at sf and comics-fan conventions are becoming a standard feature, often started by local anime fans with written permission from Claude Hill at Westchester Films to show *Star Blazers* episodes.

March: DC's highly publicized *Ronin* comic book by Frank Miller is not anime-related, but it helps to bring samurai and other Japanese cultural influences to the attention of mainstream American comics fandom.

May: The first (?) American newspaper article about how "Japanese animation isn't for kids" may be "Television Isn't Ready For This" in the 14 May issue of *The Detroit News*, in a writeup of the local anime fan club.

Summer: *Cliff Hanger*, a video game by Capcom using animation from TMS's first two *Lupin III* theatrical features, appears in video arcades throughout America.

July: Mark Hernandez in Dallas produces *Argo Notes #1*, devoted to fannish stories set in the *Star Blazers/Yamato* universe. This is the first (?) anime fan-fiction fanzine.

July: Kodansha publishes *Manga! Manga! The World of Japanese Comics*, by Frederik L. Schodt, the first major scholarly study of Japanese manga (in print and animation) to reach the American public.

August: YamatoCon I in Dallas, organized by Mark Hernandez and Don Magness, is the first independent anime mini-convention. (Earlier "anime cons", such as a "*Star Blazers* Mini-Con" run by Michael Pinto, Brian Cirulnick and Robert Fenelon at the August 1982 New York Creation Convention, were essentially elaborate anime rooms within larger sf or comic conventions.) The one-day YamatoCon has an all-*Star Blazers/ Yamato* video program, an anime dealers' room, and an attendance of 100+.

August: Phil Foglio and Nick Pollotta produce the first fan-made comedy over-dubbing of an anime video, using a *Star Blazers* episode to create the spoof *You Say Yamato*.

September: The 1983 World Science Fiction Convention, in Baltimore, features as one of its main events a 35mm screening of *Arrivederci Yamato*, arranged through Westchester Films by Robert Fenelon, Michael Pinto and Brian Cirulnick. Ardith Carlton and Robert Fenelon provide a running commentary in English for the Japanese-language film. The Mid-Atlantic C/FO chapter runs a convention-long anime video room. Twenty-two costumers wear anime costumes at a photo session on the convention center's roof.

October: Anime influences in regular comic books become apparent. A brash example is in Marvel Comics' *Star Wars #79* by Jo Duffy and Tom Palmer, where Lando Calrissian (in disguise) is drawn as a pastiche of Space Pirate Captain Harlock.

The "False Dawn" of Transforming Robots

1984 **February:** The first American edition of a Japanese-style "anime manga" appears when Books Nippan releases Vol. 1 of its *Star Blazers* anime comic album, produced in English in Japan in association with the West Cape Corporation, creator of the *Yamato* series.

February: *Highly Animated #1*, published by Collen Winters and JoLynn Horvath in Philadelphia, is devoted to anime fan-fiction in general, featuring all popular anime characters or set in any anime universes.

March: First Comics sends out press releases to announce *Dynamo Joe*, a new comic book series by Doug Rice and John Ostrander to debut as a back-up feature in *Mars #10* in July. The full page press release emphasises that "*Dynamo Joe* incorporates into its design and vision a deep admiration of the world of Japanese animation." This interstellar giant-robot series is popular enough to win its own title for a couple of years.

Spring: Japanese manga, anime books and magazines, and model kits begin to appear in American comic shops, through imports by Books Nippan through comics distributors. (Advertised in Bud Plant Inc.'s and Pacific Comics' Spring 1984 catalogs.)

Space Fanzine Yamato

Voltron begins syndication.

May: *Mekton: The Game of Japanese Robot Combat,* written by Mike Pondsmith and published by R. Talsorian Games, is the first anime-influenced fantasy role-playing game, inspired by *Mobile Suit Gundam.* An expanded, more generic and tongue-in-cheek version ("You can have green hair, just like your favorite anime hero!"), issued in March 1985 with input by Mike Jones and the Santa Clara, CA anime fans, is more popular.

September: The 1984 World Science Fiction Convention, in Los Angeles, emphasizes anime with a convention-long anime video program, an invitational guest speech by *Gundam* creator Yoshiyuki Tomino (who announces here first that there will be a *Gundam* sequel), the American premiere of Kodansha's *Lensman* feature (in 35mm with English subtitles) and the premiere of Harmony Gold's pre-*Robotech Macross* video, introduced by director Carl Macek.

September: Harmony Gold's *Macross* video feature is the first American-produced animated title to emphasize its Japanese origins and cultural influences as assets, rather than ignore or try to hide them.

September: World Events Productions' *Voltron, Defender of the Universe!* begins American syndication. This is the first Americanized anime to combine two (or more) separate programs into a single new story, casting *Go Lion* as *Lion Force Voltron* and *Dairugger-XV* as *Vehicle Team Voltron.* The *Lion Force* episodes are so popular that *Voltron* becomes the first Americanized anime to have brand-new episodes commissioned by the American producer from the original Japanese animation studio. *Voltron* also touches off (or at least symbolizes) the 1984 Christmas season mania for transforming-robot toys.

Fall: *Battledroids,* by FASA Corp., is the second, more battle-mecha-oriented, anime-inspired FRP game. It is renamed *Battletech* in March 1985 after George Lucas' lawyers point out that Lucas has trademarked the word "droid."

December: COMICO publishes an authorized *Macross* comic book ("issue #1"), the last *Macross* merchandising before it evolves into *Robotech.* The Japanese origins of *Macross* are again emphasized to American fans.

1985 High-quality but unauthorized fan-produced anime merchandise starts to appear in large quantities. T-shirts and enamelled pins are most popular, usually featuring Astro Boy, Kimba, Lum-chan, The Dirty Pair, or the *Macross* stars.

March: Harmony Gold's *Robotech,* directed by Carl Macek, begins American syndication. This is arguably the single anime title to have the greatest influence in bringing the existence of Japanese animation to the awareness of the public.

March: *Dokonjo,* another Amateur Press Association (APA), is started by Ardith Carlton for the discussion through fanzines of general anime and manga topics.

June: A translation booklet of the text in Rumiko Takahashi's *Urusei Yatsura, Vol. 1,* produced by Toren V. Smith, is the first of the anime-fan "translation guides" to the popular manga or anime titles.

July: Comico begins three separate six-weekly *Robotech* comics: *Robotech: The Macross Saga*; *Robotech Masters*; and *Robotech: The New Generation.* Unlike most licensed comic books, which are designed to be discontinued when the popularity of the original movie or video title wears out, the *Robotech* contract is designed to enable the comic book to keep going for as long as the comic book itself is successful. The *Robotech* comic books eventually move from Comico to Eternity Comics, then to Academy Comics, where they are still being published and are still helping to "keep *Robotech* alive" while most other TV cartoons of the mid 80's are forgotten.

August: The anime theatrical feature version of Nakazawa's *Barefoot Gen* has its American premiere in Los Angeles' Little Tokyo community, as part of a 40th Anniversary of Hiroshima Commemoration sponsored by Asian Americans for Nuclear Disarmament & *East Wind* magazine.

August: *Mangazine,* edited by Ben Dunn at his Antarctic Press in San Antonio, is an independent comic book devoted to fan-produced comics in the Japanese style.

September: David K. Riddick and Mario & Glen Ho produce the first translation booklet of a movie's script, *Macross: Do You Remember Love?*

September: The Ladera Travel Agency in Los Angeles begins a one-year promotion in anime fandom for the first fannish group tour to Japan, to visit Tokyo's animation studios and the anime & manga specialty shops. The "Japanimation '86" tour is the project of Ladera Travel agent Robin Schindler, an anime fan.

November: A.N.I.M.E. (Animation of Inter-Mediary Exchange) is started by Ann Schubert in the San Francisco Bay Area as an informal monthly gathering at her home. Within two years it grows to a monthly barbeque & video-watching party of sometimes 200 fans from all over Northern California. Many local anime clubs, fanzines, and other projects emerge from this group.

December: Hayao Miyazaki's *Warriors of the Wind* gets a direct-to-video release (not counting an extremely limited theatrical screening in New York City in June) by New World Video. This is arguably the first American serious anime general release video (as opposed to Harmony Gold's *Macross* specialty-release video, or various "kiddie cartoon" videos which happen to be anime).

1986

April: Starblaze Graphics/The Donning Company publishes *Robotech Art 1*, by Kay Reynolds and Ardith Carlton, a high-quality anime art book which again helps emphasize that *Robotech* is something more than "just a TV cartoon." The book describes the Japanese origins of *Robotech*, and presents a brief history of Japanese anime in America.

April: *Anime-Zine #1*, the first American attempt at an *Animage*-style professional magazine devoted to anime, is produced by Robert Fenelon (publisher/editor), Beverly Headley (co-producer), and Luke Menichelli (graphic designer).

May: BayCon '86 in San Jose, CA, presents an 80-hour, convention-long exclusive anime program in one of the hotel's major halls with a movie screen-sized projection-TV image, featuring commercial anime videos and laserdiscs for top visual quality, and with a *Japanese Animation Program Guide* of almost 100 illustrated pages of plot synopses of all titles. This "anime mini-con" is organized by Toren V. Smith.

July: The first (?) TV talk-show presentation on anime appears on Los Angeles' Group W Cable's *This is the Story*. Guests Fred Patten and Jeff Roady present a half hour show-&-tell about anime with video clips, posters, Japanese anime magazines, etc.

August: *Golgo 13 Graphic Novel Series No. 1: Into the Wolves' Lair*, by Takao Saito, is the first English translation of a major Japanese comics title intended for the American market. It is produced by Saito's own organization in Japan, for American distribution by Books Nippan.

August: Ladera Travel's "Japanimation '86" tour signs up about 30 American fans for a two-week trip to Tokyo and Osaka, with visits to many animation studios and ending at the 1986 annual Japanese National Science Fiction Convention. The tour is the first of a biannual series of fannish shopping trips to Japan's manga and anime shops and conventions.

Anime and manga influences grow more common in American independent comics, often mixed with Hong Kong martial-arts influences: e.g., Reggie Byers' *Shuriken* and Doug Bramer & Ryan Brown's *Rion 2990*.

Mid-Year: Anime fanzines become common, with such examples as *Dirty Little Girls* (devoted to the *Dirty Pair*) published by Guy Brownlee in Texas.

Mid-year: Anime APAs become common, with the start of *APA-Hashin* by Randall Stukey in Texas (May) for general discussion of anime and manga; *Lemon APA* by Scott Frazier in Colorado (May) devoted to adult anime; *Bird Scramble!* by Patricia Munson-Siter in South Dakota (August) devoted to *Gatchaman/Battle of the Planets*; *Anime Janai* by Marg Baskin in Ontario and Heather Bruton in Nova Scotia (November) for general discussions; *U.S.A. Yatsura* by Aaron Reed in Massachusetts (November) devoted to humorous anime such as *Urusei Yatsura* and *Project A-Ko*; and *Animanga* by Paul Sudlow in Tennessee (January 1987) as a fanzine workshop for anime/manga style amateur comic-art and fiction.

October: An "Official *Robotech* Convention" in Anaheim, CA, put on by the Creation Con organizers, draws approximately 4,000 fans.

November: Brian Cirulnick's *Desslock's Revenge* premieres at Philcon '86 in Philadelphia. This production, which began in 1983, is the earliest known American fan-produced anime featuring original animation.

December: Ben Dunn's *Ninja High School #1* introduces the "high school fantasy humor" influence of Rumiko Takahashi to American comics.

1987

January: U.S. Renditions is created by Nippon Shuppan Hanbai, Books Nippan's parent company, as a separate subsidiary to produce new American editions of anime merchandise (as distinct from imports from Japan). David Riddick and Robert Napton are transferred from the Books Nippan Fan Club to head the new company.

January: Anime Hasshin (originally Hasshin R.I.) is started by Lorraine Savage in Rhode Island as a correspondence-based fan club. Its high-quality fanzine, *The Rose*, attracts hundreds of members from seven countries across four continents by 1992.

February: Mike Pondsmith's *Teenagers From Outer Space* spreads the Takahashi fantasy-humor influence to FRP gaming.

March: Del Rey Books releases the first four *Robotech* paperback sf novels by Jack McKinney. The final volume, #18, is published in January 1990.

April: Panda.com, an Internet mailing list for E-mail distribution of computer discussions of *Urusei Yatsura* and related anime, is started by Mark Crispin of the A.N.I.M.E. group.

May: The Electric Holt computer bulletin board system (BBS) is started by John DeWeese, Richard Chandler, Seth Grenald and Mitch Marmel in Philadelphia. Although it is devoted to sf in general (especially *ElfQuest*), it builds up an extensive anime users' group. The BBS features anime graphics, translations of complete TV episode and movie scripts, E-mail exchanges, and open-participation storyboards (such as *Galaxy Local 999*, a spoof serial).

May: First appearance of actual American editions of Japanese manga. First Comics' edition of *Lone Wolf And Cub #1*, by Kazuo Koike and Goseki Kojima, and the joint Eclipse International/Viz Communications' editions of *Area 88 #1*, by Kaoru Shintani, *Kamui #1*, by Sanpei Shirato, and *Mai, The Psychic Girl #1*, by Kazuya Kudo and Ryoichi Ikegami, are published almost simultaneously.

July: NOW Comics publishes *Speed Racer #1*, following it a month later with *The Original Astro Boy Comics #1*, creating new comics for a nostalgia market for the TV anime of the 1960s. (Purists complain that the new comics show a lack of familiarity with the original TV story concepts.)

July: *Animag #1*, "The Magazine of Japanese Animation", is produced by Matthew Anacleto, Michael Ebert, Dana Fong, and a support team from the A.N.I.M.E. group. It becomes the closest American version yet of a professional quality *Animage*-style magazine.

November: U.S. Renditions releases the *Robotech BGM Collection, Vol. 1*, an LP record of *Robotech* background music; the first American-produced anime music record. It is later reissued as a CD.

November: rec.arts.anime is started by Ann Schubert on Internet as a computer users' anime general news group.

November: Loscon XIV in Los Angeles (Pasadena) is the first American sf convention to feature a "Daicon-style" opening ceremonies animated film, *Clearance Papers*, written by Fred Patten and animated by Michael Aguilar with stop-motion models of con guest-of-honor C.J. Cherryh's characters.

1988

January: Roy and Cathy Bruce of Richmond, VA start the Japanese Animation Network.

January: The Cal-Animage club is started at the U.C. Berkeley campus by Mike Tatsugawa. It grows into a confederation of college anime clubs linked by a computer net, mostly in California but one as far as Perth, Western Australia. Cal-Animage is organized in the manner of college fraternities, with the Alpha chapter at U.C. Berkeley, the Beta chapter at U.C. San Diego, Gamma at U.C. Santa Barbara, Theta at Stanford, etc.

Spring: *Protoculture Addicts #1*, "The Official *Robotech* Fanzine," is published by Claude Pelletier, Alain Dubreuil, Michel Gareau, and a staff of Montreal fans operating as IANVS Publications.

May: (Marvel) Epic Comics begins the American edition of Katsuhiro Otomo's *Akira*.

June *Animag* starts the Animag BBS (A.K.A. Valley of the Wind BBS), the first (?) exclusively-anime computer bulletin board system, with Takayuki Karahashi and Dana Fong as co-sysops.

Summer: GAGA Communications Inc., a Japanese-based film distributor aimed at the American movie and TV market, makes a strong promotion to sell a package of anime titles including *Crystal Triangle*, *Project A-Ko*, *Bubblegum Crisis*, *The Humanoid*, *M.D. Geist*, *Madox-01*, *Yotoden*, and many others. The promotion includes providing anime clubs with publicity materials including a video tape of trailers. GAGA presents a full-day screening, "The World Of Japanese Animation," at the July meeting of the Los Angeles Comic Book and Science Fiction Convention. GAGA is unsuccessful in selling any of its package to the American film/TV/video companies, but the attempt is highly inspirational to fans considering starting their own professional video companies.

September: Eclipse's American edition of Masamune Shirow's *Appleseed #1* is the first published project of Studio Proteus, a company started by Toren V. Smith to find the best Japanese manga and agent/translate them for American publishers.

October: Streamline Pictures is created by Carl Macek and Jerry Beck in Hollywood to import, translate, and distribute anime in America, theatrically and on video.

November: The co-publishing agreement between Eclipse International and Viz Communications ends, and Viz begins to publish its own American editions of Japanese comics. Viz is an American subsidiary of Shogakukan, one of Japan's largest manga publishers. This indicates that a major Japanese publisher feels that American interest in manga and anime is large enough to create a viable market for it.

December: Eclipse publishes *Dirty Pair #1*, by Adam Warren and Toren Smith, Studio Proteus' first original creation featuring licensed Japanese sf/anime characters.

Fandom Goes Public

1989   **February:** *Kimono My House* becomes the first authorized licensee of original American anime merchandise, starting with a Lum T-shirt licensed from Viz.

March: Streamline Pictures begins its first anime theatrical distribution, with *Laputa: The Castle in the Sky* (in Philadelphia).

May: General Products USA is started in San Francisco (Alameda) by General Products, the Japanese garage-kit company run by the fan-creators better known for the Gainax animation studio. They hire Lea Hernandez at BayCon '89 as Vice President to run the company, starting with a major publicity campaign at the 1989 San Diego Comic-Con. GP-USA's goal is to make all Japanese manga and anime merchandise available to American fans by collecting orders from the fans, buying the merchandise in Japan, and shipping it to GP-USA for re-shipment to the purchasers; in addition to importing the most popular anime merchandise for regular retail sale. The project soon fails. Two basic reasons are that American fans order (and pre-pay for) merchandise from older anime titles which are passé and no longer obtainable; and that the Japanese parent company has unreasonable expectations that the American fans will buy whatever cheap anime items they ship to America. Hernandez resigns in May 1990, turning GP-USA over to Shon Howell, who tries until December 1991 to continue the company (including taking two trips to Tokyo to try to get what the American fans want) before giving up.

Akira is released in theatres

July: The Cartoon/Fantasy Organization, torn by internal feuding during its last two years, is declared by its last leader to be dissolved. The C/FO-Los Angeles chapter (the original club) drops its "chapter" designation and continues to meet under the C/FO name as a local club.

September: The Japanese Animation Network becomes the first anime fan group to be granted official non-profit organization status by the Internal Revenue Service.

September: AnimEigo, Inc. is formed by Roe R. Adams III and Robert Woodhead in Wilmington, NC to license anime for authorized subtitled video sale in America.

December: Streamline Pictures begins the American theatrical distribution of the *Akira* anime feature.

1990   **February:** The monthly Los Angeles Comic Book and Science Fiction Convention presents the "World Premiere" of both Streamline Pictures' first videotape release, the dubbed *Akira Production Report* documentary; and U.S. Renditions' first videotape releases, the subtitled *Dangaio #1* and *Gunbuster #1*.

February: Eternity Comics' *Lensman #1*, written by Paul O'Connor and drawn by Tim Eldred and Paul Young, is a licensed comic book based upon anime which has not been released in America yet, produced by fans familiar with the Japanese versions (theatrical and TV series) through the fannish videotape trading circuit.

February: The Right Stuf, Inc., founded by Todd Fersen in Des Moines, IA, in July 1987, releases the first four authorized videos of original *Astro Boy* episodes.

April: AnimEigo releases its first subtitled videotape, *Madox-01*.

May: Eternity Comics' *Broid #1*, by Tim Eldred, is in Eternity's own publicity "conceived along the same lines as *Mobile Suit Gundam*."

July: Project A-Kon, in Dallas, is organized by Mary Wakefield and the EDC Animation Society as the first national-scale convention devoted primarily to Japanese anime, with some American animation. It is successful enough that it becomes an annual convention.

Summer: *Animenominous!* is started by Jeff Thompson, Luke Menichelli and a staff of New Jersey/Philadelphia/New York City fans as another *Animage*-style magazine devoted to profiles on fan-favorite anime titles.

August: Del Rey Books publishes the first of a three-volume edition of Yoshiyuki Tomino's *Gundam Mobile Suit* sf novel, translated by Frederik L. Schodt. In an introduction in each volume, "A Word From The Translator," Schodt informs America's sf readers of the novel's origins in Japanese animated sf.

December: With issue #10, *Protoculture Addicts* drops its *Robotech* specialization and becomes a general magazine devoted to anime and the anime fan culture in North America.

December: Streamline Pictures releases the dubbed *Akira* movie on video, as a "Video Comics" title for the comic shop specialty video market.

1991

March: The first (?) East Coast TV talk show presentation on anime appears on Manhattan Cable's *The Chronic Rift* in New York. Guests Robert Fenelon, Jo Duffy, and Felix Rodregez devote a full episode to presenting anime to the public.

July: Central Park Media, a video distribution company started by John O'Donnell in April 1990, creates its U.S. Manga Corps department (with Masumi Homma) to produce and distribute subtitled anime videos.

August: *V-MAX*, "The Anime And Manga Newsletter" is started by Matthew Anacleto and Chris Keller as a professional-quality "upgrade" of the A.N.I.M.E. group's newsletter.

August-September: AnimeCon '91 in San Jose, CA, is the first major North American convention devoted exclusively to anime and manga. AnimeCon is the result of a two year project by Toshio Okada of Gainax in Japan and Toren Smith of Studio Proteus in America, working with a committee of fans chaired by John McLaughlin, founder of the annual BayCon sf convention in San Jose. Gainax arranges for the attendance of many popular anime and manga creators as AnimeCon's guests, including Hideaki Anno, Johji Manabe, Haruhiko Mikimoto, Yoshiyuki Sadamoto and Kenichi Sonoda. There is an extensive anime program including rarities from the Tokyo animation studios. A Japanese convention style opening-ceremonies cartoon is produced by fan animators led by sf artist Rick Sternbach. An impromptu auction raises over $4,500 for the medical expenses of Ann Schubert, who suffered a massive stroke just before the con. The attendance from throughout North America is over 1,700.

October: U.S. Manga Corps' first video release is the subtitled *Dominion #1*.

1992

January: IANVS Publications begins new anime-related magazines in addition to *Protoculture Addicts*. *Mecha Press* is a bi-monthly devoted to the anime mecha hardware, covering both the fictional schematics and the model kits, plus gaming. *Cybersuit Arkadyne*, by Tim Eldred and Jonathan Jarrad, is a manga-style space adventure comic book with battle mecha.

January: Pop singer Matthew Sweet releases his music video *Girlfriend*, intercutting images of Sweet performing with clips from the anime feature *Space Adventure Cobra*. A later Sweet music video, *I've Been Waiting*, is filled with images of Lum from many of the *Urusei Yatsura* movies, TV episodes and OAVs.

February: Streamline Pictures' subtitled *Twilight of the Cockroaches* becomes the first American anime laser disc, from Lumivision.

March: Antarctic Press' *Mangazine* comic book is converted with its Vol. 2 #14 issue into an "anime & comics" magazine under editor Doug Dlin. Anime and manga news and articles on popular anime titles take precedence over the fan-drawn manga-style comic stories. An "anime classified" department allows fans to advertise their clubs and fanzines, and post requests for penpals.

March: The quantity of Japanese imports, American translations of manga as comics and anime as videos, and original American comics in the manga style has grown so large that Capital City Distribution, one of the major American specialty distributors to the comic shops, proclaims that "March is Manga Month." The one month emphasis on Japanese-influenced merchandise is so successful that Capital City repeats it next March.

April: The Atlantic Anime Alliance (AaA) is founded by Chet Jasinski and Stephen Pearl at Rutgers University as a public service anime "information brokerage". Its goals are to provide a series of free anime information sheets, to link East Coast anime fans and clubs through a loose network, to provide information at East Coast fan conventions on how to contact anime fandom, and to turn fannish public opinion against anime bootlegging. The AaA operates with a small volunteer membership/staff, and has a mailing list of over 400 for its free information sheets.

July: Anime Expo '92, at the same Red Lion Hotel in San Jose, CA, is treated by fans as the "second annual American anime convention," although it is technically a new convention, organized by Mike Tatsugawa under the auspices of a non-profit corporation, the Society for the Promotion of Japanese Animation. Anime Expo '92 also features many notable Japanese anime and manga creators as guests. A 15-minute opening ceremonies cartoon, *Bayscape 2042*, is animated by a fan team organized by David Ho of Running Ink Animation Productions. (Video copies of the cartoon and its original cels are sold at the con.) Other events include the world premieres of two Japanese OAVs, *Giant Robo #1* and *Kabuto*, and three American videos, *Guyver #1*, *Macross II #1*, and *Orguss #1*, dubbed by a new company, L.A. Hero, for release by U.S. Renditions; the premiere of the first American anime CD-ROM, *The World of U.S. Manga Corps*, produced by Brian Cirulnick and Michael Pinto, with 1,000 full-color images and 100 quicktime movies; and presentation of the first American fan awards for anime and manga, the Anime Expo Industry Awards.

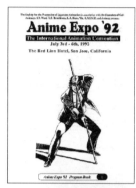

Summer: The anime specialty videos, which have been sold primarily through the comic book shops and by mail order, begin to appear in the major video retail chains and in neighborhood video rental stores. Some shops set up a separate "Japanese Animation" or "Japanimation" section. The August issue of Tower Records/Video's *Pulse!* magazine contains an article, "Moving Manga Mania: A Beginners Guide to Japanese Animation," which includes a photo of singer Matthew Sweet showing off his Lum tattoo.

August: *Manga Newswatch Quarterly* is started by Mark Paniccia in South Bend, IN as a comics-format manga and anime newsmagazine. There are now enough press releases from Viz, Dark Horse, Antarctic Press, Eternity Comics, Streamline Pictures, AnimEigo, etc., for their forthcoming anime and manga comics and videos to fill a magazine.

September: A.D. Vision, managed by Matt Greenfield in Houston, enters the subtitled-anime video field. Its first release in November is *Devil Hunter Yohko*.

October: Antarctic Press begins *Dojinshi: The World of Japanese Fanzines*, a comic book devoted to bringing the best cartoons from Japanese fanzines to America. Each issue presents Japanese fandom's impressions of popular anime titles.

November: *Animerica #0* is a preview issue of an "Anime & Manga Monthly" to begin in March 1993, edited by Seiji Horibuchi, Satoru Fujii and Trish Ledoux, published by Viz Comics. Thanks to its connections with Shogakukan, a major Japanese publisher, it is the hope of the magazine's editors that *Animerica* will be the first of several professional-quality, U.S.-produced anime magazines.

Anime Fan Clubs

Here is a listing of some of the anime fan clubs in North America. This list is by no means complete. It represents most of the major, established clubs, and the clubs that we have been able to verify. Much more extensive club listings may be found at the various Internet sites listed in this section.

AIYA! Animation Club
Meets: Tuesdays from 6-8:30 pm
Where: Western Washington University, VA462
Contact: Aiya! M-3
WWU: Viking Union 202
Bellingham, WA 98225
Robert Ketcherside
13611 6th SW
Seattle, WA 98166
E-mail: n9282081@henson.cc.wwu.edu

Akron Animation Association
Meets: 2nd & 4th Saturday of each month
Where: University of Akron (school year)
Akron-Summit County Pub. Lib. (summer)
Contact: Jay Harvey
903 Orrin St.
Akron, OH 44320
(216) 376-5401 (After 8pm EST)
E-mail: gokuu@gnu.ai.mit.edu or
bs783@cleveland.freenet.edu
Activities: Tape library, tape trading, translating and subtitling projects
Dues: $15 a year (attending members)
$20 a year for anyone in North America
$25 a year outside of North America

Animania
Meets: Saturday closest to 15th of each month,
Where: Anderson Room of Michigan Student Union on State Street
Contact: Jonathan Mayer
215 North Thayer
Ann Arbor, MI 48104
(313) 995-5539
Dave Laing (313) 333-3133
Michael Hayden (313) 348-3504
E-mail: jmayer@engin.umich.edu (J. Mayer)
Doctor_Braindamage@um.cc.umich.edu
(M. Hayden)
fingerjmayer@engin.umich.edu
to find out about next meeting.
Publication: *Animania* monthly group fanzine
Activities: Tape trading, screenings.

Animation Circle of Enthusiasts
Meets: 1st Saturday of each month
Where: Mark Keller's home
Contact: Mark D. Keller
25805 Calaroga Ave.
Hayward, CA 94545
(510) 782-1990

Animation of Nippon Inter-Mediary Exchange (ANIME)
Meets: 1st Sunday of each month
Where: Foothill College, Forum Hall #1
12345 El Monte Rd.
Los Altos, CA 94022

Anime Classic
Meets: 3rd Sunday of each month
Contact: Chris Olds or Ann Schubert
25 West Bay Shore Rd. #J5
Palo Alto, CA 94303
(415) 858-2859

Anime Club of Michigan
Meets: Monthly, check X-Trava-Con fliers
Where: X-Trava-Con Baseball & Comic Show
Knights of Columbus Hall
19801 Farmington Rd.
Livonia, MI
(810) 350-2633
Contact: Terry Williams
826 Marywood
Royal Oak, MI 48067
Publication: *Anime Club of Michigan Newsletter*
Activities: Tape trading.
Dues: $15.00 a year...$1.50 for non-members at the door.

Anime Crisis
Meets: 1st and 3rd week of the month
Where: The home of the staff
Contact: Brian Keesler
2127 Rockrose Cir.
Henderson, NV 89014
(702) 897-6936
E-mail: gogeta@wizard.com
Activities: Road trips to L.A. 2nd Sunday of every month
Dues: $20.00 a year

Anime Discovery Project (ADP)
Meets: Twice per month
Where: Univ. of Washington Student Union
Contact: David Beder / ADP
University Of Washington
Student Union Building FK-30
Room 207, Box #181
Seattle, WA 98195
E-mail: adp@hardy,u.washington.edu
Activities: Tape library, screenings
Dues: $2.50 per quarter

Anime Hasshin
Contact: Lorraine Savage
Editor/Coordinator
P.O. Box 5121
Manchester, NH 03108-5121
Publication: *The Rose* Newsletter (quarterly)
E-mail: hasshin@tiac.net
Web Site: http://www.tiac.net/users/hasshin
Activities: Correspondence between clubs, synopsis packets, tape and BGM trading, discounts on anime videos, and merchandise.
Dues: $15.00 U.S., $16 Canada, $20 elsewhere

Anime HQ Exchange
Meets: Irregularly, call for information.
Where: Elk Creek Club
Call for information
Contact: Kelly Howell, President
P.O. Box 172
Elm Creek, NE 68836
(308) 856-4342 (noon - 2pm)

Anime Niacs
Contact: Anime Niacs
P.O. Box 158392
Nashville,TN 37215
Publication: *Anime Nia*, a quarterly newsletter
Activities: 10% off on merchandise from Jellico's Interstellar Trading Co., annual fanzine
Dues: $18.00 membership

Anime Otekku (GA Tech)
Contact: Geoff Tebbetts
350673 Georgia Tech Sta.
Atlanta, GA 30332
Aaron Craig
3325568 Georgia Tech Sta.
Atlanta, GA 30332

Anime Sacramento
Meets: Odd-numbered months
Where: Laurine White's home
Contact: Laurine White
5422 Colusa Wy.
Sacramento, CA 95841
(916) 332-7461 (eves, 6 to 9pm)
Please phone for current schedule

Anime Section of Japanese Students International
Contact: Anime
c/o Japanese Students International
Johns Hopkins University
(Homewood Campus)
Baltimore, MD 21218
E-mail: tiger_sa@jhunix.hcf.jhu.edu (Shuvo Alam)
z_man@jhunix.hcf.jhu.edu (B. Hsaio)
Activities: Tape library, screenings.

Anime X
Meets: 4th Saturday of each month (except in December)
Where: Call for information or write to:
Anime X
P.O. Box 724182
Atlanta, GA 31139-1182
Contact: Lloyd Carter
727 Morosgo Dr.#7
Atlanta, GA 30324-3510
(404) 364-9773
Travis Wilborn
10116 Setter Grove Rd.
Covington, GA 30209
(707) 333-8554
Publication: *Let's Anime* fanzine $3.50 ea. or 4 for $10.00
Activities: Anime infopaks, tape library, promoting other groups.
Dues: One time $5.00 fee

Atlantic Anime Alliance
Meets: 2nd Saturday of each month
Where: School of Visual Arts (23rd & 3rd)
Contact: PO Box 10371
New Brunswick, NJ 08906-0371
Chet Jasinski
93 Hyde Ct.
Bedminster, NJ 07921-1816
(908) 781-9409
Steve Pearl
359 Lloyd Rd
Aberdeen, NJ 07747-1826
(908) 566-6842

E-mail:	c.jasinski@genie.geis.com (Chet Jasinski)
	starbuck@cybercom.com (Steve Pearl)
Publication:	*Atlantia*, a quarterly newsletter
Activities:	Organize and run the Anime East convention, publish Anime Fandom Directory, screenings.
Dues:	$16/year (incl. subscription to *Atlantia*)

Bay Area Animation Society (BAAS)

Meets:	end of each month (except in Dec.)
Where:	Empire Branch Library
	491 E. Empire St.
	San Jose, CA
Contact:	Tracy Brown, Coordinator
	Bay Area Animation Society
	P.O. Box 720244
	San Jose, CA 95172-0244
	(408) 280-7054
E-mail:	blade@netcom.com
Activities:	International correspondence.

Cal-Animage

Contact:	Mike Tatsugawa
	Cal-Animage
	2425 B Channing Way, Suite 310,
	Berkeley, CA 94704
E-mail:	mtats@ocf.berkeley.edu
	shogun@sutro.sfsu.edu
Publication:	*A-Ni-Me*: The Berkeley Journal of Animation
Activities:	Cal-Animage is a loose confederation of clubs dedicated to the goal of promoting cultural understanding through the international medium of Japanese animation. Chapters at U.C. Berkeley, U.C. San Diego, U.C. Santa Barbara, U.C. Irvine, Perth Australia, U.C.L.A., Stanford, North Dakota State U., and Western Washington.

Cal-Animage Alpha

Meets:	Mondays, 6:30 pm
Where:	2050 Valley Life Sciences Building
	U.C. Berkeley campus
E-mail:	animage@server.berkeley.edu
Web site:	www.anime.berkeley.edu/CAA/
Publication:	*Konshuu*
Activities:	Weekly screenings, tape library
Dues:	$6 per semester

Caltech Anime

Meets:	Fridays, 7 pm
Where:	Caltech Student Activity Center
Contact:	Roy Jones
	Caltech Mail Stop #673
	Pasadena, CA 91126
E-mail:	james@vlsi.cs.caltech.edu (James Cook)
Activities:	Weekly screenings

Cartoon/Fantasy Organization (C/FO)

Meets:	3rd Saturday of each month
Where:	The comics shop of Gustav Baron
	8721 Glenoaks Bl.
	Sun Valley, CA 91352
	(818) 768-4594
Contact:	Fred Patten, Secretary
	11863 Jefferson Blvd.
	Culver City, CA 90230-6322
	(310) 827-3335
Publication:	Monthly bulletin, annual membership directory, semi-annual Directory of Anime Fandom
Activities:	Auction of anime art, merchandise, and occasional visit from guests in the anime industry. 20% discount on anime merchandise at Banzai Comics and Animation with a valid C/FO membership card.
Dues:	$20.00 full membership
	$12.00 associate membership

Cartoon/Fantasy Organization- Cleveland (C/FO-Cleveland)

Meets:	2nd Sunday of each month
Where:	Michael Sherman's home
Contact:	Michael Sherman
	1200 Seneca Bl. apt.201
	Broadview Heights, OH 44147
	(216) 237-6427

Club Animaniacs SJSU

Meets:	every 3 weeks during school year
Where:	Student Activity Center, SJSU
Contact:	Ronnie Kwong
	Box 23, Student Activity Service
	One Washington Square
	San Jose, CA 95112
	(408) 259-9134
E-mail:	kwong@sparta.sjsu.edu

Club Anime West (CA West)

Meets:	2nd Saturday of each month, 11am-5pm
Where:	Empire Branch Library
	491 E. Empire St.
	San Jose, CA
Contact:	Ed Goodwin or See flyers at Nikaku Animart (408) 227-4292

Club Artistic, Neopolitical, Imaginative, Media, Exchange (Club ANIME)

Contact:	Celeste Collins
	P.O. Box 1551
	Winton, CA 95388
	(209) 357-1656
E-mail:	ccollins@koko.csustan.edu
	or: ggreene@koko.csustan.edu
Activities:	Gives shows, lectures, attends conventions

Colony Works Entertainment

Contact:	Alec Orrock
	24161-H Hollyoak
	Laguna Hills, CA 92656
	(714) 643-8352
	(714) 566-3037 Fax
E-mail:	orrock@ix.netcom.com
Activities:	Formerly known as Summer Side. Contact Alec Orrock for current information.

Corn Pone Flicks

Contact:	David Merrill
	PO Box 724182
	Atlanta, GA 30339
Publication:	*Let's Anime* fanzine

Cornell Japanese Animation Society

Meets:	Saturday nights (fall & spring semesters)
Where:	Goldwin Smith Hall, Lecture Room D
	Cornell University campus
Contact:	Ping Lin, President
	907 E. State St. Apt. B301
	Ithaca, NY 14850
	(607) 273-7805
E-mail:	pl11@cornell.edu
Publications:	weekly newsletter, New Viewer's Guide, Language & Culture Guide
Dues:	$5 per semester

Eastern Entertainment Association

Meets:	2nd Saturday of each month
Where:	274 Munich St.
	San Francisco, CA
Contact:	Peter Wong, info
	(415) 752-9267
	or Kent Johnson
	200 Van Ness #305
	San Francisco, CA 94102

Fanimation / Animania

Meets:	2nd & 4th Fridays of each month
Where:	University of Montreal
	3200 Jean Brillant St. local B-2305
	Montreal, QUEBEC
	CANADA

Foothill A.N.I.M.E.

Meets:	1st Sunday of each month
Where:	Foothill College, Room A61
	12345 El Monte Rd.
	Los Altos, CA 94022
Contact:	Michael Wright
	(408) 293-1821

The Greater Chicago Megazone

Contact:	Michael Cox
	2018 Creek Rd.
	Waukegan, IL 60087
Publication:	*Anime²*

Indiana Animation Club

Meets:	3rd Sunday of each month
Contact:	Andrew Schill
	9719 East 17th Street
	Indianapolis, IN 46229-2020
E-mail:	buaku@indy.net
	http://www.indy.net/~buaku
Activities:	Screenings, tape library

Indiana Anime Guild

Contact:	Paul McDaniels
	P.O. Box 491
	Westfield, IN 46074-0491

Inland Empire Anime Club

Meets:	Monthly
Where:	Highlander Mobile Manor
	26838 East 9th Street
	Highland, CA
Contact:	Wayne Wright
	26838 E. 9th St. #G-5
	Highland, CA 92346
	(909) 864-7140
E-mail:	beast@csnsys.com
	http://www.csnsys.com/john/iea/
Publication:	*Inland Empire Anime Bulletin*

International Animation Sodality

Meets:	Monthly, Call for information
Contact:	Roy & Cathy Bruce
	7866 Wilton Rd.
	Richmond, VA 23231-8005
	(804) 222-8403
Activities:	Promotes the understanding, culture, and growth of anime fandom through news and networking.

Japanese Animation Club of Olympic College

Contact:	Ting
	P.O. Box 45205
	Seattle, WA 98145-0205

Japanese Animation Society Of Hawaii

Meets:	2nd Sunday of each month
Contact:	Japanese Animation Society of Hawaii
	P.O. Box 22517
	Honolulu, HI 96822
	(808) 536-0519
Publication:	*Animeco* Magazine
E-mail:	animatsuri@genie.com
Dues:	$20 a year (includes subscription to Animeco Magazine). No Mail-order memberships

JC Anime

Meets: Fridays, 8:00 pm
Where: College Ave. Student Center, Room 407
Rutgers University
Contact: Alex Chen, President
E-mail: ahchen@eden.rutgers.edu
Web site: www-eden.rutgers.edu/~gsm23/JCanime
Activities: screenings

Lincoln Fantasy & Science Fiction Club

Meets: Last Sunday of each month
Where: University of Nebraska Lincoln
Contact: Garner Johnson
719 "B" St.
Lincoln, NE 68502
(402) 477-8430
Activities: Runs an annual SF convention
called MAELSTORM

Maine Animation and Gaming Association (MANGA)

Meets: Sundays bi-monthly to quarterly
Contact: John Andersen
81 Bramblewood Dr.
Portland, ME 04103-3796
(207) 797-9523
Activities: Dealer's table with anime goods,
discounts at a local comic shop,
info on conventions, fanzines.

No Name Anime

Meets: Varies, call for information
Where: Santa Teresa Library
290 International Cir.
San Jose, CA
(408) 281-1878
Contact: Matt Seitz
1170 La Terrace Cir.
San Jose, CA 95123
(408) 997-8401
Publication: *No Name Anime* Newsletter

Northern Oregon Vancouver Anime

Meets: 1st & 3rd Saturday each month
Where: Beaverton Community Center
(Corner of 5th and Hall)
Beaverton, OR
Contact: Scott Rose
10116 N.W. 29th Ave.
Vancouver, WA 98685
(206) 573-6926
Activities: Bulletin, library, meetings

Oklahoma Megazone

Contact: James Staley, info. contact
P.O. Box 268
Jones, OK 73049
(409) 399-2679

Orphaned Anime Fans (OAF)

Contact: Stephen Bennett
10511 Edenton Rd.
Partlow, VA 22534

Okating Anime Society (OAS)

Contact: Elliot Lee
(408) 554-4611 (work number)

Otaku Generation

Meets: Irregularly, call for information
Where: Manchester Mall, Community Room
(Blackstone & Shield)
Fresno, CA
Contact: Francis Fung
(209) 456-0133
Activities: Roadtrips to Anime events, parties,
give-a-ways, and more.

Otaku Shirase

Contact: Josh Ritter
457 Carlsbad Village Drive
Carlsbad, CA 92008
Publication: anime newsletter

Prince Planet Society

Contact: Dave Merrill
PO Box 724182
Atlanta, GA 31139-1182
E-mail: dave.merrill@sidnet

Rochester Institute of Technology Anime Club (RITAC)

Meets: Every Thursday at 8pm
Where: Rochester Institute of Technology
Student Union, Clark Dining Room
Contact: c/o Student Government
1 Lomb Dr.
Rochester, NY 14623

Sacramento Area Anime (SAA)

Contact: David Chan
6840 Steamboat Wy.
Sacramento, CA 95831
Tony Rubino
3715 Tallyho Dr. #10
Sacramento, CA 95826

Santa Barbara Animation Appreciation Association (SB3A)

Meets: 2nd Sunday of each month
Where: Rusty's Pizza Parlor (upstairs)
232 W. Carillo St.
Santa Barbara, CA 93101
(805) 968-7639
Contact: SB3A
P.O. Box 91729
Santa Barbara, CA 93190
(805) 964-8156
Publication: *SB3A Fanzine*

Santa Cruz Anime Media Group

Meets: 3rd Sunday of each month
Contact: Michael Wright (408) 293-1821
or Erich (408) 268-6291

Science Fiction Animation Confederation

Contact: James Meier, SFAC
9135 Alexander Road
Batavia, NY 14020
E-mail: sfac@aol.com
Publication: *Buffalo Crisis* newsletter

Southern California Animation Network (SCAN)

Meets: 2nd Saturday of each month
Where: Social Sciences Bldg., Auditorium
San Diego State University
San Diego, CA 92182-0741
Contact: Attend a meeting for info.

Summer Side

See Colony Works Entertainment

Transmasters

Contact: Joe Elbe
650 Pacific Ave
Willows, CA 95988
Activities: International Transformers fan club

Tsunami

Contact: Editor-in-Chief, Tsunami
4708 Cherokee St. #102
College Park, MD 20740-1874
E-mail: godiva@wam.umd.edu
Publication: *Anime & Manga Quarterly*

Vancouver Japanese Animation Club

Contact: William Chow
2830 East 8th Ave.
Vancouver, BC V5M 1W9 CANADA
(604) 253-4227
E-mail: BBS (604) 254-1833

Videoburn: The Club of Japanese Animation

Meets: Every Thursday (6pm to 10:30pm)
Where: University of California Riverside,
Sproul Hall #1102
Riverside, CA 92521
Contact: Justin Roby, info
6149 Bluffwood Dr.
Riverside, CA 92506
Robert Chang
955 High Peak Dr.
Riverside, CA 92521
(909) 789-8207
E-mail: habeeb@watmail.ucr.edu
changone@watmail.ucr.edu

Anime-Related Magazines

A growing number of magazines are devoting coverage to animation in general, and anime in particular. These are the major professionally published magazines (as distinct from amateur fan club "fanzines") devoted either wholly or partially to coverage of Japanese animation and/or manga.

Animation Magazine

30101 Agoura Court, Suite 110 • Agoura Hills, CA 91301
(800) 996-8666 • Fax: (818) 991-3773
E-mail: animag@aol.com • Web Site: http://www.animag.com
$4.95 (subscriptions available)
published monthly

For years, *Animation Magazine* has been the animation industry's trade journal, covering the animation scene from an insider's perspective. Averaging 60-68 pages (mostly color), the magazine covers the business and creative side of today's animation, and often features anime subjects. Anime historian Fred Patten has a regular bi-monthly column.

Animato!

The Animation Fan's Magazine
17 Spruce St. • Springfield, MA 01105
$4.50 (subscriptions available)
published quarterly

Animato! has come a long way since it was a digest-size, home-grown, fannish labor of love. These days it runs 72 pages and comes out quarterly, but its roots in fandom still remain. Lately, it has expanded its discussion of Japanese animation considerably. Highly recommended for animated cartoon buffs — anime fans included.

Anime FX

Anime • Manga • SFX • Japanese Pop Culture
This excellent 68-page, full-color British magazine, winner of the 1994 Tezuka Award for best English-language anime publication, changed its title from ***Anime U.K.*** to reflect its expanded coverage of anime in North America as well. Unfortunately, the magazine ceased publication in 1996, but it's well worth picking up back issues if you can find them.

Animeco

The Official Magazine of the Japanese Animation Society of Hawai'i
published by: Limelight Publishing Co. • 1513 Young St. #202 • Honolulu, HI 96826
E-mail: whols@aloha.net • Web Site: http://www.planet-hawaii.com/lime/
$3.95 (subscriptions available)
published quarterly

Animeco evolved from a club newsletter into a professional, 32-page magazine, earning a Tezuka Award nomination at Anime East in 1995. The presentation is attractive, and the magazine features worthwhile articles and features that are not duplicated in other anime magazines.

Animerica

Anime & Manga Monthly
published by: Viz Communications • PO Box 77010 • San Francisco, CA 94107
Web Site: http://www.viz.com
$4.95 (subscriptions available)
published monthly

Now entering its fifth year, *Animerica* is certainly the most professional of the U.S.-produced anime magazines. Each 80-page, color and black & white issue covers new anime videos in the U.S. and Japan, plus manga news, serialized manga series such as Clamp's *X/1999*, "freebies" such as posters and postcards, as well as exclusive in-depth interviews with creators such as Hayao Miyazaki, Masamune Shirow, and Rumiko Takahashi. Winner of the 1995 Tezuka Award for "Best English-language anime publication."

fps

The magazine of animation on film and video
published by: Pawn Press • PO Box 355, Station H • Montreal, QC H3G 2L1 CANADA
E-mail: emru@cam.org • Web Site: http://www.cam.org/~pawn/fps.html
$3.95 (subscriptions available)
published quarterly(ish)

fps originated as an irregular fanzine by Emru Townsend that reflected his eclectic tatses in animation. Nowadays the magazine runs 38 pages, the presentation is highly professional, and coverage has expanded to include much anime reporting. For a general-interest animation magazine, *fps* is notable for not treating anime like a poor relative. Count on it to provide considerable factual reference in addition to fan reviews.

Mangazine

Anime, Sentai and Comics
Mangazine evolved from a comic book of amateur manga-type comics by American fans into a magazine of information about the anime and manga field. Each issue was filled with "news" (a compendium of press releases from U.S. companies releasing anime or manga), an in-depth article on one or more popular anime or *sentai* (live-action masked heroes) TV programs, and an extensive "Anime Classified" section where fans could get their clubs listed, ask for pen pals, etc. Unfortunately, the magazine ceased publication in 1996, but back issues are worth searching out.

Protoculture Addicts

The Anime & Manga Magazine
P.O. Box 1433, Station B • Montreal, Quebec H3B 3L2 • Canada
Fax: (514) 527-0347
E-mail: flip@odyssee.net • Web Site: http://www.odyssee.net/~flip/PA
$4.95 (subscriptions available)
published bi-monthly

Protoculture Addicts has evolved from a 1988 *Robotech* fan publication into a fully-professional 56-page magazine which covers the complete North American anime and manga scenes. In-depth reviews of videos, theatrical releases, comic books, and mecha-oriented model kits. Their coverage of American anime conventions is particularly good.

Toon Magazine

published by: Black Bear Press • 2828 Cochran Street, Suite 152 • Simi Valley, CA 93065
$5.95 (no subscriptions)
published quarterly(ish)

TOON Magazine is devoted primarily to in-depth articles on American television animation, but there is usually at least one extensive article on an anime title such as *8 Man After*. (The Summer 1995 issue was filled by a comprehensive *Lupin III* article which was forty pages long!)

V.Max

The Anime & Manga Journal
P.O. Box 3292 • Santa Clara, CA 95055
Fax: (510) 549-1726
E-mail: vmax@aol.com
$4.50 (no subscriptions)
published quarterly(ish)

V.Max has a reputation as the magazine for the fanatically purist subtitles-only otaku. A recent editorial comments, "Unfortunately, the dubbed products available today are uniformly *bad*, compared to the Japanese originals." This obsession with accuracy means articles that are exceptionally informed and in-depth, in an attractive and well-illustrated 48-page black & white layout. Includes some coverage of the live-action *sentai* TV programs.

Additionally, at least two videophile magazines have a regular column of reviews of anime videos:

The Phantom of the Movies' VideoScope

"Animania" column by Walt James
published by PhanMedia
P.O. Box 216 • Ocean Grove, NJ 07756
$4.25 (subscriptions available)
published quarterly

Video Watchdog

"Anime Watchdog" column by Greg Barr
published by: Tim & Donna Lucas
P.O. Box 5283
Cincinnati, OH 45205-0283
$5.50 (subscriptions available)
published bi-monthly

Internet and World Wide Web

Anime fan Ann Schubert established the Internet anime newsgroup **rec.arts.anime** in late 1987. Recent measurements put the total number of people who read this newsgroup worldwide at about 70,000. It is not one of the larger newsgroups (alt.tv.simpsons has about 215,000 readers, for example), but it is definitely one of the most active, averaging more than 8,000 postings per month. By nature, the Internet and World Wide Web are growing, changing, and evolving daily, so it would be both futile and redundant for this book to attempt to list all the sites devoted to anime. Instead, we call your attention to what we consider three key electronic resources. At these sites, you will find like-minded anime fans and countless references and links to further anime-related sites.

rec.arts.anime

rec.arts.anime is an Internet newsgroup devoted solely to anime. It is a very busy site, with several hundred postings per day and tens of thousands of readers. Just checking in every couple of days and trying to catch up on the postings can consume hours each session. The newsgroup is moderated by Steve Pearl, which helps keep the chaos to a minimum, and there is an indispensible FAQ (Frequently Asked Questions) document always available. Steve also keeps a rec.arts.anime primer available, along with several handy references to just about any list or site you could want. The newsgroup has grown enough over the years to necessitate splitting off several specialized newsgroups. The major offshoots are:

rec.arts.anime.info: For the posting of anime-related news, synopses, reviews (28,600 readers; 100 messages per month).
rec.arts.anime.marketplace: Buying & selling of anime-related merchandise (37,000 readers; 1,300 messages per month).
rec.arts.anime.stories: Anime-related fan-fiction (25,000 readers; 100 messages per month).
rec.arts.manga: Devoted to the discussion of manga.
rec.games.mecha: a newsgroup devoted to mecha.

Anime Web Turnpike
http://soyokaze.biosci.ohio-state.edu/~jei/anipike/

This World Wide Web page was established in August of 1995 by Jay Fubler Harvey to provide a place where everyone could find anime and manga links in a simple and efficient manner, regardless of their browser capabilities. Firmly situated as one of the key anime hub sites, the Turnpike is now the largest organized collection of anime and manga links anywhere on the Internet... and it's growing all the time. This awesome directory of Internet sites (most of which can be accessed directly through this web page) includes anime clubs, shopping guides, fan pages, conventions, magazines, animation studios, databases, personal pages, commercial pages, reviews, Japanese and European sites, and a whole lot more.

Starbuck's Home Page
http://www.cybercomm.net/~starbuck/

Otaku is the term used (by Americans) to describe one who is fanatically obsessed with Japanese animation. Toshio Okada, the Japanese "Otaking" (king of the otaku) has declared Steve Pearl to be the American Otaking. Steve is the founder of Rutgers Anime and Megazone NJ, coordinator of The Atlantic Anime Alliance, co-chair of the Far East Expo, moderator of rec.arts.anime.info, and writes FAQs for most anime newsgroups. His home page is chock-full of knowledgable articles, and "Steve's Link Universe" is an awe-inspiring collection of Internet links and references on the order of Anime Web Turnpike.

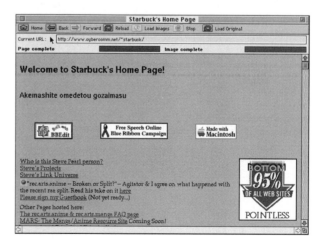

Conventions

Once upon a time, anime fans occupied tiny anime rooms at comic & sci-fi cons (when they let them). In 1990, Project A-Kon happened with a convention entirely devoted to animation including anime. Then AnimeCon came along, with both Japanese & American industry guests. Anime Expo followed the next year, filling the void left by AnimeCon. Then came Anime America. After five years, Project A-Kon finally got a Japanese guest. Then the East Coast Convention explosion occured as Otakon, Anime East, & Katsucon all debuted in the space of one year. Now, there are a number of anime-related conventions all over the country: Those that occurred during 1996 are listed here.

Anime America '96

Anime America is an annual full-featured anime and manga convention held near San Francisco, California during the summer months. Anime America is sponsored by the Foundation for Animation and Comics Education (FACE), a not-for-profit California corporation. The 1996 convention was held July 25-28 at the Red Lion Inn in San Jose, CA. Attendance was approximately 500.

1996 Guests Of Honor included:

Paul Dobson (*Ranma 1/2* Happosai voice actor, among others)

Michael Donovan (*Ranma 1/2* Ryoga voice actor, among others)

Jason Gray-Stanford (voice actor in several series)

Matt Hill (voice actor in several series)

Janyse Jaud (voice actress in several series)

Toshio Okada (founder and president of Gainax)

Ward Perry (voice actor)

Toby Proctor (voice actor)

Frederik Schodt (author of *Manga! Manga!*)

Activities included:

2 video screening rooms, manga experts panel discussion, dealer's room, workshops, cel exhibition, art contest, vocal acting tryouts, casino night, masquerade and dance party, paintball game, autograph sessions, flea market, and "artist's alley."

For information on 1997 events contact:

Anime America
929 Delbert Way
San Jose, CA 95126
E-mail: anam@rahul.net
Web site: http://scsu15.scu.edu/elec/anam.html

Anime Expo '96

Anime Expo is an annual anime and manga convention organized by the non-profit organization, Society for the Promotion of Japanese Animation(SPJA). The fifth (1996) Expo was held June 28-30 at the Anaheim Marriot and the Anaheim Convention Center. The 1996 Expo attracted some very big-name guests. Attendance was approximately 3,000.

1996 Guests of Honor included:

Hideako Anno (*Nadia, Otaku no Video, Neon Genesis Evangelion*)

Hiroyuki Kitazume (*Moldiver, Starlight Angel, L-Gaim, Char's Counterattack*)

Kenichi Sonoda (*Gunsmith Cats, Riding Bean*)

Koichi Ohata (*MD Geist, GunBuster, Genocyber*)

Mamoru Oshii (*Ghost in the Shell, Patlabor 1 and 2*)

Yoshiaki Kawajiri (*Cyber City Oedo, Demon City Shinjuku, Ninja Scroll*)

Noboru Ishiguro (*Galactic Heroes, Megazone 23*, president of Artland Studio)

Ai Orikasa (*Tenchi Muyô!* (Ryoko) voice actress)

Yumi Takada (*Tenchi Muyô!* (Ayeka) voice actress)

1996 Activities included:

90 dealers in a 16,000 square-foot hall, autograph sessions, panel discussions, video screenings, movie screenings in a 1500-seat theatre, masquerade ball, and much more.

For information on 1997 events contact:

Anime Expo
530 Showers Dr. #7-287
Mountain View, CA 94040
E-mail: info@anime-expo.org
Web Site: www.anime-expo.org
or:
SPJA
7336 Santa Monica Blvd. #640
Hollywood, CA 90046
(818) 441-3653

Anime Weekend Atlanta

Anime Weekend Atlanta was held November 1-3, 1996 at the Holiday Inn Atlanta Airport South in College Park, GA. Attendence was approximately 630.

1996 Guests of Honor included:

Steve Bennett (animator/illustrator)

Bruce Lewis (Studio Go!)

Bill Mayo (modeler)

Neil Nadelman (translator)

Lorraine Savage (Anime Hasshin)

Other guests: Greg Lane, Robert Woodhead, Ed Hill, Jeff Taterek, and more.

Activities included:

Panel discussions (including "State of the Industry", "Wings of Gainax", and "Return of Sub vs. Dub - The Revenge!"), dealers' room, three video rooms, art show, cel painting, anime model kit and costuming workshops, costume contest, and game show.

For information on 1997 events, contact:

Anime Weekend Atlanta
P.O. Box 13544
Atlanta, GA 30324-0544
E-mail: awainfo@mindspring.com
www.anime.net/~awa/
(404) 364-9773

Fanime Con

FanimeCon, The Anime Festival for the Fans, was held March 2, 1996 at the Foothill College Campus. Fanime Con is sponsored by the following local anime societies: Bay Area Animation Society, BeefBowl Anime, Eastern Entertainment Association, Foothill A.N.I.M.E., and No-Name Anime. Attendance was approximately 700.

1996 Guests of Honor included:

Greg Espinoza

Carl Horn (Associate Editor of *Animerica* magazine)

Allen Hastings (computer animator)

Fred Schodt (author of Manga! Manga!)

Toshifumi Yoshida (translator)

Toren Smith

Activities included:

3 video rooms, gaming room, costume contest, artist's row dealer's room, and much more.

For information on 1997 events contact:

Fanime Con
P.O. Box 8068
San Jose, CA 95155-8068
(408) 972-5654 Fax
E-mail: fanime@fanime.com
www.fanime.com

Far East Expo

Far East Expo is the successor to Anime East. The name change is to reflect the refocusing of the show more toward Asian pop culture in general, including anime, manga, and Hong Kong cinema. Far East Expo will continue to be the home of the Tezuka Industry Awards. It is tentatively scheduled for late October, 1997.

For information on 1997 events, contact:

Far East Expo
P.O. Box 10371
New Brunswick, NJ 08906-0371
(908) 719-9770
E-mail: fareast@net-lynx.com
www.cybercomm.net/~starbuck/FX/fx.html

I-Con XVI

I-Con, one of the largest Science Fiction & Fantasy Media conventions in the United States, has expanded its anime-related programming tracks. Although it is primarily a science fiction, fact and fantasy convention, expect plenty of guests from anime fandom and the industry. I-Con was held April 12-14, 1996 at the Stony Brook campus of the State University of New York.

For information on 1997 events contact:

I-Con XVII
PO Box 550
Stony Brook, NY 11790
E-Mail: icon@ic sunysb.edu
Phone: (516) 632-6045
FAX: (516) 632-6355

KatsuCon 2

KatsuCon is an annual small-but-spirited anime and manga convention held in the Virginia area which draws attendees from around the country. KatsuCon is sponsored by Katsu Productions, a fan-based organization. KatsuCon 2 was held March 8-10, 1996 at The Holiday Inn Executive Center in Virginia Beach, VA.

1996 Guests of Honor included:

Masakazu Katsura (*Video Girl Ai* and *D.N.A.²*)

Toren Smith

Activities included:

Video rooms, dealer's room, costume play, karaoke lounge, dance, video game room, panel discussions, and more.

For information on 1997 events contact:

Katsu Productions Ltd.
P.O. Box 11582
Blacksburg, Virginia 24062-1582
E-mail: katsucon@vtserf.cc.vt.edu
www.jurai.net/~wingman/index.html

Otakon '96

The second Otakon was held August 9-11, 1996 at Marriot's Hunt Valley Inn, Baltimore, MD. Attendance was approximately 1,000.

1996 Guests of Honor included:

Masaomi Kanzaki (Streetfighter II, Xenon manga)

1996 activities included:

Four video theatres, HK live action track, panels, artist signings, video game tournament, art show, dealers' room, masquerade, game show, cel painting workshop, artists' alley, modeling competiton, music video contest, and art auction.

For information on 1997 events contact:

Otakon c/o Dave Asher
661A Waupelani Drive
State College, PA 16801
Phone: (814) 867-3478
E-mail: dcasher@delphi.com
www.otakon.com

Project A-Kon 7

Project A-Kon was the very first national anime-based convention, is an annual event, and has been run for seven continuous years. Run professionally, by fans who believe "professional" doesn't have to mean "unapproachable" or "cold," Project A-Kon is gaining a reputation as the best party con around, drawing folks from other areas of fandom to make for a huge three-day fannish party with lots to do and lots of people to meet. The 1996 A-Kon was held May 31-June 2 at the Harvey Hotel-Addison in Dallas, TX.

1996 Guests of Honor included:

Scott Frazier (animator)

Mitsuhisa Ishikawa (producer)

Toshihiko Nishikubo (director)

Toshimichi Otsuki

1996 activities included:

24-hour video rooms, portfolio assessment, comic market, dealers' room, gaming room, panel discussions, workshops, parties, role-playing games, scavenger hunt, dance contest, costume contest, art show and auction, and more. An all-day power outage on Saturday forced cancellation of some activities, but the attendees weathered it well.

For information on 1997 events contact:

Project A-Kon
3352 Broadway, Suite 470
Garland, TX 75043
Fax: (214) 278-6935
E-mail: phoenix@cyberramp.net
www.cyberramp.net/~phoenix/akon.html

World Science Fiction Convention (WorldCon)

The annual Worldcon was one of the first to feature anime video rooms and anime costumes at its masquerade. Worldcons during the 1980s included studio-authorized screenings of *The Castle of Cagliostro* (1980), *Arrivederci Yamato* (1983) and both *Lensman* and *Robotech* (1984). *Gundam* creator Yoshiyuki Tomino was a guest speaker at the 1984 Worldcon in Anaheim, CA, and worked ingroup references to it into *Zeta Gundam*. **L.A.Con III**, the 54th annual Worldcon, was held August 29-Sept. 2, 1996 at the Anaheim Convention Center. Attendance was approximately 6,700.

1996 activities included:

24-hour anime video screening room, anime theme song karaoke, panel discussions, trivia quiz, dealer's rooms, and exhibition on Japanese fan conventions.

For information on 1997 events contact:

LoneStarCon 2
P.O. Box 27277
Austin, TX 78755-2277
(512) 453-7446

Chapter Five
Anime Resources
Video Suppliers and Retailers

Domestic Home Video Suppliers

The following is a directory of the domestic anime home video suppliers whose video releases are listed in the Video Directory. In this context, "suppliers" refers to the companies that actually hold the licences to the programs and package and duplicate the cassettes and laserdiscs. Companies that distribute the home videos are referred to as "distributors," and appear later in this chapter. The letter code used in the Video Directory for each supplier appears after the name, in parentheses.

A.D. Vision (ADV)
Southwest Plaza Building • 5750 Bintliff #217 • Houston, TX 77036-2123
(713) 977-9181 (Voice) • (713) 977-5573 (Fax)
Web site: www.advfilms.com • www.softcelpics.com/
Video labels: A.D. Vision • SoftCel Pictures
Texas-based A.D. Vision was founded by Matt Greenfield and John Ledford, releasing the subtitled version of *Devil Hunter Yohko* in December 1992. They are a specialty video supplier formed to serve the burgeoning demand for domestic versions of Japanese animation. The company is known for its line of adult-themed anime programs, and has a secondary label—SoftCel Pictures—for the release of "X-rated" programming. Formed to serve the fan community, A.D. Vision released mostly English-subtitled anime at first, but has been releasing more English-dubbed titles lately. A.D. Vision titles are distributed through a wide variety of wholesale channels. They publish a fan-oriented anime magazine titled "Fanime."
PURCHASING INFORMATION:
Direct retail sales to consumers. Consumer catalog available.
Direct wholesale sales to individual retailers.

AnimEigo, Inc. (ANI)
P.O. Box 989 • Wilmington, NC 28402-0989
(910) 251-1850 • (910) 763-2376 (Fax) • (800) 242-6463 (Orders)
E-Mail: 72447.37@compuserve.com
Web site: www.animeigo.com

AnimEigo Inc. (Anime + Eigo = "Animation In English"), a North Carolina-based company, was founded in 1989 by Robert J. Woodhead and Roe R. Adams. Their first home video release was the subtitled *Madox-01* in 1990. AnimEigo is a specialty company founded and run by anime aficionados, and has released more English-subtitled anime tapes than any other company. Their early output of multi-volume fan favorite series like the best-selling *Bubblegum Crisis*, plus *AD Police*, *Urusei Yatsura*, *Kimagure Orange Road* and *Oh My Goddess!* has diminished of late, but they have begun releasing some live-action "Samurai Cinema" films. In addition to tapes and laserdiscs, they offer licensed merchandise such as t-shirts, hats, linens, posters, original animation cels, computer screensavers and audio compact discs.
PURCHASING INFORMATION:
Direct retail sales to consumers. Consumer catalog available.
Direct wholesale sales to individual retailers. "Anime Gossip" newsletter distributed to retailers.

Best Film & Video (BFV)
108 New South Road • Hicksville, NY 11801
(516) 931-6969 • (516) 931-5959 (Fax)

Best Film and Video is a well-established "budget" video supplier. Their focus is on special-interest video titles duplicated in EP (extended play) mode, although many of their titles can be ordered in standard play as well. Unlike many of the lower-end budget video companies, BFV pays attention to quality masters, quality duplication, and quality package art (a real blight in most of this end of the market). In 1993, they licensed a package of anime titles from Streamline Pictures, including *Zillion*, *Windaria*, *Robot Carnival*, *Lensman*, and a few others. In 1995 they picked up a package of titles that had previously been licensed to Celebrity Home Entertainment, including *Dallos*, *Phoenix 2772*, *Super Dimensional Fortress Macross*, and others. They distribute both of these packages in SP (standard play), and in the case of the second package, they distribute the original uncut versions of the films under the original titles. BFV titles are carried by many of the major video wholesalers.
PURCHASING INFORMATION:
No direct retail sales to consumers.
Direct wholesale sales to individual retailers. Full catalog available.

Celebrity Home Entertainment (CEL)
22025 Ventura Blvd. • Woodland Hills, CA 91365
(818) 595-0666 • (818) 716-0168 (Fax)

Celebrity is a mainstream home video supplier with a large line-up of animated family titles under its "Just For Kids" label. They have quite a repertoire of lesser-known foreign-animated movies and TV shows that have been dubbed in English. Unfortunately, they market these films as generic kids fare, neglecting to include original credits in most cases. Sometimes their catalog contains hidden gems, revealed only to those with enough knowledge of a title to detect it through the uninformative packaging. Nonetheless, their masters are generally of good quality, and they make most titles available in both SP and EP duplication.
PURCHASING INFORMATION:
No direct retail sales to consumers.
Direct wholesale sales to individual retailers. Full catalog available.

Central Park Media (CPM)

250 West 57th Street, Suite 317 • New York, NY 10107
(800) 833-7456 (Retailers) • (800) 626-4277 (Consumers)
Web Site: www.centralparkmedia.com

Video labels: Anime 18 • CPM • US Manga Corps
Other Labels Distributed: AnimEigo, Laser Disc Entertainment, The Right Stuf, U.S. Renditions, Viz Video, Pioneer, Software Sculptors.

Central Park Media is the largest single source for anime titles — releasing 200+ titles on its three in-house labels, and acting as wholesale distributor for eight other labels. CPM was founded in 1990 by John O'Donnell, former VP of Sony Video Software. CPM got into the anime business in November 1991, inaugurating its new U.S. Manga Corps video label with the release of *Dominion Tank Police*. In 1993, CPM debuted its Anime 18 adult video label with the runaway best-seller *Urotsukidoji: Legend of the Overfiend*. That same year, CPM debuted its Central Park Media art label with *Grave of the Fireflies*. Laserdisc versions of some CPM titles are licensed to Image Entertainment and Laser Disc Entertainment. CPM was the first company to target the mainstream video channels, rather than just anime fandom and comics fans. The effort has paid off handsomely, as consumers can now go to their local Blockbuster Video and find CPM best-sellers like *Dominion Tank Police*, *Gall Force*, *Project A-Ko*, *La Blue Girl* and *MD Geist*. Central Park Media now handles the duplication and marketing of the *8th Man* videotapes from Video Rarities. Merchandising programs & POP materials available to retailers.

PURCHASING INFORMATION:
Direct retail sales to consumers are now handled for CPM by The Right Stuf. The Manga Mania Club is a direct to the consumer mail-order source for all labels distributed by CPM, and also for some labels not distributed wholesale (Manga Entertainment). An illustrated catalog is available which includes comic books, soundtracks, screensavers, CD-ROMs, posters, and phone cards.
Direct wholesale sales to individual retailers.

CQC Pictures (CQC)

405 East Wetmore Rd. #117-516 • Tucson, AZ 85705-1717
(800) 356-4386 • (520) 888-5421 • (520) 690-0442 Fax
(888) 542-5421 Toll Free Kizuna Line

PURCHASING INFORMATION:
No direct retail sales to consumers.
Wholesale sales to individual retailers.

DIC Toon Time Video (DIC)

A subsidiary of The Walt Disney Comapny
Distributed through Buena Vista Home Video
350 South Buena Vista Street • Burbank, CA 91521
(818) 295-5200 (Buena Vista Home Video)
(818) 955-5400 (DIC Entertainment)
Web Site: http://www.disney.com

DIC Entertainment has been in the business of producing TV animation for many years. Recently, they have been licensing other programming and distributing it for TV syndication, including the domestic version of the *Sailor Moon* TV series. DIC has released three volumes of *Sailor Moon* on their home video label, which is distributed exclusively through Buena Vista Home Video. So far, these tapes are sold only through mass merchants like Toys R Us.

PURCHASING INFORMATION:
No direct retail sales to consumers.
Wholesale sales to individual retailers through mainstream video distributors like Ingram and Major Video Concepts.

Family Home Entertainment (FHE)

15400 Sherman Way • PO Box 10124 • Van Nuys, CA 91410-0124
(818) 908-0303

Family Home Entertainment is the "family" label of Live Home Video, carried by all the mainstream video distributors. FHE puts out hundreds of titles each year, and occasionally some of them are Japanese animation. FHE is best known among anime fans for its fitful history of releasing *Robotech* on home video. Not too long after *Robotech* aired on television, FHE picked up the rights and made the series available on home video in the late '80s. The problems were many: they first released some individual

episodes—one per tape; then they released the *Macross* episodes four on a tape—but edited and in EP mode; then their rights expired and Streamline Pictures picked up the series. Streamline began releasing a few episodes at a time; then FHE got interested again and releases were put on hold; then FHE entered a distribution agreement with Streamline . At some point in here, Palladium Books was also releasing *Robotech New Generation* on video, but that's another story. *Finally*, in the fall of 1993, FHE released the first 20 episodes of *Robotech*—all at once, in SP, uncut, and even on laserdisc! They followed up by releasing the second 20 episodes in January '94, and the balance of the series by June '94. FHE has also released some original *Speed Racer* episodes (another story of fits and starts), and even the *Hello Kitty* series. Laserdisc versions of *Robotech* and *Speed Racer* are licensed to, and distributed exclusively through Pioneer Laserdisc.

PURCHASING INFORMATION:
No direct retail sales to consumers.
Wholesale sales to individual retailers through video wholesalers like Ingram and Baker & Taylor.

Fox Home Video (CFX)

PO Box 900 • Beverly Hills, CA 90213
(213) 236-1336 (Voice) • (213) 236-1346 (Fax)

Fox Home Video is the home video arm of Twentieth Century Fox, carried by all the mainstream video distributors. Recently they enjoyed fair success with Hayao Miyazaki's feature film *My Neighbor Totoro*. In 1995 they have had runaway best-sellers in their domestic releases of Nick Park's two *Wallace and Gromit* shorts. They also manufacture and distribute laserdisc versions of the aforementioned programs.

PURCHASING INFORMATION:
No direct retail sales to consumers.
Wholesale sales to individual retailers via video wholesalers like Ingram and Baker & Taylor.

Image Entertainment (ID)

9333 Oso Ave. • Chatsworth, CA 91311
(800) 473-3475 (Voice) • (818) 407-9111 (Fax)

Image Entertainment is one of the largest laserdisc suppliers in the country. They license titles from dozens of companies and handle the duplication and distribution themselves. They generally have an excellent in-stock inventory, and act as distributor for other laserdisc suppliers as well. They carry most anime titles, with the notable exception of Pioneer. Central Park Media and Streamline Pictures license their titles on laserdisc exclusively through Image.

PURCHASING INFORMATION:
No direct retail sales to consumers.
Direct wholesale sales to individual retailers. Monthly preview magazine available.

Lumivision (LUM)

977 Federal Blvd. • Denver, CO 80204
(800) 776-5864 (Voice) • (303) 446-0101 (Fax)

Lumivision is a special-interest laserdisc supplier that has licensed laserdisc versions of some anime programs from Streamline Pictures, The Right Stuf, and Viz Video. They are prone to order small pressings of their titles, so consumers are advised to jump on their new releases without delay. Retailers are advised to pre-book coming titles, as the number of pre-book orders determines the size and timing of their pressings. Lumivision's best-selling anime titles have been *Vampire Hunter D*, *Lensman*, *3 x 3 Eyes*, and *Nadia*. Lumivision discs are distributed by most major laserdisc outlets and wholesalers.

PURCHASING INFORMATION:
Direct retail sales to consumers. Consumer catalog available.
Direct wholesale sales to individual retailers. Catalog available.

Manga Video (MGV)

727 N. Hudson St., Suite 100 • Chicago, IL 60610
(312) 751-0020 • (312) 751-2483 (Fax)
Web site: www.manga.com/manga

Manga Video comes to the U.S. from England, where it grew out of Island Records and Pictures, which released the first anime title in the U.K., *Legend (Fist) of the North Star*. After buying up L.A. Hero (previously distributed by U.S. Renditions) its first releases in February '95 were a dubbed version of *Appleseed* and *Macross Plus*. Manga Video is something of a johnny-come-lately compared to AnimEigo or Streamline, but they have a very full slate of releases, a lot of marketing muscle, and they even co-financed the production of *Ghost in the Shell*. The marketing muscle of PolyGram (Manga Video's distributor) and Orion (Streamline's distributor) has led the transition from high-priced titles aimed at a small but fanatical fan market to affordable titles aimed at a mainstream mass market. Manga titles are distributed in the U.S. by PolyGram Video, available through all major video wholesalers.

PURCHASING INFORMATION:
No direct retail sales to consumers.
Wholesale sales to individual retailers via video wholesalers like Ingram and Baker & Taylor. Monthly new release flyers available.

Palm Beach Entertainment (PBE)

P.O. Box 7032 • Edison, NJ 08818-7032
(908) 225-8896 • (908) 225-8268 (Fax)

Palm Beach Entertainment markets the *Leo The Lion* TV series. And talk about your aggressive pricing, how about $7.95 suggested retail for Standard Play cassettes? Unfortunately, PBE titles are not handled by many wholesale distributors.

PURCHASING INFORMATION:
No direct retail sales to consumers.
Direct wholesale sales to individual retailers.

Parade Video (PRV)

Distributed by Peter Pan Industries, Inc.
88 St. Francis Street • Newark, NJ 07105
(201) 344-4214 • (201) 344-0465 (Fax)

Parade Video is a special-interest "budget" video supplier, specializing in fitness tapes, public-domain cartoons, and some licensed titles. As far as anime goes, they offer a five-tape lineup of the *Force Five* TV series (*Grandizer, Gaiking, Dangard Ace, Spaceketeers* and *Starvengers*). The tapes are duplicated in EP mode, from pretty "sad-looking" masters. Parade titles are handled by some major distributors, but can be difficult to find.

PURCHASING INFORMATION:
No direct retail sales to consumers.
Direct wholesale sales to individual retailers. Catalog available.

Pioneer Animation (PI)

P.O. Box 22782 • 2265 E. 220th Street • Long Beach, CA 90801
(800) 421-1621 • (310) 952-2791 (Fax)
E-mail: panime@primenet.com
Web site: www.pioneer-ent.com/

Pioneer is the only Japanese company with a direct presence in the U.S. anime home-video scene. They have been involved with domestic distribution of laserdiscs since the first players arrived on the consumer electronics scene in the 1980s. Pioneer has a long-standing reputation for inscrutable marketing priorities, with their title releases being somewhat fragmented and irregular. In 1994 they joined the domestic anime release party by forming an animation division, and releasing the *Tenchi Muyo!* series in simultaneous dubbed, subtitled, and multi-audio laserdisc versions—all at aggressive price points. Without question, Pioneer anime titles are of the highest quality, and the programs are interesting and diverse. Ironically (considering the powerhouse parent company), their distribution can be off-and-on, and their titles can sometimes be difficult to find through mainstream video distribution channels. Pioneer also handles pressing and distribution of FHE laserdisc titles, and has offered a commendable laserdisc-only series of anime "art" films.

PURCHASING INFORMATION:
No direct retail sales to consumers, but there is a Pioneer Animation Club that offers a newsletter and allows you to redeem "proof of purchase" coupons for anime merchandise.
Wholesale sales to individual retailers via video wholesalers like Ingram, Baker & Taylor and US Laser Distributors. Irregular new release flyers available.

The Right Stuf International (RS)

P.O. Box 71309 • Des Moines, IA 50325-1309
(800) 338-6827 (Consumer orders) • (515) 279-7434 (Fax)
Web site: www.centsys.com

The Right Stuf was founded in 1987 by Todd Ferson. Their first releases were a series of *Astro Boy* episodes in early 1990. The company is one of the early fan-oriented anime suppliers, concentrating on nostalgia shows like *Astro Boy* and *Gigantor*, with occasional releases like *Legend of the Forest* and *Toward the Terra*. Right Stuf is also the exclusive distributor of titles by Critical Mass. The Right Stuf has become a major consumer direct-mail source for anime titles from most of the major suppliers, and offers lots of licensed anime accessories. RS titles are carried by most major video wholesalers.

PURCHASING INFORMATION:
Direct retail sales to consumers. Extensive consumer catalog available, with titles from all major anime suppliers.
Direct wholesale sales to individual retailers.

Sony Music Video (Sony Wonder) (SMV)

550 Madison Avenue, Suite 1756 • New York, NY 10022
(800) 336-0248 • (212) 833-7726 Fax
Web Site: http://www.sony.com

Sony Music Video started out by marketing (what else?) music videos. They later formed a general animation/kids subsidiary label called Sony Wonder, and marketed some of the animated programming from MTV (*Beavis and Butt-Head, Ren & Stimpy, Aeon Flux*) under the new label. Their anime offering consists of the *Street Fighter II Movie* on yet another label, Renegade Home Video.

PURCHASING INFORMATION:
No direct retail sales to consumers.
Direct wholesale sales to individual retailers through video wholesalers like Ingram or Baker & Taylor.

Software Sculptors (SS)

149 Madison Avenue, Suite 202 • New York, NY 10016
(212) 245-9559 • (212) 245-7579 (Fax)
Web site: www.software-sculptors.com/

Software Sculptors began by marketing anime screensavers and CD-ROM titles for personal computers. In 1995 they released their first home video titles, beginning with the *Metal Fighters Miku* series. Their computer and home video titles are carried by some wholesale distributors.

PURCHASING INFORMATION:
Direct retail sales to consumers. Catalog available.
Direct wholesale sales to individual retailers. Catalog available

Star Anime Enterprises (SAE)

PO Box 119 • Sea Cliff, NY 11579-0119
(516) 674-3125

Star Anime Enterprises was founded by anime fan David Norell. The company's first, and to date only, video release was the two-part *Homeroom Affairs*— an adult sex comedy. SAE is very concerned with presenting anime properly (i.e. subtitled). Only two titles so far. SAE titles are distributed by most major anime wholesale companies.

PURCHASING INFORMATION:
Direct retail sales to consumers.
Direct wholesale sales to individual retailers.

Starmaker Video (STM)

151 Industrial Way East • Eatontown, NJ 07724
(800) 786-8777 • (908) 389-1020 • (908) 389-1021 Fax

Starmaker is a well-established video supplier, specializing in special-interest titles. They have distributed a few anime feature films from time to time. Until the end of 1996, they had the home video rights to *Warriors of the Wind* The company recently changed its name to Anchor Bay Entertainment.

PURCHASING INFORMATION:
No direct retail sales to consumers.
Direct wholesale sales to individual retailers.

Streamline Pictures (SPV)

2908 Nebraska Avenue • Santa Monica, CA 90404
(310) 998-0070 • (310) 998-1145 (Fax)
Web site: www.streamlinepic.com

Streamline Pictures was formed in 1988 by Jerry Beck and *Robotech* creator Carl Macek. Streamline released *Akira* theatrically in 1989 and on home video in 1990, and went on to release a multitude of (mostly dubbed) anime titles throughout the early '90s. Of late, Streamline has become active in ancillary merchandise like high-quality model kits. They signed distribution arrangements for many of their titles with other distributors, most notably a large number of titles to Orion Home Video in 1994. Presently, the bulk of SPV titles are available at wholesale only from Orion, which has wide distribution through video wholesaling channels. Carl Macek has lately been concentrating more on bringing original anime programs to the airwaves, and there has been a dramatic drop in their home video releases.

PURCHASING INFORMATION:
Direct retail sales to consumers. Consumer catalog available with videos, original cels, CDs, model kits and posters.
Wholesale sales to individual retailers are handled through Orion Home Video, available through all mainstream video wholesalers. A few titles (including the *Robotech Perfect Collections*) are still sold direct to retailers by Streamline.

Tyndale Family Video (TFV)

P.O. Box 80 • Wheaton, IL 60189-0080
(708) 668-8300 • (708) 668-9092 Fax

Tyndale Family Video is the home video arm of Tyndale House Publishers, a Christian book and video publisher. They distribute the *SuperBook* series, and, until recently, the *Flying House* series as well.

PURCHASING INFORMATION:
No retail sales to consumers.
Direct wholesale sales to individual retailers. Catalog available.

United American Video (UAV)

P.O. Box 7647 • Charlotte, NC 28241
(803) 548-7300 • (803) 548-2493 Fax

UAV is a well-established "budget" video supplier. Their focus is on EP (extended play) special interest titles. In 1995, they acquired a newly-translated version of the *Kimba* series.

PURCHASING INFORMATION:
No retail sales to consumers.
Direct wholesale sales to individual retailers.

U.S. Renditions (USR)

1123 Dominguez Street, Suite K • Carson, CA 90746
(310) 604-9701 (Voice) • (310) 604-1134 (Fax)

Video labels: U.S. Renditions • Dark Image Entertainment (DIE) • Ultra Action Video (UAV)

U.S. Renditions is the home video arm of Books Nippan, the U.S. subsidiary of Nippon Shuppan Hanbai, Inc. They were among the first U.S. companies to jump into domestic anime home video distribution, gearing their releases toward the fan market. Their first releases in 1990 were the subtitled *Dangaio* and *Gunbuster*, translated by L.A. Hero. They later added the Dark Image Entertainment label for more adult anime programs, and the Ultra Action Video label for live-action *sentai* programs. Of late, the company's output of home video titles has slowed to a trickle, perhaps due in part to the acquisition of L.A. Hero by Manga Entertainment—thereby removing their main source of programming. Parent company Books Nippan now acts as a major wholesaler supplier of nearly all domestic anime labels.

PURCHASING INFORMATION:
Direct retail sales to consumers. Consumer catalog available .
Direct wholesale sales to individual retailers. Catalog available.

Video Treasures (VT)

500 Kirts Boulevard • Troy, MI 48084
(800) 786-8777 • (313) 362-0995 • (313) 362-4454 Fax

Video Treasures is a "budget" video supplier with a large collection of second-tier animated programs (at one time, they had the entire *Terrytoons Good Guys Hour* series). They have been distributing *Samurai Pizza Cats*

for several years, long before Saban was able to get it on the air in the U.S.

PURCHASING INFORMATION:
No direct retail sales to consumers.
Direct wholesale sales to individual retailers.

Vidmark Entertainment (VMM)

2644 30th Street • Santa Monica, CA 90405
(800) 424-7070 • (310) 452-9614 Fax
Vidmark is a "budget" video supplier with a good reputation for quality. Their Kidmark line of children's videos recently began distributing home video compilations of the *Dragon Ball* TV series that began airing in North America in 1995.

PURCHASING INFORMATION:
No direct retail sales to consumers.
Direct wholesale sales to individual retailers.

Viz Video (VV)

A Subsidiary of Viz Comunications, Inc.
P.O. Box 77010 • San Francisco, CA 94107
(800) 394-3042 (Toll-Free Ordering) • (415) 546-7086 (Fax)
Editorial E-mail: viz@netcom.com
Web site: http://www.viz.com

Viz Video is the home video arm of Viz Communications, the American subsidiary of Shogakukan, one of Japan's largest publishers. Now celebrating its eleven-year anniversary as the country's leading publisher of manga in translation, Viz got into the home video game in November '93 with their release of *Ranma 1/2* and *Mermaid's Scar*. Viz anime releases are not as prolific as Central Park Media or many others, but their commitment to high-quality English renditions has earned the respect of notoriously dub-hating hardcore anime fans. Viz Video is also distributed by several major anime wholesale suppliers.

PURCHASING INFORMATION:
Direct retail sales to consumers via Viz Shop-By-Mail. Consumer catalog available. Now offering select Manga Video, Pioneer and U.S. Manga titles.
Direct wholesale sales to individual retailers. Catalog available.

The Voyager Company (VOY)

One Bridge Street • Irvington, NY 10533
(914) 591-5500 • (914) 591-6481 (Fax)

The Voyager Company is a specialty laserdisc supplier best known for their high-priced videophile line known as the Criterion Collection. Voyager releases are typically CAV multi-disc sets, and often run in the $100-$200 range. Their only anime title to date is the special 3-disc Criterion widescreen edition of *Akira*.

PURCHASING INFORMATION:
Direct retail sales to consumers. Consumer catalog available.
Direct wholesale sales to individual retailers. Catalog available.

Voyager Entertainment, Inc. (VEI)

456 Sylvan Avenue • Englewood Cliffs, NJ 07632
(800) 704-4040 (Consumers only) • (201) 569-0887 • (201) 569-2998 (Fax)

Voyager Entertainment has released the entire *Star Blazers* TV series, as well as all of the original *Yamato* theatrical movies. The company is very friendly to the fan base it serves, and sponsors the Star Blazers/Space Battleship Yamato Fan Force, a 500+ member fan club. Voyager videos are distributed through a number of wholesale channels, but some of the special collections and boxed sets are available only direct from the company.

PURCHASING INFORMATION:
Direct retail sales to consumers. Consumer catalog and fan club.
Direct wholesale sales to individual retailers. Catalog available.

Retail Businesses

The following is a partial listing of companies that sell imported and domestic anime video and audio software, manga and miscellaneous related merchandise through walk-in retail and/or mail order direct to the consumer.

A.D. Vision

Southwest Plaza Building
5750 Bintliff #217
Houston, TX 77036-2123
(713) 977-9181
[A.D. Vision videotapes and laserdiscs, certain licensed merchandise, "Fanime" magazine]

Animania!

2570 Ocean Avenue, Suite 282
San Francisco, CA 94132
(415) 759-1173
E-mail: animania@hooked.net
Hours: M-Sat: 10-6
[Laserdiscs, graphic novels and promotional items. Mail order only]

Animated Collectibles

250 West 57th Street, Suite 325
New York, NY 10107
(212) 977-7456 x242
(212) 977-8709 Fax
[This division of Central Park Media sells production cels from *Genocyber*, *Iria*, and others]

Anime Crash

13 East 4th Street
New York, NY 10003
(888) GOANIME
(212) 254-4670
(212) 254-4730 - Fax
Hours: M-Thu: 11-10, F-Sat: 11-11, Sun: 12-7
Web Site: http://www.animecrash.com
[Anime & Hong Kong cinema; big selection of tapes, LDs, imports, CDs, toys, mags, models, books, merchandise]

Anime Direct

1925 E. Dominguez St.
Long Beach, CA 90810
(800) 801-3472
(310) 952-3000 Fax
Web Site: www.lvd.com
[A division of Pioneer's laserdisc fan club. Videos, LDs, CDs, imports]

Anime Dojo

342 N. Mohawk St.
Cohoes, NY 12047
(888) 264-6348
(518) 238-0543 Fax
Web Site: www.animedojo.com/
E-mail: animedojo@magicsource.com
[Domestic videos, LDs, CDs, merchandise]

Anime Plus

8937 Reseda Blvd.
Northridge, CA 91324
(818) 773-7371
(818) 773-7372 Fax
Web Site: www.animeplus.com
[music CDs, videos, garage kits, merchandise]

Anime Wink

2959 S. Sepulveda Blvd.
Los Angeles, CA 90064
(310) 996-8823
(310) 996-8822 - Fax
M-F: 9 - 6
[Anime cels, posters, art books. Mail-orders welcome.]

Anime World

PO Box 342
Fremont CA 94537-0342
Web Site: http://www.anime-world.com
[Garage Kits & Models]

AnimEigo

PO Box 989
Wilmington, NC 28402-0989
(910) 251-1850
(910) 763-2376 - Fax
Web Site: http://www.animeigo.com
[AnimEigo videotapes and laserdiscs, shirts, hats, linens, posters, anime cels, screen savers, audio CDs]

Art Toons

PO Box 600
Northfield, OH 44067
(216) 468-2655
(216) 468-2655 - Fax
E-mail: ergezi@smtpnov.picker.com
[Anime cels]

Asahiya Bookstores U.S.A., Inc

Yaohan Plaza
333 S. Alameda St. Suite 108
Los Angeles, CA 90013
(213) 626-5650
(213) 626-1746 - Fax
[Manga and various anime magazines, books, posters, calendars, and CDs.]

Asahiya Bookstores U.S.A., Inc

100 E. Algonquin Rd.
Arlington Heights, IL 60005
(708) 956-6699
[Manga and various anime magazines, books, posters, calendars, and CDs.]

Asylum Comics

812 N. Broadway
Pittsburg, KS 66762
(316) 231-0922
[anime videos, CDs, model kits, manga, toys etc.]

Banzai Anime

2961 Sepulveda Boulevard
West Los Angeles, CA 90064
(310) 231-6080
(310) 213-6082 - Fax
Web Site: http://www.clever.net/banzai
[Anime videos, LDs, anime CDs, video games, soundtracks,toys, models, art books, manga, t-shirts, cards, posters. 20% discount to C/FO members.]

Books Nippan

605 West 7th Street
Los Angeles, CA 90017
E-mail: nippan@netcom.com
(213) 891-9636 or (800) 427-6100
(213) 891-9631 - Fax
Hours: M-F 10-7; Sat. 11-5; Closed Sun.
[Manga and various anime magazines, books, posters, calendars, and CDs. 20% discount to Fan Club members]

Books Nippan

1123 Dominguez Street, Unit K
Carson, CA 90746
(213) 604-9702
Web Site: http://club.nttca.com/nippan/
[Large selection of anime & manga merchandise. Most domestic anime video releases. 15% discount to Fan Club members]

Bud Plant Comic Art

PO Box 1689
Grass Valley, CA 95945
(800) 242-6642
[Back issues of English-translated manga. Small selection of anime/manga books and videos.]

Central Park Media

250 West 57th Street, Suite 317
New York, NY 10107
(800) 626-4277
[Manga Mania Club sells almost all domestic anime videos, manga, soundtracks, screen savers, CD-ROMs, posters, phone cards. 26-page consumer catalog available.]

Comic Planet

1950 E. Greyhound Pass #18-339
Carmel, IN 16033-7730
[anime posters, books, toys, action figures, etc.]

Event Horizon

203 Blue Ridge Drive
Old Hickory, TN 37138
[Primarily *Gundam* kits but has some *Macross*, *Orguss*, etc. as well as gaming supplies and figures. Catalog available.]

Fantasy Animation

Box 126
Marlboro, NJ 07746
(800) 863-7775
[Anime cels]

Formosa Inc. DBA Anime Market

PO Box 8126
Fort Wayne, IN 46898-8126
E-mail: thwang@mentor.cc.purdue.edu
Web Site: http://205.216.9.101/initial2.htm
[Domestically available anime at nicely discounted prices. Free catalog available.]

Galactic Trade Commission

10185 Switzer
Overland Park, KS 66212
(913) 492-2169
[One of the largest sources of plastic injection anime kits. No "garage kits." Limited stock of some kits makes some of them very, very expensive. Big catalog (12 pages at least) is $3.00]

Golden Age Collectables

1501 Pike Place Market
401 Lower Level
Seattle, WA 98101
[*Gundam*, *Aura Battler*, and a few other series kits, plus a large variety of publications. No catalog, but may be able to special order.]

Hakubundo

100 N. Beretania St.
Honolulu, HI 96817
(808) 521-3805

Hobbies

2370 Plank Road
Fredericksburg, VA 22401
(800) 241-3491
[Models, domestic videos, games, t-shirts, posters]

Horizon

912 E. 3rd Street, Suite 101
Los Angeles, CA 90013
[Models]

House of Anime

1500 Pleasant Hill Rd. #115
Duluth, GA 30136
(770) 923-2498
Web site: www.mindspring.com/~house-a
[Garage kits, soundtracks, t-shirts, free catalog]

Image Trading

68-05 Fresh Meadows Lane
Fresh Meadows, NY 11365
(718) 358-3823
(718) 358-1356 Fax
[CDs, models, garage kits, books]

Inteleg International

821 Aubrey Ave
Ardmore PA 19003
(215) 896-8177
(215) 896-1745 - Fax
[The official representative of Max Factory in the United States, stocking the full line of Max Factory products. Catalog available for SASE.]

International Disc

1125 E. Morehead St. #204
Charlotte, NC 28204
(800) 280-2990
(704) 372-0888
[imported anime LDs, videotapes, soundtracks]

IPC's Animation Company

19806 N. 4th St. #63
Phoenix, AZ 85024
(602) 581-0125
[Anime cels. Catalog available.]

Iwase Books, Honolulu

2332 Young St.
Honolulu, HI 96826
(808) 942-4949
[Manga, magazines, books, posters, CDs, calendars, video rentals.]

Iwase Books, Atlanta

3400 Woodale Dr., Unit C-510
Atlanta, GA 30326
(404) 814-0462
(404) 814-0561 Fax
[Manga and various anime magazines, books, posters, calendars, and CDs.]

Jamano

4600 Bessbourough
Montreal, Quebec H4B 2P1
Canada
(514) 482-8688
[Models. $1Can. for catalog.]

JAM Inc

Route 1, Box 742
Brogue, PA 17309
(800) 851-8309
(717) 927-9787
(717) 927-6538 - Fax
[Models, supplies, and discounted videos.]

Kimono My House

1424 62nd Street (at Hollis)
Emeryville, CA 94608
(510) 654-4627
Web Site: http://www.slip.net/~kimono
[Anime paraphernalia. Also an exclusive line of anime t-shirts.]

Kinokuniya Bookstore

665 Paularino Drive
Costa Mesa, CA 92626
(714) 434-9986
[Manga and various anime magazines, books, posters, calendars, and CDs.]

Kinokuniya Bookstore

Japan Center
1581 Webster St.
San Francisco, CA 94115
(415) 567-7625
[Manga and various anime magazines, books, posters, calendars, and CDs.]

Kinokuniya Bookstore

675 Saratoga Ave.
San Jose, CA 95129
(408) 252 1300
[Manga and various anime magazines, books, posters, calendars, and CDs.]

Kinokuniya Bookstore

(Los Angeles - Weller Court)
123 South Onizuka Street, Suite 205
Los Angeles, CA 90012
(213) 687-4447
[Manga and various anime magazines, books, posters, calendars, and CDs.]

Kinokuniya Bookstore

595 River Road,
Edgewater, NJ
(201) 941 7580
[Manga and various anime magazines, books, posters, calendars, and CDs.]

Kinokuniya Bookstore

10 West 49th Street,
New York, NY
(212) 745-1461/1462
[Manga and various anime magazines, books, posters, calendars, and CDs.]

Kinokuniya Bookstore

519 Sixth Street South
Seattle, WA
(206) 587-2477
[Manga and various anime magazines, books, posters, calendars, and CDs.]

Laser Craze

33 West Street
Boston, MA 02111
(800) 888-6086 - Orders Only
(617) 338-9820 - Questions
(617) 338-8098 - Fax
[Domestic & imported laserdiscs]

Laser Disc San Francisco

2415 Noriega Street
San Francisco, CA 94122
(415) 661-3218
[Laserdiscs, compact discs, videos, models, garage kits, and other animation products.]

Laser Perceptions

1739 Noriega Street
San Francisco, CA 94122
(415) 753-2016
E-mail: lasers@laserperceptions.com
Web Site: http://www.laserperceptions.com
[Domestic & imported laserdiscs.]

Lumivision

977 Federal Blvd.
Denver, CO 80204
(800) 776-5864
[Lumivision laserdiscs. Catalog available.]

Mikado

Japan Center, Kintetsu Building
1737 Post Street
San Francisco, CA 94115-3698
(415) 922-9450
[Japanese laserdiscs.]

Miniatures and Models

c/o Lee Cushing
6184 San Juan St.
Forest Park, GA 30050
[A variety of anime kits and publications. Catalog available.]

Musashi Enterprises

Keith Johnson
2613 S. 30th Street
Milwaukee, WI 53215
(414) 383-7791
[toys, model kits, manga, cels, search service]

NewType Toys & Hobbies

1531 10th Avenue (at Kirkham)
San Francisco, CA 94122
(415) 731-3077
[Model kits. LOTS of model kits. A catalog is
available for $2.00.]

Nichibei Anime Club

P.O. Box 12783
La Jolla, CA 92039-2783
(619) 558-8978
E-mail: cels@nichibeianime.com
Web Site: http://www.nichibeianime.com/
nichibhei
[Specializes in original animation cels and
drawings. Also carries rare toys, books, and
anime goods. Free e-mail catalog available.]

Nikaku Animart

615 N. 6th St.
San Jose, CA 95112
(408) 971-2822
E-mail: nikaku@netcom.com
Web Site: http://www.nikaku.com
[Manga, posters, CDs, laserdiscs, videotapes,
stickers, anime magazines, etc.]

Outer Limits

433 Piaget Ave. (Rte. 46 East)
Clifton, NJ 07013
(201) 340-9393
(201) 340-8885 fax
[Model kits, merchandise, videos, phone orders]

Paradigm Enterprises

2438 Durant Avenue
Berkeley, CA 94704
(510) 649-5954
(800) 790-7273
E-mail: anime@paradigm-ent.com
www: http://www.paradigm-ent.com/
[Compact discs, videos, t-shirts and toys.]

Planet Anime

2439 Times Blvd.
Houston, TX 77005
(713) 523-7122
(713) 523-3574 Fax
Web Site: www.neosoft.com/planet
[Videos, LDs, CDs, models, toys, t-shirts, cels,
posters, books, manga. Catalog available]

Psycho 5

12513 Lake City Way
Seattle, WA 98125
[*Gundam, Aura Battler*, a few *Macross*, and
publications. No catalog, but can special order
some items.]

The Right Stuf

PO Box 71309
Des Moines, IA 50325-1309
(800) 338-6827
Web Site:http://www.dwx.com/~centsys/
[Most domestic anime videos, licensed merchan-
dise, anime cels.]

Rising Sun Creations

142 Plaza Dr.
West Covina, CA 91790
(818) 337-7433
[Imported model kits, toys, cards, videos, mdse]

Sakura Japanese Bookstore

Maryland
(301) 468-0605
[Manga and various anime magazines, books,
posters, calendars, and CDs.]

Science Fiction Continuum

A division of S&J Productions, Inc.
P.O. Box 154
Colonia, NJ 07067
(800) 232-6002
[Domestically available anime & SF videos.]

Sight & Sound

27 Jones Road
Waltham, MA 02154
(617) 894-8633
Web Site: http://www.tiac.net/users/amadeus/
sslaser
[Domestic & imported laserdiscs.]

Software Sculptors

149 Madison Ave, Suite 202
New York, NY 10016
(212) 679-1171
[SS videotapes, screensavers, CD-ROMs]

Sounds Of Anime

4075 E. Holt Road Lot 19
Holt, MI 48842
(517) 694-5845
[Anime CDs, playing cards, wall scrolls, *Gundam*
toys. Has the ability to get many other products.]

Streamline Pictures

2908 Nebraska Avenue
Santa Monica, CA 90404
(310) 998-0070
[Mail-order sales of all Streamline anime videos,
CDs, theatrical posters, original anime production
cels, Streamline Modelworks resin model kits
(*Guy, Robot Carnival*, others). Free catalog.]

Studio M

247-19th Ave #6
San Francisco, CA 94121-2353
[Current & back issues of Studio Proteus
translated manga (Eclipse, Dark Horse &
Innovation).]

Super Collector

16547 Brookhurst St.
Fountain Valley, CA 92708
(714) 839-3693
(714) 839-8263 Fax
[anime tapes, LDs, soundtracks, toys, model kits,
books, magazines]

Swandive Software

5110 E. Placita Cumpas
Tucson, AZ 85718
[Domestically available anime & SF videos.
Discount prices.]

Tec Sales

P.O. Box 746
Millburn, NJ 07078
(800) 446-7775
(201) 467-1799 - Fax
[Anime videos by mail.]

Tokyo Do Shoten

18924 Brookhurst Street
Fountain Valley, CA 92708
(714) 968-9182
[Manga and anime magazines, books, posters,
calendars, and CDs.]

Tuskins

14235 Lambert Rd.
Whittier, CA 90605 USA
(213) 728-2785
E-mail: tuskins@ix.netcom.com
[Anime-related and all video games for Sony
PSX,Saturn,SFCOM,MD *Sailor-moon, Dragonball
Z,Gundam, Ranma*...and toys.]

UCI Bookstore Internet Project

(714) 824-2430
(714) 824-8545 - Fax
E-mail: anime@uci.edu or mjkiley@uci.edu
Web Site: http://www.book.uci.edu/anime.html
[Imported & Domestic Anime CDs, videos, etc]

Viz Shop By Mail

PO Box 77010
San Francisco, CA 94107
(800) 394-3042 - Toll Free Ordering
(415) 546-7086 - Fax
Worldwide Web: http://www.viz.com
[Complete line of Viz videos, Viz comics,
Animerica and *Manga Vizion* magazine back
issues. Now also offering select videos from
Manga Video, Pioneer, and U.S. Manga. Character
goods include t-shirts, embroidered logo baseball
caps, pocket organizers, cloisonné pins,
calendars, posters, screensavers, and more.
Worldwide shipping and free catalog.]

Video Online Express

5339 Prospect Road, #336
San Jose, CA 95070
(408) 364-2250
(408) 364-2251 - Fax
www: http://www.VideoExpress.com
telnet: VideoExpress.com
email: manager@VideoExpress.com
[Online video store which currently offers Anime
VHS tapes Laser Discs. Visa/MC. They have a
Netscape Secure web
server and will also accept FAXed credit card
information and even phone
orders]

Voyager Entertainment

456 Sylvan Avenue
Englewood Cliffs, NJ 07632
(800) 704-4040
[*Star Blazers* and *Yamato* videotapes.]

The Whole Toon Catalog

Facets Multimedia
1517 W. Fullerton Ave.
Chicago, IL 60614
(800) 331-6197
(773) 281-9075
(773) 929-5437 - Fax
[Mail-order catalog of animation carries every
domestic anime release. Offers rentals-by-mail,
and has a walk-in rental store]

Appendix A
Creative credits for shows discussed in this book

With its huge roster of creative talents, it should be no surprise that when it comes to bylines and credits, the Japanese animation industry is every bit as complex as the Hollywood film industry. For example, as in the case of *Star Blazers*, the titles for both Noboru Ishiguro (*enshutsu*) and Leiji Matsumoto (*kantoku*) can be translated as "director." What's a translator to do? Although the magazine *Animerica* conscientiously distinguishes Ishiguro as *Star Blazers'* "episode director" and Matsumoto as "series director," for the purposes of this book, we'll be listing directors, co-directors, episode directors and series directors interchangeably. This decision was made not because we don't appreciate the finer distinctions in directorial credit, but because of a lack of complete and accurate production information from the U.S. home video companies.

The bulk of information contained in this index is culled from the video packaging itself. It has been supplemented with credits from the TV Series chapter, credit information familiar to the authors and editor, and corrected in many cases. As discussed in the preface to this book, the romanization of Japanese names has been standardized as much as possible. Because most anime titles are part of a series, we've limited the use of this word to only those series which need to be specially distinguished (i.e. *Ranma 1/2* TV series vs. *Ranma 1/2* OAV series) or those shows which have the same name (i.e. *Orguss* vs. *Orguss 02*).

A

Abe, Hisashi .... *Dir:* Devil Hunter Yohko 2 & 3
Abe, Kunihiro .... *Anim Dir:* Armitage III; *Mecha:* Galaxy Fraulein Yuna
Abe, Yukio .... *Graphic Creation:* Keroppi Series, Hello Kitty
Adachi, Tetsu .... *Orig Work:* Weather Report Girl
Aikawa, Noboru .... *Script:* AD Police, Angel Cop, Curse of the Undead Yoma, Genocyber, Hades Project Zeorymer, The Hakkenden, Violence Jack Ep. 1
Aikawa, Sho .... *Script:* Dog Soldier
Akabori, Kanji .... *Anim Dir:* Keroppi Series, Hello Kitty
Akan, Masakazu .... *Dir:* F-3
Aketagawa, Susumu ..... *Music:* Blue Sonnet, Sohryuden
Akihiro, Masayuki .... *Dir:* Cyborg 009
Akitaka, Mika .... *Story:* Galaxy Fraulein Yuna; *Char Design:* Galaxy Fraulein Yuna
Akitsu, Toru .... *Story:* Luna Varga
Akiyama, Eiichi .... *Mecha:* Guy II
Akiyama, Katsuhito .... *Dir:* Bubblegum Crisis, BG Crisis 2: Born to Kill, BG Crisis 3: Blow Up, Gall Force, Gall Force: Earth Chapter, Rhea Gall Force, Sol Bianca; *Script:* Bubblegum Crisis 1-3
Akiyoshi, Sakai .... *Script:* Area 88
Akutsu, Junichi .... *Mecha:* Macross II
Amano, Masamichi .... *Music:* Adventure Kid, Giant Robo, Urotsuki Dôji
Amano, Wataru .... *Script:* Demon Beast Invasion Eps. 3-6
Amano, Yoshitaka .... *Char Design:* Lily C.A.T., Vampire Hunter D
Amemiya, Keita .... *Orig Work:* Iria
Amino, Tetsuro .... *Dir:* Iria; *Script:* Iria
Amiya, Masaharu .... *Script:* Blue Seed
Andrea, John .... *Music:* Street Fighter II Movie
Anno, Hideaki .... *Dir:* Aim for the Top! Gunbuster, Nadia, Neon Genesis Evangelion; *Anim Dir:* The Wings of Honneamise; *Art Dir:* Dangaio; *Mecha:* Neon Genesis Evangelion
Anno, Takashi .... *Dir:* Curse of the Undead Yoma, The Hakkenden
Anzai, Fumitaka .... *Music:* Urusei Yatsura TV series
Anzai, Tetsuo .... *Art Dir:* Dragon Century

Aoki, Tetsuro .... *Dir:* Devil Hunter Yohko; *Anim Dir:* RG Veda; *Char Design:* RG Veda
Aoki, Yuzo .... *Anim Dir:* Lupin III: Mystery of Mamo
Aoshima, Katsumi .... *Char Design:* Fire Tripper, Maris the Chôjo, One-Pound Gospel
Apapa, Mokona .... *Char Design:* RG Veda
Arai, Kazuhiro .... *Art Dir:* Hyper Doll, Dangaio, Iczer-One
Arai, Ken .... *Art Dir:* Green Legend Ran
Arai, Torao .... *Art Dir:* Tenchi in Love, Violence Jack Ep. 3, Dancougar, Fire Tripper, Guyver: Out of Control, Laughing Target, Maris the Chôjo
Araizumi, Rui .... *Story:* Slayers
Arakawa, Naruhisa .... *Script:* Iria
Araki, Hirohiko .... *Orig Work:* Baoh
Aramaki, Nobuyuki .... *Dir:* Madox-01; *Mecha:* Madox-01; *Story:* Madox-01
Aramaki, Shinji .... *Dir:* Genesis Survivor Gaiarth 1 & 2; *Mecha:* Iczer-One; *Script:* Bubblegum Crisis
Aramaki, Yoshio .... *Story:* Big Wars
Aramata, Hiroshi .... *Story:* Doomed Megalopolis
Aran, Rei .... *Story:* Iczer-One
Arisawa, Takamori .... *Music:* Sailor Moon
Asaka, Morio .... *Dir:* Mermaid's Scar, Phantom Quest Corp.
Asakura, Chitose .... *Art Dir:* Tenchi TV Series
Asamiya, Kia .... *Story:* Silent Möbius
Ashida, Toyo'o .... *Dir:* Fist of the North Star, Vampire Hunter D; *Char Design:* Crystal Triangle
Azami, Toshio .... *Planning:* Dragon Half
Azuma, Junichi .... *Art Dir:* Gall Force, Project A-Ko 2, 4

B

Bessho, Makoto .... *Anim Dir:* Genesis Survivor Gaiarth
Betsuyaku, Mijoru .... *Script:* Night on the Galactic R.R.
Buronson & Hara, Tetsuo   *Orig Work:* Fist of the North Star

C

Chigara, Koichi .... *Dir:* Phantom Quest Corp.
Chikanaga, Sanae .... *Char Design:* Countdown
Chiku, Owaya .... *Script:* Lupin III: Legend of the Gold of Babylon

Chimi, Morio .... *Story:* Hades Project Zeorymer
Cho, Kisei .... *Script:* Wicked City
Clamp .... *Orig Work:* RG Veda, Tokyo Babylon

D

Dezaki, Osamu .... *Dir:* The Professional: Golgo 13, One Pound Gospel
Dezaki, Satoshi .... *Dir:* Mad Bull
Dokite, Tsukasa .... *Char Design:* Dirty Pair

E

Ebata, Hiroyuki .... *Dir:* Dog Soldier
Egawa, Tatsuya .... *Orig Work:* Golden Boy
Eguchi, Hisashi .... *Char Design:* Roujin Z
Eguchi, Marisuke .... *Anim Dir:* Night on the Galactic R.R.
Emu, Arii .... *Script:* Bubblegum Crisis, Bubblegum Crash, Genocyber, Iczer 3
Endo, Akinori .... *Script:* 3x3 Eyes, Battle Angel, Cyber City Oedo 808, Doomed Megalopolis
Endo, Takuji .... *Dir:* Phantom Quest Corp.
Etsutomo, Hiroyuki .... *Anim Dir:* Dragon Century; *Char Design:* Dragon Century
Ezura, Hisashi .... *Char Design:* Demon Beast 3, 4

F

Fisher, Morgan .... *Music:* Twilight of the Cockroaches
Franke, Christopher ...... *Music:* Tenchi in Love
FujI, Mineo .... *Dir:* Flying House
Fujii, Wataru .... *Dir:* Dragon Pink
Fujikawa, Keisuke .... *Story:* Dancougar
Fujimoto, Yoshitaka .... *Dir:* Adventure Kid; *Anim. Dir:* Gall Force New Era
Fujishima, Kosuke .... *Orig Work:* Oh My Goddess!, You're Under Arrest
Fujita, Isaku .... *Music:* Robot Carnival
Fujiyama, Fusanobu ...... *Music:* Princess Minerva
Fukimoto, Kiyoshi .... *Dir:* Dragon Century
Fukuda, Jun .... *Dir:* Demon Beast Invasion 1,2,5 & 6, Dragon Knight
Fukuda, Kazuya .... *Art Dir:* Sohryuden
Fukuhara, Yuichi .... *Art Dir:* Marine Boy
Fukumoto, Kan .... *Dir:* La Blue Girl 3,5 & 6, Twin Dolls I & II
Fukuoka, Hajime .... *Char. Design:* Flying House

Kato, Hiroshi .... *Art Dir:* Neon Genesis Evangelion, Oh My Goddess!, Sanctuary
Kato, Michiaki .... *Music:* Big Wars, Dragon Century
Kato, Yoshio .... *Dir:* Ogre Slayer
Katoki, Hajime .... *Mecha:* Galaxy Fraulein Yuna, Patlabor 2
Katsumata, Geki .... *Art Dir:* Demon Beast Invasion 5 & 6, Odin: Photon Space Sailer Starlight, Planet Busters, Violence Jack Ep. 2
Katsumata, Hagemu .... *Art Dir:* The Humanoid
Katsumata, Tomoharu ... *Dir:* Arcadia of My Youth
Katsumata, Toru .... *Art Dir:* Windaria
Katsura, Masakazu .... *Char Design:* Iria
Kawabata, Renji .... *Dir:* Sohryuden Ep. 5
Kawahara, Yuji .... *Script:* Project A-Ko vs. Battle 2: Blue Side
Kawai, Kenji .... *Music:* Blue Seed, Burn Up!, Devilman, Ghost in the Shell, Patlabor TV, Ranma 1/2 Anything-Goes TV Series, Mermaid Forest, Patlabor 2
Kawajiri, Yoshiaki .... *Dir:* Cyber.City Oedo 808, Demon City Shinjuku, Lensman, Neo-Tokyo ("Running Man"), Ninja Scroll, Wicked City; *Char Design:* Cyber City Oedo 808, Demon City Shinjuku, Lensman; *Story:* Neo-Tokyo ("Running Man"), Ninja Scroll; *Script:* Ninja Scroll
Kawamori, Masaharu ..... *Mecha:* Patlabor 2
Kawamori, Shoji .... *Dir:* Macross Plus; *Mecha:* Dangaio, Ghost in the Shell, Macross Plus, Patlabor 2; *Story:* Macross Plus
Kawamoto, Toshihiro .... *Anim Dir:* Golden Boy; *Char Design:* Golden Boy, Mighty Space Miners
Kawamura, Eiji .... *Music:* Hades Project Zeorymer
Kawasaki, Hiroshi .... *Dir:* Record of Lodoss War
Kawasaki, Hiroyuki .... *Script:* Homeroom Affairs
Kawasaki, Masahiro ...... *Music:* Maps
Kawasaki, Tomoko .... *Script:* Project A-Ko 1, 3-4, Project A-Ko vs. Battle 1: Grey Side
Kazado, Shinsuke .... *Music:* Urusei Yatsura TV series
Kenji, Miyazawa .... *Orig Work:* Night on the Galactic RR
Kennedy, Michael .... *Music:* 8 Man After
Kichikawa, Raizo .... *Dir:* La Blue Girl
Kihei, Ryu .... *Orig Work:* Dragon Century
Kikuchi, Hideyuki .... *Orig Work:* Vampire Hunter D, Wicked City; *Story:* Demon City Shinjuku
Kikuchi, Masanori .... *Art Dir:* Giant Robo
Kikuchi, Michitaka .... *Dir:* Silent Möbius; *Char Design:* Detonator Orgun, Hades Project Zeorymer
Kikuchi, Shunsuke .... *Music:* Force Five, Dragon Ball
Kikuchi, Yasuhito .... *Script:* Crimson Wolf
Kimori, Toshiyuki .... *Music:* Arcadia of My Youth
Kimura, Shinji .... *Art Dir:* Project A-Ko
Kimura, Tetsu .... *Script:* Phantom Quest Corp.
Kinoshita, Kazuhiro .... *Art Dir:* The Heroic Legend of Arslan
Kise, Kazuchika .... *Anim Dir:* The Heroic Legend of Arslan, Patlabor 2; *Char Design:* Blue Seed
Kise, Kazuya .... *Art Dir:* Girl From Phantasia; *Char Design:* Girl From Phantasia
Kishida, Takahiro .... *Anim Dir:* Tenchi In Love; *Art Dir:* Dragon Half
Kishima, Nobuaki .... *Script:* Super Atragon, Urotsuki Dôji IV
Kishino, Yuji .... *Script:* Orguss 02
Kishiro, Yukito .... *Orig Work:* Battle Angel
Kitakubo, Hiroyuki .... *Dir:* Black Magic M-66, Golden Boy, Robot Carnival ("A Tale of Two Robots"), Roujin Z; *Char Design:* Black Magic M-66
Kitagama, Ryo .... *Music:* Hello Kitty
Kitazume, Hiroyuki .... *Dir:* Genesis Survivor Gaiarth, Moldiver, Robot Carnival ("Starlight Angel"); *Anim Dir:* Dragon Century; *Char Design:* Genesis Survivor Gaiarth, Moldiver; *Concept:* Moldiver
Kobayashi, Dan .... *Concept:* Dangard Ace, Gaiking

Kobayashi, Katsuyoshi .. *Music:* Keroppi
Kobayashi, Makoto .... *Mecha:* Super Atragon, Planet Busters
Kobayashi, Sanae .... *Anim Dir:* Roots Search; *Char Design:* Roots Search
Kobayashi, Shichiro .... *Art Dir:* Lupin III: Castle of Cagliostro, Orguss 02, Lupin III: Fuma Conspiracy, Sohryuden
Kobayashi, Takashi .... *Dir:* Slayers Ep. 12; *Char Design:* Battle Skipper
Kobayashi, Toshiaki ...... *Dir:* Magical Twilight
Kobayashi, Toshimitsu .. *Anim Dir:* Moldiver
Kochiba, Katsuhiko .... *Script:* Burn Up W
Kodaka, Kazuma .... *Orig. Work:* Kizuna
Kodama, Takao .... *Char Design:* Night on the Galactic R.R.
Kogawa, Noriyasu .... *Dir:* Ellcia; *Script:* Ellcia
Koide, Kazumi .... *Screenplay:* Big Wars
Koike, Kazuo .... *Orig Work:* Crying Freeman, Hanappe Bazooka, Mad Bull
Kojika, Kazuo .... *Art Dir:* Barefoot Gen
Komatsubara, Kazuo ...... *Anim Dir:* Arcadia of My Youth; *Char Design:* Devilman
Komoro, Tetsuya .... *Music:* Sailor Moon
Komura, Toshiaki .... *Dir:* Magical Twilight 3
Konaka, Chiaki .... *Script:* Armitage III
Kondo, Yoshifumi .... *Char Design:* Grave of the Fireflies
Kono, Dai .... *Script:* Dominion Tank Police
Kono, Jiro .... *Art Dir:* Sohryuden
Kono, Yasutaka .... *Anim Dir:* Moldiver
Konparu, Tomoko .... *Dir:* Maris the Chôjo; *Script:* Fire Tripper, Laughing Target, Maris the Chôjo, One-Pound Gospel
Koshibi, Nobuyoshi .... *Music:* Speed Racer
Koyama, Masahiro .... *Art Dir:* Dragon Half; *Char Design:* Dragon Half
Koyama, Takao .... *Script:* Project A-Ko 2
Kubawara, Norie .... *Mecha:* Genesis Survivor Gaiarth
Kubo, Hidemi .... *Anim Dir:* Sanctuary; *Char Design:* Sanctuary
Kubo, Muneo .... *Script:* Ariel, Deluxe Ariel
Kubo'oka Toshiyuki .... *Anim Dir:* Aim for the Top! Gunbuster
Kudo, Masateru .... *Char Design:* Dog Soldier
Kudo, Tadashi .... *Art Dir:* Bounty Dog
Kudo, Takashi .... *Music:* Akai Hayate, Iczer 3, Junk Boy
Kumada, Isamu .... *Dir:* Animated Classics of Japanese Literature: Grave of the Wild Chrysanthemum
Kumagai, Mitsukuni .... *Script:* Pekkle
Kume, Masao .... *Story:* Animated Classics: Student Days
Kuni, Kawachi .... *Music:* Laughing Target
Kunimoto, Yoshihiro ...... *Music:* Dirty Pair: Affair on Nolandia
Kuri, Ippei .... *Dir:* Robotech; *Anim Dir:* Speed Racer; *Art Dir:* Speed Racer; *Concept:* Tekkaman
Kuribayashi, Kyoko .... *Script:* Pochacco
Kuroda, Kazuya .... *Anim Dir:* Tenchi in Love
Kurogane, Hiroshi .... *Art Dir:* Nadia
Kusunoki, Kei .... *Orig Work:* Ogre Slayer; *Story:* Curse of the Undead Yoma
Kuwata, Jiro .... *Concept:* 8 Man After, 8th Man; *Orig Work:* 8th Man

L

Lamdo, Mao .... *Dir:* Robot Carnival ("Clouds"); *Concept:* Robot Carnival ("Clouds")
Lerios, Cory .... *Music:* Street Fighter II Movie
Levy, Shuki .... *Music:* Samurai Pizza Cats
Lida, Fumio .... *Anim Dir:* The Wings of Honneamise
Lunchfield, Horceman ... *Story:* Mighty Space Miners

M

Maeda, Mahiro .... *Art Dir:* Nadia
Maeda, Toshio .... *Orig Work:* Adventure Kid, Demon Beast Invasion, La Blue Girl, Urotsuki Dôji
Maeshima, Kenichi .... *Char Design:* Sohryuden
Magori, Mihoko .... *Art Dir:* Night on the Galactic R.R.

Maisaka, Ko .... *Orig Work:* Princess Minerva
Makaino, Koji .... *Music:* Thunderbirds 2086
Maki, Joji .... *Script:* Demon Beast Invasion
Makino, Shigeto .... *Dir:* Record of Lodoss War
Makino, Yakihiro .... *Dir:* Legend of Lyon: Flare; *Char Design:* Guy I; *Story:* Angel of Darkness
Makura, Saki .... *Dir:* One-Pound Gospel
Manabe, Johji .... *Orig Work:* Outlanders
Mandoriru-Club .... *Char Design:* Crystal Triangle
Maruyama, Masahito ...... *Music:* SuperBook
Maruyama, Masao .... *Dir:* Miyuki-chan in Wonderland; *Planning:* Devil Hunter Yohko 4
Masaki, Shinichi .... *Dir:* The Humanoid
Masayuki .... *Char Design:* Macross Plus
Mashimo, Koichi .... *Dir:* Ai (Love) City, Dominion Tank Police; *Anim Dir:* Dominion Tank Police
Mashita, Koichi .... *Dir:* Dirty Pair: Project Eden
Masuda, Toshio .... *Dir:* Odin: Photon Space Sailer Starlight; *Script:* Odin: Photon Space Sailer Starlight; *Music:* Fatal Fury: Legend of the Hungry Wolf
Masuda, Toshiro .... *Music:* Fatal Fury: Legend of the Hungry Wolf
Masunari, Koji .... *Dir:* Tenchi in Love
Masuo, Shoichi .... *Dir:* Countdown, Crimson Wolf; *Script:* Crimson Wolf
Matsubara, Hidenori ...... *Anim Dir:* Oh My Goddess!; *Char Design:* Oh My Goddess!
Matsudaira, Satoshi .... *Art Dir:* Project A-Ko 3
Matsuo, Shin .... *Anim Dir:* Judge
Matsumiya, Masazumi ... *Art Dir:* Crystal Triangle, Wanna-Be's
Matsumoto, Hajime .... *Script:* Iria
Matsumoto, Izumi .... *Orig Work:* Kimagure Orange Road
Matsumoto, Leiji .... *Dir:* Star Blazers TV Series, Spaceketeers, Dangard Ace; *Char Design:* Capt. Harlock & the Queen of a Thousand Years, Dangard Ace, Spaceketeers, Star Blazers; *Concept:* Dangard Ace, Spaceketeers, Captain Harlock and the Queen of a Thousand Years; *Orig Work:* Arcadia of My Youth, Star Blazers; *Planning:* Arcadia of My Youth
Matsumoto, Takashi ...... *Dir:* Techno Police 21C
Matsumoto, Yoshihisa ... *Dir:* Babel II
Matsuo, Shin .... *Anim Dir:* Judge; *Asst Dir:* Bounty Dog
Matsushima, Akiko .... *Dir:* Animated Classics: Student Days
Matsushita, Hiromi .... *Anim Dir:* Guyver: Out of Control
Matsushita, Makio .... *Screenplay:* Violence Jack Ep. 3
Matsu'ura, Akahisa .... *Music:* Ranma 1/2 OAV Series
Matsu'ura, Johei .... *Dir:* Crying Freeman 3, Slayers Eps. 5 & 11
Matsuzaki, Kenichi .... *Script:* Bubblegum Crisis
Matsuzono, Toru .... *Dir:* Laughing Target
Mihara, Michio .... *Char Design:* Cyber City Oedo 808
Mihashi, Ayako .... *Anim Dir:* Kizuna; *Char Design:* Kizuna
Mikamoto, Yasuyoshi ...... *Dir:* Orguss TV Series
Mikasa, Osamu .... *Dir:* 801 T.T.S. Airbats
Mikimoto, Haruhiko .... *Char Design:* Aim for the Top! Gunbuster, Macross II, Orguss TV Series
Mikuriya, Kyosuke .... *Dir:* Sohryuden Eps. 10-12
Mikuriya, Mic .... *Char Design:* Big Wars
Miller, Randy .... *Music:* Planet Busters
Minade, Koichi .... *Script:* The Humanoid
Minowa, Yutaka .... *Anim Dir:* Ninja Scroll; *Char Design:* Ninja Scroll
Minucci, Ulpio .... *Music:* Robotech
Miratsu, Takeo .... *Music:* Abashiri Family, Battle Skipper
Mita, Ryusuke .... *Orig Work:* Dragon Half
Mitsuoka, Seiichi .... *Dir:* Pochacco
Miura, Satoshi .... *Art Dir:* Kimagure Orange Road
Miura, Toru .... *Concept:* Sol Bianca
Miyagawa, Hiroshi .... *Music:* Odin: Photon Space Sailer Starlight, Star Blazers
Miyake, Bibimba .... *Art Dir:* La Blue Girl

Miyamae, Mitsuhara ...... *Art Dir:* Dirty Pair: Project Eden, Dominion Tank Police, Project A-Ko vs. Battle 1: Grey Side, Violence Jack Ep. 1

Miyamoto, Sado .... *Anim Dir:* Battle of the Planets

Miyao, Takeshi .... *Char Design:* Devil Hunter Yohko 1, 5 & 6

Miyashita, Tomoya .... *Script:* The Heroic Legend of Arislan

Miyasume, Akihiro .... *Orig. Work:* Megami Paradise

Miyatake, Kazuki .... *Mecha:* Aim for the Top! Gunbuster

Miyatake, Kazutaka .... *Mecha:* Dirty Pair: Flight 005 Conspiracy, DP: Project Eden

Miyaura, Kiyoshi .... *Music:* Lupin III: The Fuma Conspiracy

Miyazaki, Hayao .... *Dir:* Castle of Cagliostro, Lupin III TV Series, My Neighbor Totoro, Sherlock Hound, Warriors of the Wind; *Story:* My Neighbor Totoro; *Script:* Castle of Cagliostro, Lupin III TV Series, My Neighbor Totoro

Miyazaki, Kenjin .... *Char Design:* Burn Up!

Mizoguchi, Hajime .... *Music:* Please Save My Earth

Mizumura, Yoshio .... *Anim Dir:* Zillion

Mizuno, Kazunori .... *Dir:* Record of Lodoss War

Mizuno, Ryo .... *Story:* Record of Lodoss War

Mizutani, Kaoru .... *Music:* Gall Force: Earth Chapter

Mizutani, Takaya .... *Dir:* Mermaid Forest

Mizutani, Toshiharu .... *Art Dir:* Akira

Mochizuki, Mitsuru .... *Script:* Rei-Rei

Mochizuki, Tomomitsu .. *Dir:* Ranma 1/2 TV Series, Here is Greenwood; *Story:* Here is Greenwood

Mori, Eiji .... *Music:* Ranma 1/2 TV Series

Mori, Hideharu .... *Music:* Ranma 1/2 Anything-Goes Martial Arts TV Series

Mori, Masaki .... *Dir:* Barefoot Gen

Mori, Takeshi .... *Dir:* Gunsmith Cats, Kimagure Orange Road, Otaku no Video

Moriki, Yasuhiro .... *Mecha:* Lily-C.A.T.

Morimoto, Koji .... *Dir:* Robot Carnival ("Franken's Gears")

Morita, Miyoo .... *Concept:* Kizuna

Moriwaki, Makoto .... *Dir:* Hyper Doll

Moriyama, Yuji .... *Dir:* 801 T.T.S. Airbats, Project A-Ko 2, 3, 4; *Anim Dir:* Aim for the Top! Gunbuster, Macross Plus, Project A-Ko 1-4, The Wings of Honneamise; *Char Design:* 801 T.T.S. Airbats, Project A-Ko 1-4, Maison Ikkoku; *Concept:* Project A-Ko 2-4, Project A-Ko vs. Battles 1-2; *Story:* Project A-Ko 2; *Script:* Project A-Ko

Motohashi, Hideyuki ...... *Dir:* Godmars; *Anim Dir:* Goshogun, Maps, Project A-Ko vs. Battle 1: Grey Side; *Char Design:* Goshogun, Project A-Ko vs. Battle 1: Grey Side

Motohira, Ryo .... *Script:* Hyper Doll

Motoigi, Hiroaki .... *Mecha:* Iczer-One

Mukuo, Takamura .... *Art Dir:* Harmagedon

Muraki, Kazuma .... *Dir:* Angel of Darkness

Murata, Eiko .... *Mecha:* Guy II

Murata, Shunji .... *Char Design:* Sohryuden

Mutsuki, Juzo .... *Concept:* Cyber City Oedo 808, Devil Hunter Yohko 6; *Story:* Devil Hunter Yohko

Mutsuki, Mitsuo .... *Script:* New Dominion Tank Police

Mutsuki, Rika .... *Concept:* Phantom Quest Corp.

Muzuta, Mari .... *Char Design:* Demon Beast Invasion

N

Nagai, Go .... *Concept:* Abashiri Family, Cutey Honey, Grandizer, Starvengers, TranZor Z; *Orig Work:* Devilman, Hanappe Bazooka, Kekko Kamen, New Cutey Honey, Shuten Doji, Violence Jack; *Script:* Devilman

Nagaoka, Akinori .... *Dir:* Record of Lodoss War

Nagaoka, Seiko .... *Music:* El-Hazard, Tenchi Muyo TV Series

Nagaoka, Yasuchika .... *Dir:* New Cutey Honey

Nagasaka, Hideyoshi ..... *Script:* The Professional: Golgo 13

Nagashima, Yoko .... *Art:* Hello Kitty

Nagata, Shigeru .... *Music:* Here is Greenwood

Naito, Makoto .... *Script:* Lupin III: The Fuma Conspiracy

Nakada, Masao .... *Anim Dir:* The Heroic Legend of Arislan

Nakahata, Hidenori .... *Art Dir:* Macross II

Nakajima, Atsuko .... *Char Design:* Ranma 1/2 TV, OAV and Movie Series, You're Under Arrest

Nakamura, Koichiro .... *Dir:* Kimagure Orange Road

Nakamura, Manabu .... *Script:* Moldiver

Nakamura, Michitaka ..... *Art Dir:* Urusei Yatsura TV series

Nakamura, Mitsuji .... *Art Dir:* Area 88, Kishin Corps

Nakamura, Mitsuki .... *Mecha:* Battle of the Planets

Nakamura, Satoru .... *Anim Dir:* Angel Cop, Hyper Doll; *Char Design:* Hyper Doll

Nakamura, Takashi .... *Dir:* Robot Carnival ("Nightmare"); *Anim Dir:* Akira

Nakamura, Yasushi .... *Art Dir:* Iczer-One

Nakamura, Yoshinori ..... *Concept:* Dragon Knight

Nakamura, Yuma .... *Anim Dir:* Dragon Knight 2

Nakasugi, Toru .... *Char Design:* AD Police

Nakayama, Yumi .... *Char Design:* My Mai Mai

Nakaya, Kunio .... *Concept:* Gaiking

Nakayama, Shoichi .... *Char Design:* Blue Sonnet

Nakayama, Masuo .... *Art Dir:* The Guyver, RG Veda

Nakaza, Yoji .... *Art Dir:* Project A-Ko vs. Battle 2: Blue Side, RG Veda

Nakazawa, Kazuto .... *Anim Dir:* El-Hazard; *Char Design:* El-Hazard

Nakazawa, Keiji .... *Concept:* Barefoot Gen; *Orig Work:* Barefoot Gen; *Story:* Barefoot Gen; *Script:* Barefoot Gen

Nakazawa, Takehito ...... *Music:* Bubblegum Crash 1: Illegal Army, BG Crash 3: Meltdown, Genocyber, Gall Force New Era

Namba, Hiroyuki .... *Music:* Armitage III, Burn Up W

Namiki, Bin .... *Script:* Babel II

Nanba, Senji .... *Music:* Hello Kitty

Nanba, Shoji .... *Music:* Guyver: Out of Control

Nanpa, Hiroshi .... *Anim Dir:* Sukeban Deka

Nango, Yoichi .... *Art Dir:* The Hakkenden

Naoyuki, Yoshinaga .... *Dir:* Kimagure Orange Road

Nasu, Yukie .... *Orig Work:* Here is Greenwood

Negishi, Takayuki .... *Music:* Hyper Doll

Negishi, Hiroshi .... *Dir:* Bounty Dog, Burn Up W, Judge, Suikoden, Tenchi in Love; *Anim Dir:* M.D. Geist; *Script:* Tenchi in Love, Tenchi TV Series

Nemuruanzu .... *Script:* New Dominion Tank Police

Ninomiya, Tsuneo .... *Char Design:* M.D. Geist

Nishii, Masanori .... *Anim Dir:* Iczelion; *Char Design:* Iczelion

Nishii, Takafumi .... *Anim Dir:* Iczelion

Nishijima, Katsuhiko ..... *Dir:* Project A-Ko, Megami Paradise, Project A-Ko vs. Battle 1: Grey Side, Battle 2: Blue Side; *Anim Dir:* Project A-Ko vs. Battle 2: Blue Side; *Char Design:* Project A-Ko vs. Battle 2: Blue Side; *Concept:* Project A-Ko 3-4, Project A-Ko vs. Battles 1-2; *Story:* Project A-Ko 1-2; *Script:* Project A-Ko, Project A-Ko vs. Battle 1: Grey Side

Nishikawa, Masumi .... *Art Dir:* Moldiver

Nishikubo, Mizuho .... *Dir:* Zillion; *Char Design:* Zillion

Nishikubo, Toshihiko .... *Anim Dir:* Ghost in Shell

Nishimori, Akira .... *Dir:* AD Police

Nishimura, Junji .... *Dir:* Ranma 1/2 TV, OAV Series, Shuten Doji

Nishio, Daisuke .... *Dir:* 3x3 Eyes, Crying Freeman 1

Nishiyama, Akihiko .... *Dir:* El-Hazard

Nishizaki, Yoshinobu ..... *Dir:* Final Yamato, Yamato New Voyage; *Concept:* Star Blazers; *Story:* Odin: Photon Space Sailer Starlight

Nishizawa, Nobutaka ..... *Dir:* Crying Freeman 2, Shonan Bakusozoku

Nishizawa, Susumu .... *Dir:* Maps

Nitta, Ichiro .... *Music:* Area 88

Nobomuto, Keiko .... *Script:* Macross Plus

Noboru, Sugimitsu .... *Anim Dir:* Bubblegum Crash 2

Noda, Yasuyuki .... *Anim Dir:* Bubblegum Crash 3

Noriza, Makoto .... *Dir:* Slayers Eps. 2, 8

Nosaka, Akiyuki .... *Story:* Grave of the Fireflies

Nugano, Akane .... *Story:* Girl From Phantasia

O

Oba, Hideaki .... *Dir:* Genesis Survivor Gaiarth; *Anim. Dir:* Gall Force New Era

Obara, Hidekazu .... *Char Design:* Laughing Target

Obara, Shohei .... *Char Design:* The Humanoid; *Mecha:* The Humanoid

Obari, Masami .... *Dir:* Bubblegum Crisis 5, Bubblegum Crisis 6, Detonator Orgun, Fatal Fury: The Motion Picture; *Anim Dir:* Fatal Fury 1, Fatal Fury 2, Fatal Fury: The Motion Picture, Iczer-One; *Char Design:* Fatal Fury 1, Fatal Fury 2, Fatal Fury: The Motion Picture, Guy II; *Mecha:* Bubblegum Crisis 5, Bubblegum Crisis 6, Dangaio, Dancougar

Ochi, Hiroyuki .... *Dir:* Armitage III; *Char Design:* Armitage III, Explorer Woman Ray, The Hakkenden; *Mecha:* Genesis Survivor Gaiarth

Ochiai, Shigekazu .... *Planning:* Urusei Yatsura TV series

Oda, Fujio .... *Art Dir:* Hanappe Bazooka; *Char Design:* AD Police, Hanappe Bazooka

Ogawa, Tameo .... *Dir:* Hello Kitty

Ogami, Hiroaki .... *Anim Dir:* Iczer-One

Ogata, Yumiko .... *Art Dir:* Bubblegum Crash 2, Bubblegum Crash 3

Ogawa, Daisuke .... *Story:* Metal Fighters Miku

Ogura, Akira .... *Mecha:* New Dominion Tank Police

Ogura, Hiroaki .... *Art Dir:* Appleseed

Ogura, Hiromasa .... *Art Dir:* Ghost in the Shell, Giant Robo, Ninja Scroll, Patlabor 2, The Wings of Honneamise

Ohashi, Yoshimitsu .... *Char Design:* Devil Hunter Yohko 6, Green Legend Ran

Ohata, Koichi .... *Dir:* Cybernetics Guardian, Genocyber, MD Geist 2; *Mecha:* Aim for the Top! Gunbuster, Dangaio, Macross II, M.D. Geist; *Story:* M.D. Geist; *Script:* Genocyber

Ohuchi, Yoshiaki .... *Music:* M.D. Geist 2

Oji, Miyaki .... *Story:* Twin Dolls I & II; *Script:* Twin Dolls I & II

Okada, Ariaki .... *Art Dir:* Dirty Pair: Flight 005 Conspiracy

Okada, Toru .... *Music:* Dirty Pair: Flight 005 Conspiracy

Okada, Toshio .... *Story:* Aim for the Top! Gunbuster

Okada, Toshiyasu .... *Anim Dir:* Area 88, Lily-C.A.T.; *Char Design:* Area 88

Okamoto, Yukio .... *Dir:* The Hakkenden

Okamura, Kaori .... *Script:* Demon City Shinjuku

Okamura, Kenji .... *Orig Work:* Crimson Wolf

Okawa, Nanase .... *Script:* RG Veda

Okawara, Kunio .... *Mecha:* Battle of the Planets

Okazaki, Minoru .... *Dir:* Dragon Ball, (New) Gigantor

Okazaki, Takeshi .... *Orig Work:* Explorer Woman Ray

Okiura, Hiroyuki .... *Char Design:* Ghost in Shell

Oku, Koichi .... *Music:* Fire Tripper

Okubo, Masaichiro .... *Script:* Mermaid Forest

Okuda, Jun .... *Anim Dir:* Genesis Survivor Gaiarth; *Mecha:* Macross II

Okuda, Matsuri .... *Char Design:* Curse of the Undead Yoma

Okuda, Seiji .... *Dir:* Dancougar, Violence Jack; *Story:* Crystal Triangle

Okura, Masahiko .... *Char Design:* Maps

Okuwaki, Masahara .... *Dir:* Dirty Pair: Affair on Nolandia, Great Conquest: Romance of the Three Kingdoms

Omori, Hidetoshi .... *Dir:* Robot Carnival ("Deprive"); *Char Design:* The Guyver

Omori, Toshiyuki .... *Music:* The Professional: Golgo 13

Onaka, Yoichi .... *Script:* Arcadia of My Youth

Onchi, Hideo .... *Dir:* Toward the Terra

Onda, Naoyuki .... *Anim Dir:* Armitage III, Demon City Shinjuku; *Char Design:* Sol Bianca

Ono, Ryunosuke .... *Script:* Crying Freeman 5

Ono, Tatsunosuke .... *Script:* Crying Freeman 2

Ono, Yuji .... *Music:* Castle of Cagliostro, Lupin III TV Series, Mystery of Mamo, Lupin III: The Legend of the Gold of Babylon

Onuki, Kenichi .... *Char Design:* Dark Warrior

Osanai, Haruo .... *Dir:* Marine Boy; *Orig Work:* Marine Boy

Oshii, Mamoru .... *Dir:* Dallos, Ghost in Shell, Patlabor TV Series, Patlabor Movies 1-2, Urusei Yatsura TV Series; *Script:* Patlabor TV Series

Oshikawa, Shunro .... *Orig Story:* Super Atragon

Oshima, Michiru .... *Music:* Casshan: Robot Hunter

Ota, Dai .... *Art Dir:* Giant Robo

Ota, Koichi .... *Music:* My Mai Mai

Ota, Michihiko .... *Music:* Bubblegum Crash 2

Otani, Masahiro .... *Dir:* The Guyver

Otomo, Katsuhiro .... *Dir:* Akira, Neo-Tokyo ("The Order to Stop Construction"), Robot Carnival ("Opening" and "Closing"); *Char Design:* Akira, Harmagedon; *Story:* Akira, Neo-Tokyo ("The Order to Stop Construction"), Roujin Z; *Script:* Akira; *Mecha:* Roujin Z

Otonashi, Ryunosuke .... *Char Design:* End of Summer, Iria

Otsuka, Yasuo .... *Dir:* Lupin III: Mystery of Mamo; *Anim Dir:* Lupin III: Castle of Cagliostro

Oyama, Tetsunori .... *Art Dir:* Judge

Ozeki, Masayuki .... *Dir:* Lupin III: The Fuma Conspiracy

P

Pochi, Dr. .... *Concept:* Dragon Knight 2

Punch, Monkey .... *Concept:* Lupin III TV Series; *Orig Work:* Lupin III TV Series

R

Ran, Kotaro .... *Planning:* Angel of Darkness

Rasch, Torsten .... *Music:* Orguss 02

Rin, Shin .... *Char Design:* La Blue Girl, Twin Dolls I & II, New Angel

Rin, Taro .... *Dir:* Dagger of Kamui, Doomed Megalopolis, Galaxy Express 999, Harmagedon, Neo-Tokyo ("Labyrinth"); *Story:* Neo-Tokyo ("Labyrinth")

Ryu, Taiji .... *Dir:* Record of Lodoss War

S

Sadamitsu, Shinya .... *Dir:* Planet Busters; *Script:* Dragon Half

Sadamoto, Yoshiyuki ..... *Anim Dir:* Aim for the Top! Gunbuster, The Wings of Honneamise; *Char Design:* Nadia, Neon Genesis Evangelion, The Wings of Honneamise

Saezu, Shiro .... *Music:* Nadia

Saga, Satoshi .... *Dir:* Green Legend Ran

Sagisu, Shiro .... *Music:* Kimagure Orange Road, Megazone 23, Neon Genesis Evangelion

Sahara, Ako .... *Char Design:* Dragon Knight 2

Sahashi, Toshihiko .... *Music:* Fatal Fury 2: The New Battle

Saito, Masami .... *Art Dir:* Legend of the Forest

Saito, Takao .... *Orig Work:* The Professional: Golgo 13

Sakai, Akio .... *Dir:* Record of Lodoss War

Sakai, Akiyoshi .... *Script:* SuperBook, Flying House

Sakai, Shinji .... *Dir:* Sohryuden Ep. 6

Sakamoto, Ryuichi .... *Music:* The Wings of Honneamise

Sakata, Junichi .... *Dir:* 801 T.T.S. Airbats, Devil Hunter Yohko 5

Saki, Makura .... *Dir:* One-Pound Gospel

Sano, Hirotoshi .... *Anim Dir:* Bounty Dog; *Char Design:* Bounty Dog

Sakuma, Bob .... *Music:* Tekkaman, Battle of the Planets

Sanjo, Atsushi .... *Script:* The Guyver

Sanjyo, Riku .... *Script:* M.D. Geist, M.D. Geist 2

Saotome, Yusaku .... *Dir:* Junk Boy; *Art Dir:* Outlanders

Saruwatari, Tetsuya .... *Orig Work:* Dog Soldier

Sasagawa, Hiroshi .... *Anim Dir:* Speed Racer; *Art Dir:* Speed Racer

Sasaki, Hirishi .... *Art Dir:* Roujin Z

Sasamoto, Yuichi .... *Orig Story:* Ariel, Deluxe Ariel

Sato, Junichi .... *Dir:* Sailor Moon

Sato, Kazuo .... *Music:* Sailor Moon

Sato, Keiichi .... *Anim Dir:* Genesis Survivor Gaiarth

Sato, Masato .... *Dir:* Slayers Eps. 4, 10, 13

Sato, Takuya .... *Dir:* Armitage III

Sato, Yoshiharu .... *Anim Dir:* My Neighbor Totoro

Sato, Yuzo .... *Char Design:* Devil Hunter Yohko 5

Sawai, Koji .... *Dir:* Ranma 1/2 Anything-Goes Martial Arts TV Series

Sekijima, Masayori .... *Script:* Explorer Woman Ray, Orguss 02

Sekijima, Mayori .... *Script:* Megami Paradise, Bounty Dog; *Story:* Sol Bianca

Sekita, Osamu .... *Dir:* Homeroom Affairs, My Mai Mai

Seo, Ichizo .... *Music:* Gall Force

Shibata, Masahiro .... *Story:* Blue Sonnet

Shibayama, Tsutomu .... *Dir:* Ranma 1/2 TV Series

Shibuya, Yukihiro .... *Art Dir:* Maps

Shigematsu, Hidetoshi .. *Dir:* Cat Girl Nuku Nuku

Shigino, Akira .... *Anim Dir:* Saber Rider & the Star Sheriffs

Shiguma, Kenzo .... *Music:* Dirty Pair: Project Eden

Shimada, Michiru .... *Script:* Spirit of Wonder

Shimada, Mitsuru .... *Script:* Roots Search

Shimazaki, Katsumi .... *Dir:* Galaxy Fraulein Yuna; *Char Design:* Galaxy Fraulein Yuna

Shimizu, Akira .... *Dir:* Pekkle, Pochacco

Shimizu, Higashi .... *Script:* Crying Freeman 1, 3-4

Shimizu, Katsunori .... *Music:* Mad Bull

Shimizu, Keizo .... *Anim Dir:* Big Wars

Shimizu, Toshimitsu .... *Concept:* 801 T.T.S. Airbats, Rei-Rei

Shimizu, Yoshiharu .... *Anim. Dir:* Wanna-Be's; *Char Design:* Wanna-Be's

Shimono, Tetsuhito .... *Art Dir:* Dragon Century

Shin, Rin .... *Char Design:* La Blue Girl 2-6

Shinbo, Akiyuki .... *Dir:* Devil Hunter Yohko 6, Metal Fighters Miku

Shintani, Kaoru .... *Story:* Area 88

Shirado, Takashi .... *Dir:* Odin: Photon Space Sailer Starlight

Shiraishi, Kazumi .... *Concept:* Project A-Ko 3-4, Project A-Ko vs. Battles 1-2; *Story:* Project A-Ko 2

Shirasaki, Kazumi .... *Story:* Project A-Ko

Shirow, Masamune .... *Dir:* Black Magic M-66; *Story:* Appleseed, Black Magic M-66, Dominion Tank Police, New Dominion Tank Police; *Script:* Black Magic M-66

Shitamoto, Akiko .... *Char. Design:* SuperBook

Shiyuza, Isao .... *Script:* Cutey Honey, Kimagure Orange Road

Shoji, Osamu .... *Music:* Wicked City

Shudo, Takeshi .... *Story:* Goshogun; *Script:* Goshogun

Smith, E.E. "Doc" .... *Orig. Work:* Lensman

Sogo, Masashi .... *Script:* Shuten Doji

Sonoda, Hideki .... *Script:* Princess Minerva

Sonoda, Kenichi .... *Char Design:* Bubblegum Crisis, Bubblegum Crash Series, Gall Force, Gall Force: Earth Chapter, Gunsmith Cats, Rhea Gall Force, Otaku no Video, Gall Force New Era; *Story:* Riding Bean

Studio Nue .... *Mecha:* Dirty Pair: Affair on Nolandia; *Story:* Orguss TV Series

Sugii, Gisaburo .... *Dir:* Night on the Galactic R.R., Street Fighter II Movie; *Script:* Street Fighter II Movie

Sue, Nobuhito .... *Art Dir:* El-Hazard

Sugai, Hisashi .... *Dir:* Roots Search

Sugino, Akio .... *Concept:* Gaiking

Sugihara, Megumi .... *Script:* The Heroic Legend of Arislan

Sugiyama, Megumu .... *Concept:* RG Veda

Sugiyama, Takao .... *Music:* Maison Ikkoku

Suyama, Satoshi .... *Planning:* Battle of the Planets

Suzuki, Kiyoshi .... *Dir:* Lupin III: Legend of the Gold of Babylon

Suzuki, Ko .... *Dir:* Ranma 1/2 The Movie 2: Nihao My Concubine

Suzuki, Masahisa .... *Char Design:* Ariel, Deluxe Ariel

Suzuki, Michiyo .... *Anim Dir:* Tenchi in Love

Suzuki, Toshimichi .... *Story:* AD Police, Bubblegum Crisis and Crash Series, Wanna-Be's; *Planning:* AD Police, Bubblegum Crisis and Crash Series

T

Tajima, Koji .... *Music:* My Mai Mai

Tadano, Kazuko .... *Dir:* Sailor Moon; *Anim Dir:* Crystal Triangle; *Char Design:* Crystal Triangle

Takabayashi, Hisaya ...... *Script:* Devil Hunter Yohko 2

Takachiho, Haruka .... *Concept:* Dirty Pair

Takada, Akemi .... *Char Design:* Kimagure Orange Road, Patlabor 1, 2, Patlabor TV Series, Urusei Yatsura TV series

Takada, Hiroshi .... *Music:* Flying House

Takada, Kaori .... *Script:* The Heroic Legend of Arislan

Takada, Yuzo .... *Concept:* Cat Girl Nuku Nuku; *Orig Work:* 3x3 Eyes

Takagi, Hiroki .... *Char Design:* Dominion Tank Police

Takahama, Teruo .... *Music:* Demon Beast Invasion, La Blue Girl

Takahashi, Kumiko .... *Anim Dir:* Mermaid's Scar; *Char Design:* Mermaid's Scar, Maris the Chôjo

Takahashi, Rumiko .... *Orig Work:* Fire Tripper, Laughing Target, Maison Ikkoku, Maris the Chôjo, Mermaid Forest, Mermaid's Scar, One-Pound Gospel, Ranma 1/2, Urusei Yatsura (Those Obnoxious Aliens)

Takahashi, Ryosuke .... *Dir:* Armored Trooper Votoms TV Series; *Script:* Armored Trooper Votoms Stage 1 Ep. 4; *Story:* Armored Trooper Votoms TV Series

Takahashi, Shinya .... *Anim Dir:* Armitage III

Takahashi, Yuji .... *Anim Dir:* First Loves; *Char Design:* First Loves

Takahashi, Yutaka .... *Dir:* Cat Girl Nuku Nuku; *Concept:* The Heroic Legend of Arislan, RG Veda

Takahata, Isao .... *Dir:* Grave of the Fireflies; *Script:* Grave of the Fireflies

Takai, Takashi .... *Dir:* Dragon Pink 3

Takai, Tatsuo .... *Music:* Astro Boy

Takano, Fujio .... *Music:* Kizuna

Takao, Yoshinori .... *Art Dir:* M.D. Geist, Roots Search

Takaoka, Kiichi .... *Anim Dir:* RG Veda; *Char Design:* RG Veda

Takasho, Masahiko .... *Orig Work:* Crimson Wolf

Takaya, Yoshiki .... *Orig. Work:* The Guyver

Takayama, Fumihiko ...... *Dir:* Bubblegum Crisis 7, Orguss 02; *Story:* Orguss 02

Takayama, Hideki .... *Dir:* Urotsuki Dôji IV Eps. 1,2

Takayashiki, Hideo .... *Script:* Laughing Target, Maris the Chôjo, One Pound Gospel

Takechi, Masahisa .... *Music:* Robot Carnival

Takeda, Yusuke .... *Art Dir:* Dragon Half, Giant Robo

Takegami, Junki .... *Script:* Crystal Triangle

Takei, Hiroyuki .... *Music:* Homeroom Affairs

Takei, Masaki .... *Char Design:* End of Summer

Takemiya, Keiko .... *Story:* Toward the Terra

Takeshima, Sho .... *Concept:* Dark Warrior

Takeuchi, Atsushi .... *Char Design:* Armitage III; *Mecha:* Bounty Dog, Ghost in the Shell, Sol Bianca

Takeuchi, Naoko .... *Orig Work:* Sailor Moon

Takezaki, Tony .... *Char Design:* AD Police; *Story:* AD Police

Taki, Taro .... *Art Dir:* La Blue Girl

Takizawa, Toshifumi ...... *Dir:* Big Wars, Dirty Pair: Flight 005 Conspiracy

Tamano, Harumi .... *Dir:* Sohryuden Eps. 7-9

The Complete Anime Guide

Tamura, Hideki .... *Char Design:* Madox-01

Tanaka, Kiyomi .... *Art Dir:* Sohryuden; *Mecha:* Appleseed

Tanaka, Kohei .... *Music:* Aim for the Top! Gunbuster, Ariel, Deluxe Ariel, Spirit of Wonder

Tanaka, Yoshiki .... *Orig Work:* Sohryuden; *Story:* The Heroic Legend of Arislan

Tanda, Seiji .... *Anim Dir:* Genesis Survivor Gaiarth

Taniguchi, Moriyasu ...... *Anim Dir:* Violence Jack Ep. 3; *Char Design:* Violence Jack Ep. 3

Tatsuke, Noburo .... *Art Dir:* Lupin III TV series

Terada, Kenishi .... *Screenplay:* Sanctuary

Terada, Kenji .... *Script:* Baoh, Kimagure Orange Road

Terada, Norifumi .... *Script:* Ogre Slayer

Terasawa, Buichi .... *Dir:* Raven Tengu Kabuto; *Story:* Raven Tengu Kabuto; *Script:* Raven Tengu Kabuto

Tezuka, Osamu .... *Dir:* Astro Boy, Legend of the Forest; *Concept:* The Amazing Three, Ambassador Magma, Astro Boy, Kimba the White Lion, Leo the Lion, Legend of the Forest; *Orig Work:* Ambassador Magma, Astro Boy, Leo the Lion

Tobe, Atsuo .... *Anim Dir:* The Guyver

Tokushige, Takashi .... *Art Dir:* Sohryuden

Tolley, David .... *Music:* Babel II

Tomato, Aki .... *Screenplay:* Luna Varga

Tomimatsu, Yukio .... *Mecha:* Guy I

Tomioka,Yuichi .... *Script:* Gall Force: Earth Chapter

Tomita, Isao .... *Music:* Kimba the White Lion

Tomita, Sukehiro .... *Script:* Gall Force: Eternal Story

Tomita, Yoshihiro .... *Script:* Devil Hunter Yohko, End of Summer

Tomizawa, Kazuo .... *Anim Dir:* Barefoot Gen; *Char Design:* Lensman

Tomokazu, Tokoro .... *Anim Dir:* Genesis Survivor Gaiarth

Tomonaga, Kazuhide ..... *Anim Dir:* Lupin III: The Fuma Conspiracy

Toriumi, Eiko .... *Dir:* Area 88

Toriumi, Hisayuki .... *Dir:* Lily C.A.T.

Toriumi, Jinzo .... *Script:* Tekkaman, Armored Trooper Votoms Stage 1 Eps. 8,9,12,13, Armored Trooper Votoms Stage 2 Eps. 1,4,5,8,9,11; *Planning:* Battle of the Planets

Toriyama, Akira .... *Orig Work:* Dragon Ball

Totsuka, Osamu .... *Music:* Dancougar

Toyama, Kazz .... *Music:* Doomed Megalopolis

Toyo'oka, Kaoru .... *Dir:* Dragon Knight 2, New Angel

Tsuji, Masaki .... *Script:* Maps

Tsuji, Tadano .... *Art Dir:* Odin: Photon Space Sailer Starlight

Tsukabara, Setsuo .... *Music:* Marine Boy

Tsukamoto, Yumiko .... *Screenplay:* Luna Varga

Tsukimura, Ryoei .... *Script:* El-Hazard, Moldiver, Tenchi TV Series, Tenchi in Love

Tsunaki, Aki .... *Char Design:* Urotsuki Dôji IV

Tsunoda, Koichi .... *Anim Dir:* Great Conquest: Romance of the Three Kingdoms; *Char Design:* Great Conquest: Romance of the Three Kingdoms

Tsuri, Norihiro .... *Music:* The Heroic Legend of Arislan, Mermaid's Scar

Tsuru, Nobuyuki .... *Char Design:* Suikoden

Tsuruta, Kenji .... *Orig Story:* Spirit of Wonder

Tsuruyama, Osamu .... *Dir:* Akai Hayate

Tsuzurii, B. .... *Dir:* Zillion

U

Uchida, Yorihisa .... *Dir:* Guy I & II, Legend of Lyon: Flare; *Char Design:* Guy II, Legend of Lyon: Flare

Ueda, Hidehito .... *Dir:* Ambassador Magma

Ueda, Hitoshi .... *Char Design:* Phantom Quest Corp.

Ueda, Shigeru .... *Dir:* Sohryuden Eps. 1, 2

Uemura, Osamu .... *Dir:* Fire Tripper

Uetake, Sumio .... *Script:* Burn Up W

Ui, Takashi .... *Anim Dir:* Legend of the Forest

Umetsu, Yasuonori .... *Dir:* Robot Carnival ("Presence"); *Anim Dir:* Casshan: Robot Hunter, Angel Cop; *Char Design:* Casshan: Robot Hunter, Lily C.A.T.

Unozawa, Shin .... *Planning:* AD Police

Urahata, Tatsuhiko .... *Script:* Junk Boy, Mermaid's Scar, Phantom Quest Corp.

Urakami, Yasuo .... *Music:* The Heroic Legend of Arislan

Urasawa, Yoshio .... *Script:* Lupin III: The Legend of the Gold of Babylon

Urushibara, Satoshi ...... *Char Design:* Bubblegum Crisis 7, Legend of Lenmear, Plastic Little

Usami, Toshikazu .... *Char Design:* Demon Beast 5, 6

Utatane, Hiroyuki .... *Orig Story:* Countdown

W

Wada, Kaoru .... *Music:* 3x3 Eyes, Kishin Corps, Silent Möbius

Wada, Shinji .... *Orig. Work:* Sukeban Deka

Wada, Takuya .... *Dir:* Violence Jack 2; *Anim Dir:* Violence Jack 1 & 2; *Char Design:* Violence Jack 1 & 2; *Script:* Violence Jack 2

Wakakusa, Kei .... *Music:* Moldiver

Wakakusa, Megumi .... *Music:* Outlanders

Waki, Takeshi .... *Art Dir:* The Hakkenden, Raven Tengu Kabuto

Wan Yan a Gu Da .... *Concept:* F-3

Watanabe, Asami .... *Script:* Zillion

Watanabe, Hiroshi .... *Dir:* Guyver: Out of Control, Magical Princess Gigi

Watanabe, Hiroya .... *Music:* Devil Hunter Yohko

Watanabe, Jun .... *Music:* The Guyver

Watanabe, Junichi .... *Dir:* Ariel, Deluxe Ariel, Green Legend Ran; *Script:* Ariel, Deluxe Ariel

Watanabe, Kinya .... *Planning:* F-3

Watanabe, Koji .... *Mecha:* Kishin Corps

Watanabe, Makoto .... *Script:* The Guyver 4-6

Watanabe, Mami .... *Script:* Phantom Quest Corp., Record of Lodoss War

Watanabe, Michiaki .... *Music:* Dangaio, Iczer-One

Watanabe, Shinichiro .... *Dir:* Macross Plus

Watanabe, Sumio .... *Anim Dir:* The Guyver

Watanabe, Takashi .... *Dir:* Abashiri Family, Battle Skipper, Sanctuary, Slayers Ep. 1, Weather Report Girl; *Script:* Abashiri Family

Watanabe, Toshiyuki ..... *Music:* Ambassador Magma, Girl From Phantasia

Wood, Nick .... *Music:* RG Veda

Y

Yabushita, Taiji .... *Dir:* Alakazam the Great

Yamada, Katsuhisa .... *Dir:* Outlanders, Record of Lodoss War; *Script:* Devil Hunter Yohko 3

Yamada, Masaki .... *Orig Work:* Kishin Corps

Yamada, Takashi .... *Script:* Fatal Fury 1, Fatal Fury 2, Fatal Fury: The Motion Picture

Yamada, Tomoaki .... *Music:* Oh My Goddess!

Yamaga, Hiroyuki .... *Dir:* The Wings of Honneamise; *Script:* The Wings of Honneamise

Yamagata, Atsushi .... *Char Design:* Genocyber

Yamaguchi, Hiroshi .... *Script:* New Dominion Tank Police, Orguss 02

Yamaguchi, Ryota .... *Script:* Ranma 1/2 The Movie 2: Nihao My Concubine, Ranma 1/2 OAV Series

Yamaguchi, Yorifusa ..... *Dir:* Galaxy F Yuna; *Anim Dir:* Saber Rider & the Star Sheriffs

Yamaguchi, Yoshihiro .... *Dir:* Princess Minerva, Sohryuden Eps. 3-4

Yamakawa, Etsuko .... *Music:* Rhea Gall Force

Yamakawa, Hiroshi .... *Music:* Elven Bride

Yamamoto, Eiichi .... *Dir:* Odin: Photon Space Sailer Starlight, Kimba the White Lion; *Script:* Odin: Photon Space Sailer Starlight

Yamamoto, Nizo .... *Art Dir:* Grave of the Fireflies

Yamamoto, Yoshiki .... *Dir:* Rei-Rei

Yamamoto, Yoshiyuki .... *Art Dir:* Orguss TV Series

Yamamoto, Yu .... *Script:* Dark Warrior, First Loves, Green Legend Ran

Yamanaka, Kishio .... *Music:* Guy II

Yamanaka, Norimasa ..... *Music:* Appleseed, Legend of Lemnear

Yamasaki, Haruya .... *Script:* Castle of Cagliostro

Yamasaki, Seiya .... *Script:* Zillion

Yamashiro Group, Geinoh ... *Music:* Akira

Yamashita, Ikuto .... *Mecha:* Neon Genesis Eva

Yamashita, Taka'aki ...... *Dir:* Crying Freeman 5

Yamashita, Toshinari ..... *Anim Dir:* Burn Up W; *Char Design:* Burn Up W

Yamatoya, Atsushi .... *Script:* Adventure Kid, Lupin III: Mystery of Mamo

Yamauchi, Shigeyasu ..... *Dir:* Crying Freeman 4

Yamauchi, Shojuro .... *Anim Dir:* One-Pound Gospel

Yamazaki, Kazuo .... *Dir:* Maison Ikkoku, Please Save My Earth

Yamazaki, Osamu .... *Story:* Akai Hayate; *Script:* Akai Hayate

Yamazaki, Takeshi .... *Mecha:* Kishin Corps

Yamazawa, Minoru .... *Char Design:* Homeroom Affairs

Yanagawa, Shigeru .... *Planning:* SuperBook, Flying House

Yanagida, Yoshiaki .... *Art Dir:* Spirit of Wonder; *Char Design:* Spirit of Wonder

Yanagikaze, Rin'oh .... *Dir:* La Blue Girl 4, 6

Yanagisawa, Tetsuya ..... *Char Design:* Urotsuki Dôji IV

Yasuda, Hitoshi .... *Story:* Record of Lodoss War

Yatagai, Kenichi .... *Dir:* Macross II, Ten Little Gall Force

Yasuhiko, Yoshikazu ...... *Char Design:* Super Atragon

Yokayama, Seiji .... *Music:* Great Conquest: Romance of the Three Kingdoms

Yokose, Naoshi .... *Art Dir:* Blue Sonnet

Yokose, Naoto .... *Art Dir:* Demon Beast Invasion

Yokota, Osamu .... *Dir:* Slayers Eps. 3, 9

Yokoyama, Hiroyuki ...... *Dir:* Baoh

Yokoyama, Ko .... *Mecha:* Big Wars

Yokoyama, Mitsuteru ..... *Concept:* Babel II, Gigantor; *Orig Work:* Babel II, Giant Robo, Gigantor; *Story:* Giant Robo

Yoma, Juki .... *Dir:* Demon Beast 3, 4

Yoshida, Hidetoshi .... *Script:* Bubblegum Crisis 8

Yoshida, Hiroaki .... *Dir:* Twilight of the Cockroaches; *Story:* Twilight of the Cockroaches

Yoshida, Kenji .... *Concept:* Tekkaman

Yoshida, Kenjiro .... *Dir:* SuperBook

Yoshida, Noboru .... *Art Dir:* New Dominion Tank Police

Yoshida, Shigetsugu ...... *Dir:* Lupin III: Legend of the Gold of Babylon

Yoshida, Tatsuo .... *Dir:* Speed Racer; *Char Design:* Battle of the Planets, Speed Racer; *Concept:* Battle of the Planets, Speed Racer

Yoshida, Toru .... *Dir:* 801 T.T.S. Airbats

Yoshikawa, Soji .... *Dir:* Lupin III: Mystery of Mamo; *Script:* Lupin III: Mystery of Mamo, Armored Trooper Votoms Stage 1 Eps. 7,10,11, Armored Trooper Votoms Stage 2 Eps. 1-3,7,10,12-14

Yoshikawa, Soki .... *Story:* Lensman

Yoshikawa, Yoichiro ...... *Music:* Green Legend Ran, Iria, New Dominion Tank Police

Yoshimoto, Kinji .... *Dir:* End of Summer, Kekko Kamen 2, Legend of Lemnear, Plastic Little *Char Design:* La Blue Girl; *Script:* Legend of Lemnear

Yoshinari, Takamasa ...... *Story:* Great Conquest: Romance of the Three Kingdoms

Yoshino, Hiroaki .... *Music:* Crying Freeman 1-5

Yoshino, Mickey .... *Music:* Neo Tokyo

Yoshioka, Hitoshi .... *Concept:* Suikoden

Yoshizane .... *Orig. Work:* Megami Paradise

Yuki (Akane Shinshaken) .... *Concept:* Magical Twilight

Yuki, Masami .... *Char Design:* Patlabor 2; *Concept:* Patlabor TV/OAV/Movie Series

Yuki, Nobuteru .... *Char Design:* Angel Cop, Battle Angel, Sukeban Deka, Record of Lodoss War

Yumane, Kimitoshi .... *Mecha:* Madox-01

Yumeno, Rei .... *Mecha:* Gall Force 3

Yuyama, Kunihiko .... *Dir:* Goshogun, Weather Report Girl, Windaria

208

Appendix B
Guide to terms used in this book

This is a brief guide to some special terms and transliterated Japanese words employed in this guide. All the Japanese in this book (with the exception of the Video Directory, which is based on information provided by U.S. production companies) is romanized according to a modified version of the Hepburn *romaji* system. That means that, lacking a specialized macron in our character set, all long vowels are indicated with a circumflex or French "hat," as in *shôjo*, "young girl." The exception to this rule is the long *i*, which is written herein as *ii*. Double vowels can also be written with a double letter (e.g. Ootomo for Otomo), but this misleads non-Japanese speakers into pronouncing the double *o* as in "Hoover," when it should be pronounced exactly as the single vowel, but held for twice as long. Vowels appearing at the end of a Japanese word are audible. The acute French accent, sometimes employed by Western writers to indicate that the final *e* of anime is clearly pronounced (e.g. animé), is not used in romanized Japanese. Throughout the book, we have used Western-style naming, wherein the first name is first and the family name is last.

an • i • me (say "ANNIE-May") *n*. The Japanese word for animated cartoon. When used by a Japanese speaker, the term could apply to Disney's *Pocahontas* as readily as to Otomo's *Akira*. When used by Westerners, this term refers exclusively to Japanese animation.

dô • jin • shi (say "Dough-JIN-Shi") *n*. Term for amateur fan-created parody/homage comics.

man • ga (say "MAHN-Gah") *n*. The Japanese word for comics. When used by a Japanese speaker, the term could apply to Marvel's *Spider-Man* series as readily as to any comic published in Japan. When used by Westerners, this term refers exclusively to Japanese comics. In Japan, manga covers a broad range of genres, including *shojô* (girls') manga; *shônen* (boys') manga; *yakuza* (Japanese underworld) manga; salaryman (office worker) manga; samurai manga; sports manga; cooking manga; gambling manga ... the list goes on and on. Manga accounts for 40% of all Japanese publishing, and is free of the "for kids only" label with which American comics are saddled. The word is thought to have been coined in 1815 by the *Ukiyo-e* artist Hokusai for his "irresponsible pictures," or satirical drawings.

me • cha (rhymes with "Mecca") *n*. Japanese loanword (from "MECHA-nical"), used to describe not only the giant robots of anime, but its other devices as well, including but not limited to guns, vehicles and spaceships.

OAV (Original Animation Video) *n*. Term used to describe an animated film or series created specifically for release on home video, as opposed to release in movie theatres or on television. This is a common form of distribution for anime inside Japan. Only recently has American-produced animation experimented with this format for titles like *The Return of Jafar* (a sequel to Disney's *Aladdin* feature) and *The Land Before Time II* (a sequel to Don Bluth's *The Land Before Time* feature). Also referred to as *OVA*.

o • ta • ku (say "Oh-TAH-Koo") *n*. Term used to refer to fanatical devotees of anime or manga. Japanese speakers might use this term in a pejorative sense to denote someone lacking in social graces and breadth who is obsessive about a certain subject. Inside or outside Japan, this is a term to apply carefully. Some anime fans will unabashedly declare themselves otaku, while others may take offense at having the label applied to them.

sen • tai (say "SEN-Tie") *n*. Term for Japanese live-action shows about costumed heroes and martial-arts characters. Lit., "battle team."

shô • jo (say "SHOW-Joe") *n*. Term for Japanese girls' manga or anime. Lit., "young girl."

shô • nen (say "SHOW-Nehn") *n*. Lit., "small-year," meaning "young boy." This is the most widely published genre of manga in Japan, with magazines such as *Shônen Jump* ranking among the world's bestselling publications. One of the most popular *shônen* titles of all time is Rumiko Takahashi's *Ranma 1/2*, despite the fact that its creator is a woman.

ya • ku • za (say "YAH-Koo-Zah") *proper noun* A word for the criminal underworld, like "Mafia." Unlike their Western counterparts, the *yakuza* are distinguished by a code of ethics and organizational hierarchies based on the patrilinear societies defined by the samurai. *Crying Freeman* is an example of the romance associated with the *yakuza* genre.

Index

This index includes references to films, TV series, OAV releases, people, businesses, and organizations found throughout the book. Titles of books, films and series are set in *italics*, magazines and organizations are set in roman, character names are set as First Name, Last Name, and real people's names are set as Last Name, First Name. The Video Directory chapter is not included in this index.

Order Form

Phone Orders: **1-800-729-6423**
Fax Orders: (310) 532-7001
Mail Orders: **SCB Distributors**
       15612 S. New Century Drive
       Gardena, CA 90248-2129 • USA
       (310) 532-9400

THE COMPLETE ANIME GUIDE, 2ND EDITION
ISBN: 0-9649542-5-7   • $19.95

Name: _____

Address: _____

City, State, Zip Code: _____

Telephone/Fax Number: _____

Payment can be made by check, money order, or major credit card.

For wholesale orders to the book trade, please contact:
SCB Distributors
15612 S. New Century Drive
Gardena, CA 90248-2129
(800) 729-6423

To be notified of future editions, or for general inquiries, please write:
Tiger Mountain Press
P.O. Box 369
Issaquah, WA 98027 • USA
Fax: (206) 391-9064